# International Management

# Pearson

At Pearson, we have a simple mission: to help people make more of their lives through learning.

We combine innovative learning technology with trusted content and educational expertise to provide engaging and effective learning experience that serve people wherever and whenever they are learning.

We enable our customers to access a wide and expanding range of market-leading content from world-renowned authors and develop their own tailor-made book. From classroom to boardroom, our curriculum materials, digital learning tools and testing programmes help to educate millions of people worldwide — more than any other private enterprise.

Every day our work helps learning flourish, and wherever learning flourishes, so do people.

To learn more, please visit us at: www.pearson.com/uk

# International Management

Selected chapters from:

*International Management: Managing Across Borders and Cultures*
Ninth Edition and Global Edition
Helen Deresky

*International Business: The New Realities*
Fifth Edition and Global Edition
S. Tamer Cavusgil, Gary Knight and John R. Riesenberger

# Pearson

Harlow, England • London • New York • Boston • San Francisco • Toronto • Sydney • Dubai • Singapore • Hong Kong
Tokyo • Seoul • Taipei • New Dehli • Cape Town • São Paulo • Mexico City • Madrid • Amsterdam • Munich • Paris • Milan

**Pearson**
**KAO Two**
**KAO Park**
**Harlow**
**Essex CM17 9NA**

And associated companies throughout the world

Visit us on the World Wide Web at:
www.pearson.com/uk

© Pearson Education Limited 2020

Compiled from:

*International Management*: *Managing Across Borders and Cultures*
Ninth Edition and Global Edition
Helen Deresky
ISBN 978-1-292-15353-7
Pearson Education © 2017

*International Business: The New Realities*
Fifth Edition and Global Edition
S. Tamer Cavusgil, Gary Knight and John R. Riesenberger
ISBN 978-1-292-30324-6
published by Pearson Education © 2020

ISBN 978-1-83961-500-9

Printed and bound in Great Britain by Ashford Colour Press, Gosport, Hampshire.

# CONTENTS

# Chapter 1

# Globalization of Markets and the Internationalization of the Firm

**Learning Objectives** *After studying this chapter, you should be able to:*

1.1 Understand market globalization as an organizing framework.

1.2 Learn the driving forces of globalization.

1.3 Understand the impact of technological advances on globalization.

1.4 Learn the dimensions of globalization.

1.5 Understand firm-level consequences of market globalization.

1.6 Understand the societal consequences of globalization.

## Skype: A "Born Global" Business

Skype is a telecommunications application available on most major platforms and devices that provides video, audio, and text chat over the Internet between devices. It was founded in August 2003 by Niklas Zennstrom from Sweden and Janus Friis from Denmark, and it was developed in Estonia. Skype is now headquartered in Luxembourg, with offices across Europe, the United States, and Asia.

Its Swedish, Danish, and Estonian roots alone cast Skype as a business that was born to be global from the moment of its launch, but the very nature of the software and the ease of communication that it has enabled between businesses and individuals around the world speak to its position as a truly international brand.

A little over a year after its launch in October 2004, it had already been downloaded 1.5 million times. By June 2005, 10 million Skype-to-Skype calls had been made. In March 2007, its download count had reached 500 million, and by February 2008, 100 billion minutes of Skype-to-Skype calls had been made.

To the present day, Skype has grown its business strongly across the Windows, Android, and Apple platforms. This growth has been accelerated by a number of factors but predominately to its first-mover advantage, the availability of Skype across numerous platforms, and the freemium business model upon which it is built upon. This business model means that the software or application and its core features are free for users to download, but money is charged for additional features. Thanks to the size of its userbase, Skype needs only a small proportion of users to purchase premium features to generate its revenue.

*Source:* Ian Shaw/Alamy Stock Photo

Skype's astonishing global growth should perhaps not be so surprising given that the application is freely available to anyone with a compatible device—most are—and an Internet connection anywhere in the world. Skype launched at a time when it had no established competitors and was therefore unique in its offering. These factors, combined with the rise of the Internet, endless innovation in technology, and growth in service offerings has made globalization far more practicable, less expensive, and for many businesses a must. Globalization has turned Skype into the giant it is today.

As a "born global" business, Skype has succeeded in entering a number of international markets within a short space of time of its initial launch. It was able to grow exponentially thanks to its international outlook, the agility of its business and software, and the its distribution channel—the Internet. This growth and service ultimately culminated in Microsoft swooping in and acquiring the business for $8.5 billion, but the value that Microsoft has placed is well beyond that sum. Microsoft's faith in the business and underlying technology is so great that it has discontinued many of the messaging services it had developed in-house in favor of Skype.

Other born global companies include Airbnb (accommodation), HTC (smartphones), Uber (transportation), Spotify (music streaming). Skype and the "born global" businesses demonstrate that even new ventures with very limited experience but high innovation and can quickly grow internationally without having vast resources at their disposal. Our connected world makes it much easier to communicate and operate on a global basis; indeed, more companies are operating internationally today than ever before.

## Questions

**1-1.** What environmental factors create favorable conditions for businesses such as Skype to rapidly grow internationally?

**1-2.** Beyond simply increasing revenue, what advantages might a new business benefit from thanks to early international exposure and growth?

**1-3.** What are the risks associated with such rapid and dispersed growth for a new company?

*SOURCES:* "The History of Skype," Skype Blogs, August 2012, https://blogs.skype.com/wp-content/uploads/2012/08/skype-timel ne-v5-2.pdf; "Microsoft Confirms Takeover of Skype," BBC News, May 10, 2011, https://www.bbc.com/news/business-13343600.

This case was written by John Bancroft, Oxford Brookes University.

---

The opening case highlights important driving forces and causes of market globalization. These include worldwide reduction of barriers to trade and investment, market liberalization and adoption of free markets, and advances in technology.

**Globalization of markets**

Ongoing economic integration and growing interdependency of national economies.

**Globalization of markets** refers to the gradual integration and growing interdependence of national economies. Declining trade barriers and rapid changes in communications, manufacturing, and transportation technologies are enabling firms to internationalize much more rapidly and easily than ever before.

**Value chain**

The sequence of value-adding activities the firm performs in the course of developing, producing, marketing, and servicing a product.

Globalization allows companies to outsource value-chain activities to the most favorable locations worldwide. A **value chain** is the sequence of value-adding activities the firm performs in the course of developing, producing, marketing, and servicing a product. Firms source raw materials, parts, components, and service inputs from suppliers around the globe. Globalization has also made it easier for companies to sell their offerings worldwide. These trends are transforming national economies. Growing world trade and foreign direct investment (FDI) provide buyers with a wider choice of products than ever before. Global competition and innovation frequently help to lower consumer prices. Firms with cross-border business create millions of jobs that raise living standards around the world.

Globalization is not new. In early history, civilizations in the Mediterranean, Middle East, Asia, Africa, and Europe all contributed to the growth of cross-border trade. Globalization evolved out of a common desire of civilizations to reach out and touch one another.[1] It is a culmination of people's recognition, thousands of years ago, of the wonders of difference and discovery. Cross-border trading opened the world to innovations and progress by giving societies the opportunity to expand and grow. Trade through the ages fostered civilization; without it, the world would consist of warring tribes bent on getting what they need through combat.[2]

### Phases of Globalization

We can identify five distinct phases in the evolution of globalization since the 1800s. As illustrated in Exhibit 1.1, each phase was accompanied by radical technological advances and internationalization trends.

- *The first phase of globalization* began in about 1830 and peaked around 1880.[3] It was associated with the use of water and steam power to mechanize production and power ships and trains. International business became widespread due to the growth of railroads, efficient ocean transport, and the rise of large manufacturing and trading firms. Invention of the telegraph and telephone in the late 1800s enabled information flows between and within nations and aided early efforts to manage companies' supply chains.

- *The second phase of globalization* began around 1900 and was associated with the rise of electricity and steel production. Electric power was widely used to drive mass production. This phase reached its height just before the Great Depression, a worldwide economic downturn that began in 1929. In 1900, Western Europe was the most industrialized world region. Europe's colonization of countries in Asia, Africa, and the Middle East led to the establishment of some of the earliest subsidiaries of multinational enterprises (MNEs). European companies such as BASF, Nestlé, Shell, Siemens, and British Petroleum established foreign manufacturing plants by 1900.[4] In the years before World War I (pre-1914), many firms operated globally. The Italian manufacturer Fiat supplied vehicles to nations on both sides of the war.

**EXHIBIT 1.1**
**Phases of Globalization
Since the Early 1800s**

| Phase of Globalization | Approximate Period | Triggers | Key Characteristics |
|---|---|---|---|
| First phase | 1830 to late 1800s, peaking in 1880 | Introduction of railroads and ocean transport | Rise of manufacturing; cross-border trade of commodities, largely by trading companies |
| Second phase | 1900 to 1930 | Rise of electricity and steel production | Emergence and dominance of early MNEs (mainly from Europe and North America) in manufacturing, extractive, and agricultural industries |
| Third phase | 1948 to 1970s | Formation of General Agreement on Tariffs and Trade (GATT); conclusion of World War II; Marshall Plan to reconstruct Europe | Focus by industrializing Western countries to reduce trade barriers; rise of MNEs from Japan; development of global capital markets; rise of global trade names |
| Fourth phase | 1980s to about 2006 | Privatization of state enterprises in transition economies; revolution in information, communication, and transportation technologies; remarkable growth of emerging markets | Rapid growth in cross-border trade of products, services, and capital; rise of internationally active SMEs and services firms; rising prosperity of emerging markets |
| Fifth phase | 2007 to present | Rise of digital technologies, and other new technologies, which are boosting manufacturing productivity and the efficiency of international trade in services | Leveraging technology to facilitate trade and local production; rising trade in digitally enabled services but slowing growth of trade in merchandise goods |

- *The third phase of globalization* began after World War II. This phase was associated with reconstruction efforts after the war and the dismantling of trade barriers. By the war's end in 1945, substantial pent-up demand fueled markets for consumer and industrial products to rebuild Europe and Japan. Leading industrialized countries, including Australia, the United Kingdom, and the United States, sought to reduce international trade barriers to supply goods to meet this demand.

In 1947, the Bretton Woods Conference of 23 nations created the *General Agreement on Tariffs and Trade (GATT)*, which reduced barriers to international trade and investment. Participating governments recognized that liberalized trade would stimulate industrialization, modernization, and better living standards. In turn, the GATT led to the formation of the **World Trade Organization (WTO**; www.wto.org), which grew to include about 164 member nations. The WTO aims to regulate and ensure fairness and efficiency in global trade and investment. Global cooperation in the postwar era also gave birth to the International Monetary Fund and the World Bank.

Early multinationals from the third phase of globalization originated in the United States, Western Europe, and Japan. European firms such as Unilever, Philips, Royal Dutch-Shell, and Bayer organized their businesses by establishing subsidiaries around

**World Trade Organization (WTO)**
A multilateral governing body empowered to regulate international trade and investment.

the world. Many companies developed internationally recognized trade names, including Nestlé, Kraft, Lockheed, Caterpillar, Coca-Cola, and Levi's. Foreign subsidiaries of such companies operated as small versions of the parent firm, marketing their products around the world. MNEs began to seek cost advantages by locating factories in developing countries with low labor costs. International trade and investment expanded significantly in the 1960s Recovered from World War II, MNEs in Europe and Japan began to challenge the dominance of U.S. multinationals. Growing international trade coincided with increased cross-national flows of capital, leading to integration of global financial markets.[5]

- *The fourth phase of globalization* began in the early 1980s and featured the use of electronics and information technology to automate production. The phase was characterized by enormous growth in cross-border trade and investment. It was triggered by the development of personal computers, the Internet, and web browsers. It was also characterized by the collapse of the Soviet Union and the market liberalization of Central and Eastern Europe. Impressive industrialization and modernization in East Asian economies followed. International prosperity began to develop in the emerging markets, including Brazil, India, and Mexico. The 1980s witnessed huge increases in FDI, especially in capital- and technology-intensive sectors. Technological advances in information, communications, and transportation supported the rise of internationally active small and medium-sized enterprises. These advances increased the ability to organize and manage exports more efficiently and at lower cost. Modern technologies also enabled the globalization of the service sector in such areas as banking, entertainment, tourism, insurance, and retailing.

- *The fifth phase of globalization* began around 2007 with the rise of digital technologies. Technological breakthroughs in fields such as quantum computing, the Internet of Things, artificial intelligence, robotics, autonomous vehicles, 3D printing, nanotechnology, and biotechnology are blurring the lines between the physical, digital, and biological spheres. Digital and other new technologies are boosting the efficiency of international trade, especially in services. For example, much retailing is now done through giant firms such as Amazon and Alibaba, which sell their offerings around the world via online platforms. From Africa to South Asia to Latin America, as more people become digitally connected, they consume more international services. The value of world exports of services rose from about $3 trillion in 2007 to more than $5 trillion in 2017. Thanks to technological advances, national borders and traditional country-based business models are losing much of their relevance.

   Meanwhile, growth in international trade of goods has slowed during this phase. Just as new technologies support international services trade, they also increase the productivity of local manufacturing. This tendency reduces firms' cost of domestic operations and increases the attractiveness of homegrown, local manufacturing. FDI as a share of total investment has declined. Emerging market countries increasingly focus on developing local markets for locally manufactured products.[6]

**1.1** Understand market globalization as an organizing framework.

# Market Globalization: Organizing Framework

Firms expand abroad proactively to increase sales and profit through new markets, find lower-cost inputs, or obtain other advantages. Firms may also internationalize reactively because of unfavorable conditions in the home market such as regulation or declining local industry sales. Exhibit 1.2 presents an organizing framework for examining market globalization. The exhibit makes a distinction among:

- *driving forces* or causes of globalization.
- *dimensions* or manifestations of globalization.
- *firm-level consequences* of globalization.
- *societal consequences* of globalization.

   In the exhibit, the double arrows illustrate the interactive nature of the relationship between globalization and its consequences. As globalization intensifies, individual firms respond to the challenges and new advantages that it brings.

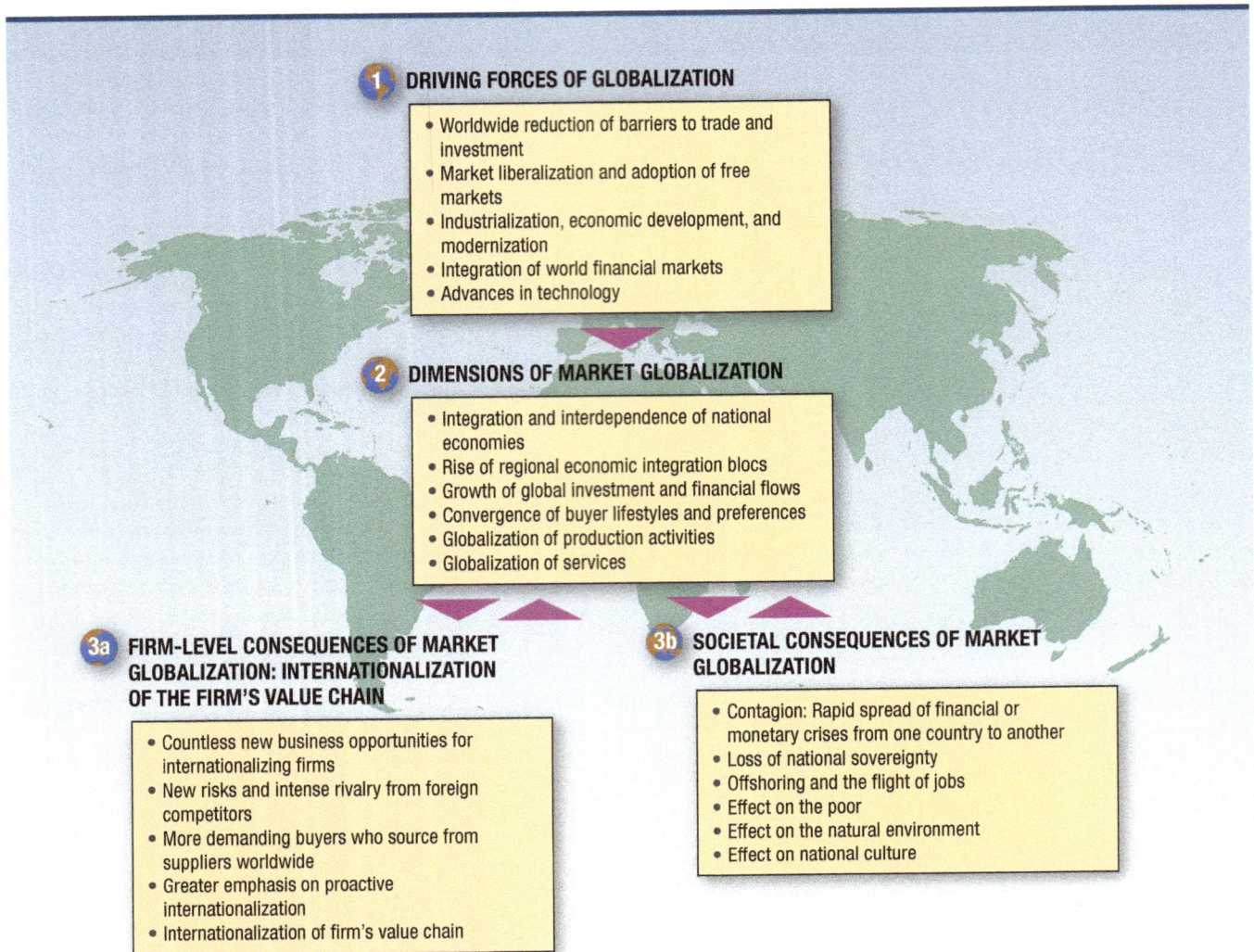

**① DRIVING FORCES OF GLOBALIZATION**

- Worldwide reduction of barriers to trade and investment
- Market liberalization and adoption of free markets
- Industrialization, economic development, and modernization
- Integration of world financial markets
- Advances in technology

**② DIMENSIONS OF MARKET GLOBALIZATION**

- Integration and interdependence of national economies
- Rise of regional economic integration blocs
- Growth of global investment and financial flows
- Convergence of buyer lifestyles and preferences
- Globalization of production activities
- Globalization of services

**③a FIRM-LEVEL CONSEQUENCES OF MARKET GLOBALIZATION: INTERNATIONALIZATION OF THE FIRM'S VALUE CHAIN**

- Countless new business opportunities for internationalizing firms
- New risks and intense rivalry from foreign competitors
- More demanding buyers who source from suppliers worldwide
- Greater emphasis on proactive internationalization
- Internationalization of firm's value chain

**③b SOCIETAL CONSEQUENCES OF MARKET GLOBALIZATION**

- Contagion: Rapid spread of financial or monetary crises from one country to another
- Loss of national sovereignty
- Offshoring and the flight of jobs
- Effect on the poor
- Effect on the natural environment
- Effect on national culture

**EXHIBIT 1.2**

**The Driving Forces, Dimensions, and Consequences of Globalization**

America Movil (www.americamovil.com) is a leading wireless phone service provider, with more than 225 million subscribers in 18 countries, that has pursued internationalization as a growth strategy. Based in Mexico, America Movil internationalized mainly through foreign direct investment (FDI) with initial operations in Brazil and Colombia. It then expanded to Ecuador, Chile, the Netherlands, and numerous other foreign markets. The firm entered into a joint venture with Citigroup to fund expansion in South America. It acquired Verizon's telephone operations in Puerto Rico. In each case, America Movil took advantage of such globalization trends as harmonizing communications technologies, converging buyer characteristics, and reduced trade and investment barriers. As emerging markets transform into sophisticated economies, they leapfrog older telecom technologies and embrace contemporary mobile phone technology—a boon to America Movil.

To minimize costs, many of the firm's cell phones are essentially identical worldwide. They are adapted only to accommodate for local languages, regulations, and telephone standards. America Movil's positioning emphasizes a global brand that is recognized everywhere. Worldwide convergence of buyer lifestyles and incomes help facilitate this transnational approach. Management coordinates operations on a global scale and applies common business processes in procurement and quality control. The strategies of product standardization, global branding, and selling to customers worldwide owe much of their success to the globalization of markets.[7]

**1.2** Learn the driving forces of globalization.

# Driving Forces of Globalization

Various trends have converged in recent years as causes of globalization. The following are particularly notable:

- *Worldwide reduction in barriers to trade and investment.* The tendency of national governments to reduce trade and investment barriers has accelerated global economic integration. For example, tariffs on the import of industrial and medical equipment and countless other products have declined nearly to zero in many countries, encouraging freer international exchange of goods and services. Falling trade barriers are facilitated by the WTO. After joining the WTO in 2001, China has made its market increasingly more accessible to foreign firms. The decrease in trade barriers is also associated with the emergence of regional economic integration blocs. The recent rise of nationalistic politicians in some countries has tended to hinder ongoing reduction of trade and investment barriers. However, the overall trend of increasing free trade continues.[8]

- *Market liberalization and adoption of free markets.* In the past three decades, free-market reforms have smoothed the integration of China, India, Russia and other formerly protectionist countries into the global economy. Numerous Asian economies—for example, India, Indonesia, Malaysia, and South Korea—embraced free market norms. These events opened much of the world to freer international trade and investment. China, India, and Eastern Europe have become some of the most cost-effective locations for producing goods and services worldwide. Privatization of previously state-owned industries in these countries has encouraged economic efficiency and attracted massive foreign capital to their national economies.

- *Industrialization, economic development, and modernization.* Many emerging markets—rapidly developing economies in Asia, Latin America, and Eastern Europe—have now moved from being low value-adding commodity producers to sophisticated, competitive producers and exporters of premium products such as electronics, computers, and aircraft.[9] For example, Brazil is now a leading manufacturer of Embraer commercial aircraft. The Czech Republic excels in producing automobiles. India is a leading supplier of software.

  Economic development results in increased incomes and living standards, an important measurement of which is *gross national income (GNI)* per person.[10] Exhibit 1.3 maps the levels of GNI worldwide. It reveals that Africa and several countries in Asia and Latin America are the lowest-income countries. These areas are also characterized by lower levels of globalization. A critical driver of rising income levels is the nation's volume of international trade. Exhibit 1.4 highlights the relationship between trade and gross domestic product (GDP). In this exhibit, trade is expressed as the volume of merchandise exports, and GDP measures the volume of goods and services production. The exhibit suggests that countries that undertake the most international trade, and whose trade levels have sharply increased in the past decade, also enjoy high and rapidly rising GDP.

- *Integration of world financial markets.* Financial market integration makes it possible for internationally active firms to raise capital, borrow funds, and engage in foreign currency transactions. Financial services firms follow their customers to foreign markets. Cross-border transactions are made easier because of the ease with which funds can be transferred between buyers and sellers. This takes place through networks of international commercial banks. For instance, the SWIFT network connects more than 11,000 financial institutions in some 200 countries. This global financial connectivity assists firms in developing and operating world-scale production and marketing operations. It enables companies to pay suppliers and collect payments from customers worldwide.

- *Advances in technology.* Technological advances are a remarkable facilitator of cross-border trade and investment. This is an important megatrend that requires greater elaboration.

# Technological Advances and Globalization

**1.3** Understand the impact of technological advances on globalization.

Perhaps the most important driving force of market globalization has been technological advances in information, communications, manufacturing, and transportation. Technological advances provide the *means* for market globalization to happen.

## Information Technology

Information technology (IT) is the science and process of creating and using information resources. Its effect on business has been revolutionary. The cost of computer processing fell by more than 30 percent per year during the past three decades and continues to fall. IT creates competitive advantages by giving companies new ways to outperform rivals.[11] Geographically distant subsidiaries of a multinational firm are now interconnected by intranets that facilitate instant sharing of data, information, and experience across company operations worldwide. MNEs use collaboration software to connect widely dispersed product development teams.

IT benefits smaller firms, too, allowing them to design and produce customized products they can target to narrow, cross-national market niches. Online search engines provide easy access to unlimited data for researching markets, competitors, and other key information. At a higher level, IT supports managerial decision making, such as the selection of qualified foreign business partners, by allowing firms to access key information and intelligence quickly.

Technology enables firms to interact with foreign partners and value-chain members in a more timely and cost-effective way. Such productivity advances provide substantial competitive advantages for the firm.[12] One result is the increased early internationalization by SMEs. Emerging markets and developing economies benefit from technological leapfrogging. For example, numerous African countries are adopting cell phone technology directly, bypassing the landline technology common to some advanced economies.

Panel (a) of Exhibit 1.5 reveals how the cost of international communications has fallen since 2000, expressed as the dramatic rise in the volume of international traffic in Voice over Internet Protocol (VoIP) calls. VoIP is the mother technology of Skype, FaceTime, and numerous other platforms that facilitate very low-cost international voice and video communications. Panel (b) of Exhibit 1.5 reveals the growth in Internet users in various regions since 2000. Africa has the fewest Internet users, whereas Europe and North America have the most, reflecting the level of economic and infrastructural development in each region.

## Digitalization

*Digitalization* refers to enabling or transforming business functions, operations, and activities by leveraging digital technologies and digitized data. Digital connectivity has become possible because of advanced IT and telecommunications technologies. Digital networks provide a global platform through which people and organizations interact, collaborate, obtain information, and develop strategies. Digital flows of information and commerce are connecting the world more than ever before. E-commerce now encompasses a vast range of platforms and applications that facilitate international buying and selling of goods and services online. For example, sharing-economy firms such as Uber and Airbnb use specialized software and the Internet to facilitate the joint creation of value and services between asset users and asset owners. Around the world, Uber allows people who need temporary transportation to hire drivers and vehicles owned by others. Airbnb allows travelers to rent other people's homes.

Digitalization is transforming interactions among customers, employees, business partners and investors by connecting locations, products, services, and data.[13] Large-scale data analysis helps uncover breakthrough business insights and develop products, services, and experiences tailored to specific customer needs. For example, automakers continuously collect data on how customers use their cars and then utilize the data to improve product quality and the driving experience. Leveraging emergent technologies such as virtual reality and artificial intelligence helps to create innovative products and services that provide competitive advantages. Robots, artificial intelligence, and IT-based automation improve operational efficiency and deliver more engaging customer experiences. For example, MNEs are introducing sensors into manufacturing operations to improve production efficiency, predict maintenance problems, and perform repairs from remote locations.

GREENLAND

CELAND

ALASKA

C A N A D A

PACIFIC
OCEAN

UNITED STATES
OF AMERICA

NORTH
ATLANTIC
OCEAN

HAWAII

MEXICO

CUBA

DOMINICAN
REPUBLIC

JAMAICA

BELIZE
GUATEMALA    HONDURAS    HAITI    PUERTO
RICO

EL SALVADOR    NICARAGUA

COSTA RICA

PANAMA

TRINIDAD &
TOBAGO

VENEZUELA

GUYANA    FRENCH
GUIANA

SURINAME

COLOMBIA

GALAPAGOS
ISLANDS

ECUADOR

B R A Z I L

PERU

SWEDEN    LATVIA

DENMARK    LITHUANIA
RUSSIA

NETHERLANDS    BELARUS

BELGIUM    GERMANY    POLAND

LUXEMBOURG    CZECH
REP.    SLOVAKIA    UKRAINE

FRANCE    LIECHTENSTEIN    AUSTRIA
SWITZERLAND    SLOVENIA    HUNGARY    MOLDOVA

CROATIA    ROMANIA

MONACO    SAN
MARINO    BOSNIA    SERBIA AND
ANDORRA    HERZEGOVINA    MONTENEGRO    BULGARIA    Black Sea

ITALY    MACEDONIA
ALBANIA

GREECE    T U R K E Y

ALGERIA

TUNISIA    MALTA    CYPRUS

LIBYA

BOLIVIA

PARAGUAY

URUGUAY

ARGENTINA

FALKLAND ISLANDS/
MALVINAS

**EXHIBIT 1.3**

**Gross National Income, in U.S. Dollars**

*Source:* Based on World Bank (2018); World Bank Development Indicator database, GNI per capita, Atlas method (current US$), www.data.worldbank.org.

Gross National Income
per Capita, in U.S. Dollars, 2017

- 20,000 or more
- 8,000–19,999
- 4,000–7,999
- 1,500–3,999
- Less than 1,500
- No data

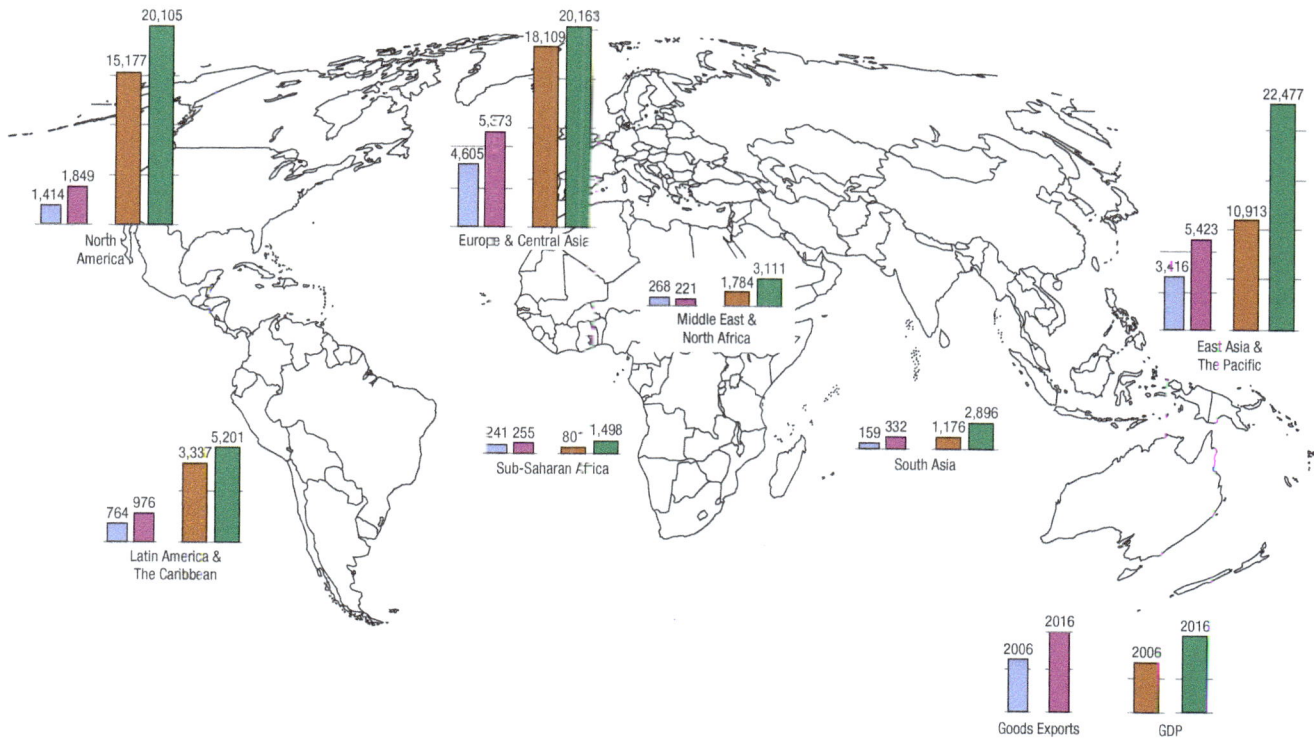

North America
1,414 | 1,849 | 15,177 | 20,105

Europe & Central Asia
4,605 | 5,573 | 18,109 | 20,163

Middle East & North Africa
268 | 221 | 1,784 | 3,111

East Asia & The Pacific
3,416 | 5,423 | 10,913 | 22,477

Sub-Saharan Africa
241 | 255 | 80 | 1,498

South Asia
159 | 332 | 1,176 | 2,896

Latin America & The Caribbean
764 | 976 | 3,337 | 5,201

Goods Exports: 2006 | 2016
GDP: 2006 | 2016

**EXHIBIT 1.4**

**Relationship Between Trade and GDP Growth, in Billions of U.S. Dollars**

*Source:* Based on World Bank, Data, 2018, www.worldbank.org.

Digitalization has numerous consequences. The marginal cost of transmitting data and information worldwide is now essentially zero. Digitalization has reduced both the importance of geographic boundaries and the costs of international interactions and transactions. Companies extensively use digital tools to support innovation and improve productivity and the effectiveness of value chains worldwide. All kinds of firms use digital platforms to connect with customers and suppliers around the world. Competition is becoming more sophisticated and global. For example, Alibaba and Amazon are connecting global suppliers and imposing competitive pressures on traditional retailers worldwide.[14]

**EXHIBIT 1.5**

**Growth of Global Communication and the Internet**

*Sources:* BridgeVoicePluto, "Disrupting Wholesale Telecom: VoIP Market Trends and Predictions," 2017, www.bridgevoice.com; IMF, *World Economic Outlook* (Washington, DC: International Monetary Fund, 2017); United Nations International Telecommunications Union, *ICT Statistics*, 2017, www.itu.int; Internet World Stats, *Internet Usage Statistics*, 2018, www.internetworldstats.com.

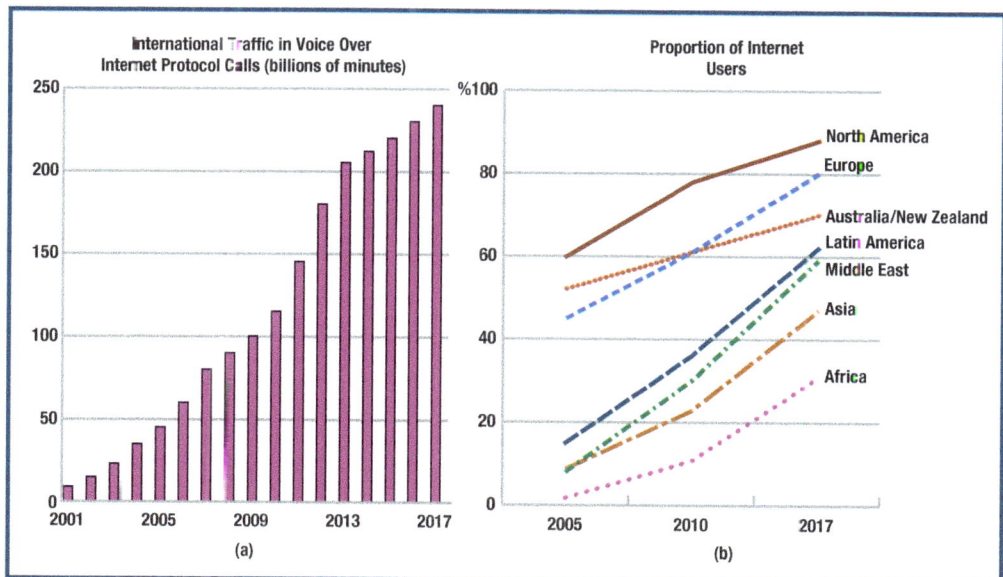

## Communications

The Internet and Internet-dependent systems such as intranets, extranets, social media, and email connect billions of people and companies. Marketers use the Internet to promote the widest range of products and services to customers worldwide. Transmitting voice, data, and images is essentially costless, making Seoul, Stockholm, and San Jose next-door neighbors. South Korea has nearly 100 percent Internet access, with one of the fastest broadband networks worldwide. Koreans use their phones to pay bills, do banking, and watch news programs.

The Internet opens the global marketplace to SMEs and other firms that would normally lack the resources to do international business. By establishing a presence on the web, even tiny enterprises can take the first step to become multinational firms. Services as diverse as designing an engine, monitoring a security camera, selling insurance, and doing secretarial work are easier to export than car parts or refrigerators. In China, thousands of rural farmers use Internet sites such as www.taobao.com to market their produce to urban consumers.[15]

## Ethical Connections

In six years, Nigeria increased its telecom infrastructure from just 500,000 phone lines to more than 30 million cellular subscribers. The result has been a dramatic rise in productivity and commerce, which has helped improve living standards. Greater access to cell phones saves wasted trips, provides access to education and health care services, and facilitates communication between suppliers and customers. MNE telecom investment in Africa allows firms to fulfill social responsibilities and improve the lives of millions of poor people.

Countries need modern infrastructure in communications, such as reliable telephone systems, to support economic development. Mobile phones are the most transformative technology in developing economies. Fortunately, cell phone infrastructure is inexpensive and relatively easy to install.

The *Internet of Things* refers to machine-to-machine connectivity online. Worldwide, mobile telephony and app development have grown enormously, creating millions of jobs, increasing productivity, and producing big GDP gains. The number of smartphone users reached 3 billion in 2017, double the figure in 2013. People everywhere are now online.[16]

Social media such as Snapchat, Instagram, and WeChat facilitate the free flow of information, deepening the pace and impact of globalization. Global communities created by platforms such as YouTube and Twitter help mobilize audiences that transcend borders and geographic distance. The "Arab Spring" in the Middle East was facilitated in large part by social media. In view of this, in some authoritarian countries, national governments restrict access to social media, fearing the role it can play in accelerating social movements. Many companies and other organizations leverage social media to communicate with their publics through direct sales, advertising, and public relations. Social media provide the means to communicate directly with millions of connected individuals in new markets. Puma uses Twitter and other platforms to market sportswear to customers in Europe and Latin America ahead of the World Cup games. McDonald's used the social media site Renren.com to market burgers and sundaes to customers in China. Social media provide various means to reach important audiences in markets around the world.[17]

## Manufacturing

Digitalization and computer-aided design (CAD) of products, robotics, and production lines have transformed manufacturing, mainly by reducing production costs. Revolutionary developments facilitate low-scale and low-cost manufacturing; firms can make products cost-effectively even in short production runs. Online platforms are increasing the productivity of business and industrial activity. Such developments benefit international business by allowing firms to adapt products more efficiently to individual

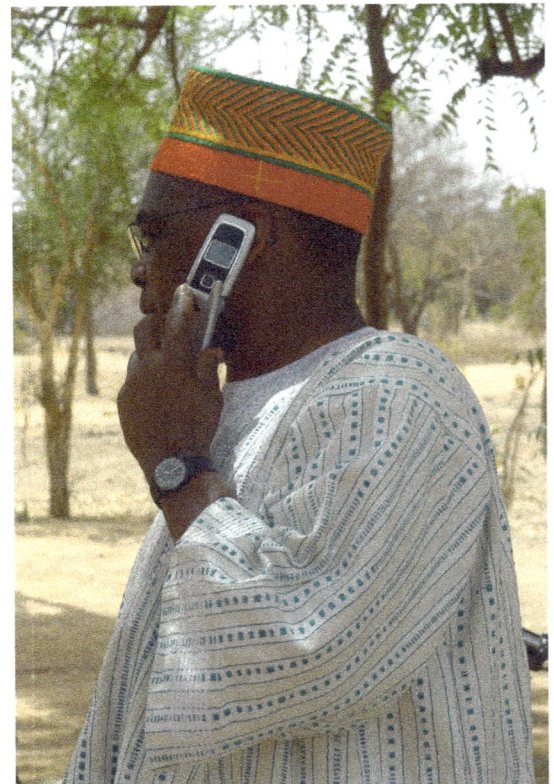

*Source:* © Gilles Paire/Fotolia

Increasing availability of cell phones in Africa has helped spur economic growth there.

*Source:* federico rostagno/123rf

Advances in transportation and low freight costs have helped spur market globalization. Triple E class ships can carry thousands of shipping containers.

foreign markets, profitably target small national markets, and compete more effectively with foreign competitors that enjoy cost advantages.[18]

## Transportation

Firms consider the cost of transporting raw materials, components, and finished products when deciding to either export or manufacture abroad. If transport costs to an important market are high, management may decide to manufacture merchandise in that market. The development of fuel-efficient jumbo jets, giant ocean-going freighters, and new transportation technology has greatly reduced shipping times and costs. In recent decades, the volume of international shipping has increased dramatically. For example, world traffic in shipping containers increased from 225 million 20-foot equivalent containers in 2000 to more than 700 million such containers in 2017, a rise of 210 percent. Containers are the big boxes, usually 40 feet long (about 12 meters), loaded on top of ships, trucks, and rail cars that carry the world's cargo. Today's ocean-going container ships hold more than 2,500 containers.[19]

Transportation of products has been revolutionized over time. However, growing transportation poses an increasing threat to the natural environment in terms of the usage of energy and other resources.

Shipbuilders, such as Maersk, have recently introduced container ships that can carry upward of 9,000 40-foot shipping containers. The vessels are so massive that only a handful of international ports can handle them, including Shanghai in China and Rotterdam in the Netherlands. These ships are used mainly to transport goods between Europe and Asia because they are too wide to pass through the Panama Canal. Technological advances in these Triple E vessels provide economies of scale that reduce the cost of transportation dramatically. They are energy efficient and environmentally friendly.[20]

**1.4** Learn the dimensions of globalization.

## Dimensions of Market Globalization

The globalization of markets can be characterized by several major dimensions.

- *Integration and interdependence of national economies.* Internationally active firms develop multi-country operations through trade, investment, geographic dispersal of company resources, and integration and coordination of value-chain activities. The collective activities of such firms give rise to *economic integration,* that is, increased trade and other commercial activities among the nations of the world. Governments assist this integration by lowering barriers to international trade and investment, harmonizing their monetary and fiscal policies within *regional economic integration* blocs, and creating *supranational* institutions. These include such organizations as the World Bank, International Monetary Fund, and World Trade Organization.
- *Rise of regional economic integration blocs.* Regional economic integration blocks consist of groups of countries that facilitate reduced trade and investment barriers among themselves. Examples include the North American Free Trade Agreement area (NAFTA), the Asia Pacific Economic Cooperation zone (APEC), and Mercosur in Latin America. In more advanced arrangements, such as a common market, the barriers to the cross-border flow of labor and capital are completely removed. A notable example is the European Union (www.europa.eu). The European Union has adopted free trade among its member countries and harmonized fiscal and monetary policies and business regulations.
- *Growth of global investment and financial flows.* In the process of conducting international transactions, firms and governments buy and sell large volumes of national currencies (such as dollars, euros, and yen). The free movement of capital around the world—the globalization of capital—extends economic activities across the globe. It further increases interconnectedness among world economies. The bond market has gained worldwide scope, with foreign bonds representing a major source of debt financing for governments and firms.

- *Convergence of consumer lifestyles and preferences.* Consumers around the world increasingly spend their money and time in similar ways. Many aspects of lifestyles and preferences are converging. Shoppers in New York, Paris, and Shanghai increasingly demand similar household goods, clothing, automobiles, and electronics. Teenagers everywhere are attracted to iPhones, Levi's jeans, and Hollywood movies. Major brands enjoy a global following encouraged by movies, global media, and the Internet. Movies such as *Transformers* and *The Hunger Games* have developed global audiences of fans. Convergence of preferences is also occurring in industrial markets, where professional buyers source raw materials, parts, and components that are increasingly *standardized*—that is, similar or identical in design and structure.
- *Globalization of production.* Intense global competition is forcing firms to reduce their costs of production. Companies cut their costs and selling prices through economies of scale, standardization of finished products, and shifting manufacturing and procurement to foreign locations with less expensive labor. For example, firms in the auto and textile industries have relocated their manufacturing to low labor-cost locations such as China, Mexico, and Poland.
- *Globalization of services.* The services sector—banking, hospitality, retailing, and other service industries—is undergoing widespread internationalization. The real estate firm REMAX has established more than 6,500 offices in some 100 countries. Firms increasingly outsource business processes and other services in the value chain to vendors located abroad. In a relatively new trend, many people go abroad to undergo medical procedures, such as cataract and knee surgeries, to save money.[21]

*Source:* Robert Harding Picture Library Ltd/Alamy

Google is one of many multinational enterprises that contribute to convergence of consumer lifestyles and preferences.

## Firm-Level Consequences of Market Globalization: Internationalization of the Firm's Value Chain

**1.5** Understand the firm-level consequences of market globalization.

The most direct consequence of market globalization is on the firm's value chain. Globalization compels firms to organize their sourcing, manufacturing, marketing, and other value-adding activities on a global scale to achieve cost advantages and time efficiencies. In a typical value chain, the firm conducts research and product development (R&D), purchases production inputs, and assembles or manufactures a product or service. Next, the firm performs marketing activities such as pricing, promotion, and selling, followed by distribution of the product in targeted markets and after-sales service. The value-chain concept is useful in international business because it helps clarify *what* activities are performed *where* in the world. For example, exporting firms perform many upstream value-chain activities (e.g., R&D and production) in the home market and many downstream activities (e.g., marketing and after-sales service) abroad.

Each value-adding activity in the firm's value chain is subject to internationalization; that is, it can be performed in locations outside the home country. Exhibit 1.6 illustrates a value chain in a typical international firm. As examples in the exhibit suggest, companies have considerable latitude regarding where in the world they can locate or configure key value-adding activities. The most typical reasons for locating value-chain activities in particular countries are to reduce the costs of R&D and production or to gain closer access to customers. Through offshoring, the firm relocates a major value-chain activity by establishing a factory or other subsidiary abroad. A related trend is global outsourcing, in which the firm delegates performance of a value-adding activity to an external supplier or contractor located abroad.

In the same month that German carmaker BMW launched a new factory in South Carolina, an aging textile plant a few miles away, Jackson Mills, closed its doors and shed thousands of workers. Globalization created a new reality for both these firms. By establishing operations in the United States, BMW found it could manufacture cars cost-effectively while more readily accessing

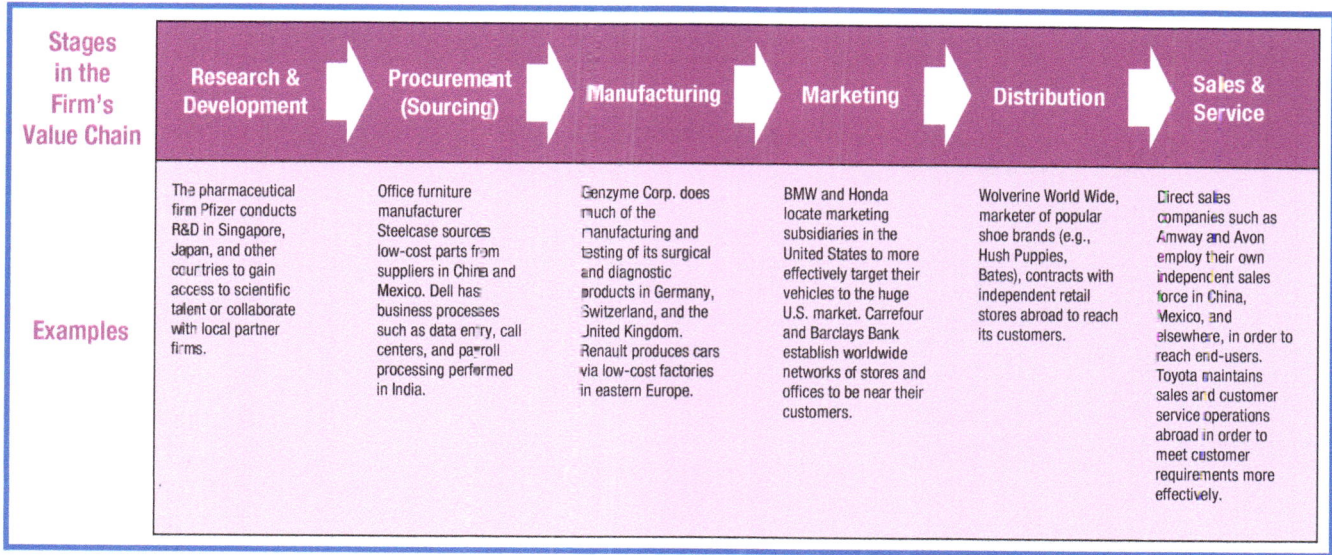

| Stages in the Firm's Value Chain | Research & Development | Procurement (Sourcing) | Manufacturing | Marketing | Distribution | Sales & Service |
|---|---|---|---|---|---|---|
| Examples | The pharmaceutical firm Pfizer conducts R&D in Singapore, Japan, and other countries to gain access to scientific talent or collaborate with local partner firms. | Office furniture manufacturer Steelcase sources low-cost parts from suppliers in China and Mexico. Dell has business processes such as data entry, call centers, and payroll processing performed in India. | Genzyme Corp. does much of the manufacturing and testing of its surgical and diagnostic products in Germany, Switzerland, and the United Kingdom. Renault produces cars via low-cost factories in eastern Europe. | BMW and Honda locate marketing subsidiaries in the United States to more effectively target their vehicles to the huge U.S. market. Carrefour and Barclays Bank establish worldwide networks of stores and offices to be near their customers. | Wolverine World Wide, marketer of popular shoe brands (e.g., Hush Puppies, Bates), contracts with independent retail stores abroad to reach its customers. | Direct sales companies such as Amway and Avon employ their own independent sales force in China, Mexico, and elsewhere, in order to reach end-users. Toyota maintains sales and customer service operations abroad in order to meet customer requirements more effectively. |

**EXHIBIT 1.6**

**Examples of How Firms' Value-Chain Activities Can Be Internationalized**

the huge U.S. market. In the process, BMW created thousands of high-paying, better-quality jobs for U.S. workers. Simultaneously, Jackson Mills had discovered it could source textiles of comparable quality more cost-effectively from suppliers in Asia. Globalization drove these firms to relocate key value-adding activities to the most advantageous locations around the world.

Without a doubt, globalization has created a crowded and intensely competitive global marketplace. As illustrated in Exhibit 1.7, globalization has meant that firms face intense rivalry from foreign competitors. This exhibit shows that in 1989 General Motors, Ford, and Chrysler together held nearly three-quarters of the market share in passenger car sales in the United States. By 2017, the percentage had fallen to 44 percent, and Chrysler had been acquired by the Italian automaker Fiat. The market shares of competitors such as Toyota, Hyundai, and others rose dramatically. Over time, the services sector also has been internationalizing at a fast pace. See the *You Can Do It: Recent Grad in IB* below featuring Terrance Rogers, who is working in the global banking industry.

---

**MyLab Management    Watch It! 2**

If your professor has assigned this, go to the Assignments section of **www.pearson.com/mylab/management** to complete the video exercise titled Rudi's Bakery Management in the Global Environment.

**EXHIBIT 1.7**

**Market Shares of Automakers in Passenger Car Sales in the United States, 1989 and 2017**

*Sources:* Based on Craig Trudell, "U.S. Automakers Seen Losing Market Share amid 2012 Growth: Cars," *Bloomberg BusinessWeek*, February 8, 2012, www.businessweek.com; J. Muller, "Automakers Gold Rush," *Forbes*, June 8, 2009, pp. 70–77; *Wall Street Journal*, "Sales and Total Share of Market by Manufacturer," February 1, 2018, www.wsj.com/mdc/public/page/2_3022-autosales.html.

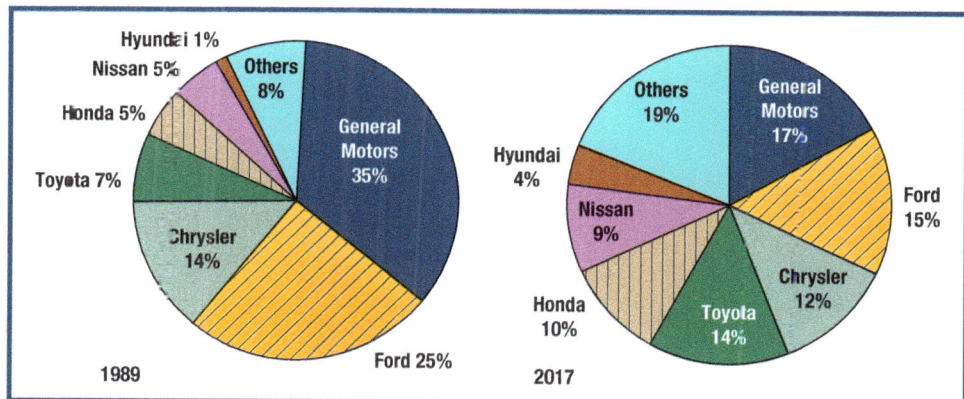

1989: Hyundai 1%, Nissan 5%, Honda 5%, Toyota 7%, Chrysler 14%, Ford 25%, General Motors 35%, Others 8%

2017: Others 19%, General Motors 17%, Ford 15%, Chrysler 12%, Toyota 14%, Honda 10%, Nissan 9%, Hyundai 4%

## You Can Do It    RECENT GRAD IN IB

### TERRANCE ROGERS

**Terrance's Majors:** Finance and international business
**Objectives:** Exploration, international perspective, self-awareness, career growth, and learning about foreign markets
**Internships during college:** Deutsche Bank
**Jobs held since graduating:**

- Business analyst at Deutsche Bank, New York
- Management associate at Deutsche Bank, New York
- Executive management rotation at Deutsche Bank, New York
- Executive management associate at Deutsche Bank, London and New York

After taking his first international business course, Terrance became fascinated with the idea of working abroad. As a university student, he enrolled in his college's International Business Certificate program. The program allowed Terrance to combine his passion for finance with his appetite for learning about culture and doing business abroad. Terrance took his first international trip through a short study abroad course. The course, "Financial and Managerial Issues in the EU," brought him to Paris and Brussels. Terrance and his classmates visited prominent businesses and the European Union offices to hear from leaders across multiple sectors. The experience allowed Terrance to believe that working abroad could be a real possibility for him.

After graduation, Terrance started his career as a business analyst with Deutsche Bank in New York. The position gave him experience in regulatory change, process improvement, and crisis management. Terrance got the opportunity to work on several global projects. After being promoted to management associate, Terrance worked directly with the chief operations officer of the Americas for his division.

After spending four years gaining experience in various areas of the bank,

Terrance took a position with numerous international responsibilities. Today, Terrance is an executive management associate, leading business strategy, finance analysis, and communications for the United Kingdom Executive Team. In this role, he splits his time between London and New York. He is responsible for interpreting financial drivers, product strategy, and operational issues that shape each business line in the region. He works directly with the head of Marketing and Communications to craft and execute communication strategy for the chief executive officer.

### Terrance's Advice for an International Career

Terrance owes his success to early exposure at his university to international business and study abroad. Terrance says that "international careers are a requirement for today's business leaders. Major clients don't just reside in the U.S. anymore, so if you want to have a long impactful career, you must find a way to gain some international exposure. Your boss will rely on you to be able to work with business associates from different cultures. Your clients will expect you to understand issues with a global perspective, and if you don't have

any global experience, your competitors (for jobs and clients) will be one step ahead of you."

### Success Factors

"If you want to work abroad, do the following things to increase your chances at securing an international role: (a) Work on projects that expose you to people in different regions across the globe; (b) mention your interest in working abroad early and bring it up in your annual review; and (c) find a way to impress the people who can make the decision. It becomes easier to make the move when the 'right people' know that you can deliver."

### Challenges

"Challenges like language barriers and cultural differences are things that should be faced as soon as you can in your career. Don't be afraid to make a mistake. It's much better to learn from cultural missteps now so that you can be a better business leader tomorrow." Globalization is a major dimension of business today.

*Source:* Courtesy of Terrance Rogers.

---

**1.6** Understand the societal consequences of globalization.

## Societal Consequences of Globalization

Our discussion so far has highlighted the far-reaching, positive outcomes of globalization. Major advances in living standards have been achieved in virtually all countries that have opened their borders to increased trade and investment.[22] Yet the transition to a global marketplace also poses challenges to individuals, organizations, and governments. Low-income countries have not been able to integrate with the global economy as rapidly as others have. Poverty remains a major problem in Africa and in populous nations such as Brazil, China, and India.[23] Let's consider some of the unintended consequences of globalization.

## Contagion: Rapid Spread of Monetary and Financial Crises

The world economy has experienced numerous financial and monetary crises. In 2008, for example, a major financial crisis was triggered by unsustainably high prices in housing and commodities. As real estate prices tumbled, many owners were left with mortgage debts greater than the value of their homes. Tens of thousands of those mortgages had been bundled and sold as investments on stock markets worldwide. As the value of these homes and securities plunged or became uncertain, stock markets also plunged.[24] The crisis began in the United States and spread around the world, like a contagious disease.

In international economics, **contagion** refers to the tendency for a financial or monetary crisis in one country to spread rapidly to other countries due to integrated national economies.[25] For example, excessive consumer borrowing can give rise to instability or overheating of national economies. Resultant crises can be aggravated by insufficient or ill-conceived regulation of the financial and banking sector or of the economy at large. As we will see later in this text, having a strong legal and regulatory framework is critical to national economic well-being.[26]

Financial or economic crises may weaken consumer confidence and reduce spending on consumer goods, services, and other consumables. Decreased spending, in turn, affects global commerce and international trade.[27] Following the crisis that began in 2008, global growth declined to levels not seen since World War II. Many national economies did not begin to recover until 2010. Economies in Japan and several countries in Europe have remained sluggish.[28]

Exhibit 1.8 shows how GDP growth in advanced, developing, and emerging economies varies over time. GDP in all three of these economies declined substantially during the recent global recession and financial crisis. One lesson of the exhibit is that, even following deep recessions, the global economy has always rebounded, and countries' GDPs have returned to growth.

## Loss of National Sovereignty

*Sovereignty* is defined as the ability of a nation to govern its own affairs; normally one country's laws cannot be applied or enforced in another country. Globalization, however, can threaten national sovereignty in various ways. MNE activities can interfere with a government's ability to control its own economy, social structure, and political system. Some corporations are bigger than the economies of small nations; Walmart's internal economy—its total revenues—is larger than the GDP of many of the world's nations, including Israel, Greece, and Poland. Large multinational firms can apply much pressure on governments through lobbying or campaign contributions and can frequently influence the legislative process.

The largest firms are constrained by market forces. In countries with many competing firms, one company cannot force customers to buy its products or force suppliers to supply it with raw materials and inputs. Resources that customers and suppliers use are made through free choice.

**Contagion**

The tendency of a financial or monetary crisis in one country to spread rapidly to other countries due to the ongoing integration of national economies.

---

**EXHIBIT 1.8**

**Percentage of Change in Annual GDP Growth**

*Sources: World Bank, Data, GDP Growth (Annual %), http:// data.worldbank.org, 2017; IMF, World Economic Outlook (Washington, DC: International Monetary Fund, September 2017); IMF, World Economic Outlook Database, 2017, www.imf.org; United Nations, UNData, "GDP Growth (annual %)," 2017, http:// data.un.org.*

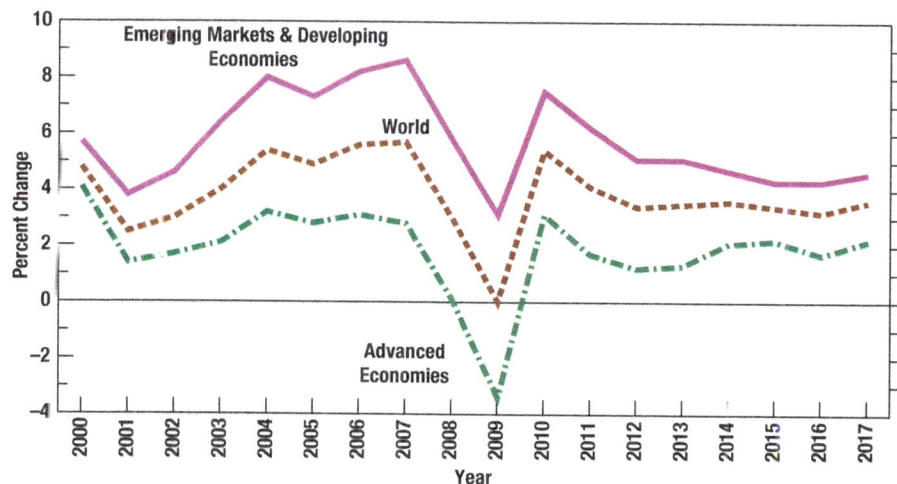

Company performance depends on the firm's skill at winning customers, working with suppliers, and dealing with competitors. Corporate dominance of individual markets is rare. In reality, market forces generally dominate companies. For example, Ford, Chrysler, and General Motors once dominated the U.S. auto market. Today, many more automotive firms—Toyota, Honda, Hyundai, Nissan, and Volkswagen—compete in the United States, along with newcomers such as Tesla. Volkswagen now leads the global market in annual unit sales. Home-country market shares of domestic U.S. automakers have tumbled.[29]

To minimize globalization's harm and reap its benefits, governments should ensure the freedom to enter and compete in markets, protect private property, enforce the law, and support voluntary exchange through markets rather than through political processes. Banks and financial institutions should be regulated appropriately. Transparency in the affairs of business and regulatory agencies is critical.

## Offshoring

Globalization has created countless new jobs and opportunities worldwide, but it also has cost many people their jobs. Ford and General Motors have laid off thousands of workers in the United States, partly the result of competitive pressures posed by carmakers from Europe, Japan, and South Korea. Ford, GM, and Volkswagen all have transferred thousands of jobs from their factories in Germany to countries in Eastern Europe.[30] *Offshoring* is the relocation of manufacturing and other value-chain activities to cost-effective locations abroad. For example, the global accounting firm Ernst & Young relocated much of its accounting support work to the Philippines. Massachusetts General Hospital has its CT scans and X-rays interpreted by radiologists in India. Many IT support services for customers in Germany are based in the Czech Republic and Romania.[31]

High-profile plant closures and manufacturing relocation have received much media attention. For example, Polaris, the U.S. manufacturer of all-terrain vehicles, moved its Wisconsin factory to Mexico to reduce production costs. In Australia, Toyota closed a Camry factory, resulting in the loss of thousands of jobs. Such closures disrupt local communities in various ways.[32]

Simultaneously, however, MNEs create millions of jobs abroad, which help raise living standards. For example, U.S. MNEs now employ about a million workers in each of Canada, China, Mexico, and the United Kingdom.[33] In developing economies and emerging markets, such positions help raise living standards.

## Reshoring

MNEs sometimes engage in *reshoring*—the return of manufacturing and services back to the home country. It is the opposite of *offshoring* which refers to the relocation of manufacturing to a foreign country, usually to take advantage of low-cost labor. For example, Ford and Boeing have reshored thousands of jobs back to the United States. Reshoring is done for various reasons, including the rise of wages and other business costs in emerging market countries as well as the desire to manage operations more effectively and locate value-chain activities closer to customers. General Electric reshored the production of energy-efficient water heaters from China back to the United States in order to manage inventory and transportation costs better. Symington's, a British food company, moved noodle production from China back to England in order to improve product quality, increase delivery speed, and manage the supply chain more effectively.[34]

## Effect on the Poor

Globalization has affected the poor in areas related to income distribution and worker exploitation by MNEs. *Income distribution* refers to the allocation of GDP and national income among the members of a society. In some countries, a relatively small minority, often less than 10 percent, holds most of the country's wealth, and the great majority of citizens live in poverty. This income inequality is substantial in several nations in Southern Africa and in Latin America, for example. Among the advanced economies, income inequality is less of a factor in Japan and most countries in Northern Europe due mainly to cultural factors and public policies. Income inequality is relatively more common in the United States, which is home to many highly paid executives and other wealthy individuals.

As nations' economies develop and per-capita incomes rise, globalization can worsen income inequality because many good-paying jobs in the manufacturing sector are lost as companies shift

Source: Peter Cook/Dorling Kindersley

Media attention and consumer concern are helping to improve wages and sweatshop conditions slowly in developing economies, such as those in South Asia.

production to low-wage countries. In the advanced economies, growing international trade coincided with falling wages in many industries as firms transferred manufacturing jobs to lower-cost countries, such as China and Mexico. However, income inequality is a complex and dynamic phenomenon. While the creation of new manufacturing jobs has increased wages for many individuals in China, Mexico, and other emerging markets, income levels among other, often larger groups in such countries have remained relatively stagnant.

In addition, automation and technology, to a large extent, have resulted in lower incomes for many people. Just as demand for high-skill workers has increased, demand for lower-skill or less-educated workers has decreased. This arises because many jobs that historically were done by low-skill workers are now performed by machines and digital platforms.[35]

Many MNEs have been criticized for paying low wages, exploiting workers, and employing child labor. Child labor is particularly troubling because it denies children educational opportunities. It is estimated there are more than 215 million children aged 5 to 17 at work around the world. About 73 million children are believed to work in hazardous conditions.[36]

Bangladesh, China, Colombia, Egypt, and the Philippines are examples of countries often characterized by poor working conditions. In Egypt, employees who strike or protest poor working conditions can be jailed. In China, many factory workers earn less than $3 per day and may have to work long hours. Companies ranging from Nike to H&M to the Gap have been accused of tolerating sweatshop conditions in their factories overseas.[37]

### MyLab Management    Watch It! 3

If your professor has assigned this, go to the Assignments section of **www.pearson.com/mylab management** to complete the video exercise titled Save the Children Social Networking.

Labor exploitation and sweatshop conditions are major concerns in many developing economies.[38] But some ask, "What other employment choices are available to poorly educated people?" A low-paying job is usually better than no job at all. Studies suggest that banning products made using child labor may produce unintended negative consequences such as reduced living standards for families.[39] Legislation passed to reduce child labor in the formal economic sector (the sector regulated and monitored by public authorities) may have little effect on jobs in the informal economic sector, sometimes called the *underground economy*. In the face of persistent poverty, abolishing formal sector jobs does not ensure that children leave the workforce and go to school.

Work conditions and salaries tend to improve, over time, in many developing countries. The growth of the footwear industry in Vietnam translated into a fivefold increase in wages. While still low by advanced economy standards, those growing wages are improving the lives of millions of workers and their families. Globalization tends to support a growing economy. Countries that liberalize international trade and investment enjoy faster per-capita economic growth. Developing economies that seek to integrate with the rest of the world tend to have faster per-capita GDP growth than those that fail to participate in the world economy.[40]

Exhibit 1.9 shows the global GDP growth rate from 2009 to 2018. Most nations are experiencing positive growth. The fastest-growing large economies are China and India. Exhibit 1.10 reveals that, on average, global poverty is declining over time.[41] This exhibit illustrates the income status of people in developing economies. Poverty remains a major factor in South Asia and sub-Saharan Africa (that part of Africa below the Saharan Desert), but even those areas have made much progress in the past decade. The Middle East and North Africa, Latin America, and East Asia are home to billions of people whose daily incomes have risen substantially. Much of these improvements are due to international trade and investment activities.[42]

## Effect on Sustainability and the Natural Environment

Globalization promotes manufacturing and economic activity that result in increased pollution, habitat destruction, and deterioration of the ozone layer. In China, for example, economic development is attracting much inward FDI and stimulating the growth of numerous industries. The construction of factories, infrastructure, and modern housing can spoil previously pristine environments. In eastern China, growing industrial demand for electricity led to construction of the Three Gorges Dam, which flooded agricultural lands and permanently altered the natural landscape. See the *Apply Your Understanding* exercise at the end of this chapter, which presents an Ethical Dilemma problem on the environmental damage done by a large oil company in Nigeria.

As globalization stimulates rising living standards, concerned citizens focus on improving their environment. Over time, governments pass legislation that promotes improved environmental conditions. For example, Japan endured polluted rivers and smoggy cities in the early decades of its economic development following World War II. As its economy grew, the Japanese passed tougher environmental standards to restore their natural environment.

Evolving company values and concern for corporate reputations have led many firms to reduce or eliminate practices that harm the environment.[43] In Mexico, for example, big automakers such as Ford and General Motors have gradually improved their environmental standards. Alcan in Canada (aluminum), Kirin in Japan (beverages), and Google in the United States (Internet services) are examples of firms that embrace practices that protect the environment, often at the expense of profits.[44] The Conservation Coffee Alliance has committed approximately $2 million to environmentally friendly coffee cultivation in Central America, Peru, and Colombia.

## Effect on National Culture

Globalization exerts strong pressures on national culture because market liberalization exposes local consumers to global brands, unfamiliar products, and different values. People worldwide are exposed to movies, television, the Internet, and other information sources that promote lifestyles of people in the United States and other advanced economies. Appetites grow for Western products and services, which are seen to signal higher living standards. For example, despite low per-capita income, many Chinese buy consumer electronics such as smartphones and TV sets. Advertising disseminates societal values modeled on Western countries. Hollywood dominates the global entertainment industry.

The flow of cultural influence often goes both ways, too. Cafe Spice is an Indian food company whose founder hails from Mumbai. The firm is transforming American tastes by selling curry dishes and other Indian favorites in cafeterias and supermarkets. Cafe Spice is helping to make Indian cuisine mainstream in the United States.[45] As the influence of the Chinese economy grows over time, Western countries will likely adopt some of China's cultural attitudes and behaviors. Chinese restaurants and some Chinese traditions are already a way of life in much of the world. Similar influences are evident from Latin America and other areas in the developing world.

*Source:* Sergey Zhukov/Shutterstock

Western companies can influence food preferences, but cultural values tend to remain stable over time. This Burger King is in Bangkok, Thailand.

**EXHIBIT 1.9**

The Growth of World GDP, Average Annual GDP Growth Rate, 2009–2018 (%)

*Source:* International Monetary Fund, World Economic Outlook database, 2018, www.imf.org.

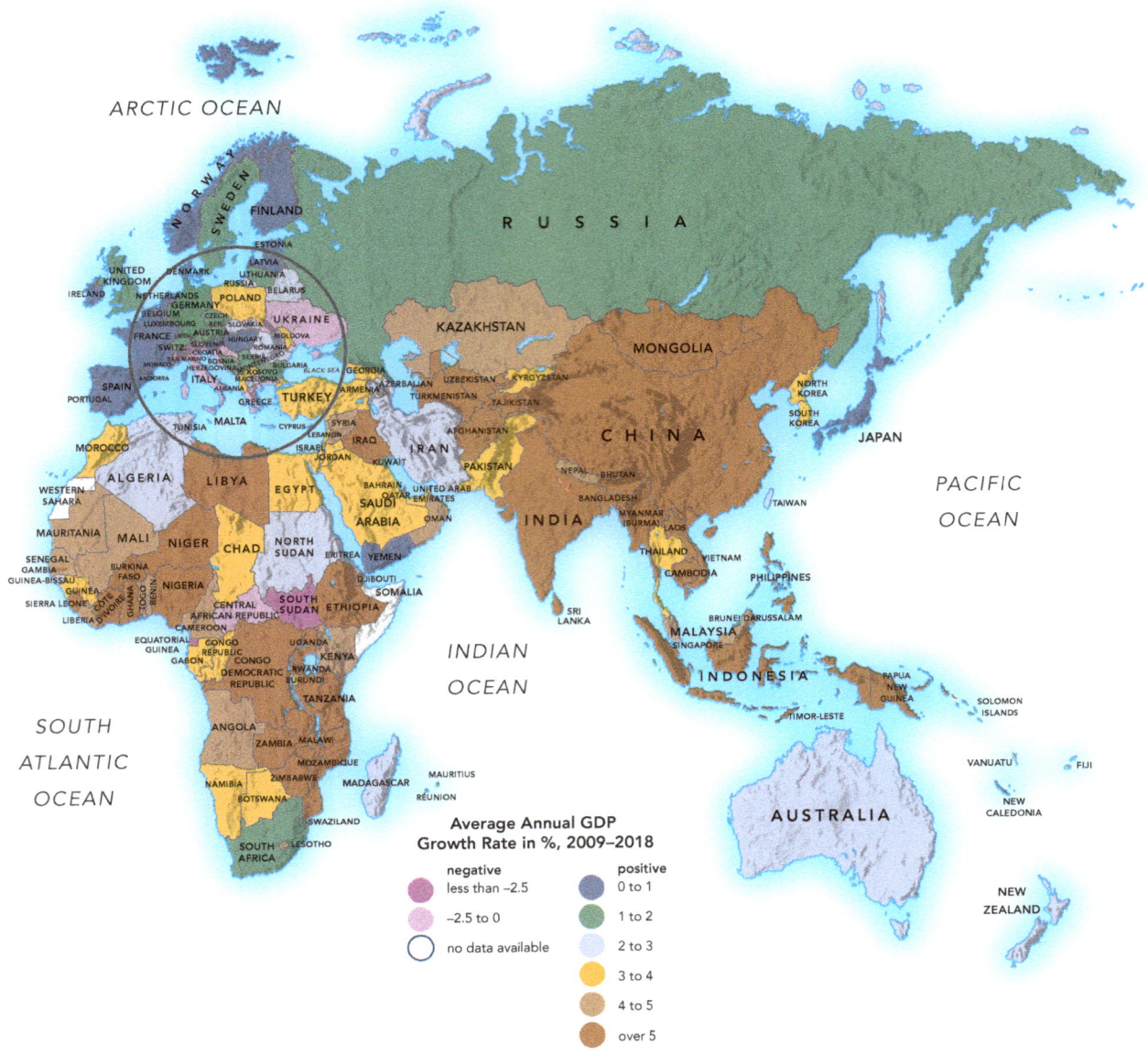

**Average Annual GDP
Growth Rate in %, 2009–2018**

negative
- less than –2.5
- –2.5 to 0
- no data available

positive
- 0 to 1
- 1 to 2
- 2 to 3
- 3 to 4
- 4 to 5
- over 5

**EXHIBIT 1.10**

**The Rise of Daily Income Levels, by Region, in U.S. Dollars**

*Sources:* L. Chandy, N. Ledlie, and V. Penciakova, *The Final Countdown: Prospects for Ending Extreme Poverty by 2030,* Policy Paper 2013–14 (Washington, DC: Brookings Institution); *Economist,* "Poverty's Long Farewell," February 28, 2015, p. 68; World Bank, GNI per capita, Atlas method (current US$), 2017, http://data.worldbank.org.

*Note:* The figures show average daily income per capita, in U.S. dollars, adjusted for inflation.

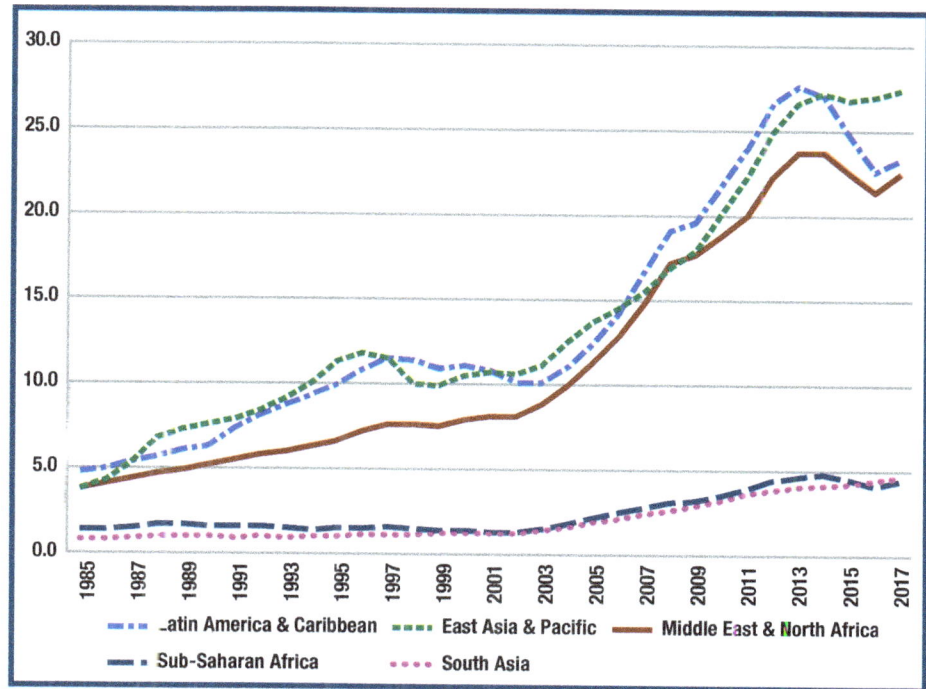

Cultural imperialism is offset by the countertrend of local nationalism. Although many products and services have become largely universal, people's behaviors and attitudes remain relatively stable over time. Religious differences are as strong as ever. Language differences are steadfast across national borders. As globalization standardizes superficial aspects of life across national cultures, people resist these forces by insisting on their national identity and taking steps to protect it. For example, laws exist to protect national language and culture in Belgium, Canada, and France

### Globalization and Africa

Africa is home to the poorest countries. The majority of its 1 billion people live on less than $5 a day. It is the area least integrated into the world economy and accounts for less than 5 percent of world trade. Although it has abundant natural resources, Africa remains underdeveloped due to many factors, including an inadequate commercial infrastructure, lack of access to foreign capital, high illiteracy, government corruption, wars, and the spread of AIDS.

Experience of the past half century suggests that traditional methods of trying to help Africa—mainly foreign aid provided by advanced economies—have achieved little success. Despite billions of dollars of aid to Africa, per-capita income is increasing relatively slowly.[45]

One of the most effective ways to alleviate African poverty is to develop more business-based models of development.[47] Several sub-Saharan African countries have recently experienced significant economic growth by increasing international trade in commodities. Africa is a major supplier of petroleum to Europe and the United States. Angola is among the top oil suppliers to China. This activity has developed a ripple effect of economic development. Because of the boom of certain sectors in Africa, there has been an increase in foreign banks, retailers, and MNE operations in the continent.[48]

Rwanda had developed business opportunities in sectors as diverse as mining, tourism, telecommunications, and real estate. China and India are beating out U.S. firms and quickly increasing their business dealings in Africa. Chinese companies are investing billions of dollars in the continent. All this international trade and investment is helping to address many of Africa's most pressing development needs.[49] Samsung has set a goal of $10 billion in African sales and is committed to training 10,000 African engineers and technicians to develop the capabilities needed for success. Even so, it will take many more years for Africa to achieve a critical mass of infrastructure and business culture sufficient to raise average incomes substantially across the continent.

Technology plays an increasing role in reducing poverty. Increasing use of mobile phones, satellite technology, and IT is helping farmers in Africa to increase crop yields and agricultural productivity. IT is being used to develop databases of information that support farmers in minimizing crop damage and improve farming methods. Data obtained from satellite technology helps farmers assess the likelihood of draught and prepare accordingly.[50]

## CLOSING CASE    A Debate on the Good and Harm of Globalization

People around the world are concerned about the impact of globalization, which they associate with job losses, declining national sovereignty, mass migration, and an intrusion of foreign values. Globalization has become a central theme in political, economic, and academic discourse. Recently, a major university sponsored a roundtable on the broader implications of globalization. The participants were an anti-globalization activist, a business executive, and a government trade official. Excerpts from the exchange provide diverse perspectives on globalization and international business.

### Activist

"One problem with international business is that it often ignores human rights and basic labor standards. Low-wage factories abroad create substandard working conditions. The activities of multinational companies not only result in job losses here at home, but also in low wages and exploited workers around the world. Just think of the sweatshops in Asia that make imported clothing. Think of the autoworkers in Mexico who live in horrible conditions and make only a few dollars a day. Also consider the poverty caused worldwide by the recent global financial and economic crisis."

### Business Executive

"Our country needs to participate in the global economy. Companies that export provide better-paying jobs, have more profits, pay higher taxes, and stimulate purchases from local suppliers. Foreign companies that invest here create new jobs, enhance local living standards, and pressure our firms to stay competitive in a challenging global marketplace. Exporters pay higher wages and provide better benefits than non-exporting firms do. Many companies need access to foreign markets because of the huge, upfront research and development costs they accumulate. One more pill is cheap; it's the cost of research to find a cure for AIDS that is prohibitive. Pharmaceutical firms can't do the necessary R&D unless they can amortize those costs over a huge, global marketplace. In the long run, uninterrupted international commerce is good."

### Trade Official

"The current administration believes in the value of free trade. The government strongly supported NAFTA, and this has already had a positive effect on the economy through increasing exports to Mexico, creating jobs, and leading to improved investment opportunities. Countries are forging ahead with international trade ties.

Canada has completed a free trade agreement with Chile. Economic ties lead to cultural ties and more peaceful relations. Also, it's hard for our government to promote freedom and democracy around the world if we're not promoting free trade."

### Activist

"We cannot overlook the detrimental effects of globalization on the natural environment. The more we trade internationally, the more irreparable harm will be done to the environment. International business means more environmentally damaging development. Companies internationalize so they can become more efficient. But if countries have weak environmental standards, then factories will be built with minimal environmental standards."

### Business Executive

"If we trade internationally, then living standards will increase everywhere. As living standards rise, awareness of and care for the environment will also increase. International business is good for the world because it creates wealth. The more affluent the people, the more they will care about their environment and pass laws to protect it. We are also becoming more responsive to concerns over social responsibility and environmental degradation. We have shown that a good economy and a clean environment are not mutually exclusive. We can have it both ways: a clean planet and a better quality of life."

### Trade Official

"I think part of the solution is to negotiate trade agreements that take environmental factors into account. International trade that disregards legitimate environmental concerns is counterproductive and defeats the political agendas of most governments around the world. It is clear that international trade must take environmental concerns into account."

### Activist

"International trade interferes with the sovereignty of national governments. When Apple or Toyota are bigger than most countries in Africa, it is harder for governments to manage policies regarding taxes, monetary policy, social issues, and exchange rates. And who are we, trying to impose our own cultural standards on the world? When I travel in Asia or Latin America, I see McDonald's all over the place. They see Western powers exploiting globalization, harming the economic, cultural, and environmental interests of the rest of the world.

"Global corporations claim they spread modern technologies around the world. But technology is good only if you have access to it. In Africa, you have no on-ramp to the Internet. You need access to a computer, which is difficult or impossible in countries where people make only a few dollars a day. When you're paid such a low wage, how can you afford technology? How can you afford to see a doctor? Globalization is widening the gap between rich and poor. As inequality grows, people have less and less in common. Multinational companies exploit poor countries and expose their people to harmful competition. Infant industries in developing economies can't make it when they're confronted with the power of giant multinational firms."

## Business Executive

"Companies increasingly recognize the importance of being good global citizens. Motorola has profited from its business in China, but it also contributes to developing educational systems in that country. There are more literate people, especially literate women, in China than ever before. Japanese MNEs invest in the communities where they do business. Companies are not all evil; they do a lot of good for the world, too. Bill Gates is doing more than any government to get people computers and connect them to the Internet. He has created the world's biggest fund to combat diseases of the poor. He and Warren Buffett are tackling many of these diseases. GlaxoSmithKline is working with the World Health Organization to find a cure for elephantiasis, a terrible disease that ravages people in Africa."

## Trade Official

"Globalization is complex and it's hard to tease out the good and the bad. Globalization has made rapid progress. Global poverty has declined and social indicators are improving around the world. It's true that income disparities have increased over the past 50 years while international trade has integrated the world economy. But the world has experienced a generally rising tide in terms of living standards. People everywhere are better off than they were

50 years ago. There are some exceptions to this, especially during recessions, but it's better to live in a world where 25 percent of the people are affluent and 75 percent are poor than a world in which nearly 100 percent of the people are poor, as was the case throughout most of history. There is a strong role for government in all this. Countries benefit from trade, but governments are responsible for protecting citizens from the negative or unintended consequences that trade may bring."

## Activist

"Governments have not done enough to regulate the excesses of capitalism. We saw this clearly in the recent global financial and economic crises."

## The Outlook for Globalization

In recent years, nationalistic sentiment has triggered an "our country first" mentality and skepticism or outright hostility toward globalization. The election of Donald Trump as president of the United States gave way to anti-trade policies and efforts to reduce immigration. After taking office, the Trump administration began renegotiating the North American Free Trade Agreement (NAFTA) and withdrew from the Trans-Pacific Partnership (TPP). In 2016, the United Kingdom voted to withdraw from the European Union. "Brexit" voters were motivated by concerns about national sovereignty and increasing immigration into the United Kingdom. Elsewhere in Europe, nationalist political parties came to power, reflecting a popular backlash against open borders and unfettered globalization.

Labor unions, human rights activists, environmentalists, and religious groups are among those opposed to globalization. Recent events represent a step backward from long-standing forward movement on free trade and global commerce. Many experts view the backlash as a predictable, temporary pause in the evolution of globalization. They argue that large-scale transformations often progress in fits and starts—one step back for every two steps forward. However, no one knows for sure what the future holds. Is globalization receding, or is it here to stay?

**AACSB:** Written and Oral Communication, Ethical Understanding and Reasoning, Reflective Thinking, Diverse and Multicultural Work Environments

### Case Questions

**1-4.** Do you think globalization and MNE activity are creating problems for the world? What kinds of problems can you identify? What are the unintended consequences of international business?

**1-5.** Summarize the arguments in favor of globalization that the business executive made. What is the role of technology in supporting company performance in a globalizing business environment?

**1-6.** What are the roles of state and federal governments in dealing with globalization? What is government's role in protecting citizens from the potential negative effects of globalization? What kinds of government actions would you recommend?

**1-7.** What is the role of education in (1) addressing the problems raised in the roundtable, (2) creating societies in which people can deal effectively with public policy issues, and (3) cultivating citizens who can compete effectively in the global marketplace?

**1-8.** Do you believe globalization is receding or advancing? Defend your answer.

*Sources:* Jacques Bughin, Susan Lund, and James Manyika, "Harnessing the Power of Shifting Global Flows," *McKinsey Quarterly*, February 2015, pp. 1–13; "The Globalization Website," retrieved from Emory University Globalization website, www.sociology.emory.edu/globalization; J. Rennie Short, "Globalization and Its Discontents: Why There's a Backlash and How It Needs to Change," *The Conversation*, November 26, 2016, http://theconversation.com; K. Ahmed, "TPP: What Is It and Why Does It Matter?", BBC, January 23, 2017, www.bbc.com; L. Elliot, "Brexit Is a Rejection of Globalisation," *The Guardian*, June 26, 2016, www.theguardian.com; N. Saval, "Globalisation: The Rise and Fall of an Idea That Swept the World," *The Guardian*, July 14, 2017, www.theguardian.com; P. Goodman, "More Wealth, More Jobs, but Not for Everyone," *New York Times*, September 28, 2016, www.nytimes.com.

This case was written by Mourad Dakhli and Gary Knight.

# END-OF-CHAPTER REVIEW

## MyLab Management

Go to **www.pearson.com/mylab/management** to complete the problems marked with this icon ⭐.

## Key Terms

contagion  18
globalization of markets  3

value chain  3
World Trade Organization (WTO)  4

## Summary

In this chapter, you learned about:

- **Market globalization as an organizing framework**

  Globalization of markets refers to the gradual integration and growing interdependence of national economies. Early civilizations in the Mediterranean, Middle East, Asia, Africa, and Europe all contributed to the growth of cross-border trade. Today's international trade was triggered by world events and technological discoveries and has progressed in phases, particularly since the early 1800s. The current phase was stimulated particularly by the rise of IT, the Internet, digital platforms, and other advanced technologies. The World Trade Organization is a multilateral governing body empowered to regulate international trade and investment.

- **The driving forces of globalization**

  Globalization is driven by several factors, including falling trade and investment barriers; market liberalization and adoption of free market economics in formerly closed economies; industrialization and economic development, especially among emerging markets; integration of world financial markets; and technological advances.

- **Technological advances and globalization**

  Advances in technology, the most important of which have occurred in information technology, digitalization, communications, the Internet, manufacturing, and transportation, are particularly important in driving globalization. These systems help create an interconnected network of customers, suppliers, and intermediaries worldwide and have made the cost of international business affordable for all types of firms.

- **The dimensions of globalization**

  Globalization can be modeled in terms of its driving forces, dimensions, societal consequences, and firm-level consequences. Globalization refers to the growing integration of the world economy from the international business activities of countless firms. It represents a growing global interconnectedness of buyers, producers, suppliers, and governments and has fostered a new dynamism in the world economy, the emergence of regional economic integration blocs, growth of global investment and financial flows, the convergence of buyer lifestyles and needs, and the globalization of both production and services. At the business enterprise level, globalization amounts to reconfiguration of company value chains—the sequence of value-adding activities, including sourcing, manufacturing, marketing, and distribution—on a global scale.

- **Firm-level consequences of market globalization**

  Globalization compels firms to organize their sourcing, manufacturing, marketing, and other value-adding activities on a global scale. Each value-adding activity can be performed in the home country or abroad. Firms choose where in the world they locate or configure key value-adding activities and internationalize value-chain activities to reduce the costs of R&D and production or gain closer access to customers.

- **Societal consequences of globalization**

  There is much debate about globalization's benefits and harm. Globalization was a major factor in the recent global recession and financial crisis. Critics complain that globalization interferes with national sovereignty, the ability of a state to govern itself without external intervention. Globalization is associated with *offshoring*, the relocation of value-chain activities to foreign locations where they can be performed at less cost by subsidiaries or independent suppliers. Globalization tends to decrease poverty, but it may also widen the gap between the rich and the poor. Furthermore, unrestricted industrialization may harm the natural environment. Globalization is also associated with the loss of cultural values unique to each nation. Nevertheless, trade and investment can help address many needs of developing countries, especially those of Africa.

## Test Your Comprehension

**AACSB and CKR Intangible Soft Skills to improve employability and success in the workplace: Written and Oral Communication, Ethical Understanding and Reasoning, Analytical Thinking, Reflective Thinking, Diverse and Multicultural Work Environments**

**1-9.** What was the precursor to globalization, and why was it important?

**1-10.** What important changes happened during the second phase of globalization?

**1-11.** Summarize the six dimensions of globalization. Which of these do you think is the most visible manifestation of globalization?

**1-12.** Describe the five driving forces of globalization.

**1-13.** What is the role of the World Trade Organization?

**1-14.** In what areas have technological advances had their greatest effect on facilitating world trade and investment?

**1-15.** How can internationalization improve value adding opportunities for a business?

**1-16.** What are the conditions under which contagion spreads from country to country?

**1-17.** It is possible for an organization to add value through overseas operations?

## Apply Your Understanding

**AACSB and CKR Intangible Soft Skills to improve employability and success in the workplace: Ethical Understanding and Reasoning, Analytical Thinking, Reflective Thinking, Application of Knowledge**

**1-18.** In 2017, the Singapore's Deputy Prime Minister Tharman Shanmugaratnam stated that the country was aiming to become a key part in the global value chain. The statement was made in the wake of the U.S. electronics firm Jabil announcing that they would be setting up a new manufacturing research and development facility in Singapore. For the minister, it showed that Singapore was well placed to provide all that was necessary to shorten value chains and enable products to be made much closer to the final marketplace. The net result was Jabil Blue Sky Singapore, which operates as an innovation and collaboration hub. How can a country secure a place in the global value chain? What are the advantages to a business in locating in such a country?

**1-19.** Globalization provides numerous advantages to businesses and consumers around the world. At the same time, some critics believe globalization is harming various aspects of life and commerce.

In what ways is globalization good for firms and consumers? In what ways is globalization harmful to firms and consumers?

**1-20.** *Ethical Dilemma:* Northern Energy, Inc. (Northern) is a large oil company with production and marketing operations worldwide. You are a recently hired manager at Northern's subsidiary in Nigeria, which provides jobs to hundreds of Nigerians and supports many local merchants and suppliers. Suppose Northern's drilling and refining practices have severely damaged the natural environment in Nigeria, polluting the air, land, and water. As a result, Northern has faced violent protests and much negative publicity in Nigeria. Develop suggestions for how Northern should address these issues. Keep in mind that top management is reluctant to invest significant new resources in Nigeria, given the firm's weakening business performance there.

## globalEDGE | INTERNET EXERCISES
Access globalEDGE™ at www.globalEDGE.msu.edu

**AACSB and CKR Intangible Soft Skills to improve employability and success in the workplace: Written and Oral Communications, Information Technology, Analytical Thinking, Diverse and Multicultural Work Environments, Application of Knowledge**

**1-21.** The KOF Swiss Economic Institute prepares the annual *KOF Index of Globalization*, which ranks the most globalized countries (enter "KOF Index of Globalization" at globalEDGE™ or other search engine). The index uses three dimensions to measure globalization: *economic globalization, political globalization*, and *social globalization*. Visit the index, and explain what each dimension represents and why each is important for a nation to achieve a substantial presence in the global economy.

**1-22.** Production in the manufacturing and services sectors increasingly has been outsourced to lower-cost locations abroad. The globalEDGE™ website has various resources that detail the nature and location of jobs that have been transferred abroad. Some experts note that the resulting foreign investment and increased demand in lower-cost countries are causing wages to rise in those countries, eliminating cost advantages from offshoring and narrowing the income gap between advanced economies and low-cost countries. In other words, offshoring is helping to reduce poverty in less developed economies. Others believe that manufacturing jobs will be consistently moved to lower-cost countries, turning China, India, and other emerging markets into top platforms for innovation and production. What do you think? Find three articles about outsourcing at globalEDGE™ by doing a search using the keywords "global outsourcing" or "offshoring," and write a report on the most likely consequences of these trends for your country, its workers, and its consumers.

**1-23.** A key characteristic of globalization is the increasingly integrated world economy. MNEs and many nations have a stake in maintaining the globalization trend. If the trend were somehow reversed, participants in international business, such as exporters, likely would suffer big economic losses. In many ways, globalization's role in the world economy is critical. But just how big is the global economy? What is the extent of international trade relative to the size of the global economy? What is the proportion of international trade in the GDPs of each of the following countries: Australia, Canada, Sweden, United Kingdom, and the United States? Consult globalEDGE™ to address these questions.

**1-24.** Globalization refers to the reduction of barriers to trade and investment, which is facilitating the internationalization of countless firms. Globalization is quickening and affecting firms around the world. However, it's also associated with various issues and challenges that confront firms as they undertake international business. Among the major issues are conditions in individual economies, indebtedness of national governments; power shifts to emerging markets, country risk in the developing economies, and environmental harm caused by industrialization. Visit globalEDGE™, and enter the keyword "globalization." Explore the information and websites that emerge from your search. Write a report on the most important contemporary issues that firms are facing as they undertake international business.

## Endnotes

1.  This discussion is based on Lawrence Beer, *Tracing the Roots of Globalization and Business Principles* (New York: Business Expert Press, 2011).

2.  The word *trade* comes from the Anglo-Saxon term *trata*, which means "to walk in the footsteps of others." Ancient trade routes were the foundation for a high level of cross-cultural exchange of ideas that led to the development of religion, science, economic activity, and government. The phrase "all roads lead to Rome" is not so much a metaphorical reference to Rome's dominance of the world 2,000 years ago but to the fact that Rome's territorial colonies were constructed as commercial resource centers to serve the needs of the Roman Empire and increase its wealth. In an empire that stretched from England to Israel and from Germany to Africa, the Romans created more than 300,000 kilometers of roads. Roman roads were the lifeblood of the state that allowed trade to flourish. The Roman Empire was so concerned about the interruption of its shipping lanes for imported goods that it dispatched army legions to protect those lanes.

In the Middle Ages, the Knights Templar acted as guardians for pilgrims making the hazardous journey to pay homage to the birthplace of the Christian religion. In addition to protecting tourists, this warrior order created the first international banking system with the use of rudimentary traveler's checks, eliminating the need for travelers to carry valuables on their person

In 1100, Genghis Khan not only united the Mongols but created an empire beyond the Chinese border that included Korea and Japan in the east, Mesopotamia (modern-day Iraq and Syria), Russia, Poland, and Hungary. He instituted common laws and regulations over his domain, most notably for the preservation of private property, to enhance and protect international trade.

Arab merchants traded in spices along land routes reaching from northern Arabia across modern-day Turkey, through Asia Minor, and finally reaching China. By concealing the origins of cinnamon, pepper, cloves, and nutmeg, traders gained a monopoly and controlled prices. Europeans came to believe that the spices came from Africa, when in fact they had merely changed hands in the region. Under the traditional trading system, spices, linen, silk, diamonds, pearls, and opium-based medicines reached Europe by indirect routes over land and sea. Representing one of the earliest systems of international distribution, the products passed through many hands on their long voyage. At every juncture, prices increased several fold. (This discussion is based on Lawrence Beer, 2011.)

3. C. Chase-Dunn, Yukio Kawano, and Benjamin D. Brewer, "World Globalization since 1795: Waves of Integration in the World-System," *American Sociological Review* 65, No. 1 (2000), pp. 77–95; Klaus Schwab, "The Fourth Industrial Revolution: What It Means, How to Respond," January 14, 2016, *World Economic Forum*, www.weforum.org.

4. Lawrence Franko, *The European Multinationals* (Stamford, CT: Greylock Publishers, 1976).

5. Credit Suisse Research Institute, "Getting Over Globalization—Outlook for 2017," January 19, 2017, www.credit-suisse.com; Louis Emmerij, "Globalization, Regionalization, and World Trade," *Columbia Journal of World Business* 27, No. 2 (1992). pp. 6–13.

6. Arindam Bhattacharya, Hans-Paul Bürkner, and Aparna Bijapurkar, "What You Need to Know About Globalization's Radical New Phase," *BCG Perspectives*, July 20, 2016, www. bcgperspectives.com; Prakash Loungani, Chris Papageorgiou, and Ke Wang, "Services Exports Open a New Path to Prosperity," *IMFBlog*, April 5, 2017, http://blogs.imf.org; World Bank, "Service Exports (BoP, current US$)," 2018, http://data.worldbank.org.

7. Company profile of America Movil, 2017, at www.hoovers. com/; Kyle Stock, "América Móvil Slims Down," *Bloomberg Businessweek*, July 14, 2014, p. 23; S.A.B. DE C.V., America Movil, *MarketLine Company Profile*, September 20, 2017, pp. 1–26.

8. Pankaj Ghemawat, "Globalization in the Age of Trump Protectionism Will Change How Companies Do Business—but Not in the Ways You Think," *Harvard Business Review*, July/August 2017, pp. 112–123.

9. Marcos Aguiar et al., *The New Global Challengers: How Top 100 Rapidly Developing Economies Are Changing the World*, Boston Consulting Group, May 25, 2006; OECD, *Economic Surveys and Country Surveillance*, 2017, www.oecd.org.

10. GNI refers to the total value of goods and services produced within a country after taking into account payments made to and income received from other countries.

11. Jacques Bughin, Susan Lund, and James Manyika, "Harnessing the Power of Shifting Global Flows," *McKinsey Quarterly* (February 2015), pp. 1–13; S. Tamer Cavusgil, "Extending the Reach of E-Business," *Marketing Management* 11, No. 2 (2002), pp. 24–29; Stephen Marshall, *The Story of the Computer: A Technical and Business History* (CreateSpace, 2017).

12. Bughin et al., 2015; Jacques Bughin, Laura LaBerge, and Anette Melbye, "The Case for Digital Reinvention," *McKinsey Quarterly*, February 2017, www.mckinsey.com.

13. McKinsey Global Institute, *Digital Globalization: The New Era of Global Flows*, 2016, www.mckinsey.com.

14. Bughin et al., 2017; Deloitte, "On the Board's Agenda: What Directors Need to Know About Digital Transformation," Deloitte Center for Board Effectiveness, October 2017, www.deloitte.com; McKinsey Global Institute, 2015.

15. Christina Larson, "In Rural China, You Don't Have to Read to Buy and Sell Online," *Bloomberg Businessweek*, February 13, 2014, pp. 17–18; Calum Turvey and Xueping Xiong, "Financial Inclusion, Financial Education, and E-Commerce in Rural China," *Agribusiness*, Spring, 2017, pp. 279–285.

16. Boston Consulting Group, "The Mobile Internet Takes Off Everywhere," *BCG Perspectives*, March 20, 2015, retrieved from www.bcgperspectives.com; International Telecommunications Union, *Measuring the Information Society 2017* (Geneva, Switzerland: International Telecommunications Union).

17. "The China Puzzle," *Journal of Advertising Research* 51, No. 4 (2011), pp. 634–642; Nicola Smith, "How to Get Fans to Cheer Your Brand On," *Marketing Week*, October 9, 2014, pp. 29–32; V. Taecharungroj, "Starbucks' Marketing Communications Strategy on Twitter," *Journal of Marketing Communications* 23, No. 6 (2017), pp. 552–571.

18. Marian Mueller, Bobby Bono, Steve Pillsbury, and Barry Misthal, *2017 Industrial Manufacturing Trends*, strategy&, www.strategyand.pwc.com.

19. Bruce Barnard, "Global Container Trade Expands at Fastest Pace Since 2010," JoC Online, May 15, 2017, p. 1; World Bank, "Container Port Traffic (TEU: 20 foot equivalent units)," http://data.worldbank.org, accessed January 5, 2018.

20. Greg Knowler, "Ready or Not, Here They Come: New Dawn Arises in Asia-Europe Trade as Mega-Ships Grow More Dominant. Are Ports Prepared?," *Journal of Commerce*, November 13, 2017, pp. 22–23.

21. Richard Barkham et al., "Globalization and Real Estate: Where Next?," *CBRE Rresearch*, May 2017, www.cbre.com; Debra Sandberg, "Medical Tourism: An Emerging Global Healthcare Industry," *International Journal of Healthcare Management* 10, No. 4 (2017), pp. 281–288.

22. Farok Contractor, "What Is Globalization? How to Measure It and Why Many Oppose It (Part 1)," *Global Business Blog*, June 3, 2017, https://globalbusiness.blog/author/fjcontractor; Stephen Fidler, "Globalization: Battered but Not Beaten," *Wall Street Journal*, January 21, 2015, p. A6.

23. Deloitte Consulting LLP, *Deloitte's Globalization Survey: Preparing for the Next Wave of Globalization*, 2014, retrieved from www.deloitte.com, March 16, 2015; World Bank, *World Bank Development Indicators*, 2017, http://data.worldbank.org.

24. F. Norris, "Crisis Is Over, but Where's the Fix?" *New York Times*, March 10, 2011, www.nytimes.com; Gabriele Parussini, "World News: Euro-Zone Economic Outlook Darkens," *Wall*

*Street Journal*, January 17, 2009, p. A7; Dave Shellock, "Signs of Deepening Recession Dent Confidence," *Financial Times*, February 14, 2009, p. 14; "When Fortune Frowned," *The Economist*, October 11, 2008, pp. 3–5.

25. "A Monetary Malaise," *The Economist*, October 11, 2008, pp. 20–25.

26. Shellock, 2009; Norris, 2011; Parussini, 2009.

27. Bin Jiang, Timothy Koller, and Zane Williams, "Mapping Decline and Recovery Across Sectors," *McKinsey on Finance*, Winter 2009, pp. 21–25; Marko Peric and Vanja Vitezic, "Impact of Global Economic Crisis on Firm Growth," *Small Business Economics* 46, No. 1 (2016), pp. 1–12.

28. "When Fortune Frowned," pp. 3–5; International Monetary Fund, www.imf.org; Shellock, 2009; Rich Miller and Simon Kennedy, "The U.S. Shops and the World Applauds," *Bloomberg Businessweek*, April 9–15, 2012, pp. 22–24; Jonathan Soble, "The Numbers Behind Japan's Sputtering Economy," *New York Times*, August 14, 2016, www.nytimes.com.

29. Liyan Chen and Andrea Murphy, "The World's Largest Public Companies," *Forbes Asia*, June 2014, pp. 50–80; Hans Greimel, "Assault on Fortress Detroit," *Automotive News*, January 19, 2015, p. 3; "When Fortune Frowned," pp. 3–5; International Monetary Fund, www.imf.org; Bertel Schmitt, "It s Official: Volkswagen Is World's Largest Automaker in 2016. Or Maybe Toyota," January 30, 2017, www.forbes.com; Shellock, 2009.

30. "The Day the Factories Stopped," *The Economist*, October 23, 2004, p. 70; Farok Contractor, "What Is Globalization? How to Measure It and Why Many Oppose It (Part 1)," Global Business Blog, June 3, 2017, https://globalbusiness.blog/author/fjcontractor.

31. Pete Engrail et al., "The New Global Job Shift," *BusinessWeek*, February 3, 2003, p. 50; Shailendra Jain and Prashant Palvia, *Global Sourcing of Services: Strategies, Issues and Challenges* (Singapore: World Scientific Publishing, 2017).

32. J. Newman, "Polaris Plant Closure to Begin in March; 484 Jobs to Be Lost," *Wisconsin State Journal*, December 23, 2010, www.host.madison.com/wsj; *The Guardian*, "Toyota Shuts Altona Plant and Leaves Thousands out of Work," October 3, 2017, www.theguardian.com.

33. *Economist*, "The Retreat of the Global Company," January 28, 2017, pp. 14–18; David Wessel, "U.S. Firms Eager to Add Foreign Jobs," *Wall Street Journal*, November 22, 2011, p. B1.

34. Filippo Albertoni, Stefano Elia, Silvia Massini, Lucia Piscitello, "The Reshoring of Business Services: Reaction to Failure or Persistent Strategy?," *Journal of World Business* 52, No. 3 (2017), pp. 417–430; Katy George, Sree Ramaswamy, and Lou Rassey, "Next-Shoring: A CEO's Guide," *McKinsey Quarterly*, January 2014; *IndustryWeek*, "Reshoring: By the Numbers," March 20, 2017, www.industryweek.com.

35. François Bourguignon, *The Globalization of Inequality* (Princeton, NJ: Princeton University Press); OECD, "Divided We Stand: Why Inequality Keeps Rising," 2011, www.oecd.org; Andrew Soergel, "Study: Globalization Has Boosted Income Inequality," *U.S. News & World Report*, May 8, 2017, www.usnews.com; World Bank, *GINI Index (World Bank Estimate)*, https://data.worldbank.org, accessed January 10, 2018.

36. International Labour Office, *Global Estimates of Child Labour: Results and trends, 2012–2016*, September 2017, www.ilo.org.

37. Christopher Blattman and Stefan Dercon, "Everything We Knew About Sweatshops Was Wrong," *New York Times*, www.nytimes.com, April 27, 2017; International Trade Union Confederation, "ITUC Global Rights Index 2017: The World's Worst Countries for Workers," www.ituc-csi.org.

38. Jörg Lindenmeier, Michael Lwin, Henrike Andersch, Ian Phau, and Ann-Kathrin Seemann, "Anticipated Consumer Guilt," *Journal of Macromarketing* 37, No. 4 (2017), pp. 444–459.

39. S. L. Bachman, "The Political Economy of Child Labor and Its Impacts on International Business," *Business Economics*, July 2000, pp. 30–41; Patrick Emerson and Andre Souza, "Is Child Labor Harmful? The Impact of Working Earlier in Life on Adult Earnings," *Economic Development and Cultural Change* 59, No. 2 (2011), pp. 345–385.

40. Farok Contractor, "Global Leadership in an Era of Growing Nationalism, Protectionism, and AntiGlobalization (Part 2)," *Global Business Blog*, June 15, 2017, https://globalbusiness.blog/author/fjcontractor; D. Dollar, "Globalization, Poverty, and Inequality Since 1980," *World Bank Policy Research Working Paper 3333*, June 2004 (Washington, DC: World Bank).

41. UNCTAD, *World Investment Report 2011* (New York: United Nations Conference on Trade And Development, 2012); World Bank, 2017.

42. Surjit Bhalla, *Imagine There's No Country: Poverty Inequality and Growth in the Era of Globalization* (Washington, DC: Peterson Institute, 2002); Contractor, 2017.

43. Keven Money, Anastasiya Saraeva, Irene Garnelo-Gomez, Stephen Pain, and Carola Hillenbrand, "Corporate Reputation Past and Future: A Review and Integration of Existing Literature and a Framework for Future Research," *Corporate Reputation Review* 20, No. 3/4 (2017), pp. 193–211; H. L. Zou, R. C. Zeng, S. X. Zeng, and Jonathan J. Shi, "How Do Environmental Violation Events Harm Corporate Reputation?," *Business Strategy and the Environment* 24, No. 8 (2015), pp. 836–854.

44. Michael Smith, "Trade and the Environment," *International Business* 5, No. 8 (1992), pp. 74; Ucilia Wang, "How Google Is Using Big Data to Protect the Environment," *The Guardian*, October 12, 2016, www.theguardian.com.

45. Richard Miller and Kelli Washington, *Restaurant, Food & Beverage Market Research Handbook*, 2016/2017, pp. 286–287.

46. "A Glimmer of Light at Last? Africa's Economy," *The Economist*, June 24, 2006, p. 71; World Bank, 2017.

47. Ans Kolk and François Lenfant, "Hybrid Business Models for Peace and Reconciliation," *Business Horizons* 59, No. 5 (2016), pp. 503–524; Dambisa Moyo, *Dead Aid* (New York: Farrar, Straus and Giroux, 2009).

48. Patrick Dupoux, Tenbite Ermias, Stéphane Heuzé, Stefano Niavas, and Mia von Koschitzky Kimani, "Winning in Africa: From Trading Posts to Ecosystems," *bcg.perspectives*, January 9, 2014, pp. 1–24; Christian Ebeke, Ntsama Etoundi, and Sabine Mireille, "The Effects of Natural Resources on Urbanization, Concentration, and Living Standards in Africa," *World Development* 96, August 2017, pp. 408–417.

49. Moyo, 2009; Irene Yuan Sun, "The World's Next Great Manufacturing Center," *Harvard Business Review*, May/June 2017, pp. 122–129.

50. Meera Senthilingam, "The Tech Solutions to End Global Hunger," *CNN*, February 24, 2017, www.cnn.com.

# Chapter 2

# Theories of International Trade and Investment

**Learning Objectives** *After studying this chapter, you should be able to:*

**2.1** Explain why nations trade.

**2.2** Learn about how nations can enhance their competitive advantage.

**2.3** Understand why and how firms internationalize.

**2.4** Explain the strategies internationalizing firms use to gain and sustain competitive advantage.

## Apple's Advantages in Global Competition

Since inception, Apple has sold more than 1.2 billion iPhones in 120 countries. Apple achieved worldwide sales of $230 billion dollars in 2017 with net income of more than $48 billion dollars. North and South America account for about 40 percent of total sales, followed by Asia with 30 percent and Europe with 25 percent. After the United States, China is Apple's best market, providing about 20 percent of total sales.

Apple products were once made entirely in the United States. Now, almost all of them are manufactured outside the United States.

Through *global sourcing*, Apple contracts with suppliers around the world, where more than 700,000 engineers build and assemble its products. One of Apple's key goals is to use comparative advantages from different countries. *Comparative advantage* is the ability of a specific country to produce a given product or service better or for a lower cost than other countries. For

example, Apple bases most of its iPhone manufacturing in China because of the country's high-quality, low-cost labor.

Consumers are one of the primary drivers of global trade, and they demand the best quality at the lowest prices. *Global sourcing* occurs when firms, striving for competitive advantage, capitalize on the comparative advantages of select countries to meet that demand. This results in increased imports through global trade.

Apple exemplifies superior *innovation*, including new product designs and more efficient production methods. It conducts most of its own research and product development in company-owned facilities in California. Innovation increases Apple's *productivity*, a gauge of how efficiently products are manufactured. Higher productivity allows firms like Apple to lower their production costs, which in turn increases profits and builds competitive advantage. An iPhone contains hundreds of parts, 90 percent of which

*Source:* humphery/Shutterstock

are produced outside the United States. Apple sources semiconductors from South Korea, memory chips from Japan, motion sensors from Italy, and rare metals from Africa. Apple then manufactures its products in China, the Czech Republic, and other low-cost locations to minimize the cost of its products. A lower price tag for iPhones or iPads stimulates sales, which in turn requires Apple to produce in high volumes. Manufacturing large quantities usually results in *economies of scale*—the larger the quantity produced, the lower the cost per unit to produce.

Global manufacturing and trade can also produce negative consequences. Apple's biggest supplier is Foxconn, a Taiwanese manufacturer that employs more than a million workers in its Chinese factories.

Employees there have complained about long hours, low wages, and crowded dormitories. Some have even committed suicide. In response, more than 250,000 protesters signed a petition demanding better labor conditions for Apple contract workers abroad.

Foxconn responded by increasing worker wages. This action reduced China's comparative advantage, but it also told the world of Foxconn's commitment to social responsibility. Apple also moved some production to India to take advantage of less expensive labor there. Apple, like many other firms, struggles with the right balance between economic considerations such as low-cost manufacturing and ethical issues such as ensuring safe and proper working conditions.

## Questions

**2-1.** Explain why most Apple products are made outside the firm's home country, the United States.

**2-2.** What is comparative advantage? How does Apple benefit from comparative advantage?

**2-3.** Describe the problems that Apple experienced with its supplier Foxconn. What steps did Apple take to resolve the problems?

*SOURCES:* Apple Inc., Form 10-K (Annual Report) 2017, retrieved from http://investor.apple.com; Eva Dou, "Why Apple Is Hiring More Engineers in China," *Wall Street Journal (Online)*, March 4, 2014, p. 1; Jamie Fullerton, "Suicide at Chinese iPhone Factory Reignites Concern over Working Conditions," *The Telegraph*, January 7, 2018, www.telegraph.co.uk; Hoovers. com, profile of Apple, Inc.; Dan Gallagher, "Apple's Bigger Smartphone Slice," *Wall Street Journal*, November 28, 2014, p. C8; Adam Lashinsky, *Inside Apple: How America's Most Admired—and Secretive—Company Really Works* (New York: Business Plus, 2012); Niall McCarthy, "Apple Has Sold 1.2 Billion iPhones over the Past 10 Years," *Forbes*, June 29, 2017, www.forbes.com; Christopher Minasians, "Where Are Apple Products Made?," *Macworld*, September 18, 2017, www.macworld.co.uk; Adam Satariano, "Apple Supplier Working Conditions to Be Targeted in Protest," *Bloomberg*, February 8, 2012, www.bloomberg.com; "Apple's Labor Practices in China Scrutinized After Foxconn," *Pegatron Reviews*, December 12, 2013, p. 2.

**Free trade**
Relative absence of restrictions to the flow of goods and services between nations.

The opening story about Apple illustrates the benefits of global free trade. International trade enables Apple to keep its manufacturing costs low and sell its desired products at competitive global prices. **Free trade** refers to the relative absence of restrictions to the flow of goods and services between nations.

Imagine a scenario in which countries did not trade with each other. What would we be missing? At a minimum, we would not have access to products and services made elsewhere. We would end up paying higher prices for offerings that other nations can produce more economically. We would waste scarce resources making some products that other countries could produce more efficiently, using fewer resources.

Similarly, try to imagine a scenario in which firms could only do business within their national borders. What would be the consequences? Paying higher prices for some domestic inputs they could have imported from other nations? What would they lose if they could not sell their products to foreign customers or gain competitive advantage by learning from foreign partners or acquiring ideas, capital, or expertise? Numerous other undesirable outcomes would follow.

Fortunately, nations and firms are generally free to do business outside their national borders. Free trade allows consumers to access the products they want at lower costs, which helps increase living standards worldwide. Although the rationale for trading and investing beyond national borders is intuitive, economists have grappled with thoughtful explanations of cross-border trade and investment.

In this chapter, we review these formal explanations or theories, many of which have been developed over time, some becoming ever more sophisticated. They address the underlying economic rationale for international business and why firms and nations trade and invest internationally. We consider questions such as:

- What is the underlying economic rationale for international business activity?
- Why does trade take place?
- What are the gains to nations and firms from international trade and investment?

**Comparative advantage**
Superior features of a nation that provide unique benefits in global competition. These features typically are derived from either natural endowments or deliberate national policies.

Central to understanding trade among nations are concepts of comparative advantage and competitive advantage, so let's explore these concepts next.

**Comparative advantage** describes superior features of a *nation* that provide unique benefits in global competition. These features typically are derived from either natural endowments or deliberate national policies. Also known as *country-specific advantage*, comparative advantage includes labor, climate, arable land, petroleum reserves and other inherited resources, such as those enjoyed by countries in the Middle East. Other types of comparative advantages are acquired over time, such as entrepreneurial orientation, availability of venture capital, and innovative capacity.

**Competitive advantage** refers to assets and capabilities of a *company* that are difficult for competitors to imitate. Such advantages help the firm enter and succeed in foreign markets. These capabilities take various forms such as specific knowledge, competencies, innovativeness, superior strategies, or close relationships with suppliers. Competitive advantage is also known as *firm-specific advantage*.

In recent years, business executives and scholars have used *competitive advantage* to refer to the advantages possessed by nations *and* individual firms in international trade and investment. To be consistent with the recent literature, we adopt this convention as well.

Exhibit 2.1 arranges leading theories of international trade and investment into two broad groups. The first group includes *nation-level* theories. These are classical theories, widely accepted since the eighteenth century. They address two questions.

- *Why* do nations trade?
- *How* can nations enhance their competitive advantage?

The second group includes *firm-level* theories. These are more contemporary theories of how firms can create and sustain superior organizational performance. Firm-level explanations address two additional questions.

- *Why* and *how* do firms internationalize?
- *How* can internationalizing firms gain and sustain competitive advantage?

We organize the remainder of our discussion according to these four fundamental questions.

> **Competitive advantage**
>
> Assets or capabilities of a firm that are difficult for competitors to imitate. They are typically derived from specific knowledge, competencies, skills, or superior strategies.

**EXHIBIT 2.1**

**Theories of International Trade and Investment**

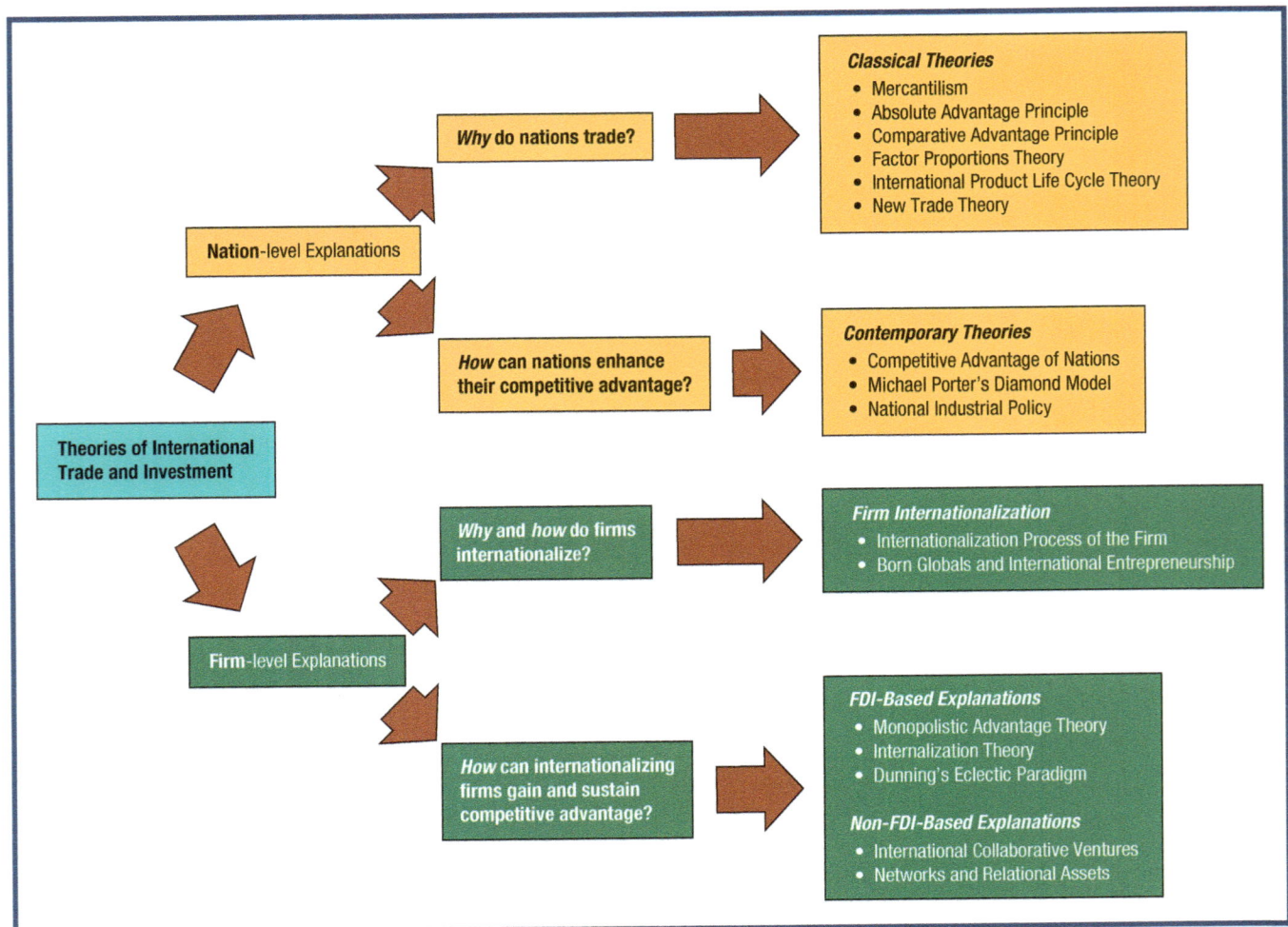

- **Theories of International Trade and Investment**
  - **Nation-level Explanations**
    - **Why** do nations trade?
      - **Classical Theories**
        - Mercantilism
        - Absolute Advantage Principle
        - Comparative Advantage Principle
        - Factor Proportions Theory
        - International Product Life Cycle Theory
        - New Trade Theory
    - **How** can nations enhance their competitive advantage?
      - **Contemporary Theories**
        - Competitive Advantage of Nations
        - Michael Porter's Diamond Model
        - National Industrial Policy
  - **Firm-level Explanations**
    - **Why** and **how** do firms internationalize?
      - **Firm Internationalization**
        - Internationalization Process of the Firm
        - Born Globals and International Entrepreneurship
    - **How** can internationalizing firms gain and sustain competitive advantage?
      - **FDI-Based Explanations**
        - Monopolistic Advantage Theory
        - Internalization Theory
        - Dunning's Eclectic Paradigm
      - **Non-FDI-Based Explanations**
        - International Collaborative Ventures
        - Networks and Relational Assets

**2.1** Explain why nations trade.

# Why Do Nations Trade?

Why do nations trade with one another? The short answer is that trade enables countries to use their national resources more efficiently through specialization and thus enables industries and workers to be more productive. These outcomes help keep the cost of many everyday products low, which translates into higher living standards. Without international trade, most nations would be unable to feed, clothe, and house their citizens at current levels. Even resource-rich countries such as the United States would suffer greatly without trade. Some types of food would become unavailable or very expensive. Coffee and sugar would be luxury items. Petroleum-based energy sources would dwindle. Vehicles would stop running, freight would go undelivered, and people would not be able to heat their homes in winter. In short, not only do nations, companies, and citizens benefit from international trade, modern life would be nearly impossible without it.

## Classical Theories

Six classical perspectives help explain the underlying rationale for trade among nations.

- Mercantilism
- Absolute advantage principle
- Comparative advantage principle
- Factor proportions theory and the Leontief Paradox
- International product life cycle theory
- New trade theory

**MERCANTILISM**   The earliest explanations of international business emerged with the rise of European nation–states in the 1500s. During this era, gold and silver were the most important sources of wealth, and nations sought to amass as much of these treasures as possible. Nations typically received payment for exports in gold, but although exports increased nations' gold stock, imports reduced it because they paid for imports with their gold. Exports were seen as good and imports as bad. Because the nation's power and strength increase as its wealth increases, **mercantilism** argues that national prosperity results from a positive balance of trade achieved by maximizing exports and minimizing or even impeding imports.

Mercantilism explains why nations attempt to run a *trade surplus*—that is, to export more goods than they import. Many people believe that running a trade surplus is beneficial; they subscribe to a view known as *neo-mercantilism*. Labor unions (which seek to protect home–country jobs), farmers (who want to keep crop prices high), and certain manufacturers (those that rely heavily on exports) all tend to support neo-mercantilism.

However, mercantilism tends to harm firms that import, especially those that import raw materials and parts used in the manufacture of finished products. Mercantilism also harms consumers because restricting imports reduces the choice of products they can buy. Product shortages that result from import restrictions may lead to higher prices—that is, inflation. When taken to an extreme, mercantilism may invite beggar-thy-neighbor policies, promoting the benefits of one country at the expense of others. By contrast, free trade is a generally superior approach.

**Mercantilism**

The belief that national prosperity is the result of a positive balance of trade, achieved by maximizing exports and minimizing imports.

---

## Free trade typically produces the following outcomes:

- Consumers and firms can more readily buy the products they want.
- Imported products may be cheaper than domestically produced products (if the exporting country benefits from some national advantages such as abundant resources).
- Lower-cost imports can help reduce company expenses, thereby raising their profits (which may be passed on to workers in the form of higher wages).
- Lower-cost imports help consumers save money, thereby increasing their living standards.
- Unrestricted international trade generally increases the overall prosperity of poor countries.

**ABSOLUTE ADVANTAGE PRINCIPLE**     Have you ever wondered why iPhones and iPads are not assembled in the United States, even though they are designed there? If you answer it is because labor cost is lower in China, you already know something about the absolute advantage principle. Because countries differ in national endowments (e.g., land, labor, technological capabilities), they are better off to specialize in the production of certain products and services and import others.

In 1776, Scottish political economist Adam Smith published *An Inquiry into the Nature and Causes of the Wealth of Nations*, a groundbreaking book. Smith attacked the mercantilist view by suggesting that nations have much to benefit from free trade. Smith argued that mercantilism deprives individuals of the ability to trade freely and to benefit from voluntary exchange. By minimizing imports and maximizing exports, a country wastes much of its national resources by having to produce products it is not suited to produce efficiently. The inefficiencies of mercantilism end up reducing the wealth of the nation as a whole while enriching a limited number of individuals and interest groups. Relative to others, each country is more efficient in the production of some products and less efficient in the production of other products. This simple idea that nations differ in their ability to produce a product efficiently is a well-accepted premise and is known as the absolute advantage principle.

Smith's **absolute advantage principle** states that a country benefits by producing primarily those products in which it has an absolute advantage—those that it can produce using fewer resources than any other country. (By "resources," early writers referred to tangible assets such as land and labor. Today, resources include intangibles such as knowledge and work ethic and capabilities such as design or zero-defect production.) Each country can increase its wealth by specializing in the production of goods in which it has unique advantages, exporting those goods, and then importing other goods in which it has no particular advantage. If every nation follows this practice, each can consume more than it otherwise could, generally at lower cost.

The absolute advantage principle applies to our daily choices as well. Consider the following scenario. Suppose you are employed as a corporate financial analyst. Imagine your car breaks down and you know nothing about repairing cars. You have the opportunity to take a leave from your job, enroll in a crash course in auto mechanics, and try to fix the car over several days. Alternatively, you can take your car to a professional mechanic. Which option would you choose? Most people will likely choose paying a professional mechanic since the alternative—forgoing wages you would have earned during the duration of the crash course—is less desirable. The professional mechanic has an absolute advantage in car repair. You have an absolute advantage in doing your financial analyst job. Using the services of a professional mechanic saves you both time and wages.

Now let's carry the absolute advantage principle to the country level. Imagine that there are only two nations: the Dairycountry, which produces and consumes only milk, and the Cattlecountry, which produces and consumes only beef. In this simplistic scenario, we ignore the cost of shipping products. Exhibit 2.2 presents the productivity of each nation. One unit of resources (labor) in Dairycountry can produce 10 gallons of milk or 8 pounds of beef. The Cattlecountry's efficiency is lower; one unit of resource produces only 2 gallons of milk or 4 pounds of beef.

We note that one unit of resources in the Dairycountry creates more of both products (10 gallons of milk or 8 pounds of beef) than the Cattlecountry (2 gallons of milk or 4 pounds of beef). Therefore, we conclude that the Dairycountry has an absolute advantage in both products; it is more efficient in the production of both milk and beef.

In the preceding example, keep in mind that we made a simplistic assumption by using a single resource: labor. Of course, in a real-world scenario, producing milk or beef requires multiple resources, labor, land, capital, appropriate climate, technical knowledge, and so on. The quantity and quality of these productive resources vary from country to country.

Even if the Dairycountry has absolute advantage in the production of both milk and beef, does it still make sense for the two nations to trade with each other? Are there benefits from trade for each nation? For the answers to these questions, we turn to the comparative advantage principle.

*Source:* creativehearts/123RF

Scottish political economist Adam Smith was among the first to articulate the advantages of international trade.

**Absolute advantage principle**
The idea that a country benefits by producing only those products it can produce using fewer resources.

**EXHIBIT 2.2**

**Productivity of the Dairycountry and the Cattlecountry in Producing Milk and Beef**

| | Quantity of products produced by one unit of resources (labor) | |
|---|---|---|
| | Milk (gallons) | Beef (pounds) |
| Dairycountry | 10 | 8 |
| Cattlecountry | 2 | 4 |

**Comparative advantage principle**

It may be beneficial for two countries to trade with each other as long as one is relatively more efficient at producing a product needed by the other

**COMPARATIVE ADVANTAGE PRINCIPLE**   In his 1817 book *The Principles of Political Economy and Taxation*, British political economist David Ricardo explained why it is beneficial for two countries to trade even though one of them may have an absolute advantage in the production of all products. Ricardo demonstrated that what matters is not the absolute cost of production but rather the *relative efficiency* with which the two countries can produce the products. Thus, the **comparative advantage principle** states that it will be beneficial for two countries to trade with each other as long as one is *relatively* more efficient at producing goods or services needed by the other. The principle of comparative advantage is the foundational logic for free trade among nations today.

To illustrate, let's recall the Dairycountry and the Cattlecountry scenario. Dairycountry has an absolute advantage in the production of both milk and beef. Therefore, you might initially conclude that Dairycountry should produce all the milk and beef it needs and not trade with Cattlecountry. However, it is still beneficial for Dairycountry to trade with Cattlecountry.

How can this be true? The answer is that rather than absolute efficiency, it is the *relative efficiency* between the two countries that matters. As we see in Exhibit 2.2, Dairycountry is five times (10/2) more efficient at producing milk but only twice (8/4) as efficient than Cattlecountry at producing beef. Although Cattlecountry is unable to produce either milk or beef more efficiently than Dairycountry, it produces beef more efficiently than it produces milk.

Conversely, Dairycountry is relatively more efficient at producing milk than beef (10/2 versus 8/4). Thus, Dairycountry should devote all its resources to producing milk and import all the beef it needs from Cattlecountry. Cattlecountry should specialize in producing beef and import its milk from Dairycountry. Each country can then produce and consume relatively more of the goods it desires for a given level of resource.

Recall the car repair example. Let's assume you are a mechanically inclined do-it-yourselfer and can fix your car faster than the professional auto mechanic. You hold absolute advantages both in car repair *and* in financial analysis. The auto mechanic, although not as efficient as you in either financial analysis or car repair, is still pretty good at repairing cars. Therefore, he should specialize in auto repair. By the same argument, you are better off focusing on your financial analyst job, no matter how talented you are at auto repair. In other words, although the car mechanic lacks absolute advantage in both tasks, he has comparative advantage in automotive repair.

Whereas a nation might conceivably have a sufficient variety of resources to provide every kind of product and service, it cannot produce all with equal proficiency. The United States could produce all the shoes its citizens need, but only at high cost. This occurs because shoes require much labor to produce, and manufacturing wages in the United States are relatively high. By contrast, producing shoes is a reasonable activity in China, where labor is abundant and wages are relatively low. It is advantageous, therefore, for the United States to specialize in a product such as patented pharmaceuticals. The production of pharmaceuticals more efficiently employs the United States' abundant supply of knowledge workers and technology in the pharmaceutical industry. The United States is better off exporting medications and importing shoes from China. (In fact, footwear marketers such as Nike and Reebok design their own shoes but source the finished product from China and other low-labor-cost countries.)

The comparative advantage view is optimistic because it implies that a nation need not be the first-, second-, or even third-best producer of a particular product to benefit from international trade. A country needs to be only *relatively* capable in producing various types of goods. In this way, the comparative advantage view implies that it is generally advantageous for *all* countries to participate in international trade.

Now, you might ask what accounts for national differences in efficiency. Initially, scholars focused on the importance of *inherited* or *natural resource advantages*, such as fertile land, abundant minerals, and favorable climate. Because South Africa has extensive mineral deposits, it produces and exports diamonds. Because Brazil has abundant fertile land and a suitable climate, it produces and exports wheat and beef.

In addition to naturally occurring advantages such as these, it has become clear that countries can also *create* or *acquire* comparative advantages. Consider the case of Japan—a few decades ago, Japan intentionally acquired many advantages (e.g., capital, specialized knowledge, and capabilities in quality assurance) that benefited its consumer electronics industry. The investments the Japanese government, banks, and manufacturing firms made paid off enormously. Companies such as Hitachi, Panasonic, and Sony invested massive resources to acquire the knowledge and skills needed to become world leaders in consumer electronics. Today, Japan accounts for a huge proportion of the industry's total world production, including digital cameras, flat panel TVs, and personal computers. More recently, South Korea has made similar investments, giving rise to such leading-edge firms as LG and Samsung.

## MyLab Management    Watch It!

If your professor has assigned this, go to the Assignments section of **www.pearson.com/mylab/management** to complete the video exercise titled InfoSys Comparative and Competitive Advantages in Global Competition.

The box highlights the limitations of traditional trade theories. Over time, scholars have introduced additional explanations of international trade, which we review next.

FACTOR PROPORTIONS THEORY    A significant contribution to explaining international trade was developed in the 1920s. Two Swedish economists, Eli Heckscher and his student, Bertil Ohlin, proposed the *factor proportions theory*, sometimes called the factor endowments theory.[1] This view rests on two premises:

- Products differ in the types and quantities of factors (labor, natural resources, and capital) required for their production.
- Countries differ in the type and quantity of production factors that they possess.

### Limitations of Absolute and Comparative Advantage Theories

Although the concepts of absolute advantage and comparative advantage provide the rationale for international trade, they overlook factors that make contemporary trade complex, such as the following:

- Government restrictions such as tariffs (taxes on imports), import barriers, and regulations can hamper international trade.
- Just as Japan has done, governments may target and invest in certain industries, build infrastructure, or provide subsidies, all to boost the competitive advantages of home–country firms.
- Large-scale production in certain industries may provide *economies of scale* and, therefore, lower prices. Economies of scale tend to compensate for weak national comparative advantages. Similarly, modern communications and the Internet tend to reduce the cost and complexity of cross-border trade.
- The main participants in international trade are individual firms that differ in significant ways. Far from being homogenous enterprises, many are highly entrepreneurial and innovative or have access to exceptional human talent, all of which support international business success.
- International shipping and insurance, critical for cross-border trade to take place, are relatively costly and make imported goods more expensive.
- Traded products are not just commodities anymore, such as milk and beef. Today, most traded goods are relatively complex. They are characterized by strong branding and differentiated features.
- Many services, such as banking and retailing, cannot be exported in the usual sense and must be internationalized through foreign direct investment.

The theory suggests that each country should export products that intensively use relatively abundant factors of production and import goods that intensively use relatively scarce factors of production. For example, the United States produces and exports capital-intensive products, such as pharmaceuticals and commercial aircraft. Argentina produces land-intensive products, such as wine and sunflower seeds.

Factor proportions theory differs somewhat from earlier theories by emphasizing the importance of each nation's factors of production. The theory states that, in addition to differences in the *efficiency* of production, differences in the *quantity* of production factors countries hold also determine international trade patterns. In this way, a country that possesses an abundance of a given production factor (e.g., labor, land) obtains a *per-unit-cost advantage* in the production of goods that use that factor intensively.

In the 1950s, research by Russian economist Wassily Leontief seemed to contradict the factor proportions theory. His *Leontief paradox* suggests that, because the United States has abundant capital, it should be an exporter of capital-intensive products. However, Leontief's analysis revealed that the United States often exported labor-intensive goods and imported more capital-intensive goods than the theory would ordinarily predict. What accounts for the inconsistency? One explanation is that numerous factors determine the composition of a country's exports and imports. Another is that, in Leontief's time, U.S. labor was relatively more productive than labor elsewhere in the world.

Perhaps the main contribution of the Leontief paradox is its suggestion that international trade is complex and cannot be fully explained by a single theory. Subsequent refinements of factor proportions theory suggested that other country-level assets—knowledge, technology, and capital—are instrumental in explaining each nation's international trade prowess. Taiwan, for example, is very strong in electronics technology and is home to a sizable population of knowledge workers in this sector.

**INTERNATIONAL PRODUCT LIFE CYCLE THEORY** In a 1966 article, Raymond Vernon sought to explain international trade based on the evolutionary process that occurs in the development and diffusion of products to markets around the world.[2] In his *International Product Life Cycle (IPLC) Theory*, Vernon observed that each product and its manufacturing technologies go through three stages of evolution: introduction, maturity, and standardization. This is illustrated in Exhibit 2.3.

Historically, in the introduction stage, a new product typically originated in an advanced economy, such as Germany or the United States. Such countries possess abundant capital and research and development (R&D) capabilities, providing key advantages in the invention of new goods. Advanced economies also have abundant, high-income consumers who are willing to try new products, which are often expensive. During the introduction stage, the new product is produced in the inventing country, which enjoys a temporary monopoly.

As the product enters the maturity phase, the product's inventors mass-produce it and seek to export it to other advanced economies. Gradually, however, the product's manufacturing becomes more routine, and foreign firms begin producing alternative versions, ending the inventor's monopoly power. At this stage, as competition intensifies and export orders begin to come from lower-income countries, the inventor may earn only a narrow profit margin.

In the standardization phase, knowledge about how to produce the product is widespread and manufacturing has become straightforward. Early in the product's evolution, production had required specialized workers skilled in R&D and manufacturing. Once standardized, however, mass production becomes the dominant activity and can be accomplished using cheaper inputs and

*Source:* Mark Agnor/123RF

Factor proportions theory describes how abundant production factors result in national advantages. Russia, for example, is an enormous land mass with abundant minerals and other natural resources.

EXHIBIT 2.3

**Illustration of Vernon's International Product Life Cycle**

*Source:* Adapted from Raymond Vernon, "International Investment and International Trade in the Product Cycle," *Quarterly Journal of Economics* 80 (May 1966), pp. 190–207 and www.provenmodels.com/583/international-product-life-cycle/raymond-vernon.

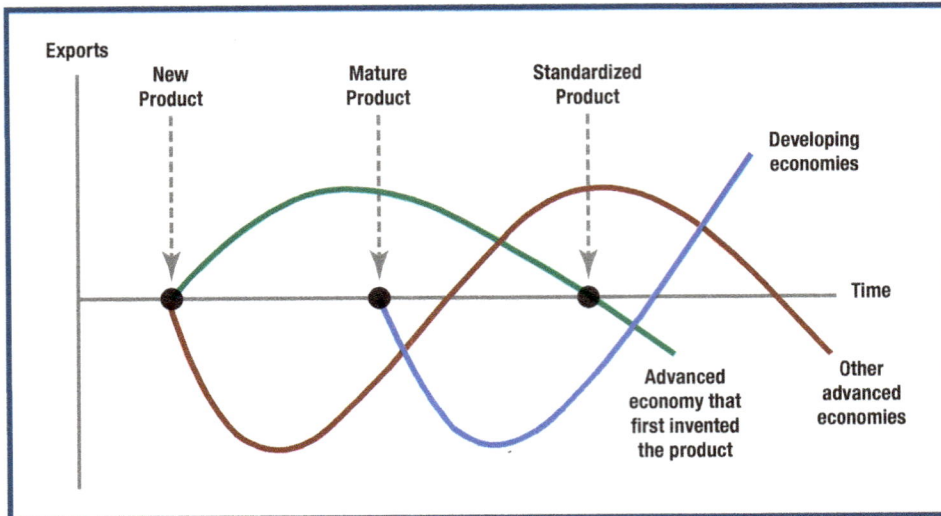

lower-cost labor. Production shifts to low-income countries where competitors enjoy low-cost advantages and can economically serve export markets worldwide. The country that invented the product eventually becomes a net importer. It and other advanced economies become saturated with imports of the good from developing economies. In effect, exporting the product has caused its underlying technology to become widely known and standardized around the world.

As an example, consider the evolution of television sets. The base technology was invented in the United States. U.S. firms began domestic production of TV sets in the 1940s. U.S. sales grew rapidly for many years. However, once TVs became a standardized product, production shifted to China, Mexico, and other countries that offered lower-cost production. Today the United States imports nearly all its television sets.

The IPLC illustrates that national advantages do not last forever. Firms worldwide are continuously creating new products, and others are constantly imitating them. The product cycle is continually beginning and ending. Vernon assumed the product diffusion process occurs slowly enough to generate temporary differences between countries in their access and use of new technologies. This assumption is no longer valid today—the IPLC has become much shorter as new products diffuse much more quickly around the world. Buyers in emerging markets are particularly eager to adopt new technologies as soon as they become available. This trend explains the rapid spread of new consumer electronics such as smartphones and tablets around the world.

**NEW TRADE THEORY** In the 1970s, economists, including Paul Krugman, observed that trade was growing fastest among industrialized countries with similar factors of production. In some new industries, there appeared to be no clear comparative advantage. The solution to this puzzle became known as the *new trade theory*. It argues that increasing returns to scale, especially *economies of scale*, are important for superior international performance in industries that succeed best as their production volume increases. For example, the commercial aircraft industry has high fixed costs that necessitate high-volume sales to achieve profitability. As a nation specializes in the production of such goods, productivity increases and unit costs fall, providing significant benefits to the local economy.

Many national markets are small, and the domestic producer may not achieve economies of scale because it cannot sell products in large volume. New trade theory implies that firms can solve this problem by exporting and gaining access to the much larger global marketplace. Industries such as generic pharmaceuticals achieve minimally profitable economies of scale by selling their output in multiple markets worldwide. The effect of increasing returns to scale allows the nation to specialize in a smaller number of industries in which it may not necessarily hold factor or comparative advantages. According to new trade theory, trade is thus beneficial even for countries that produce only a limited variety of products.

**2.2** Learn about how nations can enhance their competitive advantage.

# How Can Nations Enhance Their Competitive Advantage?

The globalization of markets has fostered a new type of competition—a race among nations to reposition themselves as attractive for business and investment. The more competitive economies today possess a combination of comparative advantages and firm-specific advantages. They feature such strengths as abundant resources, sophisticated infrastructure, well-trained workers, powerful brands, technological leadership, worldwide networks of suppliers and collaborators, and a favorable work ethic. Therefore, we conceive national competitiveness as the sum of national comparative advantages and competitive advantage of a nation's firms collectively. This notion is illustrated in Exhibit 2.4.

Now let's explore how nations can enhance their national competitiveness.

Three contemporary perspectives help explain the development of national competitive advantage: the competitive advantage of nations, the determinants of national competitiveness, and national industrial policy. Let's explain each of these in turn.

## The Competitive Advantage of Nations

How can nations position themselves in a global race for national competitiveness? An important contribution came from Professor Michael Porter in his 1990 book *The Competitive Advantage of Nations*.[3] According to Porter, the competitive advantage of a nation depends on the collective competitive advantages of the nation's firms. Over time, this relationship is reciprocal; the competitive advantages the nation holds tend to drive the development of new firms and industries with these same competitive advantages.

For example, Britain achieved a substantial national competitive advantage in the prescription drug industry due to its first-rate pharmaceutical firms, such as GlaxoSmithKline and AstraZeneca. The United States has a national competitive advantage in professional services because of such leading firms as Goldman Sachs (investment banking), Marsh & McLennan (insurance), and McKinsey (consulting). The presence of these and numerous other strong services firms, in turn, has provided the United States with overall national competencies in the global services sector.

At both the firm and national levels, competitive advantage and technological advances grow out of *innovation*.[4] Companies innovate in various ways. They develop new product designs, new production processes, new approaches to marketing, and new ways of organizing or training. Firms sustain innovation (and, by extension, competitive advantage) by continually finding better products, services, and ways of doing things.[5] For example, Australia's Vix (www.vixtechnology.com) is a world leader in fare collection equipment and software systems for the transit industry. The firm has installed systems in subways, bus networks, and other mass transit systems in such major cities as Melbourne, Rome, San Francisco, Stockholm, and Singapore. It has won numerous awards for its innovative products that have allowed the firm to internationalize quickly. Vix's investment in R&D has been significant, running as high as 23 percent of the firm's revenue.

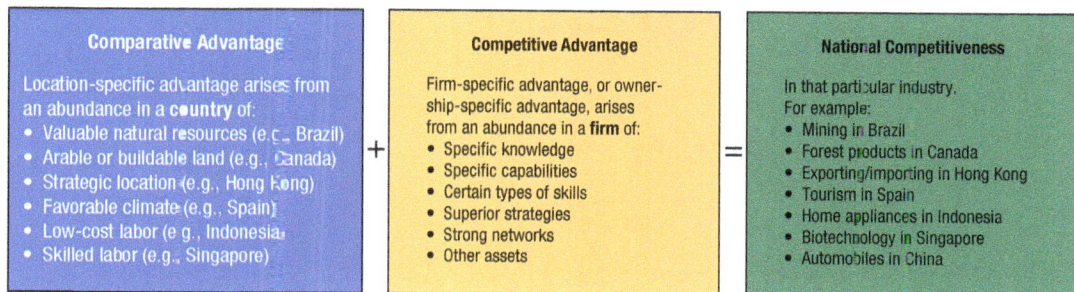

| Comparative Advantage | | Competitive Advantage | | National Competitiveness |
|---|---|---|---|---|
| Location-specific advantage arises from an abundance in a **country** of:<br>• Valuable natural resources (e.g., Brazil)<br>• Arable or buildable land (e.g., Canada)<br>• Strategic location (e.g., Hong Kong)<br>• Favorable climate (e.g., Spain)<br>• Low-cost labor (e.g., Indonesia)<br>• Skilled labor (e.g., Singapore) | + | Firm-specific advantage, or ownership-specific advantage, arises from an abundance in a **firm** of:<br>• Specific knowledge<br>• Specific capabilities<br>• Certain types of skills<br>• Superior strategies<br>• Strong networks<br>• Other assets | = | In that particular industry.<br>For example:<br>• Mining in Brazil<br>• Forest products in Canada<br>• Exporting/importing in Hong Kong<br>• Tourism in Spain<br>• Home appliances in Indonesia<br>• Biotechnology in Singapore<br>• Automobiles in China |

**EXHIBIT 2.4**

**Components of National Competitiveness: Comparative Advantage and Competitive Advantage**

Innovation results primarily from R&D. Among the industries most dependent on technological innovation are biotechnology, information technology, new materials, pharmaceuticals, robotics, medical equipment, fiber optics, and various electronics-based industries.

In a report called the *Global Innovation 1000*, the management consultancy Strategy& (www.strategyand.pwc.com) annually reports on MNEs that spend the most on R&D. Most top European, Japanese, and U.S. firms spend half or more of their total R&D in countries other than where they are headquartered. The firms do this for several reasons:

- To gain access to talent—gifted engineers and scientists reside around the world in countries such as China and India.
- To cut costs by hiring lower-paid engineers and scientists abroad to replace higher-paid personnel in the home country.
- To relocate certain R&D activities abroad where they can gain insights on specific needs of target markets.[6]

Innovation also promotes *productivity*, which is measured as output per unit of labor or capital. The more productive a firm is, the more efficiently it uses its resources. The more productive the firms in a nation are, the more efficiently the nation uses its resources.[7]

At the national level, productivity is a key determinant of the nation's long-run standard of living and a basic source of national per-capita income growth. Exhibit 2.5 depicts productivity levels in various nations over time, measured as output per hour of workers in manufacturing. Ireland and South Korea have been very successful in growing their productivity over time.

## Determinants of National Competitiveness

As part of his explanation in *The Competitive Advantage of Nations*, Michael Porter described several factors that give rise to competitive advantage at both the company and national levels. Named the Porter Diamond Model, it is composed of four major elements.

- *Demand conditions* refer to the nature of home-market demand for specific products and services. The presence of demanding customers pressures firms to innovate faster and produce better products. For example, the United States has a large population of prosperous senior citizens who suffer from various health problems. These conditions have created an enormous market for quality medical equipment and cutting-edge pharmaceutical medications.

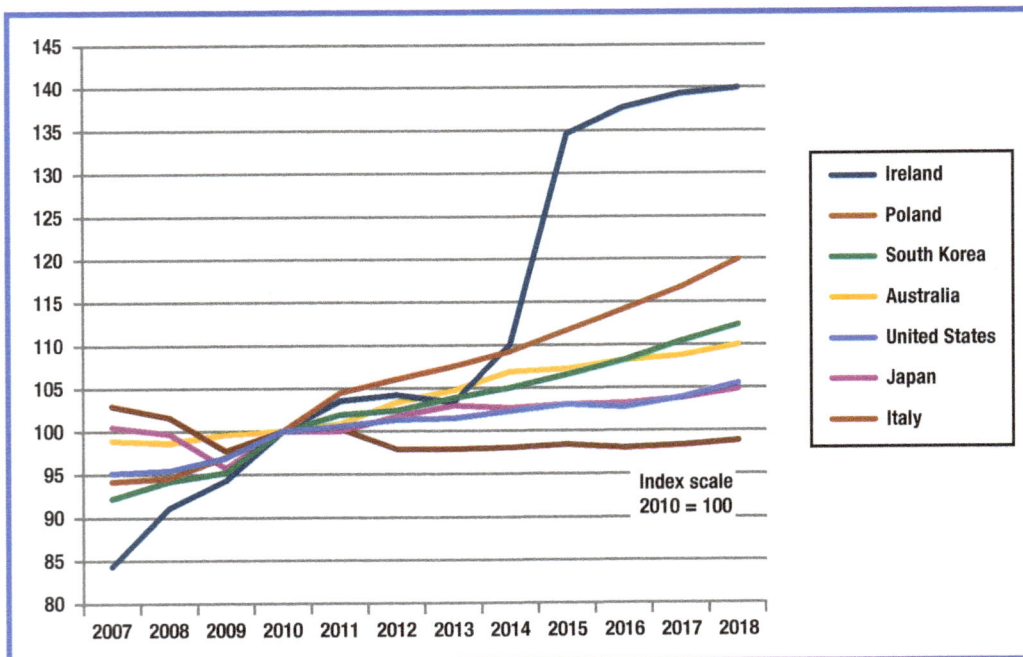

**EXHIBIT 2.5**

**Labor Productivity Levels in Selected Countries: Output per Hour in Manufacturing, 2007–2018 (index scale, 2010 = 100)**

*Source:* OECD, *OECD Data: Labour Productivity* (Organisation for Economic Cooperation and Development, 2018), https://data.oecd.org/lprdty/labour-productivity-forecast.htm#indicator-chart.

- *Firm strategy, structure, and rivalry* refer to the nature of domestic rivalry and conditions in a nation that determines how firms are created, organized, and managed. Vigorous competitive rivalry puts these firms under continual pressure to innovate and improve. They compete not only for market share but also for human talent, technical leadership, and superior product quality. The presence of strong competitors in a nation helps to create and maintain national competitive advantage. Japan has one of the world's most competitive consumer electronics industries, with major players such as Hitachi, Nintendo, Sony, and Toshiba producing semiconductors, computers, video games, and liquid crystal displays. Intense rivalry has pushed firms like Sony to a leading position in the industry worldwide and has enabled Japan to emerge as a leader in consumer electronics.
- *Factor conditions* describe the nation's resources such as labor, natural resources and advanced factors such as capital, technology, entrepreneurship, advanced workforce skills, and know-how. Each nation has a relative abundance of certain factor endowments. This helps determine the nature of its national competitive advantage. For example, Germany's abundance of workers with strong engineering skills has propelled the country to commanding heights in the global engineering and design industries.
- *Related and supporting industries* refer to the presence of clusters of suppliers, competitors, and a skilled workforce. An **industrial cluster** refers to a concentration of businesses, suppliers, and supporting firms in the same industry located at a particular geographic location.

**Industrial cluster**
A concentration of businesses, suppliers, and supporting firms in the same industry at a particular location, characterized by a critical mass of human talent, capital, or other factor endowments.

Industrial clusters are characterized by a critical mass of human talent, capital, or other factor endowments. Examples of industrial clusters include:

- The fashion industry in northern Italy.
- The pharmaceutical industry in Switzerland.
- The footwear industry in Vietnam.
- The medical technology industry in Singapore.
- Wireless Valley in Stockholm, Sweden.
- The consumer electronics industry in Japan.

Operating within a mass of related and supporting industries provides advantages through information and knowledge exchange. This results in cost-savings through economies of scale and scope.

The most important sources of national advantage are the *knowledge and skills* individuals, firms, industries, and countries possess. Knowledge and skills are the most important factors in deciding where companies will locate. Silicon Valley, California, and Bangalore, India, have emerged as leading-edge business clusters because of the availability of specialized talent. Some even argue that knowledge is the most important source of sustainable long-run competitive advantage. If correct, then future national wealth will go to those countries that invest the most in R&D, education, and infrastructure that support knowledge-intensive industries

**National industrial policy**
A proactive economic development plan a government initiates to build or strengthen a particular industry.

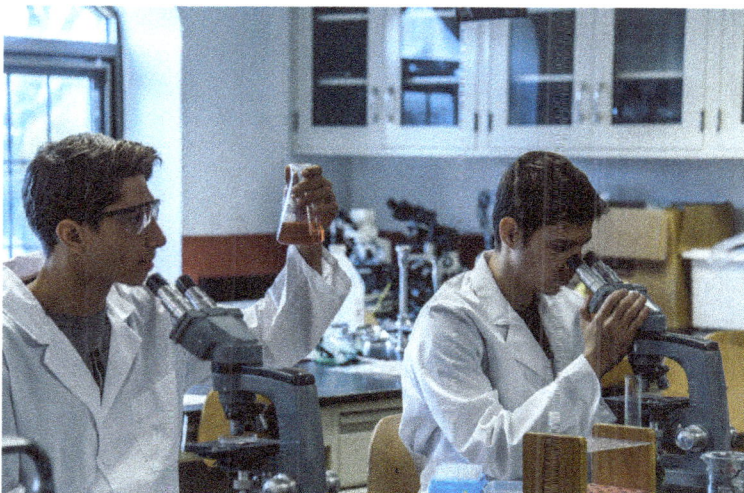

Source: StudioDin/Shutterstock
The United Kingdom enjoys a distinctive collection of comparative and competitive advantages, which have helped propel the nation to prominence in the global pharmaceutical industry.

## National Industrial Policy

Michael Porter's Diamond Model integrates country-based theories (with their focus on nation-level comparative advantages) with firm-based theories (with their focus on firm-level competitive advantages) to determine national competitiveness. Many countries develop national industrial policies. A **national industrial policy** is a proactive economic development plan a government launches to build or strengthen a particular industry, often implemented in collaboration with the private sector. Usually, governments design such policies to support high value-adding industries, those that yield higher corporate profits, better wages, and tax revenues. Historically, governments favored traditional industries, including automobiles, shipbuilding, and heavy machinery—all with long value chains that produce enormous added value.

High value–adding industries typically are knowledge-intensive industries such as IT, biotechnology, medical technology, and financial services. Dubai developed a national industrial policy to become an international commercial center in the information and communications technology (ICT) sector. Singapore's Innovation Manifesto has propelled the city–state to become a world-class center of excellence in such areas as nuclear technology.

Governments play a key role in influencing each of the four components of the Porter diamond. They can do this either positively or negatively. Governments can influence *demand conditions* and *related and supporting industries* through regulations. They can influence *factor conditions* by supporting educational initiatives and capital markets. Government tax policies and regulations can influence *firm strategy, structure, and rivalry*.

---

### Features of National Industrial Policies

- *Tax incentives.* Tax incentives encourage citizens and firms to save and invest money, which can then be used as capital for public and private investment in R&D, plant, equipment, and worker skills.
- *Monetary and fiscal policies.* These include low-interest loans that provide a stable supply of capital.
- *Educational systems.* Superior educational systems ensure a steady stream of competent workers in high technology or high value-adding industries.
- *Infrastructure.* Modern national infrastructure in areas such as IT, communication systems, and transportation enhance productivity.
- *Legal and regulatory systems.* These institutions ensure the stability of national economies.

*Sources:* Iurii Vinslav, "National Industrial Policy," *Problems of Economic Transition* 56, No. 9 (2014), pp. 16-47; Lester Thurow, *Head to Head: The Coming Economic Battle Among Japan, Europe, and America* (New York: William Morrow, 1992).

---

## National Industrial Policy in Practice

How well does national industrial policy work in practice? Let's examine the experience of New Zealand. For much of the early twentieth century, government policies limited New Zealand's ability to flourish and trade with the rest of the world. Living standards were low, and many wondered about the nation's future. In the 1980s, the New Zealand government began to develop pro-trade policies in cooperation with the private sector that resulted in national

| Statistic | New Zealand in 1993 | New Zealand in 2005 | New Zealand in 2017 |
|---|---|---|---|
| GDP per capita | $12,452 | $27,206 | $41,629 |
| NZX 50 Stock Market Index | 2,200 | 3,200 | 8,000 |
| Unemployment rate | 9.8% | 3.8% | 4.8% |
| National debt | 47% of the nation's GDP | 18% of the nation's GDP | 24% of the nation's GDP |

### EXHIBIT 2.6

### Transformation of New Zealand's Economy, 1993 to 2017

*Source:* International Monetary Fund, World Economic Outlook Databases, 2017, www.imf.org; Yahoo! Finance, http://finance.yahoo.com

*Source:* Pixsooz/Shutterstock

Following many years of poor economic performance, the government of New Zealand implemented various national industrial policies that succeeded in elevating several key economic indicators, thus raising living standards for the New Zealand people.

advantages. The government helped systematically transform the country from an agrarian, protectionist, and regulated economy to an industrialized, globally competitive, and free-market economy. New Zealand's economy grew rapidly and achieved high living standards.

These accomplishments are summarized in Exhibit 2.6. Between 1993 and 2017, New Zealand raised its per-capita GDP from $12,452 to $41,629, a 334 percent improvement in income and now among the highest in the world. During this period New Zealand's main stock market index, the NZX 50, rose from 2,200 to 8,000. The country's unemployment rate declined by more than half to 4.8 percent. Finally, the government halved its national debt as a proportion of GDP from 47 to 24 percent

As Exhibit 2.6 reveals, dynamic growth boosted real incomes and greatly improved living standards in New Zealand. The World Bank recently ranked New Zealand as the most business-friendly country in the world.[8]

### How New Zealand Successfully Transformed Its Economy Using National Industrial Policy

- Government-controlled wages, prices, and interest rates were freed and allowed to fluctuate according to market forces.
- The banking sector was liberalized, foreign exchange controls were eliminated, and the New Zealand dollar was allowed to float according to market forces.
- Most trade barriers were removed.
- Subsidies formerly granted to agriculture and other sectors were eliminated.
- The government worked earnestly with labor unions to reduce wage inflation, helping ensure that jobs remained in New Zealand and were not outsourced to lower-wage countries.
- The government initiated programs to encourage development of a knowledge economy. New Zealanders continuously upgraded skills and knowledge, providing a supply of scientists, engineers, and trained managers.
- Personal and corporate income tax rates were reduced, and the tax base was diversified to stabilize government revenues. This move fostered entrepreneurship, boosted consumer spending, and increased the nation's attractiveness for investment from abroad.
- State-owned enterprises—such as the national airline, post office, telecom, and other utilities—were sold to the private sector.

*Sources:* Dean Hyslop and Dave Mar, "Skill Upgrading in New Zealand, 1986–2001," *Australian Economic Review* 42, No. 4 (2009), pp. 422–434; Johan Christensen, "Bureaucracies, Neoliberal Ideas, and Tax Reform in New Zealand and Ireland," *Governance* 26, No. 4 (2013), pp. 563–584.

**2.3** Understand why and how firms internationalize.

# Why and How Do Firms Internationalize?

Earlier theories of international trade focused on why and how cross-national business occurs. Beginning in the 1960s, scholars turned their attention to why and how individual firms pursue internationalization. Let's examine these views.

## Internationalization Process of the Firm

Scholars developed the *internationalization process model* in the 1970s to describe how companies expand abroad. According to this model, internationalization takes place in incremental stages over a long period.[9] Initially and without much analysis or planning, firms begin exporting, the simplest foreign market entry strategy. As they become more knowledgeable, firms gradually progress to foreign direct investment (FDI), the most complex entry strategy. The relatively slow nature of internationalization often results from managers' uncertainty and uneasiness about how to proceed. They lack information about foreign markets and experience with cross-border transactions. The progression from exporting to FDI coincides with increasing levels of both risk and control.

This gradual, incremental model of internationalization is illustrated in Exhibit 2.7. Preoccupied with business in its home market, the firm starts out with a *domestic focus*. Management may be unable or unwilling to start doing international business because of concerns over its readiness or perceived obstacles in foreign markets. Eventually, the firm advances to the *pre-export stage*, often because it receives unsolicited product orders from abroad. In this stage, management investigates the feasibility of undertaking international business. Later, the firm advances to the *experimental involvement stage* by initiating limited international activity, typically through basic exporting. As managers begin to view foreign expansion more favorably, they undertake *active involvement* in international business. This occurs through the systematic exploration of international options and the commitment of resources and managerial time to achieve international success. Management may finally advance to the *committed involvement stage*. This stage is characterized by genuine interest and commitment of resources to making international business a key part of the firm's profit-making and value-chain activities. In this stage, the firm targets numerous foreign markets through various entry modes, especially FDI.[10]

To illustrate, let's examine the consumer electronics firm Samsung Corporation, headquartered in Seoul, South Korea (www.samsung.com). In the 1970s, Samsung began exporting televisions and other products to Europe and North America. In the 1990s, it entered joint ventures with various partners abroad to manufacture televisions, refrigerators, and video equipment. Around the same time, Samsung used FDI to establish regional headquarters in China, Europe, Singapore, and the United States. In the 1990s, the firm set up factories in China and other countries to manufacture consumer electronics and appliances. By 2005, Samsung had established 64 manufacturing and sales subsidiaries and 13 R&D centers around the world.[11]

## Born Global Firms

Is the gradual, cautious internationalization process previously described still valid today? Current research suggests it is not.[12] What we see today is an increasing number of young, entrepreneurial firms that intently pursue customers in foreign markets from an early age. Scholars and management consultants alike referred to this relatively novel breed of companies as *born global firms*.[13] Born globals are innovative start-ups that initiate international business soon after their founding. Mojang, maker of the Minecraft video game, is a born global. Established in 2009 in Sweden, the firm found a ready market for its popular video games. Minecraft sold 1 million games within one month of its launch to gamers worldwide. The first Minecraft convention was held in 2011 in Las Vegas, United States, and attended by 4,500 users from 24 countries. Mojang gamers are located in countries around the world.[14]

Born global firms are now found in virtually all economies. This has developed despite the scarcity of financial, human, and tangible resources that characterize most new businesses. Born globals have emerged in large numbers for two main reasons.

- Globalization has made doing international business easier than ever before.
- Advances in communication and transportation technologies have reduced the costs of operating internationally.

**EXHIBIT 2.7**

**Stages in the Internationalization Process of the Firm**

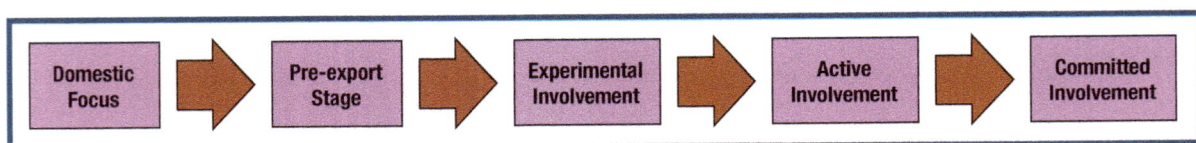

Domestic Focus → Pre-export Stage → Experimental Involvement → Active Involvement → Committed Involvement

The born global phenomenon has given rise to a new academic field, *international entrepreneurship*.[15] Current trends suggest that early internationalizing firms will become even more common in international business.

**2.4** Explain the strategies internationalizing firms use to gain and sustain competitive advantage.

# How Can Internationalizing Firms Gain and Sustain Competitive Advantage?

MNEs such as Nestlé, Unilever, Sony, Coca-Cola, and Caterpillar have all expanded abroad on a massive scale. Such MNEs have helped shape international patterns of trade, investment, and technology flows. Over time, the aggregate activities of these firms became a key driving force of globalization and ongoing integration of world economies. Let's examine how multinationals gain and sustain competitive advantage in global markets.

## FDI-Based Explanations

Most explanations of international business have emphasized FDI, the preferred entry strategy of MNEs. These large, resource-rich companies conduct business through networks of production facilities, marketing subsidiaries, regional headquarters, and other operations around the world. One way to illustrate the huge volume of FDI is to examine *FDI stock*. FDI stock refers to the total value of assets that MNEs invest abroad.

Exhibit 2.8 shows the stock and growth of inward FDI for 2006 and 2016 for a group of leading FDI destination countries. The exhibit highlights three interesting points.

- Even smaller economies such as Ireland and the Netherlands are popular destinations for direct investment.
- Both developed and developing economies are major recipients of FDI.
- Hong Kong and Singapore receive considerable FDI as important *entrepôt* ports. In such ports, merchandise can be imported without paying import duties. The goods are then transshipped to and from China, the world's largest emerging market.

Historically, most of the world's FDI was invested both by and in Western Europe, the United States, and Japan. Today, rapidly developing economies now account for a huge proportion of global FDI. An exception is Africa. It receives relatively little FDI, which hinders its ability to raise living standards in the region.[16]

Exhibit 2.9 shows the stock and growth of outward FDI for a collection of the leading FDI-providing countries. Note that firms from both advanced economies and emerging markets invest substantial FDI abroad. For example, China has greatly increased its FDI investments in recent years. Among all countries, total outward FDI stock now constitutes nearly one-third of global GDP, an impressive amount.[17]

Scholars have developed three alternative theories of how firms can use FDI to gain and sustain competitive advantage. These are the monopolistic advantage theory, internalization theory, and Dunning's eclectic paradigm. These theoretical perspectives are summarized in Exhibit 2.10.

**MONOPOLISTIC ADVANTAGE THEORY** Monopolistic advantage refers to resources or capabilities a company holds that few other firms have. Monopolistic advantage theory suggests that firms that use FDI as an internationalization strategy must own or control certain resources and capabilities not easily available to competitors. This gives them a degree of monopoly power over local firms in foreign markets. This monopolistic advantage should be specific to the MNE itself, such as a proprietary technology or a brand name, rather than to the locations where it does business.

Monopolistic advantage theory argues that at least two conditions should be present for a firm to target a foreign market over its home market. First, returns accessible in the foreign market should be superior to those available in the home market. This would provide the firm with incentives to expand abroad to take advantage of its monopoly power. Second, returns achievable in the foreign market should be superior to those earned by existing domestic competitors in the foreign market. This would give the firm an opportunity to earn monopoly profits that domestic firms in the foreign market cannot imitate.

To illustrate, let's revisit Samsung Corporation. By being on the leading edge of innovation, Samsung established many pioneering standards in the consumer electronics industry. Over time, Samsung's superior R&D and internal controls allowed the firm to acquire and keep a

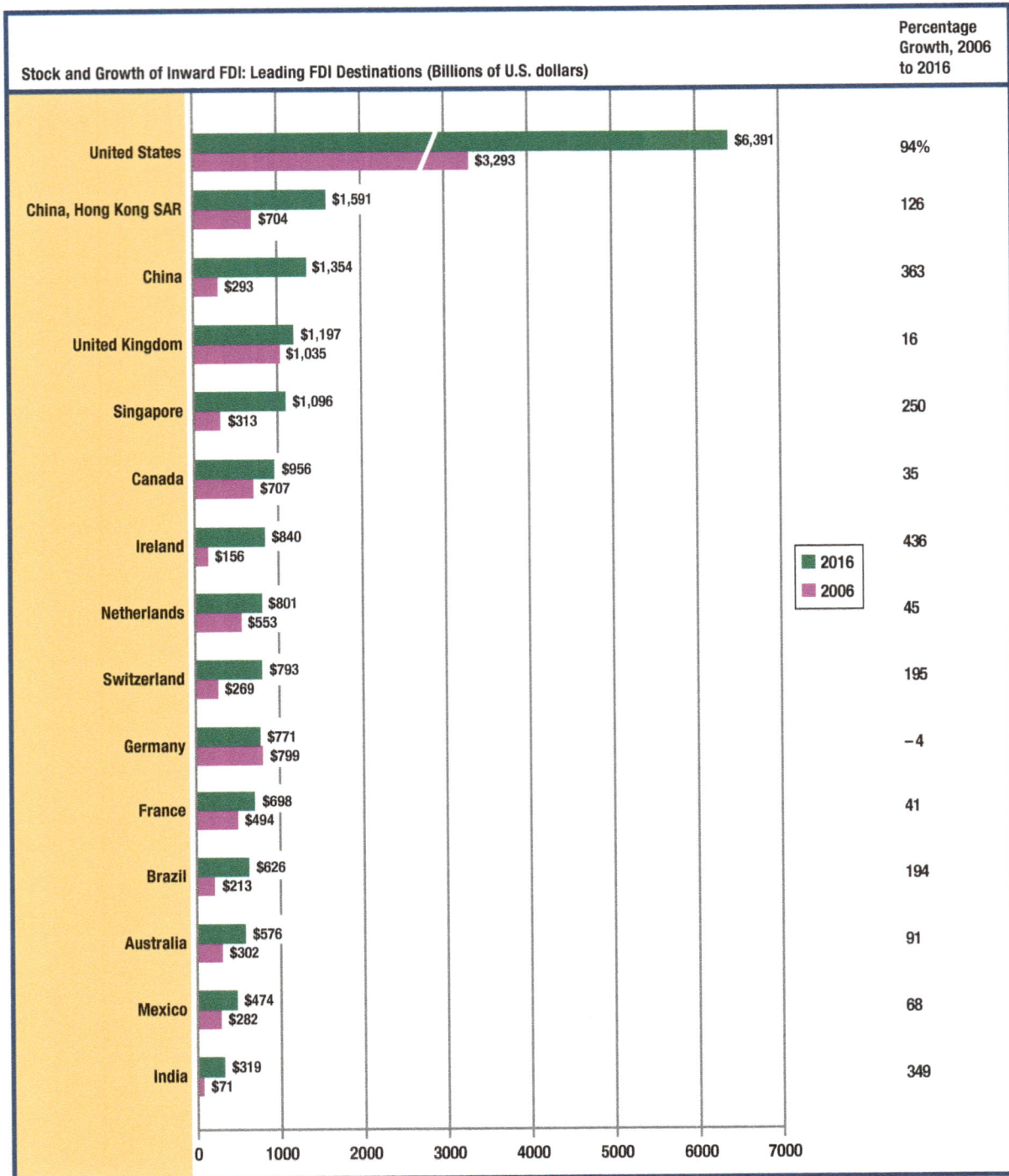

| Stock and Growth of Inward FDI: Leading FDI Destinations (Billions of U.S. dollars) | Percentage Growth, 2006 to 2016 |
|---|---|
| United States — $6,391 / $3,293 | 94% |
| China, Hong Kong SAR — $1,591 / $704 | 126 |
| China — $1,354 / $293 | 363 |
| United Kingdom — $1,197 / $1,035 | 16 |
| Singapore — $1,096 / $313 | 250 |
| Canada — $956 / $707 | 35 |
| Ireland — $840 / $156 | 436 |
| Netherlands — $801 / $553 | 45 |
| Switzerland — $793 / $269 | 195 |
| Germany — $771 / $799 | −4 |
| France — $698 / $494 | 41 |
| Brazil — $626 / $213 | 194 |
| Australia — $576 / $302 | 91 |
| Mexico — $474 / $282 | 68 |
| India — $319 / $71 | 349 |

Legend: ■ 2016  ■ 2006

**EXHIBIT 2.8**

**Stock and Growth of Inward FDI: Leading FDI Destinations (billions of U.S. dollars) and Percentage Growth, 2006 and 2016**

*Sources:* UNCTAD, *UNCTAD Stat* 2017 (New York: United Nations, 2018), http://unctad.org/en/pages/Statistics.aspx.

large body of relatively unique knowledge. This unique knowledge provided the firm with various monopolistic advantages. Samsung invented many popular products that were, for a time, relatively unique. Continuous innovation within the firm allowed Samsung to keep this uniqueness for many years. Samsung used its superior innovativeness to develop monopoly power and

| Stock of and Growth of Outward FDI: Top Sources of Outward FDI (billions of U.S. dollars) | Percentage Growth, 2006 to 2016 |
|---|---|

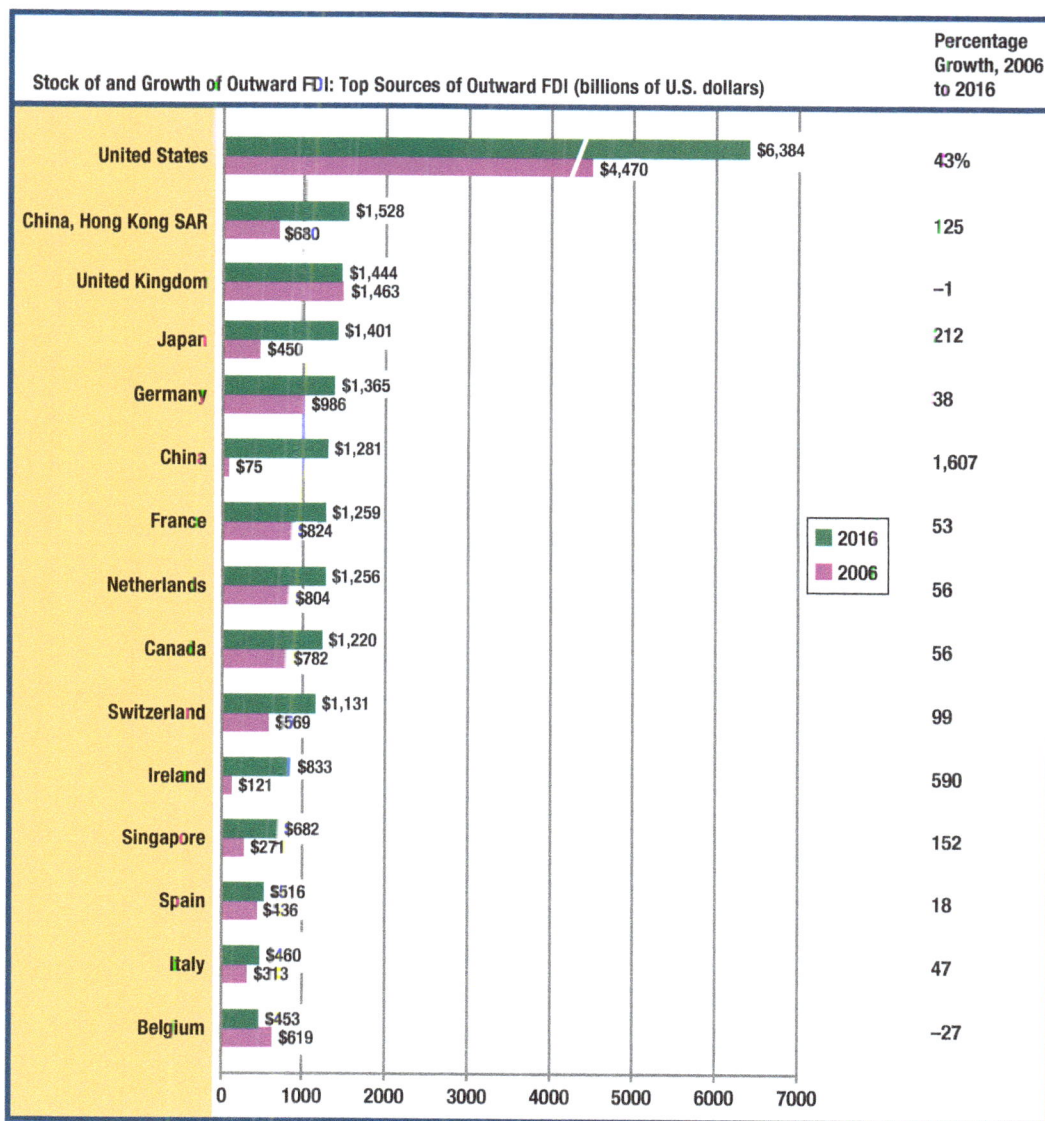

| | |
|---|---|
| United States | 43% |
| China, Hong Kong SAR | 125 |
| United Kingdom | −1 |
| Japan | 212 |
| Germany | 38 |
| China | 1,607 |
| France | 53 |
| Netherlands | 56 |
| Canada | 56 |
| Switzerland | 99 |
| Ireland | 590 |
| Singapore | 152 |
| Spain | 18 |
| Italy | 47 |
| Belgium | −27 |

United States: $6,384 (2016); $4,470 (2006)
China, Hong Kong SAR: $1,528; $680
United Kingdom: $1,444; $1,463
Japan: $1,401; $450
Germany: $1,365; $986
China: $1,281; $75
France: $1,259; $824
Netherlands: $1,256; $804
Canada: $1,220; $782
Switzerland: $1,131; $569
Ireland: $833; $121
Singapore: $682; $271
Spain: $516; $436
Italy: $460; $313
Belgium: $453; $619

Legend: ■ 2016  ■ 2006

**EXHIBIT 2.9**

**Stock of and Growth of Outward FDI: Top Sources of Outward FDI (billions of U.S. dollars) and Percentage Growth, 2006 to 2016**

*Sources:* UNCTAD, *UNCTAD Stat* 2017 (New York: United Nations, 2018), http://unctad.org/en/pages/Statistics.aspx.

**Internalization theory**
An explanation of the process by which firms acquire and retain one or more value-chain activities inside the firm. This minimizes the disadvantages of dealing with external partners and allows for greater control over foreign operations.

dominate world markets in such products as LCD panels and smartphones. As the Samsung example implies, the most important monopolistic advantages are superior knowledge and intangible skills.[18]

INTERNALIZATION THEORY    **Internalization theory** explains the process by which firms acquire and retain one or more value-chain activities inside the firm. Internalizing value-chain activities (instead of outsourcing them to external suppliers) reduces the disadvantages of dealing with outside partners for performing arms-length activities such as exporting and licensing. Internalization also gives the firm greater control over its foreign operations.

For example, the MNE might internalize manufacturing by acquiring or establishing its own plant in the foreign market. This enables the firm to produce needed inputs itself rather than sourcing from independent suppliers. Alternatively, it might internalize the marketing function by

| Theory | Key Characteristics | Benefits | Examples |
|---|---|---|---|
| **Monopolistic Advantage Theory** | The firm controls one or more resources, or offers relatively unique products and services that provide it a degree of monopoly power relative to foreign markets and competitors. | The firm can operate foreign subsidiaries more profitably than the local firms that compete in their own markets. | The Swiss pharmaceutical Novartis earns substantial profits by marketing various patent medications through its subsidiaries worldwide. |
| **Internalization Theory** | The firm acquires and retains one or more value-chain activities within the firm. | • Minimizes the disadvantages of relying on intermediaries, collaborators, or other external partners.<br>• Ensures greater control over foreign operations, helping to maximize product quality, reliable manufacturing processes, and sound marketing practices.<br>• Reduces the risk that knowledge and proprietary assets will be lost to competitors. | The Chinese MNE Lenovo:<br>• Owns and operates factories in dozens of countries to manufacture laptop computers.<br>• Controls its own manufacturing processes, ensuring quality output.<br>• Ensures its marketing activities are carried out per headquarters' plan.<br>• Retains key assets within the firm, such as leading-edge knowledge for producing the next generation of laptops. |
| **Dunning's Eclectic Paradigm** | • *Ownership-specific advantages*: The firm owns knowledge, skills, capabilities, processes, or physical assets.<br>• *Location-specific advantages*: Factors in individual countries provide specific benefits, such as natural resources, skilled labor, low-cost labor, and inexpensive capital.<br>• *Internalization advantages*: The firm benefits from internalizing foreign manufacturing, distribution, or other value-chain activities. | Provides various advantages relative to competitors, including the ability to own, control, and optimize value-chain activities—R&D, production, marketing, sales distribution, after-sales service, as well as relationships with customers and key contacts—performed at the most beneficial locations worldwide. | The German MNE Siemens:<br>• Owns factories at locations worldwide that provide optimal access to natural resources, as well as skilled and low-cost labor.<br>• Leverages the knowledge base of its employees in 190 countries.<br>• Internalizes a wide range of manufacturing activities in categories such as lighting, medical equipment, and transportation machinery. |

**EXHIBIT 2.10**
**Theoretical Perspectives on Why Firms Choose FDI**

establishing its own distribution subsidiary abroad instead of contracting with an independent foreign distributor to handle its marketing in the foreign market. The firm replaces business activities performed by independent suppliers in external markets with business activities it performs itself.

Another key reason companies internalize certain value-chain functions is to control proprietary knowledge critical to the development, production, and sale of their products and services. Because independent foreign companies are outside the MNE's direct control, they can acquire and exploit proprietary knowledge to their own advantage. They might even use the acquired knowledge to become competitors.[19]

Procter & Gamble initially considered exporting when it entered Japan. With exporting, P&G would have had to contract with an independent Japanese distributor to handle warehousing and marketing of its soap, diapers, and other products. Instead, P&G chose to enter Japan through FDI for three reasons: (1) trade barriers imposed by the Japanese government, (2) the strong market power of local Japanese firms, and (3) the risk of losing control over its proprietary knowledge. It established its own marketing subsidiary and national headquarters in Tokyo.

In the 1980s, Samsung followed a policy of exporting its products to Europe and North America. Management realized it could improve and speed up international operations by creating its own sales and production facilities in strategic markets. In the 1990s, Samsung internalized much of its production and distribution channels in Brazil, China, Mexico, and the United Kingdom. To ensure product quality, Samsung internalized production of semiconductors and circuit boards for use in making telecommunications equipment. The firm gradually transferred its manufacturing operations from Western to Eastern Europe to profit from lower-cost labor in the East. Samsung also produces various software through its subsidiary, Samsung R&D Institute in India.

## Dunning's Eclectic Paradigm

Professor John Dunning proposed the eclectic paradigm as a framework to explain the extent and pattern of the value chain operations that companies should own abroad. He drew from various theories, including comparative advantage, factor proportions, monopolistic advantage, and internalization theory. The eclectic paradigm is often viewed as the most comprehensive of FDI theories.

The eclectic paradigm specifies three conditions that determine whether a company will internationalize through FDI:

- Ownership-specific advantages
- Location-specific advantages
- Internalization advantages

Let's explain each condition in turn.

OWNERSHIP-SPECIFIC ADVANTAGES    An MNE should hold knowledge, skills, capabilities, key relationships, and other advantages that it owns and that allow it to compete effectively in foreign markets. To ensure international success, the firm's competitive advantage must be substantial enough to offset the costs that it incurs in establishing and operating foreign operations. It should also be specific to its own organization and not readily transferable to other firms. Competitive advantage may incorporate proprietary technology, managerial skills, trademarks or brand names, economies of scale, or access to substantial financial resources. The more valuable the firm's ownership-specific advantages, the more likely it is to internationalize by FDI.

Alcoa has 60,000 employees in 35 countries. The company's integrated operations include bauxite mining and aluminum refining. Its products include primary aluminum (which it refines from bauxite), automotive components, and sheet aluminum for beverage cans and Reynolds Wrap®. One of Alcoa's most important ownership-specific advantages is the proprietary technology it has acquired through its R&D activities. It has also acquired special managerial and marketing skills in the production and marketing of refined aluminum. The firm has a well-known brand name that facilitates sales. As a large firm, Alcoa also profits from economies of scale and the ability to finance expensive projects. These advantages have allowed Alcoa to generate maximal profits from its international operations.

LOCATION-SPECIFIC ADVANTAGES    The second condition that determines whether a firm will internationalize by FDI is the presence of location-specific advantages. These are the comparative advantages available in individual foreign countries that may be translated into firm competitive advantages. These may include natural resources, skilled labor, low-cost labor, or inexpensive capital. Alcoa located refineries in Brazil because of Brazil's huge deposits of bauxite, a mineral found in relatively few other locations. The Amazon and other major rivers in Brazil generate huge amounts of hydroelectric power, which is a critical ingredient in electricity-intensive aluminum refining. Alcoa also benefits from Brazil's low-cost, relatively well-educated laborers who work in the firm's refineries. The presence of these location-specific advantages helped persuade Alcoa to locate in Brazil through FDI.

INTERNALIZATION ADVANTAGES    The third condition that determines FDI-based internationalization is the presence of internalization advantages. The firm gains these benefits from internalizing foreign-based manufacturing, distribution, or other value chain activities. When profitable, the firm will transfer its ownership-specific advantages across national borders within its own organization rather than dissipating them to independent, foreign entities. The FDI decision depends on which is the best option—internalization versus using external partners and whether they are licensees, distributors, or suppliers. Internalization advantages include the ability to control how the firm's products are produced or marketed, greater control of its proprietary knowledge, and greater buyer certainty about product value.[20]

With Alcoa, the firm had five reasons to internalize many of its operations instead of letting external suppliers handle them. First, management was concerned about minimizing the dissemination of proprietary knowledge, specifically its aluminum-refining operations—knowledge the firm acquired at great expense. Second, internalization provides the best net return, allowing Alcoa to minimize the cost of operations. Third, Alcoa needs to control sales of its aluminum products to avoid depressing world aluminum prices through oversupply. Fourth, the firm wants to be able to apply a differential pricing strategy, charging different prices to different customers, a strategy it could not implement without controlling distribution. Finally, aluminum refining is complex, and Alcoa wants to maintain control of it to ensure product quality.

## Non-FDI-Based Explanations

FDI became a popular entry mode with the rise of the MNE in the 1960s and 1970s. In the 1980s, firms began to recognize the importance of collaborative ventures and other flexible entry strategies.

INTERNATIONAL COLLABORATIVE VENTURES A collaborative venture is a form of cooperation between two or more firms. There are two major types: equity-based *joint ventures* that result in a new legal entity and non-equity-based (project-based) strategic alliances in which the firms' partner, for a finite duration, to collaborate on projects related to R&D, design, manufacturing, or any other value-adding activity. In both cases, collaborating firms pool resources and capabilities and generate synergy. In other words, collaboration allows the partners to carry out activities that each might be unable to perform on its own. Collaborating firms share the risk of their joint efforts, which reduces vulnerability for any one partner.

Collaboration is critical in international business. A firm sometimes has no choice but to partner with other companies to gain access to resources and capabilities unavailable within its own organization. In addition, occasionally a government will restrict companies from entering its national market through wholly owned FDI. For example, the Chinese government prohibits foreign firms from attaining full ownership of ventures in China's health, life, and pension insurance industries, partly because local authorities intend to stimulate the development of Chinese companies in these industries. Where such restrictions exist, the firm may have no choice but to collaborate with a local partner to enter the market.[21]

A collaborative venture can give a company access to foreign partners' expertise, capital, distribution channels, marketing assets, or the ability to overcome government-imposed obstacles. By collaborating, the firm can position itself better to create new products and enter new markets. For example, Starbucks now boasts more than 1,300 coffee shops in Japan. Starbucks first entered Japan through a joint venture with a local partner, Sazaby League, Ltd. The venture allowed Starbucks to internationalize and navigate the marketplace with the help of a knowledgeable local partner.[22]

NETWORKS AND RELATIONAL ASSETS Networks and relational assets represent the economically beneficial long-term *relationships* the firm undertakes with other business entities. Such entities include manufacturers, distributors, suppliers, retailers, consultants, banks, transportation suppliers, governments, and any other organization that can provide needed capabilities. Firm-level relational assets represent a distinct competitive advantage in international business. Numerous emerging markets feature *family conglomerates*—large, highly diversified firms with interlinked ownership. A typical family conglomerate combines numerous firms in diverse industries under the control of a family or an individual owner, within a complex corporate network. In Japan, a *keiretsu* is a conglomeration of businesses linked together by cross-shareholdings to form a complex conglomerate of interlinked associations.[23] For example, the Sumitomo keiretsu comprises the SMBC Bank, Sumitomo Life (insurance), Sumitomo Realty & Development Company, Sumitomo Chemical Company, Sumitomo Corporation (trading company), Sumitomo Electric Industries, Sumitomo Heavy Industries, Mazda Motor Corporation, and numerous others. Like the keiretsu, networks are neither formal organizations with clearly defined hierarchical structures nor impersonal, decentralized markets.

The International Marketing and Purchasing (IMP) research consortium in Europe (www.impgroup.org) has driven much of the theory development on networks.[24] Network theory was proposed to compensate for the inability of traditional organizational theories to account for much that goes on in business markets.[25] In networks, buyers and sellers become bound to one another through continuous exchanges and linkages of products, services, finance, technology, and knowledge. Continued interaction among the partners results in stable relationships based on cooperation and creates value and competitive advantage even among competitors. Network linkages represent a key route by which many companies expand their business abroad, develop new markets, and develop new products. In international business, mutually beneficial and enduring strategic relationships provide real advantages to partners and reduce uncertainty and transaction costs.

The online retailer Amazon has skillfully used network connections to enter various countries. Amazon generates about 40 percent of its sales internationally. The firm entered India, a complex market, through various local connections and a partnership with a local online shopping service, Junglee. Amazon also partnered with the Indian government to facilitate Internet sales, and with digital lender Capital Float to provide loans to online sellers in India. Amazon entered China by developing a relationship with Joyo.com, a local firm highly experienced in online retailing. Amazon collaborated with Beijing Sinnet Technology, an Internet service provider in China. Amazon also partnered with Alibaba, China's largest online retailer, to sell food, kitchenware, wine, shoes and other goods.[26]

Samsung Corporation has many network connections that provide substantial benefits. The firm produces cell phones and telecommunications equipment with various partners in China. It is also well connected in the Korean financial sector. Network relationships with the Korean Industrial Bank and Korea Commercial Bank have provided Samsung with much of the financing it needs to conduct R&D and perform other key value-chain activities. In short, Samsung's network and relational assets have been critical to its success.

In the contemporary global economy, many firms have shied away from making permanent, direct investments in host countries. Instead, many firms now opt for more flexible collaborative ventures or other relationships with independent business partners abroad.

## CLOSING CASE    Unilever's Comparative and Competitive Advantages

Unilever is a multinational enterprise in the fast-moving consumer goods (FMCG) industry, with headquarters in Rotterdam, Netherlands. Unilever has 170,000 employees worldwide and generated revenue in 2017 of more than 50 billion euros (about $60 billion). Top competitors include Nestlé and Procter & Gamble. Unilever emerged in 1929 through the merger of Dutch food company Margarine Unie and British soapmaker Lever Brothers.

Today, Unilever's products fall into four main categories: personal care, food, beverages, and cleaning agents. Personal care accounts for about 38 percent of total sales and includes such products as deodorants, cosmetics, lotions, toothpaste, soap, and shampoo. Unilever's food group contributes 24 percent to total sales and comprises snacks, soups, margarines, mayonnaise, and salad dressings. Beverages and cleaning agents each contribute 18 percent to total sales. The firm's 400 brands include Ben & Jerry's, Best Foods, Dove, Flora, Knorr, Lipton, Lux, Magnum, Noxzema, Pepsodent, Vaseline, and many others.

Unilever has research and production operations in more than 100 countries. It sells products in almost 200 countries. Emerging markets—especially Brazil, China, India, Mexico, and Russia—account for more than half of total sales.

### Comparative and Competitive Advantages

Unilever's headquarters in the Netherlands, and its longstanding connection to the United Kingdom (UK), provide numerous *comparative advantages* to the firm. For example, the UK market is highly developed, sophisticated, and diversified. The Netherlands is well located to serve the world and is a key entry market for continental Europe. The Netherlands and the UK are leading platforms in new technology development, with a high concentration of knowledge workers who drive innovation in product development and operations. The UK is one of the world's leading banking centers, with an active stock market, which provides a ready supply of capital. Rotterdam is Europe's largest port. The Netherlands has leveraged its location to establish advanced infrastructure for transporting goods, people, and electronic data. Strong and stable economies in both the Netherlands and the UK ensure steady demand for Unilever products. The wide range of countries where Unilever operates provides numerous other comparative advantages.

Unilever possesses many *competitive advantages*, including thousands of patents, superior R&D capability, high-quality products, innovative technologies, economies of scale, cross-business synergies, deep distribution channels, excellent marketing capabilities, well-known brand names, customer loyalty, and access to lower-cost and superior labor through factories worldwide. Several of these strengths also provide Unilever with *monopolistic advantages*, capabilities that few other firms have. Such advantages give Unilever a degree of monopoly power over local firms in international markets.

Consistent with the Porter Diamond Model, the Netherlands and the UK are strong locations for R&D due to the presence of highly demanding consumers; superior production factors, especially in capital and labor; and numerous strong competitors that pressure Unilever to innovate. For example, Europeans are demanding consumers and push Unilever to produce high-quality products. Related and supporting industries in Europe—especially suppliers of key ingredients for food, personal care, and beauty products—provide additional advantages. Intense rivalry in the FMCG industry constantly pressures Unilever to launch new products and improve existing ones. Europe is home to numerous *industrial clusters* in the FMCG industry. Consistent with *new trade theory*, Unilever obtains massive economies of scale by selling its products throughout the world.

## Internationalization and FDI Advantages

Unilever long has pushed *internationalization* throughout its value chains, including R&D, procurement, manufacturing, distribution, and marketing and sales. The firm utilizes a full range of foreign market entry strategies, including exporting and foreign direct investment (FDI). The firm has used FDI to establish factories and marketing subsidiaries around the world. FDI allows Unilever to control international operations and reduce the risk of dealing with outside partners. For example, the firm spent $2.7 billion to acquire South Korean skin-care brand Carver Korea to extend its presence in Asia. In Colombia, Unilever acquired Quala to better target personal and home care products to Latin America. Major factories are located in Brazil, Canada, China, Indonesia, Mexico, Ireland, and Turkey. Unilever's R&D centers—in India, China, the Netherlands, the United States, and the UK—employ 6,000 scientists, engineers, and technicians. Unilever has entered many collaborative ventures to strengthen R&D, design, manufacturing, and other activities. International collaborations give the firm access to foreign partners' expertise, capital, distribution channels, marketing capabilities, and other assets.

Strategically locating R&D, production, and sales in appropriate countries provides enormous *location-specific advantages*, including access to superior labor and the ability to sell in top markets. For example, Unilever's plant in Durban, South Africa, benefits from top advantages in natural resources, physical infrastructure, and low-cost, high-quality labor. Unilever uses palm oil in the production of margarine, ice cream, soap, and shampoo. The firm's palm oil plantations in Malaysia benefit from good climate, abundant palm trees, and low-cost labor. Unilever's R&D centers in the UK leverage the country's abundant scientists and knowledge workers as well as capital needed to fund innovation.

*Factor proportions* refer to the relative concentration in countries of labor, capital, and other production factors. Unilever's plant in Hefei, China, makes personal care products under the Pond's, Dove, and Vaseline brands. China is a top manufacturing location because of plentiful low-cost, high-quality labor. The country's abundant land helps keep rents and other property-related costs low. China is also home to major stock markets and half of the world's largest 10 banks, which provide capital for Unilever's many activities there.

## Recent Events

The FMCG industry is thriving due to rapid population and income growth in emerging markets. Unilever faces many challenges, including evolving demand, complex supply chains, and uncertainty in the natural environment. Consumers increasingly shop online. Many are "going green" and demand superior value. In advanced economies, more consumers are demanding products tailored to specific and fragmented needs. Such changes erode scale advantages and provide new opportunities to small players. On the supply side, natural resource shortages are affecting the costs of chemicals, food ingredients, and other key inputs. Trade protectionism is on the rise in several top markets. Unilever's numerous comparative and competitive advantages are providing big benefits that will help the firm navigate threats and opportunities.

## AACSB and CKR Intangible Soft Skills to improve employability and success in the workplace:
### Written and Oral Communication, Analytical Thinking, Reflective Thinking, Application of Knowledge

### Case Questions

**2-4.** Unilever has used FDI extensively to internationalize its activities around the world. What advantages does FDI provide the firm? What steps can Unilever take to ensure its FDI ventures succeed?

**2-5.** What are the roles of comparative and competitive advantages in Unilever's success? Provide specific examples of natural and acquired advantages that Unilever uses to succeed in the global FMCG industry.

**2-6.** Discuss Unilever and its position in the FMCG industry in terms of the determinants of national competitiveness. What are the roles of demand conditions; firm strategy, structure, and rivalry; factor conditions; and related and supporting industries in Unilever's international success?

**2-7.** In terms of Dunning's eclectic paradigm, describe the ownership-specific advantages, location-specific advantages, and internalization advantages that Unilever holds. Which of these advantages do you believe has been most instrumental to the firm's success? Justify your answer.

*Sources:* Christopher Bartlett, "Unilever's New Global Strategy: Competing Through Sustainability," Harvard Business School case, August 24, 2016, www.hbsp.harvard.edu; Richard Benson-Armer, Steve Noble, and Alexander Thiel, "The Consumer Sector in 2030: Trends and Questions to Consider," December 2015, McKinsey & Co., www.mckinsey.com; Bhaskar Chakravorti, "Unilever's Big Strategic Bet on the Dollar Shave Club," *Harvard Business Review*, July 28, 2016, www.hbr.org; Saabira Chaudhuri, "Outfoxed by Small-Batch Upstarts, Unilever Decides to Imitate Them," *Wall Street Journal*, January 3, 2018, www.wsj.com; Saabira Chaudhuri, "Unilever and Nestlé Struggle with Cautious U.S. and European Consumers," *Wall Street Journal*, April 21, 2017, www.wsj.com; *Economist*, "Unilever Is the World's Biggest Experiment in Corporate Do-Gooding" September 2, 2017, p. 58; William George and Amram Migdal, "Battle for the Soul of Capitalism: Unilever and the Kraft Heinz Takeover Bid," Harvard Business School case, May 30, 2017, Harvard Business School Publishing, www.hbsp.harvard.edu; Vijay Mahajan, "How Unilever Reaches Rural Consumers in Emerging Markets," *Harvard Business Review*, December 14, 2016, www.cb.hbrp.harvard.edu; Marketline, "Company Profile: Unilever," February 28, 2017, www.marketline.com; Unilever, "About Unilever," 2017, www.unilever.com; U.S. Commercial Service, *Doing Business in the Netherlands: 2017 Country Commercial Guide for U.S. Companies*, www.export.gov/netherlands; U.S. Commercial Service, *Doing Business in the United Kingdom: 2017 Country Commercial Guide for U.S. Companies*, www.export.gov/unitedkingdom; Vivienne Walt, "Unilever CEO Paul Polman's Plan to Save the World," *Fortune*, February 17, 2017, www.fortune.com.

This case was written by Bohua Fu under the supervision of Gary Knight

## MyLab Management

Go to **www.pearson.com/mylab/management** to complete the problems marked with this icon ⭐.

## Key Terms

| | | |
|---|---|---|
| absolute advantage principle  37 | competitive advantage  35 | internalization theory  50 |
| comparative advantage  34 | free trade  34 | mercantilism  36 |
| comparative advantage principle  38 | industrial cluster  44 | national industrial policy  44 |

## Summary

In this chapter, you learned about:

- **Why nations trade**

  Each nation specializes in producing certain goods and services and then trades with other nations to acquire those goods and services in which it is not specialized. Classic explanations of international trade began with mercantilism, which argued that nations should seek to maximize their wealth by exporting more than they import. The absolute advantage principle argues that a country benefits by producing only those products in which it has absolute advantage or can produce using fewer resources than another country. The principle of comparative advantage contends that countries should specialize and export those goods in which they have a relative advantage compared to other countries. Comparative advantage is based on *natural advantages* and *acquired advantages*. Competitive advantage derives from distinctive assets or competencies of a firm, such as cost, size, or innovation strengths, which are difficult for competitors to replicate or imitate. *Factor proportions theory* holds that nations specialize in the production of goods and services whose factors of production they hold in abundance. *International product life cycle theory* describes how a product can be invented in one country and eventually mass-produced in other countries, with the innovating country losing its initial competitive advantage.

- **How nations enhance their competitive advantage**

  A major recent contribution to trade theory is Porter's determinants of national competitive advantage, which specify the four conditions in each nation that give rise to national competitive advantages: *demand conditions; firm strategy, structure, and rivalry; factor conditions*; and *related and supporting industries*. An industrial cluster is a concentration of companies in the same industry in a given location that interact closely with one another, gaining mutual competitive advantage. Competitive advantage of nations describes how nations acquire international trade advantages by developing specific skills, technologies, and industries. National industrial policy refers to governments' efforts to direct national resources to developing expertise in specific industries.

- **Why and how firms internationalize**

  The *internationalization process model* describes how companies expand into international business gradually, usually progressing from simple exporting to the most committed stage, FDI. Born global firms internationalize at or near their founding and are part of the emergent field of international entrepreneurship.

- **How internationalizing firms can gain and sustain competitive advantage**

  MNEs have value chains that span geographic locations worldwide. Foreign direct investment means that firms invest at various locations to establish factories, marketing subsidiaries, or regional headquarters. *Monopolistic advantage theory* describes how companies succeed internationally by developing resources and capabilities that few other firms possess. Internalization is the process of acquiring and maintaining one or more value-chain activities inside the firm to minimize the disadvantages of subcontracting these activities to external firms. Internalization theory explains the tendency of MNEs to internalize value-chain stages when it is to their advantage. The *eclectic paradigm* specifies that the international firm should possess certain internal competitive advantages, called *ownership-specific advantages, location-specific advantages*, and *internalization advantages*. Many companies engage in international *collaborative ventures*, inter-firm partnerships that give them access to assets and other advantages foreign partners hold.

## Test Your Comprehension

**AACSB:** Written and Oral Communication, Analytical Thinking, Reflective Thinking, Application of Knowledge

**2-8.** Describe the classic theories of international trade. Which theories do you believe are relevant today?

**2-9.** What is the difference between the concepts of absolute advantage and comparative advantage?

**2-10.** Summarize factor proportions theory. What factors are most abundant in China, Japan, Germany, Saudi Arabia, and the United States? Visit globalEDGE™ for helpful information.

**2-11.** How does factor proportions theory compare to international product life cycle theory?

**2-12.** Do you believe your country should adopt a national industrial policy? Why or why not?

**2-13.** There is a tendency for organizations to move from simple exporting operations to FDI over a period of time. Why is this often the case? What might slow or stop the process?

**2-14.** Industrial clusters can be valuable tools for a country's economy. Identify three global examples and describe their development. Do not choose your own country.

**2-15.** Are collaborative ventures the best option when a business has little knowledge of the market?

## Apply Your Understanding

**AACSB:** Written and Oral Communication, Ethical Understanding and Reasoning, Analytical Thinking, Reflective Thinking, Application of Knowledge

**2-16.** According to the Observatory of Economic Complexity (OEC), Australia exports 152 products that display the characteristics of comparative advantage. The OEC defines this in slightly different terms than the generally accepted definition. They suggest that a comparative advantage is revealed by a country having a larger share of global exports than would normally be expected considering the overall size of its export economy and the actual size of the products' global market. In 2016, Australia had exports of just under $200 billion. Among the products in the comparative advantage category were items as diverse as animal hides, arts and antiques, glass, and vegetables.

Examine the report on Australia's comparative advantage, which can be accessed at the website of the Australian Council of Learned Academies (https://acola.org.au/wp/reports-library). The report provides a comprehensive appraisal of the comparative advantage products and sectors; it also suggests how the country can move to secure its position in the future. What are the key steps that Australia should take? Apply this approach to your own country. Identify any comparative advantages and then suggest ways in which these can be protected and developed into the future.

**2-17.** Economist Lester Thurow once posed the question "If you were the president of your own country and could specialize in one of two industries, computer chips or potato chips, which would you choose?" When faced with this question, many people choose potato chips because "everybody can use potato chips, but not everybody can use computer chips." However, the answer is much more complex. Whether to choose computer chips or potato chips depends on such factors as the relationship between national wealth and the amount of value added in manufacturing products, the possibility that the country can benefit from monopoly power (few countries can make computer chips), and the likelihood of spin-off industries (computer chip technology gives rise to other technologies, such as computers). In light of these and other possible considerations, which would you choose, computer chips or potato chips? Justify your answer.

**2-18.** *Ethical Dilemma:* To reduce poverty in Africa, government officials want to increase African exports to Europe. Africa's top exports include agricultural products, such as meat, coffee, peanuts, and fruit, and many Africans depend on food exports for their livelihood. However, the European Union (EU) imposes high trade barriers on the import of agricultural products. Among various reasons, Europeans are concerned about food quality, and the EU has adopted rigorous agricultural safety standards. However, the tough regulations hurt African countries, which have experienced problems with food toxins and bovine diseases in the past. In addition, the agricultural lobby in Europe is powerful, and the EU subsidizes farmers heavily. Many European politicians do not want to risk angering Europe's farm lobby by supporting free international trade in agricultural products. Suppose you are part of an EU government task force investigating trade barriers on African agricultural imports. Analyze the arguments for and against agricultural trade with Africa. What should the EU do? Justify your answer.

 **globalEDGE** | **INTERNET EXERCISES**
Access globalEDGE™ at www.globalEDGE.msu.edu

**AACSB: Written and Oral Communication, Ethical Understanding and Reasoning, Information Technology, Analytical Thinking, Reflective Thinking, Application of Knowledge**

2-19. Suppose your company is interested in importing wines from Argentina. In analyzing this opportunity, you want to identify the strengths and weaknesses of the Argentine wine industry. What are the conditions that make Argentina a favorable location for wine cultivation? Provide a short description of the status of Argentina's wine exports and a list of the top importing countries of Argentine wines. In addition to globalEDGE™, some useful websites for this research include www.winesofargentina.org and www. ita.doc.gov.

2-20. Volvo (www.volvo.com) and Pilkington (www.pilkington. com) are major multinational firms with operations that span the globe. Investigate these firms by visiting their websites as well as www.hoovers.com (a site that provides specific company information) and globalEDGE™. For each company, describe its ownership-specific advantages, location-specific advantages, and internalization advantages.

2-21. The World Bank works to alleviate world poverty and provides information about conditions in developing countries, which it uses to measure progress in economic and social development. World Development Indicators (www. worldbank.org/data) is the Bank's premier source for data on international development. The Bank measures more than 800 indicators of national conditions regarding people, environment, and economy. Consult the website, click World Development Indicators or Indicators, and answer the following questions: (a) In countries with developing economies, what indicators are most associated with poverty? (b) What types of industries are most typically found in poor countries? (c) Based on comparing development indicators in poor and affluent countries, speculate on what types of actions governments in developing countries can take to help spur economic development and alleviate poverty.

## CKR Tangible Process Tools™

### What is a CKR Tangible Process Tool Exercise?

CKR Tangible Process Tools consist of practical exercises and work processes designed to familiarize you with key managerial challenges and decisions that professionals typically encounter in international business. Completing CKR Tangible Process Tool exercises in this text enables you to acquire practical, real-world work processes that will improve employability and success in the workplace. Each exercise presents a managerial challenge in a real-world scenario, the skills you will acquire in solving the exercise, and a methodology and the resources to use in solving it. The second half of the exercise is provided at the Pearson MyLab Management website (www.pearson.com/mylab/management).

### Exercise: Porter's Diamond Model and Manufacturing

The principle of comparative advantage suggests that every country possesses distinctive resources that give it advantages in the production of specific products. Michael Porter's Diamond Model, in his book, *Competitive Advantage of Nations*, argues that nations become adept at certain industries due to the presence of certain resources and four conditions: demand conditions; firm strategy, structure, and rivalry; factor conditions; and related and supporting industries. Firms establish production facilities in those countries where they can obtain the most favorable resources and advantages.

When locating value-chain activities abroad, management should try to ascertain the best location for each activity. A good approach is to (i) identify the factors that most influence company success (which tends to vary by industry) and then (ii) conduct research to find countries that offer the best combination of these factors.

In this exercise, you will gain an understanding of the factors to consider when locating company operations, learn how these factors relate to maximizing the firm's competitive advantage, and gain research skills for acquiring knowledge for planning company operations.

**Background**

Choosing the best foreign location for manufacturing provides numerous advantages, including the ability to minimize manufacturing costs, maximize the quality of produced goods, and access the best factors of production and technological resources. For example, Hoya Company, which makes eyeglass lenses, established its main factory in the Netherlands to be close to Europe's superior technology in the lens-making industry. Intel established an R&D center in Taiwan to access Taiwan's engineers and other superior knowledge in the microprocessor industry.

In this exercise, you will use the elements in Porter's Diamond Model to conduct research online to identify the best countries to establish a manufacturing plant in each of the following industries: dress shoes, flat-screen televisions, and pharmaceutical drugs. The Diamond Model states that competitive advantage results from the existence and quality in a country of four major elements.

- *Demand conditions* refer to the nature of home-market demand for specific products and services. The presence of highly demanding buyers pressures firms to innovate faster and produce better products. For example, U.S. consumers have strong spending power and suffer from various health conditions. This situation has led the United States to become one of the leading producers of patent medications and medical technology. Canadians have much experience driving in the snow in rugged conditions, which makes them demanding consumers of four-wheel-drive trucks and sport utility vehicles. Hence, Canada is a superior location for producing such products.

- *Firm strategy, structure, and rivalry* refer to the nature of domestic rivalry and conditions in a nation that govern how companies are created, organized, and managed. Here the focus is on the presence of strong competitors in the nation. When a country has numerous competitors in the same industry, the level of technology, resources, and factors of production in the nation will be relatively advanced. For example, Japan is home to some of the world's leading firms in the air conditioning industry. Constant competitive rivalry continuously pressures these firms to innovate and improve. The firms in Japan's air conditioning industry compete for managerial talent, technical leadership, and superior product quality, factors that have reached a high level in the industry in Japan.

- *Factor conditions* describe the nation's position in factors of production, such as labor, capital, infrastructure, science, and IT. Every country has more of certain factor endowments and less of others, a situation that determines the nature of national competitive advantages. For example, Germany's numerous workers with strong engineering skills have propelled the country to leadership in the global scientific instruments industry. Mexico's millions of low-wage workers have allowed the country to develop competitive advantage in the manufacture of labor-intensive industrial products, such as car parts.

- *Related and supporting industries* reflect the presence in the nation of clusters of suppliers, competitors, and complementary firms that excel in particular industries. The resulting business environment is highly supportive for the founding of particular types of firms. Operating within a mass of related and supporting industries provides advantages through information and knowledge synergies, economies of scale and scope, and access to appropriate or superior inputs. For example, Silicon Valley in California is home to hundreds of successful software companies, which collectively create synergies that make for a strong base in the industry. Southeast China is a good place to locate a factory to manufacture office furniture because of the presence there of thousands of very knowledgeable firms and workers in that industry. One city in the region is a leading capital of chair manufacturing with more than 100,000 chair workers. The firms in this industry exchange much useful knowledge about furniture manufacturing that accelerates new product development and innovations.

To complete this exercise in your MyLab, go to MyLab Management (www.pearson.com/mylab/management) and click on **Career Toolbox**.

*Note*: Some material in this exercise is based on Michael Porter, *The Competitive Advantage of Nations* (New York: Free Press, 1990).

# Endnotes

1. John Romalis, "Factor Proportions and the Structure of Commodity Trade," *The American Economic Review* 94, No. 1 (2004), pp. 67–97; Robert Zymek, "Factor Proportions and the Growth of World Trade," *Journal of International Economics* 95, No.1 (2015), pp. 42–53.

2. Raymond Vernon, "International Investment and International Trade in the Product Cycle," *Quarterly Journal of Economics* 80 (May 1966), pp. 190–207.

3. Michael Porter, *The Competitive Advantage of Nations* (New York: Free Press, 1990).

4. Jože Damijan and Crt Kostevc, "Learning from Trade Through Innovation," *Oxford Bulletin of Economics & Statistics* 77, No. 3 (2015), pp. 408–436; Leonid Kogan, Dimitris Papanikolaou, Amit Seru, and Noah Stoffman, "Technological Innovation, Resource Allocation, and Growth," *The Quarterly Journal of Economics* 132, No. 2 (2017), pp. 665–712.

5. Richard Nelson and Sidney Winter, *An Evolutionary Theory of Economic Change* (Cambridge, MA: Belknap Press, 1982); Melissa Schilling, *Strategic Management of Technological Innovation*, 5th ed. (New York: McGraw-Hill Education, 2017).

6. Barry Jaruzelski and Kevin Dehoff, "Beyond Borders: The Global Innovation 1000," *Strategy Business* 53 (2008), pp. 52–67; strategy&, *The 2017 Global Innovation 1000 study*, www.strategyand.pwc.com

7. Richard Dobbs, Jeremy Oppenheim, and Fraser Thompson, "Mobilizing for a Resource Revolution," *McKinsey Quarterly*, January 2012, www.mckinseyquarterly.com; James Manyika, Jaana Remes, and Jonathan Woetzel, "A Productivity Perspective on the Future Of Growth," *McKinsey Quarterly*, September 2014, www.mckinsey.com.

8. Andrew Mayeda, "New Zealand Dethrones Singapore as Easiest Place to Do Business," *Bloomberg*, October 25, 2016, www.bloomberg.com; OECD, *OECD Economic Surveys: New Zealand 2017* (Paris: OECD Publishing, 2017).

9. Warren Bilkey, "An Attempted Integration of the Literature on the Export Behavior of Firms," *Journal of International Business Studies* 9 (Summer 1978), pp. 3–46; S. Tamer Cavusgil, "On the Internationalization Process of Firms," *European Research* 8, No. 6 (1980), pp. 27–81; Jan Johanson and Jan-Erik Vahlne, "The Internationalization Process of the Firm—A Model of Knowledge Development and Increasing Foreign Commitments," *Journal of International Business Studies* 8 (Spring/Summer 1977), pp. 2–32.

10. Ibid.

11. Samsung, *Samsung History*, 2018, www.samsung.com; Jaeyong Song and Kyungmook Lee, *The Samsung Way* (New York: McGraw-Hill Education, 2014).

12. G. Knight and S. T. Cavusgil, "The Born Global Firm: A Challenge to Traditional Internationalization Theory," in *Advances in International Marketing*, vol. 8, ed. S. T. Cavusgil and T. Madsen (Greenwich, CT: JAI Press, 1996), pp. 11–26; S. Tamer Cavusgil and Gary Knight, "The Born-Global Firm: An Entrepreneurial and Capabilities Perspective on Early and Rapid Internationalization," *Journal of International Business Studies* 46, No. 1 (2015), pp. 3–16.

13. Cavusgil and Knight, 2015; S. T. Cavusgil and Gary Knight, *Born Global Firms: A New International Enterprise* (New York: Business Expert Press, 2009); Gary Knight and S. T. Cavusgil, "Innovation, Organizational Capabilities, and the Born-Global Firm," *Journal of International Business Studies* 35, No. 2 (2004), pp. 12–41; Benjamin Oviatt and Patricia McDougall, "Toward a Theory of International New Ventures," *Journal of International Business Studies* 25, No. 1 (1994), pp. 4–64; Michael Rennie, "Born Global," *McKinsey Quarterly* No. 4 (1993), pp. 4–52.

14. Chris Carter, "Minecraft Is Unifying Nearly All of Its Versions Across All Platforms, Except Sony," *Destructoid*, June 11, 2017, www.destructoid.com; *Minecraft Wiki*, "Timeline of Events," January 1, 2018, www.minecraft.gamepedia.com; Dave Smith, "The Top 50 Video Games of All Time, Ranked," *Business Insider*, December 11, 2016, www.businessinsider.com.

15. Marian Jones, Nicole Coviello, and Yee Kwan Tang, "International Entrepreneurship Research (1989–2009): A Domain Ontology and Thematic Analysis," *Journal of Business Venturing* 26, No. 6 (2011), pp. 632–659; Patricia McDougall and Benjamin Oviatt, "International Entrepreneurship: The Intersection of Two Research Paths," *Academy of Management Journal* 43, No. 5 (2000), pp. 902–906; Christian Schwens, Florian Zapkau, Michael Bierwerth, Rodrigo Isidor, Gary Knight, and Rudiger Kabst, "International Entrepreneurship: A Meta-Analysis on the Internationalization and Performance Relationship," *Entrepreneurship Theory and Practice*, March 2017, pp. 1–35.

16. UNCTAD, *World Investment Report 2017* (Geneva: United Nations, 2017); UNCTAD, *UNCTAD Stat 2017* (New York: United Nations, 2017).

17. Ibid.

18. Stephen Hymer, *The International Operations of National Firms* (Cambridge, MA: MIT Press, 1976); Samsung, 2018; Song and Lee, 2014.

19. Peter Buckley and Mark Casson, *The Future of the Multinational Enterprise* (London: MacMillan, 1976); Peter Buckley, Jonathan Doh, and Mirko Benischke, "Towards a Renaissance in International Business Research? Big Questions, Grand Challenges, and the Future of IB Scholarship," *Journal of International Business Studies* 48, No. 9 (2017), pp. 1045–1064; John Dunning, "The Eclectic Paradigm of International Production: A Restatement and Some Possible Extensions," *Journal of International Business Studies* 19 (1988), pp. 1–31.

20. Stephen Tallman, Yadong Luo, and Peter Buckley, "Business Models in Global Competition," *Global Strategy Journal* 7, No. 5 (2017), www.onlinelibrary.wiley.com; Dunning, 1988.

21. John Dunning, *International Production and the Multinational Enterprise* (London: Allen and Unwin, 1981); Karina R. Jensen, *Leading Global Innovation: Facilitating Multicultural Collaboration and International Market Success* (London: Palgrave Macmillan, 2017); Bruce Kogut, "Joint Ventures: Theoretical and Empirical Perspectives," *Strategic Management Journal* 9 (1988), pp. 319–332; Office of the United States Trade Representative, *2017 National Trade Estimate Report on Foreign Trade Barriers* (Washington, DC: 2017); P. Rajan Varadarajan and Margaret H. Cunningham, "Strategic Alliances: A Synthesis of Conceptual Foundations," *Journal of the Academy of Marketing Science* 23 (1995), pp. 282–296.

22. Lauren Gensler, "Piping Hot: Starbucks Sales Rise 18%," *Forbes.com*, April 23, 2015, p. 13; *Inside Retail Asia,* "Starbucks Japan Opening in Tourist Attractions," November 10, 2017, www.insideretailasia.com; Starbucks Japan, "About Us," www.starbucks.co.jp, accessed January 19, 2018.

23. Manlio Del Giudice, *Understanding Family-Owned Business Groups* (London: Palgrave McMillan, 2017); James Lincoln, Christina Ahmadjian, and Eliot Mason, "Organizational Learning and Purchase-Supply Relations in Japan," *California Management Review* 40, No. 3 (1998), pp. 244–264.

24. Del Giudice, 2017; Mats Forsgren, Ulf Holm, and Jan Johanson, *Knowledge, Networks and Power* (London: Palgrave McMillan, 2015); Hakan Hakansson, *International Marketing and Purchasing of Industrial Goods: An Interaction Approach* (New York: Wiley, 1982).

25. Forsgren, Hoom, and Johanson, 2015; Hakansson, 1982.

26. *Amazon*, "Government of Telangana Partners with Amazon India to Help Weavers Sell Online," August 7, 2017, www.amazon.in; Amy Nguyen-Chyung and Elliot Fault, *Amazon in Emerging Markets* (Ross School of Business, University of Michigan and WDI Publishing, 2014); *The Economic Times,* "Capital Float Partners with Amazon India to Disburse Loans to E-sellers," March 20, 2017, www.economictimes.indiatimes.com; *Wall Street Journal,* "Amazon Sells Hardware to Cloud Partner in China," November 14, 2017, www.wsj.com; Yue Wang, "To Boost China Sales, Amazon Tries Alibaba Partnership," *Forbes*, March 5, 2015, www.forbes.com.

# Chapter 3

# Political and Legal Systems in National Environments

**Learning Objectives** *After studying this chapter, you should be able to:*

3.1 Describe political and legal environments in international business.

3.2 Understand political systems.

3.3 Understand legal systems.

3.4 Describe the participants in political and legal systems.

3.5 Identify the types of country risk produced by political systems.

3.6 Identify the types of country risk produced by legal systems.

3.7 Know about managing country risk.

## Galileo: Regional Disintegration and Its Consequences

A lot has been written about Brexit since the referendum in June 2016 in terms of both the threats and the opportunities it may entail, but there are a few points that are inarguable. The challenges it poses to transnational businesses and initiatives is one major point, and in no other case this is more evident than in the case of Galileo.

Galileo is the all-European satellite navigation system that, once fully operational in mid 2020s, will surpass any existing geo-localization in terms of accuracy and precision, GPS included. But it is Galileo's sophistication that creates issues in light of Brexit. Galileo's Public Regulated Service (PRS), a feature designed to serve as a secure, encrypted navigation system, is considered by the European Union as a back-up system vital for both civil and military purposes—and due to EU laws, it is available only to EU member states.

The United Kingdom has been involved since day one in the design and the construction of Galileo through the UK-based Surrey Satellite Technology Ltd., a subsidiary of both Germany's OHB and France's Airbus. This company manufactures a critical piece for Galileo's satellites: its "brain," or payload.

However, once the United Kingdom leaves the European Union, it may also find itself outside the Galileo project due to the restrictions mentioned above. Endless disputes around Galileo's membership and manufacturing contracts have been raging since January 2018, when the supplier contracts for Galileo had to be renewed and the renewal bidding procedure started.

Threatened with exclusion, the United Kingdom might decide to withdraw from the project and build a system on its own for which it has the technical capabilities. It could even go to the extent of stopping British companies from manufacturing components for Galileo's systems. Moreover, the

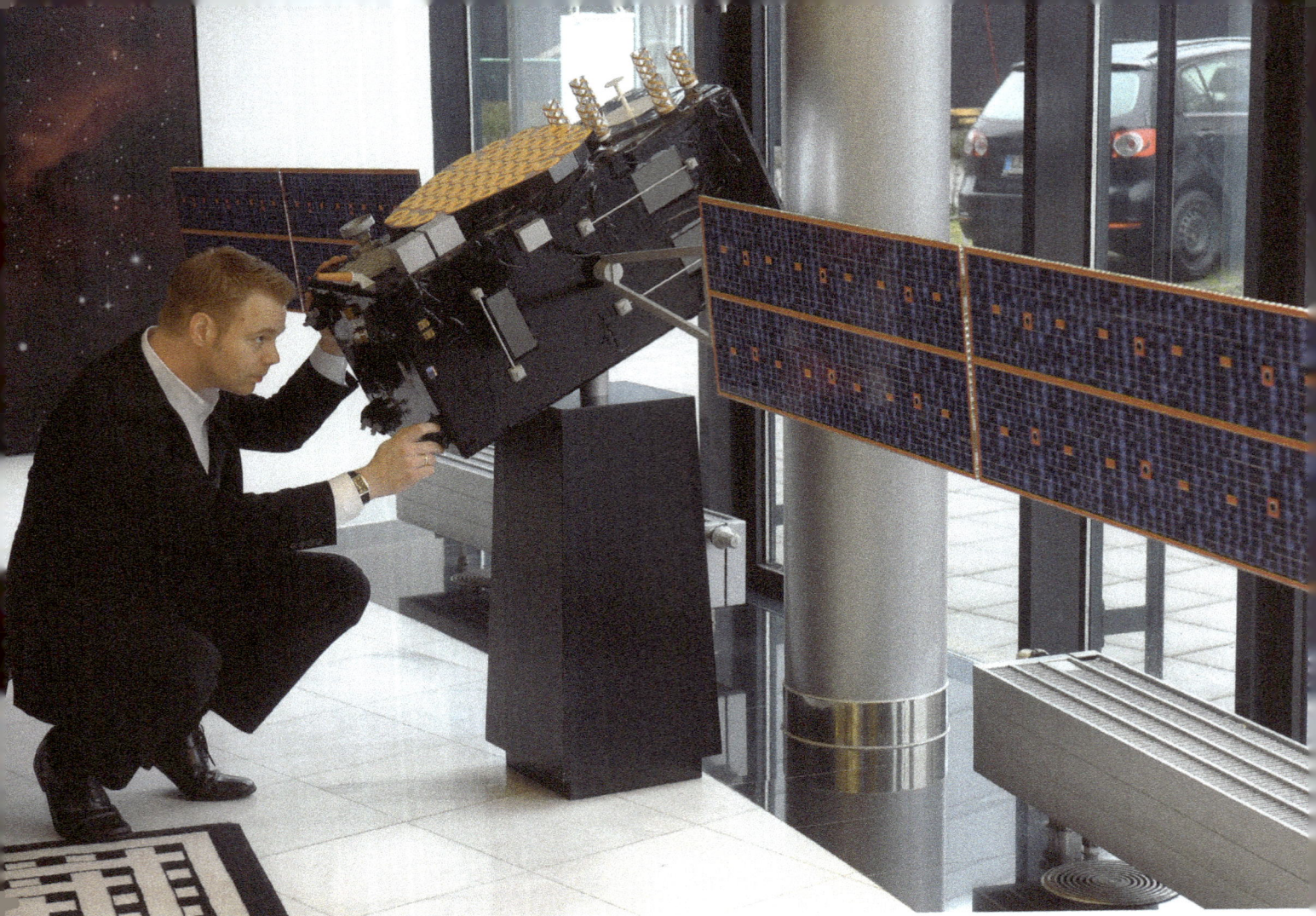

Source: dpa picture alliance archive/Alamy Stock Photo

country could also seek to reclaim the £1.2 billion spent so far on developing the new navigation system.

It is still unclear how this issue will be handled, and Galileo is one of many troubling areas of the Brexit divorce settlement, but there are precedents for non-EU participation in the navigation system. It is certain, however, that the project itself is very likely to be delayed in any circumstance other than full cooperation, proving yet again that the political landscape can have a massive effect on businesses.

## Questions

**3-1.** Galileo is one of many ongoing EU initiatives in aerospace that the United Kingdom, as a member state, takes part. Why has Galileo attracted all this attention and controversy compared to others, such as Copernicus, which receives even more funding from the European Union? Illustrate the major difference and explain what specific issues affect Galileo.

**3-2.** The United Kingdom's reactions to the EU stance have been varied, but all of them amount to strong disagreement. What claim can the United Kingdom put forward in opposition to this position? Is anybody else supporting it?

**3-3.** What are the possible ways forward in the Galileo dilemma if the United Kingdom leaves the European Union as planned? Discuss the available options and their likelihood.

SOURCES: ESA, "Norway Signs Galileo Agreement with Commission," September 22, 2010, https://www.esa.int/Our_Activities/Navigation/Norway_signs_Galileo_agreement_with_Commission, accessed May 24, 2018; Stefania Paladini, "Brexit and the EU Space Industry," Centre for Brexit Studies Blog, May 29, 2018, https://centreforbrexitstudiesblog.wordpress.com/2018/05/29/brexit-and-the-eu-space-industry-the-galileo-conundrum/; "UK Makes Galileo Satellite a Condition for EU Defence Collaboration," *Financial Times*, 2018, https://www.ft.com/content/e8d45d26-5f34-11e8-9334-2218e7146b04, accessed May 24, 2018; M. Busby, "UK Plans Own Space Programme After Dispute with EU over Galileo Project, Defence Secretary Announces," *The Independent*, May 21, 2018, https://www.independent.co.uk/news/uk/home-news/brexit-galileo-satellite-programme-space-dispute-williamson-barnier-clarke-a8360276.html, accessed September 14, 2018; J. Amos, "UK Ups the Ante on Galileo Sat-nav Project," *BBC News*, http://www.bbc.com/news/science-environment-44116085, accessed May 24, 2018; Space Growth Partnership, "Prosperity from Space: A Partnership Strategy for UK," UK Space Agency, http://www.ukspace.org/wp-content/uploads/2018/05/Prosperity-from-Space-strategy_2May2018.pdf, accessed May 24, 2018.

This case was written by Stefania Paladini, Birmingham City University.

Most of us expect a familiar business landscape when we conduct business at home. Yet foreign markets differ in terms of political and legal systems as well as business norms. As illustrated by the opening case, foreign markets often pose major challenges and create vulnerabilities for the firm. Managers must be able to navigate difficult regulations and practices and avoid unethical or questionable conduct.

At the same time, the political and legal context may also present opportunities for companies. Preferential subsidies, government incentives, and protection from competition reduce business costs and influence strategic decision making. Many governments encourage domestic investment from foreign MNEs by offering tax holidays and cash incentives to employ local workers.

**Country risk** is defined as exposure to potential loss or adverse effects on company operations and profitability caused by developments in a country's political and/or legal environments. Sometimes termed *political risk,* it is one of four major types of international business risks. Although the immediate cause of country risk is a political or legal factor, underlying such factors may be economic, social, or technological developments. Exhibit 3.1 identifies dimensions of country risk prevalent in international business. We address them in this chapter. Government intervention, protectionism, and barriers to trade and investment are particularly notable in international business. Mismanagement or failure of the national economy can lead to financial crises, recessions, market downturns, currency crises, and inflation. Such events usually arise from business cycles, poor monetary or fiscal policies, a defective regulatory environment, or imbalances in the underlying economic fundamentals of the host country.

Political or legislative actions can harm business interests, such as laws that are unexpectedly strict or result in unintended consequences. Many laws favor host-country interests—that is, interests in foreign countries where the firm has direct operations. For example, Coca-Cola's business suffered in Germany after the German government enacted a recycling plan that required consumers to return non-reusable soda containers to stores for a refund of 0.25 euros. Rather than coping with unwanted returns, big supermarket chains responded by yanking Coke

**Country risk**

Exposure to potential loss or adverse effects on company operations and profitability caused by developments in a country's political and/or legal environments.

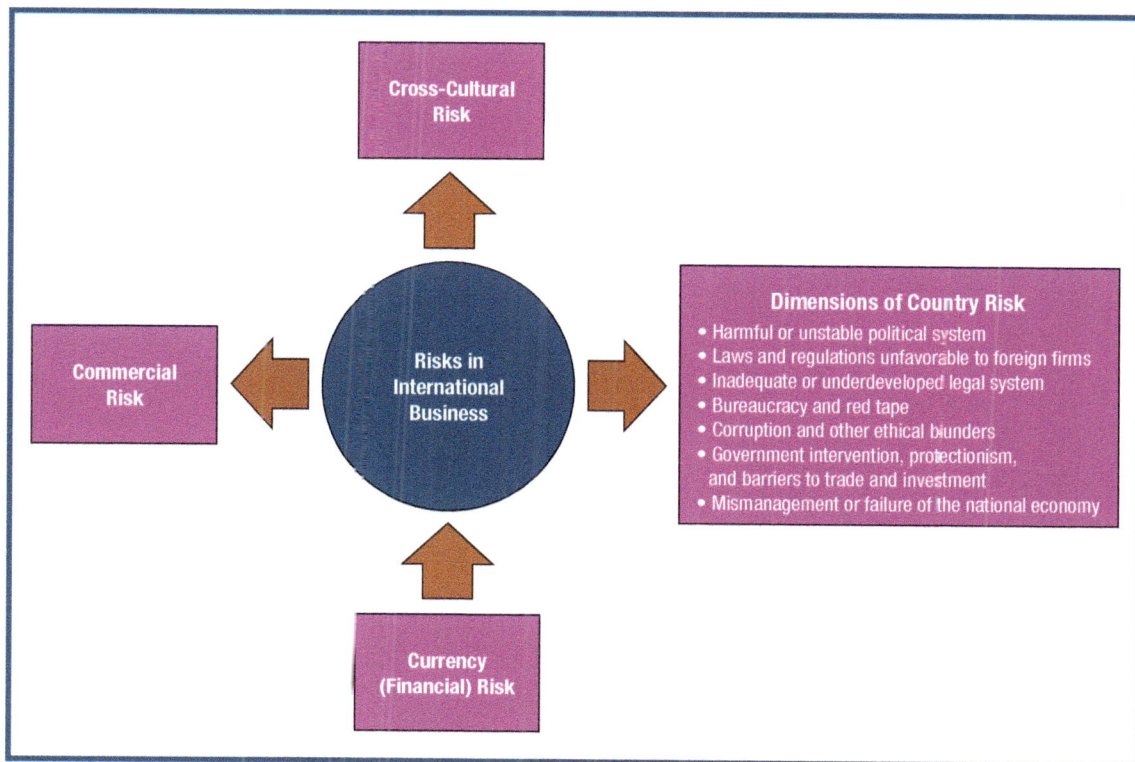

**EXHIBIT 3.1**

**Country Risk as One of Four Major Risks in International Business**

from their shelves and pushing their own store brands instead. The Hilton Hotel chain was fined $700,000 in 2017 for data breaches that compromised more than 350,000 credit card numbers. The European Union enacted a new law, the General Data Protection Rule (GDPR). Under the GDPR, if the breaches had occurred in 2018, Hilton would have had to pay about $420 million— or $1,200 for every compromised record. In China, the government has censored TV programs such as *Downton Abbey, House of Cards*, and *The Walking Dead*, whose content is considered inappropriate for Chinese citizens. Chinese authorities forbid the broadcast of Western shows that feature sex, violence, extramarital affairs, and content critical of the Chinese government.[1]

## How Prevalent Is Country Risk?

Exhibit 3.2 presents the level of country risk in selected countries, measured as political stability, legal environment, economic indicators, and tax policy. Venezuela is dominated by an unpredictable, dictatorial government. Zimbabwe remains under authoritarian rule. Libya is risky in the wake of civil war and political instability. Such countries suffer from unstable governments, underdeveloped legal systems, or biased law enforcement. Conversely, countries such as Canada, Japan, and Singapore are characterized by stable, transparent, and well-founded political and legal systems. Exhibit 3.2 indicates that risk tends to be lower in countries with a favorable legal climate and political stability. In contrast, risks are higher in countries with political instability and substantial government intervention. Many of the riskiest states are poor countries that would benefit enormously from direct investment and integration into the world economy.[2] For the complete list of countries ranked by risk, visit the Risk Briefing site at the Economist Intelligence Unit (www.viewswire.eiu.com).

Country risk may affect all firms in a country equally or only a subset. For example, unrest in Zimbabwe has tended to affect all firms in that country. By contrast, in 2017 the Venezuelan government seized a factory owned by General Motors despite the presence of several competitors in Venezuela, such as Toyota and Fiat Chrysler.[3]

The government of India imposes many restrictions on imports and inward foreign investment. Strict regulations limit imports of agricultural products, chemicals, motor vehicles, and many other products. For example, high tariffs on crude edible oils affect imports of processed

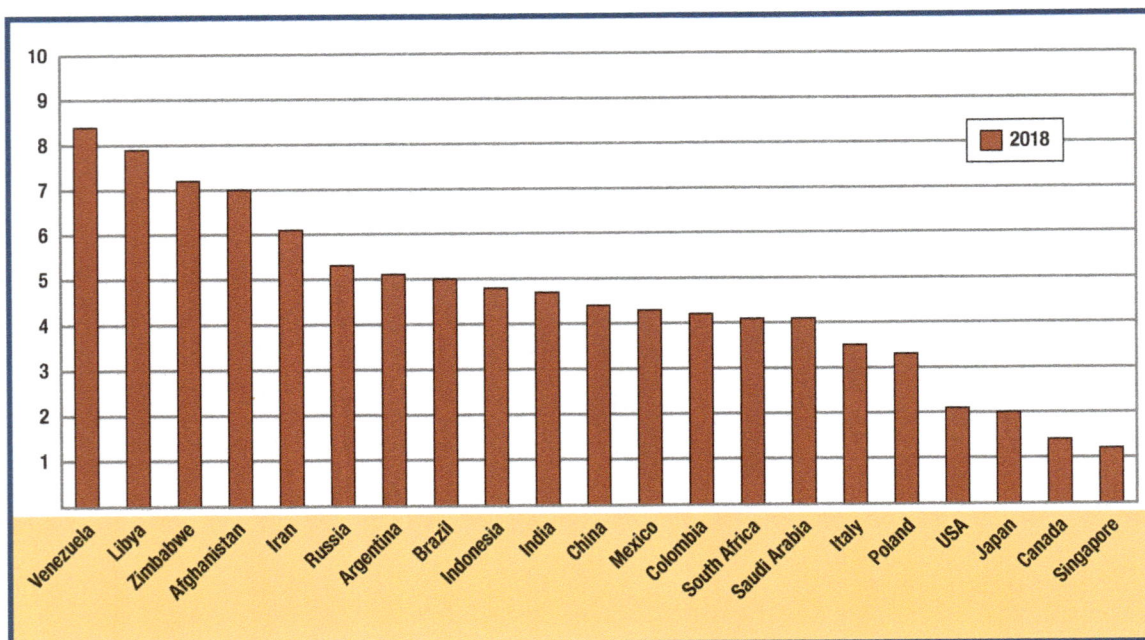

**EXHIBIT 3.2**

**Country Risk in Selected Countries, 2018 (ranked 0 to 10; a high number indicates greater risk)**

*Sources:* Based on *Economist Intelligence Unit*, "Risk Briefing," 2018, http://viewswire.eiu.com/index.asp?layout=homePubTypeRK; *Euler Hermes Country Risk Ratings*, 2017, www.eulerhermes.com/economic-research/country-risks/Pages/country-reports-risk-map.aspx; *Euromoney*, "Euromoney Country Risk," 2018, www.euromoneycountryrisk.com/.

foods and ingredients used in quick-service restaurants. Product sales are subject to substantial value-added and sales taxes, as well as various fees, at both the federal and state levels. India's system of tariffs and fees is complex and lacks transparency. Barriers to inward FDI limit the investment activities of foreign firms, particularly in the services sector. ArcelorMittal, Nissan, Walmart, and numerous other firms have faced delays in establishing operations in India due to government bureaucracy and Indian activist groups, which often oppose industrial development.[4]

**3.1** Describe political and legal environments in international business

## Political and Legal Environments in International Business

A **political system** is a set of formal institutions that constitute a government. It includes legislative bodies, political parties, lobbying groups, and trade unions. The principal functions of a political system are to:

**Political system**
A set of formal institutions that constitute a government that include legislative bodies, political parties, lobbying groups, and trade unions.

- Provide protection from external threats.
- Ensure stability based on laws.
- Govern the allocation of valued resources among the members of a society.
- Define how a society's members interact with each other.

Each country's political system is unique, having evolved within a particular historical, economic, and cultural context. Political systems are also constantly evolving in response to constituent demands and the evolution of the national and international environments. *Constituents* are the people and organizations that support the political system and receive government resources.

**Legal system**
A system for interpreting and enforcing laws.

A **legal system** is a system for interpreting and enforcing laws. Laws, regulations, and rules establish norms for conduct. A legal system includes institutions and procedures that:

- Ensure order.
- Resolve disputes in civil and commercial activities.
- Tax economic output.
- Provide protections for private property, including intellectual property and other company assets.

Exhibit 3.3 identifies the aspects of political and legal systems that contribute to country risk. Political and legal systems are dynamic and constantly changing. The two systems are interdependent—changes in one affect the other. Adverse developments in political and legal systems give rise to country risk. They can result from installation of a new government, shifting values or priorities in political parties, initiatives special interest groups develop, and the creation

**EXHIBIT 3.3**

**Sources of Country Risk**

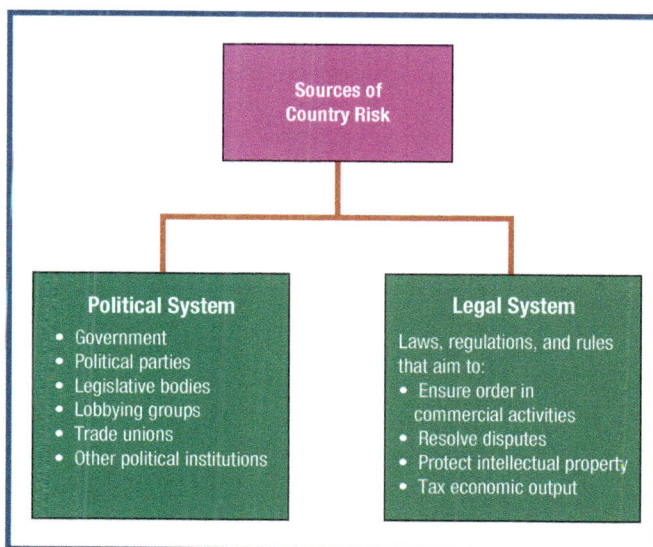

Sources of Country Risk

Political System
- Government
- Political parties
- Legislative bodies
- Lobbying groups
- Trade unions
- Other political institutions

Legal System
Laws, regulations, and rules that aim to:
- Ensure order in commercial activities
- Resolve disputes
- Protect intellectual property
- Tax economic output

of new laws or regulations. Gradual change is easier for the firm to accommodate; sudden change is harder to deal with and poses greater risk to the firm.

Unfavorable developments give rise to new conditions that may threaten the firm's products, services, or business activities. For example, a new import tariff may increase the cost of a key component used to manufacture a product. A change in labor law may alter the hours the firm's employees are allowed to work. Installing a new political leader may lead to government takeover of corporate assets.

Country risk is *always* present, but its nature and intensity vary over time and from country to country. In China, for example, the government is currently overhauling the national legal system, making it more harmonious with Western systems. Some new regulations have been poorly formulated or are confusing or contradictory. Foreign high-tech firms like Google, eBay, Amazon, and Facebook are all confronted with laws and regulations that restrict their entry and activities in the Chinese market. In disputes between local and foreign firms, governments are often inclined to protect local interests. Even where Western firms obtain favorable judgments in the courts, they may not be enforced.[5] Let's delve into political and legal systems in more detail.

## Political Systems

**3.2** Understand political systems.

The world is characterized by three major types of political systems: authoritarianism, socialism, and democracy. Exhibit 3.4 highlights countries that exemplify these systems. These categories are not mutually exclusive. Many democracies also include some elements of socialism. Many former authoritarian regimes now embrace a mix of socialism and democracy. To address sluggish economic conditions, governments in Europe have implemented relatively socialistic policies such as nationalizing firms in the banking industry. China has applied some democratic approaches, such as land reforms and open markets, to stimulate commercial activity.

### Authoritarianism

Under authoritarianism, the state attempts to regulate most aspects of public and private behavior. Well-known authoritarian states from the past include China (1949–1980s) and the Soviet Union (1918–1991). Authoritarianism centralizes power in the government. The state may seek to control not only all economic and political matters but also the attitudes, values, and beliefs of the citizenry. Often, the entire population is mobilized in support of the state and a political or religious ideology. Authoritarian states are generally either theocratic (religion-based) or secular (non–religion-based). Usually there is a state party led by a dictator, such as Kim Jong-un in North Korea. Party membership is mandatory for those seeking to advance within the social and economic hierarchy. Power typically is maintained by means of secret police, propaganda disseminated through state-controlled mass media, regulation of free discussion and criticism, and/or the use of terror tactics. Authoritarian states usually do not tolerate activities by individuals or groups such as churches, labor unions, or political parties that are not directed toward the state's goals.[6]

Many authoritarian states have either disappeared or evolved toward democracy and capitalism. China initiated major reforms in the 1980s, and the Soviet Union collapsed in 1991. Agricultural land and state enterprises were sold to private interests, and entrepreneurs gained the right to establish their own businesses. The transition has not been easy, and former authoritarian

| Elements of Authoritarianism Found in | Elements of Socialism Found in | Largely Democratic |
|---|---|---|
| Afghanistan | Bolivia | Australia |
| Iran | China | Canada |
| North Korea | Egypt | Japan |
| Venezuela | India | New Zealand |
| Several Countries in Africa (such as Equatorial Guinea, Eritrea, Sudan, Zimbabwe) | Romania | United States |
| | Russia | Most European countries |
| | Tanzania | Most Latin American countries |

**EXHIBIT 3.4**

**Examples of Countries Under Various Political Systems**

*Source:* Leonid Andrenov/123RF

By protecting private property rights, democracies promote entrepreneurship. The proprietors of the stores on this street in Madrid, Spain enjoy the benefits of their ownership.

states continue to maintain political control, including government intervention in business. Former Soviet Union states and China are still characterized by substantial red tape and bureaucracy that hinder economic activity (for examples, see the World Bank's www.doingbusiness.org). Today, numerous states exhibit elements of authoritarianism, particularly in Africa, Asia, and the Middle East. Several countries are controlled by heads of state with substantial dictatorial powers, such as Omar al-Bashir in Sudan, Emomali Rahmon in Tajikistan, and Nicolas Maduro in Venezuela.

## Socialism

Socialism's fundamental principle is that capital and wealth should be vested in the state and used primarily as a means of production rather than for profit. Socialism is based on a collectivist ideology. Collective welfare of people is seen to outweigh the welfare of the individual. Socialists argue that capitalists receive a disproportionate amount of society's wealth relative to workers. They believe that in a capitalist society, the pay of workers does not represent the full value of their labor. They argue government should control the basic means of production, distribution, and commercial activity.

Socialism takes the form of *social democracy* in much of the world. Social democracy is an ideology that supports economic and social interventions to promote social justice through democratic means. Social democracies incorporate both capitalist and socialist practices and often feature highly developed welfare systems, distributing aid to those in need. Social democracy has been most successful in Western Europe and also plays a major role in the political systems of several large countries such as Brazil and India. Social democratic governments frequently intervene in the private sector and in business activities, as in Italy and Norway. Corporate income tax rates are often relatively high, as in France and Sweden. A few countries, such as Germany, have experienced net outflows of FDI as businesses seek to escape extensive regulation.

## Democracy

Democracy is characterized by two major features:

- *Private property rights.* Individuals can own property and assets and increase one's asset base by accumulating private wealth. Property includes tangibles, such as land and buildings, as well as intangibles, such as stocks, contracts, patent rights, and intellectual assets. Democratic governments devise laws that protect property rights. People and firms can acquire property, use it, buy or sell it, and bequeath it to whomever they want. These rights are important because they encourage individual initiative, ambition, and innovation as well as thrift and the desire to accumulate wealth. People are less likely to have these qualities if there is uncertainty about whether they can control their property or profit from it.
- *Limited government.* The government performs essential functions that serve all citizens. These include national defense; maintenance of law and order and diplomatic relations; and constructing and maintaining infrastructure such as roads, schools, and public works. State control and intervention in the economic activities of private individuals or firms is minimal. By allowing market forces to determine economic activity, the government ensures that resources are allocated with maximal efficiency.[7]

Democracy is closely associated with *openness*, or lack of excessive regulation or barriers to the entry of firms in foreign markets. The greater the openness, the fewer the constraints placed on foreign firms. Absence of excessive regulations also benefits buyers because openness increases the quantity and variety of products available. Competition pressures firms to improve product quality continually. Increased efficiency and lower prices may follow. After India's government lowered entry barriers in the Indian automobile market, foreign automakers steadily entered the market. Their presence increased the number of models available for sale, raised the quality of available cars, and lowered prices. A similar response occurred in the mobile telephone market in China.[8]

Under democracy, the individual pursuits of people and firms are sometimes at odds with equality and justice. Because people have differing levels of personal and financial resources, each performs with varying degrees of success, leading to inequalities. Critics of pure democracy argue that when these inequalities become excessive, government should step in to correct them. Each society balances individual freedom with broader social goals. In democracies such as Japan and Sweden, the democracy's rights and freedoms are construed in larger societal terms rather than on behalf of individuals.

Virtually all democracies include elements of socialism, such as government intervention in the affairs of individuals and firms. Socialism emerges because of abuses or negative externalities that occur in purely democratic or capitalistic systems. For the past two decades, Japan has been striving to achieve the right balance between democracy and socialism. Poor management practices and an economic recession led to the bankruptcy of thousands of Japanese firms. To maintain jobs and economic stability, the Japanese government intervened to support numerous large firms and banks that, under pure capitalism, would have failed. However, such policies led to inflexibility in the Japanese economy and a delay of needed structural improvements.

Many countries, including Australia, Canada, the United States, and those in Europe, are best described as having a mixed political system—characterized by a strong private sector and a strong public sector, with considerable government regulation and control.

## National Governance and Economic Prosperity

**National governance** refers to the system of policies and processes by which nations are governed. It reflects the manner in which public institutions develop laws and regulations, conduct public affairs, and manage public resources.[9] Exhibit 3.5 reveals that national governance is closely related to economic prosperity, measured as per-capita GDP. In the exhibit, national governance is assessed using six variables: public accountability, political stability and absence of violence, government effectiveness, regulatory quality, rule of law, and control of corruption.[10] As the quality of national governance rises, so does economic prosperity, leading to higher living standards for citizens. Nations with the highest living standards—for example, Canada, Ireland, and Singapore—also tend to have higher quality national governance. By contrast, countries with the lowest living standards—for example, North Korea, Pakistan, Venezuela—tend to score lowest on national governance.

National governance is related to *political freedom* and *economic freedom*.[11] Political freedom is characterized by:

- Free and fair elections.
- The right to form political parties.
- Fair electoral laws.
- Existence of a parliament or other legislative body.
- Freedom from domination by the military, foreign powers, or religious hierarchies.
- Self-determination for cultural, ethnic, and religious minorities.

Economic freedom is related to:

- The extent of government interference in business.
- The strictness of the regulatory environment.
- The ease with which commercial activity is carried out according to market forces.

Economic freedom flourishes when governments support the institutions necessary for that freedom, such as freely operating markets and the rule of law.

**National governance**
The system of policies and processes by which nations are governed and the manner in which they develop laws and regulations, conduct public affairs, and manage public resources.

**EXHIBIT 3.5**

**Relationship Between Quality of National Governance and Per-Capita GDP (in US$)**

*Sources:* International Monetary Fund, *World Economic Outlook Databases*, 2017, www.imf.org; Daniel Kaufmann, Aart Kraay, and Massimo Mastruzzi, "The Worldwide Governance Indicators: A Summary of Methodology, Data and Analytical Issues," World Bank Policy Research, Working Paper No. 5430, 2010, www.worldbank. org; World Bank, *Worldwide Governance Indicators*, 2018, www. info.worldbank.org.

*Note:* On the horizontal access, a high score indicates better quality national governance.

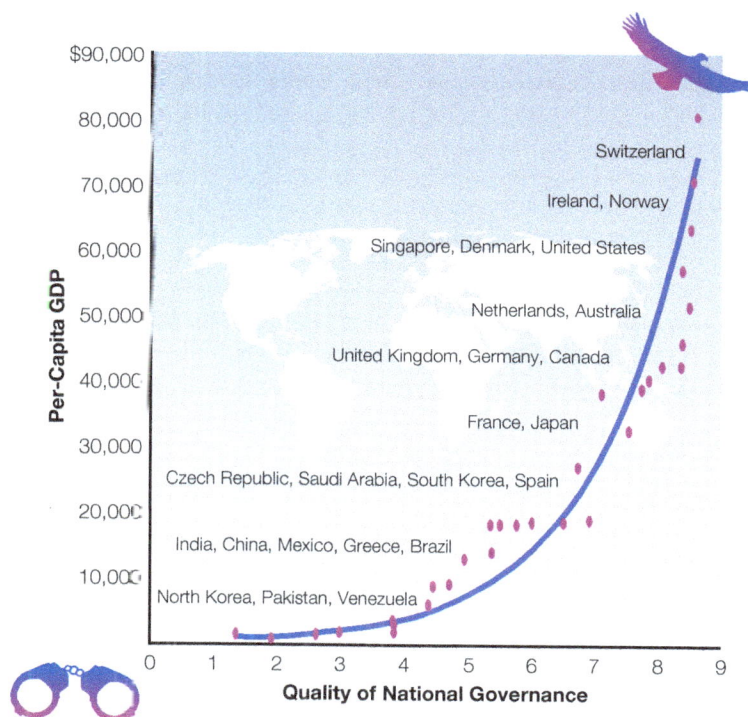

## The Relationship Between Political Systems and Economic Systems

Each political system tends to be associated with a particular type of economic system. Generally speaking, authoritarianism is associated with command economies, democracy with market economies, and socialism with mixed economies. Let's review these economic systems.

COMMAND ECONOMY Also known as a centrally planned economy, a command economy makes the state a dominant force in the production and distribution of goods and services. Central planners make resource allocation decisions, and the state owns major sectors of the economy. In command economies, sizable bureaucracy thrives, and central planning tends to be less efficient than market forces in synchronizing supply and demand. For example, goods shortages have been so common in Venezuela that people often wait in lines for hours to buy basic necessities such as sugar and bread. China and Russia continue to exhibit some characteristics of command economies. However, the system is gradually dying out and being replaced by market economies and mixed economies.

MARKET ECONOMY Market forces—the interaction of supply and demand—determine prices in a market economy. Government intervention in the marketplace is limited, and economic decisions are left to individuals and firms. Market economies are closely associated with capitalism, in which the means of production are privately owned and operated. Participants typically exhibit a market-oriented mentality and entrepreneurial spirit. The task of the state is to establish a legal system that protects private property and contractual agreements. However, the government may also intervene to address the inequalities that market economies sometimes produce.

MIXED ECONOMY A mixed economy exhibits the features of both a market economy and a command economy. It combines state intervention and market mechanisms for organizing production and distribution. Most industries are under private ownership, and entrepreneurs freely establish, own, and operate corporations. But the government also controls certain functions, such as pension programs, labor regulation, minimum wage levels, and environmental regulation. State-owned enterprises operate in key sectors such as transportation, telecommunications, and energy. In France, for example, the government partly owns dozens of companies, mainly in the transportation, communication, and energy industries. Peugeot and Renault are partially state owned. In Germany, Japan, Norway, Singapore, and Sweden, the government often works closely with business and labor groups to determine industrial policy, regulate wage rates, and/or provide subsidies to support specific industries.[12]

The past century saw a large increase in the number of mixed economies and a concurrent rise in government involvement in economic matters. For example, in the United States, combined government spending increased from about 27 percent of GDP in 1960 to roughly 40 percent today and is expected to attain 50 percent by 2038. In Belgium, Denmark, France, Greece, and several other countries in Europe, annual government spending now exceeds 50 percent of GDP. In recent years, governments in Europe, Japan, and North America have imposed many new regulations on private firms.[13] Regulations were adopted that covered workplace safety, minimum wages, pension benefits, and environmental protection.

## Legal Systems

**3.3** Understand legal systems.

Legal systems provide a framework of rules and norms of conduct that mandate, limit, or permit specified relationships among people and organizations and provide punishments for those who violate these rules and norms. Laws require or limit specific actions while empowering citizens to engage in others, such as entering into contracts and seeking remedies for contract violations. Legal systems are dynamic—they evolve over time to represent each nation's changing social values and the evolution of their social, political, economic, and technological environments.

Political systems—authoritarianism, socialism, and democracy—tend to influence their respective legal systems. Democracies tend to encourage market forces and free trade. In countries with well-developed legal systems, such as Australia, Canada, Japan, the United States, and most European countries, laws are widely known and understood. In such countries, laws are effective and legitimate because they are:

- Applied to all citizens equally.
- Issued through formal procedures by recognized government authorities.
- Enforced systematically and fairly by police forces and formally organized judicial bodies.

In these countries, a tradition of law exists in which citizens consistently respect and follow the rule of law. **Rule of law** refers to a legal system in which rules are clear, publicly disclosed, fairly enforced, and widely respected by individuals, organizations, and the government. International business flourishes in societies where the rule of law prevails. In the United States, for example, the Securities and Exchange Act encourages confidence in business transactions by requiring public companies to disclose their financial indicators to investors frequently. Legal systems can be eroded by declining respect for the law, weak government authority, or burdensome restrictions that attempt to forbid behavior prevalent in the society. In the absence of the rule of law, firms must contend with great uncertainty, and economic activity can be impeded.

**Rule of law**
A legal system in which rules are clear, publicly disclosed, fairly enforced, and widely respected by individuals, organizations, and the government.

Nations are primarily governed by one of four basic legal systems: common law, civil law, religious law, or mixed. These legal systems are the foundation for laws and regulations. Exhibit 3.6 provides examples of countries where these legal systems are dominant.

### Common Law

Also known as case law, common law is a legal system that originated in England and spread to Australia, Canada, the United States, and former members of the British Commonwealth. The basis of common law is tradition, previous cases, and legal precedents set by the nation's courts through interpretation of statutes, legislation, and past rulings. The national legislature in common-law countries (such as Parliament in Britain and Congress in the United States) holds ultimate power to pass or amend laws. In the United States, because the constitution is difficult to amend, the Supreme Court and even lower courts have much flexibility to interpret the law. Common law is more flexible than other legal systems because it is more open to interpretation by courts. Judges in a common-law system have substantial power to interpret laws based on the unique circumstances of individual cases.

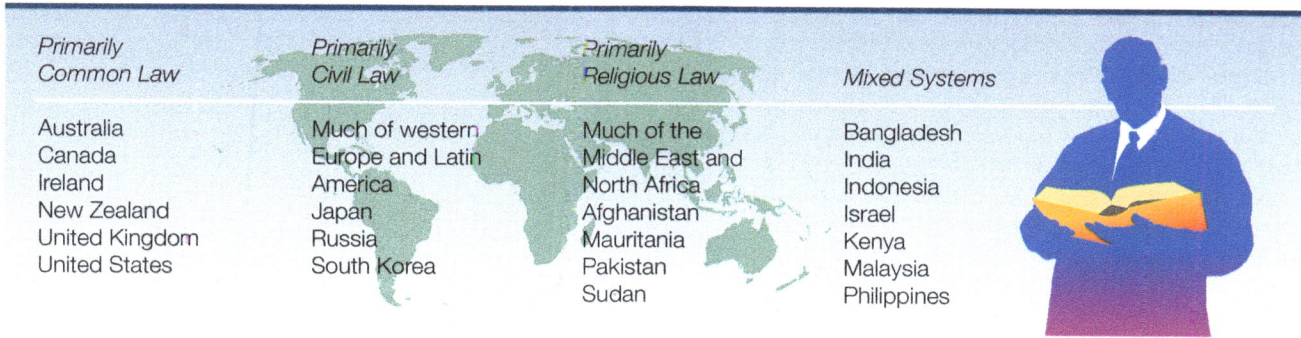

| Primarily Common Law | Primarily Civil Law | Primarily Religious Law | Mixed Systems |
|---|---|---|---|
| Australia | Much of western | Much of the | Bangladesh |
| Canada | Europe and Latin | Middle East and | India |
| Ireland | America | North Africa | Indonesia |
| New Zealand | Japan | Afghanistan | Israel |
| United Kingdom | Russia | Mauritania | Kenya |
| United States | South Korea | Pakistan | Malaysia |
|  |  | Sudan | Philippines |

**EXHIBIT 3.6**

**Dominant Legal Systems in Selected Countries**

*Source:* Based on World Legal Systems at www.jurigiobe.ca.

## Civil Law

Also known as code law, civil law is found in France, Germany, Italy, Japan, Turkey, and Latin America. Its origins go back to Roman law and the Napoleonic Code. Civil law is based on an all-inclusive system of laws that have been codified; the laws are clearly written and accessible. It is divided into three codes: commercial, civil, and criminal. Civil law is considered complete as a result of catchall provisions found within the law. Rules and principles form the starting point for legal reasoning and administering justice. The codified rules emerge as specific laws and codes of conduct produced by a legislative body or some other supreme authority.

Both common law and civil law systems originated in Western Europe and represent the common values of Western Europeans. A key difference between the two systems is that common law is primarily judicial in origin and based on court decisions, whereas civil law is primarily legislative in origin and based on laws passed by national and local legislatures. Differences in common and civil law give rise to differing business approaches in different countries. These are highlighted in Exhibit 3.7. In reality, common-law systems generally contain elements of civil law and vice versa. The two systems complement each other, and countries that employ one also tend to employ some elements of the other.

## Religious Law

This legal system is strongly influenced by religious beliefs, ethical codes, and moral values viewed as mandated by a supreme being. The most important religious legal systems are based on Hindu, Jewish, and Islamic law. Among these, the most widespread is Islamic law, found mainly in the Middle East and North Africa. In addition to these areas, other countries with substantial populations of Muslims (followers of Islam) include Indonesia (about 205 million Muslims), Pakistan (180 million), India (175 million), and Nigeria (75 million).

| Legal Issues | Civil Law | Common Law |
|---|---|---|
| Ownership of intellectual property | Determined by registration. | Determined by prior use. |
| Enforcing agreements | Commercial agreements become enforceable only if properly notarized or registered. | Proof of agreement is sufficient for enforcing contracts. |
| Specificity of contracts | Contracts tend to be brief because many potential problems are already covered in the civil code. | Contracts tend to be very detailed, with all possible contingencies spelled out. Usually more costly to draft a contract. |
| Compliance with contracts | Noncompliance is extended to include unforeseeable human acts such as labor strikes and riots. | Acts of God (floods, lightning, hurricanes, etc.) are the only justifiable excuses for noncompliance with the provisions of contracts. |

**EXHIBIT 3.7**

**Examples of Differences Between Common Law and Civil Law**

Islamic law, also known as the *shariah*, is based on the Qur'an, the holy book of Muslims, and the teachings of the Prophet Mohammed. Adherents generally do not differentiate between religious and secular life. Islamic law governs relationships among people, between people and the state, and between people and a supreme being. It spells out norms of behavior regarding politics, economics, banking, contracts, marriage, and many other social issues. Thus, Islamic law might be said to encompass all possible human relationships. Because it is seen as divinely ordained, it is relatively static and absolute. Unlike other legal systems, it evolves very little over time.[14]

Most Muslim countries currently maintain a dual system, in which both religious and secular courts coexist. Other countries with large Muslim populations, such as Indonesia, Bangladesh, and Pakistan, have secular constitutions and laws. Turkey, another country with a majority Muslim population, has a strongly secular constitution. Saudi Arabia and Iran are unusual in that religious courts have authority over all aspects of jurisprudence.

Contemporary liberal movements within Islam oppose traditional views of religious law. For example, strict interpretation of Islamic law prohibits the giving and receiving of interest on loans or investments. To comply with Islamic law, financial institutions employ a variant of international banking known as Islamic finance, based on the principles of shariah law. Many Western banks—for example, JP Morgan and Deutsche Bank—have subsidiaries in Islamic countries that comply with shariah laws. Instead of requiring interest payments, they charge administrative fees or take equity positions in the projects they finance. Many issue *sukuks*, Islamic-compliant bonds that offer revenue from an asset, such as a rental property, rather than interest. The global market for shariah-compliant financial instruments now exceeds two trillion U.S. dollars.[15]

*Source:* Zurijeta/Shutterstock

Islamic law specifies norms of behavior regarding commercial relations, contracts, banking, and other areas. This mosque is in Mecca, Saudi Arabia.

### Mixed Systems

Mixed systems consist of two or more legal systems operating together. In most countries, legal systems evolve over time, adopting elements of one system or another that reflect their unique needs. The contrast between civil law and common law has become blurred as many countries combine them. For example, legal systems in South Africa and the Philippines mix elements of civil law and common law. Legal systems in Indonesia and most Middle Eastern countries share elements of civil law and Islamic law.

Historically, socialist law was a legal system found in the former Soviet Union, China, and a few states in Africa. It was based on civil law, with elements of socialist principles that emphasized state ownership of property. The rights of the state dominated those of the individual. When the Soviet Union collapsed and China began transitioning to capitalism, socialist law gave way to other legal systems, especially civil law.

**MyLab Management   Watch It!**

If your professor has assigned this, go to the Assignments section of **www.pearson.com/mylab/management** to complete the video exercise titled Anthony Shadid Unrest in the Middle East and North Africa.

## Participants in Political and Legal Systems

Political and legal systems evolve from the interplay among various societal institutions at both the national and international levels. Five types of participants are active in transforming political and legal systems.

**3.4** Describe the participants in political and legal systems.

### Government

The government, or the public sector, is the most important participant, operating at national, state, and local levels. Governments have the power to enact and enforce laws. They strongly influence how firms enter host countries and how they conduct business there. Governments regulate international business activity through a complex system of institutions, agencies, and public officials. Agencies that possess such powers in the United States include the U.S. Trade Representative and the International Trade Administration (www.ita.doc.gov). In Canada, such functions are handled by the Ministry of Foreign Affairs (www.international.gc.ca), the Ministry of Finance, and the Export and Import Controls Bureau. Similar agencies operate in Australia, Britain, and virtually all other countries.

### International Organizations

Supranational agencies such as the World Trade Organization (www.wto.org), the United Nations (www.un.org), and the World Bank (www.worldbank.org) strongly influence international business. For example, the United Nations Conference on Trade and Development (UNCTAD, www.unctad.org) helps oversee international trade and development in the areas of investment, finance, technology, and enterprise development. Such organizations facilitate free and fair trade by providing administrative guidance, governing frameworks, and, occasionally, giving financial support.

### Regional Trade Organizations

Regional economic integration refers to the growing economic interdependence that results when two or more countries within a geographic region form an alliance whose goal is to reduce barriers to trade and investment. Regional trade organizations, such as the European Union (EU), the North American Free Trade Agreement (NAFTA), and the Association of Southeast Asian Nations (ASEAN), aim to advance the economic and political interests of their members. The EU is especially well developed, with its own executive, legislative, and bureaucratic bodies. It enacts and enforces laws and regulations that directly affect business. For example, in 2018 the EU implemented the Markets in Financial Instruments Directive, to better regulate financial markets and improve investor protections. The Directive restricts banks' ability to charge fees and increases reporting requirements for brokers and other financial institutions. Preparations associated with the new regulations were expected to cost banks, brokers, and other firms billions of dollars.[16]

### Special Interest Groups

Special interest groups operate to advance the goals of a particular community. Numerous special interest groups serve the interests of specific countries, industries, or causes. For example, the Organisation for Economic Co-operation and Development (OECD, www.oecd.org) supports the economic developmental and business goals of advanced economies. The Organization of Petroleum Exporting Countries (OPEC, www.opec.org) is a powerful cartel that controls global oil prices, which, in turn, affect consumer prices and the cost of doing business. OPEC emerged as a powerful voice for oil-producing countries, including Saudi Arabia, Iran, Venezuela, Nigeria, and Indonesia. Other groups exercise similar control over the production and allocation of commodities such as sugar, coffee, and iron ore.

Special interest groups engage in political activity to advance specific causes, ranging from labor rights to environmental protection. They often influence national political processes and produce outcomes with far-reaching consequences for business. Many target industries and affect individual firms. In China, activists are pressuring the government to reduce pollution. Industrialization and a sharp rise in the use of fossil fuels are contaminating China's air, water, and soil.[17] In the United States, Greenpeace and other environmentalist groups opposed construction of the Keystone pipeline, fearing it would produce oil spills, polluting ground water and killing wildlife. Environmentalist groups were instrumental in halting construction of the pipeline.[18] Exhibit 3.8 provides a sample of interest groups and their likely stance toward various business issues.

### Competing Firms

Rival domestic firms with a strong presence in the host country naturally have an interest in opposing the entry of foreign firms into the local market and may lobby their government for protection. For example, host-country competitors often complain when foreign firms

| Group | Typical Issue | Example |
|---|---|---|
| Labor unions | Oppose imported goods and global sourcing | U.S. United Steelworkers union opposed imports of steel from China |
| Competing businesses | Dislike competition from foreign firms | Japanese rice producers opposed imports of rice from the United States |
| Customers | May avoid foreign-made products. Dislike improper marketing practices. | Motorists in Australia accused BP of unfair pricing of petroleum products |
| Conservationists | Fight against wildlife loss and destruction of the natural environment | Environmentalists oppose lumber imports from countries with tropical rain forests |

**EXHIBIT 3.8**

**Issues of Concern to Special Interest Groups**

receive financial support from the parent or host-country governments. Asterix, a French theme park, opposed French government support for U.S.-based Disney when the latter established Disneyland Paris. Similarly, U.S. automakers in Detroit opposed BMW's construction of a factory in South Carolina. However, the state government of South Carolina supported the BMW facility on the grounds that it would generate jobs and increase tax revenues.

## Types of Country Risk Produced by Political Systems

**3.5** Identify the types of country risk produced by political systems.

How do political systems create challenges for firms engaged in international business? Let's examine the specific risks produced by political systems.

### Government Takeover of Corporate Assets

Governments occasionally seize the assets of corporations. The industry sectors most often targeted by government seizure are natural resources (for example, mining and petroleum), utilities, and manufacturing. Fortunately, aggressive seizure is less common these days as governments in many developing countries have adopted institutional reforms that aim to attract FDI from abroad and foster economic growth.

---

### Government seizure takes on various forms

- *Confiscation* is the seizure of corporate assets without compensation. Beginning in the 1980s, for example, the government of Zimbabwe systematically seized more than 5,000 farms mostly owned by farmers of European descent and redistributed the land to native Zimbabweans.
- *Expropriation* is seizure with compensation. In Venezuela, ExxonMobil and ConocoPhillips were forced to abandon multibillion-dollar investments in the local oil industry. The government of Bolivia seized Sabsa, a Spanish airline operating in the country. Gradual yet persistent pressure from the Russian government led TNK-BP, a Russian subsidiary of British energy giant BP, to sell a major stake in its oil business to the national gas monopoly Gazprom.
- *Nationalization* describes government seizure of an entire industry, with or without compensation. For example, the government of Bolivia nationalized much of the oil and gas industry in that country. President Hugo Chavez nationalized the cement industry in Venezuela. Nationalization occurs in advanced economies as well. Following the global financial crisis, the federal government of Iceland nationalized most of the country's banking industry.

*Sources:* Conor Gaffey, "In Zimbabwe, White Farmers Are Suing President Robert Mugabe over Land Seizures," *Newsweek,* August 22, 2017, www.newsweek.com; Carlos Quiroga, "Bolivia Nationalizes Spanish-Owned Airports Operator," *Reuters,* February 18, 2013, www.reuters.com; Robert Wade and Silla Sigurgeirsdottir, "Iceland's Rise, Fall, Stabilisation and Beyond," *Cambridge Journal of Economics* 36, No. 1 (2012), pp. 127–144.

"Creeping expropriation" is a subtle form of country risk in which governments modify laws and regulations after foreign MNEs have made substantial local investments in property and plants.[19] Examples include abrupt termination of contracts and the creation of new laws that favor local firms. Corporate raiders and government officials in Russia occasionally raid the offices of competitors and subject them to questionable criminal investigations. Such tactics can force foreign MNEs to cede control of their operations to local interests.[20] Governments in Bolivia, Kazakhstan, Russia, and Venezuela have modified tax regimes to extract revenues from foreign coal, oil, and gas companies. Troops stormed the Kazakhstan offices of U.S. mining company AES to enforce an alleged tax fine amounting to some $200 million. One of the country's largest providers of electricity, AES reduced its operations in Kazakhstan in the wake of persistent abuse by the Kazakh government.[21] Subtle or devious approaches to government takeover make country risk harder to predict.

### Embargoes and Sanctions

Most countries are signatories to international treaties and agreements that specify rules, principles, and standards of behavior in international business. Nevertheless, governments may unilaterally resort to sanctions and embargoes to respond to offensive activities of foreign countries. A *sanction* is a type of trade penalty imposed on one or more countries by one or more other countries. Sanctions typically take the form of tariffs, trade barriers, import duties, and import or export quotas. They generally arise in the context of an unresolved trade or policy dispute, such as a disagreement about the fairness of some international trade practice. There is much evidence suggesting that sanctions often do not achieve desired outcomes. For example, the United States imposed trade sanctions on Iran and Syria. However, goods continue to flow in and out of both countries from China, Germany, Japan, and numerous other trading partners. The European Union and the United States imposed trade sanctions on Russia following the latter's military intervention in Ukraine. The sanctions contributed to collapse of the Russian ruble and to the Russian financial crisis and caused economic damage to many firms in the EU.[22]

An *embargo* is an official ban on exports to or imports from a particular country to isolate it and punish its government. It is generally more serious than a sanction and is used as a political punishment for some disapproved policies or acts. For example, the United States has enforced embargoes against Iran and North Korea, at times labeled as state sponsors of terrorism. The European Union has enacted embargoes against Belarus, Sudan, and China in certain areas, such as foreign travel, to protest human rights and weapon-trading violations.

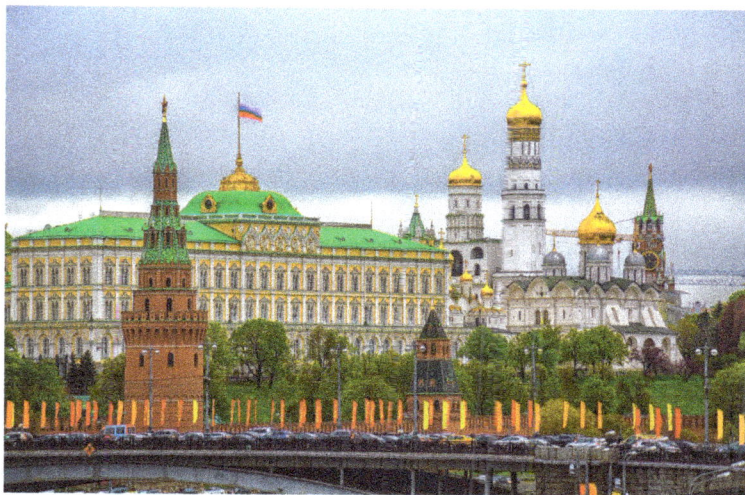

*Source:* Igor Sobolev/123RF

Activists called for a boycott of Russian products and the Sochi Winter Olympics over charges that Russia's government discriminated against gays and lesbians. Pictured is the Kremlin in Moscow, site of the official residence of Russia's president.

### Boycotts Against Firms or Nations

Consumers and special interest groups occasionally target particular firms perceived to have harmed local interests. Consumers may refuse to patronize firms that behave inappropriately. A *boycott* is a voluntary refusal to engage in commercial dealings with a nation or a company. Boycotts and public protests result in lost sales and increased costs (for public relations activities needed to restore the firm's image). Disneyland Paris and McDonald's have been the targets of boycotts by French farmers, who believe these firms represent U.S. agricultural policies and globalization, which many French citizens oppose. Activists in numerous countries organized a boycott of petroleum company BP following its oil spill in the Gulf of Mexico.[23] During the 2014 Winter Olympics in Sochi, Russia, activist groups advocated boycotting Russian products over concerns that Russia's government discriminates against gays and lesbians.[24]

### Terrorism

Terrorism is the threat or actual use of force or violence to attain a political goal through fear, coercion, or intimidation.[25] It is sometimes sponsored by national governments. Terrorism has escalated in much of the world, as exemplified by attacks in France, India, the Philippines, Spain, the United Kingdom, and the United States as well as various countries in Africa and the Middle East. In India, more than 30,000 people have died in terrorist attacks in the past two decades.[26] Major terrorist attacks have occurred recently in Afghanistan, Iraq, Nigeria, Pakistan, and Syria. In addition to causing loss of life, terrorism can severely damage commercial infrastructure and disrupt business activities. It induces fear in consumers, who reduce their purchasing, potentially leading to economic recession. The transportation and retailing industries are particularly affected. Terrorism also affects financial markets. In the days following the September 11, 2001, attacks in New York, the value of the U.S. stock market dropped some 14 percent.[27]

### War, Insurrection, and Violence

War, insurrection, and other forms of violence pose significant problems for business operations. Although such events usually do not affect companies directly, their indirect effects can be disastrous. Violent conflict among drug cartels and security services along the U.S.–Mexico border has led some firms and financiers to withdraw investments from Mexico because of perceived heightened risks and political instability. In India, Tata Motors (www.tatamotors. com) shifted the location of a major new factory due to violent protests by local farmers who feared the loss of their livelihood.[28] To minimize losses from violent acts, firms can purchase risk insurance.

## Types of Country Risk Produced by Legal Systems

**3.6** Identify the types of country risk produced by legal systems.

In addition to political concerns, country risk also arises due to peculiarities of national legal systems. Especially relevant to international business are *commercial law*, which specifically covers business transactions, and *private law*, which regulates relationships between persons and organizations, including contracts and liabilities that may arise due to negligent behavior. In many countries, the legal system favors home-country nationals. Laws are designed to promote the interests of local businesses and the local economy.

Legal systems in both the host country and the home country pose various challenges to firms, which we review next.

### Country Risk Arising from the Host-Country Legal Environment

Governments in host countries impose various laws and regulations on foreign companies doing business there.

**FOREIGN INVESTMENT LAWS** These laws affect the type of entry strategy firms choose as well as their operations and performance. Many nations impose restrictions on inward FDI. For example, Indonesia restricts foreign investment in certain industries, such as tourism, alcoholic beverages, and some chemical manufactures, to protect the country's security or cultural assets. Investment in several other industries requires obtaining special permission from Indonesia's central government.[29] The United States restricts foreign investments that might affect national security. Proposed investments can be reviewed by the U.S. Committee on Investments. In 2017, following the committee's recommendation, the U.S. government blocked a Chinese company's attempt to acquire Lattice Semiconductor Corporation.[30]

**CONTROLS ON OPERATING FORMS AND PRACTICES** Governments impose laws and regulations on how firms can conduct production, marketing, and distribution activities within their borders. Such restrictions can hinder company performance abroad. For example, host countries may require companies to obtain permits to import or export. They may devise complex regulations that complicate transportation and logistical activities or limit the options for entry strategies. In China's huge telecommunications market, the government requires foreign investors to seek joint ventures with local firms; local operations cannot be wholly owned by foreigners. The government's goal is to ensure that China maintains control of its telecommunications industry but obtains inward transfer of technology, knowledge, and capital. In 2014, U.S. authorities banned Huawei, a giant Chinese telecommunications company, from bidding on U.S. government contracts for network equipment because of concerns over the possibility of espionage.[31]

Shibuya is a popular shopping district in Tokyo. In Japan, foreign-owned large stores such as Carrefour and Walmart have faced restrictive laws designed to protect local retailers.

**MARKETING AND DISTRIBUTION LAWS** These laws determine which practices are allowed in advertising, promotion, and distribution. For example, Finland, France, and Norway prohibit cigarette advertising on television. Germany largely prohibits comparative advertising, in which a product is promoted as superior to a competing brand. Many countries cap the prices of critical goods and services, such as food and health care. Such constraints affect firms' marketing and profitability. Product safety and liability laws hold manufacturers and sellers responsible for damage, injury, or death defective products cause. In the case of violations, firms and company executives are subject to legal penalties, such as fines or imprisonment, as well as civil lawsuits. Product liability laws in developing countries are generally weak. Some firms take advantage of these weaknesses. For example, as litigants pursued tobacco companies in Europe and the United States, these companies shifted much of their marketing of cigarettes to developing countries.

**LAWS ON INCOME REPATRIATION** MNEs earn profits in various countries and typically seek ways to transfer these funds back to their home country. However, in some countries, governments devise laws that restrict such transfers. The action is often taken to preserve hard currencies, such as euros, U.S. dollars, or Japanese yen. Repatriation restrictions limit the amount of net income or dividends that firms can remit to their home-country headquarters. Although such constraints often discourage inward FDI, they are common in countries experiencing a shortage of hard currencies.

Governments around the world are contemplating ways to tax and regulate e-commerce and the Internet.

**ENVIRONMENTAL LAWS** Governments enact laws to preserve natural resources; to combat pollution and the abuse of air, earth, and water resources; and to ensure health and safety. In Germany, for example, companies must follow strict recycling regulations. Manufacturers and distributors bear the burden of recycling product packaging. Governments usually try to balance environmental laws against the impact such regulations may have on employment, entrepreneurship, and economic development. For example, environmental standards in Mexico are looser or less well enforced than in some other countries, but the Mexican government is reluctant to strengthen them for fear that foreign MNEs may reduce their investments there.

**CONTRACT LAWS** International contracts attach rights, duties, and obligations to the contracting parties. Contracts are used in five main types of business transactions:

- Sale of goods or services, especially large sales.
- Distribution of the firm's products through foreign distributors.
- Licensing and franchising—that is, a contractual relationship that allows a firm to use another company's intellectual property, marketing tools, or other assets for a fee.
- FDI, especially in collaboration with a foreign entity, to create and operate a foreign subsidiary.
- Joint ventures and other types of cross-border collaborations.

Numerous countries are attempting to develop an international standard for international sales contracts. The United Nations Convention on Contracts for the International Sale of Goods (CISG) is a uniform text of law for international sales contracts. More than 75 countries are now party to the CISG, covering about three-quarters of all world trade. Unless excluded by the express terms of a contract, the CISG is deemed to supersede any otherwise applicable domestic law(s) regarding an international sales transaction.

**INTERNET AND E-COMMERCE REGULATIONS**    Internet and e-commerce regulations are the new frontier in legal systems and continue to evolve.[32] Firms that undertake e-commerce in countries with weak laws face considerable risk. In China, for example, the government has developed legislation to ensure security and privacy due to the rapid spread of the Internet and e-commerce. Many consumer-privacy laws have yet to be enacted, and progress has been delayed on the development of methods to protect private data from criminal or competitive eyes. Protections for online contracting methods have been implemented with the recent adoption of e-signature laws. Emergent e-signature laws offer protections for online contracting.

**INADEQUATE OR UNDERDEVELOPED LEGAL SYSTEMS**    Just as laws and regulations can lead to country risk, an underdeveloped regulatory environment or poor enforcement of existing laws can also pose challenges for the firm. Worldwide, safeguards for intellectual property are often inadequate. Regulations to protect intellectual property may exist on paper but not be adequately enforced. When an innovator invents a new product, develops new computer software, or produces some other type of intellectual property, another party may copy and sell the innovation without paying the inventor. Russia's legal framework is relatively weak and inconsistent. Russian courts lack substantial experience ruling on business matters. Due to the unpredictable and potentially harmful legal environment, Western firms frequently abandon joint ventures and other business initiatives in Russia.[33]

Inadequate legal protection is most common in developing economies but can be a factor in developed economies as well. The recent global financial crisis was precipitated, in part, by insufficient regulation in the financial and banking sectors of the United States, Europe, and other regions. Government authorities have been considering how regulatory structures can be revamped to provide a sounder footing for connecting global savers and investors as well as reliable methods for managing financial instability. Governments seek to expand regulation, provide new means to increase transparency and information flows, and find ways to harmonize regulatory policies and legal frameworks across national borders. Banks and other financial institutions are revising disclosure rules to make information more specific and consistent. Some experts believe the financial crisis does not imply that more regulation is needed. Rather, they argue for more intelligent regulation, better enforcement of existing regulation, and better supervision of financial institutions.[34]

Read the *You Can Do It: Recent Grad in IB*, which features Christopher Johnson. Chris enhanced his knowledge about the international regulatory and taxation environment through study abroad.

## Country Risk Arising from the Home-Country Legal Environment

Does country risk arise only due to the host country's legal environment? No, home-country legal systems also play a role. **Extraterritoriality** refers to the application of home-country laws to persons or conduct outside national borders. In most cases, such laws are intended to prosecute individuals or firms located abroad for some type of wrongdoing.

Examples of extraterritoriality in international business abound. A French court ordered Yahoo! to bar access to Nazi-related items on its website in France and to remove related messages and images from its sites accessible in the United States. In 2018, the European Union fined Qualcomm $1.2 billion for unfair and anti-competitive practices because, for several years, Qualcomm had paid billions of dollars to Apple to ensure Apple would use only Qualcomm's chipsets in the production of iPhones and iPads. In effect, the European Union fined Qualcomm for unfairly favoring Apple, at the expense of Intel, even though all three companies are based in the United States. Businesses generally oppose extraterritoriality because it tends to increase the costs and uncertainty of operating abroad.[35]

**THE FOREIGN CORRUPT PRACTICES ACT (FCPA)**    The U.S. government passed the Foreign Corrupt Practices Act (FCPA), which bans firms from offering bribes to foreign parties to secure or retain business. The FCPA was enacted after more than 400 U.S. companies admitted paying bribes to foreign government officials and politicians. The Act also covers foreign firms and managers who act in furtherance of corrupt payments while in the United States. The FCPA requires

**Extraterritoriality**
Application of home-country laws to persons or conduct outside national borders.

## CHRISTOPHER JOHNSON

- **Education:** Bachelor's and master's in accounting
- **Objectives:** Develop a career as a tax practitioner in the financial services industry
- **Internships during college:** State of Georgia, Georgia Lottery; Deloitte Tax LLP
- **Jobs held since graduating:** Deloitte Tax LLP in Chicago, IL, and Atlanta, GA; The Ayco Company: A Subsidiary of Goldman Sachs

*Source:* Christopher Johnson

During his junior year, Christopher participated in a two-week study abroad program in Istanbul, Turkey. The program gave Chris a global business perspective and inspired a passion to work for a multinational organization in the financial industry. Meetings with business executives and with students from a local university proved invaluable. The experience whetted Chris' desire to learn as much as possible about global business. Chris learned about various aspects of the political and legal environment in international business.

After graduation, Chris interned with Deloitte Tax. There he gained technical, analytical, and enhanced communication skills. Following his internship, Chris entered graduate school and earned a Master's in Accountancy. Upon graduation, he took a full-time position with Deloitte in their tax division. Initially he worked in domestic compliance and global jurisdictional exposure. After two years with the firm, Chris began consulting with multiple clients. Christopher consults on taxation with various multinational firms, including projecting tax implications of business combinations or acquisitions, managerial changes, proposed or enacted legislation, or other market factors.

## Christopher's Advice for International Exposure

"Capitalizing on an opportunity to broaden your educational and professional horizon is not only enjoyable but essential in an ever-changing global society. Understanding the role that international business plays across cultural variations will allow for a well-developed global commerce perspective. Such exposure will also assist with determining your specific career path of choice."

## Professional Success Factors

"The transition from college to corporate America has the potential to be extremely difficult. My advice to those that are approaching this milestone is to *have a strong sense of self*. Knowing your strengths and limitations will allow you to succeed anywhere your career takes you, domestically or abroad. Don't hesitate to step into unfamiliar situations, countries, or cultures. This experience will only give you more self-confidence. I believe exposing myself to a remarkably different country such as Turkey turned out to be more instructive than studying in London or Rome.

"The most important part of your career is the execution. Practical and skillful application of diverse knowledge is what employers seek worldwide. In many ways, the workplace is a classroom. I would advise new graduates that continuous learning will prove invaluable in professional roles and personal endeavors. Written and oral communication skills are important. Knowing my field is only half the battle; being an effective communicator is critical too. When communicating with foreign clients, it is important to develop interpersonal relations and teamwork, and seek to understand diverse and multicultural work environments."

## Challenges

"The biggest challenge I faced in my early professional career was to learn how to take time for personal interests such as family, friends, and the study of cultures. Often, young professionals who are new to the corporate setting view themselves as working machines rather than actual human beings that require more than their employer's support. I have learned to enjoy the journey of success."

*Source:* Courtesy of Christopher Johnson.

companies with securities listed in the United States to meet U.S. accounting provisions. Such firms must devise and maintain accounting systems that control and record all company expenditures.[36] One problem with the FCPA is that "bribe" is not clearly defined. For example, the Act draws a distinction between bribery and facilitation payments; the latter may be permissible if making such payments does not violate local laws.[37]

Some U.S. managers argue the FCPA harms their interests because foreign competitors often are not constrained by such laws. FCPA criminal and civil penalties are increasingly harsh. Firms can be fined up to $2 million, and individuals can be fined up to $100,000 and face imprisonment. In 2017, the U.S. energy services company Halliburton agreed to pay a $29 million fine to settle charges related to payments made to a company in Angola. Halliburton had paid the Angolan firm in order to win lucrative oilfield services contracts.[38]

**ACCOUNTING AND REPORTING LAWS**  Accounting practices and standards differ greatly around the world, posing difficulties for firms. For example, when assigning value to stocks and other securities, most countries use the lower of cost or market value. Brazil, however, encourages firms to adjust portfolio valuations because of historically high inflation. When valuing physical assets such as plant and equipment, Canada uses historical costs. Some Latin American countries use inflation-adjusted market value. Although firms can write off uncollectible accounts in the United States, the allowance is not permitted in France, Spain, and South Africa. Research and development costs are expensed as incurred in most of the world but capitalized in South Korea and Spain. Belgium, Malaysia, and Italy use both conventions.

**TRANSPARENCY IN FINANCIAL REPORTING**  The timing and transparency of financial reporting vary widely around the world. **Transparency** is the degree to which firms regularly reveal substantial information about their financial condition and accounting practices. In the United States, public firms are required to report financial results to stockholders and to the Securities and Exchange Commission each quarter. In much of the world, however, financial statements are prepared annually or less often, and they often lack transparency. Transparency improves business decision making and the ability of citizens to hold companies accountable.

Recently, the U.S. Congress passed the Dodd–Frank Wall Street Reform and Consumer Protection Act, which aims to increase transparency in the United States financial sector. Passed in response to the late-2000s recession, the Act created an oversight board that monitors banking activities. It aims to reduce financial risk-taking by restricting certain banking activities and requiring bank executives to be responsible for compliance. Running to more than 2,000 pages of new regulations, banks have condemned the Act for imposing too many regulatory costs. U.S. affiliates of foreign multinational banks must comply with the Act's provisions. In an effort to avoid rigid financial requirements, some European banks are reducing their banking activities in the United States. Recently, the European Union introduced the Basel III global regulatory standard, which aims to increase the quality and transparency of the capital base of European banks. U.S. banks will be required to comply with the new Basel III rules.[39]

**Transparency**
The degree to which companies regularly reveal substantial information about their financial condition and accounting practices.

## Ethical Connections

Many countries lack antibribery laws for international transactions. The Organisation for Economic Co-operation and Development recently called for a ban on grease payments, small-scale bribes intended to speed up telephone hookups, government paperwork, and other everyday matters in international commerce. A culture of grease payments and other corruption is corrosive, harming the rule of law and sustainable economic development.

## Managing Country Risk

**3.7** Know about managing country risk.

How should managers respond to country risk? In the discussion that follows, we highlight several specific strategies managers can employ to manage country risk.

### Proactive Environmental Scanning

Anticipating country risk requires advance research. Initially, managers develop a comprehensive understanding of the political and legal environment in target countries. They then engage in *scanning* to assess potential risks and threats to the firm. Scanning allows the firm to improve practices in ways that conform to local laws and political realities and to create a positive environment for business success.

One of the best sources of intelligence in the scanning process is employees working in the host country. They are knowledgeable about evolving events and can evaluate them in the context of local history, culture, and politics. Embassy and trade association officials regularly develop and analyze intelligence on the local political scene. Some consulting firms, such as Verisk Maplecroft (www.maplecroft.com) and Business Entrepreneurial Risk Intelligence (www.beri.com), specialize in country-risk assessment and provide guidelines for appropriate strategic responses. Once the firm has researched the political climate and contingencies of the target environment, it develops and implements strategies to facilitate effective management of relations with policymakers and other helpful contacts in the host country. The firm then takes steps to minimize its exposure to country risks that threaten its performance.

### Strict Adherence to Ethical Standards

Ethical behavior is important not only for its own sake but also because it helps insulate the firm from some country risks that less-conscientious firms encounter. Those companies that engage in questionable practices or operate outside the law naturally invite redress from the governments of the host countries where they do business.

### Alliances with Qualified Local Partners

A practical approach to reducing country risk is to enter target markets in collaboration with a knowledgeable and reliable local partner. Qualified local partners are better informed about local conditions and better situated to establish stable relations with the local government. Western firms often enter China and Russia by partnering with local firms that assist in navigating complex legal and political landscapes.

### Protection Through Legal Contracts

A legal contract spells out the rights and obligations of each party. Contract law varies widely from country to country, and firms must adhere to local standards. For example, a Canadian firm doing business in Belgium generally must comply with the laws of both Belgium and Canada as well as with the evolving laws of the European Union.

---

**Firms generally employ any of three approaches for resolving international disputes.**

- *Conciliation* is the least adversarial method. It is a formal process of negotiation with the objective to resolve differences in a friendly manner. The parties in a dispute employ a conciliator, who meets separately with each in an attempt to resolve their differences. Parties can also employ mediation committees—groups of informed citizens—to resolve civil disputes.
- *Arbitration* is a process in which a neutral third party hears both sides of a case and decides in favor of one party or the other based on an objective assessment of the facts. Compared to litigation, arbitration saves time and expense while maintaining the confidentiality of proceedings. Arbitration is often handled by supranational organizations such as the International Chamber of Commerce in Paris or the Stockholm Chamber of Commerce.
- *Litigation* is the most adversarial approach and occurs when one party files a lawsuit against another to achieve desired ends. Litigation is most common in the United States; most other countries favor arbitration or conciliation.

---

## CLOSING CASE    The Global Biopharmaceutical Industry: Political, Legal, and Ethical Dilemmas

The global biopharmaceutical industry develops, produces, and markets medications. The industry includes a dozen large firms, including Pfizer (based in the United States, www.pfizer.com), Roche (Switzerland, www.roche.com) Sanofi (France, www.sanofi.com), and AstraZeneca (United Kingdom, www.gsk.com). Europe and North America account for most of global pharmaceutical sales, but emerging market countries like Brazil and China are experiencing rapid sales growth and show much promise. The industry achieved worldwide sales of over $1.1 trillion in 2017. The industry is confronted with several challenges.

## High Cost of Research and Development

Among all industries, the biopharmaceutical industry invests the most in R&D, creating and marketing medications meant to treat everything from cancer to hair loss. Thousands of biopharmaceutical medications allow people to live longer and healthier lives. Europe and the United States benefit from strong patent protection laws and abundant investment capital. According to industry statistics, it takes 10 to 15 years from initial discovery to approval of a new medicine. For every 5,000 to 10,000 compounds that enter the research pipeline, only one receives approval. The average R&D investment for each new approved medicine, including the cost of failures, exceeds $1.2 billion. Some estimates are much higher. Only three out of every 10 newly approved medicines are successful enough to recover their R&D costs. For their successful products, biopharmaceutical firms must charge prices high enough not only to recover the high costs of product development but also to recover the cost of products that never achieve profitability.

## Limited Protection for Intellectual Property

Protecting property rights is a key objective of legal systems. Governments grant patents and provide other types of protections for intellectual property. In practice, such protection is often inadequate, especially in developing countries, where biopharmaceutical firms encounter substantial country risk. India has a history of weak intellectual property protection, which has discouraged R&D and innovation. Most people in India have low incomes, and few Indians can afford medications. India has a long history of producing counterfeit and pirated medications, often by violating the drug patents of foreign pharmaceutical firms. Illicit laboratories in India have freely infringed on drug patents and engaged in a selling free-for-all in the huge Indian biopharmaceutical market. They reverse-engineered patented compounds developed by European and U.S. companies and began selling the pirated generics at drastically lower prices. Foreign biopharmaceutical firms routinely pursue legal action against these violations, but given limited patent protection, India's generic drug manufacturers have flourished.

## The Challenge from Generic Brands

Under World Trade Organization (WTO) rules, a patent protects a drug inventor from competition for up to 20 years. In reality, when the lengthy testing and approval phase is factored in, the effective life of a drug patent is often less than 12 years. The manufacturer typically has only five to eight years of patent protection in which to recover its investment before generic manufacturers can legally enter the market. Once a patent expires, generic manufacturers have the right to produce medications originally invented by major pharmaceuticals. Generic manufacturers typically sell the medications that they produce at very low prices. Patent protections are important because they encourage innovation by allowing inventors a limited opportunity to recover their R&D investments. However, patent protection laws governing biopharmaceuticals differ substantially around the world.

Each year biopharmaceutical firms invest some 20 percent of revenues in R&D to invent new compounds, used to develop new medications. The main reason that generic manufacturers can charge lower prices is that they do not incur the high costs of R&D to develop new medications. Because the medications are already established in the marketplace, generic manufacturers also incur substantially lower marketing and sales expenses.

In the world of generic drugs, Israel-based Teva (www.tevapharm.com) is the largest manufacturer with global sales of more than $22 billion. In the United States, generic medications account for more than half of all dispensed prescriptions. Once a branded compound's patent expires, generic manufacturers begin producing generic versions. Retail prices for the compound can fall by as much as 90 percent within 12 to 18 months.

## Counterfeit Drugs

Worldwide, enforcement of intellectual property law varies. Many governments fail to ensure the quality of imported medicines. As a result, a growing industry of counterfeit and bio-inequivalent medications has emerged worldwide. A counterfeit ring from China supplied 1 million fake OneTouch Test Strips (used to treat diabetes) to hundreds of pharmacies in Canada, India, the United States, and numerous other countries. In Niger, some 2,500 people died after receiving fake vaccines for meningitis. European Union officials seized more than 35 million fake pills at ports around Europe, including drugs intended to treat malaria, cancer, cholesterol, and pain.

The World Health Organization estimates that up to 30 percent of medicines sold in developing economies may be counterfeit. In sub-Saharan Africa, counterfeits contribute to 115,000 deaths from malaria annually. Fake drugs are a factor in as many as 300,000 deaths each year in China. Up to 160,000 children die annually from pneumonia after receiving counterfeit medications. Sales of counterfeit biopharmaceuticals exceed $500 billion each year. Counterfeiting is greatest in countries where regulatory oversight is weakest.

Internet-based pharmacies are especially dubious. MarkMonitor, an industry watchdog, found that only a fraction of several thousand online pharmacies it examined were legitimate. Many of the pharmacies claiming to be based in Canada and the United States were in fact traced to China, Russia, and India. It is estimated that more than 50 percent of medicines sold through the Internet are fake—often containing no or too little of the active ingredient.

Because of the threats that counterfeit manufacturers pose, branded biopharmaceutical firms spend significant resources to protect their patents and intellectual property around the world. Branded manufacturers have pursued legal actions at the WTO and against individual nations. The WTO's agreement on Trade-Related Aspects of Intellectual Property Rights (TRIPS) was approved by approximately 150 WTO member countries.

## Neglected Therapeutic Areas

A large portion of biopharmaceutical research is focused on developing treatments for diseases that can return the cost of capital and generate profits. For these reasons, biopharmaceutical firms tend to target the most attractive markets. For example, these firms are more likely to develop a drug for cancer and cardiovascular diseases than for ailments common to poor countries such as tuberculosis. R&D to develop drugs common in poor countries is often perceived as too costly and risky.

At the same time, governmental and private initiatives have begun to address these market realities by providing incentive packages and public–private partnerships. For example, the Bill and Melinda Gates Foundation (www.gatesfoundation.org) is investing billions of dollars to fight AIDS, tuberculosis, and various infectious diseases that affect developing countries.

## Public Scrutiny

The biopharmaceutical industry's actions are often subject to public scrutiny within national political and legal systems. For example, the government of South Africa got into a tussle with several manufacturers of branded AIDS drugs. Because of high prices, the government sanctioned the importation of nonapproved generics. The reaction from branded biopharmaceutical manufacturers was to sue South Africa, which created an international backlash against the firms. Not only did the episode generate much negative publicity for the branded pharmaceutical firms, it made people more aware of the generic drug industry and its potential for helping those the AIDS pandemic affects. In the wake of the South African debacle, Brazil and several other countries threatened to break patents if biopharmaceutical firms did not make their drugs more affordable. In the interest of good public relations, several branded biopharmaceutical firms began to offer their AIDS drugs at lower prices in Africa. The United States and various European governments have provided billions of dollars in subsidies to support AIDS treatment in Africa.

## The Future

Without adequate intellectual property protection, the biopharmaceutical industry has fewer incentives to invent new drugs. At the same time, consumers in poor countries need access to drugs but can't afford them. Lax intellectual property laws facilitate the production of cheap generic drugs, but without these protections, major biopharmaceutical firms have fewer incentives to fund the R&D that results in new treatments for the diseases that plague the world. As selling prospects in Brazil, China, and other emerging markets develop over time, biopharmaceutical firms increasingly target those markets but face enormous challenges.

## AACSB and CKR Intangible Soft Skills to improve employability and success in the workplace:
Written and Oral Communication, Ethical Understanding and Reasoning, Information Technology, Analytical Thinking, Diverse and Multicultural Work Environments, Reflective Thinking, Application of Knowledge, Interpersonal Relations and Teamwork

### Case Questions

**3-4.** Specify the types of country risks that biopharmaceutical firms face in international business. How do the political and legal systems of countries affect the global biopharmaceutical industry?

**3-5.** People need medications, but the poor often cannot afford them. Governments may not provide subsidies for health care and medications. Meanwhile, biopharmaceutical firms focus their R&D on compounds likely to provide the best returns. What is the proper role of the following groups in addressing these dilemmas: national governments, branded biopharmaceutical firms, and generic manufacturers?

**3-6.** Consult www.phrma.org, the Pharmaceutical Research and Manufacturers of America. What steps is the branded industry taking to address the various ethical issues it faces, such as providing affordable drugs to poor countries?

**3-7.** Consult the TRIPS agreement at the WTO portal (www.wto.org). What are the latest developments regarding this treaty? What types of protection does this treaty provide to pharmaceutical firms? What enforcement mechanisms does TRIPS provide for ensuring that these protections will be carried out?

**3-8.** Recommend a strategy that management at a large biopharmaceutical firm should employ to reduce the likelihood of political and legal risks that such firms face. What steps should management take to minimize its exposure to such risks?

*Sources:* Kate Baggaley, "Counterfeit Drugs Are Putting the Whole World at Risk," *Popular Science,* March 2, 2017, www.popsci.com; Robert Coopman, "The Road Ahead for Research-Based Drug Companies," *Chain Drug Review,* January 2, 2012, p. 71; IFPMA, *The Pharmaceutical Industry and Global Health* (Geneva: International Federation of Pharmaceutical Manufacturers & Associations, 2017); IMAP, *Pharmaceuticals & Biotech Industry Global Report—2016,* www.imap.com; P. Jayakumar, "Patently Justified," *Business Today,* March 15, 2015, pp. 58–64; PhRMA, *2016 Profile: Biopharmaceutical Research Industry* (Washington, DC: Pharmaceutical Research and Manufacturers of America, 2017), www.phrma.org; European Federation of Pharmaceutical Industries and Associations, "The Value of the Pharmaceutical Industry; Key to Europe's Economy," January 16, 2017, www.efpia.eu; U.S. Food and Drug Administration, "Counterfeit Medicine," 2018, www.fda.gov; Leonora Walet, "Fighting Fake Drugs," *Chemical & Engineering News,* February 23, 2015, p. 28–29; World Health Organization, "Counterfeit and Falsified Medical Products," Fact Sheet, January 2018, www.wto.int.

*Note:* Kevin McGarry assisted in the development of this case.

# END-OF-CHAPTER REVIEW

## MyLab Management

Go to **www.pearson.com/mylab/management** to complete the problems marked with this icon ⭐.

---

## Key Terms

country risk   64
extraterritoriality   79
legal system   66

National governance   69
political system   66

rule of law   71
transparency   81

---

## Summary

In this chapter, you learned about:

- **Political and legal environments in international business**

  International business is influenced by political and legal systems. Country risk refers to exposure to potential loss or to adverse effects on company operations and profitability caused by developments in national political and legal environments. A political system is a set of formal institutions that constitute a government. A legal system is a system for interpreting and enforcing laws. Adverse developments in political and legal systems increase country risk. These can result from events such as a change in government or the creation of new laws or regulations.

- **Political systems**

  The three major political systems are authoritarianism, socialism, and democracy. They provide frameworks within which laws are established and nations are governed. Democracy is characterized by private property rights and limited government. Socialism occurs mainly as social democracy. Today, most governments combine elements of socialism and democracy. Authoritarianism is associated with command economies, socialism with mixed economies, and democracy with market economies.

- **Legal systems**

  There are four major legal systems: common law, civil law, religious law, and mixed systems. The rule of law implies a legal system in which laws are clear, understood, respected, and fairly enforced.

- **Participants in political and legal systems**

  Actors include government, which exists at the national, state, and municipal levels. The World Trade Organization and the United Nations are typical of international organizations that influence international business. Special interest groups serve specific industries or country groupings and include labor unions, environmental organizations, and consumers that promote particular viewpoints. Companies deal with competing firms in foreign markets, which may undertake political activities aimed at influencing market entry and firm performance.

- **Types of country risk produced by political systems**

  Governments impose constraints on corporate operating methods in areas such as production, marketing, and distribution. Governments may expropriate or confiscate the assets of foreign firms. Governments or groups of countries also impose embargoes and sanctions that restrict trade with certain countries. Boycotts are an attempt to halt trade or prevent business activities and are usually pursued for political reasons. War and revolution have serious consequences for international firms. Terrorism has become more salient recently.

- **Types of country risk produced by legal systems**

  Foreign investment laws restrict FDI in various ways. Such laws include controls on operating forms and practices, regulations affecting marketing and distribution, restrictions on income repatriation, environmental laws, and Internet and e-commerce regulations. Extraterritoriality is the application of home-country laws to conduct outside of national borders. Accounting and reporting laws vary around the world. Transparency is the degree to which firms reveal substantial and regular information about their financial condition and accounting practices.

- **Managing country risk**

  Successful management requires developing an understanding of the political and legal context abroad. The firm should scan the environment proactively and strictly adhere to ethical standards. Country risk is also managed by allying with qualified local partners abroad. The firm should seek protection through legal contracts.

## Test Your Comprehension

**AACSB:** Written and Oral Communication, Ethical Understanding and Reasoning, Analytical Thinking, Diverse and Multicultural Work Environments, Reflective Thinking, Application of Knowledge, Interpersonal Relations and Teamwork

**3-9.** Adverse and sudden developments in political and legal systems can create country risk. Suggest three examples of such adverse developments.

**3-10.** Define the concept of national governance. What are the common characteristics and the associate economic freedoms of national governance?

**3-11.** What are the specific characteristics of market economies and mixed economies? Which is more common?

**3-12.** What are the pillars upon which effective and legitimate laws are based?

**3-13.** Special interest groups operate in most countries. They tend to have distinctive agendas. What is their role in the political and legal system?

**3-14.** Why should an organization strictly adhere to ethical standards wherever it operates?

## Apply Your Understanding

**AACSB:** Written and Oral Communication, Ethical Understanding and Reasoning, Information Technology, Analytical Thinking, Diverse and Multicultural Work Environments, Reflective Thinking, Application of Knowledge, Interpersonal Relations and Teamwork

**3-15.** Country risk refers to the ways governments restrict or fail to restrict business activities. The nature of such restrictions varies around the world. In each country, national economic success substantially depends on the quality of laws and regulations. Government must strike the right balance—too little regulation promotes uncertainty; too much causes hardship. Country risk is revealed in various ways.

- Foreign investment laws
- Controls on operating forms and practices
- Environmental laws
- Contract laws
- E-commerce laws
- Underdeveloped legal systems
- Accounting and reporting laws

   Conduct research online, and give specific examples of each type of country risk. Describe how each might help or hinder company activities.

**3-16.** Suppose you get a job at Aoki Corporation, a firm that manufactures glass for industrial and consumer markets. Aoki is a large firm but has little international experience. Senior managers are considering a plan to move Aoki's manufacturing to China, Mexico, or Eastern Europe and to begin selling its glass in Latin America and Europe. However, they know little about the country risks that Aoki may encounter. Describe how each of the following factors might contribute to country risk as Aoki ventures

abroad: foreign investment laws, controls on operating forms and practices, and laws regarding repatriation of income, environment, and contracts.

**3-17.** *Ethical Dilemma*: The United States imposed a trade and investment embargo on Iran. U.S. citizens were barred from doing business with Iran. Proponents argued the embargo was justified because Iran has supported terrorism, is developing nuclear weapons, and is a disruptive force in the Middle East. However, critics condemned the trade sanctions for several reasons. First, they argued the sanctions represented a double standard because the United States supports other countries that have engaged in terrorism and other bad behaviors. Second, the best way to nurture healthy dissent and civil society in Iran may be to engage the country rather than restrict economic relationships. Third, the sanctions harmed the Iranian people, who were deprived of the benefits of trade with the United States. Fourth, the sanctions were largely ineffective because other countries supply Iran with products it needs. Finally, the sanctions harmed U.S. companies, especially oil and gas firms, which were prevented from doing business with Iran. What is your view? Analyze the arguments for and against trade with Iran. Can the United States, acting alone, compel desired changes in Iran by imposing sanctions? Justify your answer.

## globalEDGE | INTERNET EXERCISES

Access globalEDGE™ at www.globalEDGE.msu.edu

**AACSB:** Written and Oral Communication, Ethical Understanding and Reasoning, Information Technology, Analytical Thinking, Diverse and Multicultural Work Environments, Reflective Thinking, Application of Knowledge, Interpersonal Relations and Teamwork

**3-18.** Supranational organizations such as the World Bank (www.worldbank.org) and the World Trade Organization (www.wto.org) oversee much of the legal framework within which the world trading system operates. Political frameworks for industries or country groupings are influenced by organizations such as the Organization of Petroleum Exporting Countries (www.opec.org) and the Organisation for Economic Co-operation and Development (www.oecd.org). Using globalEDGE™ and the online portals cited here, address the following question: What is the goal of each organization, and how does it go about achieving its goal? By viewing the news and press releases at each website, summarize the latest initiatives of each organization.

**3-19.** When companies venture abroad, managers seek information on the legal and political environments in each country. This information is available from various web sources, as illustrated in the following exercises. (a) Suppose you want to sign up distributors in the European Union and want to learn about EU contract law. What should you do? Consult the globalEDGE™ portal to learn about EU trade and contract laws. Try the following: At globalEDGE™, click Reference Desk, Global Resource Directory, and then Trade Law. Describe the resources there for learning about contract law in Europe. (b) The Central Intelligence Agency's portal provides up-to-date information about national governments and political environments. Go to www.cia.gov, click World Factbook, and summarize the political environment in each of China, Colombia, France, and Russia.

**3-20.** Freedom House is a nonprofit organization that monitors the state of freedom worldwide. It conducts an annual Freedom in the World Survey, which you can view at www.freedomhouse.org. The survey compares the state of political rights and civil liberties in nearly 200 countries over time. Visit the site, and answer the following questions. (a) What is the role of political rights and civil liberties in the Freedom House rankings? (b) What can governments in these countries do to facilitate more rapid social and political development? (c) What are the implications of the rankings for companies doing international business?

# Endnotes

1. BBC News, "Hilton Hotels Fined for Credit Card Data Breaches," November 1, 2017, www.bbc.com; Scott Cendrowski, "China's Censors Target Streaming," *Fortune,* March 1, 2015, pp. 18–20; Jack Ewing, "Germany: A Cold Shoulder for Coca-Cola," *BusinessWeek,* May 2, 2005, p. 52; James Griffiths, "Banned on Chinese TV: 'Western Lifestyles,' Cleavage and Time Travel," August 31, 2016, www.cnn.com; Alex Hickey, "Hilton to Pay $700K in Data Breach Fines, but It Could Be Much Worse," *CIODive,* November 6, 2017, www.ciodive.com.

2. "Country Risk," *The Economist,* February 26, 2005, p. 102; Edward Mansfield and Eric Reinhardt, "International Institutions and the Volatility of International Trade," *The Political Economy of International Trade* 46, August (2005), pp. 65–96; Joakim Reiter, "5 Ways to Make Global Trade Work for Developing Countries," *World Economic Forum,* September 29, 2016, www.weforum.org; UNCTAD, *World Investment Report 2017* (Geneva: United Nations Conference on Trade and Development, 2017).

3. BBC News, "GM Says Venezuelan Car Plant Is Seized by Government," April 20, 2017, www.bbc.com; Anna Rosenberg and William Attwell, "What Investors Need to Know About Zimbabwe After Mugabe," *Harvard Business Review,* December 28, 2017, pp. 2–6.

4. S. Tamer Cavusgil, Pervez Ghauri, and Ayse Akcal, *Doing Business in Emerging Markets* (Thousand Oaks, CA: Sage, 2013); International Trade Administration, *India Country Commercial Guide* (Washington, DC: U.S. Department of Commerce, 2017, www.export.gov); Mehul Srivastava, "What's Holding India Back," *Business Week,* October 19, 2009, pp. 38–44; USTR, *2017 National Trade Estimate Report on Foreign Trade Barriers* (Washington DC: Office of the United States Trade Representative, 2017).

5. David Pierson, "Why U.S. Tech Companies Can't Figure Out China," *Los Angeles Times,* August 1, 2016, www.latimes.com; David Ramli, "Where Facebook Has No Friends, Tech Bends to China's Will," *Bloomberg,* December 5, 2017, www.bloomberg.com.

6. James Danziger and Charles Anthony Smith, *Understanding the Political World,* 12th ed. (New York: Pearson Education, 2016); Milan W. Svolik, *The Politics of Authoritarian Rule* (New York: Cambridge University Press, 2012).

7. Milton Friedman and Rose Friedman, *Free to Choose* (New York: Harcourt Brace Jovanovich, 1980); Robert Genetski, *Rich Nation, Poor Nation: Why Some Nations Prosper While Others Fail* (Amazon Digital Services, www.amazon.com, 2017).

8. Robert Dahl and Ian Shapiro, *On Democracy: Second Edition,* 2nd ed. (New Haven, CT: Yale University Press, 2015); Joseph Johnson and Gerald Tellis, "Drivers of Success for Market Entry into China and India," *Journal of Marketing* 72 (May 2008), pp. 1–13; Priyam Saraf, "How Do Import Tariffs on Cars Affect Competitiveness? The Case of India and Pakistan," *World Bank,* August 28, 2017, www.worldbank.org.

9. Mark Bevir, *Governance: A Very Short Introduction* (Oxford, UK: Oxford University Press, 2012); Francis Fukuyama, "What Is Governance?," *Governance* 26, No. 3 (2013), pp. 347–368; Robert Rotberg, *On Governance* (Waterloo, ON: Centre for International Governance Innovation, 2015); UNESCAP, "What Is Good Governance," United Nations Economic and Social Commission for Asia and the Pacific, 2015, www.unescap.org.

10. Daniel Kaufmann, Aart Kraay, and Massimo Mastruzzi, "The Worldwide Governance Indicators: A Summary of Methodology, Data and Analytical Issues," World Bank Policy Research, Working Paper No. 5430, 2010, www.worldbank.org; World Bank, *Worldwide Governance Indicators,* 2018, www.info.worldbank.org.

11. María J. Angulo-Guerreroa, Salvador Pérez-Morenob, and Isabel M. Abad-Guerreroa, "How Economic Freedom Affects Opportunity and Necessity Entrepreneurship in the OECD Countries," *Journal of Business Research* 73, No. 3 (2017), pp. 30–37; James Gwartney et al., *Economic Freedom of the World: 2017 Annual Report* (Vancouver, Canada: Fraser Institute, 2017); Freedom House, Freedom in the World 2017 (Washington, DC: Freedom House, 2017).

12. Barry Clark, *The Evolution of Economic Systems: Varieties of Capitalism in the Global Economy* (New York: Oxford University Press, 2016); *Economist,* "Setting Out the Store," January 11, 2014, pp. 18–21.

13. Arthur Brooks, "The Debt Ceiling and the Pursuit of Happiness," *Wall Street Journal,* July 25, 2011, www.wsj.com; OECD, *General Government Spending* (Organisation for Economic Cooperation and Development, www.data.oecd.com, 2018); Proquest and Bernan Press, *Statistical Abstract of the United States* (Lanham, Maryland: Bernan Press, 2017).

14. Jason Boyett, *12 Major World Religions: The Beliefs, Rituals, and Traditions of Humanity's Most Influential Faiths,* (Berkeley, CA: Zephyros Press, 2016); Lewis Hopfe and Brett Hendrickson, *Religions of the World,* 13th ed. (New York: Pearson, 2015).

15. International Monetary Fund, "Islamic Finance and the Role of the IMF," February 2017, www.imf.org; Mansur Masih, "Islamic Finance and Banking," *Emerging Markets Finance & Trade* 53, No. 7 (2017), pp. 1455–1457; Maha Khan Phillips, "Doing God's Work; Islamic Finance Is Meant to Reconcile Both Commercial and Religious Ideals," *Wall Street Journal,* March 1, 2010, www.wsj.com.

16. Dick Schumacher, "MiFID II," *Bloomberg,* January 3, 2018, www.bloomberg.com; Philip Stafford, "What Is Mifid II and How Will It Affect EU's Financial Industry?," *Financial Times,* September 15, 2017, www.ft.com.

17. *Bloomberg Business,* "China's Pollution Assault Boosting Solar, Electric Vehicles," April 7, 2015, www.bloomberg.com; Anthony Kuhn, "For Some in China's Middle Class, Pollution Is Spurring Action," *NPR,* March 2, 2017, www.npr.org.

18. BBC News, "Keystone XL Pipeline: Why Is It So Disputed?," January 24, 2017, www.bbc.com; Sarah Chacko, "XL Pipeline Clogged by Politics," *CQ Weekly,* December 8, 2014, p. 1462.

19. Philipp Harms and Philipp an de Meulen, "Demographic Structure and the Security of Property Rights: The Role of Development and Democracy," *European Journal of Political Economy* 29 (March 2013), pp. 73–89; David Khachvani, "Compensation for Unlawful Expropriation: Targeting the Illegality," *Foreign Investment Law Journal* 32 No. 2 (2017), pp. 385–403.

20. Ibid.

21. Jason Bush, "Russia's Raiders," *BusinessWeek*, June 16, 2008, pp. 67–71; *National Law Review*, "Kazakhstan Ordered to Pay $506 Million for Crude Expropriation of Oil and Gas Investments," January 18, 2017, www.natlawreview.com; N. Vardi, "Power Putsch," *Forbes*, June 2, 2008, pp. 84–92.

22. Francesco Giumelli, "EU-Russia Trade Bouncing Back Despite Sanctions," *EUObserver*, October 17, 2017, www.euobserver. com; Matthew Philips, "What Trade Sanctions?" *Bloomberg BusinessWeek*, January 30–February 5, 2012, p. 16.

23. John Chipman, "Why Your Company Needs a Foreign Policy," *Harvard Business Review*, September 2016, pp. 36–43; Nicola Clark, "BP Hit by Boycott Threat amid US Oil-Spill Crisis," *Marketing*, May 12, 2010, p. 1.

24. Michele Rivkin-Fish and Cassandra Hartblay, "When Global LGBTQ Advocacy Became Entangled with New Cold War Sentiment," *Brown Journal of World Affairs* 21, No. 1 (2014), pp. 95–111.

25. Yonah Alexander, David Valton, and Paul Wilkinson, *Terrorism: Theory and Practice* (Boulder, CO: Westview, 1979); Martin Miller, *The Foundations of Modern Terrorism: State, Society and the Dynamics of Political Violence* (Cambridge, UK: Cambridge University Press, 2013); Jonathan White, *Terrorism and Homeland Security* (Boston: Cengage Learning, 2017).

26. Institute for Economics & Peace, *Global Terrorism Index 2014* (Sydney, Australia: Institute for Economics & Peace, 2015); U.S. Department of State, *Country Reports on Terrorism*, July 2017, www.state.gov; M. Srivastava and N. Lakshman, "How Risky Is India?" *BusinessWeek*, December 4, 2008, www.businessweek.com; White, 2017.

27. Institute for Economics & Peace, 2015; Jonathan Laing, "Aftershock," *Barron's*, September 9, 2002, p. 23; Randall Filer and Dragana Stanisic, "The Effect of Terrorist Incidents on Capital Flows," *Review of Development Economics* 20, No. 2 (2016), pp. 502–513; Daniel Meierrieks and Thomas Gries, "Causality Between Terrorism and Economic Growth," *Journal of Peace Research* 50, No. 1 (2013), pp. 91–104.

28. Rina Chandran, "India's Top Court Calls Land Deal for Tata Motors Factory a 'Farce,'" *Reuters*, August 31, 2016, www. reuters.com; V. Nair, "Tata Nano, World's Cheapest Car, Won't Help Pay Debt," *Bloomberg*, 2009, www.bloomberg.com; Srivastava, 2009.

29. V. Sreeja, "Indonesia's Government to Relax Foreign Direct Investment Norms to Boost Economy as Growth Sputters," *International Business Times*, April 19, 2015, www.ibtimes. com/indonesias-government-relax-foreign-direct-investment-norms-boost-economy-growth-sputters-1519258; USTR, 2017.

30. Kate O'Keeffe, "Trump Blocks China-Backed Fund from Buying Lattice Semiconductor," *Wall Street Journal*, September 13, 2017, www.wsj.com.

31. Arjun Kharpal, "We're Still Keen to Set Up in the US: Huawei," *CNBC*, February 24, 2016; www.cnbc.com; Linda Yueh, "Huawei Boss Says U.S. Ban 'Not Very Important,'" BBC, October 16, 2014, www.bbc.com/news/business-29620442; USTR (2017).

32. *Bloomberg Businessweek*, "How Not to Regulate the Internet," November 7, 2016, p. 16; Tom Fairless and Stephan Fidler, "Europe Wants the World to Embrace Its Internet Rules," *Wall Street Journal*, February 25, 2015, www.wsj.com; Craig MacKinder and Michael Carroll, *Security and Privacy in an IT World: Managing and Meeting Online Regulatory Compliance in the 21st Century* (Georgetown, ON: Kinetics Design, 2017).

33. Cavusgil, Ghauri, and Akcal, 2013; USTR, 2017.

34. J. Fox, "New World Order," *Time*, February 16, 2009, p. 29; "Krise des Bankensystems: Zu viel Finanzinnovationen, zu wenig Regulierung?" *Ifo Schnelldienst*, November 14, 2008, pp. 3–15; Laura Kodres, "What Is to Be Done," *Finance & Development*, March 2009, pp. 23–27; Marc Labonte, *Who Regulates Whom? An Overview of the U.S. Financial Regulatory Framework* (Washington, DC: Congressional Research Service, 2017).

35. International Chamber of Commerce, "Policy Statement: Extraterritoriality and Business," July 13, 2006; European Commission, "Antitrust: Commission Fines Qualcomm €997 Million for Abuse of Dominant Market Position," press release, January 24, 2018, http://europa.eu/rapid/press-release_IP-18-421_en.htm.

36. U.S. Department of Justice, *A Resource Guide to the U.S. Foreign Corrupt Practices Act (FCPA)* (Washington, DC: US Department of Justice, 2017).

37. Judith Scott, Debora Gilliard, and Richard Scott, "Eliminating Bribery as a Transnational Marketing Strategy," *International Journal of Commerce & Management* 12, No. 1 (2002), pp. 1–17; U.S. Department of Justice, 2017.

38. Paul Pelletier, "The Foreign-Bribery Sinkhole at Justice," *Wall Street Journal*, April 21, 2015, p. A17; *Soap, Perfumery & Cosmetics*, "Avon to Shell Out $135m Fine in China Bribery Case," January 2015, p. 11; US Securities and Exchange Commission, "SEC Enforcement Actions: FCPA Cases," 2017, www.sec.gov.

39. Bank for International Settlements, "Basel III: International Regulatory Framework for Banks," 2017, www.bos.org; John Heltman, "Volcker, Inc.: How One Rule Became a Cottage Industry," *American Banker*, March 30, 2015, p. 1.

# Chapter 4

# The Cultural Environment of International Business

**Learning Objectives** *After studying this chapter, you should be able to:*

4.1 Understand culture and cross-cultural risk.

4.2 Learn the dimensions of culture

4.3 Describe the role of language and religion in culture.

4.4 Describe culture's effect in international business.

4.5 Learn models and explanations of culture.

4.6 Understand managerial implications of culture.

## *Hallyu* and the Rising Influence of the Korean Global Culture

Culture matters in international business. Some of the ways it intersects with business are immediately evident; others are less so. Diasporas are often the first to spread the customs of their countries of origin, often shaping the cities they exist in to a degree that far surpasses the size of their communities. In more recent times, the proliferation of expats (short for "expatriates," meaning professionals living far from home for reasons of work) clearly display the importance of culture in the business environment.

Other kinds of cultural impact go in a different direction. Sometimes, it is not the flows of populations bringing with them their nation's products to their new home or its values to the job market; it is the country itself that manufactures iconic products or exports cultural products of worldwide appeal, thereby branding itself at a global level. If the United States is the most obvious example of this, there are recent ones to have attracted the world's attention. South Korea and the phenomenon named *hallyu* offer a textbook case in this sense.

While the country is certainly a powerhouse in terms of GDP and export performance (especially when its geographic and demographic composition are taken into account), the size of its expat community and long-term diaspora is smaller in comparison to other, more established overseas communities. A quick look at the number of Koreans overseas—7.4 million in 2017, according to the South Korean Ministry of Foreign Affairs—will show that they are considerably less numerous than, say, the Chinese (about 9 million in Thailand alone).

Yet one cannot on this count underestimate the growing appeal of Korean culture on groups of youth across the world, in other Asian countries but also as far away as Europe and the Americas. There is a growing literature, both in academia and in the press, that analyzes South Korea's so-called "soft power," a concept

based on a debate about China's growing outreach in the 2000s. Soft power is an approach in international relations where a country uses its economic and cultural attractiveness instead of military power. And South Korea's soft power can be full of surprises.

*Hallyu* is a Chinese term that translates as "Korean Wave." It is a collective term that refers to fashion, films, music, cuisine, and an overarching "country image" that spread through Asia in the first decades of the 21st century. South Korean manufacturing led the way, with products that span from cars to electronics to home appliances. The Samsung Galaxy smartphones are probably the most famous, but car brands like Hyundai and Kia are increasingly popular. Food like kimchi-flavored pot noodles, Korean beers like Hite and Cass, and Korean BBQ restaurants can be found across the world.

But media and other artistic events are also very important, especially when it comes to spreading cultural values. K-pop (Korean pop music) is an example of a cultural product that exploded in popularity around the world, especially among younger listeners. Perhaps the most famous example is Psy's 2012 K-pop single "Gangnam Style"; though the song is specifically about the new generation of Seoul nouveaux-riches who live in Gangnam, with its

2 billion YouTube views, it has been a worldwide phenomenon. The country earning $5 billion from its pop-culture exports—mainly K-Pop music, movies, and TV series—in 2013. It doubled that figure by 2017.

It has not always been like that. Up to 1985, one would be hard pressed to find the country setting any sort of worldwide trend. Music bands were censored by the government, all forms of protests were banned, and television shows were considered boring even at home. But the 1997 Asian crisis forced the country and its big conglomerates to reorganize to survive. Many of them profited from state subsidies and tax incentives and massively diversified their operations. Samsung was one of the first, moving into digital TVs and mobile phones. Without the upheaval provoked by the Asian Crisis, there would probably have been no *hallyu*.

Thanks to the government's strong support of this export of cultural values, South Korea has managed to surpass Japan to become Asia's biggest trendsetter in fashion and culture, from Hong Kong, with its profusion of Korean BBQ restaurants, to Manila, where viewers are such big fans of Korean dramas that they have even produced local remakes in Tagalog. One Korean drama, *Winter Sonata*, managed to reach countries as far away as Iraq and Uzbekistan. When it comes to television programming, South Korea has something of an edge compared to other countries: being rather more conservative, South Korean cultural values have proved to be more adaptable than those of modern Japan and China, and are therefore easier to identify with. This may also account for K-pop's stronger global appeal over Japan's J-pop.

The triumph of *Hallyu* is illustrated by the fact that Japan, a country that was once regarded as the trendsetter of the region, is now studying the South Korean model and success strategy to the point of setting up a government-sponsored fund of $500 million named "Cool Japan" to realize its own soft power.

## Questions

**4-1.** The rise of South Korea has attracted a lot of attention over the last decade due to its unusual characteristics. What does make South Korea a special case?

**4-2.** The success of Korean manufacturing created a favorable environment the world over for *hallyu*. What are, in your opinion, the most remarkable examples of Korean industries, and why?

**4-3.** Inspired by the Korean model, Japan has started promoting a similar country campaign around the world named Cool Japan, targeting young people and emphasizing its culture. Why is this outcome surprising to many analysts?

*SOURCES:* Korean Ministry of Foreign Affairs, http://www.mofa.go.kr/www/brd/m_3454/list.do; *The Economist,* "Soap, Sparkle and Pop. How a Really Uncool Country Became the Tastemaker of Asia," August 14, 2014, https://www.economist.com/books-and-arts/2014/08/09/soap-sparkle-and-pop, retrieved December 5, 2018; Euny Hong, *The Birth of Korean Cool: How One Nation Is Conquering the World Through Pop Culture* (NY: Picador, 2014).

This case was written by Stefania Paladini, Birmingham City University.

The opening case highlights the opportunities of leveraging national cultures. In international business, success requires sensitivity to national interests and cultural expectations. The framework in Exhibit 4.1 identifies the essential concepts for understanding culture and its importance in international business. In this chapter, we will examine these concepts in detail.

**4.1** Understand culture and cross-cultural risk.

**Culture**
The values, beliefs, customs, arts, and other products of human thought and work that characterize the people of a given society.

## Culture and Cross-Cultural Risk

As reflected in the opening case, **culture** refers to the values, beliefs, customs, arts, and other products of human thought and work that characterize the people of a given society. Culture shapes our behavior. Although as human beings we share many similarities, as groups of people

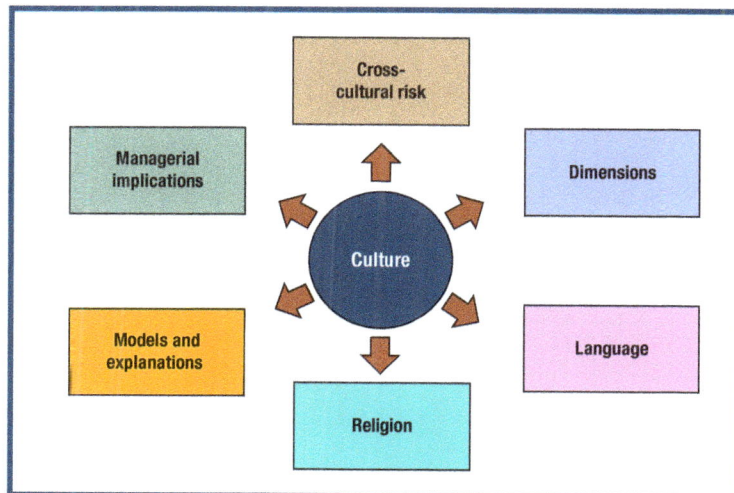

**EXHIBIT 4.1**

**Framework on the Essential Elements of Culture**

or societies, we exhibit many differences. Culture even affects the common rituals of daily life. Greeting ceremonies are a deeply embedded cultural marker and have evolved over many centuries. They specify such behaviors as whether to shake hands, what to say, and how far apart to stand. These cultural conventions may vary as a function of the age, gender, or status of the greeters. In China, friends express thoughtfulness by asking each other whether they have had their meal yet. In Turkey, a typical greeting is "What is new with you?" In Japan, elaborate greeting and parting rituals are the norm, and individuals routinely apologize to the other party just before ending a telephone conversation.

Culture captures how the members of the society live—for instance, how we feed, clothe, and shelter ourselves. Culture explains how we behave toward each other and with other groups. Culture defines our values and attitudes and the way we perceive the meaning of life.

Food is among the most interesting aspects of national culture. In Japan, pizza is often topped with fish and seaweed. In the United States, pizza can be piled high with meat. In France, it often comes with various cheeses. Look at Exhibit 4.2, which depicts numerous menu items at McDonald's fast-food restaurants around the world. McDonald's attempts to offer a relatively standardized menu worldwide but often varies offerings to suit tastes in individual countries. Many cultures are complex. As reflected in the opening case, some are relatively individualistic, whereas others are more collectivist. Some impose many norms and rules on social behavior; others are less imposing.[1]

Why should we concern ourselves with culture in cross-border business? The answer is that culture introduces new risks. We highlight these risks in Exhibit 4.3. **Cross-cultural risk** is a situation or event in which a cultural misunderstanding puts some human value at stake. Misunderstanding and miscommunication arise because people have differing values and expectations. They do not always communicate (verbally or nonverbally) what the other party is anticipating or may have diverse ways of communicating. For example, a head nod has different meanings in India and the United Kingdom. Cross-cultural misunderstandings can ruin business deals, hurt sales, or harm the corporate image. Today, developing an appreciation of and sensitivity for cultural differences is an imperative. Managers who are well informed about cross-cultural differences have advantages in managing employees, marketing products, and interaction with customers and business partners.

**Cross-cultural risk**
A situation or event in which a cultural misunderstanding puts some human value at stake.

**EXHIBIT 4.2**
**McDonald's Menu Items Around the World**
*Source:* sytnik/123rf

**Japan:** *Ebi Burger*—made of shrimp

**Canada:** *My Poutine*—French fries topped with gravy and cheese curds

**Morocco:** *Recette Moutarde*—burger in ciabatta bread, slathered in mustard

**Germany:** Beer is a beverage choice

**Hong Kong:** *Rice Burger*—two patties of sticky rice instead of buns

**Norway:** *McLaks*—sandwich made of grilled salmon and sour cream dill sauce

**Saudi Arabia:** *McArabia*—grilled beef with spices, lettuce, tomato, onion, garlic sauce, in a pita wrap

**Japan:** *McHotdog Mega Breakfast*—hotdog with scrambled eggs and ketchup

**France:** Wine is a menu favorite

**Philippines:** *McSpaghetti*—spaghetti noodles in a sweet tomato-based sauce

**India:** *Paneer Salsa Wrap*—cottage cheese wrap, cabbage, celery, with mayonnaise and salsa

**Malaysia:** *Bubur Ayam*—chicken porridge, a local favorite

**EXHIBIT 4.3**

**The Four Major Risks in International Business**

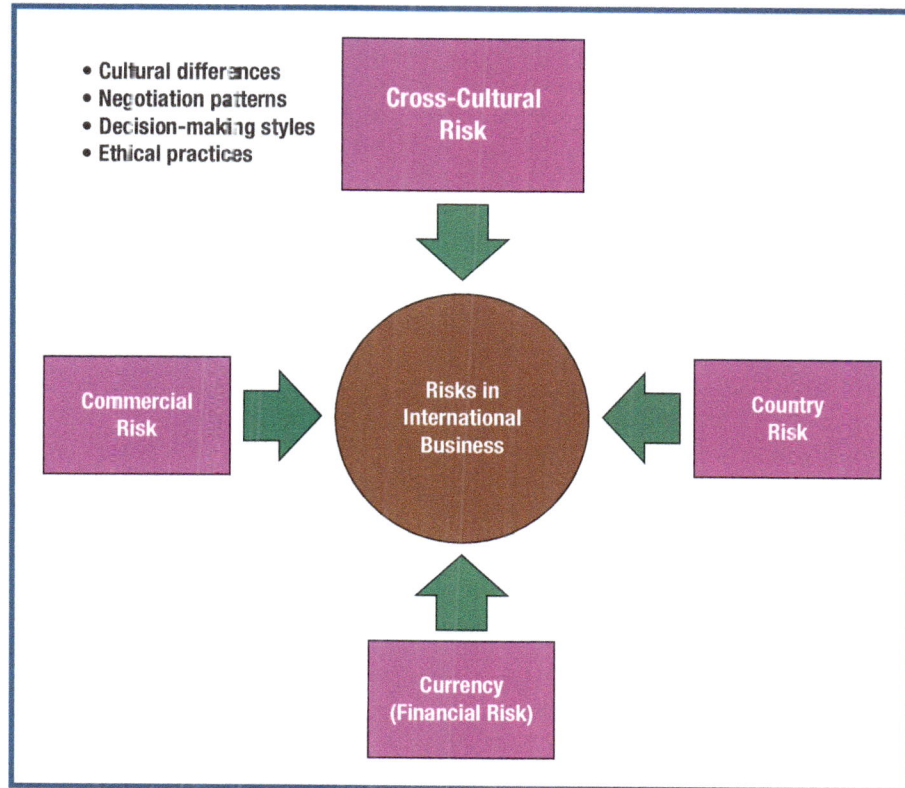

- Cultural differences
- Negotiation patterns
- Decision-making styles
- Ethical practices

Cross-Cultural Risk

Commercial Risk

Risks in International Business

Country Risk

Currency (Financial Risk)

*Source:* Dinodia/123RF

This Indian farm family is wearing traditional attire

Today, firms conduct business in environments characterized by unfamiliar languages as well as unique beliefs, norms, and behaviors. Managers need to be able to reconcile these differences to create profitable ventures. They must not only understand cultural differences—they must also develop international cultural competence.

## What Culture Is *Not*

Now that you have an idea of what culture is, let us define what it is *not*. Culture is:

- *Not right or wrong*. Culture is relative. People of different nationalities simply perceive the world differently. Each culture has its own notions of acceptable and unacceptable behavior. For example, in some Islamic cultures, a wife cannot divorce her husband. In many countries, nudity is entirely acceptable on TV. In Japan and Turkey, wearing shoes in the home is taboo.
- *Not about individual behavior*. Culture is about groups. It refers to a collective phenomenon of shared values and meanings. Thus, whereas culture defines the collective behavior of each society, individuals often behave differently.
- *Not inherited*. Culture comes from people's social environment. No one is born with a shared set of values and attitudes. Rather, children gradually acquire specific ways of thinking and behaving as they are raised in a society. In the United States, for example, children usually learn to value individualism. In China, children learn to depend on family members and acquire values based on Confucianism. Culture is passed from generation to generation by parents, teachers, mentors, peers, and leaders. Modern methods of communication, including the media, play an enormous role in transmitting culture.

## Socialization and Acculturation

This process of learning the rules and behavioral patterns appropriate to one's society is called **socialization**. Each society has rules—do's, don'ts, expectations, and preferences that guide behavior particularly of children as they the mature.[2] In Indonesia, for example, children are socialized to value cooperation, group harmony, and emotional restraint. Children are taught to avoid conflicts with others. In France, young people are socialized to appreciate cooking, fine cuisine, and wine.[3] The rules of socialization may be explicitly stated—for example, "We don't do things that way around here"—or they may be implicit, that is, everyone is expected to know how to function at work, at school, with friends, and so forth. Breaking a rule amounts to a failure to conform. As each of us matures, failing to follow society's rules provides opportunities for learning what the rules are. Socialization is cultural learning and provides the means to acquire cultural understandings and orientations that a particular society shares. It is a subtle process; we often adapt our behavior unconsciously and unwittingly.

**Acculturation** is the process of adjusting and adapting to a culture other than one's own. It is commonly experienced by people who live in other countries for extended periods, such as expatriate workers. In many ways, acculturation is challenging because adults are often less flexible than children.[4]

**Socialization**
The process of learning the rules and behavioral patterns appropriate for living in one's own society.

**Acculturation**
The process of adjusting and adapting to a culture other than one's own.

## Dimensions of Culture

More than any other feature of human civilization, culture illustrates the differences among societies based on language, habits, customs, and modes of thought. Yet most of us are not completely aware of how culture affects our behavior until we encounter people from other cultures.

Anthropologists use the iceberg metaphor to call attention to the many dimensions of culture, some obvious and some not so obvious. Above the surface, certain characteristics are visible, but below, invisible to the observer, is a massive base of assumptions, attitudes, and values. These invisible characteristics strongly influence decision making, relationships, conflict, and other dimensions of international business. We are usually unaware of the nine-tenths of our cultural makeup that exists below the surface. In fact, we are often not aware of our own culture unless we meet another one. Exhibit 4.4 illustrates the *iceberg concept of culture*, using three layers of awareness: high culture, folk culture, and deep culture.

Culture emerges through the integration of our values and attitudes; manners and customs; time and space perceptions; symbolic, material, and creative expressions; education; social structure; language; and religion. Let's examine these in more detail.

**4.2** Learn the dimensions of culture.

### Values and Attitudes

*Values* represent a person's judgments about what is good or bad, acceptable or unacceptable, important or unimportant, and normal or abnormal.[5] Values are the basis for our motivation and behavior. Our values guide the development of our attitudes and preferences. They guide us in the decisions we make and in how we lead our lives. Typical values in North America and northern Europe include work, or output orientation; being on time; and the acquisition of wealth. People from such countries may misjudge those from, say, Latin America, who may not hold such values. *Attitudes* are similar to opinions but are often unconsciously held and may not be based on logical facts. Prejudices are rigidly held attitudes, usually unfavorable and usually aimed at particular groups of people.

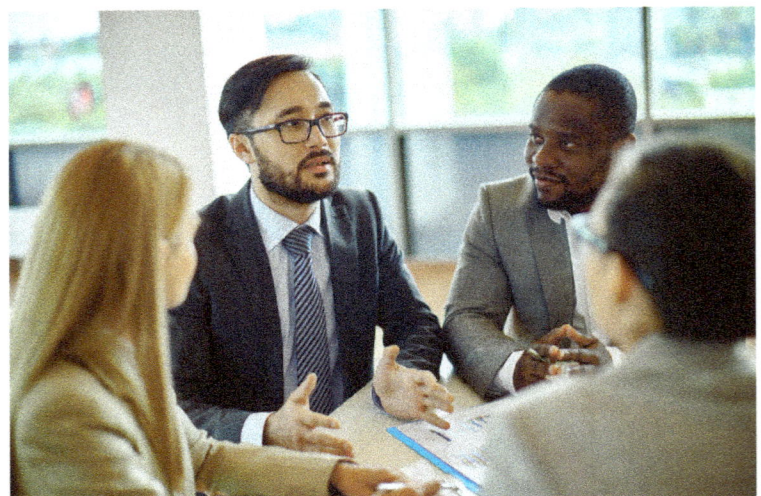

*Source:* Dmitriy Shironosov/123rf
Cross-cultural meetings are increasingly common.

### Manners and Customs

Manners and customs are ways of behaving and conducting oneself in public and business situations. Some countries are characterized by informal cultures; people treat each other as equals and work together cooperatively. In other countries, people tend to be more formal; status, power, and respect are relatively more important.

Although you may see more people around the world developing a taste for sushi and tacos, preferences for food, eating habits, and mealtimes are still varied. Customs that vary most worldwide relate to work hours and holidays, drinking and toasting, appropriate behavior at social gatherings, gift giving, and women in the workforce. Gift giving is complex in much of the world. In Japan, it is usually a mistake not to offer a gift in initial meetings. The Middle East is characterized by generous gift giving.

Handshaking varies across the world: limp handshakes, firm handshakes, elbow-grasping handshakes, and no handshake at all. In some parts of the world, people greet by kissing each other on both cheeks. In Southeast Asia, greeting involves placing the palms together in front of the chest, as in praying. In Japan, bowing is the norm.[6]

### Perceptions of Time

Time has a strong influence on business. It affects people's expectations about planning, scheduling, profit flows, and promptness in arriving for work and meetings. Japanese managers tend to prepare strategic plans for extended periods, such as a decade. The planning horizon for Western companies is much shorter, typically a few years. Some societies are more oriented to the past, others to the present, and still others to the future.

People in past-oriented cultures believe plans should be evaluated in terms of their fit with established traditions, customs, and wisdom. Innovation and change do not occur very often and are justified to the extent they fit with experience. Europeans are relatively past-oriented and prefer to conserve traditional ways of doing things.

Young countries such as Australia, Canada, and the United States are relatively focused on the present. They tend to have a **monochronic** orientation to time—a rigid orientation in which people are focused on schedules, punctuality, and time as a resource. They view time as *linear*, like a river flowing into the future, carrying workers from one activity to the next.

In such cultures, where people are highly focused on the clock, managers make commitments, set deadlines, and follow a strict schedule in meetings. Punctuality is a virtue, and time is money. Throughout the day, workers glance at their watches, their computer's clock, or the clock on the wall. Investors are impatient and want quick returns. Managers have a relatively short-term perspective when it comes to investments and making money. Company profitability is measured on a quarterly basis. In this way, people in the United States have acquired a reputation for being hurried and impatient. Indeed, the word *business* was originally spelled *busyness*.

Some cultures have a **polychronic** perspective on time. In such societies, instead of performing single tasks serially, people are inclined to do many things at once. In this way, members of polychronic cultures are easily distracted. They can change plans often and easily, and lengthy delays are sometimes needed before taking action. Punctuality per se is relatively unimportant, and managers consider time commitments flexible. They do not strictly follow the clock and schedules. They put more value on relationships and spending time with people.[7]

Chinese and Japanese firms typically are future-oriented. They focus not on how the firm will perform next quarter but on how it will perform a decade from now. Many large Japanese firms offer lifetime employment and invest heavily in employee training. They expect workers to remain with the firm for decades. Latin Americans have a flexible perception of time and may not arrive exactly at the predetermined time for appointments. In the Middle East, strict Muslims view destiny as the will of God ("Inshallah," or "God willing," is a frequently used phrase). They tend to downplay the importance of future planning. They perceive appointments as relatively vague future obligations.

### Perceptions of Space

Cultures also differ in their perceptions of physical space. We have our own sense of personal space and feel uncomfortable if others violate it. Conversational distance is closer in Latin America than in northern Europe or the United States. When a North American talks to a Latin American, he or she may unconsciously back up to maintain personal space. Those who live in crowded Japan or Belgium have smaller personal space requirements than those who live in land-rich Russia or the United States. In Japan, it is common for employee workspaces to be crowded together in the same room, desks pushed against each other. One large office space might contain desks for fifty employees. U.S. firms

**Monochronic**

A rigid orientation to time, in which the individual is focused on schedules, punctuality, and time as a resource.

**Polychronic**

A flexible, nonlinear orientation to time, in which the individual takes a long-term perspective and emphasizes human relationships.

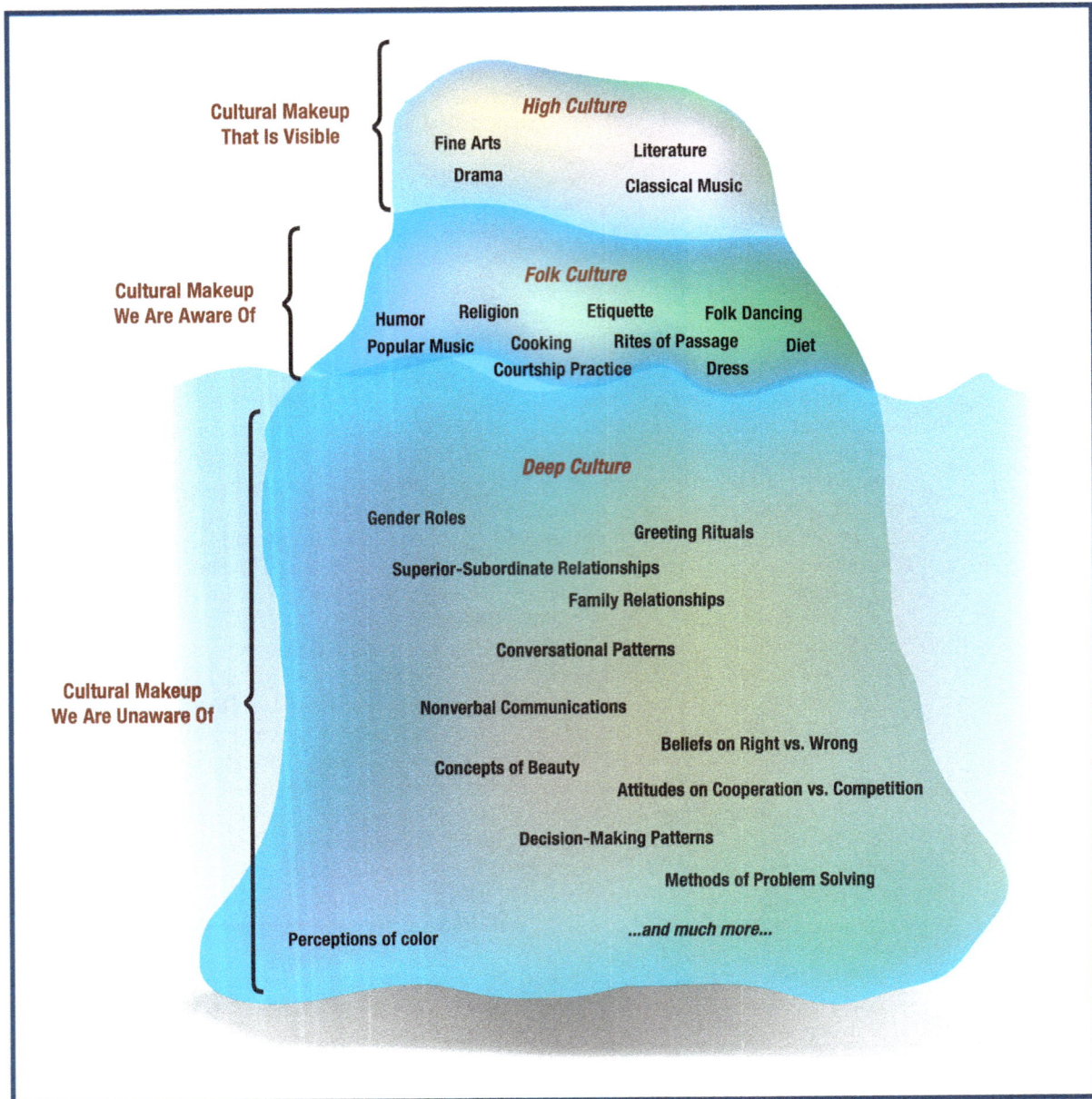

**Cultural Makeup That Is Visible**

**High Culture**

Fine Arts

Literature

Drama

Classical Music

**Cultural Makeup We Are Aware Of**

**Folk Culture**

Humor    Religion    Etiquette    Folk Dancing

Popular Music    Cooking    Rites of Passage    Diet

Courtship Practice    Dress

**Cultural Makeup We Are Unaware Of**

**Deep Culture**

Gender Roles

Greeting Rituals

Superior-Subordinate Relationships

Family Relationships

Conversational Patterns

Nonverbal Communications

Beliefs on Right vs. Wrong

Concepts of Beauty

Attitudes on Cooperation vs. Competition

Decision-Making Patterns

Methods of Problem Solving

Perceptions of color

*...and much more...*

**EXHIBIT 4.4**

**Culture as an Iceberg**

partition individual workspaces and provide private offices for more important employees. In Islamic countries, close interaction between men and women is not encouraged in public places.

## Symbolic Productions

A *symbol* can be letters, figures, colors, or other characters that communicate a meaning. For example, the cross is the main symbol of Christianity. The red star was the symbol of the former Soviet Union. National symbols include flags, anthems, seals, monuments, and historical myths. Symbols can represent nations, religions, or corporations, and they can help to unite people. Mathematicians and scientists use symbols as their language. Businesses have many types of symbols, in the form of trademarks, logos, and brands. Think how easy it is to identify popular company logos such as Tesla's T-shaped badge, Apple's apple, and Cadbury's unique lettering.

Colors carry diverse meanings in different cultures, as summarized in Exhibit 4.5. Color meanings in each country are based on spiritual, social, cultural, historic and political influences. Black is frequently associated with death in Western culture, but white is associated with death

**EXHIBIT 4.5**

**The Meaning of Colors Around the World**

*Sources:* Xiao-Ping Gao and John H. Xin, "Investigation of human's emotional responses on colors," *Color Research and Application*, 31, No. 5 (2006), pp. 411–417; John Gage, *Color and Culture: Practice and Meaning from Antiquity to Abstraction* (Oakland, CA: University of California Press, 1999); Mabel Weaver, *Color Symbolism* (Amazon Digital Services, 2014, www.amazon.com).

|       | Europe and North America          | China                             | Japan                           | Middle East                    |
|-------|-----------------------------------|-----------------------------------|---------------------------------|--------------------------------|
| Red   | Danger, stop, anger, love, passion | Good luck, joy, celebration, long life | Celebration, danger, anger | Danger, anger, evil |
| White | Purity, peace, brides             | Mourning, death, humility         | Mourning, death, purity         | Mourning, death, purity        |
| Black | Death, evil, mourning             | Evil, color for young boys        | Evil                            | Evil                           |
| Green | Money, safety, luck, prosperity   | Youth, growth, adultery           | Life, energy, freshness, youth  | Strength, luck, fertility      |
| Blue  | Sadness, calm, trust, masculinity | Strength, power, immortality      | Purity, cleanliness             | Protective                     |

in much of Asia. Red is often associated with danger in the United States but signifies happiness and celebration in China. Red is the traditional bridal color in China, but white is the more traditional bridal color in Western culture. Blue is a safe color choice with many positive associations. In Europe and North America, blue represents trust and security and is considered soothing and peaceful. Elsewhere, blue symbolizes love, healing, and good health. In Western cultures, green represents luck, freshness, and environmental awareness. In some Eastern cultures, green symbolizes youth and new life. Purple is often associated with royalty, wealth, honor, and spirituality. In Brazil and Thailand, purple is the color of mourning.

Colors are important and powerful communication tools that express emotions and feelings. Colors are one of the most influential factors that affect perceptions in branding and advertising. Companies must choose color schemes carefully when developing product features, advertising, packaging, and marketing programs. When buyers encounter a product for the first time, the perception of the product is significantly influenced by its color.[8]

## Material Productions and Creative Expressions

*Material productions* are artifacts, objects, and technological systems that people construct to function within their environments. They are integral to human life and provide the means to accomplish objectives as well as communicate and conduct exchanges within and between societies. The most important technology-based material productions are the infrastructures that supply energy, transportation, and communications. Others include social infrastructure (systems that provide housing, education, and health care), financial infrastructure (systems for managing means of exchange in banks and other financial institutions), and marketing infrastructure (systems that support marketing-related activities such as ad agencies). Creative expressions of culture include arts, folklore, music, dance, theater, and high cuisine. Education is an especially important system that emerges within cultures.

## Education

Cultural values, ideas, beliefs, traditions, and attitudes are passed from one generation to the next through education. Education takes place in many ways, especially through lessons and behavior acquired from parents, family, and peers; participation in groups (social, business, and religious); and formal schooling. In most countries, academic education usually occurs through schooling. Available talent and skill base of a region or country influences where corporations will locate international ventures such as factories or call centers. Better-educated locations tend to attract higher paying and higher skilled positions such as outsourced call centers and accounting functions. Literacy, the ability to read, is an important indicator of education level and varies substantially around the world. Exhibit 4.6 shows literacy rates in selected countries.

The literacy rate is higher for men than for women in many developing economies. This arises for various reasons, often related to culture, religion, nation-level conflicts, and socioeconomic factors. In the African country of Sudan, for example, 82 percent of men are literate compared to 66 percent of women. This disparity results partly because Sudan is a male-dominated

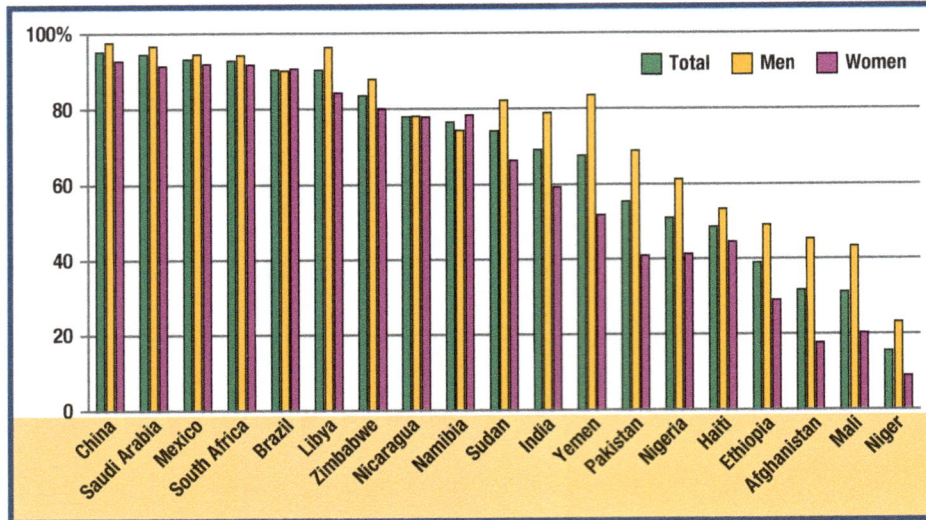

**EXHIBIT 4.6**

**Literacy Rates by Gender in Selected Countries (percent of those who can read)**

*Sources:* Central Intelligence Agency, *The World Factbook 2018* (Washington, DC: Central Intelligence Agency, 2018); United Nations, UNICEF Global Databases, 2017, http://data. unicef.org; UNESCO, *Effective Literacy and Numeracy Practices Database (LitBase)*, http:// litbase.uil.unesco.org/, accessed January 5, 2018.

society in which women tend to take on subordinate roles and have limited opportunities to attend school. Women are expected to bear and raise children and perform domestic chores in the home. Educational opportunities in Sudan also have been hindered by war and ethnic strife. In Namibia, another African country, the literacy rate is higher for women than for men, at 78 and 74 percent, respectively. This has resulted partly from government efforts such as the National Literacy Programme to increase citizens' literacy and communications skills. Programs often target Namibian women, while men concentrate on traditional labor-intensive jobs such as fishing, mining, and agriculture.[9]

## Social Structure

Social structure refers to the pattern of social arrangements and organized relationships that characterize a society. It refers to how a society is organized in terms of individuals, families, groups, and socioeconomic strata. All cultures have a social structure that influences our status or class in society. Understanding the social structure of international employees, clients, and suppliers is vital for avoiding cultural misunderstandings and optimizing business transactions.

*Individuals.* Because Western cultures emphasize individualism and individual success, social status often is determined by individual performance. This helps explain the high degree of worker mobility and entrepreneurial activity typical in Western societies. Excessive individualism, however, can reduce the effectiveness of teams, particularly in collectivist cultures typical of Asia.

*Family.* In many cultures, immediate and extended family holds particular importance in the nation's social structure. In such cultures, the family often plays a substantial role in the formation and structure of business activities. In China, for example, family-owned and family-run businesses are relatively common, and ownership often passes on to successive generations.

*Reference groups.* In some societies, people's social status is defined by group or employer affiliation rather than by individual performance. When meeting business people in Tokyo, for instance, they typically will identify themselves in terms of the companies where they work rather than by their function or job title at that firm. In Japanese firms, objectives and strategies are typically decided by groups rather than by individual managers.

*Social stratification.* In most cultures, individuals are classified within classes or social layers depending on their occupation, income level, or family history. However, societies differ in the importance they place on social strata and on the ease with which people can advance to higher strata. In most countries, senior business and government leaders typically occupy the highest social strata. The middle strata usually consist of business managers and medical or scientific professionals. Those in the lowest strata typically work in manual labor, basic services such as retailing, or lower-level administrative positions.

*Social mobility.* Social mobility refers to the ease with which a person can move up within social strata. The most rigid type of social mobility operates in a *caste system* in countries such as India. In a caste system, a person's social status is determined by birth, and he or she has little opportunity for social mobility. Individuals are often restricted to working in a specific occupation, such as a farmer or factory worker, depending on the caste they were born into. Understanding social norms in caste system countries is necessary to successfully manage employees who work at different levels of the social strata. Advanced economies are characterized by the *class system*, a more flexible form of social stratification within which people usually have greater mobility to move to higher strata and change their social status. Social mobility in caste and class systems alike influences people's attitude toward work, entrepreneurship, and labor relations.

**4.3** Describe the role of language and religion in culture.

## Role of Language and Religion in Culture

Language and religion are among the most important manifestations of culture. Often described as the expression or *mirror* of culture, verbal language is not only essential for communications, it also provides insights into culture. It's a major differentiator between cultural groups and castes and provides an essential means for business leaders to communicate effectively with employees, suppliers, and customers. Language can be classified as verbal and nonverbal.

### Verbal Language

The world has approximately 7,000 active languages, including more than 2,000 in each of Africa and Asia. Most of these languages have only a few thousand speakers.[10] Just 23 languages are spoken by half the world's population. Exhibit 4.7 displays the world's most spoken languages.

**EXHIBIT 4.7**

**The Most Common Primary Languages in the World**

*Sources:* Gary Simon and Charles Fennig (eds.), *Ethnologue: Languages of the World*, 20th ed., 2017, www.ethnologue.com; Central Intelligence Agency, *CIA World Factbook*, 2017, www.cia.gov.

| World Rank | Language | Approximate Number of Native Speakers (Millions) | Countries with Substantial Number of Native Speakers |
|---|---|---|---|
| 1 | Mandarin Chinese | 900 | China, Singapore |
| 2 | Spanish | 435 | Argentina, Mexico, Spain |
| 3 | English | 370 | Australia, Canada, United Kingdom, United States |
| 4 | Arabic | 290 | Egypt, Saudi Arabia, United Arab Emirates |
| 5 | Hindi | 260 | India, Pakistan |
| 6 | Bengali | 240 | Bangladesh, India |
| 7 | Portuguese | 220 | Brazil, Portugal |
| 8 | Russian | 150 | Russia, Kazakhstan, Ukraine |
| 9 | Japanese | 130 | Japan |
| 10 | Punjabi | 90 | Pakistan, India |
| 11 | Javanese | 84 | Indonesia |
| 12 | Wu Chinese | 80 | China |
| 13 | Korean | 77 | South Korea, North Korea |
| 14 | German | 77 | Germany, Austria |
| 15 | French | 76 | France, Ivory Coast, Gabon, Canada |

| Company and Location | Intended Ad Slogan | Literal Translation |
|---|---|---|
| Parker Pen Company in Latin America | "Use Parker Pen, avoid embarrassment!" | "Use Parker Pen, avoid pregnancy!" |
| Pepsi in Germany | "Come Alive with Pepsi" | "Come out of the grave with Pepsi." |
| Pepsi in Taiwan | "Come Alive with Pepsi" | "Pepsi brings your ancestors back from the dead." |
| Fisher Body (car exteriors) in Belgium | "Body by Fisher" | "Corpse by Fisher" |
| Salem cigarettes in Japan | "Salem—Feeling Free" | "Smoking Salem makes your mind feel free and empty." |

**EXHIBIT 4.8**

**Blunders in International Advertising**

National languages, dialects, and translation tend to complicate verbal communication. It is sometimes difficult to find words to convey the same meaning in a different language. For example, a one-word equivalent to *aftertaste* does not exist in many languages. Even when a word can be translated well into other languages, its concept and meaning may not be universal. For example, the Japanese word *muzukashii* can be variously translated as "difficult," "delicate," or "I don't want to discuss it," but in business negotiations, it usually means "out of the question." Advertising themes often lose their original meaning in translation or give the wrong impression.

Exhibit 4.8 shows how the popular slogans of some languages translate into unintended phrases in other languages. Pepsi's mistranslation in Taiwan is an example. Taiwanese people knew Pepsi could not bring their ancestors back from the grave, but many were surprised at Pepsi's apparent carelessness in rendering a poor translation. Even people from different countries who speak the same language may experience communication problems because some words are unique to a particular language. Exhibit 4.9 shows how two English-speaking countries interpret the same word in very different ways and how misinterpretations can hamper intended meaning.[11]

Sometimes business jargon—vocabulary unique to a particular country—can cause communication problems. Examples of English jargon that puzzle nonnative speakers include "the bottom line," "to beat around the bush," "shooting from the hip," "feather in your cap," and "get down to brass tacks." Imagine the difficulty that professional interpreters encounter in translating such phrases!

An **idiom** is an expression whose symbolic meaning is different from its actual or literal meaning. It is a phrase you cannot understand by knowing only what the individual words in the phrase mean. For example, to "roll out the red carpet" is to welcome a guest extravagantly—no red carpet is actually used. The phrase is misunderstood when interpreted in a literal way. In Spanish, the idiom "no está el horno para bolos" literally means "the oven isn't ready for bread rolls," but the phrase is understood as "the time isn't right." In Japanese, the phrase "uma ga au" literally means "our horses meet," but the everyday meaning is "we get along with each other."

**Idiom**
An expression whose symbolic meaning is different from its literal meaning.

| Word | Meaning in U.S. English | Meaning in British English |
|---|---|---|
| Scheme | A somewhat devious plan | A plan |
| Redundant | Repetitive | Fired or laid off |
| Sharp | Smart | Conniving, unethical |
| To table | To put as issue on hold | To take up an issue |
| To bomb | To fail miserably | To succeed grandly |
| Windscreen | A screen that protects against wind | Automobile windshield |

**EXHIBIT 4.9**

**Differences in Meaning Between American and British English**

Idioms exist in virtually every culture, and people often use them as a short way to express a larger concept. Managers should study national idioms to gain a better understanding of cultural values. Exhibit 4.10 offers several expressions that reveal cultural traits of different societies.

## Nonverbal Communication

Nonverbal communication is unspoken and includes facial expressions and gestures.[12] In fact, nonverbal messages accompany most verbal ones. These include facial expressions, body movements, eye contact, physical distance, posture, and other nonverbal signals. Exhibit 4.11 lists several types of nonverbal communication.

Nonverbal communications frequently can lead to confusion and misunderstandings because of cultural differences. Certain facial expressions and hand gestures have different meanings in different cultures, and a lack of awareness of the meanings of these gestures in the local culture can lead to negative consequences. For example, standing side by side with someone can

**EXHIBIT 4.10**

**Idioms That Symbolize Cultural Values**

| Country | Expression | Underlying Value |
|---|---|---|
| Japan | "The nail that sticks out gets hammered down." | Group conformity |
| Australia and New Zealand | "The tall poppy gets cut down." (Criticism of a person who is perceived as presumptuous, attention-seeking, or without merit.) | Egalitarianism |
| Sweden and other Scandinavian countries | "*Janteloven*" or "Jante Law." "Don't think you're anyone special or that you're better than us." | Modesty |
| Korea | "A tiger dies leaving its leather, a man dies leaving his name." | Honor |
| Turkey | "Steel that works does not rust." | Hard work |
| United States | "Necessity is the mother of invention." | Resourcefulness |
| Thailand | "If you follow older people, dogs won't bite you." | Wisdom |

**EXHIBIT 4.11**

**Nonverbal Communication**

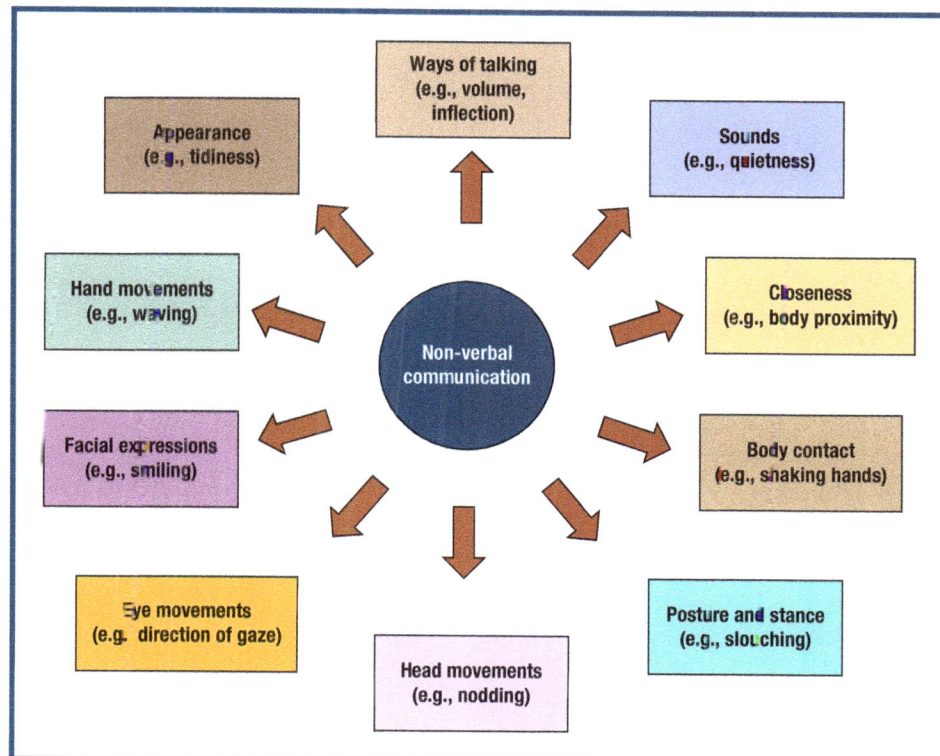

indicate cooperation, whereas a face-to-face posture might indicate competition or opposition. Touching tends to indicate levels of intimacy, from shaking hands to patting the back to hugging.

## Religion

Religion is a system of common beliefs or attitudes concerning a being or a system of thought that people consider sacred, divine, or the highest truth and includes the moral codes, values, institutions, traditions, and rituals associated with this system. Religious concepts of right and wrong have played a key role in the development of ethical values and social responsibility. Almost every culture is underpinned by religious beliefs.[13] Religion influences culture and, therefore, managerial and customer behavior in many ways. Exhibit 4.12 shows the dominant religions worldwide but only the most common religion in each location; most countries are home to people of various faiths.

Although there are thousands of distinct faith groups worldwide, four major religions dominate: *Christianity* with roughly 2 billion adherents, *Islam* with about 1.5 billion followers, and *Hinduism* and *Buddhism*, each with about 1 billion adherents. Other belief systems include *Confucianism* and *Judaism*.

Religion appears to have a positive effect on economic activity.[14] Religious affiliations help create bonds of trust and shared commitment, which facilitate lending and trade. Furthermore, religion can boost GDP in a country by reducing corruption and increasing respect for law and order. Religion that promotes moral values should help foster successful economic systems. Conversely, a lack of ethical values tends to coincide with economic decay; a lawless society cannot sustain normal business activities for long. It is noteworthy, however, that some societies with strong religious values—for example, many Middle Eastern countries and their embrace of Islam or southern Africa and its many Christian devotees—have not produced high living standards for their citizens. This implies religion alone is insufficient to support economic development. Other factors, such as strong private property rights, political and economic freedom, and an entrepreneurial spirit, are also important. Let's review each of the four major religions.

CHRISTIANITY.    Followers of Jesus Christ, Christians are concentrated in the Americas, Europe, Australia, South Korea, and southern Africa. Christianity is divided into three major groups: Catholic, Protestant, and Eastern Orthodox. Catholics account for more than half of all Christians; Protestants encompass numerous denominations, including Baptists and Methodists; and Eastern Orthodox Christianity is practiced mainly in Greece and Russia.

Although the number of adherents has declined over time, particularly in Europe and North America, the cultural effects of Christianity have largely endured. For one, Sunday is still regarded as a day of rest when most people do not work. German sociologist Max Weber and other scholars have suggested a relationship between Protestantism and capitalism. Protestantism long emphasized individual effort, orderliness, and hard work to achieve worldly success and as a duty that benefits both the individual and society. As a revolutionary movement that broke with the Catholic Church, Protestantism also long emphasized religious freedom and independent thinking. Such views are consistent with the political and economic freedoms that encouraged the rise of capitalism in the advanced economies, especially in Northern Europe and North America. Eventually, capitalism's accumulation of wealth came to be viewed as an outward symbol of the individual's hard and God-given work during his or her earthly life.[15] The Catholic notion of "good works" also contributes to arduous work and economic development, especially when adherents believe their labor contributes to a greater good.

ISLAM.    Islam is based on the *Qur'an*, the religion's holy book, which Muslims believe was revealed by God to the prophet Muhammed in the seventh century. Most Muslims belong to one of two denominations: Sunni and Shia. Although most Muslims live in the Middle East, North Africa, and South Asia, the most populous Muslim country is Indonesia. Adherents engage in daily ritual prayers and fasting during the month of Ramadan. The *Qur'an* strongly encourages charitable giving. Strict Muslims believe the purpose of life is to worship God (known as Allah). In most Middle East countries, Islam is the basis for government and legal systems as well as the social and cultural order; however, globalization has exposed the Islamic world to outside cultural influences. Strict Islamists tend to view Western ideals as a threat to their values, whereas liberal Muslims seek to reconcile religious tradition with Western values and secular governance. Muslim immigrants have established communities in Europe and the United States, importing values and customs rooted in Islamic faith.

Sharia, the Islamic law based on the *Qur'an*, influences the legal code to varying degrees in Muslim countries. Its influence in secular states such as Turkey is much less than in orthodox Islamic countries such as Saudi Arabia. Sharia law covers all aspects of daily life, economic activity, and public governance. Non-secular societies do not distinguish between church and state. Family is at the center of Muslim life, and Islam specifies obligations and legal rights of family members.

Islam encourages free trade through rules that prohibit restraints on market-based exchange such as monopolies and price fixing. Islam encourages the free flow of information that facilitates

Christianity
Judaism
Hinduism
Islam

Buddhism
Nature religion
Chinese religion
Other groups

efficient demand and supply. The *Qur'an* condemns charging interest for money loaned. Thus, banks in Islamic countries have devised methods for financing debt without violating Sharia law.

The *Qur'an* prohibits drinking alcohol, gambling, and showing too much skin. These restrictions affect firms that deal in alcoholic beverages, resorts, entertainment, and women's clothing. Many multinational firms are reaching out to Muslim communities. Nokia launched a mobile phone application that shows Muslims the direction toward Mecca, Islam's holiest site, when they pray. Heineken, the Dutch brewing giant, rolled out the nonalcoholic malt drink *Fayrouz* for the Islamic market. In general, MNEs are allowed to operate as long as they abide by Sharia law, do not exploit people, and earn profits fairly.[16]

HINDUISM.    A unique faith practiced in South Asia, especially India, Hinduism emerged from various ancient traditions. Unlike Christianity and Islam, Hinduism is not connected to any one prophet and lacks a unified belief system. To its adherents, it is a traditional way of life and an

**EXHIBIT 4.12**
**World Religions**

*Sources:* Based on Godweb, 2018, www.godweb.org/ religionsofworld.htm and World Religion Map, 2018, https://worldmap.harvard.edu/data/ geonode:wrd_province_religion_ qg0.

open-hearted faith that fully accepts other faiths. *Dharma* is a central concept that encourages behavior that is just and harmonious and promotes joyful living. Hindus believe in reincarnation, a cycle of birth, life death, and rebirth. The nature of actions taken during one's lifetime, *karma*, determines future destiny. In this life and the next, evil actions lead to future suffering; good deeds bring about *nirvana* (paradise). Hindus believe that kindness in action fosters a better world. The religion values spiritual rather than material achievements.

Karma implies that people are born into a social level, or *caste*, through their good or bad deeds in earlier lives. Critics argue that the caste system promotes slower economic growth because it hinders advancement from one social level to another in organizational settings;[17] thus company advancement can be based on a person's social level rather than on merit or potential. Ambition is dampened if followers believe they are destined to remain at a particular level at work. The caste system can also promote disharmony because followers may discriminate against employees whom they perceive to fit different social levels. In Hofstede's typology, India is characterized by high power distance because a sharp distinction is often drawn between upper and lower caste workers.

Hinduism's focus on spiritual enlightenment and selfless working for the greater good of society can influence the conduct of business. A devotion to positive karma and ascetic lifestyle are potentially at odds with the relatively materialistic pursuits of business.[18] However, some argue that business performance can be enhanced by embracing Hinduism's teachings in areas such as self-control, discipline, and devotion to duty.[19]

**BUDDHISM.**    Buddhism is a belief system that encompasses various traditions and practices and is based on the teachings of the prophet Buddha. It is common in Asia, especially China and Japan. Buddhists subscribe to Four Noble Truths: Life is beset by suffering and pain; desire and greed are the root of all human suffering; personal suffering can be reduced by controlling desire and greed; and the way to end suffering is through righteous living, which includes good conduct, wisdom, and mental development.

Buddhism promotes harmony to achieve inner happiness and peaceful relations with others. In this way, it supports harmony and stability in commercial relations. Buddhism also encourages cooperation and tolerance for others, which are good for business. It is permissible in Buddhism to pray for security and good fortune. In this way, followers are comfortable with acquiring wealth as long as it is done with patience and harmony. Buddhism promotes a life centered on spiritual rather than worldly matters. Accordingly, it is seen to support ethical and responsible behavior in business. However, as in Hinduism, Buddhism's focus on spirituality and moderation might restrain entrepreneurial action.

**CONFUCIANISM.**    Confucianism is a way of life taught by the philosopher Confucius, who lived about 2,500 years ago in present-day China. More a philosophy than a religion, Confucianism does not prescribe any specific rituals or practices. The main belief system of the Chinese people, it has influenced culture in China and other parts of Asia, especially Korea, Japan, and Vietnam, for thousands of years. Although East Asians profess various faiths, especially Shintoism, Taoism, and Buddhism, most also embrace some aspects of Confucianism.

Confucianism has an optimistic view of human nature and a strong emphasis on ethical behavior. Adherents believe that people are teachable, improvable, and perfectible through personal and communal efforts that emphasize learning and self-renewal. They believe it is best to behave with fairness, humanity, and charity toward others. *Ren* is a Confucian virtue that refers to doing honorable deeds and being kind to others. Other important qualities include loyalty, social harmony, and respect for one's parents and ancestors.

**JUDAISM.**    Judaism was founded more than 3,000 years ago in the Middle East. Today the world's 14 million Jews primarily reside in Israel, Europe, and North America. Many migrated around the world in the wake of persecution or the pursuit of business opportunities.[20] Judaism strongly influenced early Christianity and Islam. Jews believe in one God and that that God is concerned with the actions of humankind. Jews attempt to conduct themselves accordingly. Strict adherents aim to apply their faith in every aspect of their lives.

The Jewish attitude toward business is positive, and much business conduct is rooted in Jewish law, which prohibits dishonest behavior. The accumulation of wealth is acceptable and even encouraged. Simultaneously, Jews are expected to be generous and charitable. Businesses should operate responsibly, emphasizing ethics and fair play beyond that required by local law.

# Culture's Effect in International Business

4.4 Describe culture's effect in international business.

Culture can differ sharply, even between neighboring countries. Exhibit 4.13 examines cultural differences between Mexico and the United States. Effective handling of the cross-cultural interface is a critical source of firms' competitive advantage. Managers not only need to develop empathy and tolerance toward cultural differences but also must acquire a sufficient degree of factual knowledge about the beliefs and values of foreign counterparts. Cross-cultural proficiency is paramount in many managerial tasks, including:

- Managing employees
- Communicating and interacting with foreign business partners
- Negotiating and structuring international business ventures
- Developing products and services
- Preparing advertising and promotional materials

| DIMENSION | MEXICO | UNITED STATES |
|---|---|---|
| Role of context | High-context culture that values social trust, personal goodwill, and ritualized business | Low-context culture that emphasizes efficiency, explicit communications, and "getting down to business" |
| Individualism versus collectivism | Relatively group oriented. Extended families, teamwork, and group loyalty are valued. | Relatively individualistic. Emphasis on personal freedom and working alone. Group loyalty is less valued. |
| Time orientation | Fluid and polychronic. Long-term relationships are valued. Mexicans emphasize the past and believe they have little control over the future. | Rigid and monochronic. Business is short-term oriented and values profit above all else. Americans believe they can control the future. |
| Space perceptions | Conversational distance is close. Personal space is less valued. | Conversational distance is ample. Personal space is highly valued. |
| Religion | Christianity is influential in daily life and often in business. | Americans' religious orientation is diverse and declining. |
| Language | Spanish dominates with little linguistic diversity. | While English dominates, there is much linguistic diversity. |
| Negotiations | Tend to progress slowly. Decisions take time. Legalism is avoided in agreements. | Emphasis on efficiency and quick decision making. Agreements are often legalistic. |
| Business relations | Relationship-oriented. Mexicans are easygoing, valuing personal bonds. | Deal-oriented. Business performance takes precedence over relationships. |
| Business meetings | Arriving late is acceptable. Meetings are informal and usually don't follow a strict agenda. | Americans are time-oriented, arriving promptly to meetings, which often follow a formal agenda. |
| Superior–subordinate relations | Firms are hierarchical, with much power distance. Senior managers are relatively authoritarian. | Lower power distance. Firms are "flatter" with less hierarchy. Relations with superiors are informal and easygoing. |
| Style of dress in business | Conservative, emphasizing dark suits. High-status personnel are expected to dress the part. | Business casual is widely accepted. "Dressing the part" is less important. |

**EXHIBIT 4.13**

**Perceived Cultural Attributes of Mexico and the United States**

*Sources:* Based on Geert Hofstede, *Culture's Consequences* (Beverly Hills, CA: Sage, 1980); Boye De Mente, *The Mexican Mind* (Beverly Hills, CA: Phoenix Books, 2011); Lucila Ortiz, *A Primer for Spanish Language, Culture and Economics* (Bloomington, IN: Xlibris, 2011); Russell Maddicks, *Mexico—Culture Smart!: The Essential Guide to Customs & Culture* (London: Kuperard, 2017).

- Preparing for international trade fairs and exhibitions
- Screening and selecting foreign distributors and other partners
- Interacting with current and potential customers from abroad

Let's consider specific examples of how cross-cultural differences may complicate company activities.

*Developing products and services.* Cultural differences necessitate adapting marketing activities to suit the specific needs of target markets. Johnson & Johnson developed different varieties of its mouthwash, Listerine, for foreign markets. For instance, it created alcohol-free Listerine Zero for Muslim countries where spirits are forbidden. For Asian markets, it launched Green Tea Listerine. In Europe, consumers want their mouthwash to solve more complex problems than just bad breath, so the firm developed an advanced gum treatment rinse.[21]

*Providing services.* Firms that engage in services such as lodging and retailing substantially interact with customers, implying greater cultural interaction and the potential for cognitive and communication gaps. Imagine a Western lawyer who tries to establish a law office in China or a Western restaurant chain operating in Russia. Both firms will encounter substantial cultural challenges. Differences in language and national character have the same effect as trade barriers.[22]

*Organizational structure.* Some companies prefer to delegate authority to country managers, which results in a decentralized organizational structure. Other firms have centralized structures, in which power is concentrated at regional or corporate headquarters. Firms may be bureaucratic or entrepreneurial. How do you deal with a bureaucratic partner or manage distantly located, decentralized subsidiaries?

*Teamwork.* Cooperating with partners and host-country nationals to achieve common organizational goals is critical to business success. But what should managers do if foreign and domestic nationals don't get along? The Chinese home appliance manufacturer Haier (www.haier.com) delayed acquiring overseas firms because management felt it lacked the ability to manage foreign nationals and integrate differing cultural systems.

*Pay-for-performance system.* In some countries, merit is not the main basis for promoting employees. In China and Japan, a person's age is the most important determinant, but how do such workers perform when Western firms evaluate them using performance-based measures?

*Lifetime employment.* In some Asian countries, firms are very protective of their employees, who may work for the same company all their lives. The expectations that arise from such devoted relationships can complicate dealings with outside firms. Western managers may struggle to motivate employees who expect they will always have the same job.

*Union–management relationships.* In Germany, union bosses hold the same status as top-level managers and can sit on corporate boards. Many European firms have a business culture in which workers are relatively equal to managers. This approach can reduce the flexibility of company operations because it makes it harder to lay off workers.

*Attitudes toward ambiguity.* In some countries, people have a hard time tolerating *ambiguity*, which refers to situations in which information can be understood in more than one way. For example, some bosses give exact and detailed instructions, whereas others give vague and incomplete instructions. If you're not comfortable working with minimum guidance or taking independent action, you may not fit well into some cultures.

*Negotiations.* Negotiations arise in virtually all aspects of business, as when the firm takes on a partner or a supplier–buyer relationship. Goals, interests, ethics, and cultural assumptions vary cross-culturally, which can complicate forming and maintaining business relationships. In most of Northern Europe, negotiations are relatively efficient, impersonal, and unsociable; negotiators get down to business quickly.

*Technology.* In the past, distinct cultures developed because regions had limited contact with each other. Today, digital, information, communications, and transportation technologies bring people into close contact. The Internet and other communications technologies imply greater likelihood of cross-cultural miscommunications and blunders. To help reduce problems, managers use software that instantly converts messages into any of dozens of languages.[23]

## Models and Explanations of Culture

Scholars have developed several explanations for gaining deeper insights into the role of culture. In this section, we review cultural metaphors, E. T. Hall's high and low context cultures, and Hofstede's dimensions of culture.

### Cultural Metaphors

Martin Gannon offered an insightful analysis of cultural orientations.[24] In his view, a **cultural metaphor** refers to a distinctive tradition or institution that is strongly associated with a particular society. It is a guide to deciphering people's attitudes, values, and behavior.

For example, American football is a cultural metaphor for traditions in the United States, such as being a team player and having a strong leader who moves an organization aggressively toward a desired goal. The Swedish *stuga* (cottage or summer home) is a cultural metaphor for Swedes' love of nature and desire for individualism through self-development. The Brazilian concept of *jeitinho Brasileiro* refers to an ability to cope with the challenges of daily life through creative problem solving or navigating the country's demanding bureaucracy. In the Brazilian context, manipulation and smooth talking are not necessarily viewed negatively because individuals may need to resort to these methods to conduct business.

Anthropologists and other social scientists have studied culture for centuries. Two leading interpretations of national culture are those of E. T. Hall and Geert Hofstede. Hall's contribution was to make a distinction between high- and low-context cultures. Hofstede's influential research led him to distinguish important dimensions of culture.

### High- and Low-Context Cultures

Anthropologist Edward T. Hall classified cultures as low context and high context.[25] When communicating, people in **low-context cultures** rely heavily on spoken words and detailed verbal explanations. As Exhibit 4.14 shows, Europeans and North Americans tend to be low-context with long traditions of writing and speech making. In such cultures, the main function of speech is to express ideas and thoughts clearly, logically, and convincingly; communication is direct, and meaning is straightforward. In negotiations, for example, Americans typically come to the point quickly. Low-context cultures tend to value expertise and performance. Managers conduct negotiations as efficiently as possible. These cultures use specific, legalistic contracts to conclude agreements.

Germany and the United States are leading examples of low-context cultures. International managers sometimes complain that presentations by their U.S. counterparts are too detailed. Everything is spelled out, even when meanings seem perfectly obvious. In Germany, business planning is detailed and explicit. Key information is explained in relatively great detail. Laws, rules, and procedures are thorough and clear and allow people to know what is expected so that they can plan their activities accordingly. Much emphasis is placed on leading a structured and ordered life.[26]

By contrast, **high-context cultures**, such as China and Japan, emphasize nonverbal messages and view communication as a means to promote smooth, harmonious relationships. They prefer an indirect and polite style that emphasizes mutual respect and care for others. They are on guard not to embarrass or offend others. This helps explain why Japanese people hesitate to say *no* even when they disagree with what someone is saying. They are more likely to say "it is different," a softer response. In East Asian cultures, showing impatience, frustration, irritation, or anger disrupts harmony and is considered rude and offensive. Asians tend to be soft-spoken, and people typically are sensitive to context and body language. At a business luncheon in Tokyo, for example, the boss is almost always the senior-looking individual seated farthest from the entrance to the room. In Japan, superiors are given such favored seating to show

**4.5** Learn models and explanations of culture.

**Cultural metaphor**
A distinctive tradition or institution strongly associated with a particular society.

**Low-context culture**
A culture that relies on elaborate verbal explanations, putting much emphasis on spoken words.

**High-context culture**
A culture that emphasizes nonverbal messages and views communication as a means to promote smooth, harmonious relationships.

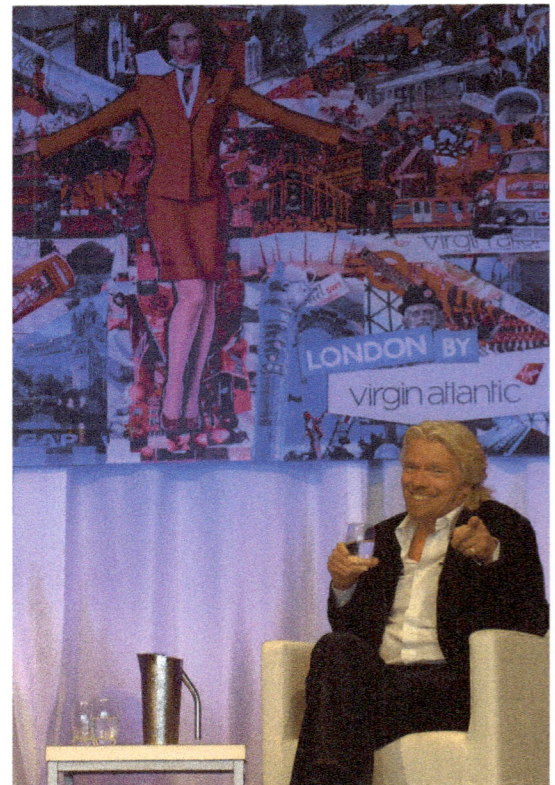

*Source:* Sergei Bachlakov/Shutterstock

The edgy, risk-taking culture of companies under the Virgin brand owes much to the independent and flamboyant spirit of company founder Richard Branson and contrasts sharply with the conservative cultures of other British firms despite the companies sharing the same national culture.

**EXHIBIT 4.14**

**Hall's High- and Low-Context Typology of Cultures**

*Source:* Based on *Beyond Culture* by Edward T. Hall, 1976. 1981 by Edward T. Hall. Doubleday, a division of Random House, Inc. For online information about other Random House, Inc. books and authors, see the Internet website at http://www.randomhouse.com; Mark Cleveland, Michel Laroche, and Nicolas Papadopoulos, "You Are What You Speak? Globalization, Multilingualism, Consumer Dispositions and Consumption," *Journal of Business Research* 68, No. 3 (2015), pp. 542–552; Donghoon Kim, Yigang Pan, and Heung Soo Park, "High-Versus Low-Context Culture: A Comparison of Chinese, Korean and American Cultures," *Psychology & Marketing* 15, No. 6 (1998), pp. 507–521.

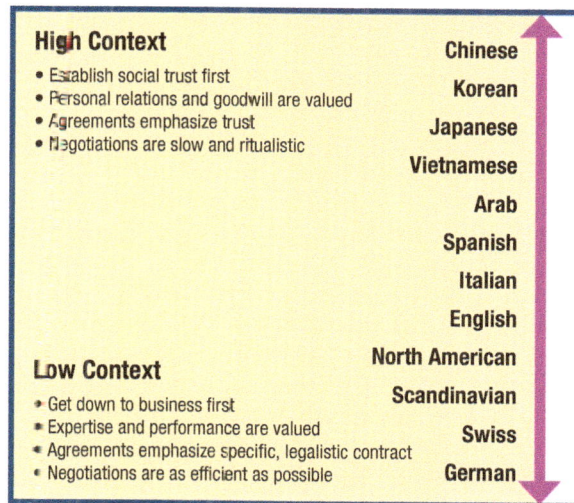

| High Context | |
| --- | --- |
| • Establish social trust first | Chinese |
| • Personal relations and goodwill are valued | Korean |
| • Agreements emphasize trust | Japanese |
| • Negotiations are slow and ritualistic | Vietnamese |
| | Arab |
| | Spanish |
| | Italian |
| | English |
| | North American |
| **Low Context** | Scandinavian |
| • Get down to business first | Swiss |
| • Expertise and performance are valued | German |
| • Agreements emphasize specific, legalistic contract | |
| • Negotiations are as efficient as possible | |

respect. Negotiations tend to be slow and ritualistic, and agreement is founded on trust. To succeed in Asian cultures, it is critical to have a keen eye for nonverbal signs and body language.

## Hofstede's Research on National Culture

Dutch anthropologist Geert Hofstede conducted one of the early studies of national cultural traits. He collected data on the values and attitudes of 116,000 employees at IBM, a diverse company in terms of nationality, age, and gender. Based on this research, Hofstede identified six independent dimensions of national culture, described next.[27]

**Individualism versus collectivism** refers to whether a person functions primarily as an individual or as part of a group. In individualistic societies, each person tends to focus on his or her own self-interest, and ties among people are relatively loose. These societies prefer individualism over agreement within the group. Competition for resources is the norm, and those who compete best are rewarded financially. Australia, Canada, the United Kingdom, and the United States tend to be strongly individualistic societies.

By contrast, in collectivist societies, ties among individuals are highly valued. Business is conducted in the context of a group in which others' views are strongly considered. The group is all-important because life is a cooperative experience. Conformity and compromise help maintain group harmony. China, Panama, and South Korea are examples of strongly collectivist societies.

**Power distance** describes how a society deals with the inequalities in power that exist among people. In societies with *low* power distance, the gaps between the powerful and weak are small. In Denmark and Sweden, for example, governments have set up tax and social welfare systems that ensure their citizens are relatively equal in terms of income and power. The United States also scores relatively low on power distance.

Societies characterized by *high* power distance do not care very much about inequalities and allow them to grow over time. There are substantial gaps between the powerful and the weak. Guatemala, Malaysia, the Philippines, and several Middle Eastern nations are examples of countries with high power distance. In high-power-distance firms, autocratic management styles focus power at the top and grant little self-rule to lower-level employees. In low-power-distance firms, managers and subordinates are relatively equal and cooperate to achieve organizational goals. **Uncertainty avoidance** refers to the extent to which individuals can tolerate risk and uncertainty in their lives. People in societies with high uncertainty avoidance create institutions that minimize risk and ensure financial security. Companies emphasize stable careers and produce many rules to regulate worker actions and minimize uncertainty. Managers may be slow to make decisions as they investigate the nature and potential outcomes of several options. Belgium, France, and Japan are countries that score high on uncertainty avoidance.

Societies that score low on uncertainty avoidance socialize their members to accept and become accustomed to uncertainty. Managers are entrepreneurial and relatively comfortable taking risks, and they make decisions relatively quickly. People accept each day as it comes and

**Individualism versus collectivism**
Describes whether a person functions primarily as an individual or as part of a group.

**Power distance**
Describes how a society deals with the inequalities in power that exist among people.

**Uncertainty avoidance**
The extent to which people can tolerate risk and uncertainty in their lives.

take their jobs in stride because they are less concerned about ensuring their future. They tend to tolerate behavior and opinions different from their own because they do not feel threatened by them. India, Ireland, Jamaica, and the United States are leading examples of countries with low uncertainty avoidance.

**Masculinity versus femininity** refers to a society's orientation based on traditional male and female values. In masculine cultures, both men and women put high priority on achievement, ambition, and economic growth. Society values competitiveness and boldness. In the workplace, men and women alike are assertive and focused on career and earning money. Typical examples include Australia and Italy. The United States is a moderately masculine society. Hispanic cultures are relatively masculine and display a zest for action, daring, and competitiveness. In business, the masculinity dimension reveals itself as self-confidence and leadership.

In feminine cultures, such as the Scandinavian countries, gender roles overlap. Both men and women emphasize nurturing roles, interdependence among people, and caring for less fortunate people. Welfare systems are highly developed and education is highly supported. Men and women alike are relationship oriented, minimizing conflict, and putting emphasis on the quality of life. In business as well as in private life, they strive for consensus. Work is viewed as necessary to earn money, which is needed to enjoy life.

**Long-term versus short-term orientation**[28] refers to the degree to which people and organizations defer pleasure or gratification to achieve long-term success. Firms and people in cultures with a long-term orientation tend to take the long view to planning and living. They focus on years and decades. The long-term dimension is best illustrated by the so-called Asian values—traditional cultural orientations of several Asian societies, including China, Japan, and Singapore. These values are partly based on the teachings of the Chinese philosopher Confucius. They include discipline, loyalty, hard work, regard for education, respect for family, focus on group harmony, and control over one's desires. Scholars credit these values for the *East Asian miracle*, the remarkable economic growth and modernization of East Asian nations during the past several decades.[29] By contrast, the United States and most other Western countries emphasize a short-term orientation.

**Indulgence versus restraint** is the extent to which people try to control their desires and impulses. Indulgent cultures focus on individual happiness, having fun, and enjoying life. People feel greater freedom to express their own emotions and desires. In the workplace, people feel freer to express their opinions, give feedback, and even change jobs. They aim to be happy on the job and project a positive attitude. Mexico, Sweden, and the United States are examples of indulgent societies.

By contrast, restrained societies try to suppress needs gratification. Happiness of the individual is less valued, and people are reluctant to express their own emotions and needs. People avoid expressing personal opinions, and job mobility is often limited. Basic drives are often controlled by strict social norms. China, Egypt, and Russia exemplify restrained countries.

Although useful, the Hofstede framework has its weaknesses. The original research was based on data collected around 1970. Much has changed since then, including successive phases of globalization, widespread exposure to global media, technological advances, and changes in the role of women in the workforce. In addition, Hofstede's findings are based on the employees of a single company—IBM—in a single industry, making it difficult to generalize. Hofstede's data were collected using questionnaires, which is not effective for probing some of the deep issues that surround culture. Finally, Hofstede did not capture all potential dimensions of culture. Nevertheless, Hofstede's framework is useful as a general guide and for gaining deeper understanding in cross-national interactions with business partners, customers, and value-chain members.[30]

**Masculinity versus femininity**
Refers to a society's orientation based on traditional male and female values. Masculine cultures tend to value competitiveness, assertiveness, ambition, and the accumulation of wealth. Feminine cultures emphasize nurturing roles, interdependence among people, and taking care of less fortunate people.

**Long-term versus short-term orientation**
Refers to the degree to which people and organizations defer pleasure and gratification to achieve long-term success.

**Indulgence versus restraint**
The extent to which people try to control their desires and impulses.

*Source:* Ivan Paunovic/123RF

Mexico emphasizes collectivism and loyalty to the group. Business is characterized by long-term, easygoing relationships. Substantial power distance is the norm in larger companies, where the dress code is typically conservative.

## Deal Versus Relationship Orientation

Another important dimension of culture concerns the nature of business relationships. In deal-oriented cultures, managers focus on the task at hand and prefer getting down to business. At the extreme, such managers may even avoid small talk and other preliminaries. They prefer to seal agreements with a legalistic contract and take an impersonal approach to settling disputes. Leading examples of deal-oriented cultures include those of Australia, northern Europe, and North America.

In relationship-oriented cultures, managers put more value on relationships with people. To these managers, it is important to build trust and understanding and get to know the other party in business interactions.

For example, it took nine years for Volkswagen to negotiate the opening of a car factory in China, a strong relationship-oriented society. For the Chinese, Japanese, and many in Latin America, relationships are as important as the deal.[31] As noted in the opening case, in China, the concept of *guanxi* (literally, "connections") is deeply rooted in ancient Confucian philosophy and values a social chain of command and people's responsibilities to each other. It stresses the importance of relationships within the family and between superiors and subordinates.

**4.6** Understand managerial implications of culture.

# Managerial Implications of Culture

Although culture shapes behavior generally, it also plays a major role in cross-border business. Let's consider the nature of culture at three distinct levels. Exhibit 4.15 suggests that company employees are socialized by three cultures: *national culture, professional culture,* and *corporate culture.*[32] Working effectively within these overlapping cultures is challenging. The influence of professional and corporate culture tends to grow as people are socialized into a profession and workplace.

Most companies have a distinctive set of norms, values, and modes of behavior that distinguish them from other organizations. Such differences are often as distinctive as national culture, so that two firms from the same country can have vastly different organizational cultures. For example, Standard Chartered (www.standardchartered.com), a time-honored British bank, has a conservative culture that may be slow to change. By contrast, Virgin (www.virgin.com), the much younger British music and travel provider, has an experimental, risk-taking culture.

These cultural layers present yet another challenge for the manager: To what extent is a particular behavior caused by national culture? In companies with a strong organizational culture, it is hard to determine where the corporate influence begins and the national influence ends.

In the French cosmetics firm L'Oreal (www.loreal.com), the distinction between national and corporate cultures is not always clear. The French have a great deal of experience in the cosmetics and fashion industries, but L'Oreal is a global firm staffed by managers from around the

**EXHIBIT 4.15**

**National, Professional, and Corporate Culture**

*Source:* Based on V. Terpstra and K. David, *Cultural Environment of International Business*, 3rd ed. (Cincinnati, OH: South-Western, 1991).

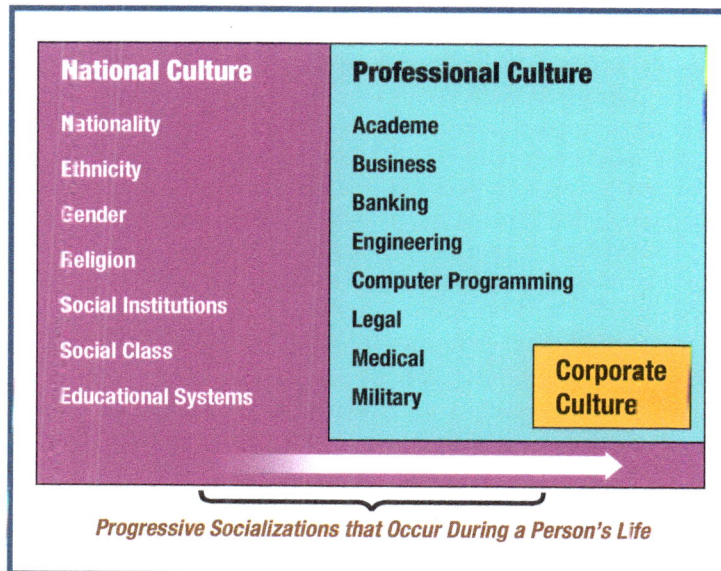

| National Culture | Professional Culture |
|---|---|
| Nationality | Academe |
| Ethnicity | Business |
| Gender | Banking |
| Religion | Engineering |
| Social Institutions | Computer Programming |
| Social Class | Legal |
| Educational Systems | Medical |
| | Military |
| | **Corporate Culture** |

*Progressive Socializations that Occur During a Person's Life*

world. Their influence, combined with management's receptiveness to world culture, has shaped L'Oreal into a unique organization, distinctive within French culture.

## Cultural Orientations

One aspect of cross-cultural risk is **ethnocentric orientation**—using our own culture as the standard for judging other cultures. It is also known as home-country orientation.[33] Most managers are raised in a single culture and tend to view the world mainly from their own perspective. Ethnocentric managers usually believe their own race, religion, or ethnic group is somehow superior to others. Although the tendency to be ethnocentric is widespread, the most effective international managers avoid it; instead, they adopt a polycentric or geocentric orientation. A **polycentric orientation** refers to a host-country mind-set in which the manager develops a strong attachment to the country in which she or he conducts business. **Geocentric orientation** refers to a global mind-set through which the manager can understand a business or market without regard to country boundaries. A geocentric orientation implies an openness to, and awareness of, diversity across cultures.[34] Managers with a geocentric orientation possess a cosmopolitan view and acquire skills for successful social behavior in cross-cultural encounters.[35] They adopt new ways of thinking and learn to analyze cultures. They avoid the temptation to judge different behavior as somehow inferior.[36]

**Ethnocentric orientation**
Using our own culture as the standard for judging other cultures.

**Polycentric orientation**
A host-country mind-set in which the manager develops a strong attachment to the country in which she or he conducts business.

**Geocentric orientation**
A global mind-set by which the manager can understand a business or market without regard to country boundaries.

### MyLab Management   Watch It!

If your professor has assigned this, go to the Assignments section of **www.pearson.com/mylab/management** to complete the video exercise titled Impact of Culture on Business a Spotlight on China.

## How to Acquire Cross-Cultural Competence

Managers are more effective in cross-cultural encounters when they keep an open mind, are inquisitive, and don't jump to conclusions about others' behaviors. Even experienced managers undergo cultural training that emphasizes people-watching skills and human relations techniques. Skills are more important than pure information because skills can be transferred across countries, whereas information is often country-specific. Planning that combines informal mentoring from experienced managers and formal training through seminars, courses, and simulations abroad and at home can go far in helping managers meet cross-cultural challenges.

Although every culture is unique, certain basic guidelines are appropriate for gaining cross-cultural competence. Let's review three guidelines managers can follow to prepare for successful cross-cultural encounters.

*GUIDELINE 1: Acquire factual knowledge about the other culture and try to speak the language.* Successful managers acquire a base of knowledge about the values, attitudes, and lifestyles of the cultures that they encounter. Managers study the political and economic background of target countries—their history, current national affairs, and perceptions about other cultures. Such knowledge increases understanding about the partner's mind-set, organization, and objectives. Decisions and events become easier to interpret. Sincere interest in the target culture helps establish trust and respect. It helps lay the foundation for open and productive relationships. Even modest attempts to speak the local language are welcome. Superior language skills help ensure international business success. In the long run, managers who can converse in multiple languages are more likely to negotiate successfully and have positive business meetings.

*GUIDELINE 2: Avoid cultural bias.* Problems arise when managers simply assume that foreigners think and behave just like the folks back home. Such ethnocentric assumptions lead to poor business strategies in both planning and execution. Managers new to international business can find the behavior of a foreigner odd and perhaps improper. For example, it is easy to be offended when a foreigner does not appreciate our food, history, entertainment, or everyday traditions. In this way, cultural bias can be a significant barrier to successful interpersonal communication.

A person's own culture conditions how he or she reacts to different values, behavior, or systems, so most people unconsciously assume that people in other countries experience the world as they do. They view their own culture as the norm; everything else may seem strange. This is known as the **self-reference criterion**—the tendency to view other cultures through the lens of our own culture. Understanding the self-reference criterion is a critical first step to avoiding cultural bias and ethnocentric mistakes.

To compete effectively, companies must continually improve ways to communicate with and manage customers and partners around the world. Global teams with members from various cultural backgrounds enable firms to profit from knowledge amassed across the organization's worldwide operations. Such teams function best when the members engage in high-quality communications, minimizing miscommunications caused by differences in language and culture. Nevertheless, inexperienced managers often misunderstand the behavior of foreign counterparts, which hinders the effectiveness of cross-cultural meetings. One way to minimize such problems is critical incident analysis.

**Critical incident analysis** is a useful technique that managers use to analyze awkward situations in cross-cultural encounters. It encourages a more effective approach to cultural differences by helping managers become more objective and develop empathy for other points of view. Critical incident analysis involves the following steps:

- Identify the situations where you need to be culturally aware to interact effectively with people from another culture, including socializing, working in groups, and negotiating.
- When confronted with seemingly strange behavior, discipline yourself to avoid making hasty judgments. Instead, try to view the situation or the problem in terms of the unfamiliar culture. Make observations and gather objective information from native citizens or secondary sources.
- Learn to make a variety of interpretations of others' behavior, to select the most likely one in the cultural context, and only then to formulate your own response.
- Learn from this process and improve continually.

**Self-reference criterion**

The tendency to view other cultures through the lens of our own culture.

**Critical incident analysis**

A method for analyzing awkward situations in cross-cultural encounters by becoming more objective and developing empathy for other points of view.

*Source:* rawpixel/123RF

In Japan and South Korea, bowing is common in business and personal settings.

*GUIDELINE 3: Develop cross-cultural skills.*
Working effectively with counterparts from other cultures requires you to make an investment in your professional development. Each culture has its own ways of conducting business and negotiations and solving disputes. You're exposed to high levels of uncertainty. Concepts and relationships can be understood in a variety of ways.[37] To be successful in international business, you should strive for cross-cultural proficiency. Cross-cultural proficiency is characterized by four key personality traits:

- *Tolerance for ambiguity*: The ability to tolerate uncertainty and apparent lack of clarity in the thinking and actions of others.
- *Perceptiveness*: The ability to observe closely and appreciate hard-to-see information in the speech and behavior of others.
- *Valuing personal relationships*: The ability to recognize the importance of interpersonal relationships, which is often much more important than achieving one-time goals or winning arguments.
- *Flexibility and adaptability*: The ability to be creative in finding innovative solutions, to be open-minded about outcomes, and to show grace and kindness under pressure.

Managers with a geocentric or cosmopolitan view of the world are generally better at understanding and dealing with similarities and differences among cultures. Successful multinational firms seek to instill a geocentric cultural mind-set in their employees and use a geocentric staffing policy to hire the best people for each position, regardless of national origin. Over time, such firms develop a core group of managers who are comfortable in any cultural context.

One way for managers to determine the skills they need to approach cultural issues is to measure their cultural intelligence.[38] *Cultural intelligence (CQ)* is a person's capacity to function effectively in situations characterized by cultural diversity. It focuses on specific capabilities important for high-quality personal relationships and effectiveness in culturally diverse settings and work groups.

*Source:* **Mark Bowden/123RF**

Cross-cultural proficiency increases the effectiveness of meetings and other encounters in international business.

## Ethical Connections

Ethical norms and values vary by culture. A survey of 23,000 managers worldwide found that compared to firms in Italy, companies in the United Kingdom are more likely to be led by senior managers who support high standards of ethical conduct. Compared to Japan, employees in Australia stated that if they witnessed a violation of ethical standards, they would feel relatively comfortable reporting it. Compared to firms in Russia, employees in India believed that Indian companies are committed to ethical conduct.

*Source:* A. Ardichvili, D. Jondle, B. Kowske, "Dimensions of Ethical Business Cultures: Comparing Data from 13 Countries of Europe, Asia, and the Americas," *Human Resource Development International* 15, No. 3 (2010), pp. 299–315.

## CLOSING CASE    Hollywood Movies and Global Culture

The most commercially successful filmmaker of all time, Steven Spielberg, is synonymous with U.S. cinema. He has directed and produced international blockbusters such as *Jurassic Park*, *Transformers*, and the Indiana Jones movies. But critics complain that his movies promote American values and reflect the larger trend of the Americanization of beliefs and lifestyles around the world.

Take the case of Hollywood's depiction of Africa. Hollywood movies—for example, *Beasts of No Nation* and *Blood Diamond*—consistently have portrayed Africa as scenically beautiful but terrible in other ways. Other films, for example, *Independence Day*, depict Africa as a land of backward villagers and tribal warriors. The popular movie *Lost in Translation* came under fire for portraying Japanese people as robotic characters who mix up their L's and R's. The image-conscious Japanese were disappointed by their depiction as comic relief. In a scene in which Bill Murray's character is taking a shower in a five-star hotel, he must bend and contort to get his head under the showerhead. Another scene, in which Murray is shown towering at least a foot above an elevator full of local businessmen, mocks the smaller physique of the Japanese. The film was seen to reinforce negative stereotypes about the Japanese.

Today, American studios produce 70 percent of the films viewed internationally. Hollywood is one of the United States' major exporting industries. In contrast, the European film industry is now about one-ninth the size it was in 1945, and today, foreign films hold less than 2 percent of the U.S. market. The copyright-based industries, which also include software, books, music, and TV, contribute enormously to the U.S. economy. Although the United States imports few foreign films, Hollywood's output remains in high demand worldwide.

Fans worldwide increasingly stream movies on their smartphones, tablets, and other personal devices. Netflix is a leading supplier, with more than 100 million subscribers in 190 countries. Other suppliers include Amazon, Apple, Disney, and Hulu. Netflix has subsidiaries in Brazil, India, Japan, South Korea, and the Netherlands. Netflix streams movies from major film companies and also produces its own programs like the popular series *House of Cards*.

### Stereotypes and Religious Values

Under attack since their origin, Hollywood films are widely accused of presenting biased accounts of reality. *Borat* was seen to portray Muslims negatively and was banned throughout the Arab world. Similarly, *The Dictator* was thought to offer negative stereotypes of

Arabs. Critics felt *The Love Guru* made fun of Hinduism, the main religion of South Asia. *Slumdog Millionaire,* while very popular in Western countries, was much criticized in South Asia where many felt the film presented negative stereotypes about India. Some believed the portrayal of urban poverty in India was exaggerated and inaccurate. Nations with deep religious values were offended by *Brokeback Mountain,* which portrayed a homosexual relationship between two cowboys in the United States.

Crucial to U.S. dominance of world cinema is widespread acceptance of the cultural associations inherent in Hollywood films, an obstacle competitors must overcome. U.S. stars and Hollywood directors are well established in the international movie scene with worldwide drawing power.

## Movies and Comparative Advantage

According to the theory of comparative advantage, countries should specialize in producing what they do best and import the rest. Economists argue this theory applies to films as much as to any industry. As a former Canadian prime minister remarked, "Movies are culture incarnate. It is mistaken to view culture as a commodity... Cultural industries, aside from their economic impact, create products that are fundamental to the survival of Canada as a society." Thus, some countries attempt to block imports of movies from the United States in an effort to protect their own film industries.

## A Cultural Dilemma

Despite plenty of arguments on both sides of this ongoing debate, many big-budget Hollywood movies are in fact multinational productions. The James Bond thriller *Quantum of Solace*, with its German-Swiss director and stars hailing from Britain, Ukraine, and France, was filmed in Britain, Panama, Chile, Italy, and Austria. Russell Crowe, Charlize Theron, Penelope Cruz, Nicole Kidman, and Daniel Craig are just a few of the many global stars not from the United States. Two of the seven major film companies collectively known as *Hollywood* aren't even U.S. firms. Hollywood is not as American as it once was.

As the lines connecting Hollywood with the United States are increasingly blurred, protectionists should not abandon their quest to save the intellectual and artistic quality of films. In an interview with the *New York Times*, French director Eric Rohmer stated that his countrymen should fight back with high-quality movies, not protection. "I am a commercial film maker. I am for free competition and am not supported by the state."

## AACSB and CKR Intangible Soft Skills to improve employability and success in the workplace: Analytical Thinking, Diverse and Multicultural Environments, Reflective Thinking

### Case Questions

**4-4.** Most aspects of foreign culture, such as language, religion, gender roles, and problem-solving strategies, are hard for the casual observer to understand. In what ways do Hollywood movies affect national culture outside the United States? What aspects of U.S. culture do Hollywood films promote around the world? Can you observe any positive effects of Hollywood movies on world cultures?

**4-5.** Culture plays a key role in business. In what ways have movies influenced managerial tasks, company activities, and other ways of doing business around the world? Can watching foreign films be an effective way of learning how to do business abroad? Justify your answer.

**4-6.** Hollywood movies are very popular abroad, but foreign films are not viewed much in the United States. What factors determine the high demand for Hollywood films? Why are they so popular in Europe, Japan, Latin America, and elsewhere? Why are foreign films demanded so little in the United States? What can foreign filmmakers do to increase demand for their movies in the United States?

*Sources:* Harriet Alexander, "Why *Beasts of No Nation* Fails to Tell the Whole Story About Child Soldiers," *The Telegraph,* October 16, 2015, www.telegraph.co.uk; Sam Ali, "*Borat* Panders to Muslim Hatred," *The Spokesman-Review*, November 21, 2006, www.spokesman.com; Hillary Busis, "Blame Canada: The 5 Greatest Pop Culture Insults to America's Hat," *Entertainment Weekly*, January 18, 2015, retrieved from www.ew.com/article/2012/10/12/canada-jokes; Ben Child, "Sacha Baron Cohen Criticised over 'Negative Stereotypes' of Arabs," *The Guardian*, May 17, 2012, www.theguardian.com; Hyun-key Kim Hogarth, "The Korean Wave: An Asian Reaction to Western-Dominated Globalization," *Perspectives on Global Development & Technology* 12, No. 1/2 (2013), pp. 135–151; K. Lee, "The Little State Department: Hollywood and the MPAA's Influence," *Northwestern Journal of International Law & Business* 28, No. 2 (2008), pp. 371–383; K. Day, "Totally Lost in Translation," *The Guardian*, January 24, 2004, www.theguardian.com; Duncan Gilchrist and Michael Luca, "How Netflix's Content Strategy Is Reshaping Movie Culture," *Harvard Business Review Digital Articles*, August 31, 2017, pp. 2–5; Tom Pollard, "Hollywood's Asian-Pacific Pivot: Stereotypes, Xenophobia, and Racism," *Perspectives on Global Development & Technology* 16, No. 1–3 (2017), pp. 131–144; Salman Rushdie, "A Fine Pickle," *The Guardian*, February 28, 2009, www.theguardian.com; Alissa Wilkinson, "Hollywood's Ideas About Audiences Are Outdated. Wonder Woman's Record-Smashing Debut Proves It," *Vox*, June 5, 2017, www.vox.com.

This case was written by Sonia Prusaitis under the supervision of Dr. Gary Knight.

# END-OF-CHAPTER REVIEW

## MyLab Management
Go to **www.pearson.com/mylab/management** to complete the problems marked with this icon ⭐.

## Key Terms

acculturation   95
critical incident analysis   114
cross-cultural risk   93
cultural metaphor   109
culture   92
ethnocentric orientation   113
geocentric orientation   113
high-context culture   109

idiom   101
individualism versus
collectivism   110
Indulgence versus restraint   111
long-term versus short-term
orientation   111
low-context culture   109
masculinity versus femininity   111

monochronic   96
polycentric orientation   113
polychronic   96
power distance   110
self-reference criterion   114
socialization   95
uncertainty avoidance   110

## Summary
In this chapter, you learned about:

- **Culture and cross-cultural risk**

  Culture is the values, beliefs, customs, arts, and other products of human thought and work that characterize the people of a given society. Cross-cultural risk arises from a situation or event in which a cultural misunderstanding puts some human value at stake. Values and attitudes are shared beliefs or norms that individuals have internalized.

- **Dimensions of culture**

  Culture is reflected by various dimensions, including our values and attitudes; manners and customs; time and space perceptions; symbolic, material, and creative expressions; education; and social structure. Social structure is characterized by individuals, family, and groups as well as by social stratification and mobility. Monochronic cultures exhibit a rigid orientation to time in which the individual is focused on schedules, punctuality, and time as a resource. Polychronic cultures have a flexible, nonlinear orientation to time in which the individual takes a long-term perspective.

- **Role of language and religion in culture**

  There are nearly 7,000 active languages in the world, of which Mandarin Chinese, Hindi, English, Spanish, and Arabic are among the most common. Language has both verbal and nonverbal characteristics and is conditioned by our environment. Sometimes it is hard to find words to convey the same meaning in different languages. Religion provides meaning and motivation that define people's ideals and values and affects culture and international business deeply.

The four main religions are Christianity, Islam, Hinduism, and Buddhism.

- **Culture's effect in international business**

  In international business, culture affects management of employees, marketing activities, and interaction with customers and partners. Culture influences the design of products and services. It affects the firm's internal environment and how managers perceive and deal with business tasks.

- **Models and explanations of culture**

  Culture can be interpreted through cultural metaphors, distinctive traditions or institutions that serve as a guide or map for deciphering attitudes, values, and behavior. An idiom is an expression whose symbolic meaning is different from its literal meaning. Low-context cultures rely on elaborated verbal explanations, putting much emphasis on spoken words. High-context cultures emphasize nonverbal communications and a more holistic approach to communication that promotes harmonious relationships. Hofstede's typology of cultural dimensions consists of individualism versus collectivism, power distance, uncertainty avoidance, masculinity versus femininity, long-term versus short-term orientation, and indulgence versus restraint.

- **Managerial implications of culture**

  Most corporations exhibit a distinctive set of norms, values, and beliefs that distinguish them from other organizations. Managers can misinterpret the extent to which a counterpart's behavior is attributable to national, professional, or corporate culture. Ethnocentric orientation refers to using one's own culture as the standard for judging other cultures. Polycentric orientation refers to a host country mind-set that gives the manager greater affinity with the country in which she or he conducts business. Geocentric orientation refers to a global mind-set by which the manager can understand a business or market without regard to country boundaries. National culture influences consumer behavior, manage-

rial effectiveness, and the range of value-chain operations such as product and service design and marketing activities. Managers need to develop understanding and skills in dealing with other cultures and should avoid cultural bias and engage in critical incident analysis to avoid the self-reference criterion.

## Test Your Comprehension

**AACSB and CKR Intangible Soft Skills to improve employability and success in the workplace: Analytical Thinking, Diverse and Multicultural Work Environments, Reflective Thinking**

**4-7.** Describe culture and cross-cultural risk.

**4-8.** Describe the characteristics of high- and low-context cultures.

**4-9.** What are cultural metaphors, and why are they significant?

**4-10.** What are the two major perceptions of time, and how does each affect international business?

**4-11.** How are values and attitudes internalized?

**4-12.** What are the major religions, and how do they affect international business?

**4-13.** What are the elements of language?

**4-14.** Distinguish the three layers of culture. What are the major elements of country-level and professional culture?

**4-15.** How can a manager use critical incident analysis in order to avoid the self-reference criterion? Why is this an important factor?

**4-16.** How does a manager with a deal orientation differ from a manager with a relationship orientation?

**4-17.** What are the four key personality traits that characterize cross-cultural proficiency?

## Apply Your Understanding

**AACSB and CKR Intangible Soft Skills to improve employability and success in the workplace: Written and Oral Communication, Ethical Understanding and Reasoning, Diverse and Multicultural Work Environments, Reflective Thinking**

**4-18.** Suppose you get a job at Kismet Indemnity, a life insurance company. In its 45-year history, Kismet has never done any international business. Now its president, Randall Fraser, wants to expand abroad. You have noted in meetings that he seems to lack much awareness of the role of culture. Write a memo to him in which you explain why culture matters in international business. Be sure to speculate on the effects of various dimensions of culture on sales of life insurance.

**4-19.** People tend to see other cultures from their own point of view. They accept their own culture and its ways as the norm; everything else seems foreign, or even mysterious. This chapter described an approach called self-reference criterion (SRC), which is the tendency to view other cultures through the lens of one's own culture. How would you go about defining the nature of SRC? Suggest an example of how it could emerge in an international context. Explain the possible problems in this approach in the context of international business operations and

outline the importance of the concept of SRC for a firm planning to enter international markets for the first time.

**4-20.** *Ethical Dilemma*: Suppose you work for a multinational firm and are posted to Bogotá, Colombia. After renting a house in a posh neighborhood, you hire a full-time housekeeper to perform household chores, a common practice among wealthy Colombians. A colleague at work tells you that local housekeepers are typically poor women who live in Bogotá's slums and earn about $200 a month. As an executive, you feel guilty about paying such a cheap wage when you can afford much more, but for cultural and socioeconomic reasons, your colleague insists you cannot pay more than the going rate. Doing so might embarrass your housekeeper and risk upsetting the economic balance in her community. Analyze this dilemma. Do you pay your housekeeper the customary local rate or a higher wage? Justify your decision. Can you think of any creative solutions to this dilemma?

## globalEDGE | INTERNET EXERCISES
Access globalEDGE™ at www.globalEDGE.msu.edu

### AACSB and CKR Intangible Soft Skills to improve employability and success in the workplace: Information Technology, Analytical Thinking, Diverse and Multicultural Work Environments, Application of Knowledge

4-21. Ethnologue (www.ethnologue.com/web.asp) is a site that lists the world's known languages. It is an excellent resource for scholars and others with language interests and contains statistical summaries of the number of language speakers by language size, family, and country. Using Ethnologue, try the following:

   a. Visit the China page. What is the population of China? Of the country's nearly 300 languages, which has the largest number of speakers? Which has the second-largest number of speakers? How do these figures compare to the total number of English speakers in the English-speaking countries of Australia, Britain, Canada, New Zealand, and the United States?

   b. Visit the Spain page. How many people live in Spain? How many native Spanish speakers are in Spain? How many languages altogether are spoken in Spain?

   c. Switzerland is one of the smallest European countries. What are the major languages of Switzerland, and how many speakers does each have?

   d. Ethnologue's Statistics section shows the distribution of living languages as a percentage of world population. Which world region has the most languages? Which region has the fewest? Why do you suppose those regions evolved in such a way?

4-22. Cultural intelligence is a person's ability to function effectively in situations characterized by cultural diversity. globalEDGE™ and other online resources feature cultural intelligence scales. What are the components of cultural intelligence? Answer the questions on this scale, and calculate your score on cultural intelligence. Compare your score to those of your classmates.

4-23. Various websites list cultural blunders or faux pas (false steps) people make in their international interactions. Neglecting to develop relationships (as in "Just sign the contract, I'm in a hurry!") and making too-casual use of first names (as in "Just call me Bill!") are examples of such blunders. Research online sources such as Kwintessential (www.kwintessential.co.uk) or simply enter "cultural blunders" in an Internet search engine to identify examples of improper cultural behaviors. How can managers avoid these errors?

---

**CKR Career Preparation Kit™**

**CKR IB Process Knowledge and Tools©**

**Country Cultural Awareness Checklist**

Traveling internationally requires thorough, early preparation, including actions not normally required for purely domestic travel.

A critical checklist, based on this chapter, is the **CKR: Country Cultural Awareness Checklist.**

Every country is different. For any country that you intend to visit, it is best to develop your awareness of the its background, appropriate manners and etiquette, and verbal and nonverbal communication.

For a more detailed treatment of this topic, visit the Pearson MyLab Management website (www.pearson.com/mylab/management), and click on the **CKR: Country Cultural Awareness Checklist**. It contains a comprehensive list of the details that you need to prepare before traveling abroad.

---

# Endnotes

1. Yoree Koh and Daisuke Wakabayashi, "The Land of the Rising Crust," *Wall Street Journal,* September 20, 2014, p. D8; Preetika Rana, "In India, Forget Doughnuts, It's Time to Make the Tough Guy Chicken Burger," *Wall Street Journal,* November 29, 2014, pp. A1 and A4; Harry C. Triandis *Culture and Social Behavior* (New York: McGraw-Hill, 1994).

2. F. Kluckhohn and F. Strodbeck, *Variations in Value Orientations* (Evanston, IL: Row Peterson, 1961).

3. Dante Chicchetti (ed.), *Developmental Psychopathology,* 3rd ed., Vol. 4 (Hoboken, NJ: Wiley, 2016); Charles Sowerwine, *France Since 1870: Culture, Politics and Society,* 3rd ed. (London: Palgrave Macmillan, 2018).

4. James Neuliep, *Intercultural Communication: A Contextual Approach* (Thousand Oaks, CA: Sage, 2018).

5. Alice Eagly and Shelly Chaiken, *The Psychology of Attitudes* (New York: Harcourt Brace Jovanovich, 1993); Geert Hofstede, "Attitudes, Values and Organizational Culture: Disentangling the Concepts," *Organization Studies* 19, No. 3 (1998), pp. 477–493.

6. Roger Axtell, *The Do's and Taboos of International Trade* (New York: Wiley, 1994).

7. Edward T. Hall, *The Silent Language* (Garden City, NY: Anchor, 1981); Neuliep, 2018.

8. Della Moty. *Colors Talk! Meanings of Colors,* Amazon Digital Services, www.amazon.com, 2017; Christina Wang, "Symbolism of Colors and Color Meanings Around the World," *Shutterstock Blog,* April 3, 2015, www.shutterstock.com.

9. Valerie Berenger and Audrey Verdier-Chouchane, "Child Labour and Schooling in South Sudan and Sudan: Is There a Gender Preference?," *African Development Review* 28, No. S2 (2016), pp. 177–190; UNESCO (2017), "National Literacy Programme," UNESCO Institute for Lifelong Learning, http://litbase.uil.unesco.org.

10. "Babel Runs Backwards," *The Economist,* January 1, 2005, pp. 58–60; M. Paul Lewis et al. (ed.), *Ethnologue· Languages of the World,* 18th ed. (Dallas, TX: SIL International, 2015), www.ethnologue.com; *Ethnologue,* "How Many Languages Are There in the World?," 2017, www.ethnologue.com.

11. Erin Moore and Lynne Truss, *That's Not English: Britishisms, Americanisms, and What Our English Says About Us* (New York: Gotham, 2015).

12. Hall, 1981; Neuliep, 2018.

13. John Esposito and Darrell Fasching, and Todd Lewis, *World Religions,* 6th ed. (New York: Oxford University Press, 2017).

14. Rachel McCleary, "Religion and Economic Development," *Policy Review* (April/May 2008), pp. 45–57; Rachel McCleary and Robert Barro, "Religion and Economy," *Journal of Economic Perspectives* 20, No. 2 (2006), pp. 49–72; Jeaney Yip and Susan Ainsworth, "Whatever Works" *Journal of Macromarketing* 36, No. 4 (2016), pp. 443–456.

15. Adrian Furnham, *The Protestant Work Ethic* (London: Routledge, 1990); Max Weber, *The Protestant Ethic and the Spirit of Capitalism* (New York: Charles Scribner's Sons, 1930; Vigeo Press Reprint, 2017).

16. Meg Carter, "Muslims Offer a New Mecca for Marketers," *Financial Times,* August 11, 2005, p. 13; Laura Colby, "Tired of Halal Chicken? Try the Eyeshadow," *Bloomberg Businessweek,* December 26, 2016, p. 24.

17. *Economist,* "Untouchable and Unthinkable," October 6, 2007, pp. 15–16; Ira Gang, Kunal Sen, and Myeong-Su Yun, "Is Caste Destiny? Occupational Diversification among Dalits in Rural India," *European Journal of Development Research* 29, No. 2 (2017), pp. 476–492.

18. Esposito et al., 2017; Furnham, 1990; Sethi S. Prakash and P. Steidlmeier, "Hinduism and Business Ethics," *Wiley Encyclopedia of Management* 2 (2015), pp. 1–5; Weber, 1959.

19. Esposito et al., 2017; Charles Hee, "A Holistic Approach to Business Management: Perspectives from the Bhagavad Gita," *Singapore Management Review* 29, No. 1 (2007), pp. 73–84; Sethi and Steidlmeier, 2015.

20. Esposito et al., 2017; Hershey Friedman, "The Impact of Jewish Values on Marketing and Business Practices," *Journal of Macromarketing* 21 (June 2001), pp. 74–80.

21. Rachel Abrams, "Adapting Listerine to a Global Market," *New York Times*, September 12, 2014, retrieved March 28, 2015, from www.nytimes.com/2014/09/13/business/adapting-listerine-to-a-global-market.html?_r=0.

22. James Agarwal, Naresh Malhotra, and Ruth Bolton, "A Cross-National and Cross-Cultural Approach to Global Market Segmentation: An Application Using Consumers' Perceived Service Quality," *Journal of International Marketing* 18, No. 3 (2010), pp. 18–40; J. Andrew Petersen, Tarun Kushwaha, and V. Kumar, "Marketing Communication Strategies and Consumer Financial Decision Making: The Role of National Culture," *Journal of Marketing* 79 (2015), pp. 44–63.

23. Bangaly Kaba and K. Osei-Bryson, "Examining Influence of National Culture on Individuals' Attitude and Use of Information and Communication Technology: Assessment of Moderating Effect of Culture Through Cross Countries Study," *International Journal of Information Management* 33, No. 3 (2013), pp. 441–452; *Forbes*, "This Translation Tool Is Helping Break Global Language Barriers," May 17, 2017, www.forbes.com; Erin Meyer, "When Culture Doesn't Translate," *Harvard Business Review* 93, No. 10 (2015), pp. 66–72; Sengun Yeniyurt and Janell Townsend, "Does Culture Explain Acceptance of New Products in a Country? An Empirical Investigation," *International Marketing Review* 20, No. 4 (2003), pp. 377–396.

24. Martin Gannon and Raj Pillai, *Understanding Global Cultures: Metaphorical Journeys Through 34 Nations*, 6th ed. (Thousand Oaks, CA: Sage, 2015).

25. Edward T. Hall, *Beyond Culture* (New York: Anchor, 1976); Edward T. Hall and Mildred Reed Hall, *Understanding Cultural Differences* (Boston: Intercultural Press, 1990).

26. Craig Storti, *The Art of Doing Business Across Cultures: 10 Countries, 50 Mistakes, and 5 Steps to Cultural Competence* (Boston: Intercultural Press, 2017).

27. Sjoerd Beugelsdijk, Tatiana Kostova, and Kendall Roth, "An Overview of Hofstede-Inspired Country-Level Culture Research in International Business Since 2006," *Journal of International Business Studies* 48, No. 1 (2017), pp. 30–47; Geert Hofstede, *Culture's Consequences* (Beverly Hills, CA: Sage, 1980); Geert Hofstede, Gert Jan Hofstede, and Michael Minkov, *Cultures and Organizations: Software of the Mind*, 3rd ed. (New York: McGraw-Hill, 2010).

28. Ibid.

29. Kazimierz Poznanski, "Confucian Economics: How Is Chinese Thinking Different?," *China Economic Journal* 10, No. 3 (2017), pp. 362–384; Richard Priem, Leonard Love, and Margaret Shaffer, "Industrialization and Values Evolution: The Case of Hong Kong and Guangzhou, China," *Asia Pacific Journal of Management* 17, No. 3 (2000), pp. 473–482.

30. Beugelsdijk, Kostova, and Roth, 2017; Hofstede, 1980; Hofstede, Hofstede, and Minkov, 2010.

31. Joyce Osland, Silvio De Franco, and Asbjorn Osland, "Organizational Implications of Latin American Culture: Lessons for the Expatriate Manager," *Journal of Management Inquiry* 8, No. 2 (1999), pp. 219–238; David C. Thomas and Mark F. Peterson, *Cross-Cultural Management: Essential Concepts*, 4th ed. (Thousand Oaks, CA: Sage, 2017).

32. Hofstede, 1998; Vern Terpstra and Kenneth David, *The Cultural Environment of International Business,* 3rd ed. (Cincinnati, OH: Southwestern, 1991); Thomas and Peterson, 2017.

33. Neuliep (2018); Howard Perlmutter, "The Tortuous Evolution of the Multinational Corporation," *Columbia Journal of World Business* 4, No. 1 (1969), pp. 9–18.

34. V. Govindarajan and A. Gupta, *The Quest for Global Dominance* (San Francisco: Jossey-Bass/Wiley, 2001); Joana Story, John Barbuto Jr., Fred Luthans, and James A. Bovaird, "Meeting the Challenges of Effective International HRM: Analysis of the Antecedents of Global Mindset," *Human Resource Management* 53, No. 1 (2014), pp. 131–155.

35. Robert Boyd and Peter Richerson, *Culture and Evolutionary Process* (Chicago: University of Chicago Press, 1985); Story et al., 2014; Thomas and Peterson, 2017.

36. Story et al., 2014; Thomas and Peterson, 2017; Harry C. Triandis, *Culture and Social Behavior* (New York: McGraw-Hill, 1994).

37. Tomasz Lenartowicz and James P. Johnson, "A Cross-National Assessment of the Values of Latin America Managers: Contrasting Hues or Shades of Gray?" *Journal of International Business Studies* 34, No. 3 (2003), pp. 266–281; Thomas and Peterson, 2017; Neuliep, 2018.

38. Soon Ang, Linn Van Dyne, and Christine Koh, "Personality Correlates of the Four-Factor Model of Cultural Intelligence," *Group & Organization Management* 31, No. 1 (2006), pp. 100–123; Kevin Groves, Ann Feyerherm, and Minhua Gu, "Examining Cultural Intelligence and Cross-Cultural Negotiation Effectiveness," *Journal of Management Education* 39, No. 2 (2015), pp. 209–243; David C. Thomas and Kerr Inkson, *Cultural Intelligence: Surviving and Thriving in the Global Village* (Oakland, CA: Berrett-Koehler Publishers, 2017).

CHAPTER

# 5 Communicating Across Cultures

## OUTLINE

## OBJECTIVES

**5-1.** To recognize the communication process and how cultural differences can cause noise in that process

**5-2.** To appreciate the cultural variables that affect communication for both the sender and the listener.

**5-3.** To be aware of the impact of IT on cross-border communications.

**5-4.** To learn how to manage cross-cultural business communications successfully.

## Opening Profile: The Impact of Social Media on Global Business

*[I]t's becoming more and more evident to enterprises that the social web actually does make sense for businesses.[1]*

K. ANANTH KRISHNAN (TATA CONSULTANCY SERVICES)
April 27, 2011

*BNP Paribas, the French bank, launched its Facebook and Twitter sites in 2010 and has one of the largest followings, with about 120,000 Facebook "fans."[2]*

FINANCIAL TIMES
January 10, 2011

Managers in international businesses or nonprofit enterprises around the world are grappling with the question of how to benefit from the burgeoning use of social media networks—through the Internet, video, audio, and phone—both external and internal to the organization. The networks, such as Facebook, are directly and indirectly linking people and business around the world. (Facebook, for example, had 1.44 billion monthly users around the world as of April 2015.) The power of such linkages for political and social motives was made clear during the Arab Spring in 2011, started by one person in Egypt protesting the government by using YouTube, iPhones, and other media.

Global business managers are realizing that these social media are potential sources of rich information, outside the normal chain of communication, that their companies could use to find out more about what customers want, how new ideas might be received, what competitors are doing, what problems might be lurking and how to deal with them, and so on. As an example, K. Ananth Krishnan, the chief technology officer (CTO) of Tata Consultancy Services, observed in an interview that, "Increasingly, data is coming at businesses in *unstructured ways*. It's coming from outside of companies, in the kinds of networking and SMS messaging habits that customers have. And it's coming from unstructured sources *inside* companies, from in-house blogs to internal knowledge markets."[3] (Tata Consultancy Services, based in India, has 198,000 IT consultants in 42 countries.) Krishnan notes, however, that concerns about privacy of information gathered through such sources must be taken into account.

Another challenge to the effective use of social media is how to measure the effectiveness of each source as a benefit to the company, given the considerable investment their use would require. Firms such as Target, Dell, and Burger King are trying to find what works best for them as social media applications such as Google+, Facebook, LinkedIn, YouTube, blogs, microblogs such as Twitter, and so on, have changed the way consumers interact with companies and friends about brands and services—with both positive and negative feedback.[4]

*39 percent of companies we've surveyed already use social-media services as their primary digital tool to reach customers, and that percentage is expected to rise to 47 percent within the next four years.*

McKINSEY QUARTERLY
April 2012[5]

**FIGURE 5-1** Social Media

*Source:* arrow/Fotolia

*(Continued)*

Although many companies are trying out social media to market their products or services and get feedback, others feel that the audience is too general and does not work as well as being able to target their message to specific demographic markets.[6]

Regardless of how companies interact with and use social media networks, it is clear that they are here to stay. that they can have considerable impact on global businesses, and that they are affecting political and social trends as well. In China, for example, more than 300 million people use social media, which is very popular because it is less likely to be monitored by the government. Years ahead of the West, with social media such as Renren and Sina Weibo, China's online users spend more than 40 percent of their time online on social media, a figure that continues to rise rapidly, according to McKinsey and Company consultants. There is no Facebook, YouTube, or Twitter. However, in spite of the complexities and challenges, the sheer numbers of users present considerable opportunity for marketing

*Cultural communications are deeper and more complex than spoken or written messages. The essence of effective cross-cultural communication has more to do with releasing the right responses than with sending the "right" messages.*

HALL AND HALL[8]

*Multi-local online strategy…is about meeting global business objectives by tuning in to the cultural dynamics of their local markets.*

"THINK GLOBALLY, INTERACT LOCALLY," NEW MEDIA AGE[9]

As the opening profile suggests, communication in all its forms is a critical factor in the cross-cultural management issues, particularly those of an interpersonal nature, involving motivation, leadership, group interactions, and negotiation. Culture is conveyed and perpetuated through communication in one form or another. Culture and communication are so intricately intertwined that they are, essentially, synonymous.[10] By understanding this relationship, managers can move toward constructive intercultural management. Nardon et al. point out that although global managers cite multicultural communication as a serious challenge, at the same time, it can open up important sources of business opportunity. "It is through communication that relationships are formed, conflicts are resolved, and innovative ideas are created and shared."[11]

Managers doing business around the world invariably complain that cross-cultural communication challenges have led to lost business, unintended offenses, and embarrassment—in particular in countries where it is crucial to develop relationships and trust. Communication, whether in the form of writing, talking, listening, or through the Internet, is an inherent part of a manager's role and takes up the majority of a manager's time on the job. Studies by Mintzberg demonstrate the importance of oral communication; he found that most managers spend between 50 and 90 percent of their time talking to people.[12] The ability of a manager to communicate effectively across cultural boundaries will largely determine the success of international business transactions or the output of a culturally diverse workforce. It is useful, then, to break down the elements involved in the communication process, both to understand the cross-cultural issues at stake and to maximize the opportunities to establish common meaning among the parties communicating.

## THE COMMUNICATION PROCESS

The term **communication** describes the process of sharing meaning by transmitting messages through media such as words, behavior, or material artifacts. Managers communicate to coordinate activities, to disseminate information, to motivate people, and to negotiate future plans. It is of vital importance, then, for a receiver to interpret the meaning of a particular communication in the way the sender intended. Unfortunately, the communication process (see Exhibit 5-1) involves stages during which meaning can be distorted. Anything that undermines the communication of the intended meaning is typically referred to as **noise**.

The primary cause of noise is that the sender and the receiver each exists in a unique, private world thought of as her or his life space. The context of that private world, largely based on culture, experience, relations, values, and so forth, determines the interpretation of

**EXHIBIT 5-1** The Communication Process

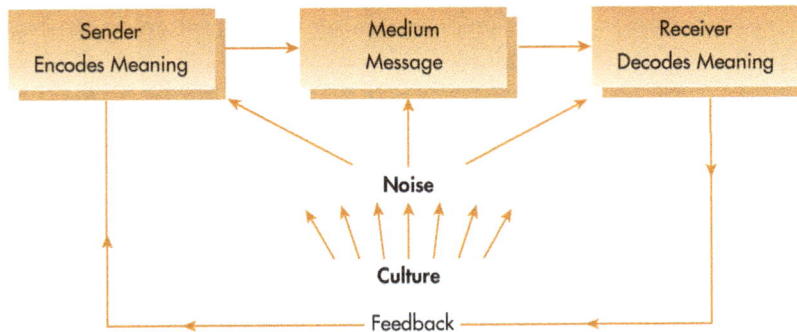

meaning in communication. People filter, or selectively understand, messages consistent with their own expectations and perceptions of reality and their values and norms of behavior. The more dissimilar the cultures of those involved, the greater the likelihood of misinterpretation. In this way, as Samovar, Porter, and Jain state in their book, *Understanding Intercultural Communication*, cultural factors pervade the communication process:

> *Culture not only dictates who talks with whom, about what, and how the communication proceeds, it also helps to determine how people encode messages, the meanings they have for messages, and the conditions and circumstances under which various messages may or may not be sent, noticed, or interpreted. In fact, our entire repertory of communicative behaviors is dependent largely on the culture in which we have been raised. Culture, consequently, is the foundation of communication. And, when cultures vary, communication practices also vary.[13]*

Communication, therefore, is a complex process of linking up or sharing the perceptual fields of sender and receiver; the perceptive sender builds a bridge to the life space of the receiver.[14] After the receiver interprets the message and draws a conclusion about what the sender meant, he or she will, in most cases, encode and send back a response, making communication a circular process.

The communication process is rapidly changing, however, as a result of technological developments; therefore it is propelling global business forward at a phenomenal growth rate. These changes are discussed later in this chapter.

## Cultural Noise in the Communication Process

> *In Japanese there are several words for "I" and several words for "you" but their use depends on the relationship between the speaker and the other person. In short, there is no "I" by itself; the "I" depends on the relationship.[15]*

Because the focus in this text is on effective cross-cultural communication, it is important to understand what cultural variables cause noise in the communication process. This knowledge of **cultural noise**—the cultural variables that undermine the communication of intended meaning—will enable us to take steps to minimize that noise and so improve communication.

When a member of one culture sends a message to a member of another culture, **intercultural communication** takes place. The message contains the meaning the encoder intends. When it reaches the receiver, however, it undergoes a transformation in which the influence of the decoder's culture becomes part of the meaning.[16] Exhibit 5-2 provides an example of intercultural communication in which the meaning got all mixed up. Note how the attribution of behavior differs for each participant. **Attribution** is the process by which people look for an explanation of another person's behavior. When they realize that they do not understand another person, they tend, say Hall and Hall, to blame their confusion on the other's "stupidity, deceit, or craziness."[17]

In the situation depicted in Exhibit 5-2, the Indian employee becomes frustrated and resigns after experiencing communication problems with his German boss. How could this outcome have been avoided? We do not have much information about the people or the context of the situation, but we can look at some of the variables that might have been involved and use them as a basis for analysis.

**EXHIBIT 5-2** **Cultural Noise in International Communication**[18] The vice president for operations of a German manufacturing company headquartered in Munich became concerned about satisfying an important client in France with an order that he had outsourced to a subsidiary in India. He decided to visit the local manager and confirm the importance of delivering the order on time. The following is what transpired in his interaction with the local production manager.

| Behavior | | Attribution | |
|---|---|---|---|
| *German:* | "What can be done to make sure this project is completed on time?" | *German:* | I am giving him some responsibility. |
| | | *Indian:* | Doesn't he know what to do? He is the boss. Why is he asking me? |
| *Indian:* | "I don't know. What do you suggest?" | *German:* | Can't he take responsibility? |
| | | *Indian:* | I asked him for instructions. |
| *German:* | "You know the scheduling and staffing situation here better than me." | *German:* | I want to train him to make some decisions. |
| | | *Indian:* | What kind of manager is he? Well, he expects me to say something. |
| *Indian:* | "I'll hire another worker, then we should be ready in two weeks." | *German:* | One more worker is totally insufficient; he doesn't know how to schedule properly. I need a definite deadline commitment—not "should be ready." |
| *German:* | "Hire three workers and give them a deadline of three weeks. Are we agreed on that deadline?" | *German:* | I offer a contract. |
| | | *Indian:* | These are my orders: three weeks. |

**The German returned to his office in Munich, confident that the project would be completed on time and the order delivered on schedule, which he conveyed to the client. After four weeks, the customer called to complain that he had not received the order. The German VP immediately called the Indian manager:**

| | | | |
|---|---|---|---|
| *German:* | "Why hasn't the order been sent out as we agreed?" | *German:* | I am holding him responsible for our agreement. |
| | | *Indian:* | He wants to know why it is not ready. |
| *Indian:* | "It will be completed next week." | (Both attribute that it is not ready.) | |
| *German:* | "But you told me it would be sent out in three weeks." | *German:* | I must teach him to take responsibility for deadlines. |
| | | *Indian:* | This person does not know how to manage; it was not possible to complete the project in three weeks. I am going to get another job where the boss knows how to manage! |

# THE CULTURE–COMMUNICATION LINK

The following sections examine underlying elements of culture that affect communication. The degree to which one is able to communicate effectively largely depends on how similar the other person's cultural expectations are to our own. However, cultural gaps can be overcome by prior learning and understanding of those variables and how to adjust to them.

## Trust in Communication

*The key ingredient in a successful alliance is trust.*

JAMES R. HOUGHTON, FORMER CHAIRMAN, CORNING, INC.[19]

Effective communication, and therefore effective collaboration in alliances across national boundaries, depends on the informal understandings among the parties that are based on the trust that has developed between them. However, the meaning of trust, and how it is developed and communicated, varies across societies. In China and Japan, for example, business transactions are based on networks of long-standing relationships based on trust rather than on the formal contracts and arm's-length relationships typical of the United States. When there is trust between parties, implicit understanding arises within communications. This understanding has numerous benefits in business, including encouraging communicators to overlook cultural differences and minimize problems. It allows communicators to adjust to unforeseen circumstances with less conflict than would be the case with formal contracts, and it facilitates open communication in exchanging ideas and information.[20] From his research on trust in global collaboration, John Child suggests the following guidelines for cultivating trust:

- Create a clear and calculated basis for mutual benefit. There must be realistic commitments and good intentions to honor them.
- Improve predictability: Strive to resolve conflicts and keep communication open.
- Develop mutual bonding through regular socializing and friendly contact.[21]

What can managers anticipate with regard to the level of trust in communications with people in other countries? If trust is based on how trustworthy we consider a person to be, then it must vary according to that society's expectations about whether that culture supports the norms and values that predispose people to behave credibly and benevolently. Are there differences across societies in those expectations of trust? Research on 90,000 people in 45 societies by the World Values Study Group provides some insight on cultural values regarding predisposition to trust. When we examine the percentage of respondents in each society who responded that "most people can be trusted," we can see that the Nordic countries and China had the highest predisposition to trust, followed by Canada, the United States, and Britain, whereas Brazil, Turkey, Romania, Slovenia, and Latvia had the lowest level of trust in people.[22]

## The GLOBE Project

Results from the GLOBE research on culture provide some insight into culturally appropriate communication styles and expectations for the manager to use abroad. GLOBE researchers Javidan and House make the following observations:[23] For people in societies that ranked high on performance orientation—for example, the United States—presenting objective information in a direct and explicit way is an important and expected manner of communication; this contrasts with people in Russia or Greece—societies that ranked low on performance orientation—for whom hard facts and figures are not readily available or taken seriously. In those cases, a more indirect approach is preferred. People from countries ranking low on assertiveness, such as Sweden, also recoil from explicitness; their preference is for much two-way discourse and friendly relationships.

People ranking high in the humane dimension, such as those from Ireland and the Philippines, make avoiding conflict a priority and tend to communicate with the goal of being supportive of people rather than of achieving objective results. This contrasts with people from France and Spain, whose agenda is achievement of goals.

The foregoing provides examples of how to draw implications for appropriate communication styles from the research findings on cultural differences across societies. Astute global managers have learned that culture and communication are inextricably linked and that they should prepare themselves accordingly. Most will also suggest that you carefully watch and listen to how your hosts are communicating and then follow their lead.

## Cultural Variables in the Communication Process

On a different level, it is also useful to be aware of cultural variables that can affect the communication process by influencing a person's perceptions; some of these variables have been identified by Samovar and Porter and discussed by Harris and Moran and others.[24] These variables are as follows: attitudes; social organization; thought patterns; roles; language (spoken or written); nonverbal communication (including kinesic behavior, proxemics, paralanguage, and object language); and time. Although these variables are discussed separately in this text, their effects are interdependent and inseparable—or, as Hecht, Andersen, and Ribeau put it, "Encoders and decoders process nonverbal cues as a conceptual, multichanneled gestalt."[25] As you read the explanations of these variables in the discussion that follows, consider how they apply in the context of communicating and managing in India, as outlined in the nearby feature, "Under the Lens: Communicating in India—Language, Culture, Customs, and Etiquette."

## UNDER THE LENS

*Communicating in India—Language, Culture, Customs and Etiquette*

### FACTS AND STATISTICS

**Location**    Southern Asia, bordering Bangladesh, 4,053 km; Bhutan, 605 km; Burma, 1,463 km; China, 3,380 km; Nepal, 1,690 km; and Pakistan, 2,912 km

**Capital**    New Delhi

**Climate**    Varies from tropical monsoon in south to temperate in north

**Population**    1.28 billion (as of August 12, 2015.)

**FIGURE 5-2** Map of India

*Source:* © Dorling Kindersley/Dorling Kindersley Limited

**FIGURE 5-3** Indian Flag

*Source:* Malgorzata Kistryn/Fotolia LLC

**Ethnic Make-up**   Indo-Aryan, 72%; Dravidian, 25%; Mongoloid and other, 3% (2000)

**Religions**   Hindu, 81.3%; Muslim, 12%; Christian, 2.3%; Sikh, 1.9%; other groups, including Buddhist, Jain, and Parsi, 2.5% (2000)

**Government**   Federal republic

## LANGUAGES IN INDIA

The different states of India have different official languages, some of them not recognized by the central government. Some states have more than one official language. Bihar in east India has three official languages—Hindi, Urdu, and Bengali—that are all recognized by the central government. But Sikkim, also in east India, has four official languages, of which only Nepali is recognized by the central government. Besides the languages officially recognized by central or state governments are other languages that don't have this recognition, and their speakers are waging political struggles to obtain this recognition. The central government decided that Hindi was to be the official language of India, and therefore, it also has the status of official language in the states.

You can learn some useful Hindi phrases by visiting http://www.kwintessential.co.uk/resources/language/hindi-phrases.html.

## INDIAN SOCIETY AND CULTURE

### Hierarchy

- The influences of Hinduism and the tradition of the caste system have created a culture that emphasizes established hierarchical relationships.

- Indians are always conscious of social order and their status relative to other people, whether family, friends, or strangers.

- All relationships involve hierarchies. In schools, teachers are called *gurus* and are viewed as the source of all knowledge. The patriarch, usually the father, is considered the leader of the family. The boss is seen as the source of ultimate responsibility in business. Every relationship has a clear-cut hierarchy that must be observed for the social order to be maintained.

*(Continued)*

FIGURE 5-4  **The Taj Mahal**

*Source:* olgagomenyuk/Fotolia LLC

## The Role of the Family

- People typically define themselves by the groups to which they belong rather than by their status as individuals. Someone is deemed to be affiliated to a specific state, region, city, family, career path, religion, and so on.
- This group orientation stems from the close personal ties Indians maintain with their family, including the extended family.
- The extended family creates a myriad of interrelationships, rules, and structures. Along with these mutual obligations comes a deep-rooted trust among relatives.

## Just Can't Say No

- Indians do not like to express "no," whether verbally or nonverbally.
- Rather than disappoint you, for example, by saying something isn't available, Indians will offer you the response that they think you want to hear.
- This behavior should not be considered dishonest. An Indian would be considered terribly rude if he did not attempt to give a person what had been asked.
- Because they do not like to give negative answers, Indians may give an affirmative answer but be deliberately vague about any specific details. This will require you to look for nonverbal cues, such as a reluctance to commit to an actual time for a meeting or an enthusiastic response.

## Etiquette and Customs in India

### Meeting Etiquette

- Religion, education, and social class all influence greetings in India.
- This is a hierarchical culture, so greet the eldest or most senior person first.
- When leaving a group, each person must be bade farewell individually.
- Shaking hands is common, especially in the large cities among the more educated who are accustomed to dealing with Westerners.
- Men may shake hands with other men, and women may shake hands with other women; however, there are seldom handshakes between men and women because of religious beliefs. If you are uncertain, wait for him or her to extend his or her hand.

## Naming Conventions

Indian names vary based on religion, social class, and region of the country. The following are some basic guidelines to understanding the naming conventions.

### Hindus

- In the north, many people have both a given name and a surname.
- In the south, surnames are less common, and a person generally uses the initial of his or her father's name in front of their own name.
- The man's formal name is their name s/o (son of) and the father's name. Women use d/o to refer to themselves as the daughter of their father.
- At marriage, women drop their father's name and use their first name with their husband's first name as a sort of surname.

### Muslims

- Many Muslims do not have surnames. Instead, men add the father's name to their own name with the connector "bin," so "Abdullah bin Ahmed" is "Abdullah, the son of Ahmed."
- Women use the connector binti.
- The title Hajji (m) or Hajjah (f) before the name indicates that the person has made his or her pilgrimage to Mecca.

### Sikhs

- Sikhs all use the "Singh" name. It is either adopted as a surname or as a connector name to the surname.

## Gift-Giving Etiquette

- Indians believe that giving gifts eases the transition into the next life.
- Gifts of cash are given to friends and members of the extended family to celebrate life events such as birth, death, and marriage.
- It is not the value of the gift, but the sincerity with which it is given, that is important to the recipient.
- If invited to an Indian's home for a meal, it is not necessary to bring a gift, although one will not be turned down.
- Do not give frangipani or white flowers because they are used at funerals.
- Yellow, green, and red are lucky colors, so try to use them to wrap gifts.
- A gift from a man should be said to come from both him and his wife, mother, sister, or some other female relative.
- Hindus should not be given gifts made of leather.
- Muslims should not be given gifts made of pigskin or alcoholic products.
- Gifts are not opened when received.

## Dining Etiquette

- Indians entertain in their homes, restaurants, private clubs, or other public venues, depending on the occasion and circumstances.
- Although Indians are not always punctual themselves, they expect foreigners to arrive close to the appointed time.
- Take off your shoes before entering the house.
- Dress modestly and conservatively.
- Politely turn down the first offer of tea, coffee, or snacks. You will be asked again and again. Saying no to the first invitation is part of the protocol.

There are diverse dietary restrictions in India, and these may affect the foods that are served:

- Hindus do not eat beef, and many are vegetarians.
- Muslims do not eat pork or drink alcohol.
- Sikhs do not eat beef.
- Lamb, chicken, and fish are the most commonly served main courses for nonvegetarian meals because they avoid the meat restrictions of the religious groups.

*(Continued)*

Table manners are somewhat formal, but this formality is tempered by the religious beliefs of the various groups.

- Much Indian food is eaten with the fingers.
- Wait to be told where to sit.
- If utensils are used, they are generally a tablespoon and a fork.
- Guests are often served in a particular order; the guest of honor is served first, followed by the men, and the children are served last. Women typically serve the men and eat later.
- You may be asked to wash your hands before and after sitting down to a meal.
- Always use your right hand to eat, whether you are using utensils or your fingers.
- In some situations, food may be put on your plate for you, whereas in other situations, you may be allowed to serve yourself from a communal bowl.
- Leaving a small amount of food on your plate indicates that you are satisfied. Finishing all your food means that you are still hungry.

## Business Etiquette and Protocol in India

### Relationships and Communication

- Indians prefer to do business with those they know.
- Relationships are built on mutual trust and respect.
- In general, Indians prefer to have long-standing personal relationships prior to doing business.
- It may be a good idea to go through a third-party introduction. This gives you immediate credibility.

## Business Meeting Etiquette

- If you will be traveling to India from abroad, it is advisable to make appointments by letter at least one month and, preferably, two months in advance.
- It is a good idea to confirm your appointment because they can be cancelled at short notice.
- The best time for a meeting is late morning or early afternoon. Reconfirm your meeting the week before and call again that morning; it is common for meetings to be cancelled at the last minute.
- Keep your schedule flexible so that it can be adjusted for last-minute rescheduling of meetings.
- You should arrive at meetings on time because Indians are impressed with punctuality.
- Meetings will start with a great deal of getting-to-know-you talk. In fact, it is quite possible that no business will be discussed at the first meeting.
- Always send a detailed agenda in advance. Send back-up materials, charts, and other data as well. This allows everyone to review and become comfortable with the material prior to the meeting
- Follow up a meeting with an overview of what was discussed and the next steps.

## Business Negotiating

- Indians are nonconfrontational. It is rare for them to disagree overtly, although this is beginning to change in the managerial ranks.
- Decisions are reached by the person with the most authority.
- Decision making is a slow process.
- If you lose your temper, you lose face and prove you are unworthy of respect and trust.
- Delays are to be expected, especially when dealing with the government.
- Most Indians expect concessions in both price and terms. It is acceptable to expect concessions in return for those you grant.
- Never appear overly legalistic during negotiations. In general, Indians do not trust the legal system, and someone's word is sufficient to reach an agreement.
- Do not disagree publicly with members of your negotiating team.
- Successful negotiations are often celebrated by a meal.

### Dress Etiquette

- Business attire is conservative.
- Men should wear dark-colored, conservative business suits.
- Women should dress conservatively in suits or dresses.
- The weather often determines clothing. In the hotter parts of the country, dress is less formal, although dressing as previously suggested for the first meeting will indicate respect.

### Titles

- Indians revere titles such as Professor, Doctor, and Engineer.
- Status is determined by age, university degree, caste, and profession.
- If someone does not have a professional title, use the honorific title "Sir" or "Madam."
- Titles are used with the person's name or the surname, depending on the person's name. (See Social Etiquette for more information on Indian naming conventions.)
- Wait to be invited before using someone's first name without the title.

### Business Cards

- Business cards are exchanged after the initial handshake and greeting.
- If you have a university degree or any honor, put it on your business card.
- Use the right hand to give and receive business cards.
- Business cards need not be translated into Hindi.
- Always present your business card so the recipient may read the card as it is handed to him or her.

*Source:* http://www.kwintessential.co.uk/resources/global-etiquette/India-country-profile.html, September 5, 2011. Used with permission of www.kwintessential.co.uk.

## ATTITUDES

We all know that our attitudes underlie the way we behave and communicate and the way we interpret messages from others. Ethnocentric attitudes are a particular source of noise in cross-cultural communication. In the incident described in Exhibit 5-2, both the Indian and the German are clearly attempting to interpret and convey meaning based on their own experiences of that kind of transaction. The German is probably guilty of stereotyping the Indian employee by quickly jumping to the conclusion that he is unwilling to take responsibility for the task and the scheduling.

This problem, **stereotyping**, occurs when a person assumes that every member of a society or subculture has the same characteristics or traits. Stereotyping is a common cause of misunderstanding in intercultural communication. It is an arbitrary, lazy, and often destructive way to find out about people. Astute managers are aware of the dangers of cultural stereotyping and deal with each person as an individual with whom they may form a unique relationship.

## SOCIAL ORGANIZATIONS

Our perceptions can be influenced by differences in values, approach, or priorities relative to the kind of social organizations to which we belong. These organizations may be based on one's nation, tribe, or religious sect, or they may consist of the members of a certain profession. Examples of such organizations include the Academy of Management or the United Auto Workers (UAW).[26]

## THOUGHT PATTERNS

The logical progression of reasoning varies widely around the world and greatly affects the communication process. Managers cannot assume that others use the same reasoning processes, as illustrated by the experience of a Canadian expatriate in Thailand, related in a book by Harris and Moran.

*While in Thailand a Canadian expatriate's car was hit by a Thai motorist who had crossed over the double line while passing another vehicle. After failing to establish that the fault lay with the Thai driver, the Canadian flagged down a policeman. After several minutes of seemingly futile discussion, the Canadian pointed out the double line in the middle of the road and asked the policeman directly, "What do these lines signify?" The policeman replied, "They indicate the center of the road and are there so I can establish just how far the accident is from that point." The Canadian was silent. It had never occurred to him that the double line might not mean "no passing allowed."[27]*

In the Exhibit 5-2 scenario, perhaps the German did not realize that the Indian employee had a different rationale for his time estimate for the job. Because the Indian was not used to having to estimate schedules, he just took a guess, which he felt he had been forced to do.

## ROLES

Societies differ considerably in their perceptions of a manager's role. Much of the difference is attributable to their perceptions of who should make the decisions and who has responsibility for what. In the Exhibit 5-2 example, the German assumes that his role as manager is to delegate responsibility, to foster autonomy, and to practice participative management. He prescribes the role of the employee without any consideration of whether the employee will understand that role. The Indian's frame of reference leads him to think that the manager is the boss and should give the order about when to have the job completed. He interprets the German's behavior as breaking that frame of reference, and therefore he feels that the boss is "stupid and incompetent" for giving him the wrong order and for not recognizing and appreciating his accomplishments. The manager should have considered what behaviors Indian workers would expect of him and then either should have played that role or discussed the situation carefully, in a training mode.

## LANGUAGE

Spoken or written language, of course, is a frequent cause of miscommunication, stemming from a person's inability to speak the local language, a poor or too-literal translation, a speaker's failure to explain idioms, or a person missing the meaning conveyed through body language or certain symbols. Even among countries that share the same language, problems can arise from the subtleties and nuances inherent in the use of the language, as noted by George Bernard Shaw: "Britain and America are two nations separated by a common language." This problem can exist even within the same country among different subcultures or subgroups.[28]

Many international executives tell stories about lost business deals or lost sales because of communication blunders.

*When Pepsi Cola's slogan "Come Alive with Pepsi" was introduced in Germany, the company learned that the literal German translation of "come alive" is "come out of the grave."*

*A U.S airline found a lack of demand for its "rendezvous lounges" on its Boeing 747s. They later learned that "rendezvous" in Portuguese refers to a room that is rented for prostitution.[29]*

More than just conveying objective information, language also conveys cultural and social understandings from one generation to the next. Examples of how language reflects what is important in a society include the 6,000 Arabic words that describe camels and their parts and the 50 or more classifications of snow the Inuit, the Eskimo people of Canada, use.

In as much as language conveys culture, technology, and priorities, it also serves to separate and perpetuate subcultures. In India, 14 official and many unofficial languages are used, and more than 800 languages are spoken on the African continent.

Because of increasing workforce diversity around the world, the international business manager will have to deal with a medley of languages. For example, assembly-line workers at the Ford plant in Cologne, Germany, speak Turkish and Spanish as well as German.

In Malaysia, Indonesia, and Thailand, many of the buyers and traders are Chinese. Not all Arabs speak Arabic; in Tunisia and Lebanon, for example, French is the language of commerce.

International managers need either a good command of the local language or competent interpreters. The task of accurate translation to bridge cultural gaps is fraught with difficulties: Joe Romano, a partner of High Ground, an emerging technology-marketing company in Boston, found out on a business trip to Taiwan how close a one-syllable slip of the tongue can come to torpedoing a deal. He noted that one is supposed to say to the chief executive "Au-ban," meaning "Hello, No. 1. Boss." Instead, he accidentally said "Lau-ban ya," which means "Hello, wife of the boss." Essentially, Mr. Romano called him a woman in front of 20 senior Taiwanese executives, who all laughed; but the boss was very embarrassed because men in Asia have a very macho attitude.[30]

Even the direct translation of specific words does not guarantee the congruence of their meaning, as with the word "yes" used by Asians, which usually means only that they have heard you, and, often, that they are too polite to disagree. The Chinese, for example, through years of political control, have built into their communication culture a cautionary stance to avoid persecution by professing agreement with whatever opinion was held by the person questioning them.[31]

Sometimes even a direct statement can be misinterpreted instead as an indirect expression, as when a German businessman said to his Algerian counterpart, "My wife would love something like that beautiful necklace your wife was wearing last night. It was beautiful." The next day the Algerian gave him a box with the necklace in it as a gift to his wife. The Algerian had interpreted the compliment as an indirect way of expressing a wish to possess a similar necklace. The German was embarrassed, but had to accept the necklace. He realized he needed to be careful how he expressed such things in the future—such as asking where that kind of jewelry is sold.[32]

In much of the world, politeness and a desire to say only what the listener wants to hear create noise in the communication process. Often, even a clear translation does not help a person understand what is meant because the encoding process has obscured the true message. With the poetic Arab language—replete with exaggeration, elaboration, and repetition—meaning is attributed more to how something is said than to what is actually said.

For the German supervisor and Indian employee cited in Exhibit 5-2, it is highly likely that the German could have picked up some cues from the employee's body language that probably implied problems with the interpretation of meaning. How might body language have created noise in this case?

## Nonverbal Communication

Clearly, as explained by Roger Axtel in his book, *Essential Do's and Taboos*,[33] the nonverbal signal that, in the U.S., is interpreted as "okay" is absolutely not "okay" in many countries. Axtel gives the example of when Vice President Richard Nixon flew to Brazil in an attempt to improve relations between the two countries. As reported in the newspapers, when Nixon stepped off the plane in Sao Paulo, he gave the "A-okay" sign—with both hands! The crowd at the airport booed—of course—given the meaning in Brazil (a private part of a woman's body); not surprisingly, photos of this incident were in the paper the next day!

Behavior that communicates without words (although it often is accompanied by words) is called **nonverbal communication**. People will usually believe what they see over what they hear—hence the expression, "A picture is worth a thousand words." Studies show that these subtle messages account for between 65 and 93 percent of interpreted communication.[34] Even minor variations in body language, speech rhythms, and punctuality, for example, often cause mistrust and misperception of the situation among cross-national parties.[35] The media for such nonverbal communication can be categorized into four types: (1) kinesic behavior, (2) proxemics, (3) paralanguage, and (4) object language.

The term **kinesic behavior** refers to communication through body movements—posture, gestures, facial expressions, and eye contact, as illustrated in the accompanying "Under the Lens: Communicating Italian Style" feature. Although such actions may be universal, often

*Communicating Italian Style*[36]

When traveling around Europe, you will probably notice that Italians use the most body language when communicating; they seem to be walking down the street mumbling while their hands are going all over wildly, typically while on their *telefonini*. In fact, it is difficult for the person listening on the phone to interpret sometimes because the speaker's hand gestures and other nonverbal signals are invisible. Their hands convey much meaning, and Italians commonly make about 250 gestures when talking and doing other things simultaneously such as conversing on the cell phone. Examples are that of wagging the hands downward, meaning "come here"; slowly drawing a circle with the hand, meaning "whatever"; pressing a finger into the cheek, meaning that something tastes good; and brushing the back of the hand outward across the chin meaning "I don't give a damn." Gestures can convey that the person feels pride, or shame, or desperation, or fear, giving more meaning than the words alone. Of course, gestures are culture-specific (varying also according to the area within Italy, those in the south tending to be louder and more effusive than those in the north) so you should be careful to be aware that their meanings may differ significantly around the world and may cause offense. Women should realize that flirtatious behavior from Italian men is common and part of their culture. This behavior, along with the close-talking nature of Italians, including sitting close and perhaps lightly touching the arm of the other person, can make it uncomfortable for women who are used to more personal space in communicating.

Italians tend to be gregarious and loud but interrupt one another anyway. They are uncomfortable with silence but do not seem to lack interesting subjects to discuss, such as their architecture and art, Italian history and football, and especially their families.

Italians' dress is conservative and chic and formal for business meetings. One is expected to use formal titles and last names until requested to do otherwise; and women use their maiden names in business. Present your business cards face up, and be sure to read theirs before putting them away.

One is expected to shake hands with everyone present when arriving and when leaving, and it is customary to kiss friends on both cheeks, left first. Eye contact is essential when talking to an Italian; otherwise, you would be viewed as unfriendly and perhaps untrustworthy. Italians do not observe personal space when conversing, so one should expect close contact and much hand movement even with business contacts. People from reserved cultures such as the British will likely be perceived as disinterested by Italians since they tend to be very emotionally engaged with the conversation.

their meaning is not. Because kinesic systems of meaning are culturally specific and learned, they cannot be generalized across cultures. Most people in the West would not correctly interpret many Chinese facial expressions; for example, sticking out the tongue expresses surprise, a widening of the eyes shows anger, and scratching the ears and cheeks indicates happiness.[37] Research has shown for some time, however, that most people worldwide can recognize displays of the basic emotions of anger, disgust, fear, happiness, sadness, surprise, and contempt.[38]

As illustrated previously, visitors to other countries must be careful about their gestures and how they might be interpreted. For example, people in Japan may point with their middle finger, which is considered an obscene gesture to others. To Arabs, showing the soles of one's feet is an insult; recall the reporter who threw his shoe at President Bush in late 2008 during his visit to Iraq. This was, to Arabs, the ultimate insult.

Many businesspeople and visitors react negatively to what they feel are inappropriate facial expressions, without understanding the cultural meaning behind them. In his studies of cross-cultural negotiations, Graham observed that the Japanese feel uncomfortable when faced with the Americans' eye-to-eye posture. They are taught since childhood to bow their heads out of humility, whereas the automatic response of Americans is, "look at me when I'm talking to you!"[39]

Subtle differences in eye behavior (called *oculesics*) can throw off a communication badly if they are not understood. Eye behavior includes differences not only in eye contact but also in the use of eyes to convey other messages, whether or not that involves mutual gaze. For example, during speech, Americans will look straight at you, but the British keep your attention by looking away. The British will look at you when they have finished speaking, which signals that it is your turn to talk. The implicit rationale for this is that you can't interrupt people when they are not looking at you.[40]

It is helpful for U.S. managers to be aware of the many cultural expectations regarding posture and how they may be interpreted. In Europe or Asia, a relaxed posture in business meetings may be taken as bad manners or the result of poor upbringing. In Korea, you are expected to sit upright, with feet squarely on the floor, and to speak slowly, showing a blending of body and spirit.

**Proxemics** deals with the influence of proximity and space on communication—both personal space and office space or layout. Americans expect office layouts to provide private space for each person and, usually, a larger and more private space as one goes up the hierarchy. In much of Asia, the custom is open office space with people at all levels working and talking in close proximity to one another. Space communicates power in both Germany and the United States, evidenced by the desire for a corner office or one on the top floor. The importance of French officials, however, is made clear by a position in the middle of subordinates, communicating that they have a central position in an information network, where they can stay informed and in control.[41] The following "Under the Lens" feature illustrates the connections between beliefs about the variables of proxemics and business decisions.

Do you ever feel vaguely uncomfortable and start moving backward slowly when someone is speaking to you? This is because that person is invading your bubble—your personal space. Personal space is culturally patterned, and foreign spatial cues are a common source of misinterpretation. When someone seems aloof or pushy, it often means that she or he is operating under subtly different spatial rules.

Hall and Hall suggest that cultural differences affect the programming of the senses and that space, perceived by all the senses, is regarded as a form of territory to be

## UNDER THE LENS

*How Feng Shui Affects Business*

Feng Shui (pronounced "fung shway") is an ancient Chinese system of aesthetics believed to use the laws of both heaven and earth to help one improve life by receiving positive *qi*. Feng shui translates into English as "wind-water."[42] Qi (pronounced "chee" in English) is "a movable positive or negative life force which plays an essential role in feng shui."[43]

Throughout history, Asian experts have read these energy patterns and discerned how to benefit by facing their buildings and offices in a particular direction, by designing gardens and entrances in a positive way, and by using Qi in rooms to influence aspects in an individual's life. "The quality of Qi is expressed through form, shape, color, direction, time, and the feeling it generates within us."[44] Various methods to establish beneficial settings have included compass directions, dowsing (commonly known as using a rod to move over the earth to find underground water, buried metals, and so on), and geomancy (loosely referred to as attempting to interpret meanings from patterns or markings in the soil or sand).

Westerners also use Feng shui, often in the process of building or decorating offices and homes—although not always following expert advice. When Donald Trump lost some important Asian clients due to his properties' apparently bad feng shui, he hired a feng shui master to analyze the auspiciousness of Trump Towers. In fact, feng shui and other beliefs from Chinese culture can drastically influence business deals. Michael Rudder, a real-estate broker in New York, found this out the hard way and now integrates feng shui in his planning—especially because most of his recent sales of office buildings and condominiums have been to Asians.[45] Also, as found by many others involved in real-estate, certain numbers have specific meanings in different cultures. In Chinese, Japanese, and Korean, for example, the pronunciation of the number four sounds the same as the word for death. No wonder many buildings in Asia do not have a fourth floor. In Chinese, the number eight is a homophone for the word for getting rich. The eighth floor, and building numbers with eights in them, often sell at a premium.[46]

protected.[47] South Americans, southern and eastern Europeans, Indonesians, and Arabs have **high-contact cultures**, preferring to stand close, touch a great deal, and experience a close sensory involvement. Latin Americans, for example, have a highly physical greeting such as putting their arms around a colleague's back and grabbing him by the arm. On the other hand, North Americans, Asians, and northern Europeans have **low-contact cultures** and prefer much less sensory involvement, standing farther apart and touching far less. They have a distant style of body language. In France, a relationship-oriented culture, good friends greet members of the opposite sex with a peck on each cheek; a handshake is a way to make a personal connection.

Interestingly, high-contact cultures are mostly located in warmer climates, and low-contact cultures in cooler climates. Americans are relatively nontouching, automatically standing at a distance so that an outstretched arm will touch the other person's ear. Standing any closer than that is regarded as invading intimate space. However, Americans and Canadians certainly expect a warm handshake and maybe a pat on the back from closer friends, though not the very warm double handshake of the Spaniards (clasping the forearm with the left hand). The Japanese, considerably less **haptic** (touching), do not shake hands; an initial greeting between a Japanese businessperson and a Spanish businessperson would be uncomfortable for both parties if they were untrained in cultural haptics. The Japanese bow to one another—the depth of the bow revealing their relative social standing.

*Imagine the smartphone app that would ask your identity, the identity of the other greeter, where you both are and how many times you have greeted each other. It would then propose a compromise—a namaste followed by a handshake, perhaps, or a bow punctuated by a slap on the back.[48]*

When considering high- and low-contact cultures, we can trace a correlation between Hofstede's cultural variables of individualism and collectivism and the types of kinesic and proxemic behaviors people display. Generally, people from individualistic cultures are more remote and distant, whereas those from collectivist cultures are interdependent; they tend to work, play, live, and sleep in close proximity.[49]

The term **paralanguage** refers to how something is said rather than the content—that is, the rate of speech, the tone and inflection of voice, other noises, laughing, or yawning. The culturally aware manager learns how to interpret subtle differences in paralanguage, including silence. Silence is a powerful communicator. It may be a way of saying "no," of being offended, or of waiting for more information to make a decision. There is considerable variation in the use of silence in meetings. Whereas Americans become uncomfortable after 10 or 15 seconds of silence, Chinese prefer to think the situation over for 30 seconds before speaking. The typical scenario between Americans and Chinese, then, is that the American gets impatient, says something to break the silence, and offends the Chinese by interrupting his or her chain of thought and comfort level with the subject.[50]

The term **object language**, or **material culture**, refers to how we communicate through material artifacts, whether architecture, office design and furniture, clothing, cars, or cosmetics. Material culture communicates what people hold as important. In the United States, for example, someone wishing to convey his important status and wealth would show guests his penthouse office or expensive car. In Japan and China, a businessman presents his business card to a new contact and expects the receiver to study it and appreciate his position. The cards are called name cards in China and are an essential aspect of doing business—a way to build networks. The exchange of cards occurs as soon as you meet, and visitors should be careful to get an appropriate translation for their cards.[51] In Mexico, a visiting international executive or salesperson is advised to take time out, before negotiating business, to show appreciation for the surrounding architecture, which Mexicans prize. The importance of family to people in Spain and much of Latin America would be conveyed by family photographs around the office and, therefore, an expectation that the visitor would enquire about the family.

## TIME

Another variable that communicates culture is the way people regard and use time. To Brazilians, relative punctuality communicates the level of importance of those involved. To Middle Easterners, time is something controlled by the will of Allah.

To initiate effective cross-cultural business interactions, managers should know the difference between *monochronic time systems* and *polychronic time systems* and how they affect

**EXHIBIT 5-3** Forms of Nonverbal Communication

- Facial expressions
- Body posture
- Gestures with hands, arms, head, etc.
- Interpersonal distance (proxemics)
- Touching, body contact
- Eye contact
- Clothing, cosmetics, hairstyles, jewelry
- Paralanguage (voice pitch and inflections, rate of speech, and silence)
- Color symbolism
- Attitude toward time and the use of time in business and social interactions
- Food symbolism and social use of meals

communications. Hall and Hall explain that in **monochronic cultures** (Switzerland, Germany, and the United States), time is experienced in a linear way, with a past, a present, and a future, and time is treated as something to be spent, saved, made up, or wasted. Classified and compartmentalized, time serves to order life. This attitude is a learned part of Western culture, probably starting with the Industrial Revolution. Monochronic people, found in individualistic cultures, generally concentrate on one thing at a time, adhere to time commitments, and are accustomed to short-term relationships.

In contrast, **polychronic cultures** tolerate many things occurring simultaneously and emphasize involvement with people. Two Latin friends, for example, will put an important conversation ahead of being on time for a business meeting, thus communicating the priority of relationships over material systems. Polychronic people—Latin Americans, Arabs, and those from other collectivist cultures—may focus on several things at once, be highly distractible, and change plans often.[52]

The relationship between time and space also affects communication. Polychronic people, for example, are likely to hold open meetings, moving around and conducting transactions with one party and then another, rather than compartmentalizing meeting topics, as do monochronic people.

The nuances and distinctions regarding cultural differences in nonverbal communication are endless. The various forms are listed in Exhibit 5-3; wise intercultural managers will take careful account of the role that such differences might play.

What aspects of nonverbal communication might have created noise in the interactions between the German supervisor and the Indian employee in Exhibit 5-2? Undoubtedly, some cues could have been picked up from the kinesic behavior of each person. It was the responsibility of the manager, in particular, to notice any indications from the Indian that could have prompted him to change his communication pattern or assumptions. Face-to-face communication permits the sender of the message to get immediate feedback, both verbal and nonverbal, and thus to have some idea as to how that message is being received and whether additional information is needed. What aspects of the Indian employee's kinesic behavior or paralanguage might have been evident to a more culturally sensitive manager? Did both parties' sense of time affect the communication process?

## Context

*East Asians live in relatively complex social networks with prescribed role relations; attention to context is, therefore, important for their effective functioning. In contrast, westerners live in less constraining social worlds that stress independence and allow them to pay less attention to context.*

RICHARD E. NISBETT[53]

A major differentiating factor that is a primary cause of noise in the communication process is that of context—which actually incorporates many of the variables discussed earlier. The **context** in which the communication takes place affects the meaning and interpretation of the interaction. Cultures are known to be high- or low-context cultures, with a relative range in between.[54] In **high-context cultures** (Asia, the Middle East, Africa, and the Mediterranean), feelings and thoughts are not explicitly expressed; instead, one has to read between the lines and interpret meaning from one's general understanding. Two such high-context cultures are the South Korea and Arab cultures. In such cultures, key information is embedded in the context rather than made explicit. People make assumptions about what the message means through their knowledge of the person or the surroundings. In these cultures, most communication takes place within a context of extensive information networks resulting from close personal relationships. See the following "Management in Action" feature for further explanation of the Asian communication style.

In **low-context cultures** (Germany, Switzerland, Scandinavia, and North America), where personal and business relationships are more compartmentalized, communication media have to be more explicit. Feelings and thoughts are expressed in words, and information is more readily available. Westerners focus more on the individual and therefore tend to view events as the result of specific agents, whereas Easterners view events in a broader and longer-term context.[55]

In cross-cultural communication between high- and low-context people, a lack of understanding may preclude reaching a solution, and conflict can arise. Germans, for example, will expect considerable detailed information before making a business decision, whereas Arabs will base their decisions more on knowledge of the people involved—the information is present, but it is implicit. People in low-context cultures, such as those in Germany, Switzerland, Austria, and the United States, convey their thoughts and plans in a direct, straightforward communication style, saying something like, "We have to make a decision on this today." People in high-context cultures, such as in Asia and, to less extent in England, convey their thoughts in a more indirect, implicit manner; this means that someone from Germany needs to have more patience and tact and be willing to listen and watch for clues—verbal and nonverbal—about his or her colleagues' wishes.

People in high-context cultures expect others to understand unarticulated moods, subtle gestures, and environmental clues that people from low-context cultures simply do not process. Misinterpretation and misunderstanding often result.[56] People from high-context cultures perceive those from low-context cultures as too talkative, obvious, and redundant. Those from low-context cultures perceive high-context people as secretive, sneaky, and mysterious. Research indicates, for example, that Americans find talkative people more attractive, whereas the Koreans—a high-context people—perceive less-verbal people as more attractive. (These conflicts are illustrated in the accompanying "Management in Action" feature). Finding the right balance between low- and high-context communications can be tricky, as Hall and Hall point out: "Too much information leads people to feel they are being talked down to; too little information can mystify them or make them feel left out."[57] Exhibit 5-4 shows the relative level of context in various countries.

The importance of understanding the role of context and nonverbal language to avoid misinterpretation is illustrated in the accompanying feature, *Comparative Management in Focus: Communicating with Arabs.*

**EXHIBIT 5-4** Cultural Context and Its Effects on Communication

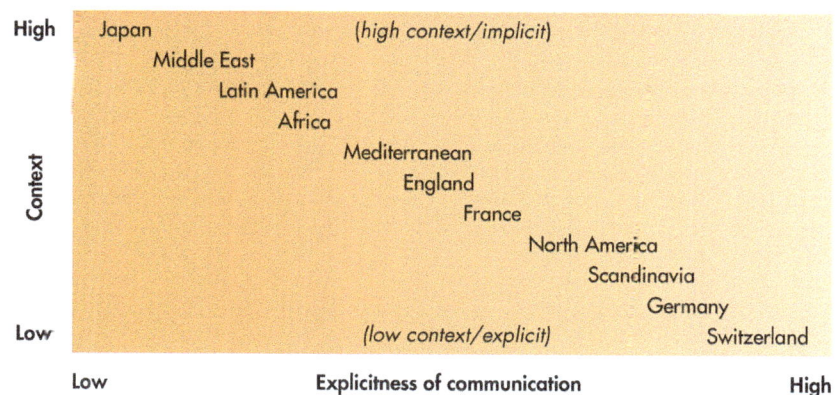

*Source:* Based on information drawn from E. T. Hall and M. R. Hall, *Understanding Cultural Differences* (Yarmouth, ME: Intercultural Press, 1990); and Martin Rosch, "Communications: Focal Point of Culture," *Management International Review* 27, No. 4 (1987).

## MANAGEMENT IN ACTION
*Oriental Poker Face: Eastern Deception or Western Inscrutability?*

Among many English expressions that are likely to offend those of us whose ancestry may be traced to the Far East, two stand out quite menacingly for me: "Oriental poker face" and "idiotic Asian smile." The former refers to the supposedly inscrutable nature of a facial expression that apparently reflects no particular state of mind, while the latter pokes fun at a face fixed with a perpetually friendly smile. Westerners' perplexity, when faced with either, arises from the impression that these two diametrically opposed masquerading strategies prevent them from extracting useful information—at least the type of information that at least they could process with a reasonable measure of confidence—about the feelings of the person before them. An Asian face that projects no signs of emotion, then, seems to most Westerners nothing but a facade. It does not matter whether that face wears an unsightly scowl or a shining ray; a facial expression they cannot interpret poses a genuine threat.

Compassionate and sympathetic to their perplexity as I may be, I am also insulted by the Western insensitivity to the significant roles that subtle signs play in Asian cultures. Every culture has its unique modus operandi for communication. Western culture, for example, apparently emphasizes the importance of direct communication. Not only are the communicators taught to look directly at each other when they convey a message, but they also are encouraged to come right to the point of the message. Making bold statements or asking frank questions in a less than diplomatic manner (i.e., "That was really a very stupid thing to do!" or "Are you interested in me?") is rarely construed as rude or indiscreet. Even embarrassingly blunt questions such as "President Clinton, did you have sexual intercourse with Monica Lewinsky?" are tolerated most of the time. Asians, on the other hand, find this direct communicative communication style quite unnerving. In many social interactions, they avoid direct eye contact. They "see" each other without necessarily looking directly at each other, and they gather information about inner states of mind without asking even the most discreet or understated questions. Many times they talk around the main topic, and, yet, they succeed remarkably well in understanding one another's position. (At least they believe they have developed a reasonably clear understanding.)

To a great extent, Asian communication is listening-centered; the ability to listen (and a special talent for detecting various communicative cues) is treated as equally important as, if not more important than, the ability to speak. This contrasts clearly with the American style of communication that puts the utmost emphasis on verbal expression; the speaker carries most of the burden for ensuring that everyone understands his or her message. An Asian listener, however, is prone to blame himself or herself for failing to reach a comprehensive understanding from the few words and gestures performed by the speaker. With this heavier burden placed on the listener, an Asian speaker does not feel obliged to send clearly discernible message cues (at least not nearly so much as he or she is obliged to do in American cultural contexts). Not obligated to express themselves without interruption, Asians use silence as a tool in communication. Silence, by most Western conventions, represents discontinuity of communication and creates a feeling of discomfort and anxiety. In the Orient, however, silence is not only comfortably tolerated but is considered a desirable form of expression. Far from being a sign of displeasure or animosity, it serves as an integral part of the communication process, used for reflecting on messages previously exchanged and for carefully crafting thoughts before uttering them.

It is not outlandish at all, then, for Asians to view Americans as unnecessarily talkative and lacking in the ability to listen. For the Asian, it is the American who projects a mask of confidence by being overly expressive both verbally and nonverbally. Since the American style of communication places less emphasis on the act of listening than on speaking, Asians suspect that their American counterparts fail to pick up subtle and astute communicative signs in conversation. To one with a cultural outlook untrained in reading those signs, an inscrutable face represents no more than a menacing or amusing mask.

*Source:* Dr. Jin Kim, State University of New York–Plattsburgh. Copyright © 2003 by Dr. Jin Kim. Used with permission of Dr. Kim.

## Comparative Management In Focus
*Communicating with Arabs*

In the Middle East, the meaning of a communication is implicit and interwoven and, consequently, much harder for Americans, accustomed to explicit and specific meanings, to understand.

Arabs are warm, emotional, and quick to explode: sounding off is regarded as a safety valve. In fact, the Arabic language aptly communicates the Arabic culture, one of emotional extremes. The language contains the means for overexpression, many adjectives, words that allow for exaggeration, and metaphors to emphasize a position. What is said is often not as important as *how* it is said. Eloquence and flowery speech are admired for their own sake, regardless of the content. Loud speech is used for dramatic effect.

At the core of Middle Eastern culture are friendship, honor, religion, and traditional hospitality. Family, friends, and connections are very important on all levels in the Middle East and will take precedence over business transactions. Arabs do business with people, not companies, and they make commitments to people, not contracts. A phone call to the right person can help to get around seemingly insurmountable obstacles. An Arab expects loyalty from friends, and it is understood that giving and receiving favors is an inherent part of the relationship; no one says no to a request for a favor. A lack of follow-through is assumed to be beyond the friend's control.[58]

Because hospitality is a way of life and highly symbolic, a visitor must be careful not to reject it by declining refreshment or rushing into business discussions. Part of that hospitality is the elaborate system of greetings and the long period of getting acquainted, perhaps taking up the entire first meeting. Although the handshake may seem limp, the rest of the greeting is not. Kissing on the cheeks is common among men, as is handholding between male friends. However, the Arab social code strictly forbids any public display of intimacy between men and women.

Women play little or no role in business or entertainment; the Middle East is a male-dominated society, and it is impolite to inquire about women. Other nonverbal taboos include showing the soles of one's feet and using the left (unclean) hand to eat or pass something. In discussions, slouching in a seat or leaning against a wall communicates a lack of respect.

The Arab society also values honor. Harris and Moran explain, "Honor, social prestige, and a secure place in society are brought about when conformity is achieved. When one fails to conform, this is considered to be damning and leads to a degree of shame."[59] Shame results not just from doing something wrong but from others finding out about that wrongdoing. Establishing a climate of honesty and trust is part of the sense of honor. Therefore, considerable tact is needed to avoid

MAP 5.1  **Saudi Arabia and the Arabian Peninsula**

**FIGURE 5-5** Westerner Meeting with Arab Businessman

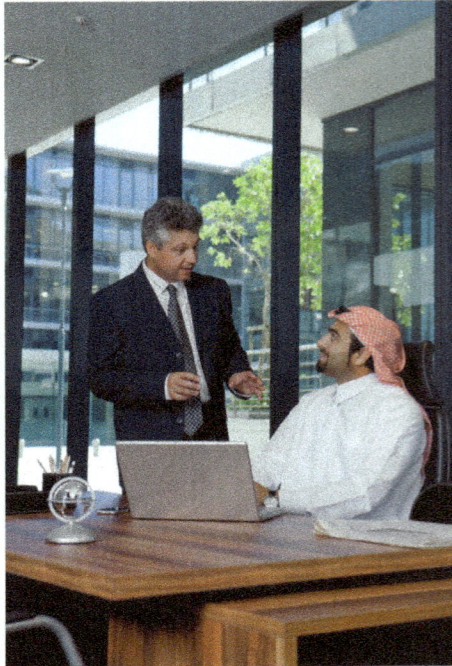

*Source:* Hi Brow Arabia/Alamy

conveying any concern or doubt. Arabs tend to be quite introverted until a mutual trust is built, which takes a long time.[60]

In their nonverbal communication, most Arab countries are high-contact cultures. Arabs stand and sit closer and touch people of the same sex more than Westerners. They do not have the same concept of public and private space or, as Hall puts it, "Not only is the sheer noise level much higher, but the piercing look of the eyes, the touch of the hands, and the mutual bathing in the warm moist breath during conversation represent stepped-up sensory inputs to a level which many Europeans find unbearably intense. On the other hand, the distance preferred by North Americans may leave an Arab suspicious of intentions because of the lack of olfactory contact."[61]

The Muslim expression *Bukra insha Allah*—"Tomorrow if Allah wills"—explains much about the Arab culture and its approach to business transactions. A cultural clash typically occurs when an American tries to give an Arab a deadline. "'I am going to Damascus tomorrow morning and will have to have my car tonight,' is a sure way to get the mechanic to stop work," explains Hall, "because to give another person a deadline in this part of the world is to be rude, pushy, and demanding."[62] In such instances, the attitude toward time communicates as loudly as words.

In verbal interactions, managers must be aware of different patterns of Arab thought and communication. Compared to the direct, linear fashion of American communication, Arabs tend to meander. They start with social talk, discuss business for a while, loop around to social and general issues, then back to business, and so on.[63] American impatience and insistence on sticking to the subject will cut off their loops, triggering confusion and dysfunction. Instead, Westerners should accept that considerable time will be spent on small talk and socializing, with frequent interruptions, before getting down to business.

Exhibit 5-5 illustrates some of the sources of noise that are likely to interfere in the communication process between Americans and Arabs, thereby causing miscommunications and misunderstandings.

For people doing business in the Middle East, the following are some useful guidelines for effective communication.

- Be patient. Recognize the Arab attitude toward time and hospitality—take time to develop friendship and trust because these are prerequisites for any social or business transactions.

- Recognize that people and relationships matter more to Arabs than the job, company, or contract—conduct business personally, not by correspondence or telephone.

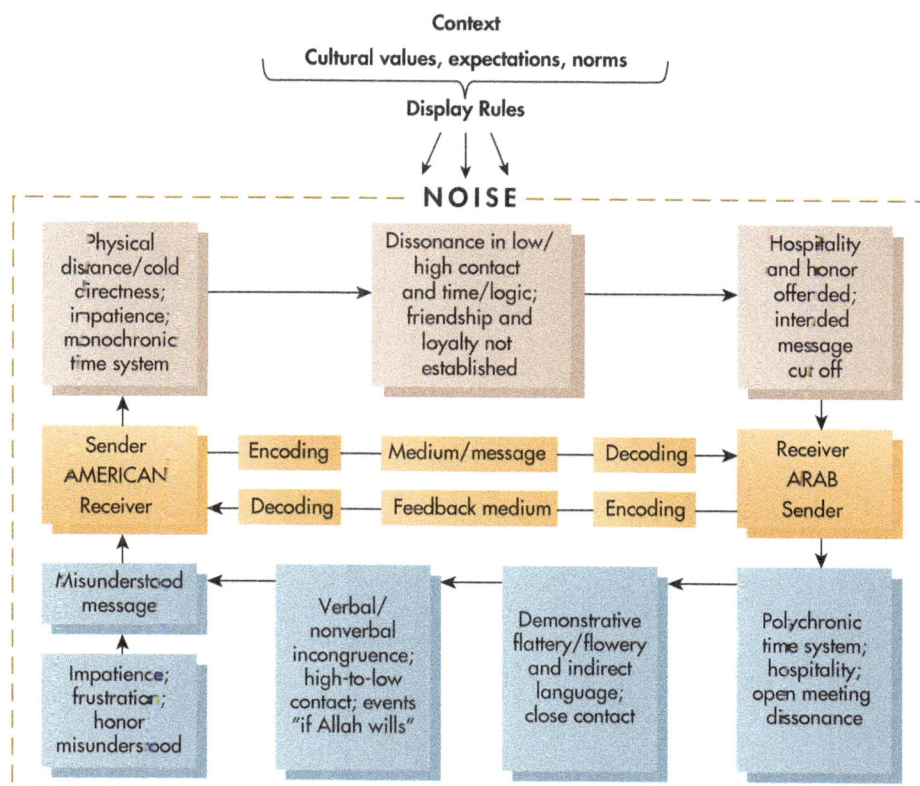

**EXHIBIT 5-5** Miscommunication between Americans and Arabs Caused by Cross-Cultural Noise

- Avoid expressing doubts or criticism when others are present—recognize the importance of honor and dignity to Arabs.
- Adapt to the norms of body language, flowery speech, and circuitous verbal patterns in the Middle East and don't be impatient to get to the point.
- Expect many interruptions in meetings, delays in schedules, and changes in plans.[64]

## Communication Channels

In addition to the variables related to the sender and receiver of a message, the variables linked to the channel itself and the context of the message must be taken into consideration. These variables include fast or slow messages and information flows as well as different types of media.

### INFORMATION SYSTEMS

Communication in organizations varies according to where and how it originates, the channels and the speed at which it flows, whether it is formal or informal, and so forth. The type of organizational structure, the staffing policies, and the leadership style will affect the nature of an organization's information system.

As an international manager, it is useful to know where and how information originates and the speed at which it flows, both internally and externally. In centralized organizational structures, as in South America, most information originates from top managers. Workers take less responsibility for keeping managers informed in a South American company than in a typical company in the United States, where delegation results in information flowing from the staff to the managers. In a decision-making system in which many people are involved, such as the **ringi system** of consensus decision making in Japan, the expatriate needs to understand that there is a systematic pattern for information flow.

Context also affects information flow. In high-context cultures (such as in the Middle East), information spreads rapidly and freely because of the constant close contact and the implicit ties among people and organizations. Information flow is often informal. In low-context cultures (such as Germany or the United States), information is controlled and focused and thus does not flow so freely.[65] Compartmentalized roles and office layouts stifle information channels; information sources tend to be more formal.

It is crucial for an expatriate manager to find out how to tap into a firm's informal sources of information. In Japan, employees usually have a drink together on the way home from work, and this becomes an essential source of information. However, such communication networks are based on long-term relationships in Japan (and in other high-context cultures). The same information may not be readily available to outsiders. A considerable barrier in Japan separates strangers from familiar friends, a situation that discourages communication.

Americans are more open and talk freely about almost anything, whereas Japanese will disclose little about their inner thoughts or private issues. Americans are willing to have a wide public self, disclosing their inner reactions verbally and physically. In contrast, the Japanese prefer to keep their responses largely to their private self. The Japanese expose only a small portion of their thoughts; they reduce, according to Barnlund, "the unpredictability and emotional intensity of personal encounters."[66] In intercultural communication between Americans and Japanese, cultural clashes between the public and private selves result when each party forces its cultural norms of communication on the other. In the American style, the American's cultural norms of explicit communication impose on the Japanese by invading the person's private self. The Japanese style of implicit communication causes a negative reaction from the American because of what is perceived as too much formality and ambiguity, which wastes time.[67]

Cultural variables in information systems and context underlie the many differences in communication style between Japanese and Americans. Exhibit 5-6 shows some specific differences. The Japanese *ningensei* (human beingness) style of communication refers to the preference for humanity, reciprocity, a receiver orientation, and an underlying distrust of words and analytic logic.[68] The Japanese believe that true intentions are not readily revealed in words or contracts but are, in fact, masked by them. In contrast to the typical American's verbal agility and explicitness, Japanese behaviors and communications are directed to defend and give face for everyone concerned; to do so, they avoid public disagreements at all costs. In cross-cultural negotiations, this last point is essential.

The speed with which we try to use information systems is another key variable that needs attention to avoid misinterpretation and conflict. Americans expect to give and receive information very quickly and clearly, moving through details and stages in a linear fashion to the conclusion. They usually use various media for fast messages—IMs, emails, Skype, faxes, social media, and familiar relationships—to give all the facts up front. In contrast, the French use the slower message channels of deep relationships, culture, and sometimes mediators to exchange information. A French written communication will be tentative, with subsequent letters slowly building up to a new proposal. The French preference for written communication, even for informal interactions, echoes the formality of their relationships—and results in slowing a message transmission down that often seems unnecessary to Americans.[69]

In short, it behooves Americans to realize that, because much of the world exchanges business information through slower message media, it is wise to schedule more time for transactions, develop patience, and learn to get at needed information in more subtle ways—after building rapport and taking time to observe the local system for exchanging information.

We have seen that cross-cultural misinterpretation can result from noise in the actual transmission of the message—the choice or speed of media. Interpreting the meaning of a message can thus be as much a function of examining the transmission channel (or medium) as it is of examining the message itself.

**EXHIBIT 5-6** Differences between Japanese and American Communication Styles

| Japanese Ningensei Style of Communication | U.S. Adversarial Style of Communication |
|---|---|
| 1. Indirect verbal and nonverbal communication | 1. More direct verbal and nonverbal communication |
| 2. Relationship communication | 2. More task communication |
| 3. Discourages confrontational strategies | 3. Confrontational strategies more acceptable |
| 4. Strategically ambiguous communication | 4. Prefers more to-the-point communication |
| 5. Delayed feedback | 5. More immediate feedback |
| 6. Patient, longer-term negotiators | 6. Shorter-term negotiators |
| 7. Uses fewer words | 7. Favors verbosity |
| 8. Distrustful of skillful verbal communicators | 8. Exalts verbal eloquence |
| 9. Group orientation | 9. More individualistic orientation |
| 10. Cautious, tentative | 10. More assertive, self-assured |
| 11. Complementary communicators | 11. More publicly critical communication |
| 12. Softer, heart-like logic | 12. Harder, analytic logic preferred |
| 13. Sympathetic, empathetic, complex use of pathos | 13. Favors logos, reason |
| 14. Expresses and decodes complex relational strategies and nuances | 14. Expresses and decodes complex logos, cognitive nuances |
| 15. Avoids decision making in public | 15. Frequent decision making in public |
| 16. Makes decisions in private venues, away from public eye | 16. Frequent decision in public at negotiating tables |
| 17. Decisions via *ringi* and *nemawashi* (complete consensus process) | 17. Decisions by majority rule and public compromise is more commonplace |
| 18. Uses go-betweens for decision making | 18. More extensive use of direct person-to-person, player-to-player interaction for decisions |
| 19. Understatement and hesitation in verbal and nonverbal communication | 19. May publicly speak in superlatives, exaggerations, nonverbal projection |
| 20. Uses qualifiers, tentativeness, humility as communicator | 20. Favors fewer qualifiers, more ego-centered |
| 21. Receiver/listening–centered | 21. More speaker- and message-centered |
| 22. Inferred meanings, looks beyond words to nuances, nonverbal communication | 22. More face-value meaning, more denotative |
| 23. Shy, reserved communicators | 23. More publicly self-assertive |
| 24. Distaste for purely business transactions | 24. Prefers to "get down to business" or "nitty gritty" |
| 25. Mixes business and social communication | 25. Tends to keep business negotiating more separated from social communication |
| 26. Utilizes *matomari* or "hints" for achieving group adjustment and saving face in negotiating | 26. More directly verbalizes management's preference at negotiating tables |
| 27. Practices *haragei* or "belly logic" and communication | 27. Practices more linear, discursive, analytical logic; greater reverence for cognitive than for affective |

*Source:* A. Goldman, "The Centrality of 'Ningensei' to Japanese Negotiating and Interpersonal Relationships. Implications for U.S.–Japanese Communication," *International Journal of Intercultural Relations* 18, No. 1 (1994), with permission from the *International Journal of Intercultural Relations*, 2011.

# INFORMATION TECHNOLOGY: GOING GLOBAL AND ACTING LOCAL

*Microsoft has struck a deal with the biggest Chinese search engine, Baidu.com, to offer Web search services in English.*

WWW.NYTIMES.COM
*JULY 4, 2011*[70]

*All information is local; IT systems can connect every corner of the globe, but IT managers are learning they have to pay attention to regional differences.*

COMPUTERWORLD[71]

Using the Internet as a global medium for communication has enabled companies of all sizes to develop a presence quickly in many markets around the world—and, in fact, has enabled them to go global. However, their global reach cannot alone translate into global business. Those companies are learning that they have to adapt their e-commerce and their enterprise resource planning (ERP) applications to regional idiosyncrasies beyond translation or content management issues; for example, even asking for a name or an email address can incur resistance in many countries where people do not like to give out personal information.[72] Although communication over the Internet is clearly not as personal as face-to-face, cross-cultural communication, those transactions must still be regionalized and personalized to adjust to differences in language, culture, local laws, and business models as well as differences in the level of development in the local telecommunications infrastructure. Yet, if the Internet is a global medium for communication, why do so many U.S. companies treat the web as a U.S.-centric phenomenon? Giving preference to some geographic regions, languages, and cultures is "a short-sighted business decision that will result in diminished brand equity, market share, profits and global leadership."[73]

When Baidu.com—China's leading search engine—made a business decision in July 2011 to partner with Microsoft to offer web search services in English, it had clearly realized that it needed to go beyond Chinese because of the 10 million per day searches for English terms on its site.

*"More and more people here are searching for English terms," Kaiser Kuo, the company's spokesman, said Monday. "But Baidu hasn't done a good job. So here's a way for us to do it."*[74]

For its part, Microsoft's expansion of Bing in China gave it access to the world's largest Internet population of more than 470 million users. Both companies realized that the English-language search results would be censored (as happened to Google, which pulled out of the mainland and went to Hong Kong), and it is reported that Microsoft is cooperating with China's government on censorship rules regarding the content that can be accessed.[75] Beijing requires Internet companies operating on the mainland to censor results the government considers threatening, including references to human rights issues and dissidents.[76] Clearly, both going global and acting local can be fraught with difficulties.

It seems essential, then, for a global online strategy also to be multilocal. The impersonal nature of the web must somehow be adapted to local cultures to establish relationships and create customer loyalty. Effective technological communication requires even more cultural sensitivity than face-to-face communication because of the inability to assess reactions and get feedback or, in many cases, even retain contact. It is still people, after all, who respond to and interact with other people through the medium of the Internet, and those people interpret and respond according to their own languages and cultures as well as their local business practices and expectations. In Europe, for example, significant differences in business cultures and e-business technology have slowed e-business progress there. However, some companies are making progress in pan-European integration services, such as leEurope, which aims to cross language, currency, and cultural barriers. Specifically, leEurope is building a set of services "to help companies tie their back-end e-business systems together across European boundaries through a series of mergers involving regional e-business integrators in more than a dozen countries."[77]

# MANAGING CROSS-CULTURAL COMMUNICATION

Steps toward effective intercultural communication include the development of cultural sensitivity, careful encoding, selective transmission, careful decoding, and appropriate follow-up actions.

## Developing Cultural Sensitivity

When acting as a sender, a manager must make it a point to know the receiver and encode the message in a form that will most likely be understood as intended. On the manager's part, this requires an awareness of his or her own cultural baggage and how it affects the communication process. In other words, what kinds of behaviors does the message imply, and how will they be perceived by the receiver? The way to anticipate the most likely meaning that the receiver will attach to the message is to internalize honest cultural empathy with that person. What is the cultural background—the societal, economic, and organizational context—in which this communication is taking place? What are this person's expectations regarding the situation, what are the two parties' relative positions, and what might develop from this communication? What kinds of transactions and behaviors is this person used to? Cultural sensitivity is really just a matter of understanding the other person, the context, and how the person will respond to the context. Americans, unfortunately, have a rather negative reputation overseas of not being culturally sensitive. One not-for-profit group, called Business for Diplomatic Action, has the following advice for Americans when doing business abroad, in its attempts to counteract the stereotypical American traits such as boastfulness, loudness, and speed.

- **Read a map** Familiarize yourself with the local geography to avoid making insulting mistakes.
- **Dress up** In some countries, casual dress is a sign of disrespect.
- **Talk small** Talking about wealth, power, or status—corporate or personal—can create resentment.
- **No slang** Even casual profanity is unacceptable.
- **Slow down** Americans talk fast, eat fast, move fast, live fast. Many cultures do not.
- **Listen as much as you talk** Ask people you're visiting about themselves and their way of life.
- **Speak lower and slower** A loud voice is often perceived as bragging.
- **Religious restraint** In many countries, religion is not a subject for public discussion.
- **Political restraint** Steer clear of this subject. If someone is attacking U.S. politicians or policies, agree to disagree.[78]

## Careful Encoding

In translating his or her intended meaning into symbols for cross-cultural communication, the sender must use words, pictures, or gestures that are appropriate to the receiver's frame of reference. Of course, language training is invaluable, but senders should also avoid idioms and regional sayings (such as "Go fly a kite" or "Foot the bill") in a translation, or even in English when speaking to a non-American who knows little English.

Literal translation, then, is a limited answer to language differences. Even for people in English-speaking countries, words can have different meanings. Ways to avoid problems are to speak slowly and clearly, avoid long sentences and colloquial expressions, and explain things in several ways and through several media if possible. However, even though English is in common use around the world for business transactions, the manager's efforts to speak the local language will greatly improve the climate. Sometimes people from other cultures resent the assumption by English-speaking executives that everyone else will speak English.

Language translation is only part of the encoding process; the message also is expressed in nonverbal language. In the encoding process, the sender must ensure congruence between the nonverbal and the verbal message. In encoding a message, therefore, it is useful to be as objective as possible and not to rely on personal interpretations. To clarify their messages further, managers can hand out written summaries of verbal presentations and use visual aids such as graphs or pictures. A good general guide is to move slowly, wait, and take cues from the receivers.

## Selective Transmission

The type of medium chosen for the message depends on the nature of the message, its level of importance, the context and expectations of the receiver, the timing involved, and the need for personal interaction, among other factors. Typical media include instant messaging (IM), email, letters or memos, reports, meetings, telephone calls, teleconferences, videoconferences, or face-to-face conversations. The secret is to find out how communication is transmitted in the local organization—how much is downward versus upward or vertical versus horizontal, how the grapevine works, and so on. In addition, the cultural variables discussed earlier need to be considered: whether the receiver is from a high- or low-context culture, whether he or she is used to explicit or implicit communication, and what speed and routing of messages will be most effective.

For the most part, it is best to use face-to-face interaction for relationship building or for other important transactions, particularly in intercultural communications, because of the lack of familiarity between parties. Personal interactions give the manager the opportunity to get immediate verbal and visual feedback and make rapid adjustments in the communication process.

International dealings are often long-distance, of course, limiting the opportunity for face-to-face communication. However, personal rapport can be established or enhanced through telephone calls or videoconferencing and through trusted contacts. Modern electronic media and social networks can be used to break down communication barriers by reducing waiting periods for information, clarifying issues, and allowing instant consultation, such as through Skype, for one-on-one or group video-chat. Ford Europe uses videoconferencing for engineers in Britain and Germany to consult about quality problems. Through the video monitors, they examine one another's engineering diagrams and usually find a solution that gets the factory moving again in a short time.

## Careful Decoding of Feedback

Timely and effective feedback channels can also be set up to assess a firm's general communication about the progression of its business and its general management principles. The best means for getting accurate feedback is through face-to-face interaction because this allows the manager to hear, see, and immediately sense how a message is being interpreted. When visual feedback on important issues is not possible or appropriate, it is a good idea to use several means of attaining feedback, in particular by employing third parties.

Decoding is the process of translating the received symbols into the interpreted message. The main causes of incongruence are because (1) the receiver misinterprets the message, (2) the receiver encodes his or her return message incorrectly, or (3) the sender misinterprets the feedback. Two-way communication is thus essential for important issues so that successive efforts can be made until an understanding has been achieved. Asking other colleagues to help interpret what is going on is often a good way to break a cycle of miscommunication.

Perhaps the most important means for avoiding miscommunication is to practice careful decoding by improving one's listening and observation skills. A good listener practices projective listening, or empathic listening—listening, without interruption or evaluation, to the full message of the speaker; attempting to recognize the feelings behind the words and nonverbal cues; and understanding the speaker's perspective.

At the multinational corporation (MNC) level, avenues of communication and feedback among parent companies and subsidiaries can be kept open through telephone calls, regular meetings and visits, reports, and plans, all of which facilitate cooperation, performance control, and the smooth running of the company. Communication among far-flung operations can be managed best by setting up feedback systems and liaison people. The headquarters people should maintain considerable flexibility in cooperating with local managers and allowing them to deal with the local context as they see fit.

## Follow-up Actions

Managers communicate through both action and inaction. Therefore, to keep open the lines of communication, feedback, and trust, managers must follow through with action on what has been discussed and then agreed upon—typically a contract, which is probably the most important formal business communication. Unfortunately, the issue of contract follow-through is a particularly sensitive one across cultures because of the different interpretations regarding what constitutes a contract (perhaps a handshake, perhaps a full legal document) and what actions should result. Trust, future communications, and future business are based on such interpretations, and it is up to managers to understand them and follow through on them.

The management of cross-cultural communication depends largely on a manager's personal abilities and behavior. Behaviors that researchers indicate to be most important to intercultural communication effectiveness (ICE) are listed here, as reviewed by Ruben.

- Respect (conveyed through eye contact, body posture, voice tone, and pitch)
- Interaction posture (the ability to respond to others in a descriptive, nonevaluative, and nonjudgmental way)
- Orientation to knowledge (recognizing that one's knowledge, perception, and beliefs are valid only for oneself and not for everyone else)
- Empathy
- Interaction management
- Tolerance for ambiguity
- Other-oriented role behavior (one's capacity to be flexible and adopt different roles for the sake of greater group cohesion and group communication)[79]

Researchers have established a relationship between personality traits and behaviors and the ability to adapt to the host-country's cultural environment.[80] What is seldom pointed out, however, is that communication is the mediating factor between those behaviors and the relative level of adaptation the expatriate achieves. The communication process facilitates cross-cultural adaptation, and, through this process, expatriates learn the dominant communication patterns of the host society. Therefore, we can link personality factors shown by research to ease adaptation with those necessary for effective intercultural communication.

Kim has consolidated the research findings of these characteristics into two categories: (1) **openness**—traits such as open-mindedness, tolerance for ambiguity, and extrovertedness—and (2) **resilience**—traits such as having an internal locus of control, persistence, a tolerance of ambiguity, and resourcefulness.[81] These personality factors, along with the expatriate's cultural and racial identity and the level of preparedness for change, comprise that person's potential for adaptation. The level of preparedness can be improved by the manager before his or her assignment by gathering information about the host country's verbal and nonverbal communication patterns and norms of behavior. However, we must remember the practicalities of situational factors that can affect the communication process—variables such as the physical environment, time constraints, the degree of structure, and feelings of irritability or overwork, among others.

## CONCLUSION

Effective intercultural communication is a vital skill for international managers and domestic managers of multicultural workforces. Because miscommunication is much more likely to occur among people from different countries or racial backgrounds than among those from similar backgrounds, it is important to be alert to how culture is reflected in communication—in particular through the development of cultural sensitivity and an awareness of potential sources of cultural noise in the communication process. A successful international manager is thus attuned to these variables and is flexible enough to adjust his or her communication style to address the intended receivers best—that is, to do it their way.

Cultural variables and the manner in which culture is communicated underlie the processes of negotiation and decision making. How do people around the world negotiate? What are their expectations and their approach to negotiations? What is the importance of understanding negotiation and decision-making processes in other countries?

## Summary of Key Points

- Communication is an inherent part of a manager's role, taking up the majority of the manager's time on the job. Effective intercultural communication largely determines the success of international transactions or the output of a culturally diverse workforce.
- Culture is the foundation of communication, and communication transmits culture. Cultural variables that can affect the communication process by influencing a person's perceptions include attitudes, social organizations, thought patterns, roles, language, nonverbal language, and time.
- Language conveys cultural understandings and social norms from one generation to the next. Body language, or nonverbal communication, is behavior that communicates without words. It accounts for 65 to 93 percent of interpreted communication.
- Types of nonverbal communication around the world are kinesic behavior, proxemics, paralanguage, and object language.
- Effective cross-cultural communication must take into account whether the receiver is from a country with a monochronic or a polychronic time system.

- Variables related to channels of communication include high- and low-context cultures, fast or slow messages and information flows, and various types of media.
- In high-context cultures, feelings and messages are implicit and must be accessed through an understanding of the person and the system. In low-context cultures, feelings and thoughts are expressed, and information is more readily available.
- The effective management of intercultural communication necessitates the development of cultural sensitivity, careful encoding, selective transmission, careful decoding, and follow-up actions.
- Certain personal abilities and behaviors facilitate adaptation to the host country through skilled intercultural communication.
- Communication through the Internet must still be localized to adjust to differences in language, culture, local laws, and business models.

## Discussion Questions

**5-1.** How does culture affect the process of attribution in communication? Can you relate this to some experiences you have had with your classmates?

**5-2.** How will the perceptions of international managers' roles affect the way they manage their subordinates?

**5-3.** What are the potential problems an international manager with a low-context culture will face when working or negotiating with their counterpart in a high-context culture?

**5-4.** Give some examples of cultural differences in the interpretation of body language. What is the role of such nonverbal communication in business relationships?

**5-5.** Explain the differences between high- and low-context cultures, giving some examples. What are the differential effects on the communication process?

**5-6.** Discuss the role of information systems in a company, how and why they vary from country to country, and the effects of these variations.

## Application Exercises

**5-7.** Form small groups of three to four students, preferably from different cultural backgrounds. Show them the product catalogs or promotion material of four different brands of automobiles from four different countries—America, Japan, Germany, and India. Have them write down their perceptions of the brands and ask them to present their ideas. Discuss whether the students have stereotyped perceptions of these automobiles.

**5-8.** Invite some students who are from other countries to your class. Ask them to bring photographs, slides, and so forth of people and events in their native countries. Have them explain the meanings of various nonverbal cues such as gestures, dress, voice inflections, architecture, and events. Discuss with them any differences between their explanations and the attributions you assigned to those cues.

**5-9.** Check with your family, relatives, or friends to identify someone with overseas working experience. Talk to this person and ask him or her to identify the benefits and problems of working abroad. What lessons can you get from this experience? Set out a brief plan for yourself, assuming you will be assigned to work overseas in the same country where the person you spoke to worked.

## Experiential Exercise

**5-10.** Form two or three pairs to enact skits—separately—in front of the class and then ask your class for feedback and to guess where you are from.

Each person in each pair decides on a different cultural profile to enact—for example, act as if one of you is, say, Japanese or Arab, and the other is, say, German or Mexican. Set up a five-to-

ten minute skit, presumably for an intended business transaction. Research and practice with your partner the typical communication style, both verbal and nonverbal (use English for everyone).

Both you and your class will see how difficult it is to put yourself in the persona of someone from a different cultural background.

## CASE STUDY

### Miscommunications with a Brazilian Auto Parts Manufacturer

The Brazilian sun beat down steadily on the tarmac outside as Alessandro Silva and Agosto Ventura stood inside the São Paulo-Guarulhos International Airport. They were awaiting the arrival of two representatives from Lucky Auto Parts Company, a regional wholesaler and retailer based in Ames, Iowa.

Mr. Silva, the president of a mid-sized auto parts manufacturer in São Paulo, and Mr. Ventura, the company's sales manager, were looking forward to a new business relationship with Henry Williams, president of Lucky Auto Parts Company. A few weeks previously, in an initial phone call, President Silva invited President Williams to visit the Brazilian manufacturing facility, a potential source of after-market auto parts for Lucky. This would be the American company's first venture into buying parts directly from a foreign manufacturer. Williams planned to take his new vice president of purchasing, Wally Astor, who also happened to be his son-in-law, on this first trip. Mr. Williams thought this exploratory buying trip would be a good introduction to the auto parts business for Wally; although Wally had experience as a new car salesman, he had no experience in the auto parts field.

Unfortunately, a few days before the trip, Williams had to cancel his trip to be available for a deposition on a court case pending against his company. It had taken a long time to get the appointment with Mr. Silva, and Williams did not think it wise to cancel the trip. Because Wally was eager to prove himself in his new role, Williams decided to let him handle this mission without the old man looking over his shoulder. In the rush to review the legal documents for the deposition, Williams forgot to notify his Brazilian counterpart that he would not be coming on this visit.

As he was preparing for the trip, Wally Astor realized that it was summer in Brazil and that it was a long flight to Brazil from Ames through Miami. Based on this, he decided to dress as informally and comfortably as possible.

At the airport, both Mr. Silva and Mr. Agosto were dressed as usual when conducting business or in the public eye for social occasions, that is, in suits and ties. As they stood outside the door of the international arrivals area, Agosto held a neatly printed sign with Wally Astor's name on it. Soon a young man in his late twenties approached them and announced that he was Wally Astor; both Mr. Silva and Mr. Ventura were visibly surprised, especially because the young man was dressed in faded blue jeans, sneakers, and a checked shirt with the sleeves rolled up.

"Hey, thanks for picking me up," Wally said as the three shook hands. "You must be Alexander and Agosto? My father-in-law said you were going to meet us at the airport."

"I am President Alessandro Silva, and this is my Marketing Director, Mr. Ventura," Mr. Silva said icily. "We expected to see President Williams. Will he be coming on a later flight?"

"No, he had something important come up, so he sent me to take care of the visit to Brazil," Wally replied. "Oh, here, let me give you my business card so you'll know I really am who I say I am."

President Silva read the card carefully and turned to Agosto with a frown. The card had the U.S. flag emblazoned on it with an italicized inscription under it: "An American-owned business."

Agosto turned to Wally and said politely, "I'm certain you are tired from your long journey. Shall we drop you at your hotel and then pick you up for dinner about nine o'clock?"

"Nine o'clock! Isn't that a little late for dinner?" Wally exclaimed. "No, let's just go to your office and get right to it, shall we? I have a contract drawn up by the lawyer-types in my department. I think you'll find it covers all the details and is more than fair."

President Silva spoke up more forcefully than he intended, "Mr. Astor …"

"Please call me Wally."

"No, Mr. Astor. I don't know you or your company well enough to call you by your first name and certainly not well enough to look at an important contract with you today. I was impressed with the phone conversation I had with President Williams, but *he* is not here today, so let's drop you at your hotel and begin our discussion over dinner later this evening."

Wally was surprised and uncomfortable to see Mr. Silva standing very close to him, staring intently into his eyes and gesticulating to emphasize his words. Wally took a step back, but Mr. Silva took a step toward him to close the gap between them.

"OK, Mr. Silva. Maybe I sounded like I was trying to rush things a bit. But you see, I booked my flight out for tomorrow evening so I can spend a couple days in Rio to see what that's about."

There was an uncomfortable silence during which no one spoke. Finally, Wally said, "I guess I would like to go to my hotel and rest up. Then we can have dinner at 9:00. OK?"

Ventura knew that President Silva was not warming to Wally, so he decided to see whether he could get the relationship back on track. Because he and Wally were about the same age and held the same status within their respective organizations, he felt comfortable doing this.

"That sounds very good, Wally," Ventura said. "We will pick you up at 9:00. And please, call me Agosto."

Once he was settled in his hotel room, Wally phoned Henry Williams to check in as instructed.

"Yeah, Dad," Wally said. "I met with them at the airport. They drove me to the hotel and we're going to dinner tonight to get acquainted. Can you believe they want to eat at 9 P.M.?"

"That's good," Williams replied. "Did you see their facility yet?"

"No. The president, Mr. Silva, is kinda stiff. He said he wants to get to know us better before he talks business. I think he's doing the Latin American thing about *mañana*. I tried to get the ball rolling this afternoon, but he wouldn't hear of it."

"Well, he's just being cautious, like I am. I like to know a man personally before I enter into a long-term contract with him, too. Wally, this isn't like selling cars. It's building relationships that have to work day after day. I'm sorry I threw you into this situation alone."

"You know," Wally said, "I think he's upset that you aren't here."

"I hope you conveyed my apology to him," Williams replied, "and explained that this deposition came up at the last minute."

"I sure did."

"OK. Call me tomorrow afternoon to let me know how the dinner conversation went. How long do you think you'll be out there?"

"Well, I made reservations to leave for Rio tomorrow evening for a couple days," Wally said.

"Why are you going to Rio? Who is out there?" Williams asked.

"I promised Mindy I'd check out Rio as a possible vacation spot for later this year."

"Wally, you don't work for Mindy. You work for me. If Mr. Silva wants to talk with you for the next few days, that's exactly what you're going to do. Forget about going to Rio!"

That evening at the restaurant, Mr. Silva insisted that Wally sit across the table from him and Mr. Agosto.

"Mr. Astor, I want to thank you for joining us for a Brazilian business dinner this evening," said Mr. Silva. "We always start with cafezinho, a very strong espresso. We think it helps the conversation to flow."

For the next hour, Wally found himself talking freely about his wife, their relationship, his in-laws, his childhood and parents, and many other topics that would never find their way into a business discussion in the U.S. To encourage Wally, Mr. Silva and Agosto shared humorous stories about themselves and shared their favorite sports, movies, pastimes, wines, and vacation areas.

Their free exchange about themselves continued throughout the dinner, and as the three men were served cafezinho after the meal, they began to talk business for the first time that evening. President Silva introduced the topic.

"Wally, I think tomorrow morning you should join us to see the plant. I want you to meet with our purchasing and quality assurance managers. We pride ourselves on using the best materials and maintaining the strictest tolerance standards. After you are more familiar with how we do things, we will meet again for dinner before your flight to Rio and discuss when Mr. Williams can visit us to resume exploring our potential business partnership."

"Sir," Wally began, "I cancelled my trip to Rio so I can learn more about your operation, your products, and where our mutual interests may lie. Perhaps we can have dinner again tomorrow night and decide what our next steps should be for the following few days."

"I'm very happy to hear you say that. And please, call me Alessandro."

# Case Questions

**5-11.** What are three of the cultural missteps that Wally Astor and his father-in-law, Henry Williams, made in this scenario? Why do you think this happened?

**5-12.** If you were a native of Brazil and advising American business representatives about what to do when talking with Brazilian business partners, what would you tell the Americans about Brazilian culture?

**5-13.** Imagine that the situation in this case study was reversed, that is, the Brazilian businessmen were coming to the United States to look for a supplier. What would you tell the Brazilians about American business culture to prepare them for success?

*Source:* Linda Catlin. Ms. Catlin is an organizational anthropologist and the co-author of *International Business: Cultural Sourcebook and Case Studies*. She consults with clients on projects related to cross-cultural business communications, organizational culture, and organizational change dynamics. Her clients include the Mayo Clinic, the Kellogg Foundation, General Motors, Ascension Health, and BASF.

Linda Catlin, Claymore Associates. Used with permission.

# Endnotes

1. K. Ananth Krishnan (Tata Consultancy Services), interviewed by Michael S. Hopkins, "The 'Unstructured Information' Most Businesses Miss Out On," *MIT Sloan Management Review: The Magazine*, April 27, 2011.

2. Sharlene Goff, "Lenders Eye Social Media Angles," *Financial Times*, London (UK), January 10, 2011, p. 18.

3. Krishnan.

4. Donna L. Hoffman and Marek Fodor, "Can You Measure the ROI of Your Social Media Marketing?" *MIT Sloan Management Review* 52 (Fall 2010), p. 1.

5. Roxane Divol, David Edelman, and Hugo Sarrazin, "Demystifying Social Media," *McKinsey Quarterly*, April 2012; "What Marketers Say about Working Online: McKinsey Global Survey Results," mckinseyquarterly.com, November 2011.

6. "Facebook Takes a Dive: Why Social Networks Are Bad Businesses," http://www.time.com/time/business/article/0,8599,1888796,00.html#ixzz1RosHjXUq, accessed July 10, 2011.

7. Cindy Chiu, Chris Ip, and Ari Silverman, "Understanding Social Media in China," *McKinsey Quarterly*, April 2012.

8. E. T. Hall and M. R. Hall, *Understanding Cultural Differences* (Yarmouth, ME: Intercultural Press, 1990), p. 4.

9. E. Wilmott, "New Media Vision," *New Media Age*, September 9, 1999, p. 8.

10. Hall and Hall; K. Wolfson and W. B. Pearce, "A Cross-Cultural Comparison of the Implications of Self-discovery on Conversation Logics," *Communication Quarterly* 31 (1983), pp. 249–256.

11. L. Nardon, R. M. Steers, and C. J. Sanchez-Runde, "Seeking Common Ground: Strategies for Enhancing Multicultural Communication," *Organizational Dynamics*. 2011, in press, http://dx.doi.org/10.1016/j.orgdyn.2011.01.002.

12. H. Mintzberg, *The Nature of Managerial Work* (New York: Harper and Row, 1973).

13. L. A. Samovar, R. E. Porter, and N. C. Jain, *Understanding Intercultural Communication* (Belmont, CA: Wadsworth Publishing, 1981).

14. P. R. Harris and R. T. Moran, *Managing Cultural Differences*, 3rd ed. (Houston: Gulf Publishing, 1991).

15. H. C. Triandis, quoted in *The Blackwell Handbook of Cross-Cultural Management*, M. Gannon and K. Newman, eds. (Oxford, UK: Blackwell Publishers, 2002).

16. Samovar, Porter, and Jain.

17. Hall and Hall, p. 15.

18. Based on H. C. Triandis, *Interpersonal Behavior* (Monterey, CA: Brooks/Cole, 1997), p. 248.

19. James R. Houghton, former chairman of Corning, Inc., quoted in Organizational Dynamics 29, No. 4 (2001).

20. J. Child, "Trust: The Fundamental Bond in Global Collaboration," *Organizational Dynamics* 29, No. 4 (2001), pp. 274–288.

21. Ibid.

22. World Values Study Group, *World Values Survey, ICPSR Version* (Ann Arbor, MI: Institute for Social Research, 1994); R. Inglehart, M. Basanez, and A. Moreno, *Human Values and Beliefs: A Cross-Cultural Sourcebook* (Ann Arbor: University of Michigan Press, 1998).

23. Mansour Javidan and Robert J. House, "Cultural Acumen for the Global Manager," *Organizational Dynamics* 29, No. 4 (2001), 289–305.

24. Samovar and Porter; Harris and Moran.

25. M. L. Hecht, P. A. Andersen, and S. A. Ribeau, "The Cultural Dimensions of Nonverbal Communication, in *Handbook of International and Intercultural Communication*, M. K. Asante and W. B. Gudykunst, eds. (Newbury Park, CA: Sage Publications, 1989), pp. 163–185.

26. H. C. Triandis, *Interpersonal Behavior* (Monterey, CA: Brooks/Cole, 1977).

27. Harris and Moran.

28. Adapted from N. Adler, *International Dimensions of Organizational Behavior*, 2nd ed. (Boston: PWS-Kent, 1991).

29. D. A. Ricks, *Big Business Blunders: Mistakes in Multinational Marketing* (Homewood, IL: Dow Jones–Irwin, 1983).

30. P. Garfinkel, "On Keeping Your Foot Safely Out of Your Mouth," www.nytimes.com, July 13, 2004.

31. Jiatao Li, Katherine R. Xin, Anne Tsui, and Donald C. Hambrick, "Building Effective International Joint Venture Leadership Teams in China," *Journal of World Business* 34, No. 1 (1999), pp. 52–68.

32. D. Walker, T. Walker, and J. Schmitz, *Doing Business Internationally* (New York: McGraw-Hill, 2003).

33. Roger E. Axtell, *Essential Do's and Taboos*," (Hoboken, NJ: John Wiley and Sons, Inc., 2007).

**34.** R. L. Daft, *Organizational Theory and Design*, 3rd ed. (St. Paul, MN: West Publishing, 1989).

**35.** Li et al., 1999.

**36.** Rachel Donadio, "When Italians Chat, Hands and Fingers Do the Talking," www.nytimes.com, *Rome Journal*, June 30, 2013; www.ediplomat.com, accessed July 8, 2014; http://www.theguardian.com/world/shortcuts/2013/jul/02/how-speak-italian-with-hand-gestures; http://acad.depauw.edu/mkfinney_web/teaching/Com227/culturalPortfolios/ITALY/Italy%20Nonverbal.html, accessed July 8, 2014; http://www.goinglobal.com/articles/1112/, accessed July 8, 2014.

**37.** O. Klineberg, "Emotional Expression in Chinese Literature," *Journal of Abnormal and Social Psychology* 33 (1983), pp. 517–530.

**38.** P. Ekman and W. V. Friesen, "Constants Across Cultures in the Face and Emotion," *Journal of Personality and Social Psychology* 17 (1971), pp. 124–129.

**39.** J. Pfeiffer, "How Not to Lose the Trade Wars by Cultural Gaffes," *Smithsonian* 18, No. 10 (January 1988).

**40.** E. T. Hall, *The Silent Language* (New York: Doubleday, 1959).

**41.** Hall and Hall.

**42.** Random House, American Heritage, Merriam Webster; *feng-shui*, Oxford English Dictionary, 2nd ed. (Oxford University Press, 1989); Tina Marie, *"Feng Shui Diaries, Esoteric Feng Shui* (2007–2009); "Baidu Baike," *Huai Nan Zi*; Stephen L. Field, *The Zangshu, or Book of Burial*.

**43.** http://www.instituteoffengshui.com/fengshui.html, accessed June 24, 2011.

**44.** Ibid.

**45.** Jonathan Vatner, "When Feng Shui Helps Determine a Deal's Fate," www.nytimes.com, August 24, 2010.

**46.** Ibid.

**47.** Hall and Hall.

**48.** Anand Giridharada, "How to Greet in a Global Microcosm," New York Times Online, October 15, 2010.

**49.** Hecht, Andersen, and Ribeau.

**50.** Li et al., 1999.

**51.** "The Name Game: Business Cards an Essential Part of Operating in China," *The International Herald Tribune*, January 10, 2011.

**52.** Hall and Hall.

**53.** Robert Matthews, "Where East Can Never Meet West," *Financial Times*, October 21, 2005.

**54.** Hall and Hall.

**55.** Matthews, 2005.

**56.** Hecht, Andersen, and Ribeau.

**57.** Hall and Hall.

**58.** M. K. Nydell, *Understanding Arabs* (Yarmouth, ME: Intercultural Press, 1987).

**59.** Harris and Moran.

**60.** E. T. Hall, *The Hidden Dimension* (New York: Doubleday, 1966), p. 15.

**61.** Hall and Hall.

**62.** Ibid.

**63.** Based largely on the work of Nydell; and R. T. Moran and P. R. Harris, *Managing Cultural Synergy* (Houston: Gulf Publishing, 1982), pp. 81–82.

**64.** Ibid.

**65.** Hall and Hall.

**66.** D. C. Barnlund, "Public and Private Self in Communicating with Japan," *Business Horizons* (March–April 1989), pp. 32–40.

**67.** Hall and Hall.

**68.** A. Goldman, "The Centrality of 'Ningensei' to Japanese Negotiating and Interpersonal Relationships: Implications for U.S.–Japanese Communication," *International Journal of Intercultural Relations* 18, No. 1 (1994).

**69.** Jean-Louis Barsoux and Peter Lawrence, "The Making of a French Manager," *Harvard Business Review* (July–August 1991), pp. 58–67.

**70.** D. Barboza, "Microsoft Forms Partnership with China's Leading Search Engine," www.nytimes.com, July 4, 2011.

**71.** D. Shand, "All Information Is Local: IT Systems Can Connect Every Corner of the Globe, But IT Managers Are Learning They Have to Pay Attention to Regional Differences," *Computerworld* 88 No. 1 (2000).

**72.** Shand.

**73.** Wilmott.

**74.** Barboza, July 4, 2011.

**75.** Doug Tsuruoka, "Hudong to Help Microsoft's Bing in Chinese Search," *Investor's Business Daily*," June 6, 2012.

**76.** Barboza, July 4, 2011.

**77.** T. Wilson, "B2B Links, European Style: Integrator Helps Applications Cross Language, Currency and Cultural Barriers," *InternetWeek*, October 9, 2000, p. 27.

**78.** Based on www.Businessfordiplomaticaction.org, accessed August 19, 2006.

**79.** R. B. Ruben, "Human Communication and Cross-Cultural Effectiveness," in *Intercultural Communication: A Reader*, L. Samovar and R. Porter, eds. (Belmont, CA: Wadsworth, 1985), p. 339.

**80.** D. Ruben and B. D. Ruben, "Cross-Cultural Personnel Selection Criteria, Issues and Methods," in *Handbook of Intercultural Training*, vol. 1, *Issues in Theory and Design*, D. Landis and R. W. Brislin, eds. (New York: Pergamon, 1983), pp. 155–175.

**81.** Young Yun Kim, *Communication and Cross-Cultural Adaptation: An Integrative Theory* (Clevedon, UK; Multilingual Matters, 1988).

# Chapter 6

# Exporting and Global Sourcing

**Learning Objectives** *After studying this chapter, you should be able to:*

**6.1** Understand exporting as a foreign market entry strategy.

**6.2** Describe how to manage export-import transactions.

**6.3** Explain identifying and working with foreign intermediaries.

**6.4** Understand outsourcing, global sourcing, and offshoring.

**6.5** Describe the benefits and risks of global sourcing.

**6.6** Understand global sourcing strategies and supply-chain management.

## Maersk and the Global Container Business

Despite huge technological change over recent decades, including advances in aviation technology, some 90 percent of traded goods are still shipped in large standard-sized containers. Indeed, the shipping container itself is one of the key innovations of the past century. Invented by U.S. trucking magnate Malcolm McLean in 1956, containers meant that goods were no longer shipped loose in wooden crates. This allowed goods to be shipped in huge volumes, slashing costs for exporters. It has driven global sourcing and offshoring of production and led to the globalization of supply chains, resulting in sharp reductions in production costs and prices to consumers.

Container shipping companies are key intermediaries in the exporting process and have made this an extremely attractive market entry strategy. The giant of this sector is Maersk Line—in 2018, it transported some 21 percent of global seaborne container freight. Founded in Denmark in 1904, Maersk is a conglomerate with activities across the transport and energy sector subsidiaries and offices in over 130 countries, and some 88,000 employees.

The resilience of the shipping container in an era of very rapid technological change is a testimony to its dramatic impact on export–import transactions. Nonetheless, the sector is vulnerable to downturns in global trade and fluctuating oil prices. Indeed, Maersk consolidated its dominant position as an intermediary for exporters during the financial crisis. It exploited its size to take advantage of overcapacity and buy ships at a discount and to optimize route networks. This allows it to operate at the lowest possible costs, passing on some of these efficiencies to customers through reduced prices and forcing rivals to operate at a loss to compete.

However, this resilience does not necessarily mean that the dominance of container shipping will continue. Enormous cargo ships emit huge amounts of greenhouse gases and are likely to come under increasing pressure to be more environmentally friendly. Indeed, pressure to be more fuel-efficient is affecting the speed at which vessels travel, which is slowing down shipping times considerably.

Although Maersk's management shares the sector's general pessimism about the future of container shipping,

*Source:* tcly/Shutterstock

it is positioning itself to remain competitive, ordering a new fleet of state-of-the-art larger ships in a bid to cut costs further. However, it faces the threat of rivals seeking to exploit its tactics, which risks eroding its dominance over coming years.

Container ships can still transport vastly greater volumes of goods than alternatives in air, rail, and road transport—there is little prospect of the container ceasing to be the key tool in managing global supply chains. This means that Maersk will remain a key intermediary for exporters around the world.

However, for it to continue to withstand competition from alternatives bolstered by improved infrastructure and technological innovation, the container shipping business will need to innovate. Its challenge over the coming decades is likely to be building larger and faster vessels that emit drastically reduced levels of greenhouse gases.

**AACSB and CKR Intangible Soft Skills to improve employability and success in the workplace:** Reflective Thinking, and Application of Knowledge.

## Questions

**6-1.** Why has container shipping been such a revolutionary and resilient phenomenon?

**6-2.** How has Maersk gained a competitive edge in this sector, and what are the key threats it is likely to face over the short to medium term?

**6-3.** Why might container shipping be more useful and important for exporters in some sectors than others?

*SOURCES:* Maersk, http://www.maersk.com/en/industries/transport; "Why Have Containers Boosted Trade So Much?," *The Economist*, May 21, 2013, http://www.economist.com/blogs/economist-explains/2013/05/economist-explains-14; "About Us—The Maersk Group, " http://www.maersk.com/en/the-maersk-group/about-us; "Denmark's Maersk Line Sticks to Its Market-leading Course," *Financial Times*, July 8, 2015, http://www.ft.com/cms/s/0/4a171548-2558-11e5-bd83-71cb60e8f08c.html#axzz3oo9t8ckx; "High-Tech Shipping Containers: Boxing Clever," *The Economist*, March 1, 2014, http://www.economist.com/news/science-and-technology/21597878-engineers-are-trying-upgrade-humble-shipping-container-boxing-clever; John Vidal, "True Scale of CO2 Emissions from Shipping Revealed," *The Guardian*, February 13, 2008, http://www.theguardian.com/environment/2008/feb/13/climate-change.pollution; John Vidal, "Modern Cargo Ships Slow to the Speed of the Sailing Clippers," *The Guardian*, July 25, 2010 http://www.theguardian.com/environment/2010/jul/25/slow-ships-cut-greenhouse-emissions; Sam Chambers, "Grim Outlook for Container Sector," Splash 24/7, October 9, 2015, http://splash247.com/grim-outlook-for-container-sector/; "Fast Container Ships: How to Shrink the World," The *Economist*, August 13, 2001, http://www.economist.com/node/738336.

This case was written by Neil Pyper, Coventry University.

Most economic activity takes place outside the home country; thus, it makes sense for firms to engage in international business. Internationalization helps companies grow and become more competitive. In this chapter, we provide a detailed overview on exporting. We examine the advantages and disadvantages of exporting and the steps that experienced firms follow to ensure success. We explore the nature of export intermediaries and examine the various methods that buyers use to pay for imported goods. We also examine exporting's counterpart: importing and global sourcing. Firms access enormous advantages by sourcing parts, finished products, and services from suppliers around the world. Let's begin by examining exporting.

**6.1** Understand exporting as a foreign market entry strategy.

**Exporting**
The strategy of producing products or services in one country (often the producer's home country) and selling and distributing them to customers located in other countries.

## Exporting as a Foreign Market Entry Strategy

**Exporting** refers to the strategy of producing products or services in one country (often the producer's home country) and selling and distributing them to customers located in other countries.

Because it entails limited risk, expense, and knowledge of foreign markets and transactions, most companies prefer exporting as their primary foreign market entry strategy. In a classical scenario, the focal firm retains its manufacturing activities in its home market but conducts marketing, distribution, and customer service activities in the export market. Today, many MNEs based in advanced economies locate manufacturing in another country—usually an emerging market such as China, Mexico, or Poland—and may then export these products to target markets. The firm may carry out marketing, distribution, and customer service in the export market, or commission an independent distributor to perform these activities on its behalf.

Exporting is the entry strategy responsible for the massive inflows and outflows that constitute global trade. Exporting generates enormous foreign-exchange earnings for nations. Japan has benefited from export earnings for years. China has become the leading exporter in various sectors, providing huge revenues to its economy. Smaller economies such as Belgium and Finland also add much to their foreign-exchange reserves from exporting and use them to pay for their sizable imports of foreign goods.

Exporting is a common entry strategy even among firms that have extensive international operations. Some of the world's largest exporters include aircraft manufacturers Airbus and Boeing. Big trading companies that deal in commodities, such as Cargill and Marubeni, are also large-scale exporters. Large manufacturing firms typically account for the largest overall value of exports and make up about three-quarters of the total value of exports from the United States. However, most exporting firms—more than 90 percent in most countries—are small and medium-sized enterprises (SMEs) with fewer than 500 employees.

As an entry strategy, exporting is very flexible. The exporter can both enter and withdraw from markets fairly easily with minimal risk and expense. Firms can develop production facilities at various foreign locations and export products to other countries.

The volume of world exports has grown enormously. As revealed in Exhibit 6.1, various manufacturing industries and firms depend heavily on international trade. The analysis is limited to large, publicly traded manufacturing companies in the United States. The data represent international sales from both the headquarters country and the firm's foreign subsidiaries. As reflected in the exhibit, many industries generate half or more of their total sales from foreign markets. Alongside Exxon Mobil, Advanced Micro Devices, Corning, and Abbott Laboratories, foreign markets account for more than two-thirds of the international sales of such firms as Apple, AstraZeneca, BHP Billiton, Bombardier, Daimler, Electrolux, and Rio Tinto.[1]

**EXHIBIT 6.1**

**International Sales Intensity of Typical U.S. Industries**

*Sources:* Patti Domm, "Shrinking Dollar Could Boost the Market and Make These Stocks Big Winners," *CNBC*, July 24, 2017, www.cnbc.com; *Forbes*, "The Global 2000," 2017, www.forbes.com; Hoovers corporate profiles, 2018, www.hoovers.com.

| Industry | Average International Sales in the Industry (as percentage of total sales) | Example Firm in the Industry | Example Firm's International Sales (as percentage of total sales) |
|---|---|---|---|
| Energy | 59% | Exxon Mobil | 66% |
| Information Technology | 57 | Advanced Micro Devices | 78 |
| Materials | 53 | Corning | 72 |
| Industrials | 45 | Caterpillar | 59 |
| Healthcare | 37 | Abbott Laboratories | 69 |
| Consumer Discretionary | 35 | Mattel | 40 |
| Consumer Staples | 34 | General Mills | 28 |

## Service Sector Exports

In most advanced economies, services are the largest component of economic activity. Services marketed abroad include travel, construction, engineering, education, banking, insurance, and entertainment. Hollywood film studios earn billions by exporting their movies and videos. Construction firms send their employees abroad to work on major construction projects. Accountants and engineers often provide their services through the Internet, by telephone and mail, and by visiting customers directly in their home countries. Insurance packages are created in a central location, such as London, and then exported by mail and the Internet to customers in other countries.

However, many *pure* services cannot be exported because they cannot be transported. You cannot box up a haircut and ship it overseas. Most retailing firms, such as Home Depot and Marks & Spencer, offer their services by establishing retail stores in their target markets. They internationalize through FDI because retailing requires direct contact with customers. Many services firms export *some* of what they produce but rely on other entry strategies to provide other offerings abroad. For example, Ernst & Young (www.ey.com) exports *some* accounting services by sending its employees abroad. It also undertakes FDI by setting up offices overseas and hiring local personnel to perform local accounting services.

International travel is usually considered a service export. When a Canadian citizen stays in a hotel in Brazil, the hotel is said to have exported its service to the foreigner. When an Australian citizen visits India to undergo a cataract operation—a trend known as medical tourism—it is counted as exporting in India's national accounts. In China, France, Spain and the United States, tourism generates more foreign exchange than exports of most categories of merchandise.[2]

Most services are delivered to foreign customers either through local representatives or agents or in conjunction with other entry strategies such as FDI, franchising, or licensing. The Internet provides the means to export some types of services, from airline tickets to architectural services. The Internet has helped make services the fastest-growing exporting sector.[3]

*Source:* eduardo gonzalez diaz/123rf

Vellus Products Inc. is a U.S.-based producer of grooming products for dogs, and exports to countries worldwide. It is one of many small and medium-sized enterprises that find success by internationalizing their unique products.

## Advantages of Exporting

- Increases overall sales volume and market share, and generates profit margins that are often more favorable than in the domestic market.
- Increases economies of scale, reducing per-unit costs of manufacturing.
- Diversifies customer base, reducing dependence on home markets.
- Stabilizes fluctuations in sales associated with economic cycles or seasonality of demand.
- Minimizes the cost of foreign market entry; the firm can use exporting to test new markets before committing greater resources through FDI.
- Minimizes risk and maximizes flexibility compared to other entry strategies.
- Leverages the capabilities of foreign distributors and other business partners located abroad.

## Disadvantages of Exporting

- Offers fewer opportunities to learn about customers, competitors, and other unique aspects of the foreign market because the firm does not establish a physical presence there (in contrast to FDI).
- The firm must acquire and dedicate capabilities to conduct complex transactions, which can strain organizational resources. Exporters must become proficient in international sales contracts and transactions, new financing methods, and logistics and documentation.
- Exposes the firm to tariffs and other trade barriers as well as fluctuations in exchange rates. Exporters can be priced out of foreign markets if shifting exchange rates make their products too costly to foreign buyers. For example, the U.S. dollar lost 10 percent in value against the European euro in 2017–2018. As the euro became more expensive in dollar terms, U.S. buyers reduced their imports of goods from Europe.

### A Systematic Approach to Exporting

Experienced managers use a systematic approach to successful exporting. Exhibit 6.2 highlights the steps in this process. Let's examine each in detail.

STEP ONE: ASSESS GLOBAL MARKET OPPORTUNITY    As a first step, management assesses the various global market opportunities available to the firm. Managers analyze the readiness of the firm to carry out exporting. They screen for the most attractive export markets. They identify qualified intermediaries and other foreign business partners. They estimate industry market

**EXHIBIT 6.2**

**A Systematic Approach to Exporting**

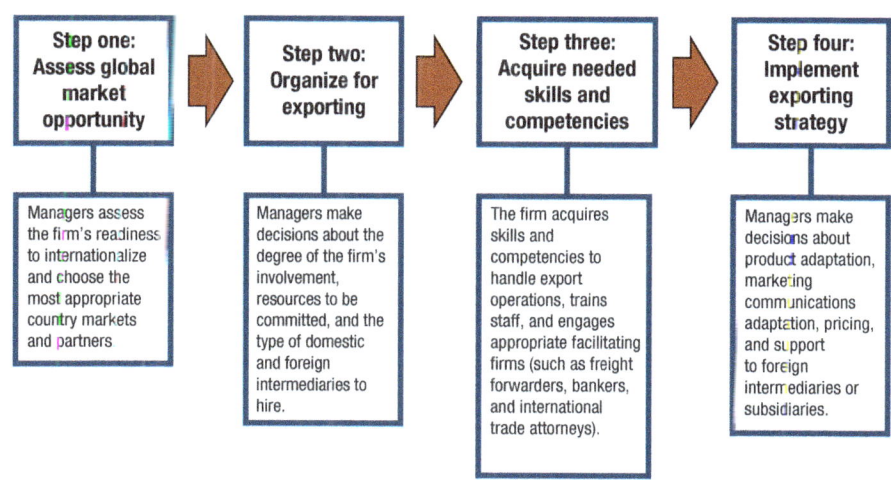

| Step one: Assess global market opportunity | Step two: Organize for exporting | Step three: Acquire needed skills and competencies | Step four: Implement exporting strategy |
|---|---|---|---|
| Managers assess the firm's readiness to internationalize and choose the most appropriate country markets and partners | Managers make decisions about the degree of the firm's involvement, resources to be committed, and the type of domestic and foreign intermediaries to hire. | The firm acquires skills and competencies to handle export operations, trains staff, and engages appropriate facilitating firms (such as freight forwarders, bankers, and international trade attorneys). | Managers make decisions about product adaptation, marketing communications adaptation, pricing, and support to foreign intermediaries or subsidiaries. |

potential and company sales potential. Participating in foreign trade shows is useful for identifying market potential and foreign intermediaries.

**STEP TWO: ORGANIZE FOR EXPORTING**   Next, managers ask: What types of managerial, financial, and productive resources should the firm commit to the export venture? What timetable should the firm follow to achieve exporting goals? To what degree should the firm rely on domestic and foreign intermediaries to implement exporting?

Exhibit 6.3 illustrates alternative organizational arrangements in exporting. **Indirect exporting** is accomplished by contracting with intermediaries located in the firm's home market. Smaller exporters, or those new to international business, typically hire an export management company or a trading company based in their home country. These intermediaries assume responsibility for finding foreign buyers, shipping products, and getting paid. For most firms, indirect exporting's main advantage is the ability to internationalize with lower risk, less complexity, and at lower cost, than direct exporting.

In contrast, **direct exporting** is typically achieved by contracting with intermediaries located in the foreign market. The foreign intermediaries serve as an extension of the exporter, negotiating on behalf of the exporter and assuming such responsibilities as local supply-chain management, pricing, and customer service. The main advantage of direct exporting is that it gives the exporter greater control over the export process, and potential for higher profits, as well as a closer relationship with foreign buyers and the marketplace. However, the exporter also must dedicate substantial time, personnel, and corporate resources to developing and managing export operations.

Key considerations for choosing between direct or indirect exporting are:

- The time, capital, and expertise that management is willing to commit.
- Strategic importance of the foreign market.
- Nature of the firm's products, including the need for after-sales support.
- Availability of capable foreign intermediaries in the target market.

Note that many firms do both direct and indirect exporting.

**Indirect exporting**
Exporting that is accomplished by contracting with intermediaries located in the firm's home market.

**Direct exporting**
Exporting that is accomplished by contracting with intermediaries located in the foreign market.

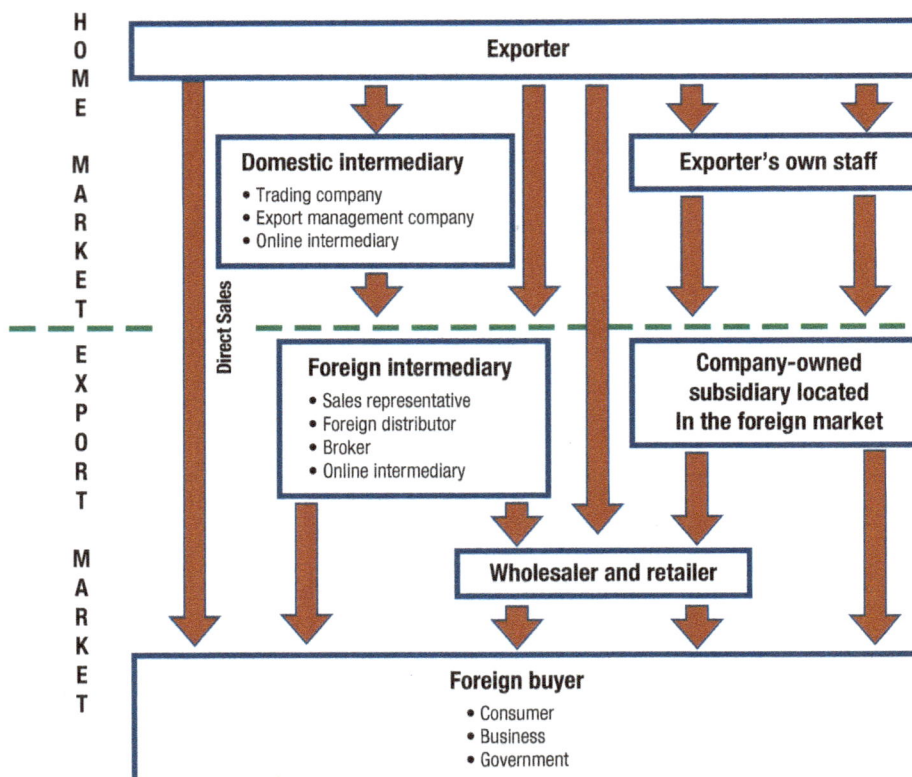

**EXHIBIT 6.3**

**Alternative Organizational Arrangements for Exporting**

*Source:* Jules Selmes/Pearson Education Ltd

China is a major exporter of machinery, furniture, and other goods. Galeria Kaufhof and other department stores worldwide source much of their apparel and footwear from exporting manufacturers in China.

**Company-owned subsidiary**

A representative office of the focal firm that handles marketing, physical distribution, promotion, and customer service activities in the foreign market.

At a more advanced stage, the firm may establish a sales office or a **company-owned subsidiary** in the foreign market to handle marketing, physical distribution, promotion, and customer service activities. Such a subsidiary allows the firm to manage major tasks in the market directly, such as attending trade fairs, doing market research, engaging distributors, and finding and serving customers. Companies tend to establish subsidiaries in markets that are large or strategically important. At the extreme, the firm may establish distribution centers and warehouses or a full-function marketing subsidiary staffed with a local sales force.

**STEP THREE: ACQUIRE NEEDED SKILLS AND COMPETENCIES** Export transactions require specialized skills and competencies in areas such as product development, distribution, logistics, finance, contract law, and currency management. Also useful are foreign language skills and the ability to interact well in foreign cultures. Fortunately, *facilitators* are available to assist firms that lack specific competencies. They include companies such as banks, freight forwarders, and international trade consultants.

**STEP FOUR: IMPLEMENT EXPORTING STRATEGY** In the final stage, the firm implements and manages its exporting strategy, often requiring management to refine approaches to suit market conditions. *Product adaptation* means modifying a product to make it fit the needs and tastes of the buyers in the target market. When Microsoft markets computer software in Japan, the software must be written in Japanese. Even Vellus, which makes dog-grooming products, must vary the ones it sells abroad due to differing conditions. The dog brushes and shampoos that Vellus sells in the United States may not sell in the United Kingdom, and vice versa. In export markets with many competitors, the exporter needs to adapt its products to gain competitive advantage. In addition to adapting products, the firm also might adapt its pricing and distribution approaches.

### Importing

**Importing or global sourcing**

The procurement of products or services from independent suppliers or company-owned subsidiaries located abroad for consumption in the home country or a third country

The counterpart of exporting is **importing** or **global sourcing**, also known as *global procurement*, or global purchasing, the strategy of buying products and services from foreign sources and bringing them into the home country or a third country. The fundamentals of exporting, payments, and financing also apply to importing. Exporting and importing collectively refer to *international trade*. Exhibit 6.4 summarizes the top trading partners of selected countries and the European Union (EU), counting their combined imports and exports. As single countries, Canada and the United States are each other's top trading partners, suggesting that much international trade is regional rather than global. China is a top trading partner with the United States, mostly due to its massive merchandise exports. The EU trades most with China and the United States. Overall, the exhibit reveals that most international trade occurs among the advanced economies and increasingly between the advanced economies and emerging markets.

**6.2** Describe how to manage export-import transactions.

## Managing Export-Import Transactions

When comparing domestic and international business transactions, key differences arise in documentation and shipping.

**Documentation**

Official forms and other paperwork required in export transactions for shipping and customs procedures.

### Documentation

**Documentation** refers to the official forms and other paperwork required in export transactions for shipping and customs procedures. The exporter usually first issues a *quotation* or *pro forma invoice* upon request by potential customers. It informs them about the price and description of the exporter's product or service. The *commercial invoice* is the actual demand for payment the exporter issues when a sale is made.

## Canada: Top Trading Partners

## China: Top Trading Partners

## European Union: Top Trading Partners

## United States: Top Trading Partners

**EXHIBIT 6.4**

**Top Trading Partners of Selected Countries**

*Note:* Values shown represent the sum of merchandise exports and imports in billions of U.S. dollars for 2017.

*Sources:* European Commission at http://ec.europa.eu; Statistics Canada at www.statcan.gc.ca/tables-tableaux/sum-som/l01/cst01/gblec02a-eng.htm; U.S. Department of Commerce at www.census.gov/foreign-trade; U.S.–China Business Council at www.uschina.org; World Trade Organization, at http://stat.wto.org

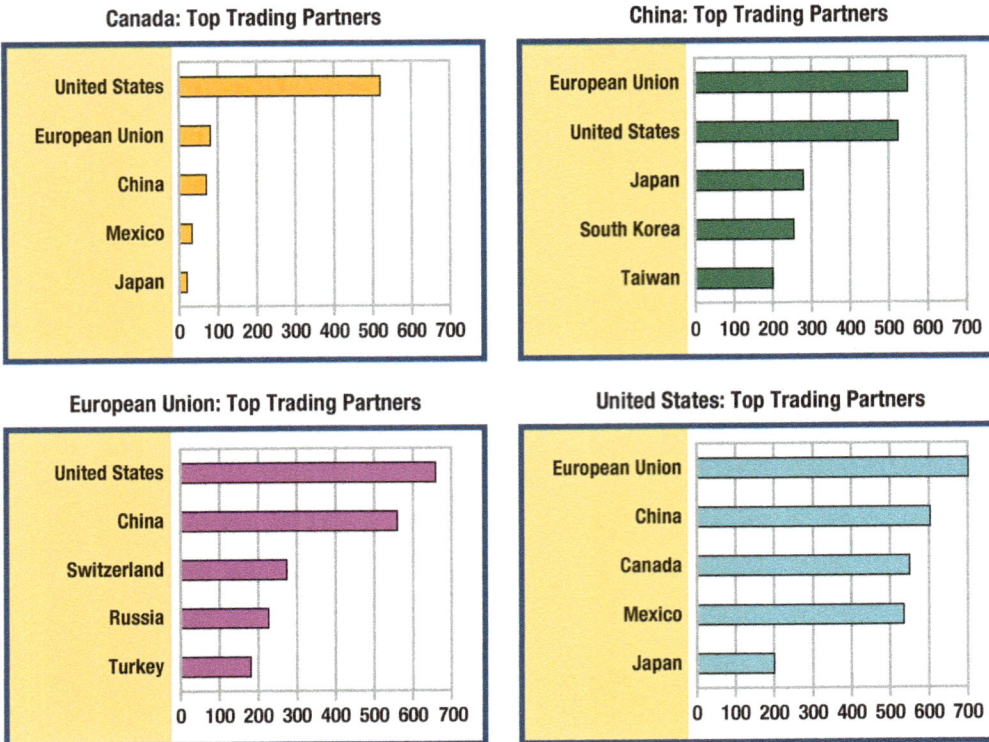

Firms typically distribute exported goods by ocean transport, although some use air transport. The *bill of lading* is the basic contract between exporter and shipper. It authorizes a shipping company to transport the goods to the buyer's destination and serves as the importer's receipt and proof of title for purchase of the goods. The *certificate of origin* is the birth certificate of the goods being shipped and indicates the country of origin. In addition, exporters usually must provide a full description of the products being shipped. Government authorities use this information to find out the content of shipments, to control exports, and to compile statistics on the goods entering and leaving the country. Exporters usually purchase an *insurance certificate* to protect the exported goods against damage, loss, pilferage (theft), and, in some cases, delay. The exporter typically entrusts the preparation of documents to an international freight forwarder. Freight forwarders function like travel agents for cargo.

### Shipping and Incoterms

Export transactions involve shipping products from the exporter's factory to a nearby seaport or airport. From there they travel by ship or airplane to a foreign port and are then transferred to land-based transportation and delivered to the customer. Some shipments to bordering countries are transported entirely overland by rail or truck. Exporters incur transportation costs and carry insurance against damage or loss during transit.

In the past, disputes sometimes arose over who should pay the cost of freight and insurance in international transactions, the foreign buyer or the seller (that is, the exporter). To eliminate such disputes, the International Chamber of Commerce (www.iccwbo.org) developed a system of universal, standard terms of sale and delivery, known as **Incoterms** (short for "International Commerce Terms"). Commonly used in international sales contracts, Incoterms specify how the buyer and the seller share the cost of freight and insurance and at which point the buyer takes title to the goods.

For example, *EXW* is an Incoterm that refers to "ex works (named place)." It implies that delivery of the goods takes place at the seller's premises or another named place, such as a factory or a warehouse. EXW represents minimal obligation for the seller because the buyer bears all costs and risks involved in claiming the goods from the seller's premises. The buyer arranges all shipping.

*FOB* refers to "free on board (port of shipment)." It means that delivery will take place when the goods pass the ship's rail at the named port of shipment, that is, the port of origin in the seller's

**Incoterms**
Universally accepted terms of sale that specify how the buyer and the seller share the cost of freight and insurance in an international transaction and at which point the buyer takes title to the goods.

*Source:* Martin Sookias/Pearson Education Ltd

Large-scale exporting results in global trade and generates enormous earnings. Airbus is Europe's leading exporter of commercial aircraft. These aircraft are at Leipzig Airport, Germany.

home country. In this case, the buyer bears all the costs and risks of shipping from the point of delivery. The seller clears the goods for export, but the buyer must arrange shipping from the port of shipment and onward.

*CIF* is an Incoterm that means "cost, insurance, and freight (named port of destination)." It implies that the seller pays the cargo insurance and delivery of goods to a named port of destination. At that point, responsibility for the goods transfers from the seller to the buyer. From that point onward, the buyer is responsible for customs clearance and other costs and risks.

## Payment Methods in Exporting and Importing

In the course of business transactions, receiving payment is relatively complicated in international business. Foreign currencies may be unstable. Governments may be reluctant to allow funds to leave the country. In the event of disputes, local laws and enforcement systems may favor local companies over foreign firms.

In advanced economies and many emerging markets, firms may extend credit to buyers with the assurance that they will be paid. It is typical for exporters to allow these customers several months to make payments or to structure payment on *open account*. In trading with some developing economies, however, exporters extend credit cautiously because of the risk that some customers may fail to pay.

There are several payment methods in international business. Listed roughly in order from most to least secure from the exporter's perspective, they are: *cash in advance, letter of credit, open account*, and *countertrade*. We explain each of these payment methods next.

**CASH IN ADVANCE**   When the exporter receives cash in advance, payment is collected before the goods are shipped to the customer. This approach is advantageous to the exporter, which need not worry about collection problems and can access the funds almost immediately upon concluding the sale. From the buyer's standpoint, however, cash in advance is risky and may cause cash-flow problems. The buyer may hesitate for fear the exporter will not follow through with shipment, particularly if the buyer does not know the exporter well. For these reasons, cash in advance is unpopular with buyers and tends to discourage sales. Exporters who insist on it tend to lose out to competitors who offer more favorable payment terms.

**Letter of credit**
Contract between the banks of a buyer and a seller that ensures payment from the buyer to the seller upon receipt of an export shipment.

**LETTER OF CREDIT**   A documentary letter of credit, or simply a letter of credit, resolves most of the problems associated with cash in advance. Letter of credit is popular with experienced exporters because it protects the interests of both seller and buyer. Essentially, a **letter of credit** is a contract between the banks of the buyer and the seller that ensures payment from the buyer to the seller upon receipt of an export shipment. It amounts to a substitution of each bank's name and credit for the name and credit of the buyer and the seller. The system works because virtually all banks have established relationships with correspondent banks around the world.

An *irrevocable letter of credit* cannot be canceled without agreement by both buyer and seller. The selling firm will be paid as long as it fulfills its part of the agreement. The letter of credit immediately establishes trust between buyer and seller. The letter of credit also specifies the documents the exporter is required to present, such as a bill of lading, commercial invoice, and certificate of insurance. Before making a payment, the buyer's bank verifies that all documents meet the requirements the buyer and seller agreed to in the letter of credit. If not, the discrepancy must be resolved before the bank makes the payment.

Exhibit 6.5 presents the typical cycle of an international sale through a letter of credit. As shown in the exhibit:

1. An Exporter signs a contract for sale of goods to a foreign buyer, the Importer.
2. The Importer asks its bank (the Importer's Bank) to open a letter of credit in favor of the Exporter, the beneficiary of the credit.

**EXHIBIT 6.5**
**Letter of Credit Cycle**

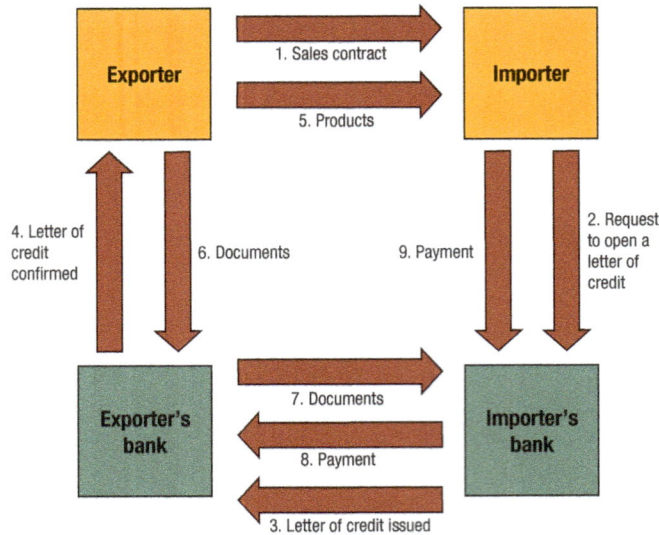

3. The Importer's Bank notifies the Exporter's Bank that a letter of credit has been issued.
4. The Exporter's Bank confirms the validity of the letter of credit.
5. The Exporter prepares and ships the products to the Importer as specified in the letter of credit.
6. The Exporter presents the shipment documents to its bank, the Exporter's Bank, which examines them to ensure that they fully comply with the terms of the letter of credit. The documents typically include an invoice, bill of lading, and insurance certificate, as specified in the letter of credit.
7. The Exporter's Bank sends the documents to the Importer's Bank, which similarly examines them to ensure that they comply fully with the letter of credit.
8. Upon confirmation that everything is in order, the Importer's Bank makes full payment for the goods to the Exporter through the Exporter's Bank.
9. The Importer makes full payment to its bank within the time period granted, which, in many countries, can extend to several months.

A related payment method is the *draft*. Similar to a check, the draft is a financial instrument that instructs a bank to pay a precise amount of a specific currency to the bearer on demand or at a future date. For both letters of credit and drafts, the buyer must make payment upon presentation of documents that convey title to the purchased goods and confirm that specific steps have been taken to prepare the goods and their shipment to the buyer. Letters of credit and drafts can be paid immediately or at a later date. In addition, the exporter can sell any drafts and letters of credit in its possession to avoid having to wait weeks or months to be paid for its exports.

**OPEN ACCOUNT**   When the exporter uses an *open account*, the buyer pays the exporter at some future time following receipt of the goods. It is similar to the way a retail customer pays a department store on account for products he or she has purchased. Because of the risk involved, exporters use this approach only with customers of long-standing or excellent credit, or with a subsidiary the exporter owns. The exporter simply bills the customer, who is expected to pay under agreed terms at some future time. Open accounts are risky, and the firm should structure such payment methods with care.

**COUNTERTRADE**   **Countertrade** refers to paying for goods or services using other goods or services when conventional means of payment are difficult or unavailable. Similar to barter, countertrade is especially common when dealing with governments in developing economies and emerging markets. In a typical deal, the focal firm is a Western company, say General Electric (GE). It wishes to sell its products or technology—for example, jet engines—to a developing-country government. If a developing economy's government falls short of hard currency, for example, it may require a foreign seller to accept some local products as partial payment for purchased goods.

Typically, the products that companies in developing countries offer are commodities such as agricultural grains, minerals, or manufactured goods. If a firm agrees to take these products, it

**Countertrade**
An international business transaction where all or partial payments are made in kind rather than cash.

**Barter**
A type of countertrade in which goods are directly exchanged without the transfer of any money.

**Compensation deals**
A type of countertrade in which payment is in both goods and cash.

**Counterpurchase**
A type of countertrade with two distinct contracts. In the first, the seller agrees to a set price for goods and receives cash from the buyer. This first deal is contingent on a second in which the seller agrees to purchase goods from the buyer for the same amount as in the first contract or a set percentage of same.

**Buy-back agreement**
A type of countertrade in which the seller agrees to supply technology or equipment to construct a facility and receives payment in the form of goods the facility produces.

must arrange to sell them to convert the goods to cash. Compared to transactions in which buyers pay with cash, countertrade is complicated. Transactions can take years to complete. Philip Morris exported cigarettes to Russia for which it received industrial chemicals as payment. It shipped the chemicals to China and received glassware in exchange that it then sold for cash in North America.

Some experts claim that countertrade accounts for as much as one-third of all world trade. Countertrade deals are common in large-scale government procurement projects. Firms based in developing economies that want to do international business often need to develop countertrade capabilities.

There are four main types of countertrade:

- **Barter** is the direct exchange of goods without any money. Though less common today, barter is still used (even in domestic trade) in straightforward, one-shot deals. It requires a single contract (rather than two or more contracts typical of other forms), has a short time span (other countertrade deals may stretch over several years), and is less complicated (other forms usually require managerial commitment and additional resources).
- **Compensation deals** include payment in both goods and cash. For example, a company may sell its equipment to the government of Brazil and receive half the payment in hard currency and the other half in Brazilian merchandise.
- **Counterpurchase**, also known as a back-to-back transaction or offset agreement, requires two distinct contracts. In the first, the seller agrees to a set price for goods and receives cash from the buyer. This first deal is contingent on a second contract in which the seller also agrees to purchase goods from the buyer (or produce and assemble a certain proportion of goods in the buyer's country) for the same cash amount as the first transaction or a set percentage of it. If the two exchanges are not of equal value, the difference can be paid in cash. Counterpurchase is common in the defense industry in sales of military hardware.
- **Buy-back agreement** arises when the seller agrees to supply technology or equipment to construct a facility and receives payment in the form of goods the facility produces. For example, the seller might design and build a factory in the buyer's country to manufacture tractors. The seller is compensated by receiving finished tractors from the factory it built, which it then sells in world markets. In essence, the original transaction trades goods and services that produce other goods and services, which are then received in payment. Product buy-back agreements may require several years to complete and therefore entail substantial risk.

---

### Firms can encounter numerous problems in countertrade

- The goods the customer offers may be inferior in quality, with limited sales potential in international markets.
- Putting a market value on the goods the customer offers may prove difficult, especially if they are commodities or of low quality. In addition, the buyer may not have the opportunity to inspect the goods or analyze their marketability before the sale.
- The parties to countertrade transactions tend to pad their prices. As a result, the cash the seller receives upon selling received goods may prove less than expected.
- Countertrade is usually complex, cumbersome, and time-consuming. Deals are often difficult to bring to conclusion.
- Government rules can make countertrade highly bureaucratic and often prove frustrating for the exporting firm.

---

If countertrade is so risky, why do many firms use it? First, the alternative may be no trade at all. For example, some national governments require countertrade as a means of obtaining needed goods. Some firms use countertrade to get a foothold in new markets or to access new sources of supply. In the mining industry, for example, certain types of minerals are available only in developing economies. Mining rights may be available only to firms willing to countertrade. Finally, many firms use countertrade as a way to repatriate profits frozen in a foreign subsidiary's blocked accounts. Otherwise unable to access its funds, the firm will scout the local market for products it can successfully export. General Motors' former Motors Trading subsidiary was created to generate trade credits—that is, sell its vehicles in return for contributing to exports of merchandise originating from that country.

## Financing

Exporters often need to obtain financing to support international sales. Financing implies that the buyer or seller obtains a short-term loan to fulfill an export sale. The ability to offer attractive payment terms is often necessary to generate sales. If an SME receives a large order from a foreign buyer, access to the working capital provided from financing can determine the firm's ability to fill the order.

Exporters typically obtain financing from commercial banks, distribution intermediaries, buyers, or suppliers. In some cases, the exporter can sell its accounts receivable to a specialized financial institution, a process known as *forfaiting*.

Large exporters with foreign subsidiaries often employ *intra-corporate financing*. The MNE may allow its subsidiary to retain a higher-than-usual level of its own profits to finance export sales. The parent firm may provide loans, equity investments, and trade credit (such as extensions on accounts payable) as funding for the international selling activities of its subsidiaries. The parent can also guarantee loans obtained from foreign banks by its subsidiaries. Finally, large MNEs can often access equity financing by selling corporate bonds or shares in stock markets.

Numerous government agencies offer programs to assist exporters with their financing needs. Some provide loans or grants to the exporter. Others offer guarantee programs that require the participation of a bank or other approved lender. Under such arrangements, the government pledges to repay a loan a commercial bank makes if the importer cannot repay.

In the United States, the *Export-Import Bank* (Ex-Im Bank; www.exim.gov) is a government agency that issues credit insurance to protect firms against default on exports sold under short-term credit. Canada's *Export Development Corporation* (www.edc.ca), Brazil's *Banco Nacional de Desenvolvimento Economico e Social* (www.bndes.gov.br), and India's *Export Credit & Guarantee Corporation* (www.ecgc.in) provide services similar to those of the Ex-Im Bank. Government assistance programs are especially useful to SMEs, which often cannot obtain financing from other sources. For example, the U.S. *Small Business Administration* (www.sba.gov) helps small exporters obtain trade financing.

Four key factors influence the ability of an exporter or importer to obtain financing for export sales.

- *Creditworthiness of the exporter.* Small or inexperienced firms may encounter difficulty in obtaining bank financing, especially large loans.
- *Creditworthiness of the importer.* Some buyers, particularly from developing economies or countries with currency controls, may be unable to secure financing.
- *Riskiness of the sale.* Banks are reluctant to loan funds for risky transactions. International sales are usually more risky than domestic ones. Riskiness depends the value and marketability of the good being sold, uncertainty of the sale, conditions in the buyer's country, and likelihood that the loan will be repaid.
- *Timing of the sale* influences the cost of financing. The exporter usually wants to be paid as soon as possible, whereas the buyer prefers to delay payment. Banks may hesitate to finance a sale if the time to complete it is considerable.

Creditworthiness, risk, and timing also affect the cost of financing, which in turn affects the pricing and profitability of sales and the payment terms the exporter can offer.

## Identifying and Working with Foreign Intermediaries

**6.3** Explain identifying and working with foreign intermediaries.

As the opening case highlights, success in exporting usually depends on establishing strong relationships with distributors, sales representatives, and other foreign market intermediaries. Distribution channel intermediaries are physical distribution and marketing service providers in the value chain for focal firms. They move products and services in the home country and abroad and perform key downstream functions in the target market. For most exporters, relying on an independent foreign distributor is a low-cost way to enter foreign markets. The intermediary's intimate knowledge, contacts, and services in the local market can provide a strong support system, especially for small or inexperienced exporters. Intermediaries can be based in the foreign target market or in the home country, or they might operate through the Internet.

Most intermediaries are based in the exporter's target market. They provide many services, including conducting market research, appointing local representatives, exhibiting products at trade shows, arranging local transportation for cargo, and clearing products through customs. Intermediaries organize local marketing activities, including product adaptation, advertising, selling, and after-sales service. Many finance sales and extend credit. In short, intermediaries based in the foreign market can function like the exporter's local partner, handling all needed local business functions.

A **foreign distributor** is a foreign market–based intermediary that works under contract for an exporter. The foreign distributor takes title to and distributes the exporter's products in a national market or territory. It often performs marketing functions such as sales, promotion, and after-sales service. Foreign distributors are essentially independent wholesalers that purchase merchandise from exporters (at a discount) and resell it after adding a profit margin. They promote, sell, and maintain an inventory of the exporter's products in the foreign market. They also typically maintain substantial physical resources and provide financing, technical support, and after-sales service for the product, relieving the exporter of these functions abroad.

A **manufacturer's representative** is an intermediary contracted by the exporter to represent and sell its merchandise or services in a designated country or territory. Manufacturer's representatives go by various names—agents, sales representatives, or service representatives. In essence, they act as contracted sales personnel in a designated target market on behalf of the exporter. They are usually given broad powers and autonomy. Manufacturer's representatives do not take title to the goods they represent and are most often compensated by commission. They do not maintain physical facilities, marketing, or customer support capabilities, so the exporter must handle these functions.

Some intermediaries are domestically based. Wholesaler importers bring in products or commodities from foreign countries for sale in the home market, re-export, or use in the manufacture of finished products. Manufacturers also import a range of raw materials, parts, and components used in the production of higher value-added products. They may also import a complementary collection of products and services to supplement or augment their own product range. Retailers such as department stores, specialized stores, mail-order houses, and catalogue firms import many of the products they sell. A trip to retailers such as Best Buy, Canadian Tire, or Marks & Spencer reveals that most of their offerings are sourced from abroad, especially from low labor-cost countries.

A **trading company** serves as an intermediary that engages in import and export of various commodities, products, and services. It assumes the international marketing function on behalf of producers, especially those with limited international business experience. Manufacturers that lack the will or resources to sell their products internationally often employ trading companies. Large trading companies operate much like agents, coordinating sales of countless products in markets worldwide. Typically, they are high-volume, low-margin resellers compensated by adding profit margins to what they sell. In Japan, large trading companies are known as *sogo shosha*. In Japan and China alike, trading companies usually engage in both exporting and importing and are specialists in low-margin, high-volume trading.

A domestically based intermediary is the **export management company (EMC)**, which acts as an export agent on behalf of a (usually inexperienced) client company. In return for a commission, an EMC finds export customers on behalf of the client firm, negotiates terms of sale, and arranges for international shipping. Although typically much smaller than a trading company, some EMCs have well-established networks of foreign distributors in place that allow exported products immediate access to foreign markets. Because of the indirect nature of the export sale, the manufacturer runs the risk of losing control over how its products are marketed abroad, with possible negative consequences for its international image.

Some focal firms use the Internet to sell products directly to customers rather than going through traditional wholesale and retail channels. By eliminating traditional intermediaries, companies can sell their products more cheaply and faster. This benefits SMEs in particular because they usually lack the substantial resources needed to undertake conventional international operations.

Countless online intermediaries broker transactions between buyers and sellers worldwide. Emergent technologies offer—and sometimes require—new roles that intermediaries have not taken previously. Many traditional retailers establish websites or link with online service

**Foreign distributor**
A foreign market–based intermediary that works under contract for an exporter, takes title to, and distributes the exporter's products in a national market or territory, often performing marketing functions such as sales, promotion, and after-sales service.

**Manufacturer's representative**
An intermediary contracted by the exporter to represent and sell its merchandise or services in a designated country or territory.

**Trading company**
An intermediary that engages in import and export of a variety of commodities, products, and services.

**Export management company (EMC)**
A domestically based intermediary that acts as an export agent on behalf of a client company.

providers to create an electronic presence. The electronic sites of retailers such as Tesco (www. tesco.com) and Walmart (www.walmart.com) complement existing physical distribution infrastructure and bring more customers into physical outlets.

## Finding Foreign Intermediaries

Direct exporters often struggle to find appropriate intermediaries in target countries. Various sources are available for finding intermediaries abroad, including:

- Country and regional business directories, such as Kompass (Europe), Bottin International (worldwide), and the Japanese Trade Directory.
- Trade associations that support specific industries, such as the National Furniture Manufacturers Association or the National Association of Automotive Parts Manufacturers.
- Government departments, ministries, and agencies charged with assisting economic and trade development, such as Austrade in Australia (www.austrade.gov.au), Export Development Canada (www.edc.ca), and the International Trade Administration of the U.S. Department of Commerce (www.trade.gov).
- Commercial attachés in embassies and consulates abroad.
- Freight forwarders and trade consultants with specific knowledge about the exporter's target markets.

The exporter should consider attending a trade fair in the target country. Trade fairs are not only excellent sites to meet potential intermediaries, they also provide the means to become familiar with key players in the local industry and generally to learn about the target market. Visiting the target market is often the best way to identify and qualify intermediaries. On-site visits afford managers direct exposure to the market and opportunities to meet prospective intermediaries. Managers can also inspect the facilities as well as gauge the capabilities, technical personnel, and sales capabilities of prospective intermediaries. Once they have narrowed the choices, experienced exporters often request prospective intermediaries to prepare a business plan for the proposed venture. Its quality and sophistication provide a basis for judging the candidate's true capabilities.

## Working with Foreign Intermediaries

In exporting, the most typical intermediary is the foreign-based independent distributor. The exporter relies on the distributor for much of the marketing, physical distribution, and customer service activities in the export market. Experienced exporters go to great lengths to build relational assets—that is, high-quality, enduring business and social relationships—with key intermediaries and facilitators abroad. Sharon Doherty (in the opening case) succeeded in exporting by developing close relationships with qualified foreign distributors. Although competitors can usually replicate the exporter's other competitive attributes, such as product features or marketing skills, strong ties with competent foreign intermediaries are built over time and provide the exporter with an enduring competitive advantage.

The firm should strive to cultivate mutually beneficial, bonding relations with key intermediaries. To create a positive working relationship, the exporter should be sensitive to the intermediary's objectives and aspirations. The exporter should build solidarity by demonstrating solid commitment, remaining reliable, and building trust. This requires developing a good understanding of the intermediary's needs and working earnestly to address them. In general, foreign intermediaries expect exporters to provide:

- Good, reliable products for which there is a ready market.
- Products that provide significant profits.

Source: james3035/123RF GB Ltd

Working closely with foreign intermediaries helps green car manufacturers sell electric vehicles around the world. This charging station is in Korea.

- Opportunities to handle other product lines.
- Support for marketing communications, advertising, and product warranties.
- A payment method that does not unduly burden the intermediary.
- Training for intermediary staff and the opportunity to visit the exporter's facilities (at the exporter's expense) to gain firsthand knowledge of the exporter's operations.
- Help establishing after-sales service facilities, including training of local technical representatives and the means to replace defective parts, as well as a ready supply of spare parts, to maintain or repair the products.

The exporter in turn has expectations its intermediaries should meet. Exhibit 6.6 summarizes the selection criteria that experienced exporters use to qualify prospective intermediaries.

## When Intermediary Relations Go Bad

Despite good intentions, disputes can arise between the exporter and its intermediaries on issues such as compensation, marketing practices, after-sales service, inventory levels, and adapting the product for local customers. In anticipation of such disagreements, exporters generally establish a contract-based, legal relationship with the partner. Some firms require candidate intermediaries to undergo a probationary period during which they evaluate performance. If it is suboptimal or if disputes appear likely to emerge, the exporter may impose special requirements or even end the relationship.

The contract between an exporter and its intermediary contains various elements. A typical contract specifies the:

- Duration of the relationship between the exporter and the intermediary.
- Sales territory granted to the intermediary.
- Manner in which the intermediary is expected to handle the product (e.g., regarding adaptation, pricing, advertising).
- Tasks and performance goals that the intermediary is expected to achieve.
- Tasks and responsibilities that the exporter is expected to perform.
- Process to be followed for resolving disputes.
- Conditions under which the relationship with the intermediary can be terminated.

**EXHIBIT 6.6**

**Criteria for Evaluating Export Intermediaries**

*Sources:* Based on Davide Papa and Lorna Elliott, *International Trade and the Successful Intermediary* (New York: Routledge, 2016); International Trade Administration, *Basic Guide to Exporting: The Official Government Resource for Small and Medium-Sized Businesses* (Washington, DC: International Trade Administration, 2016); International Trade Administration, "Finding Foreign Buyers: Choosing a Sales Channel," March 16, 2018, www.export.gov.

| Intermediary Dimension | Evaluation Criteria |
|---|---|
| *Organizational Strengths* | • Ability to finance sales and growth in the market<br>• Ability to provide financing to customers<br>• Management team quality<br>• Reputation with customers<br>• Connections with influential people or government agencies in the market |
| *Product-Related Factors* | • Knowledge about the exporter's product<br>• Quality and superiority of all product lines handled by the intermediary<br>• Ability to ensure security for patents and other intellectual property rights<br>• Extent to which intermediary handles competing product lines |
| *Marketing Capabilities* | • Experience with the product line and target customers<br>• Extent of geographic coverage provided in the target market<br>• Quality and quantity of sales force<br>• Ability to formulate and implement marketing plans |
| *Managerial Commitment* | • Percent of intermediary's business consisting of a single supplier<br>• Willingness to maintain inventory sufficient to fully serve the market<br>• Commitment to achieving exporter's sales targets |

Exporters should find out about the legal requirements for termination in advance and specify the intermediary's rights for compensation. In many countries, commercial regulations favor local intermediaries and may require the exporter to indemnify—that is, compensate—the intermediary even if there is just cause for termination. In some countries, legal contracts may prove insufficient to protect the exporter's interests. Many countries in Africa and Latin America lack strong legal frameworks, which can make contracts hard to enforce.

Just as in their domestic operations, exporters occasionally encounter problems with buyers or intermediaries who default on payment. In terms of payment mechanisms, cash in advance or a letter of credit is usually best. The exporter can also buy insurance to cover commercial credit risks. If a default happens, the exporter's best recourse is to negotiate with the offending party. At the extreme, the exporter may pursue litigation, arbitration, or other legal means for enforcing payment on a sale.

## Outsourcing, Global Sourcing, and Offshoring

When firms import needed goods or services, they engage in global sourcing. Before delving into this important topic, let's first review outsourcing. Specifically, **outsourcing** refers to the procurement of selected value-adding activities, including production of intermediate goods or finished products, from external independent suppliers. Firms outsource because they are not superior at performing *all* value-chain activities, and it is more cost effective to outsource these activities. For example, Harley Davidson sources motorcycle helmets from suppliers in China.

**Business process outsourcing (BPO)** refers to the procurement of services. When firms engage in BPO, they procure services such as accounting, human resource functions, IT services, or technical support, from external suppliers.[4] Firms contract with third-party service providers to reduce the cost of performing service tasks. Typically, such tasks fall outside the firm's core competencies or are not critical to maintaining its competitive position in the marketplace. BPO can be divided into two categories. *Back-office activities* include internal, upstream business functions such as payroll and billing. *Front-office activities* include downstream, customer-related services such as marketing or technical support.

In undertaking outsourcing, managers face two key decisions: which, if any, value-chain activities should be outsourced; and where in the world these activities should be performed.

Let's consider these choices.

### Decision 1: Outsource or Not?

Managers must decide between *internalization* and *externalization*—whether each value-adding activity should be conducted in house or by an external, independent supplier. In business, this is traditionally known as the *make* or *buy* decision: "Should we make a product or perform a value-chain activity ourselves, or should we obtain it from an outside contractor?"

Firms usually internalize those value-chain activities they consider part of their *core competencies*, those that they perform particularly well or that use proprietary knowledge they want to control. Canon uses its core competencies in precision mechanics, fine optics, and microelectronics to produce some of the world's best cameras, printers, and copiers. It usually performs R&D and product design itself to reduce the risk of divulging proprietary knowledge to competitors and to generate continuous improvement in these competencies. By contrast, firms will usually source from *external* suppliers when they can obtain non-core products, components, or services at lower cost or from suppliers specialized in providing them.

### Decision 2: Where in the World Should Value-Adding Activities Be Located?

A second key decision that firms face is whether to keep each value-adding activity in the home country or locate it in a foreign country. **Configuration of value-adding activity** refers to the pattern or geographic arrangement of locations where the firm carries out value-chain activities.[5] Instead of concentrating value-adding activities in their home country, many firms configure

**6.4** Understand outsourcing, global sourcing, and offshoring.

**Outsourcing**
The procurement of selected value-adding activities, including production of intermediate goods or finished products, from independent suppliers.

**Business process outsourcing (BPO)**
The outsourcing to independent suppliers of business service functions such as accounting, payroll, human resource functions, travel services, IT services, customer service, or technical support.

**Configuration of value-adding activity**
The pattern or geographic arrangement of locations where the firm carries out value-chain activities.

them across the world to save money, reduce delivery time, access factors of production, or extract maximum advantages relative to competitors.

This helps explain the migration of manufacturing industries from Europe, Japan, and the United States to emerging markets in Asia, Latin America, and Eastern Europe. Depending on the firm and the industry, management may decide to concentrate certain value-adding activities in just one or a handful of locations while dispersing others to numerous countries. External suppliers are typically located in countries characterized by low-cost labor, competent production processes, and specific knowledge about relevant engineering and development activities.[6]

German automaker BMW (www.bmw.com) operates 17 factories in six countries to manufacture sedans, coupes, and convertibles. Workers at the Munich plant build the BMW 3 Series and supply engines and key body components to other BMW factories abroad. BMW has plants in the United States, China, and India, where it manufactures automobiles from imported parts and components. Management configures BMW's sourcing at the best locations worldwide to minimize costs (for example, by producing in China), hire skilled people (by producing in Germany), remain close to key markets (by producing in China, India, and the United States), and succeed in the intensely competitive global car industry.[7]

## Global Sourcing

*Global sourcing* relies on a contractual relationship between the buyer (the focal firm) and a foreign source of supply. It is also called *importing, global procurement*, or *global purchasing*. Dell (www.dell.com) relies on a manufacturing network composed largely of independent suppliers

Display from an American-owned factory in Taiwan (Corning) or a Singapore-owned factory in India (Flextronics)

Battery from a Chinese factory (Shenzhen Desay Battery Technology) or a Korean-owned factory in India (Samsung)

Memory card from a German-owned factory in Malaysia (Infineon) or an American-owned factory in China (SanDisk)

Microprocessor from an American-owned factory in Taiwan (Qualcomm) or a Taiwanese factory (MediaTek)

Sensor from a Japanese-owned factory in Ireland (Alps Electric) or from an Austrian-owned factory in Singapore (AMS)

Power supply from a Taiwanese-owned factory in Thailand (Delta) or an American-owned factory in Mexico (Kemet)

Modem from an American-owned factory in China (Ixntel) or an American-owned factory in India (Broadcom)

Speaker from a Japanese-owned factory in Vietnam (Foster Electric) or a Netherlands-owned factory in the United States (NXP)

**EXHIBIT 6.7**

**Global Sourcing for a Typical Smartphone**

*Source:* scanrail/123RF

located around the world. Exhibit 6.7 details the sourcing required for parts and components of a typical smartphone, from suppliers located worldwide.[8]

Global sourcing is a low-control strategy in which the focal firm sources from independent suppliers through contractual agreements as opposed to the high-control strategy of buying from company-owned subsidiaries. Global sourcing frequently represents the firm's initial involvement in international business. For many firms, it increases management's awareness about other international opportunities.[9] Retailers usually obtain a substantial portion of their merchandise from foreign suppliers. Retailers such as Carrefour, Canadian Tire, and Home Depot are large-scale importers. Walmart accounts for a substantial proportion of U.S. imports from China, more than $30 billion per year. Steinway procures parts and components from a dozen foreign countries to manufacture grand pianos. HP provides technical support to its customers from call centers based in India.

In many cases, firms move entire sections of their value chains abroad, such as R&D, manufacturing, or technical support. In the sports apparel industry, firms such as Nike and Reebok subcontract nearly all their athletic shoe production to lower-cost foreign manufacturers. Clothing retailer Gap sources more than 80 percent of its apparel from suppliers in Asia. The Gap, Nike, and Reebok function primarily as brand owners and marketers, not as manufacturers. Apple sources some 70 percent of its production from abroad while focusing internal resources on continuously improving its software and product designs. This allows Apple management to optimize usage of the firm's finite capital resources and focus on its core competencies.

The total worldwide sourcing market for product manufacturing and services is massive, amounting to trillions of dollars annually. Global sourcing employs more than 1 million people in the Philippines alone. Worldwide, the most frequently outsourced business processes include logistics and procurement, sales and marketing, and customer service, followed by finance and accounting. Global sourcing by the private sector now accounts for more than half of all imports by major countries. Contractors such as Softtek in Mexico help banks around the world develop customized software, manage IT systems, and perform support and maintenance for commercial finance operations. Softtek (www.softtek.com) has 12,000 employees, mostly engineers. The firm has outsourcing facilities in Brazil, Colombia, Peru, and several other countries.

India is the current leader in the processing of advanced economies' relocated business services. The country has 2.5 million people working in the BPO industry. Indian BPO service providers have developed business relationships with 75 percent of *Fortune* 500 companies. Global competition and economic volatility have pressured advanced-economy firms to seek further ways to reduce costs, to the benefit of service suppliers in India.

---

### The growth of global sourcing has been driven by three key factors

- *Technological advances in communications, especially the Internet and international telecommunications.*  Access to vast online information means focal firms can quickly find suppliers that meet specific needs anywhere in the world. Firms can communicate continuously with foreign suppliers at very low cost.
- *Falling costs of international business.*  Tariffs and other trade barriers have declined substantially. Efficient communication and transportation systems have made international procurement cost effective and accessible to any firm.
- *Entrepreneurship and rapid economic transformation in emerging markets.*  China, India, and other emerging markets have quickly developed as important suppliers of various products and services. Entrepreneurial suppliers aggressively pursue sourcing partnerships with foreign buyers.

---

The decisions about whether and where to outsource are shown in the framework in Exhibit 6.8. The focal firm can source from independent suppliers (wherein the activity is externalized, or outsourced), from company-owned subsidiaries and affiliates (wherein the activity is internalized), or from both. In the exhibit, Cells C and D represent the global sourcing scenarios. Although global sourcing implies procurement from foreign locations, in some cases the focal firm may source from its own wholly owned subsidiary or an affiliate jointly owned with another firm (Cell C). This is **captive sourcing**. Genpact was a captive sourcing unit of General Electric (GE),

**Captive sourcing**
Sourcing from the firm's own production facilities.

| | Value-adding activity is internalized | Value-adding activity is externalized (outsourced) |
|---|---|---|
| Value-adding activity kept in home country | A<br><br>Keep production in-house, in home country | B<br><br>Outsource production to third-party provider at home |
| Value-adding activity conducted abroad (global sourcing) | C<br><br>Delegate production to foreign subsidiary or (captive sourcing) | D<br><br>Outsource production to a third-party provider abroad (contract manufacturing or global sourcing from independent suppliers) |

**EXHIBIT 6.8**

**The Nature of Outsourcing and Global Sourcing**

*Sources:* Based on B. Kedia and D. Mukherjee, "Understanding Offshoring: A Research Framework Based on Disintegration, Location and Externalization Advantages," *Journal of World Business* 44, No. 3 (2009), pp. 250–261; *Information Economy Report 2009* (New York: United Nations, 2009); *World Investment Report 2004* (New York: UNCTAD, 2004).

with annual revenues of more than $1 billion and more than 37,000 employees worldwide. Now an independent company based in India, Genpact (www.genpact.com) is one of the largest providers of business-process outsourcing services.[10]

The relationship between the focal firm and its foreign supplier (Cell D in Exhibit 6.8) may take the form of **contract manufacturing**, an arrangement in which the focal firm contracts with an independent supplier to manufacture products according to well-defined specifications. Once it has manufactured the products or components, the supplier delivers them to the focal firm, which then markets, sells, and distributes them. In essence, the focal firm rents the manufacturing capacity of the foreign contractor. Contract manufacturing accounts for more than half of all manufacturing in the toy, sporting goods, consumer electronics, and automotive industries. It is also common in the pharmaceuticals, furniture, semiconductor, apparel, and footwear industries.[11]

Have you ever heard of Taiwan's Hon Hai Precision Industry Company? Also known as Foxconn, Hon Hai is a leading contract manufacturer in the global electronics industry, with annual sales of more than $130 billion. Hon Hai (www.foxconn.com) works under contract for many well-known companies, churning out PlayStations for Sony; iPods, iPhones, and iPads for Apple; printers and PCs for Hewlett-Packard; and thousands of other products. The firm employs more than one million people in dozens of contract factories worldwide, from Malaysia to Mexico.[12]

**Offshoring** is the relocation of a business process or entire manufacturing facility to a foreign country. It is common in the service sector, including banking, software code writing, legal services, and customer-service activities.[13] Large legal hubs have emerged in India that provide services such as drafting contracts and patent applications, conducting research and negotiations, and performing paralegal work, all on behalf of Western clients. With lawyers in Europe and North America costing $300 an hour or more, law firms in India can cut Western companies' legal bills by up to 75 percent.[14]

**Contract manufacturing**
An arrangement in which the focal firm contracts with an independent supplier to manufacture products according to well-defined specifications.

**Offshoring**
The relocation of a business process or entire manufacturing facility to a foreign country.

**Industries that benefit most from global sourcing are characterized by:**

- Large-scale manufacturing whose primary competitive advantage is efficiency and low cost.
- High labor intensity in product and service production, such as garment manufacturing and call centers.
- Uniform customer needs and standardized technologies and processes in production and other value-chain activities, such as automobiles and machine parts.
- Established products with a predictable pattern of sales, such as components for consumer electronics.
- Information intensity whose functions and activities can be easily transmitted through the Internet, such as accounting, billing, and payroll.
- Outputs that are easily codified and transmitted over the Internet or by telephone, such as software preparation, technical support, and customer service.

Companies headquartered in the advanced economies outsource the most services by volume. Emerging markets and developing economies are the most popular destinations by far, especially India, China, Mexico, Indonesia, Egypt, Chile, and the Philippines. Key criteria for evaluating destinations include the availability of an appropriate labor force, wage rates, worker skill level, language and culture compatibility, quality of infrastructure, the country's legal system, economic environment, tax rates, and regulatory costs. In addition to large firms, global sourcing provides big benefits for small and medium-sized enterprises (SMEs). SMEs from car dealerships to real estate firms increasingly farm out accounting, support services, and design work to suppliers around the world.[15]

Exhibit 6.9 explains the strategic implications of sourcing and location decisions. The exhibit portrays a typical value chain, ranging from R&D and design to customer service. The first row indicates the degree to which management considers each value-adding activity a strategic asset to the firm. The second row indicates whether the activity tends to be internalized inside the focal firm or outsourced to a foreign supplier. The third row indicates where management typically locates an activity.

*Source:* qdxjw/123rf

Global sourcing facilitates the procurement of intermediate and finished products from suppliers worldwide. This container ship is preparing to depart Qingdao, a top shipping port in China.

**MyLab Management   Watch It! 1**

If your professor has assigned this, go to the Assignments section of **www.pearson.com/ mylab/management** to complete the video exercise titled Toyota Outsourcing and Logistics.

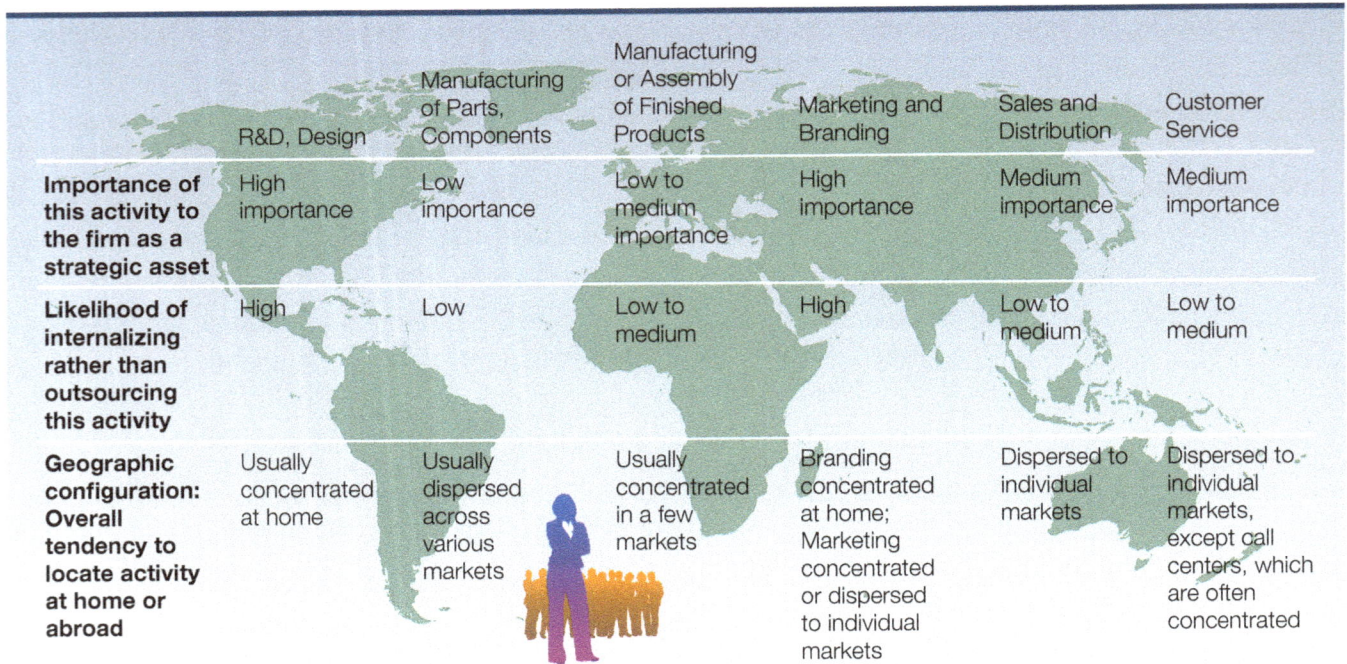

| | R&D, Design | Manufacturing of Parts, Components | Manufacturing or Assembly of Finished Products | Marketing and Branding | Sales and Distribution | Customer Service |
|---|---|---|---|---|---|---|
| **Importance of this activity to the firm as a strategic asset** | High importance | Low importance | Low to medium importance | High importance | Medium importance | Medium importance |
| **Likelihood of internalizing rather than outsourcing this activity** | High | Low | Low to medium | High | Low to medium | Low to medium |
| **Geographic configuration: Overall tendency to locate activity at home or abroad** | Usually concentrated at home | Usually dispersed across various markets | Usually concentrated in a few markets | Branding concentrated at home; Marketing concentrated or dispersed to individual markets | Dispersed to individual markets | Dispersed to individual markets, except call centers, which are often concentrated |

**EXHIBIT 6.9**

**Typical Choices of Outsourcing and Geographic Dispersion of Value-Chain Activities Among Firms**

**6.5** Describe the benefits and risks of global sourcing.

# Benefits, Risks, and Responsibilities of Global Sourcing

Global sourcing brings enormous benefits to firms, primarily leading to improved performance and superior competitive advantages. However, global sourcing also entails various risks. Firms that undertake global sourcing are confronted with challenges and opportunities for corporate social responsibility.

## Benefits of Global Sourcing

The main benefits of global sourcing are cost efficiency and the ability to achieve strategic goals. Let's examine these.

COST EFFICIENCY  The primary rationale for global sourcing is to reduce the firm's costs of inputs and operations. Exhibit 6.10 reveals typical manufacturing wages per hour of workers in various countries with low labor costs. For comparison, in 2017 manufacturing wages averaged about $34 and $22 per hour in the European Union and the United States, respectively. As shown in the exhibit, 2017 hourly wages ranged from $1.20 in Vietnam to $7.50 in Poland, far lower than in the advanced economies. This wage discrepancy explains why MNEs source inputs from emerging markets. Note that wages in China, Poland, and Turkey have been rising fairly rapidly. This improves living standards in those countries but is also making them less attractive as sourcing destinations. MNEs are shifting much of their manufacturing to Indonesia, Vietnam and other countries that feature very low labor costs.[16]

ABILITY TO ACHIEVE STRATEGIC GOALS  The strategic view of global sourcing is called *transformational outsourcing*. It suggests that just as the firm achieves cost efficiencies, it also obtains the means to restructure operations, speed up innovation, and fund otherwise-unaffordable development projects.[17] Global sourcing allows the firm to free expensive analysts, engineers, and managers from routine tasks to spend more time on important tasks. These tasks include researching, innovating, managing, and generally undertaking high-value-adding activities that contribute more productively to increasing company performance.[18] Global sourcing becomes a catalyst to overhaul organizational processes and company operations and increase the firm's overall competitive advantages. It allows the firm to achieve large, longer-term strategic goals.

Numerous fashion merchandisers—for example, Gap, H&M, Kate Spade, Nike, UNIQLO—outsource the production of their apparel to specialized, independent suppliers. These suppliers are located in such countries as Bangladesh, China, and India. The strategy allows apparel firms to focus on their core competencies, including design, marketing, and distribution.[19]

**EXHIBIT 6.10**

**Average Wage per Hour of Workers in Manufacturing, in U.S. Dollars**

*Sources:* Sharon Chen, "U.S. Wages Will Be 58 Times Indonesia's By 2019," *Bloomberg,* April 5, 2015, www.bloomberg.com; "Eurostat: Hourly Labour Costs," 2018, ec.europa.eu; International Labour Organisation, "Statistics and Databases," 2018, www.ilo.org; Labour Bureau, Government of India, 2018, http://labourbureau.nic.in; *The Economist Intelligence Unit,* "Still Making It: An Analysis of Manufacturing Labour Costs in China," 2014, www.eiu.com.

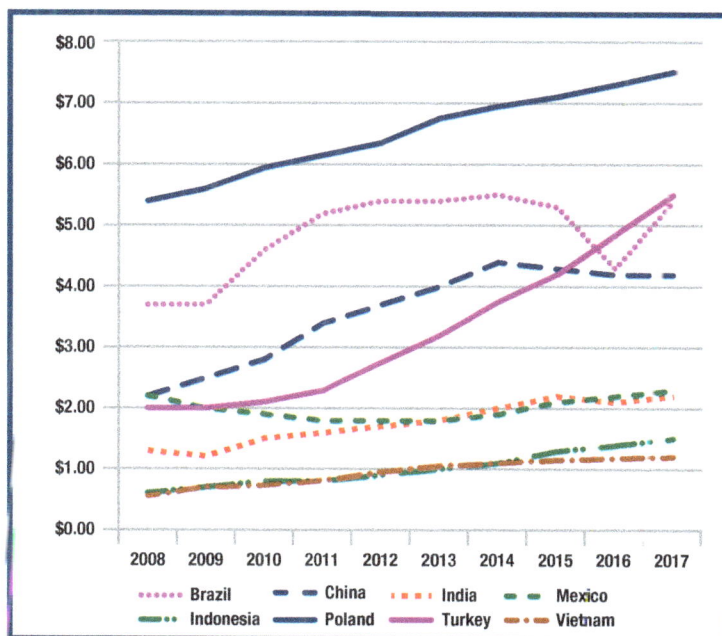

The twin objectives of cost efficiency and strategic goal achievement are often both present in a particular global sourcing activity. Global sourcing can provide other benefits as well, including:

- *Faster corporate growth.* Firms can focus their resources on performing more-profitable activities such as R&D or building relationships with customers. For example, they can expand their staff of engineers and researchers while keeping constant their cost of product development as a percentage of sales.
- *Access to qualified personnel abroad.* Countries such as China, India, and Ireland offer abundant pools of educated engineers, managers, and other specialists to help firms achieve their goals. Disney has much of its animation work done in Japan, home to world-class animators.
- *Improved productivity and service.* Manufacturing productivity and other value-chain activities can be improved by suppliers that specialize in these activities. Penske Truck Leasing improved its efficiency and customer service by outsourcing dozens of business processes to Mexico and India.
- *Business process redesign.* By reconfiguring their value-chain systems or reengineering their business processes, companies can improve their production efficiency and resource usage. MNEs see offshoring as a means to overhaul outdated company operations.[20]
- *Increased speed to market.* By shifting software development and editorial work to India and the Philippines, the U.S.-Dutch publisher Wolters Kluwer was able to produce a greater variety of books and journals and publish them faster. Pharmaceutical firms get new medications to market faster by outsourcing clinical drug trials.
- *Access to new markets.* Sourcing provides an entrée to the market, an understanding of local customers, and the means to initiate marketing activities there. By moving many of its R&D operations to Russia, the telecommunications firm Nortel gained an important foothold in a market that needs telephone switching equipment and other communications infrastructure.[21]
- *Technological flexibility.* Leveraging independent suppliers abroad provides firms the flexibility to quickly change sources of supply, employing whichever suppliers offer the most advanced technologies. In this way, sourcing provides greater organizational flexibility and faster responsiveness to evolving buyer needs.[22]

Combined, these benefits give firms the ability to renew their strategic positions continuously. Outsourcing specialists such as Accenture and Genpact meticulously dissect the workflow of other firms' human resources, finance, or IT departments. This helps the specialists build new IT platforms, redesign all processes, and administer programs, acting as virtual subsidiaries to their client firms. The specialists then disperse work among global networks of staff from Asia to Eastern Europe and elsewhere.[23]

## Risks of Global Sourcing

In addition to potential benefits, global sourcing also brings unexpected complications. As many as half of all outsourcing arrangements are terminated earlier than planned. Global sourcing entails the following major risks.[24]

- *Lower-than-expected cost savings.* International transactions are often more complex and costly than expected. Conflicts and misunderstandings may arise from differences in the national and organizational cultures between the focal firm and foreign supplier. Establishing an outsourcing facility can be surprisingly expensive due to the need to upgrade poor infrastructure or locate it in a large city to attract sufficient skilled labor.[25]
- *Environmental factors.* Environmental challenges include currency fluctuations, tariffs and other trade barriers, high energy and transportation costs, adverse macroeconomic events, labor strikes, and natural disasters. Firms that source from countries whose currencies are strengthening experience higher costs. Many countries suffer from poor public infrastructure, as exemplified by power outages and poor road and rail networks. India is characterized by periodic shortages of electrical power. In 2012, a massive power outage in India left several hundred million people without power and disrupted businesses and transport systems.
- *Weak legal environment.* Many popular locations for global sourcing (for example, China, India, and Russia) have weak intellectual property laws and poor enforcement, which can

erode key strategic assets. Inadequate legal systems, red tape, convoluted tax systems, and complex business regulations complicate local operations in many countries.

- *Inadequate or low-skilled workers.* Some foreign suppliers may be staffed by employees who lack appropriate knowledge about the tasks with which they are charged. Other suppliers suffer rapid turnover of skilled employees. The mean education level of workers in many developing economies is sometimes insufficient to support the manufacturing needs of companies in high-tech industries. In many such countries, educational institutions are lacking and may not produce a sufficient number of workers with superior skills. Such challenges affect the productivity and economic growth of numerous countries.[26]
- *Overreliance on suppliers.* Unreliable suppliers may put earlier work aside when they gain a more important client. Suppliers occasionally encounter financial difficulties or are acquired by other firms with different priorities and procedures. Management at the focal firm may find itself scrambling to find alternate suppliers. Overreliance can reduce the focal firm's control of important value-chain tasks.
- *Risk of creating competitors.* As the focal firm shares its intellectual property and business-process knowledge with foreign suppliers, it also runs the risk of creating future rivals. Schwinn, long the leader in the global bicycle industry, transferred much of its production and core expertise to lower-cost foreign suppliers, which acquired sufficient knowledge to become competitors, eventually forcing Schwinn into bankruptcy (from which it later recovered).
- *Erosion of morale and commitment among home-country employees.* Global sourcing can leave employees caught in the middle between their employer and their employer's clients. When outsourcing forces retained and outsourced staff to work side by side, tensions and uncertainty may diminish employee commitment and enthusiasm.

### Reshoring and Nearshoring

**Reshoring**
The return of a business process or entire manufacturing facility to the home country.

In Europe and the United States, many firms have reestablished formerly foreign-based manufacturing back to the home country. Known as **reshoring**, it is the opposite of offshoring, and refers to the return of a business process or entire manufacturing facility to the home country. Historically, many advanced economy firms located their manufacturing operations in emerging markets or developing economies to access lower-cost labor. In addition to labor costs, however, MNE managers consider a range of variables when siting production facilities, including product quality, workforce productivity, availability of key inputs, and proximity to key markets. After offshoring production, many firms in Europe and the United States have found such conditions lacking. Dissatisfaction with global sourcing has led such companies to return production operations to the home country. For example, Boeing, Ford, and General Electric each have reshored several thousand jobs back to the United States in recent years. Adidas, British Telecom, and Santander are examples of MNEs that have reshored production back to Europe.

Other factors that have encouraged MNEs to reshore production back to the home country include rising labor costs in China and other emerging markets, flat labor costs in the advanced economies, and increased automation. For example, firms in the automotive, electronics, and machinery industries have greatly increased the use of robots in their manufacturing, which reduces per-unit production costs. When such factors are included, higher labor costs in the advanced economies become less relevant in decisions about where to locate production. Reshoring benefits the home economy through job creation, industrial development, and improving the balance of trade.

Many MNEs have underestimated the costs and logistical planning required to locate production abroad. The reshoring phenomenon underscores the importance of carefully weighing the pros and cons of global sourcing. It also highlights the importance of following a strategic approach to global sourcing.[27]

**Nearshoring**
The offshoring or relocation of business processes or manufacturing facilities to a nearby country, often sharing a border with the home country.

**Nearshoring** refers to the offshoring or relocation of business processes or manufacturing facilities to a nearby country, often sharing a border with the home country. Nearshoring has gained popularity because production is located close to the home market while still offering access to lower-cost labor and other advantages. For example, many MNEs in Western Europe now site production facilities in Poland, Romania, and other Eastern European countries in order to take advantage of close proximity combined with cheaper labor. Mexico and Central America serve a similar function for Canada and the United States.[28]

## Corporate Social Responsibility

The business community sees global sourcing as a way to maintain or increase business competitiveness and enhance long-term company sustainability. Others view it negatively, focusing on the loss of local jobs. After IBM workers in Europe went on strike against offshoring, shareholders at IBM's annual meeting argued for an anti-offshoring resolution. In the United States, 45,000 Verizon workers went on strike to protest the telecom company's decision to outsource support services jobs to Mexico and the Philippines. In Ireland, Cadbury workers struck to protest global outsourcing of confectionary manufacturing from local factories.[29]

Critics of global sourcing point to three potential problems.

- Job losses in the home country
- Reduced national competitiveness
- Declining standards of living

Regarding the last two concerns, critics worry that, as more tasks are performed at lower cost with comparable quality in other countries, high-wage countries will lose their national competitiveness. Long-held knowledge and skills will eventually drain away to other countries, they fear, and the lower wages paid abroad will eventually pull down wages in the home country, leading to lower living standards.

*Source:* a katz/Shutterstock

Global sourcing has sparked protests in many countries. Here, trade union members at Verizon telecommunications company in the United States protest the outsourcing of jobs to Mexico and other countries.

A major concern is job losses. The advanced economies have outsourced millions of jobs to emerging markets in the past decade. Job losses rise when companies increase their sourcing of input and finished goods from abroad. Walmart sources as much as 70 percent of its finished merchandise from abroad. This has led citizens to form a protest group called Walmartwatch.com, which claims millions of U.S. jobs have been lost due to Walmart's global sourcing.[30] Job losses are occurring in developing economies as well. For example, in the textile industry, Honduras, Indonesia, and Turkey have seen jobs gradually transferred to India and Pakistan.[31]

Outsourcing and offshoring represent a process of *creative destruction*, a concept first proposed by the Austrian economist Joseph Schumpeter.[32] According to this view, firms' innovative activities tend to make mature products obsolete over time. The introduction of personal computers essentially eliminated the typewriter industry, the DVD player eliminated the VCR, and so on. Just as offshoring results in job losses and adverse effects for particular groups and economic sectors, it also creates new advantages and opportunities for firms and consumers alike. Sourcing usually enhances company sustainability for the long term. New industries created through creative destruction will create new jobs and innovative products.

> **MyLab Management    Watch It! 2**
>
> If your professor has assigned this, go to the Assignments section of **www.pearson.com/ mylab/management** to complete the video exercise titled Bringing Jobs Back to the United States.

## Global Sourcing Strategies and Supply-Chain Management

**6.6** Understand global sourcing strategies and supply-chain management.

Firms can reduce much of the risk in global sourcing by employing appropriate strategies. Skillful supply-chain management reduces the costs and enhances the advantages available from global sourcing.

## Managerial guidelines for global sourcing

- *Go offshore for the right reasons.* The best rationale is strategic. Most companies cite cost cutting as the main reason for global sourcing. After the first year, however, the amount of money saved tends to decline. Global sourcing provides the means to achieve more beneficial, long-term goals. Management should analyze its value-chain activities and outsource those in which it is relatively weak, that offer relatively little value to the bottom line, or that can be performed more effectively by others, yet are not critical to the firm's core competencies.
- *Get employees on board.* Global sourcing can demoralize employees and other organizational stakeholders. Senior management should seek employee support by reaching a consensus of managers and labor, developing alternatives for redeploying laid-off workers and soliciting employee help in choosing foreign partners.
- *Choose carefully between a captive operation and contracting with outside suppliers.* Managers should be vigilant about striking the right balance between the organizational activities they retain inside the firm and those they source from outside. Many firms establish their own sourcing operations abroad to maintain control of outsourced activities and technologies.
- *Choose suppliers carefully.* Finding and managing foreign suppliers is complex. The focal firm may have limited influence over suppliers' manufacturing and processes. Suppliers may engage in opportunistic behavior or act in bad faith. To ensure the success of sourcing ventures, the focal firm must exercise great care to identify and screen potential suppliers and then monitor the activities of those suppliers from which it sources.
- *Emphasize communications and collaboration with suppliers.* Global sourcing may fail if buyers and suppliers spend too little time getting well acquainted. Rushing into a deal before clarifying each other's expectations produces misunderstandings and poor results. Managers at the focal firm may need to monitor manufacturing processes closely. Partners must share necessary information.[33] Close collaboration with suppliers in development activities enables the focal firm to tap ideas for new products, technologies, and improvements. Efforts to build strong relationships foster a moral contract between the focal firm and the supplier, often more effective than a formal legal contract.
- *Safeguard interests.* The focal firm should protect its interests in the supplier relationship. It can advise the supplier against engaging in activities that harm the firm's reputation. The firm can share costs and revenues by building a stake for the supplier so that, in case of failure to meet expectations, the supplier also suffers costs or forgoes revenues. Management should maintain flexibility by keeping open its options for finding alternate partners if needed. The focal firm should withhold access to intellectual property and key assets. If conflicts are unresolved by negotiations, one option is to acquire full or partial ownership of the supplier.

Public policy should strive to mitigate the potential harm global sourcing can cause.[34] Governments can use economic and fiscal policies to encourage the development of new technologies by helping entrepreneurs reap the financial benefits of their work and keeping the cost of capital for financing R&D low. A strong educational system, including technical schools and well-funded universities, supplies engineers, scientists, managers, and knowledge workers. A strong educational system provides firms with pools of high-quality labor.

**Global supply chain**
The firm's integrated network of sourcing, production, and distribution, organized on a worldwide scale and located in countries where competitive advantage can be maximized.

## Global Supply-Chain Management

A key reason sourcing products from distant markets has become a major business phenomenon is the efficiency with which goods can be physically moved from one part of the globe to another.

A **global supply chain** is the firm's integrated network of sourcing, production, and distribution, organized on a worldwide scale and located in countries where competitive advantage can be maximized. Global supply-chain management includes both upstream (supplier) and downstream (customer) flows.

The concepts of supply chain and value chain are related but distinct. Recall that the value chain is the collection of activities intended to design, produce, market, deliver, and support a product or service. By contrast, the supply chain is the collection of logistics specialists and activities that provides inputs to manufacturers or retailers.

Skillful supply-chain management serves to optimize value-chain activities. Sourcing from numerous suppliers scattered around the world is neither economical nor feasible without an efficient supply-chain system. Casual observers are impressed by the vast collection of products in a supermarket or department store that originated from dozens of countries. The speed with which these products are delivered to end users is equally impressive.

Consider a customer in Canada who orders a Dell laptop computer. The order is typically routed to the Dell factory in Malaysia, where workers must access 30 distinct component parts that originate with Dell suppliers scattered around the world. Indeed, the total supply chain for a typical Dell computer, including multiple tiers of suppliers, typically includes some 400 companies in Asia, Europe, and the Americas. Dell is so skilled at managing all this complexity that customers typically receive their computers within two weeks of submitting an order.

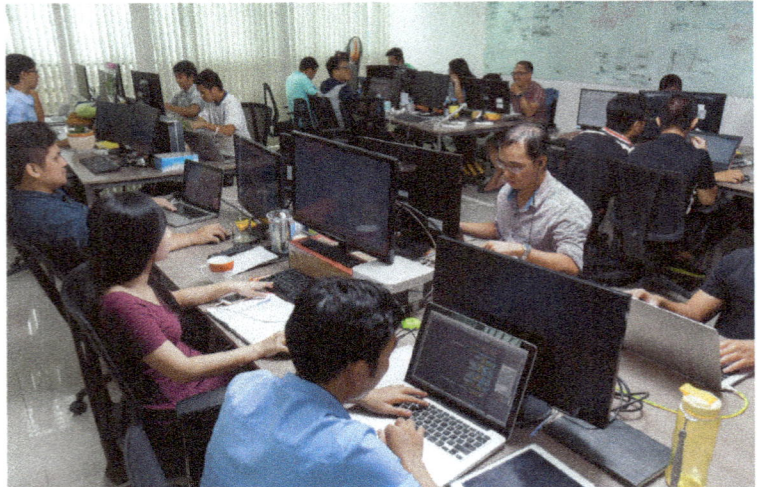

*Source:* ProStockStudio/Shutterstock

Minimizing the risks of global sourcing entails several critical strategies. Following a careful selection process, the focal firm should invest in collaborating and communicating with suppliers, such as these software developers in Asia.

Networks of supply-chain hubs and providers of global delivery service are an integral part of global supply chains. Many focal firms delegate supply-chain activities to such independent logistics service providers as DHL, FedEx, and TNT. Consulting firms that manage the logistics of other firms are called *third-party logistics providers (3PLs)*. Using a 3PL is often the best solution for international logistics, especially for firms that produce at low volumes or lack the resources and expertise to create their own logistics network.

Exhibit 6.11 illustrates the stages, functions, and activities in the supply chain. It reveals how suppliers interact with the focal firm and how these, in turn, interact with distributors and retailers.

Costs of physically delivering a product to an export market may account for as much as 40 percent of the good's total cost. Skillful supply-chain management reduces this cost while increasing customer satisfaction. Firms use information and communications technologies (ICTs) to streamline supply chains, reducing costs and increasing distribution efficiency. For example, *electronic data interchange (EDI)* automatically passes orders directly from customers to suppliers through a sophisticated ICT platform. ICTs enhance information sharing and improve efficiency by allowing the firm to track international shipments and clear customs. In efficient systems, suppliers are connected through automated, real-time communications. The focal firm and its supply-chain partners continuously share information to meet marketplace demands constantly.

Logistics physically moves goods through the supply chain. It incorporates information, transportation, inventory, warehousing, materials handling, and similar activities associated with the delivery of raw materials, parts, components, and finished products. Managers seek to reduce moving and storage costs by using just-in-time inventory systems. Internationally, logistics are complex due to wide geographic distances, multiple legal environments, and the often inadequate and costly nature of distribution infrastructure in individual countries. The more diverse the firm's global supply chain, the greater the cost of logistics.

Competent logistics management is critical, especially for just-in-time inventory systems. The California ports of Los Angeles (www.portoflosangeles.org) and Long Beach (www.polb.com) handle more than 40 percent of imports into the United States, processing more than 24,000 shipping containers per day. Infrastructure deficiencies and increasing demand can result in long delays, which translate into longer transit times and higher costs for U.S. importers. Because of delays, Toys "R" Us had to build 10 extra days into its supply chain.[35] As a result of

EXHIBIT 6.11

Stages, Functions, and
Activities in the Global
Supply Chain

| | Suppliers | Focal Firm | Intermediaries and/or Retailers |
|---|---|---|---|
| Stage in supply chain | Sourcing, from home country and abroad | Inbound materials; outbound goods and services | Distribution to domestic customers or foreign customers (exports) |
| Major functions | Provide raw materials, parts, components, supplies, as well as business processes and other services to focal firm | Manufacture or assemble components or finished products, or produce services | Distribute and sell products and services |
| Typical activities | Maintain inventory, process orders, transport goods, deliver services | Manage inventory, process orders, manufacture or assemble products, produce and deliver services, distribute products to customers, retailers, or intermediaries | Manage inventory, place or process orders, produce services, manage physical distribution, provide after-sales service |

poor supply-chain planning, the Microsoft Xbox 360 games console sold out soon after launch. Scarcity led to high prices in unofficial channels. On eBay, Xbox consoles sold for as much as $1,000, compared with the official price of about $400.[36]

International logistics usually use multiple *transportation modes*, including land, ocean, and air transport. Land transportation is conducted on highways and railroads, ocean transport is by container ships, and air transport is on commercial or cargo aircraft. Transportation modes involve several trade-offs. The three main considerations are *cost, transit time* to deliver the goods, and *predictability*, the match between anticipated and actual transit times.

## Comparison of ocean, land, and air transport

- Ocean transport accounts for about 90 percent of international shipments. It is slower than air but far cheaper. It was revolutionized by the development of 20- and 40-foot shipping containers, the big boxes that sit atop seagoing vessels. A modern ship's ability to carry thousands of containers yields economies of scale, making ocean transport very cost effective, often accounting for only 1 percent of a product's final price.
- Land transport is usually more expensive than ocean transport but cheaper than air. Exporters often opt for ocean shipping even when land transport is available. For example, some Mexican firms send goods to Canada by ship.
- Air transport is fast and extremely predictable but expensive. It is used mostly to transport perishable products (such as food and flowers), products with a high value-to-weight ratio (such as fine jewelry and laptop computers), and urgently needed goods (such as medicines and emergency supplies). Although the use of air freight has increased because of gradually declining cost, it still accounts for only 1 percent of international shipments.

## CLOSING CASE — Inditex and Zara: A Tale of Comparative Advantages

Zara is one of the best-known fashion brands around the world as well as the subject of a sizable body of literature analyzing its astonishing success in terms of its capillary, just-in-time distribution, and its attentive marketing campaigns. However, it can be argued that is Zara's parent company, Inditex, that has mastered the game of comparative advantages; that is, the ability of a business to produce goods and services at a lower opportunity cost than that of their trade partners on a global scale, leveraging the global supply chain with precision and sophistication, earning accolades for marketing strategy as well as sustainability.

Inditex (which stands for Industria de Diseño Textil, S.A.) is a Spanish multinational clothing company headquartered in Arteixo, Galicia. It started out in the 1960s with a small family business of cloth makers in the Galician regional capital of A Coruña. Their first shop, named Zara, opened in 1975, establishing its formula of tasteful fashion at affordable prices. The year after, the firm incorporated and continued setting up shops across Spain. In the 1980s, the company hired a computer expert and set up a new supply chain design that shortened the time-to-market drastically, allowing the company to respond very quickly to the fashion's mutable tastes. Inditex's revolutionary model was born.

Inditex now claims to be the biggest fashion group in the world, and not without good reason: it operates over 7,200 stores across five continents and 96 markets, using as many as 1,824 suppliers worldwide. Inditex owns a number of other fashion brands, such as Massimo Dutti, but Zara accounts for about a third of the total number of stores, at 2,238.

Zara's success—and that of Inditex—is that it does not rely on market surveys to learn about its customers' preferences; it learns directly at the shops, where the managers act as marketing surveyors themselves, recording what is picked up, what is tried on, and what is discarded. The stock changes twice a week and orders take as little as 48 hours to reach the shelves, so the brand is capable to react almost in real time to any changes.

To achieve this, the supply chain must not only be reactive and slick in its operations but also "short," which means low lead times (the period from the moment an order is placed to the moment it is delivered to the customer). This can be a major advantage. China has been—and still is—the global leader in suppliers of clothing, though it has recently been challenged in some low-end segments by even cheaper competitors in Vietnam, Indonesia, and Bangladesh. Geographically, however, it is still far away, and this does matter to shops in Europe.

Asian producers do enjoy an absolute advantage in clothing; nobody can beat their pricing, after all. Nevertheless, more sophisticated and expensive producers can still maintain a comparative advantage if there are more important considerations than

production costs or sheer pricing. Timing is one of them, and of paramount importance for Zara. A container ship takes between 30 and 45 days to reach Europe from producers from Asia, so the lead time of an Asian producer can vary from three to six months. This may be acceptable for "wholesale" clothing items, but it will not do for the model Inditex has set up.

Inditex's solution is to use global sourcing in a smarter and more flexible way, buying from producers and factories close to wherever the shops are located, which guarantees low time-to-market. About 57 percent of their 7,210 factories are located in proximity to their headquarters in Arteixo; 645 of those suppliers guarantee a production of over 20,000 units for Inditex. This makes sense considering that, global brand or not, the core of Inditex's business is still very much Europe-oriented. Most of its 7,200 stores are still based in Europe: Zara leads the way with 1,342, Pull&Bear has 686, and Massimo Dutti has 517. As the majority of Inditex's suppliers are based in Galicia, its products can reach any destination in Europe by truck in 48–72 hours, beating whatever competitive advantage Chinese and other Asian producers could have in terms of pure pricing.

Of course, when it comes to selling in the Asian markets, Asian suppliers are more competitive than their European counterparts due to the reduced distance, and this is where the lowest price factor offered by the many Chinese and South-East Asian factories can be fully exploited. With 1,655 shops in Asia, Inditex manages to do well enough for itself. Zara leads here again with 564 shops, and you can find the brand in many East Asian cities. Hong Kong has long been a flagship city for the brand since 2004, and when Inditex reached China two years later, it set up more than 200 stores. South Korea is a major market too, with 39 stores in big cities such as Seoul, Busan, Daegu, and Kwangju—Inditex has a total of 58 stores under five major brands. Japan is another huge market; since the first shop opened in 1997, there have been more than 50 openings.

Inditex's global sourcing strategy, which mixes in-house design and flexible outsourcing, has allowed its brands to offer a larger number of retail items than its competitors even when they have the same strategy of a worldwide presence and over a thousand small and large shops each, like H&M, for example, or UNIQLO. This variety, coupled with the rapid turnover on its shelves to adapt to changing tastes and preferences, has become one of the keys to Zara's continuous success.

This is especially apparent when comparing some of the recent results of H&M, which owns over 4,800 stores in 71 markets, with those of Inditex. While the Spanish group reported a 7 percent increase in profit in 2017, H&M saw a further drop of 62 percent in the first quarter of 2018 after another bad year in 2017—a sign that some adjustments in overall strategy are likely on the way.

### AACSB and CKR Intangible Soft Skills to improve employability and success in the workplace:
Analytical Thinking, Diverse and Multicultural Work Environments, Reflective Thinking, and Application of Knowledge

### Case Questions

**6-4.** Why is Inditex considered a special case in terms of its approach to the global supply chain? Discuss the typical global supply chain model and explain how Inditex is different.

**6-5.** What does the law of comparative advantages state, and why does Inditex serve as a good example?

**6-6.** Asia represents the universal powerhouse of production but only features partially in Inditex's approach. What made Asia the first world's supplier of fashion products and a main sourcing spot in the first place?

**6-7.** Name some of Inditex's competitors. What is their strategy?

6-8. Sustainability is becoming an important component in both Inditex and its competitors' marketing strategy, and it has in turn changed the way that production—and therefore the companies' global supply chains—are structured. How did this come about, and what are Inditex and the other groups doing in this area?

6-9. Online shopping is picking up, and digital-first sellers such as Amazon and Zappos have started selling fashion items as well. What could Inditex do to strengthen its unique grip on its customers and beat the competition?

*Sources:* Inditex.com, official website; Rick Frasch, "Sourcing Goods and Suppliers in China: A How to Guide for Small Businesses," *Forbes*, January 6, 2014, https://www.forbes.com/sites/allbusiness/2014/01/06/sourcing-goods-and-suppliers-in-china-a-how-to-guide-for-small-businesses/#7752360f6d34; Tim Worstall, "Inditex's Zara and the Power of Comparative Advantage," *Forbes*, June 7, 2015, https://www.forbes.com/sites/timworstall/2015/06/07/inditexs-zara-and-the-power-of-comparative-advantage/#6b746707e279; H&M Group, "At a Glance," http://about.hm.com/en/about-us/h-m-group-at-a-glance.html; Jessica Tyler, "We Visited H&M and Zara to See Which Was a Better Fast-Fashion Store, and the Winner Was Clear for a Key Reason," *Business Insider*, June 15, 2018, https://www.businessinsider.com/hm-zara-compared-photos-details-2018-5?r=US&IR=T#i-went-to-zara-next-it-was-directly-across-from-the-top-level-of-hm-16.

This case was written by Stefania Paladini, Birmingham City University.

# END-OF-CHAPTER REVIEW

## MyLab Management
Go to **www.pearson.com/mylab/management** to complete the problems marked with this icon ⭐.

## Key Terms

barter 166
business process outsourcing (BPO) 171
buy-back agreement 166
captive sourcing 173
company-owned subsidiary 162
compensation deals 166
configuration of value-adding activity 171
contract manufacturing 174

counterpurchase 166
countertrade 165
direct exporting 161
documentation 162
exporting 158
export management company (EMC) 168
foreign distributor 168
global sourcing 162
global supply chain 180

importing 162
Incoterms 163
indirect exporting 161
letter of credit 164
manufacturer's representative 168
nearshoring 178
offshoring 174
outsourcing 171
reshoring 178
trading company 168

## Summary
In this chapter, you learned about:

- **Exporting as a foreign market entry strategy**

Exporting is producing at home and then shipping products abroad, to be sold and delivered to foreign customers through intermediaries. It is the strategy most firms favor when they first internationalize. It is also a relatively flexible entry strategy, allowing the firm to withdraw readily in case of problems in the target market. A systematic approach to exporting requires managers to perform a global market opportunity assessment, make organizational arrangements for exporting, acquire needed skills and competencies, and design and implement the export strategy. Among the organizational arrangements for exporting are indirect exporting, direct exporting, and establishing a company-owned subsidiary.

- **Managing export-import transactions**

Management must become familiar with customs clearance, international goods transportation, and **documentation**, the required forms and other paperwork used to conclude international sales. The exporter typically entrusts preparation of documents to a freight forwarder. **Incoterms** are universally accepted terms of sale that effectively specify what is and is not included in the price of a product sold internationally. Exporting also requires knowledge of payment methods, such as cash in advance, letter of credit, open account, and countertrade. For most firms, letter of credit is best because it establishes immediate trust and protects both buyer and seller. Intense competition drives exporters to offer attractive payment terms to their customers.

- **Identifying and working with foreign intermediaries**

Managers can identify intermediaries, such as sales representatives and distributors, from a variety of public and private information sources. It is best to develop long-term relationships with these business partners, who perform a variety of functions abroad on behalf of the exporter by cultivating mutually beneficial bonds, genuinely responding to distributor needs, and encouraging loyalty.

- **Outsourcing, global sourcing, and offshoring**

Global sourcing refers to the procurement of products or services from suppliers or company-owned subsidiaries located abroad for consumption in the home country or a third country. Business process outsourcing refers to the outsourcing of business functions such as finance, accounting, and human resources. Procurement can be from either independent suppliers or company-owned subsidiaries or affiliates. Offshoring refers to the relocation of a business process or entire manufacturing facility to a foreign country. Managers make two strategic decisions regarding value-adding activities: whether to *make* or *buy* inputs and where to locate value-adding activity—that is, the geographic configuration of value-adding activity.

- **Benefits and risk of global sourcing**

Global sourcing aims to reduce the cost of doing business or to achieve other strategic goals. Global sourcing has provided the means to turn around failing businesses, speed up the pace of innovation, or fund development projects that are otherwise unaffordable. Risks include failing to realize anticipated cost savings, dealing with environmental uncertainty, creating competitors, engaging suppliers with insufficient training, relying too much on suppliers, and eroding the morale of existing employees. Many MNEs engage in **reshoring** and **nearshoring** of production.

- **Global sourcing strategies and supply-chain management**

Firms should develop a strategic perspective in making global sourcing decisions. In addition to cost cutting, global sourcing is also a means to create customer value and improve the firm's competitive advantages. The efficiency with which goods can be physically moved from one part of the globe to another makes global sourcing feasible. Global supply chain refers to the firm's integrated network of sourcing, production, and distribution, organized on a world scale and located in countries where competitive advantage can be maximized.

## Test Your Comprehension

**AACSB and CKR Intangible Soft Skills to improve employability and success in the workplace: Diverse and Multicultural Work Environments, Reflective Thinking, and Application of Knowledge**

**6-10.** Why might services be the most significant form of export for advanced economies?

**6-11.** What is meant by global procurement, and what are the implications of this type of transaction?

**6-12.** Why is knowledge of incoterms important to importers and exporters?

**6-13.** Explain the payment methods that exporters typically use. What is the most reliable payment method, and how do exporters carry it out?

**6-14.** Explain the nature, role, and risks involved in countertrade.

**6-15.** What steps should the exporter take to ensure success in working with intermediaries?

**6-16.** Identify the benefits that companies receive from global sourcing. Why do firms outsource to foreign suppliers?

**6-17.** What are the implications for company strategy and performance of business process outsourcing?

**6-18.** What are the risks that firms face in global sourcing?

**6-19.** What are the main benefits to a business of global sourcing?

**6-20.** Is global sourcing really about cost-cutting?

**6-21.** How can global sourcing help ensure a competitive advantage?

# Apply Your Understanding

**AACSB and CKR Intangible Soft Skills to improve employability and success in the workplace: Written and Oral Communication, Ethical Understanding and Reasoning, Analytical Thinking, Reflective Thinking, and Application of Knowledge**

**6-22.** Moose & Walrus (M&W) is a manufacturer of a popular line of clothing for young people. M&W is firmly established in its home market, which is relatively saturated and has little prospects for future sales growth. Top management has decided to export M&W's clothing line to Japan, Turkey, and various European countries. Suppose M&W hires you to assist with internationalization. Prepare a briefing for senior managers that describes:

- The advantages and disadvantages of exporting.
- A systematic approach to exporting.
- A systematic approach to managing export-import transactions.
- Export payment methods.

What factors should M&W consider regarding the possible need to adapt its clothing styles for its target markets?

**6-23.** A Dubai-owned, Turkey-based manufacturer of refrigerators has come to the conclusion that, in order to expand into Europe and other markets, it needs to set up a direct exporting department. To date, the business has been hugely successful in the domestic market and has sold reasonably well through distributors in some neighboring countries such as Greece, Georgia, Armenia, and Bulgaria. You have been appointed as their new direct exporting manager. The intention is to target the European Union first. Your first task is to find distributors in the target markets. How will you approach this task? What resources should you access to find distributors in these markets? Once established, what is the best way to maintain solid relations with foreign distributors? Finally, what payment method should the business use for most of its prospective markets?

**6-24.** *Ethical Dilemma:* Suppose that you have been hired by GM Global, a technology company specializing in the creation of pest- and drought-resistance plants. They are in a delicate industry, so GM Global emphasizes social responsibility in its business dealings and uses three foreign market entry strategies: exporting, joint ventures, and FDI. Exporting means the sale of products to customers located abroad, usually under contract with foreign intermediaries that organize marketing and distribution activities in local markets. Using joint ventures, GM Global partners with foreign firms to access their technology, expertise, production factors, and existing permissions to grow and market GM products. Using FDI, GM Global invests funds to establish factories or other subsidiaries overseas. Each of the strategies—exporting, joint venture, and FDI—is vulnerable to particular types of ethical dilemmas, and top management has directed you to identify and describe the most typical ones. What types of ethical problems might arise in each type of entry strategy? Which entry strategy is most likely to give rise to ethical problems? Justify your answer.

**globalEDGE** | **INTERNET EXERCISES**
Access globalEDGE™ at www.globalEDGE.msu.edu

**AACSB and CKR Intangible Soft Skills to improve employability and success in the workplace: Written and Oral Communication, Ethical Understanding and Reasoning, Information Technology, Analytical Thinking, Diverse and Multicultural Work Environments, Reflective Thinking, and Application of Knowledge**

6-25. You work for a firm that manufactures children's toys. Despite little international experience, management wants to start exporting. Your boss understands the importance of using strong distributors abroad but knows little about how to find them. You are aware that many national governments offer programs that help new exporters find intermediaries in foreign countries. Examples include trade missions, trade shows, and matchmaker programs (in which the exporter is matched with foreign intermediaries). In the United States, the International Trade Administration (ITA) provides various services to help exporters find foreign distributors. Visit the ITA website (www.ita.doc.gov) or the main trade support agency of your country (through globalEDGE™), and see what programs are available. Then prepare a memo to your boss in which you describe specific programs to help your firm get started in exporting.

6-26. Suppose you work for a major trading company exporting timber from Canada, petroleum from Britain, and processed food products from the United States. To enhance your career prospects, you want to learn more about the export of these goods from their respective countries. Visit globalEDGE™, and research current international news about these industries in the countries indicated. Based on your findings, prepare a brief report on the status of each in the context of your firm's exporting efforts.

6-27. Suppose your employer wants to export its products and be paid through letter of credit (LC). You have volunteered to become the company's LC expert. One way to accomplish this is to visit globalEDGE™ and do a search on the keywords "letter of credit." Another is to visit the websites of major banks to learn about procedures and instructions to receive payment through LC. Visit the websites of CIBC (www.cibc.com), the National Australia Bank (www.nab.com.au), and HSBC (www.hsbc.com) to see what you can learn about LCs. For each bank, what are the requirements for getting an LC? What services does the bank offer regarding LCs? Can you get training in LCs from these banks?

6-28. International labor standards are complex and closely related to global sourcing. In particular, the use of sweatshops has attracted much attention. A sweatshop is a factory characterized by very low wages, long hours, and poor working conditions. Some sweatshops employ children in unsafe conditions. Pro-labor groups advocate for minimum labor standards in foreign factories. Suppose your future employer wants to outsource a portion of its production to certain developing countries but is concerned about the possibility of employing sweatshop labor. Visit the websites of groups that encourage minimum standards in labor conditions (for example, www.workersrights.org, www.usas.org, or www.corpwatch.org or enter the keywords "labor conditions" at globalEDGE™), and prepare a memo to your employer that discusses the major concerns of those who advocate minimum labor standards.

**CKR Tangible Process Tool Exercise™**
**Identifying an Attractive Export Market**

Exporters seek the best markets for their products and services. Managers do market research to identify potential export markets. They examine such factors as market size, growth rate, economic status, competition, and the degree of political stability. The task of choosing the best export markets is complex. What makes an ideal market? What market potential indicators should be considered? Many firms follow a systematic process of international market research. In this exercise, you will learn the important indicators used to assess potential export markets, access information needed to develop international business plans, and research country-level barriers that firms face in exporting.

**Background**

Exporting is the most widely used entry mode. This is especially true for smaller firms or those new to international business. Research is vital to small and medium-sized enterprises, which usually lack the resources to sustain significant losses from failed exporting efforts.

Successful exporting requires developing knowledge about appropriate target markets. It involves identifying market opportunities and understanding the characteristics and conditions of target markets. Research provides insights about customer requirements, competitor activity, and appropriate ways of doing business.

Exporters need to learn about the technology level of potential target markets. In countries with low technological knowledge, distributors or customers may need to be trained in the product's features and usage. A country's attractiveness as a target market is reduced if distributors and customers require extensive training.

In this exercise, assume you work for a firm that makes and markets microwave ovens. Initially, the firm wants to sell compact microwave oven models. Assume they retail for about $50. Your task is to conduct research to find attractive export markets.

To complete this exercise, go to MyLab Management (www.pearson.com/mylab/management) and click on **Career Toolbox**.

# Endnotes

1. International Trade Administration, "Trade Statistics," 2018, www.trade.gov; The Times, "Exploring Global Export Markets," www.thetimes.co.uk, accessed April 7, 2013; UNCTAD, *Handbook of Statistics 2017* (New York: United Nations, 2018).

2. Anne Smith, "Health Care Bargains Abroad," *Kiplinger's Personal Finance*, January 2012, pp. 65–68; Oliver Smith, "The 51 Destinations Where Tourists Outnumber Locals," *The Telegraph,* September 27, 2017, www.telegraph.co.uk.

3. UNCTAD, 2018.

4. Matthew Alexander, *Outsourcing 365* (Amazon Digital Services, 2017, www.amazon.com); "Outsourcing: Time to Bring It Back Home?" *Economist*, March 5, 2005, p. 63.

5. Oystein Fjeldstad and Charles Snow, "Business Models and Organization Design," *Long Range Planning* 51, No. 1 (2018), pp. 32–39; Michael E. Porter, *Competition in Global Industries* (Boston: Harvard Business School Press 1986).

6. Benito Arrunada and Xose H. Vazquez, "When Your Contract Manufacturer Becomes Your Competitor," *Harvard Business Review,* September 2006, pp. 135–145; Peter J. Buckley, *The Global Factory: Networked Multinational Enterprises in the Modern Global Economy* (Northampton, MA: Edward Elgar, 2018); McKinsey & Co., "The Great Re-make: Manufacturing for Modern Times," June 2017, www.mckinsey.com.

7. Neal Boudette and William Boston, "BMW Readies U.S. Factory Expansion," *Wall Street Journal*, March 25, 2014, www.wsj.com; BMW Group, *Locations: The BMW Group—A Global Company*, www.bmw.com, April 8, 2018.

8. *China Daily,* "Top 10 Global Smartphone Suppliers," June 30, 2017, www.usa.chinadaily.com.cn; Geoffrey Fowler, "How Was Your Smartphone Made? Nobody Really Knows," *Wall Street Journal,* July 8, 2016, www.wsj.com; Wilhelm Kohler and Erdal Yalcin, *Developments in Global Sourcing* (Cambridge, MA: MIT Press, 2018).

9. Kohler and Yalcin, 2018; UNCTAD, 2017.

10. Andrew Baxter, "GE Unit Plugs into the Outside World," *Financial Times*, September 28, 2005, p. 8; *Marketline*, Genpact Limited, August 30, 2017, www.marketline.com; Don Lee, "The Philippines Has Become the Call-Center Capital of the World," *Lost Angeles Times,* February 1, 2015, www.latimes.com; Angelika Zimmermann, Ilan Oshri, Eleni Lioliou, and Alexandra Gerbasi, "Sourcing In or Out: Implications for Social Capital and Knowledge Sharing," *The Journal of Strategic Information Systems* 27 No. 1 (2018), pp. 82–100.

11. McKinsey & Co., 2017; UNCTAD, 2017.

12. Ruth Alexander, "Which Is the World's Biggest Employer?" *BBC News Magazine*, March 19, 2012, www.bbc.co.uk; Lorraine

Luk, "Hon Hai Shifts Its Chinese Work Force," *Wall Street Journal*, August 19, 2010, p. B8.

13. Masaaki Kotabe, Janet Murray, and Rajshekhar Javalgi, "Global Sourcing of Services and Market Performance: An Empirical Investigation," *Journal of International Marketing* 6 (1998), pp. 10–31; Masaaki Kotabe and Janet Murray, "Outsourcing Service Activities," *Marketing Management* 10 (2001), pp. 40–46.

14. Joshua Freedman, "Distance Earning," *Lawyer*, November 21, 2011, pp. 14–16; Amy Kazmin, "Outsourcing: Law Firms Fuel the Demand for Offshore Services," *Financial Times*, January 30, 2009, www.ft.com; Jan Stentoft et al., "Performance Outcomes of Offshoring, Backshoring and Staying at Home Manufacturing," *International Journal of Production Economics* 199 (May 2018), pp. 199–208.

15. Alexander, 2017; Richard Frasch and Charlotte Westfall, "Sourcing Goods and Suppliers in China: A How-To Guide for Small Businesses," *Forbes,* January 26, 2014, www.forbes.com; Kohler and Yalcin, 2018; Poh-Lin Yeoh, "Internationalization and Performance Outcomes of Entrepreneurial Family SMEs," *Thunderbird International Business Review* 56, No. 1 (2014), pp. 77–96.

16. International Labour Organization, *Global Wage Report 2016/17* (Geneva: International Labour Organization, 2015); Sophia Yan, "'Made in China' Isn't So Cheap Anymore, and That Could Spell Headache for Beijing," *CNBC*, February 27, 2017, www.cnbc.com.

17. Alexander, 2017; Fu Jia, Guido Orzes, Marco Sartor, and Guido Nassimbeni, "Global Sourcing Strategy and Structure: Towards a Conceptual Framework," *International Journal of Operations & Production Management* 37, No. 7 (2017), pp. 840–864; Kohler and Yalcin, 2018.

18. Ibid.

19. Jung Ha-Brookshire, *Global Sourcing in the Textile and Apparel Industry* (New York: Fairchild Books, 2017).

20. Alexander, 2017; Jia, Orzes, Sartor, and Nassimbeni, 2017; Kohler and Yalcin, 2018.

21. Ibid.

22. Alexander, 2017; Kohler and Yalcin, 2018; Hokey Min, *The Essentials of Supply Chain Management* (Upper Saddle River, NJ: Pearson FT Press, 2015).

23. Alexander, 2017; Jia, Orzes, Sartor, and Nassimbeni, 2017; Kohler and Yalcin, 2018.

24. John Fernie and Leigh Sparks, *Logistics and Retail Management: Emerging Issues and New Challenges in the Retail Supply Chain* (London: Chartered Institute of Logistics and Transport, 2018); Masaaki Kotabe and Janet Murray, "Global Sourcing Strategy and Sustainable Competitive Advantage," *Industrial Marketing Management* 33 (2004), pp. 7–14; Min, 2015.

25. Harold Sirkin, Michael Zinser, and Douglas Hohner, *Made in America, Again* (Boston: Boston Consulting Group, August 2011).

26. Deloitte, "2018 Global Manufacturing Competitiveness Index," 2018, www.deloitte.com.

27. Leigh Buchanan, "Why U.S. Manufacturers Are Turning Their Attention to 'Reshoring,'" *Inc.*, October 26, 2017, www.inc.com; James Hagerty and Mark Magnier, "Companies Tiptoe Back Toward 'Made in the U.S.A.,'" *Wall Street Journal*, January 13, 2015, www.wsj.com; *IndustryWeek*, "Reshoring: By the Numbers," March 20, 2017, www.industryweek.com; *International Labour Organization*, "Re-Shoring in Europe: Trends and Policy Issues," September 23, 2015, www.ilo.org; McKinsey & Co., 2017; Michele Nash-Hoff, "Reshoring Has Become an Economic Development Strategy," *IndustryWeek*, May 19, 2016, www.industryweek.com; Alessandra Vecchi, *Reshoring of Manufacturing: Drivers, Opportunities, and Challenges* (New York: Springer, 2017).

28. Paul Hartman, Jeffrey Ogden, Joseph Wirthlin, and Benjamin Hazen, "Nearshoring, Reshoring, and Insourcing: Moving beyond the total cost of ownership conversation," *Business Horizons* 60, No. 3 (2017), pp. 363–373; Ilan Oshri and Julia Kotlarsky, *The Handbook of Global Outsourcing and Offshoring* (Basingstoke, UK: Palgrave Macmillan, 2015); Luca Ventura, "Nearshoring Tide Rises," *Global Finance*, September 2016, p. 65; *Wall Street Journal*, "Why 'Nearshoring' Is Replacing 'Outsourcing,'" June 4, 2014, www.wsj.com.

29. David Goldman and Aaron Smith, "36,000 Verizon Workers Go on Strike," *CNN tech*, April 13, 2016, www.money.cnn.com; Dan Griffin and Mark Hilliard, "Cadbury's Staff in Dublin Go on Indefinite Strike," *Irish Times*, March 3, 2016, www.irishtimes.com.

30. "To Start Up Here, Companies Hire Over There," *USAToday*, February 11, 2005, pp. 1B–2B; Gilly Wright, "Will Reshoring Production Reverse Job Losses?," *Global Finance*, January 2017, p. 56.

31. Grace Kunz, Elena Karpova, and Myrna Garner, *Going Global: The Textile and Apparel Industry* (New York: Fairchild Books, 2016); John Thoburn, Kirsten Sutherland, and Thi Hoa Nguyen, "Globalization and Poverty: Impacts on Households of Employment and Restructuring in the Textiles Industry of Vietnam," *Journal of the Asia Pacific Economy* 12, No. 3 (2007), pp. 345–362.

32. Leonid Kogan, Dimitris Papanikolaou, Amit Seru, and Noah Stoffman, "Technological Innovation, Resource Allocation, and Growth," *The Quarterly Journal of Economics* 132, No. 2 (2017), pp. 665–712; Joseph A. Schumpeter, *Capitalism, Socialism, and Democracy* (New York: Harper, 1942).

33. Alexander, 2017; Kohler and Yalcin, 2018; Nada R. Sanders, *Supply Chain Management: A Global Perspective* (Hoboken, NJ: Wiley, 2017).

34. Kohler and Yalcin (2018).

35. Jeffrey Sparshott, "Trade Gap Shrinks by Most in 6 Years," *Wall Street Journal*, June 4, 2015, p. A2; Laura Stevens, Suzanne Kapner and Leslie Josephs, "Port Delays Starting to Damage Businesses," *Wall Street Journal*, www.wsj.com.

36. Alison Maitland, "Make Sure You Have Your Christmas Stock In," *Financial Times*, December 19, 2005, p. 11; Sanders, 2017.

# Chapter 7

# Foreign Direct Investment and Collaborative Ventures

**Learning Objectives** *After studying this chapter, you should be able to:*

7.1 Understand international investment and collaboration.

7.2 Describe the characteristics of foreign direct investment.

7.3 Explain the motives for FDI and collaborative ventures.

7.4 Identify the types of foreign direct investment.

7.5 Understand international collaborative ventures.

7.6 Discuss the experience of retailers in foreign markets.

## Huawei Invests in Africa

Africa is the world's second most populous continent, with a population just over one billion. Much of Africa is troubled by poor economic conditions. Most people in sub-Saharan Africa live on less than four dollars per day. Recently, Africa has begun to grow economically in part due to increased investment from abroad.

China is investing billions in Africa. The investments are targeting extractive industries, such as petroleum and mining, as well as higher-value industries, such as textiles and telecommunications. African demand for mobile communications is growing rapidly. In Ghana, Kenya, and South Africa, for example, about 85 percent of citizens own a cell phone, compared to 90 percent in the United States.

Huawei Technologies is China's largest telecommunications equipment manufacturer, with annual revenues exceeding $90 billion. The firm generates about 60 percent of its sales outside of China. It is a key player in African development. Huawei (pronounced who-ah-way) employs more than 180,000 people, including more than 10,000 in Africa. Huawei established a presence in Africa in the 1990s. It has developed cell phone networks throughout the continent. In the past decade, Huawei has invested more than $2 billion in Africa. The region now accounts for about 15 percent of Huawei's annual revenue.

Huawei leveraged foreign direct investment (FDI) and collaborative ventures in Africa to establish two R&D facilities, four regional headquarters, six training centers, and 20 representative offices. Despite various challenges, Huawei's operations there have proven very profitable. The firm leverages economies of scale, inexpensive labor, and numerous other advantages to keep

costs low. Efficient operations allow Huawei to price its cell phones lower than Ericsson, Nokia, and other competitors. The ability of Chinese firms to operate profitably in poor countries is a primary reason China's companies are outpacing firms from Europe, Japan, and North America in expanding their presence in Africa.

In Uganda, Huawei developed a government data center and several large-scale projects connecting agencies to a central network. In Ghana, Huawei invested more than $100 million to develop telecom facilities. In Northern Africa, Huawei entered a joint venture with ZTE Corporation to expand mobile networks in nine cities and build 800,000 phone lines. In Algeria, Huawei established a mobile network to complement a cell network completed by ZTE. Recently, Huawei and Global Marine Systems formed a joint venture to develop telecommunications infrastructure in Africa.

In addition to developing telecommunications infrastructure, Huawei's investments contribute directly to economic development. The expansion of cell networks allows Africans, many of whom live in isolated areas, to find jobs and interact with important contacts. Connecting to the Internet further enhances commercial growth. China's Africa investments benefit not only Africans, but also European and U.S. firms. These companies benefit from the roads, railways, telephony, energy systems, and other infrastructure that Chinese firms have helped to develop.

As manufacturing costs in China rise and the African middle class expands, Chinese firms will likely invest much more in Africa. China is playing a key role by financing and providing needed development expertise. Various African countries are streamlining regulations and creating business-friendly environments, increasing their attractiveness for more FDI.

## Questions

**7-1.** What are the main characteristics of Africa as a market for mobile telephones?

**7-2.** What benefits does foreign investment bring to Africa?

**7-3.** Describe the various ways Huawei has invested in Africa.

SOURCES: *Africa Research Bulletin*, "Telecommunications: Africa," January 16, 2013, pp p19650C–19851C; *China Daily*, "Huawei Promotes Digital Transformation in Egypt, North Africa," December 8, 2017, www.chinadaily.cn; Huawei, "Africa Fact Sheet," December 10, 2011, www.huawei.com; Huawei, *2017 Annual Report*, www.huawei.com; Olusegun Ogundeji, "Huawei Leads New Efforts to Develop Cable Infrastructure in Africa," *PCWorld*, March 19, 2015, www.pcworld.com; Pew Research Center, "Cell Phones in Africa: Communication Lifeline," April 15, 2015, www.pewglobal.org; Claire Van Den Heever, "Huawei's Quest for Hearts and Minds in Africa," October 16, 2016, www.atimes.com; Hejuan Zhao and Zhang Yuzhe, "China's Telecoms and Wireless Drums for Africa," *Caixin Online*, February 22, 2012, http://english.caixin.com.

---

The opening case highlights the benefits of foreign direct investment (FDI) and collaborative ventures to both firms and nations. The worldwide spread of capital and ownership through FDI is one of the remarkable facets of globalization.

Consider Tata Motors (www.tatamotors.com), India's largest automaker. Tata earns about 65 percent of its sales from abroad. Tata paid $2.3 billion to purchase Jaguar and Land Rover from the Ford Motor Company. Tata owns many Jaguar and Land Rover car factories in Asia and Europe. Tata developed the Nano—the world's cheapest car. Renault and Nissan partnered with Tata to distribute the Nano in Europe. Tata also acquired 50 percent of Miljo, a Norwegian electric vehicle maker. In South Korea, Tata purchased Daewoo Commercial Vehicle Company, a leading manufacturer of trucks and tractors.[1]

Internationalizing through FDI enables the firm to maintain a physical presence in key markets, secure direct access to customers and partners, and perform critical value-chain activities in the market. FDI is an equity or ownership form of foreign market entry. It is the entry strategy most associated with large MNEs—such as Bombardier, Ford, and Unilever—that have extensive physical operations around the world. As they venture abroad, firms that specialize in products usually establish manufacturing plants. Firms that offer services, such as banks, cruise lines, and restaurant chains, usually establish agency relationships and retail facilities.

In this chapter, we examine the nature of FDI and collaborative ventures. We explain the motives that drive companies to use these entry strategies. We highlight numerous companies engaged in FDI as well as best practices for investment and partnering success. We also examine retailers, a distinctive category of foreign investors in the services sector.

## International Investment and Collaboration

**7.1** Understand international investment and collaboration.

**Foreign direct investment (FDI)**
An internationalization strategy in which the firm establishes a physical presence abroad through acquisition of productive assets such as capital, technology, labor, land, plant, and equipment.

**International portfolio investment**
Passive ownership of foreign securities such as stocks and bonds to generate financial returns.

**Foreign direct investment (FDI)** is an internationalization strategy by which the firm establishes a physical presence abroad through direct ownership of productive assets such as capital, technology, labor, land, plant, and equipment. FDI is the most advanced and complex foreign market entry strategy. Firms use FDI to establish manufacturing plants, marketing subsidiaries, or other facilities in target countries. Because this involves investing substantial resources to establish a physical presence abroad, FDI is riskier than other entry strategies.

Do not confuse FDI with **international portfolio investment**, which refers to passive ownership of foreign securities, such as stocks and bonds, to generate financial returns. International portfolio investment is a form of international investment, but it is not FDI, which seeks ownership control of a business abroad and represents a long-term commitment. The United Nations uses the benchmark of at least 10 percent ownership in the enterprise to differentiate FDI from portfolio investment. However, this percentage may be misleading because control is not usually achieved unless the investor owns at least 50 percent of a foreign venture.

An **international collaborative venture** is a cross-border business partnership in which collaborating firms pool their resources and share costs and risks of a new venture. Here the focal firm partners with one or more companies to pursue a joint project or initiative. International collaborative ventures are also sometimes called international partnerships or international strategic alliances.

A **joint venture** is a form of collaboration between two or more firms to create a new, jointly owned enterprise. Unlike collaborative arrangements in which no new entity is created, the partners in a joint venture typically invest money to create a new enterprise. Joint ventures (JVs) may last for many years. A partner in a joint venture may enjoy minority, equal, or majority ownership.

Consider the following example from the beer industry. In 2004, Brazilian private equity firm 3G Capital launched the Belgium-based brewer InBev. In 2008, Inbev established a major presence in the U.S. beer market by purchasing Anheuser-Busch for $52 billion. The new firm, called Anheuser-Busch InBev, in 2016 acquired SABMiller, based in London, which itself had been formed when South African Breweries purchased the American firm Miller Brewing. In 2013, Anheuser-Busch InBev also acquired Mexico's largest brewer, Grupo Modelo, known for its Corona and Modelo Especial brands of beer. In 2017, Anheuser-Busch InBev formed a joint venture with Anadolu Efes, a Turkish brewery, with the goal of marketing beer in Russia.[2] Through numerous FDI and collaborative ventures, Anheuser-Busch InBev has become the world's largest brewer and operates more than 140 breweries across Asia, Europe, and North and South America. Brazilian investor 3G Capital maintains a 23 percent stake in the firm.[3]

## Volume of Foreign Direct Investment and Collaborative Ventures

Literally hundreds of cross-border direct investments and collaborative ventures take place each year. In 2017, the value of such investments or acquisitions surpassed $1.5 trillion worldwide. The top five recipients of FDI were China, United States, Netherlands, Ireland, and Australia.[4] Recent examples of cross-border investments include:

- Volkswagen spent $1 billion to build a factory in Poland to manufacture delivery vans.
- The British pharmaceutical firm GlaxoSmithKline purchased the global Vaccines division of Switzerland's Novartis for $5.25 billion.
- Denmark's LEGO Group spent more than 100 million euros to build a toy factory in China.
- China's Haier paid $5.4 billion to acquire the home appliances division of General Electric.
- Johnson Controls, a U.S. maker of car batteries and heating and ventilation equipment, acquired Ireland-based peer Tyco International for $16.5 billion, a deal that allows Johnson Controls to relocate to Ireland and substantially reduce its income tax obligations.
- Japan's Toshiba formed a joint venture with the U.S. firm United Technologies to establish R&D centers in Europe and India to support joint innovation in the heating and air conditioning industry.

These and other examples illustrate several trends:

- Firms from both advanced economies and emerging markets are active in FDI.
- Destination or recipient countries for such investments are both advanced economies and emerging markets.
- Companies use various strategies to enter foreign markets, including acquisitions and collaborative ventures.
- Firms from all types of industries, including services, are active in FDI and collaborative ventures. Retailers began expanding abroad in the 1970s, including Metro AG (Germany), Royal Ahold (Netherlands), Tesco (United Kingdom), and Walmart (United States).
- Direct investment by foreign firms occasionally inflames citizens' patriotic feelings. In the United States, for example, Chinese oil company CNOOC attempted to buy Unocal Corporation. The action raised concerns about a Chinese state enterprise gaining control of a key U.S. firm in the energy sector. Strong opposition drove the U.S. Congress to ban the deal.

## Most Active Firms in FDI

Exhibit 7.1 provides a sample of leading MNEs engaged in FDI. Royal Dutch Shell, Toyota, and other firms in the exhibit are listed based on the value of factories, subsidiaries, and other assets they own in foreign countries. For example, Toyota has numerous subsidiaries around the world. Individual Toyota subsidiaries engage in various value-chain activities, including R&D,

### International collaborative venture

A cross-border business alliance in which partnering firms pool their resources and share costs and risks to undertake a new business venture; also referred to as an international partnership or an international strategic alliance.

### Joint venture

A form of collaboration between two or more firms to create a new, jointly owned enterprise.

| Company | Home Country | Industry | Approximate Sales (billions of U.S. dollars) | | Approximate Assets (billions of U.S. dollars) | |
|---|---|---|---|---|---|---|
| | | | Foreign | Total | Foreign | Total |
| Royal Dutch Shell | United Kingdom | Petroleum | 349 | 411 | 152 | 233 |
| Toyota Motor | Japan | Motor vehicles | 303 | 436 | 173 | 255 |
| BP | United Kingdom | Petroleum | 235 | 263 | 141 | 183 |
| Total | France | Petroleum | 233 | 243 | 110 | 141 |
| Anheuser-Busch InBev | Belgium | Food and beverages | 208 | 258 | 39 | 45 |
| Volkswagen Group | Germany | Motor vehicles | 197 | 432 | 192 | 240 |
| Chevron | United States | Petroleum | 189 | 260 | 54 | 110 |
| General Electric | United States | Electrical and electronic equipment | 178 | 365 | 70 | 124 |
| Exxon Mobil | United States | Petroleum | 165 | 330 | 122 | 219 |
| Softbank | Japan | Telecommunications | 145 | 220 | 45 | 82 |

**EXHIBIT 7.1**

**World's Most International Nonfinancial MNEs, Based on Value of Foreign Assets**

*Sources:* Based on Hoovers company database at www.hoovers.com, 2018; UNCTAD, "Annex Table 24. The World's Top 100 Non-Financial TNCs, Ranked by Foreign Assets," in *World Investment Report 2017* (New York: United Nations, 2017), accessed April 12, 2018, at www.unctad.org.

manufacturing, marketing, sales, and customer service. The most internationally active MNEs are in the automotive and petroleum industries.

### Service Firms and FDI

Most companies in the services sector, such as retailing, construction, and personal care, must offer their services where they are consumed. This usually requires establishing either a permanent presence through FDI (as in retailing) or a temporary relocation of the service company personnel (as in the construction industry).[5] Management consulting is a professional service usually embodied in experts who interact directly with clients to provide advice. To reach their customers, consulting firms such as McKinsey and Accenture establish offices in key international markets. Many support services, such as advertising, insurance, accounting, legal work, and overnight package delivery, are also best provided at the customer's location. FDI is vital for internationalizing services.[6]

Intrawest, Inc. has established offices and other facilities in China where it aims to build ski resorts. HSBC Bank has established branches around the world because banking services are usually provided directly to customers wherever banks do business. Exhibit 7.2 portrays the world's largest MNEs in the services sector. Many such firms are concentrated in the retailing, banking, and financial services industries.

### Leading Destinations for FDI

Advanced economies such as Australia, Canada, Japan, Netherlands, the United Kingdom, and the United States long have been popular destinations for FDI. These countries all share high per capita GDP, strong GDP growth, high density of knowledge workers, and superior business infrastructure, such as telephone systems and energy sources.[7] In recent years, however, developing economies and emerging markets have gained much appeal as FDI destinations. This is illustrated by data from the United Nations Conference on Trade and Development. It suggests that, between 2005 and 2017, the volume of FDI flowing into emerging markets and developing economies has generally increased. Meanwhile, since 2005, the amount of FDI flowing into advanced economies has mostly declined. This continuing trend bodes well for less-developed economies because FDI is a key determinant of economic development and living standards.[8]

| Company | Home Country | Industry | Revenues (billions of U.S. dollars) |
|---|---|---|---|
| Walmart | United States | Retailing | 486 |
| AT&T | United States | Telecommunications, media | 164 |
| EXOR Group | Italy | Investments | 155 |
| ICBC | China | Banking, financial services | 148 |
| AmerisourceBergen | United States | Drug wholesaling | 147 |
| China State Construction Engineering | China | Construction | 145 |
| AXA | France | Financial services | 144 |
| Amazon.com | United States | Online retailing | 136 |
| China Construction Bank | China | Banking, financial services | 135 |
| Allianz | Germany | Insurance | 122 |
| Costco | United States | Retailing | 119 |
| Walgreens Boots Alliance | United States | Retailing | 117 |
| Agricultural Bank of China | China | Banking, financial services | 117 |
| Ping An Insurance | China | Insurance | 117 |
| Bank of China | China | Banking, financial services | 114 |

**EXHIBIT 7.2**

**World's Largest MNEs in the Services Sector, Based on Annual Revenues**

*Sources: Forbes*, "Global 2000," 2017, www.forbes.com; *Fortune*, "Global 500," 2017, www.fortune.com; Hoovers company database at www.hoovers.com, 2018; UNCTAD, "Annex Table 24. The World's Top 100 Non-Financial TNCs, Ranked by Foreign Assets," in *World Investment Report 2017* (New York: United Nations, 2017), accessed April 12, 2018, at www.unctad.org.

According to A. T. Kearney's FDI Confidence Index, China ranks among the top destinations for foreign investment (www.atkearney.com). China is popular because of its size, rapid growth rate, and low labor costs. It is an important platform where MNEs manufacture products for export to key markets in Asia and elsewhere.[9] China also holds strategic importance for its long-term potential as a target market and source of competitive advantage.

## Factors to Consider in Choosing FDI Locations

Exhibit 7.3 lists the criteria firms use to evaluate countries as potential targets for FDI projects. Suppose Taiwan-based Acer (www.acer.com) wants to build a new computer factory. Its managers will research the best country in which to build it, looking at country and regional factors, infrastructural factors, political factors, profit retention factors, and human resource factors.

As an example, consider the attractiveness of Eastern European nations as FDI destinations. Several of the selection criteria noted in Exhibit 7.3 have attracted foreign firms to these countries. In the Czech Republic, giant Chinese electronics manufacturer Sichuan Changhong (www.changhong.com) built a $30 million factory that produces up to one million flat-screen televisions per year. Numerous automakers, from Ford to Nissan, have built factories in the region. Wages in Eastern Europe are relatively low; engineers in Slovakia earn half of what Western

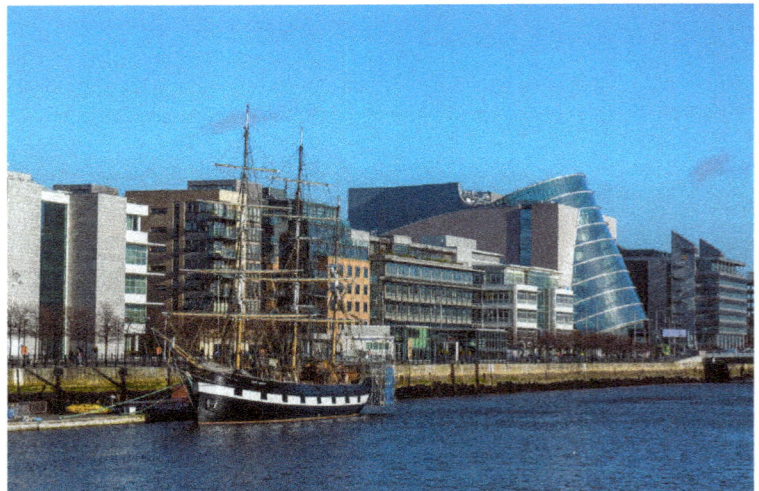

*Source:* LMspencer/Shutterstock

Business-friendly Ireland is one of the world's top FDI destinations. Pictured here is Dublin, home to European operations of Google, Intel, and numerous other multinational technology firms.

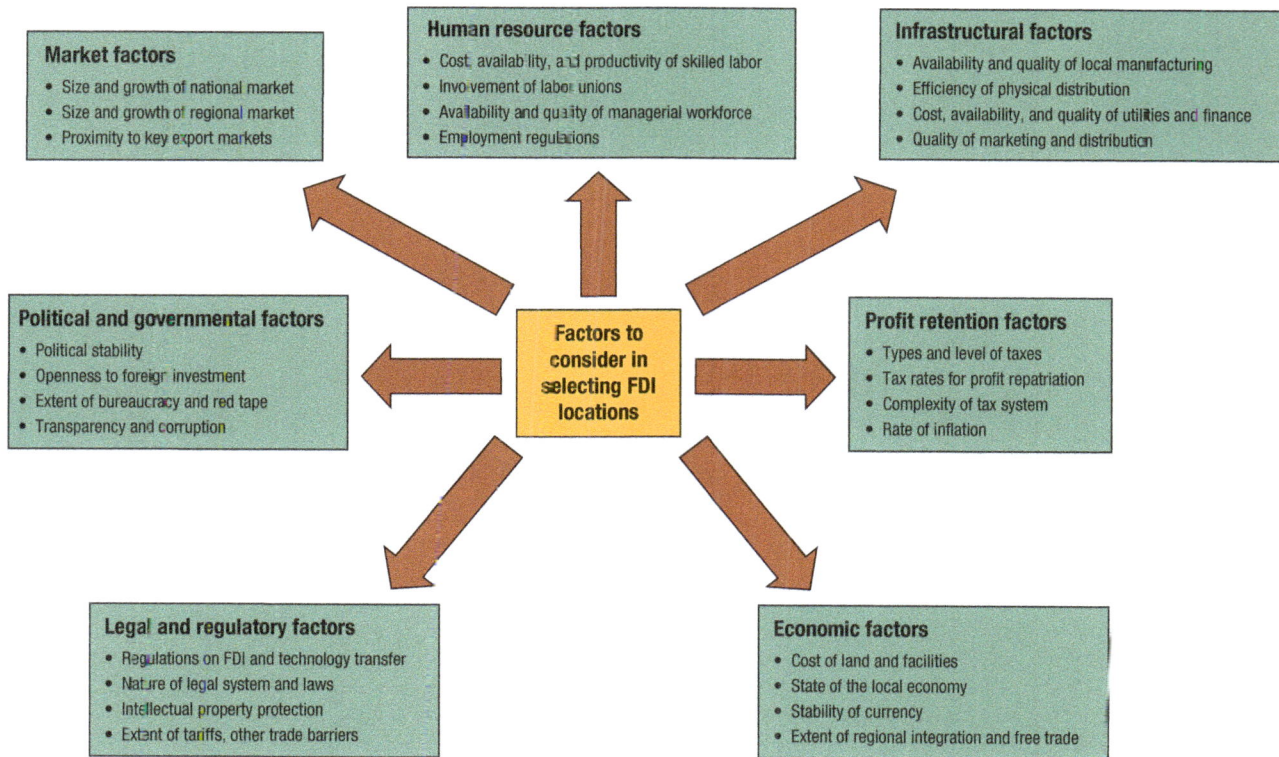

**Market factors**
- Size and growth of national market
- Size and growth of regional market
- Proximity to key export markets

**Human resource factors**
- Cost, availability, and productivity of skilled labor
- Involvement of labor unions
- Availability and quality of managerial workforce
- Employment regulations

**Infrastructural factors**
- Availability and quality of local manufacturing
- Efficiency of physical distribution
- Cost, availability, and quality of utilities and finance
- Quality of marketing and distribution

**Political and governmental factors**
- Political stability
- Openness to foreign investment
- Extent of bureaucracy and red tape
- Transparency and corruption

**Factors to consider in selecting FDI locations**

**Profit retention factors**
- Types and level of taxes
- Tax rates for profit repatriation
- Complexity of tax system
- Rate of inflation

**Legal and regulatory factors**
- Regulations on FDI and technology transfer
- Nature of legal system and laws
- Intellectual property protection
- Extent of tariffs, other trade barriers

**Economic factors**
- Cost of land and facilities
- State of the local economy
- Stability of currency
- Extent of regional integration and free trade

**EXHIBIT 7.3**

**Factors to Consider in Selecting Foreign Direct Investment Locations**

*Sources:* John H. Dunning, *Explaining International Production* (New York: Routledge, 2015); Daniel Hoi Ki Ho and Peter Tze Yiu Lau, "Perspectives on Foreign Direct Investment Location Decisions: What Do We Know and Where Do We Go from Here?," *International Tax Journal* 33 No. 3 (2007), pp. 39–48; Robert Green and William Cunningham, "The Determinants of US Foreign Investment: An Empirical Examination," *Management International Review*, 15 No. 2–3 (1975), pp. 113–120; Franklin Root, *Entry Strategies for International Markets*, (Hoboken, NJ: John Wiley & Sons, 1994).

engineers make, and assembly-line workers one-third to one-fifth. In addition, East European governments offer incentives, from financing to low taxes, as in Slovakia, where all income taxes add up to a simple 19 percent. By comparison, personal income tax rates often exceed 30 percent in Germany. Eastern Europe also provides ready access to the huge EU market.[10] Managers examine a combination of criteria when making decisions about where in the world to establish operations through FDI.

**7.2** Describe the characteristics of foreign direct investment.

## Characteristics of Foreign Direct Investment

FDI is an advanced form of foreign market entry with distinctive characteristics. Key features of FDI include:

- *Substantial resource commitment.* As the ultimate internationalization strategy, it is far more taxing on the firm's resources and capabilities than any other entry strategy. For example, the U.S. firm General Electric owns more than $300 billion in factories, subsidiaries, and other operations outside the United States.[11]
- *Local presence and operations.* With FDI, the firm establishes itself directly in the market, leading to direct contact with customers, intermediaries, facilitators, and governments. Some firms concentrate operations in one or a few locations; others disperse their FDI among many countries. The MNE network may become so extensive that the firm effectively loses its nationality. Nestlé, for example, is based in Switzerland but generates more than 90 percent of its sales from abroad. The Indian MNE Tata Consultancy Services

generates most of its revenues in North America, whereas rival IBM, a U.S. company, obtains nearly two-thirds of its sales from abroad.[12]

- *Investment in countries that provide specific comparative advantages.* Managers invest in countries based on the advantages these locations offer. Thus, firms tend to perform R&D in countries with leading-edge knowledge for their industry, source from countries home to suppliers that provide superior goods, build factories in locations with low labor costs, and establish marketing subsidiaries in countries with excellent sales potential.

- *Intense dealings in the host market.* Firms that enter through FDI necessarily deal more intensely with culture and other aspects of the host country. MNEs with high-profile, conspicuous operations are especially vulnerable to close public scrutiny of their actions. To minimize potential problems, managers often favor investing in countries that are culturally and linguistically familiar. When setting up shop in continental Europe, for example, U.S. firms frequently choose the Netherlands because English is widely spoken there.[13]

*Source:* maridav/123RF

Vodafone is one of the most international firms due to its very extensive FDI activities. This mobile phone service provider invests to establish retail outlets in Africa, Asia-Pacific, Europe, the Middle East, and the Americas.

- *Substantial risk and uncertainty.* Establishing a permanent, fixed presence abroad makes the firm vulnerable to country risk and intervention by local governments. In addition to local labor practices, direct investors also must contend with local economic conditions such as inflation and recessions. French automaker Renault recently acquired a 25 percent stake in Russian automaker AvtoVAZ to produce Lada brand cars in Russia. However, the 40-year-old AvtoVAZ plant is plagued by inefficient operations, a slow workforce, and a history of organized crime.[14] Business in Russia often requires paying bribes, and the country has a history of high inflation and other macroeconomic concerns. The Russian government often intervenes in the private sector.

Even a large, well-established company such as Disney (www.disney.com) experienced several failures in its foreign investing.[15] When Disney established Tokyo Disneyland, its management assumed the Disneyland experience could not be successfully transferred to Japan. So instead of investing, Disney opted to license rights in Japan for nominal profits. Tokyo Disneyland proved to be a huge success. Not wanting to repeat the same mistake, management opted for an FDI stake in its next theme park—Disneyland Paris. However, it proved to be a financial sinkhole. Having learned from these experiences, Disney made its Hong Kong Disneyland park more successful. Disney owns 47 percent of the venture, making the Hong Kong government the major partner. Management wants to expand the park, but negotiations with the Hong Kong government have been tense and complicated. After receiving permission from the Chinese government, Disney in 2016 launched its most recent theme park, Shanghai Disneyland. Management is worried about intellectual property violations in China, which may reduce profits from licensing Disney movies, animated characters, and other valuable properties.[16]

## Ethics, Social Responsibility, Sustainability, and FDI

Companies that internationalize through FDI are often criticized for ethical lapses and irresponsible behavior because such firms can exert substantial power in the markets where they are most heavily invested. For example, some MNEs operate foreign factories under harsh working conditions. Others engage in bribery to advance their interests. Some MNEs market shoddy products or employ questionable marketing practices through their foreign subsidiaries.

At the same time, the strong local presence implied by FDI offers opportunities to conduct business in ways that ensure high ethical standards and social responsibility. Many MNEs invest in local communities and seek to establish global standards of fair treatment for workers.

Unilever (www.unilever.com), the giant Dutch-British producer of consumer products, demonstrates its corporate social responsibility (CSR) by:

- Operating a free community laundry in a slum in São Paulo, Brazil.
- Funding a hospital that offers free medical care to the needy in Bangladesh.
- Teaching palm oil producers to reuse plant waste in Ghana.
- Providing small loans to help women in remote villages start small-scale businesses in India.[17]

Many MNEs are responding to global *sustainability* agendas. For example, automakers such as Toyota, Renault, and Volkswagen are investing in fuel-efficient and clean technologies. Nokia is a leader in phasing out toxic materials. Dell was among the first to accept old PC hardware from consumers and recycle it for free. Suncor Energy assists Native Americans to deal with social and ecological issues in Canada's far north.

## Ethical Connections

FDI offers numerous benefits to recipient countries. However, FDI may produce side effects that harm the natural environment, especially in countries with weak environmental laws. Pollution and ecological destruction may result alongside rapid economic growth. One MNE, a manufacturer of food additives, allowed untreated wastewater to flow into the ThiVai River in Vietnam. Resulting pollution nearly destroyed the livelihood of thousands of downstream farmers. Firms must behave responsibly in their international dealings. Governments must not allow development goals to compromise citizens' well-being.

**7.3** Explain the motives for FDI and collaborative ventures.

## Motives for FDI and Collaborative Ventures

The ultimate goal of FDI and international collaborative ventures is to enhance company competitiveness in the global marketplace. Various motives explain why firms pursue these entry strategies. In Exhibit 7.4, we classify the motives for FDI and collaborative ventures into three categories: market-seeking, resource- or asset-seeking, and efficiency-seeking.[18] In many cases, firms aim to satisfy several motives simultaneously. Let's examine these motives in more detail.

### Market-Seeking Motives

Managers may seek new market opportunities as a result of either unfavorable developments in their home market (that is, they may be pushed into international markets) or attractive opportunities abroad (they may be pulled into international markets). There are three primary market-seeking motivations.

- *Gain access to new markets or opportunities.* The existence of a substantial market motivates many firms to produce offerings at or near customer locations. Local production improves customer service and reduces the cost of transporting goods to buyer

**EXHIBIT 7.4**

**Firm Motives for Foreign Direct Investment and Collaborative Ventures**

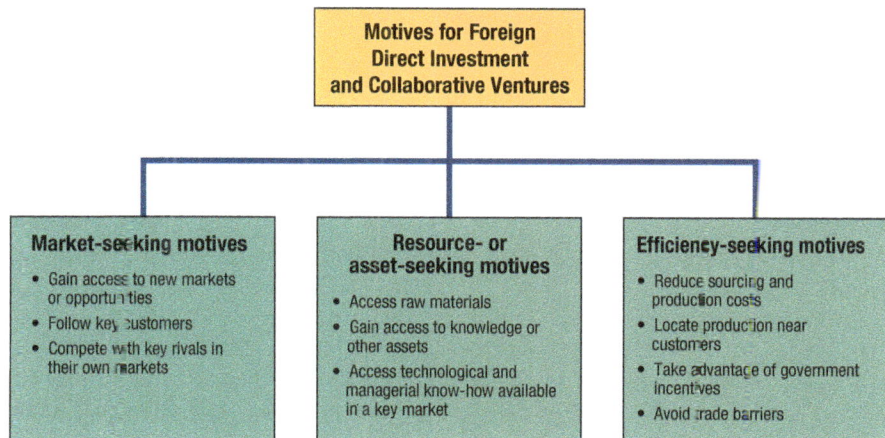

**Motives for Foreign Direct Investment and Collaborative Ventures**

**Market-seeking motives**
- Gain access to new markets or opportunities
- Follow key customers
- Compete with key rivals in their own markets

**Resource- or asset-seeking motives**
- Access raw materials
- Gain access to knowledge or other assets
- Access technological and managerial know-how available in a key market

**Efficiency-seeking motives**
- Reduce sourcing and production costs
- Locate production near customers
- Take advantage of government incentives
- Avoid trade barriers

locations. Coca-Cola, IBM, Samsung, and Siemens all generate more sales abroad than in their home markets. The opening case highlights Huawei Technologies, a Chinese firm that has invested billions in Africa to gain access to fast-growing mobile phone markets there.

- *Follow key customers.* Firms often follow their key customers abroad to preempt other vendors from serving them. Establishing local operations also positions the firm to serve customer needs better. Tradegar Industries supplies the plastic that its customer, Procter & Gamble, uses to manufacture disposable diapers. When P&G built a plant in China, Tradegar followed P&G there, establishing production in China as well.
- *Compete with key rivals in their own markets.* Some MNEs may choose to confront current or potential competitors directly, in the competitors' home market. The strategic purpose is to weaken the competitor by forcing it to expend resources to defend its market. In the earth-moving equipment industry, Caterpillar entered a joint venture with Mitsubishi to put pressure on the market share and profitability of their common rival, Japan's Komatsu. The need to spend substantial resources to defend its home market reduced Komatsu's ability to expand abroad.[19]

## Resource- or Asset-Seeking Motives

Firms frequently want to acquire production factors that are more abundant or less costly in a foreign market. They may also seek complementary resources and capabilities of partner companies headquartered abroad. Specifically, FDI or collaborative ventures may be motivated by the firm's desire to attain the following assets.

- *Raw materials needed in extractive and agricultural industries.* Firms in the mining, oil, and crop-growing industries have little choice but to go where the raw materials are. In the wine industry, companies establish wineries in countries suited for growing grapes, such as France and Chile. Oil companies establish refineries in countries with abundant petroleum reserves such as Kuwait.
- *Knowledge or other assets.*[20] By establishing a local presence through FDI, the firm is better positioned to deepen its understanding of target markets. FDI provides the foreign firm better access to market knowledge, customers, distribution systems, and control over local operations. By collaborating in R&D, production, and marketing, the focal firm can benefit from the partner's know-how. When Whirlpool entered Europe, it partnered with Philips to benefit from the latter's well-known brand name and distribution network. Royal Dutch Shell and PetroChina established a $1.3 billion joint venture to extract gas and oil from the Changbei gas field in China. Through this venture, PetroChina is acquiring knowledge about Shell's advanced technologies for extracting fossil fuels from deep shale deposits. In turn, Shell gained access to the gas field and is learning from PetroChina how to navigate the complex Chinese energy market.[21]
- *Technological and managerial know-how.*[22] The firm may benefit by establishing a presence in a key industrial cluster. Examples include the robotics industry in Japan, chemicals in Germany, fashion in Italy, and software in the United States. Companies can obtain many advantages from locating at the hub of knowledge development and innovation in a given industry. Denmark, Finland, Israel, New Zealand, Sweden, and the United States are considered ideal for R&D in the biotechnology industry because they have abundant biotech knowledge workers.[23] Many firms enter a collaborative venture abroad as a prelude to wholly owned FDI. Collaboration with a local partner reduces the risks of entry and provides the entrant local expertise before launching operations of its own in the market.

## Efficiency-Seeking Motives

International expansion enables the firm to achieve *economies of scale*. International expansion allows the firm to increase sales and employ company assets across a larger number of products and markets. As the quantity of productive output increases, the per-unit cost of production tends to decline. In turn, profits rise as the firm's average cost of operations falls. Similarly, with increasing output, the per-unit cost of other productive activities declines—R&D, marketing, distribution, and customer support.

> ## When firms expand into international markets, they obtain economies of scale. This occurs for various reasons.
>
> - *Falling fixed costs.* Many industries and productive tasks have high per-unit fixed costs that decline the more the task is performed. For example, imagine the per-unit cost of the first car that rolls off an assembly line—production cannot occur unless the firm builds a factory. To increase international sales, the firm must produce more cars. As more cars are produced, the cost to build the factory is amortized across many cars, and the average cost per car declines.
> - *Managerial resource efficiencies.* International expansion implies that the firm must employ a relatively fixed number of headquarters staff across more subsidiaries and affiliates. In this way, managerial talent is used more efficiently.
> - *Specialization of labor.* When productive output increases, the firm hires more workers, who become more specialized in their tasks. As they specialize, workers become more efficient and produce more output per hour worked.
> - *Volume discounts.* Suppliers usually offer discounts for large-quantity purchases. Per-unit sourcing costs fall as the firm buys more parts, components, and other inputs.
> - *Financial economies.* Compared to small firms, large companies usually can access capital at lower cost. This arises because large firms are relatively powerful and tend to borrow large sums.

Internationalization also increases *economies of scope*. Economies of scope refers to the cost savings that arise from using a relatively fixed base of managerial talent, facilities, and other company assets across a larger marketplace. For example, Unilever uses the same base of managers and marketing experts at its Netherlands headquarters to develop advertising for numerous product lines for many countries in Europe. This is more efficient than delegating the task to individual managers in each European country. The cost-reducing benefits of doing business in numerous countries simultaneously are substantial. MNEs frequently concentrate production in only a few locations to increase the efficiency of manufacturing.[24] Many firms develop global brands to increase the efficiency of marketing activities.

In addition to attaining economies of scale and scope, firms engage in international business to achieve four major efficiency-seeking goals:

- *Reduce sourcing and production costs by accessing inexpensive labor and other cheap inputs to the production process.*[25] This motive accounts for the massive investment by foreign firms in factories and service-producing facilities in China, Mexico, Eastern Europe, and India. MNEs establish factories in such locations to reduce production costs.
- *Locate production near customers.* In industries that need to be especially sensitive to customer needs or in which tastes change rapidly, companies often locate factories or assembly operations near important customers. H&M and Zara locate much of their garment production close to customers in Europe. Compared to costs in China or Latin America, manufacturing clothing in Europe is more expensive. But the clothing gets into shops faster and more closely represents the latest fashion trends.[26]
- *Take advantage of government incentives.* In addition to restricting imports, governments

*Source:* Samot/Shutterstock

Firms in the wine industry engage in foreign direct investment and collaborative ventures to access raw materials, in this case, farm land suitable for cultivating wine grapes. Pictured is a vineyard in Italy.

frequently offer subsidies and tax concessions to foreign firms to encourage them to invest locally. Governments encourage inward FDI because it provides local jobs and capital, increases tax revenue, and transfers skills and technologies.[27]

- *Avoid trade barriers.* Companies often enter markets through FDI to avoid tariffs and other trade barriers because these usually apply only to exporting. By establishing a physical presence inside a country or an economic bloc, the foreign company obtains the same advantages as local firms. Partnering with a local firm also helps overcome regulations or trade barriers and satisfy local content rules. The desire to avoid trade barriers helps explain why numerous Japanese automakers established factories in the United States. However, this motive is declining in importance because trade barriers have fallen substantially in many countries.

## Types of Foreign Direct Investment

One way to illustrate the pattern of FDI worldwide is to examine FDI stock. FDI stock refers to the total value of assets that MNEs own in foreign countries. The map in Exhibit 7.5 portrays the volume of FDI stock per capita by country. High levels of FDI stock suggest that a country is a popular investment destination and that MNE managers are confident about the country's economic health and prospects. We can classify FDI activities by form (greenfield versus mergers and acquisitions), nature of ownership (wholly owned versus joint venture), and level of integration (horizontal versus vertical).

### Greenfield Investment Versus Mergers and Acquisitions

**Greenfield investment** occurs when a firm invests to build a new manufacturing, marketing, or administrative facility as opposed to acquiring existing facilities. As the name *greenfield* implies, the investing firm typically buys an empty plot of land and builds a production plant, marketing subsidiary, or other facility there for its own use. This is exactly what Ford did when it established its large factory in Rayong, Thailand, to manufacture small cars for emerging markets.

An **acquisition** is the purchase of an existing company or facility. For example, Brazil's Natura Cosmeticos acquired the Body Shop, a British retailer of cosmetics and skin care products, in order to expand Natura's reach into advanced economy markets.[28] The Chinese personal computer manufacturer Lenovo made an ambitious acquisition of IBM's PC business, which now accounts for some two-thirds of Lenovo's annual revenue. The deal provided Lenovo with valuable strategic assets such as brands and distribution networks and helped it rapidly extend its market reach and become a global player.[29]

A **merger** is a special type of acquisition in which two companies join to form a larger firm. Like joint ventures, mergers can generate many positive outcomes, including inter-partner learning and resource sharing, increased scale economies, cost savings from eliminating duplicative activities, a broader range of products and services for sale, and greater market power. Cross-border mergers confront many challenges due to national differences in culture, competition policy, corporate values, and operating methods. Success requires substantial advance research, planning, and commitment. *Merger and acquisition* (M&A) activity is substantial in international business. The largest international M&As in recent years include the Kraft Foods (United States) merger with Cadbury (United Kingdom), Suntory's (Japan) purchase of Beam (United States) in the liquor industry, and Telefonica's (Spain) purchase of Brasilcel (Brazil) in the telecommunications sector.[30]

Multinational enterprises may favor acquisition over greenfield FDI because, by acquiring an existing company, they gain ownership of existing assets such as plant, equipment, and human resources as well as access to existing suppliers and customers. Unlike greenfield FDI, acquisition provides an immediate stream of

**7.4** Identify the types of foreign direct investment.

**Greenfield investment**
Direct investment to build a new manufacturing, marketing, or administrative facility as opposed to acquiring existing facilities.

**Acquisition**
Direct investment to purchase an existing company or facility.

**Merger**
A special type of acquisition in which two firms join to form a larger enterprise.

*Source:* malevic/123RF

More companies are investing in Africa to develop power plants and renewable energy. In addition to providing capital for local economies, such investments supply needed infrastructure. This solar panel is helping power a farm in Africa.

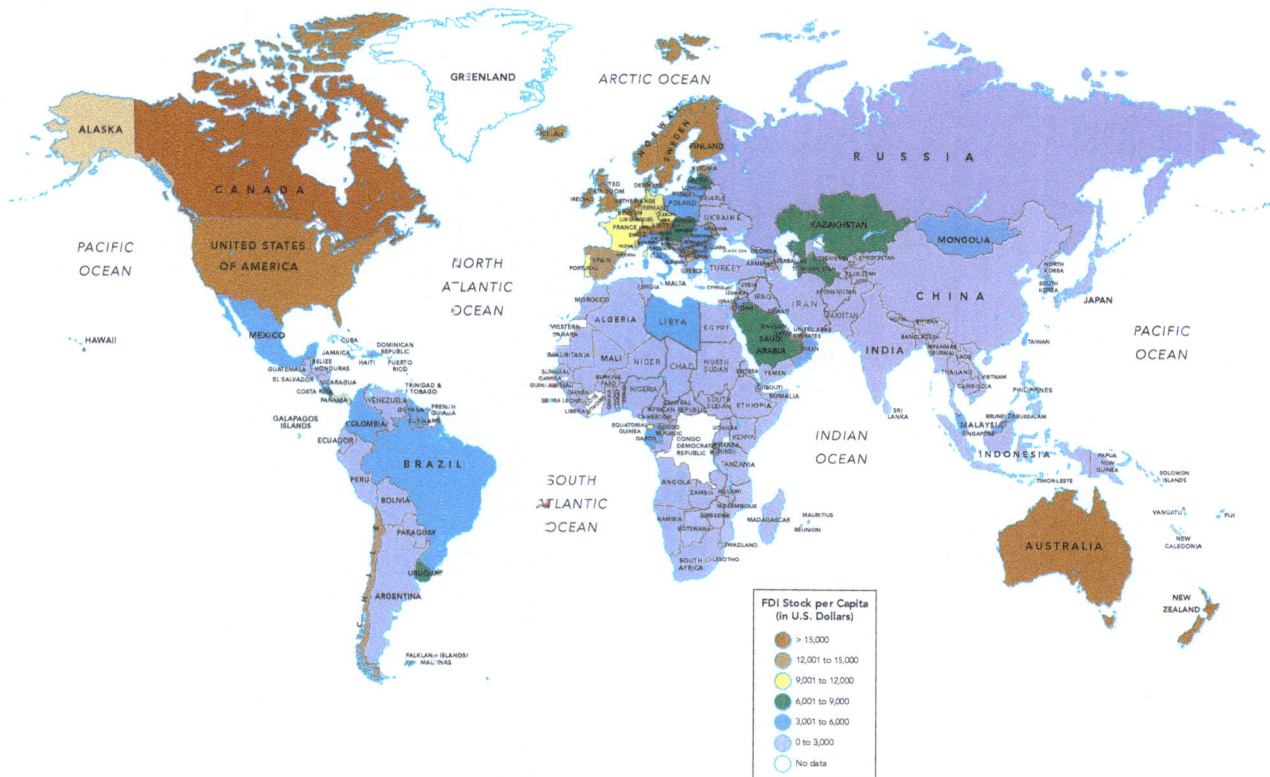

**EXHIBIT 7.5**

**Stock of Foreign Direct Investment per Capita**

*Sources:* Based on data from UNCTAD, "Foreign Direct Investment Flows and Stock," 2018, http://unctadstat.unctad.org; and World Bank, "Population, Total," https://data.worldbank.org.

**Equity participation or equity ownership**
Acquisition of partial ownership in an existing firm.

**Wholly owned direct investment**
A foreign direct investment in which the investor fully owns the foreign assets.

**Equity joint venture**
A type of partnership in which a new firm is created through the investment or pooling of assets by two or more parent firms that gain joint ownership of the new legal entity.

revenue and accelerates the MNE's return on investment. However, host-country governments often pressure MNEs to undertake greenfield FDI. Greenfield FDI creates new jobs and production capacity, facilitates technology and know-how transfer to locals, and improves linkages to the global marketplace. Many governments offer incentives to encourage greenfield investments. They may be sufficient to offset the advantages of acquisition-based entry.

## The Nature of Ownership in FDI

Foreign direct investors also choose their degree of control in the venture. This is accomplished through full or partial ownership, resulting in a commensurate degree of control over decision making on such issues as product development, expansion, and profit distribution. Firms can choose between a wholly owned or joint venture to secure control, which also determines the extent of their financial commitment. If the focal firm is pursuing partial ownership in an existing firm, this is known as **equity participation or equity ownership**.

**Wholly owned direct investment** is FDI in which the investor assumes 100 percent ownership of the business and secures complete managerial control over its operations. Foreign automakers, for example, typically established fully owned manufacturing plants in the United States to serve the large U.S. market from within.[31]

In contrast to wholly owned direct investment, an **equity joint venture** is a type of partnership in which a separate firm is created through the investment or pooling of assets by two or more parent firms that gain joint ownership of the new legal entity.[32] A partner in a joint venture may hold majority, equal (50–50), or minority ownership. Minority ownership provides little control over the operation.

A joint venture is an attractive entry strategy because many foreign markets are complex. Collaborating with a local partner enhances the foreign entrant's ability to navigate the local market. Collaborative ventures benefit small and medium-sized enterprises by providing them with needed capital and other assets. For example, Shanghai-based Tri Star International acquired a majority stake in Illinois-based Adams Pressed Metals, a manufacturer of parts for tractors and other earth-moving equipment. The cash infusion saved 40 jobs at Adams and gave Tri Star access to the U.S. market and marketing know-how.[33]

A joint venture with a local partner may sometimes be the only entry strategy available to the focal firm. This can occur when the government of a target country seeks to protect its important industries by prohibiting 100 percent foreign ownership in local enterprises. Mexico's government, for example, requires foreign MNEs to form joint ventures with local Mexican firms when entering the country's oil industry, which is considered vital to Mexico's economic security. However, governments are relaxing such regulations in most industries, and most are receptive to FDI.

## Vertical Versus Horizontal Integration

A third way of classifying FDI is by whether integration takes place vertically or horizontally. **Vertical integration** is an arrangement whereby the firm owns or seeks to own multiple stages of a value chain for producing, selling, and delivering a product or service. The firm may acquire:

- *downstream* value-chain facilities, such as marketing and selling operations, or
- *upstream* value-chain facilities, such as factories or assembly plants.

**Horizontal integration** is an arrangement in which the firm owns or seeks to own the activities performed in a single stage of its value chain. Microsoft's primary business is developing computer software. In addition to producing word processing and spreadsheet software, it has developed foreign subsidiaries that make other types of software, such as a Montreal-based firm that produces software for creating movie animations. Horizontal integration implies that the firm invests in its own industry to expand its capacity and activities.

Let's illustrate the difference between vertical and horizontal integration. In 2014, Korean appliance manufacturer Samsung Electronics acquired Quietside Corporation, a leading distributor of air conditioners in North America. Samsung bought Quietside to enhance its ability to distribute its own air conditioners in a key foreign market. The acquisition exemplifies downstream vertical integration because appliance distribution is outside Samsung's normal sphere of operations. Subsequently, Samsung acquired the manufacturing plants of Amica, a home appliance company in Poland. This acquisition represents horizontal integration because Samsung Electronics' core business is manufacturing appliances and electronic products. By buying Amica's manufacturing plants, Samsung invested in its own industry to expand its production capacity.[34]

Read the "You Can Do It: Recent Grad in IB" profile featuring Jennifer Knippen. She acquired valuable international business experience by working for a foreign-owned company in her home country.

## International Collaborative Ventures

Collaborative ventures, sometimes called *international partnerships* or *international strategic alliances*, are essentially partnerships between two or more firms.[35] They help companies overcome together the often substantial risks and costs involved in achieving international projects that might exceed the capabilities of any one firm operating alone. Groups of firms sometimes form partnerships to accomplish large-scale projects such as developing new technologies or completing major undertakings such as power plants. By collaborating, the focal firm can draw on a range of complementary technologies, accessible only from other companies, to innovate and develop new products. Advantages such as these help explain why such partnerships have become enormously popular in recent decades.[36]

Although collaboration can take place at similar or different levels of the value chain, it is typically focused on R&D, manufacturing, or marketing. International collaborative ventures greatly increase R&D productivity in high-technology sectors such as robotics, semiconductors, aircraft manufacturing, medical instruments, and pharmaceuticals.

Two basic types of collaborative ventures are equity joint ventures and project-based, nonequity ventures. *Equity joint ventures* are traditional collaborations of a type that has existed for decades. Recent years have seen a proliferation of nonequity, *project-based collaborations*. Let's examine these ventures in detail.

**Vertical integration**
An arrangement whereby the firm owns or seeks to own multiple stages of a value chain for producing, selling, and delivering a product or service.

**Horizontal integration**
An arrangement whereby the firm owns or seeks to own the activities performed in a single stage of its value chain.

**7.5** Understand international collaborative ventures.

### JENNIFER KNIPPEN

**Jennifer's majors:** Economics and international business
**Jobs held since graduating:**
* Sales engineer, KONE, Inc.

*Source:* Jennifer Knippen

Jennifer Knippen was inspired to pursue an international career after participating in a study-abroad program in Valencia, Spain. After graduating with dual majors in economics and international business, she returned to Spain for five months of intensive training in Spanish and traveled through various regions to broaden her education.

When she returned home, Jennifer attended a career fair, which led to a sales engineer position with the U.S. subsidiary of KONE, Inc., a leading manufacturer of elevators and escalators based in Finland. Her experience at KONE was both challenging and inspiring. Jennifer had to learn a technical product in the demanding construction industry.

As a sales engineer, she consulted architects in the design stages of a project—cost analysis, equipment specifications, building integration, and code compliance. She next generated a proposal to the general contractor working on the project. She managed the application of the above knowledge for the project through completion (more than a year). Jennifer managed multiple projects at a time while still meeting annual and quarterly sales budgets.

Managers at KONE praised Jennifer's strong interpersonal relations and teamwork skills. She began working on high-rise projects with some of the top architectural and construction firms. Through pre-selling, with KONE's global support and resources, Jennifer stimulated substantial demand. Eventually, she was awarded Best in Class for the highest-volume sales in her region.

Jennifer experienced the benefits and challenges of working in diverse and multicultural environments that come with working for a local subsidiary of an international parent company. KONE has enjoyed big success in Europe and other parts of the world and has applied a similar approach in the United States. One of the challenges Jennifer faced was strict U.S. building code regulations. She also had to monitor fluctuations in the euro–dollar exchange rate because these greatly affect the sales price of imported equipment.

### What's Ahead?

Jennifer returned to school to complete an MBA in international business. She thought her experience, coupled with an advanced degree in international management, would position her well for an exciting international career.

### Success Factors for a Career in International Business

Foreign travel and a study-abroad program in college inspired Jennifer to pursue an international career. Learning Spanish enhanced her credentials to secure an international business job. Jennifer set career goals and worked hard to achieve them.

*Source:* Photo courtesy of Jennifer Knippen.

### Equity Joint Ventures

Joint ventures are normally formed when no one party possesses all the assets needed to exploit an available opportunity. In a typical international deal, the foreign partner contributes capital, technology, management expertise, training, or some type of product. The local partner contributes the use of its factory or other facilities, knowledge of the local language and culture, market navigation know-how, useful connections to the host-country government, or lower-cost production factors such as labor or raw materials. Western firms often seek joint ventures to gain access to markets in Asia. The partnership allows the foreign firm to access key market knowledge, gain immediate access to a distribution system and customers, and attain greater control over local operations.

Starbucks is in a joint venture with Tata Global Beverages, an Indian tea and coffee producer. Under the deal, Tata has established more than 100 Starbucks shops around India, leveraging the local strength of its brand name and deep knowledge of Indian beverage retailing.[37] The partnership provides both firms superior access to each other's strategic assets in innovation, branding, distribution, and market knowledge.

Samsung, the Korean electronics firm, began internationalizing in the 1970s through joint ventures with foreign-technology suppliers such as NEC, Sanyo, and Corning Glass Works. The partnerships allowed Samsung to acquire product designs and marketing outlets and gave management increasing confidence in foreign operations. As its capabilities grew, Samsung ventured into international production. Its earliest foreign manufacturing effort was a joint venture in Portugal, launched in 1982. In the 1990s, Samsung formed a joint venture with British supermarket chain Tesco to establish a chain of hypermarkets in South Korea. Samsung's 2013 joint venture with the U.S. company Corning produces glass displays for televisions. In 2017, Samsung formed a joint venture with Kerry Logistics to leverage Samsung software and other technological platforms to offer logistical services in China.[38]

### Project-Based, Nonequity Ventures

Increasingly common in cross-border business, the **project-based, nonequity venture** is a collaboration in which the partners create a project with a relatively narrow scope and a well-defined timetable, without creating a new legal entity. Combining staff, resources, and capabilities, the partners collaborate on new technologies or products until the venture bears fruit or they no longer consider collaboration valuable. Such partnering reduces the enormous fixed costs of R&D, especially in technology and knowledge-intensive industries, and helps firms catch up with rivals. For example, Russia's Rusnano and U.S. firm Crocus Technology entered a venture to research and produce advanced versions of MRAM chips. These chips function as memory chips in smart electronics such as digital cameras and smartphones.[39]

Hewlett-Packard formed a nonequity joint venture with Taiwanese contract manufacturer Foxconn to conduct research on hyperscale computing and storage technologies. The venture reflects HP's desire to gain market share in the large-scale data center market. The venture is a strategic commercial agreement that aims to produce advanced computer servers for customers such as Amazon, Google, and Facebook. Such Internet service companies operate large-scale data centers to run their applications for online sales, search services, cloud storage, and social networking. For example, Facebook uses hyperscale technology to store images in its massive photo archive. Amazon uses the technology to store information about millions of its customers. The nonequity venture will leverage the computing and brand leadership of HP with the high-volume design and low-cost manufacturing expertise of Foxconn. HP and Foxxconn jointly will design and eventually manufacture the hyperscale storage technologies. In 2016, HP and Foxconn launched a new joint venture to make computer servers that support cloud computing services.[40]

> **Project-based, nonequity venture**
> A collaboration in which the partners create a project with a relatively narrow scope and a well-defined timetable without creating a new legal entity.

### Differences Between Equity and Project-Based, Nonequity Ventures

In contrast to traditional equity joint ventures, project-based collaborations share the following distinctive characteristics:

- No new legal entity is created. Partners carry on their activity within the guidelines of a contract.
- Parent companies do not necessarily seek ownership of an ongoing enterprise. Instead, they contribute their knowledge, expertise, staff, and monetary resources to derive knowledge or other benefits.
- Collaboration tends to have a well-defined timetable and end date; partners go their separate ways once they have accomplished their objectives or have no further reason for continuation.
- Collaboration is narrower in scope than in equity joint venturing, typically emphasizing a single project, such as development, manufacturing, marketing, or distribution of a new product.
- Exhibit 7.6 highlights advantages and disadvantages of the two types of international collaborative ventures.

### Consortium

A **consortium** is a project-based, usually nonequity venture initiated by multiple partners to fulfill a large-scale project. It is typically formed with a contract that delineates the rights and obligations of each member. Work is allocated to the members on the same basis as profits. In a three-partner consortium, for example, if each party performs one-third of the work, then

> **Consortium**
> A project-based, nonequity venture initiated by multiple partners to fulfill a large-scale project.

| | Advantages | Disadvantages |
|---|---|---|
| Equity joint ventures | • Afford greater control over future directions<br>• Facilitate transfer of knowledge between the partners<br>• Common goals drive the joint venture | • Complex management structure<br>• Coordination between the partners may be a concern<br>• Difficult to terminate<br>• Greater exposure to political risk |
| Project-based nonequity ventures | • Easy to set up<br>• Simple management structure; can be adjusted easily<br>• Takes advantage of partners' respective strengths<br>• Can respond quickly to changing technology and market conditions<br>• Easy to terminate | • Knowledge transfer may be less straightforward between the partners<br>• No equity commitment; thus, puts greater emphasis on trust, good communications, and developing relationships<br>• Conflicts may be harder to resolve<br>• Division of costs and benefits may strain relationship |

each earns one-third of the profits. Consortia are popular for innovation in industries such as commercial aircraft, computers, pharmaceuticals, and telecommunications, where the costs of developing and marketing a new product often reach hundreds of millions of dollars and require wide expertise. Boeing, Fuji, Kawasaki, and Mitsubishi joined forces to design and manufacture major components of the Boeing 767 aircraft. In China, South Korea's Doosan Group and the U.S. firm Westinghouse partnered with China's State Nuclear Power Technology Corporation to build nuclear power plants. Westinghouse is majority owned by Japan's Toshiba Corporation.[41]

Often, several firms pool their resources to bid on a major project such as building a power plant or a high-tech manufacturing facility. Each brings a unique specialty to the project but would be unable to win the bid on its own. No formal legal entity is created; each firm retains its individual identity. In this way, if one party withdraws, the consortium can continue with the remaining participants. iNavSat is a consortium formed among several European firms to develop and manage Europe's global satellite navigation system.

### Cross-Licensing Agreements

A **cross-licensing agreement** is a project-based, nonequity venture in which the partners agree to allow access to licensed intellectual property developed by the other on preferential terms. Microsoft entered such an agreement with Japan's JVC to share patented knowledge on software and other products. Two firms also might enter a cross-distribution agreement, in which each partner has the right to distribute products or services produced by the other on preferential terms. The Star Alliance is an agreement among more than 25 airlines—including Air Canada, United, Lufthansa SAS, Singapore Airlines, and Air New Zealand—to market each other's airline flights (www.staralliance.com).

### Potential Risks in Collaboration

Firms that collaborate have decided partnering is preferred to going it alone. In short, the potential benefits outweigh potential risks. In analyzing a possible collaboration, management should address the following questions.

- Are we likely to grow dependent on or become dominated by the partner firm?
- By partnering, will we stifle growth and innovation in our own organization?
- Will we share our competencies excessively, to the point that corporate interests are threatened? How can we safeguard our core competencies?
- Will we be exposed to significant commercial, political, cultural, or currency risks?
- How effectively can we integrate the cultures and operations of the partner firms?
- Will we close off any growth opportunities by participating in this venture?
- Will managing the venture place an excessive burden on our corporate resources, such as managerial, financial, or technological resources?

**Cross-licensing agreement**
A type of project-based, nonequity venture in which partners agree to access licensed technology developed by the other on preferential terms.

The potential partner may be a current or potential competitor, is likely to have its own agenda, and will likely gain important competitive advantages from the relationship.[42] Management must protect its hard-won capabilities and other organizational assets to preserve its bargaining power and ability to compete. The firm does not want to become too dependent on its partner. Harmony is not necessarily the most important goal, and accepting some conflict and tension between the partners may be preferable to surrendering core skills. For example, Westinghouse shared thousands of technical documents and other intellectual property during its partnership with Chinese firms to build nuclear reactors in China. Intellectual property rights in China are weaker than in some other countries, and the Chinese aim to become major developers of nuclear energy. Western industrial knowledge is certain to seep out to potential competitors, which will hurt future prospects of Westinghouse and other non-Chinese firms in the market.[43]

## Managing Collaborative Ventures

The initial decision in internationalization is to choose the most appropriate target market because the market determines the characteristics needed in a business partner. If the firm plans to enter an emerging market, for example, it may need a partner with political clout or connections. In this way, country targeting and partner selection are interdependent choices.

Exhibit 7.7 outlines the process for identifying and working with a suitable business partner.[44] It reveals that managers need to draw on their cross-cultural competence, legal expertise, and financial planning skills.

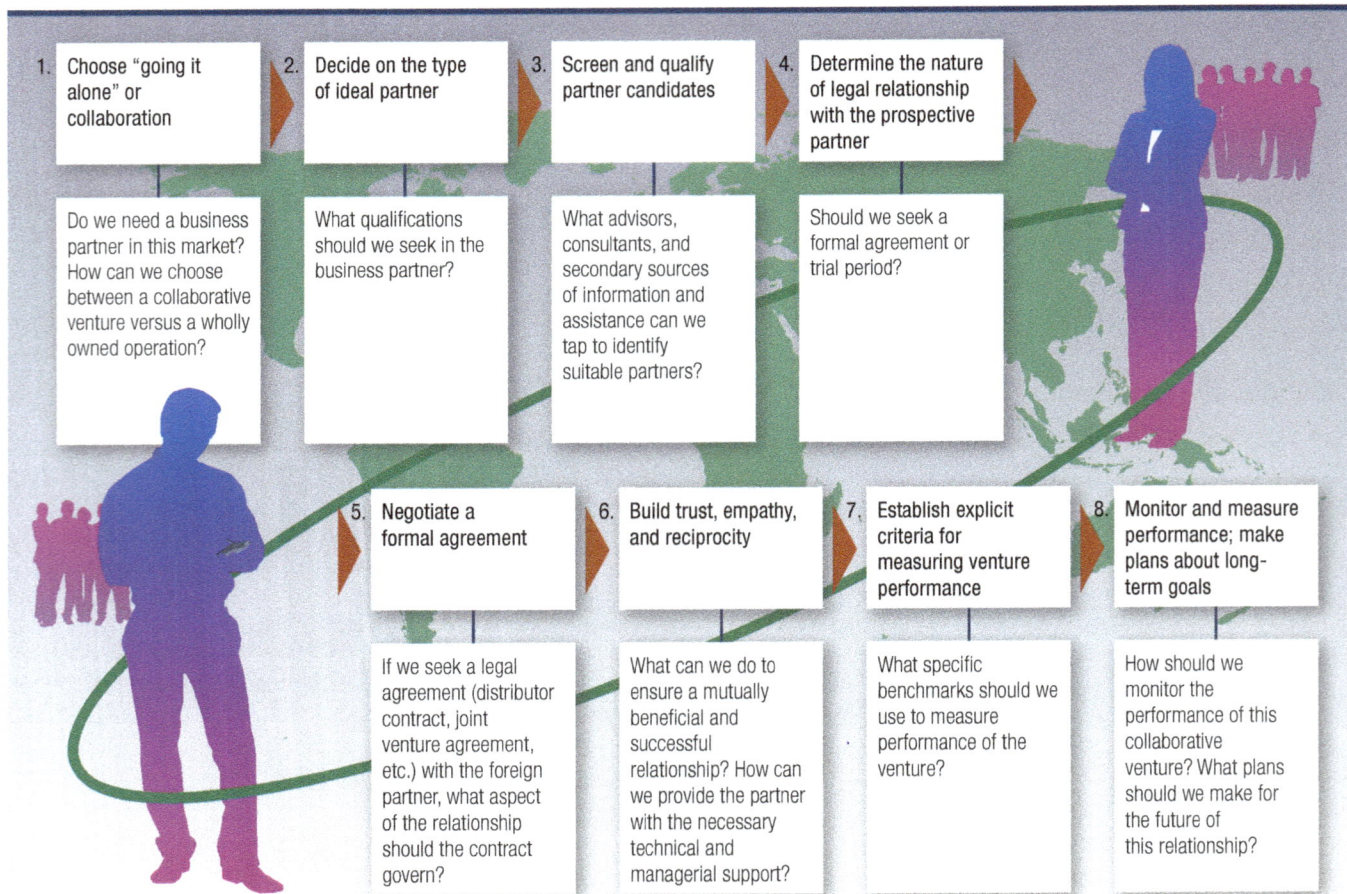

1. Choose "going it alone" or collaboration

Do we need a business partner in this market? How can we choose between a collaborative venture versus a wholly owned operation?

2. Decide on the type of ideal partner

What qualifications should we seek in the business partner?

3. Screen and qualify partner candidates

What advisors, consultants, and secondary sources of information and assistance can we tap to identify suitable partners?

4. Determine the nature of legal relationship with the prospective partner

Should we seek a formal agreement or trial period?

5. Negotiate a formal agreement

If we seek a legal agreement (distributor contract, joint venture agreement, etc.) with the foreign partner, what aspect of the relationship should the contract govern?

6. Build trust, empathy, and reciprocity

What can we do to ensure a mutually beneficial and successful relationship? How can we provide the partner with the necessary technical and managerial support?

7. Establish explicit criteria for measuring venture performance

What specific benchmarks should we use to measure performance of the venture?

8. Monitor and measure performance; make plans about long-term goals

How should we monitor the performance of this collaborative venture? What plans should we make for the future of this relationship?

**EXHIBIT 7.7**

**A Systematic Process for International Business Partnering**

When managers first contemplate internationalization through FDI, they usually think in terms of a wholly owned operation. Many are accustomed to retaining the control and sole access to profits that come with 100 percent ownership. Although the nature of the industry or product can make partnering less desirable, management should consider collaboration an option. Typically, the firm enters a collaborative venture when it discovers a weak or missing link in its value chain and chooses a partner that can remedy the deficiency. China is an increasingly popular venue for collaboration in the Internet service-provider industry. Both Microsoft and Google entered this huge market through joint ventures with local partners, but eBay and Yahoo! entered China primarily through wholly owned FDI. Each firm chose the entry strategy most appropriate for its situation.[45]

About half of all collaborative ventures fail within the first five years of operation because of unresolved disagreements, confusion about venture goals, and other problems. International ventures are particularly challenging because, in addition to complex business issues, managers must contend with differences in culture and language as well as in political, legal, and economic systems. The failure rate of collaborative ventures is higher in developing economies than in advanced economies. Companies as diverse as Avis, Daewoo, General Motors, and Virgin have experienced such failures.[46]

French food giant Danone (www.danone.com) terminated its joint venture with a local Chinese partner after years of contentious relations. Danone had formed the partnership at a time when the Chinese government often required such ventures from foreign firms.[47] In later years, however, the Chinese partner established a mirror business in which it sold, on the side, the same products the joint venture was marketing. The partner claimed that contract terms were unfair and accused Danone of trying to gain control of its other businesses.

### Success in collaborative ventures is attained by following several guidelines

- *Be cognizant of cultural differences.* International collaborations require both parties to learn and appreciate each other's corporate and national cultures. Cultural incompatibility can cause anger, frustration, and inefficiency. The partners may never arrive at a common set of values and organizational routines, especially if they are from very distinct cultures—say, Norway and Nigeria. Establishing cultural compatibility is a must.
- *Pursue common goals.* When partners have differing goals for the venture or their goals change over time, they can find themselves operating at cross-purposes. Japanese firms tend to value market share over profitability, whereas U.S. firms value profitability over market share. Because different strategies are required to maximize each of these performance goals, a joint venture between Japanese and U.S. firms may fail. To overcome such challenges, partners need to interact regularly and communicate at three levels of the organization: senior management, operational management, and the workforce.
- *Give due attention to planning and management of the venture.* Without agreement on questions of management, decision making, and control, each partner may seek to control all the venture's operations, which can strain the managerial, financial, and technological resources of both. In some cases, equal governance and a sense of shared enterprise are best because they help partners view themselves as equals and reach consensus. In other cases, having a dominant partner in the relationship helps ensure success. When one of the partners is clearly the driver or the leader in the relationship, there is less likelihood of a stalemate or prolonged negotiations.
- *Safeguard core competencies.* Collaboration takes place between current or potential competitors that must walk a fine line between cooperation and competition. Volkswagen and General Motors succeeded in China by partnering with the Chinese firm Shanghai Automotive Industry Corporation (SAIC; www.saicmotor.com). The Western firms transferred much technology and know-how to their Chinese partner. Having learned much from them, SAIC is now becoming a significant player in the global automobile industry and even a competitor to its earlier partners.[48]

- *Adjust to shifting environmental circumstances.* When environmental conditions change, the rationale for a collaborative venture may weaken or disappear. An industry or economic downturn may shift priorities in one or both firms. Cost overruns can make the venture untenable. New government policies or regulations can increase costs or eliminate anticipated benefits. Flexibility is key for adjusting to changing conditions.

**MyLab Management   Watch It!**

If your professor has assigned this, go to the Assignments section of **www.pearson.com/mylab/ management** to complete the video exercise titled Entering the Chinese Market.

## The Experience of Retailers in Foreign Markets

**7.6** Discuss the experience of retailers in foreign markets.

Retailers represent a special case of international service firms that internationalize substantially through FDI and collaborative ventures. Retailing takes various forms and includes department stores (Marks & Spencer, Macy's), specialty retailers (Body Shop, Gap), supermarkets (Sainsbury, Safeway), convenience stores (7-Eleven, Tom Thumb), discount stores (Zellers, Target), and big-box stores (Home Depot, IKEA). Walmart has more than 425 stores and about 100,000 employees in China. It sources almost all its merchandise locally, providing jobs for thousands more Chinese.[49]

The major drivers of retailer internationalization include saturation of home-country markets, deregulation of international investment, and opportunities to benefit from lower costs abroad. Home Depot expanded abroad because the home improvement market in Canada and the United States is becoming saturated.[50] Most emerging markets exhibit pent-up demand, fast economic growth, a growing middle class, and increasingly sophisticated consumers. In densely populated developing countries, consumers are flocking to discount retailers that sell a wide selection of merchandise at low prices.

Retailers usually choose between FDI and franchising as a foreign market entry strategy. The larger, more experienced firms, such as Carrefour, Royal Ahold, and Walmart, tend to internationalize through FDI. They typically own their stores and maintain direct control over operations and proprietary assets. Smaller and less internationally experienced firms such as Anytime Fitness tend to rely on networks of independent franchisees. In franchising, the franchisee adopts a business system from, and pays an ongoing fee to, a franchisor. Other firms may employ a dual strategy—using FDI in some markets and franchising in others. Although franchising facilitates rapid internationalization, compared to FDI, it affords the firm less control over its foreign operations, which can be risky in countries with unstable political or economic situations or weak intellectual property laws.

Many retailers have floundered in foreign markets.[51] When the French department store Galleries Lafayette opened in New York City, it could not compete with the city's numerous posh competitors. In its home market in the United Kingdom, Marks & Spencer succeeds with store layouts that blend food and clothing offerings in relatively small spaces, a formula that translated poorly in Canada and the United States. IKEA experienced problems in Japan where consumers value high-quality furnishings, not the low-cost products IKEA offers. Most recently, Home Depot abandoned the Chinese market after only a few years there.

*Source:* Yury Gubin/123rf

Retailers are a distinctive category of international service firms that usually internationalize through FDI and collaborative ventures. Pictured is a department store in Russia.

As another example, Walmart (www.walmart.com) is the world's largest retailer but failed in Germany because it could not compete with local competitors and eventually exited the market. In Mexico, Walmart constructed massive U.S.-style parking lots for its new super centers. However, most Mexicans don't have cars, and city bus stops were too far away, so shoppers could not haul their goods home. In Brazil, most families do their big shopping once a month on payday. Walmart built aisles too narrow and crowded to accommodate the rush and stocked shelves in urban São Paulo with some items that were not needed such as leaf blowers. Walmart's red, white, and blue banners, reminiscent of the U.S. flag, offended local tastes in Argentina. Sam's Club, Walmart's food discounting operation, failed in Latin America partly because its huge multipack items were too big for local shoppers with low incomes and small apartments. Today Walmart is one of Latin America's most successful retailers. It took Walmart many years to learn to adapt to local market needs.[52]

So, what are the typical challenges faced by retailers when they expand overseas?

### Challenges of International Retailing

- *Culture and language* are a significant obstacle. Compared to most businesses, retailers are close to customers. They must respond to local market requirements by customizing their product and service portfolio, adapting store hours, modifying store size and layout, training local workers, and meeting labor union demands.
- Consumers tend to develop strong *loyalty to indigenous retailers*. As Best Buy in Turkey, Home Depot in China, and Walmart in Germany discovered, local firms usually enjoy great allegiance from local consumers.
- Managers must address *legal and regulatory barriers* that can be idiosyncratic. Germany limits store hours, and most retailers are closed on Sundays. IKEA has been wary of entering India due to excessive restrictions placed on foreign retailers. China's government introduced regulations that restricted online publishing, which especially affected foreign vendors. The new regulations led Apple to end online sales of iBooks and iTunes Movies.[53]
- When entering a new market, retailers must develop *local sources* for thousands of products, including some that local suppliers may be unwilling or unable to provide. When Toys "R" Us entered Japan, local toy manufacturers were reluctant to work with the U.S. firm. Some retailers end up importing many of their offerings, which requires establishing complex and costly international supply chains.

### How Retailers Succeed in International Markets

Following Walmart's various failures in Latin America, the firm revised its approaches and eventually achieved considerable success. Walmart and other successful retailers follow a systematic approach to foreign expansion. Let's examine how retailers succeed in international markets.

- *Advanced research and planning.* A thorough understanding of the target market combined with a sophisticated business plan allows the firm to anticipate potential problems and prepare for success. In the run-up to launching stores in China, management at the giant French retailer Carrefour spent 12 years building up its business in Taiwan, where it developed a deep understanding of Chinese culture. It also learned how to forge alliances with local governments. These preparations helped Carrefour become China's biggest foreign retailer, rapidly developing a network of hypermarkets in 25 cities.[54]
- *Efficient logistics and purchasing networks.* Scale economies in procurement are especially critical. Retailers need to organize sourcing and logistical operations to ensure they always maintain adequate inventory while minimizing the cost of operations. In Mexico, Walmart substantially reorganized its supply chains and developed highly efficient and localized purchasing networks. The firm now obtains more than 80 percent of the merchandise sold in its Mexico stores from local suppliers. Resultant lower costs combined with scale economies allows the chain to offer a huge range of products at low prices.
- *An entrepreneurial, creative approach to foreign markets.* The most successful retailers devise novel and innovative approaches. Virgin Megastore is a good example. Starting

from one London location, founder Richard Branson expanded Virgin to numerous markets throughout Europe, North America, and Asia. The stores were big and well lit and stocked music albums in a logical order, all innovations at the time. Sales turnover was much faster than that of smaller music retailers. Zara has devised various creative approaches in international markets, including quickly picking up new fashion trends, responding to local factors like weather and pop culture, and turning stock briskly, which keeps customers coming back for new product.

- *Business model to suit local conditions.* Home Depot offers merchandise in Mexico that suits the small budgets of do-it-yourself builders. It has introduced payment plans and promotes the do-it-yourself mind-set in a country where most cannot afford to hire professional builders.[55] The major dimensions along which retailers differentiate themselves abroad include selection, price, marketing, store design, and the ways in which goods are displayed. They must proceed cautiously while adapting to local conditions to avoid diluting or destroying the unique features that first made them successful.

IKEA, the world's largest furniture retailer, has enjoyed great success, launching more than 200 furniture megastores in dozens of countries. Superior performance derives from strong leadership and skillful management of human resources and from the careful balancing of global integration of operations with responsiveness to local tastes. In each store, IKEA (www.ikea.com) offers as many standardized products as possible while maintaining sufficient flexibility to accommodate specific local conditions. In the United States, for example, IKEA increased the size of its beds to suit American tastes better. In China, IKEA cut its prices to accommodate customer income levels better. IKEA tests the waters first and learns in smaller markets before entering big markets. For example, IKEA perfected its retailing model in German-speaking Switzerland before entering Germany.[56]

## CLOSING CASE    China's "Going Out" Strategy

### Chinese OFDIs: A General Outlook

There have been a lot of discussions, especially after China's entry into the WTO, about the continuous increase of outward foreign direct investments (OFDIs) from China into every area of the globe, a phenomenon that has been referred to as "China's going-out strategy." According to the China Council for the Promotion of International Trade (CCPIT), in 2017, China's outbound FDI flows attained the absolute high of $124.63 billion (growing at an average annual rate of 27.2 percent since 2007), placing China among the world's three largest source of FDIs, after the United States and Japan, with a global share of 10.14 percent. Chinese FDIs, which have been pouring into the different sectors and countries fairly copiously, have not always been welcomed positively. This is due to several complex reasons.

First of all, the sectors these investments have targeted have in some cases have attracted worries that behind them lies a clear political strategy of the Chinese government to take control in sensitive sectors. This has been the reason why some tentative acquisitions by China that targeted strategic materials and critical infrastructures have been blocked in recent years. For instance, over the past 10 years, in the United States, a number of acquisitions by Chinese companies have been blocked by Congress. A famous example from the energy sector is UNOCAL, which was acquired by Chevron after the China National Offshore Oil Corporation retracted its higher competing bit in the face of political resistance. Another country that has indicated its suspicion of Chinese FDIs in strategic sectors is Australia, where the acquisition of Lynas, a company dealing in rare-earth elements, by Chinalco was vetoed.

On the other hand, Europe—the European Union in particular—has only recently begun to examine this complex issue, an interest spurred by the increase in investments from China, which has traditionally been cautious about entering the EU market. This increase in Chinese investment continued through the global financial crisis and the sovereign debt crisis, and it is still ongoing.

In order to analyze the importance and characteristics of Chinese FDIs in Europe, it will be useful to compare them with the U.S. market, given that two phenomena seem to be connected, even when they were not influencing each other, since 2008.

As shown in the chart, after a different start in terms of amount and timeframe, the two flows have taken different directions, with Europe receiving almost double the amount of incoming FDI as the United States did in 2011–2012. According to the analysts, this trend was due to the numerous business opportunities arising from the sovereign debt crisis in the euro zone, which opened interesting opportunities to Chinese shoppers.

### Chinese OFDI in Europe

To determine whether the Chinese government has a grand strategy to occupy strategic locations in Europe or this renewed interest from the Asian giant is purely dictated by commercial motivations (and pursued independently by Chinese companies), it is important to examine the character of the Chinese FDIs in Europe over the years, from their modest start to their present surge. First, we must quantify this presence and gauge how it has been changing over the years.

Chinese investments in Europe are a fairly recent phenomenon. They were not substantial until 2004, amounting to less than $1 billion annually. The surge started in 2008, and in 2009 FDIs reached in flows of $3 billion before tripling in 2010, reaching a level of more than $10 billion. A better idea of their consistence can be obtained by looking at them in terms of stock.

Chinese investors in particular have taken the opportunity to enter the capital of companies that are short of cash but able to guarantee stable returns over the long-term, as is normally the case with infrastructure and public services. In terms of geographic presence, four countries have been consistently preferred as target countries (though this has been changing more recently): the United Kingdom, Italy, Netherlands, and Germany.

In individual sectors, energy seems to be a favorite target, accounting for $17 billion in stock between 2000 and 2014. This should not come as a surprise; natural resources have always represented one of the primary objectives of Chinese investment abroad. In Europe, Chinese companies have spent about €5 billion on oil and gas companies, including upstream and exploration JVs (as in the case of Sinopec-Talisman), refineries (PetroChina-INEOS), and projects with a broader scope (Sinopec-Emerald Energy).

In sectors like food, real estate, manufacturing, and public utilities, penetration has been more intense recently, and this is one of the main differences with the policy of Chinese acquisitions in the United States. The motivations of Chinese FDIs here have been not of a resource seeker but more in terms of acquisition of technologies to modernize Chinese domestic enterprises and to advance in the global value chain. In this sense, the economic crisis in Europe has given Chinese companies a precious opportunity to acquire knowhow and technology that is indispensable for their future. For example, during the period 2000–2014, mechanical engineering (especially automotives) became the second most popular sector for OFDI from China, worth $7.7 billion. In 2016, China's COSCO Shipping (the largest shipping company in the world) bought a 51 percent stake in the Piraeus Port Authority (the port of the Greek capital, Athens). China State Grid also acquired a 24 percent stake in Greece's Independent Power Transmission Operator (IPTO).

## The European Union's Position on Chinese Investments

Over the last decade, the European Union has generally welcomed Chinese investments, and cases of regulatory vetoes to acquisitions are unheard of. It is also true, however, that the European Union lacks a coherent policy and, instead of a regulatory framework at the Commission's level, there is a fragmentary approach where each member state decides on its own. Moreover, and partly for the same reason, not all countries have benefited from Chinese money the same way. Countries that have implemented transparent legislation, such as Germany, Sweden, and the United Kingdom have also been more successful in attracting foreign capital—and China is only one country among many.

However, this enhanced interest and growing Chinese presence has reignited debate at a continental level over FDIs, though it has generally been more in the sense of devising and implementing a more consistent policy of attracting Asian investments in Europe than restricting them, which has been the case in other countries.

The general view is that the Chinese approach in Europe seems driven primarily by the search for commercial gains and is therefore not threatening at a strategic level. Moreover, the OFDIs are generally the initiative of individual companies and not politically directed by the Chinese government. This was also noted in the case of public enterprises in China, which have shown a clear tendency to act according to the logic of profit.

## Outlook

The latest data shows that Chinese FDIs have continued to flow into the European Union despite its improved economic and financial situation. They have changed character, however, and the data reveals an increase in greenfield investments with significant capital expenditure, such as food plants in France and machinery production in Germany, and targeting of small and medium enterprises that are generally left outside this kind of acquisitions. Finally, it is important to point out that, despite this upward trend, the economic importance of Chinese investment in the European Union is still limited (about 2 percent of the European total), and further efforts by both parts are needed to align investments to the level of importance of foreign trade between two partners.

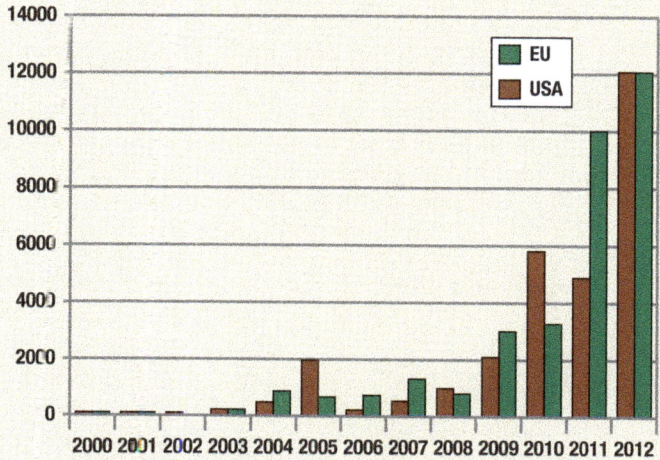

**Chinese FDIs to the United States and the European Union (in $ million)**
(*Source*: Author's elaboration on: ICE 2013; Rhodium Group 2013; MOFCOM 2013)

## AACSB and CKR Intangible Soft Skills to improve employability and success in the workplace:
Written and Oral Communication, Analytical Thinking, Diverse and Multicultural Work Environments, Reflective Thinking, and Application of Knowledge

### Case Questions

**7-4.** Analyze the overall trends among Chinese FDIs and compare the case of the United States and the European Union. How do they relate to each other?

**7-5.** With regard to Chinese FDIs, what are the motivating factors behind the Chinese presence in Europe? How do they compare to the FDI doctrine studied in the rest of the chapters?

**7-6.** What are the main countries and sectors where Chinese FDIs have been concentrated in the last five years? What are the reasons behind these choices?

**7-7.** Consider the trends as analyzed in the last section. Why, in your opinion, are greenfield investments are on the rise? What other changes can be expected in the coming years in terms of the Chinese presence in Europe?

**7-8.** Over the last decade, Chinese investments in the European Union have been welcomed. What do you think the latter's likely attitude toward Chinese investment in the longer term would be?

*Sources:* "Australia Rejects China Nonferrous's Acquisition of Lynas," September 25, 2009, http://www.china.org.cn/business/highlights/2009-09/27/content_18609842.htm; World Resource Institute, "China's Overseas Investments, Explained in 10 Graphics," January 28, 2015, http://www.wri.org/blog/2015/01/china%E2%80%99s-overseas- investments-explained -10-graphics; "Chinese Investment into Europe Hits Record High in 2014," Baker & McKenzie, February 11, 2015, http://www.bakermckenzie.com/news/Chinese-investment-into-Europe-hits-record-high-in-2014-02-11-2015/; Ministry of Commerce of the People's Republic of China, National Bureau of Statistics of the People's Republic of China, State Administration of Foreign Exchange (2014), 2013 Annual Statistical Bulletin of China's Outward Foreign Direct Investment, Beijing, China: China Statistics Press; European Union website, Foreign Direct Investment Statistics 2014, http://ec.europa.eu/eurostat/statistics-explained/index.php/Foreign_direct_investment_statistics.

This case was written by Stefania Paladini, Birmingham City University.

# END-OF-CHAPTER REVIEW

### MyLab Management
Go to **www.pearson.com/mylab/management** to complete the problems marked with this icon: ⭐.

## Key Terms

acquisition 201
consortium 205
cross-licensing agreement 206
equity joint venture 202
equity participation or equity ownership 202
foreign direct investment (FDI) 192
greenfield investment 201
horizontal integration 203
international collaborative venture 193
international portfolio investment 192
joint venture 193
merger 201
project-based, nonequity venture 205
vertical integration 203
wholly owned direct investment 202

## Summary
In this chapter, you learned about:

- **International investment and collaboration**

Foreign direct investment (FDI) is an internationalization strategy by which the firm establishes a physical presence abroad through ownership of productive assets such as capital, technology, labor, land, plant, and equipment. An international collaborative venture is a cross-border business alliance in which partnering firms pool their resources and share costs and risks of the venture. A joint venture is a form of collaboration between two or more firms that leads to minority, equal, or majority ownership.

- **Characteristics of foreign direct investment**

FDI is the most advanced and complex entry strategy and involves establishing manufacturing plants, marketing subsidiaries, or other facilities abroad. For the firm, FDI requires substantial resource commitment, local presence and operations in target countries, and the ability to access comparative advantages. It also entails greater risk compared to other entry modes. FDI is most commonly used by MNEs—large firms with extensive international operations. Services are intangible and typically cannot be exported. Services are usually location-bound and require firms to establish a foreign presence, generally through FDI. International portfolio investment is passive ownership of foreign securities such as stocks and bonds.

- **Motives for FDI and collaborative ventures**

Firms employ FDI for various reasons, including *market-seeking motives*, to enter new markets and gain new customers; *resource/asset-seeking motives*, to acquire production factors that may be cheaper or more abundant in foreign markets; and *efficiency-seeking motives*, to enhance the efficiency of the firm's value-adding activities. These motives often occur in combination. Motivations for international collaborative ventures include the ability to gain access to new markets, opportunities, or knowledge; to undertake international activities too costly or risky for one firm alone; to reduce costs; to meet government requirements; and to prevent or reduce competition.

- **Types of foreign direct investment**

FDI can be wholly owned direct investment, in which the firm owns 100 percent of foreign operations, or an equity joint venture with one or more partners. Firms may engage in greenfield investment by building a facility from scratch or by acquiring an existing facility from another firm through acquisition. With vertical integration, the firm seeks to own multiple stages of its value chain. With horizontal integration, the firm seeks to own activities involved in a single stage of its value chain. A merger is a special type of acquisition in which two companies join to form a new, larger firm.

- **International collaborative ventures**

Joint ventures (JVs) are normally formed when no one party possesses all the assets needed to exploit an opportunity. Joint ventures are an example of ownership-based collaborations. The project-based, nonequity venture emphasizes a contractual relationship between the partners and is formed to pursue certain goals or meet an important business need while the partners remain independent. A consortium is a project-based, nonequity venture initiated by multiple firms to undertake a large-scale activity that is beyond the capabilities of the individual members. Collaboration requires management to define its goals and strategies clearly. It requires much research and analysis up front as well as strong negotiation skills. Decisions are made regarding allocation of responsibilities in management, production, finance, and marketing as well as how to handle day-to-day operations and plans for the future. Because many collaborative ventures fail prematurely, firms should choose their partners carefully and follow a systematic process.

- **The experience of retailers in foreign markets**

Because retailing requires intensive customer interaction, it is particularly susceptible to culture, income levels, and other conditions abroad. Success depends on adapting to local conditions while maintaining the retailer's unique features and value proposition. International retailers face cultural and language barriers, strong customer loyalty to local retailers, legal and regulatory barriers, and the need to develop local supply sources. Retailer success also depends on advanced research and planning, establishing efficient logistics and purchasing networks, using an entrepreneurial and creative approach to foreign markets, and adjusting the business model to suit local needs.

## Test Your Comprehension

**AACSB and CKR Intangible Soft Skills to improve employability and success in the workplace:**
**Analytical Thinking, Written and Oral Communication, Reflective Thinking, Diverse and Multicultural Work Environments, and Application of Knowledge**

7-9. What are the three different options as far as joint ventures are concerned?

7-10. How can FDI be seen as efficiency seeking?

7-11. Many MNEs are adhering to global sustainability agendas. What does this mean, and what are the implications for businesses?

7-12. Identify the different types of collaborative ventures. What type of venture is best for entering a culturally distant market such as Malaysia or Uzbekistan? For the next generation of products in its industry? For undertaking a short-term project, such as building infrastructure (e.g., highway, dam) abroad?

7-13. What are the major motives for undertaking FDI for a small firm whose sales are dwindling in its home market? For a firm that wants to enter a country with high trade barriers? For a firm with high manufacturing costs in its home market? For a hotel chain? For a large, diversified firm seeking to enter various markets worldwide for a variety of reasons?

7-14. What factors should management consider when deciding where in the world to establish a factory? A marketing subsidiary? A regional headquarters?

7-15. What is a project-based non-equity venture, and how are the partners' independence protected?

7-16. How can a global retailer ensure that they adapt to conditions in an overseas market while retaining their unique features and value proposition?

## Apply Your Understanding

**AACSB and CKR** Intangible Soft Skills to improve employability and success in the workplace: Written and Oral Communication, Ethical Understanding and Reasoning, Analytical Thinking, Diverse and Multicultural Work Environments, Reflective Thinking, and Application of Knowledge.

**7-17.** Suppose you get a job at MobileTV, a small manufacturer of TV sets installed in cars and boats. Business has declined recently, foreign rivals from emerging markets are increasing competition, and management is worried. Because MobileTV does all its manufacturing in Canada and the United Kingdom, it lacks cost advantages, and its prices are relatively high. After studying the problem, you conclude that MobileTV should move much of its production to Mexico, but senior management knows little about FDI. Prepare a report to management detailing the advantages of establishing a production base in Mexico. Why should the firm be interested in foreign manufacturing? Recommend which type of FDI MobileTV should use in Mexico. Finally, what advantages and disadvantages should the venture expect from manufacturing in Mexico?

**7-18.** Suppose you work for Aoki Corporation, a producer of processed foods. Your boss, Hiroshi Aoki, heard there is a big market for processed foods in Europe but does not know how to enter or do business there. You recommend entering Europe through a joint venture with a local European firm. Prepare a memo to Aoki explaining the objectives and risks of internationalizing through collaborative ventures. Explain why a collaborative venture might be a better entry strategy than wholly owned FDI. Keep in mind that processed food is a culturally sensitive product that entails various complexities in marketing and distribution. What type of European partner should Aoki seek?

**7-19.** *Ethical Dilemma*: Censorship standards vary worldwide. What is acceptable in some countries, such as nudity on television, criticizing authority, or revealing government secrets that affect national security, is unacceptable in others. Google is an Internet service multinational that used FDI to establish operations in China. Google enjoyed growing market success for several years. Eventually, however, Chinese government officials blocked Google from the market because Google refused to censor links to websites on sensitive topics such as independence for Taiwan and criticism of the Chinese government. Government censorship requirements eventually forced Google to withdraw from mainland China, a move that ceded market share to Chinese competitors and hurt Google's profits. Suppose you are an international manager at Google. Should Google have exited China, or should it reestablish its presence there and comply with Chinese censorship rules? Analyze the arguments for and against Google's withdrawal from China. What can Google do to address the problem effectively?

# globalEDGE | INTERNET EXERCISES

Access globalEDGE™ at www.globalEDGE.msu.edu

## AACSB and CKR Intangible Soft Skills to improve employability and success in the workplace: Information Technology, Written and Oral Communication, Analytical Thinking, Diverse and Multicultural Work environments, Reflective Thinking, and Application of Knowledge

7-20. Suppose your company wants to establish a factory in Latin America to make and sell products in the region. It has narrowed the pool of candidate countries to Argentina, Brazil, and Chile. Your task is to write a report that compares the FDI environments of these countries. One approach is to obtain the country fact sheet for each nation from UNCTAD (www.unctad.org), a UN agency that gathers FDI data. You can access this data either through globalEDGE™ or the UNCTAD site. By examining the fact sheets, answer each of the following questions individually for Argentina, Brazil, and Chile.

  a. What nations are the major trading partners of each country in the region? (This indicates the size and stability of existing trading relationships with key partners.)

  b. Which companies are the leading firms now pursuing FDI in each country? (This helps identify key competitors.)

  c. What is each country's rating on the FDI Performance Index? (This rating indicates the performance that typical firms have experienced when investing in each country.)

  d. What is the level of merger and acquisition activity in each country? (This shows the maturity of each country for acquisition-based FDI.) Elaborate and justify your findings.

7-21. Suppose your firm wants to identify prospective countries for direct investment. Your boss has requested a report on the attractiveness of alternative locations based on

their potential FDI return. A colleague mentions a tool called the FDI Confidence Index. Consult this resource and write a report in which you identify the top FDI destinations as well as the criteria used to construct the index. The Confidence Index is published by the consulting firm A. T. Kearney, based on an annual survey of CEOs at the world's top MNEs. Access the index by entering "FDI Confidence Index" at globalEDGE™ or directly at www.atkearney.com. Download the PDF file to do your research.

7-22. Assume you own a company that manufactures medical products in the biotechnology industry. You want to establish a foreign plant to manufacture your products and are seeking countries with a high concentration of knowledge workers. Thus, you decide to collect information about the knowledge economy abroad. The World Bank highlights the state of the knowledge economy in various countries. The data are accessible by visiting the World Bank site (www.worldbank.org) and entering the keywords "Knowledge Economy Index" in the search engine. You will be able to find several articles and retrieve information about these countries. Visit the site and prepare a report on the knowledge economy for each of the following: Singapore, South Korea, and Spain.

## CKR Tangible Process Tool Exercise™

### Selecting a Site for a Manufacturing Plant

Manufacturing involves various activities, including developing products, managing the inflow of parts and other inputs, organizing logistics, maintaining quality standards, and actual manufacturing operations. To gain comparative advantages, firms use foreign locations to manufacture the products that they offer their customers. For firms that manufacture abroad in company-owned factories, the most important first step is to find the right location to build a factory.

Decisions regarding where to locate factories are complex. For large production projects, numerous decision makers perform complex analyses. Building or acquiring a foreign factory involves FDI, usually the most expensive foreign entry strategy. Given limited resources, managers establish factories in locations that maximize organizational advantages. The best approach to selecting a location is to narrow the possible countries by using a systematic research process.

In this exercise, assume you work for a company (e.g., Grohe, Kohler) that makes bathroom fixtures, for example, sinks, bathtubs, and shower systems. Your firm wants to expand its presence in the huge European market with these products. The European Union is very attractive due to 500 million affluent consumers in a concentrated area. To serve this region better, companies establish manufacturing plants in Europe through direct investment. However, because production costs are high in Western Europe, many firms establish plants in Eastern Europe, home to lower-cost, high-quality labor. Your task is to identify the most suitable Eastern European country to establish a manufacturing plant.

**Background**

Finding the best location to establish a foreign factory requires much research and planning. Initially, companies establish factories at foreign locations to minimize production costs. Other objectives include the ability to improve the value added to products, to be close to key foreign customers, and to access production factors not available at home. In a world of intense competition, manufacturing in countries that offer low-cost, high-quality labor makes the firm more competitive and helps it survive and thrive.

Management wants to access low-cost labor that has sufficient knowledge and skills to carry out manufacturing in ways that meet quality standards and performance objectives. Often the most important criteria for establishing foreign production is the level of workforce productivity. Productivity implies that the firm can generate maximal output of production for minimal cost. Productivity hinges on various factors, including the skill level of workers.

In the research phase, management accounts for numerous factors, including those related to each country's economy, political system, level of government intervention, legal protections, quality and cost of labor, presence of labor unions, and the level of infrastructure in the target country. In general, the firm wants to locate its manufacturing in countries where factors are optimal.

To complete this exercise, go to MyLab Management (www.pearson.com/mylab/management) and click on **Career Toolbox**.

## Endnotes

1. Company profile of Tata at www.hoovers.com; Peter Harrop, "India Buys More of the UK Electric Vehicle Industry Cambridge, UK," *Automotive Industries*, January 2012, www.dallasnews.com; Andrew Saunders, "Jaguar Land Rover's Indian Adventure," *Management Today*, February 2014, pp. 30–34; Ketan Thakar, "Tata Motors Crosses 1-million Sales Mark in FY18," *The Economic Times,* April 13, 2018, www.economic-times.indiatimes.com.

2. Hoovers, profile on Anheuser-Busch InBev, 2018, www.hoovers.com.

3. Lisa Brown, "A-B InBev Finalizes $100 Billion Acquisition of SABMiller, Creating World's Largest Beer Company," *Chicago Tribune,* October 11, 2016, www.chicagotribune.com; Geoff Colvin, "The Brazilian Investors Who Control Kraft Heinz Are Applying Their Proven Formula to Construct a New Global Food Colossus. What Will They Buy Next?," *Fortune,* January 19, 2017, www.fortune.com; Hoovers, 2018.

4. UNCTAD, "Global FDI Flows Slipped Further in 2017," *Investment Trends Monitor*, January 2018, www.unctad.org.

5. UNCTAD, *World Investment Report* (Geneva: UNCTAD, 2018, www.unctad.org); M. S. Castaño, M. T. Méndez, and M. Á. Galindo, "Innovation, Internationalization and Business-Growth Expectations Among Entrepreneurs in the Services Sector," *Journal of Business Research* 69, No. 5 (2016), pp. 1690–1695.

6.  Rajshekhar Javalgi, David A. Griffith, and D. Steven White, "An Empirical Examination of Factors Influencing the Internationalization of Service Firms," *Journal of Services Marketing* 17 (2003), pp. 185–201; UNCTAD, 2018.

7.  Paul Laudicina and Erik Peterson, *The 2017 A. T. Kearney Foreign Direct Investment Confidence Index* (A. T. Kearney, 2018), www.atkearney.com; UNCTAD, 2018.

8.  UNCTAD, "Global FDI Flows Slipped Further in 2017," *Investment Trends Monitor*, January 2018, www.unctad.org.

9.  Laudicina and Peterson, 2018.

10. Neil Buckley, "Opportunities and Risks for Investors in Central and East Europe," May 7, 2017, www.ft.com; Federation of European Employers, *Pay in Europe* (London Federation of European Employers, 2013), www.fedee.com

11. UNCTAD, *World Investment Report* (Geneva: UNCTAD, 2018, www.unctad.org).

12. Steve Hamm, "IBM vs. Tata: Which Is More American?" *BusinessWeek*, May 5, 2008, p. 28; *The Economic Times*, "Tata Consultancy Says It Plans to Step Up Local Hiring in US," March 23, 2017, www.economictimes.indiatimes.com.

13. *EY Attractiveness Survey: The Netherlands 2017*, May 2017, www.ey.com; Thomas C. Head and P. Sorensen, "Attracting Foreign Direct Investment: The Potential Role of National Culture," *Journal of American Academy of Business* 6 (2005), pp. 305–309.

14. *Automotive News Europe,* "AvtoVAZ's New Boss Faces a Tough Job at Russian Carmaker," March 16, 2016, www.euro-peautonews.com; *Business Eastern Europe.* "Russia: The Joke Misfires," March 14, 2011, p. 9.

15. Clay Chandler, "Mickey Mao," *Fortune,* April 18, 2005, pp. 170–178; Denise Tsang and Cannix Yau, "Hong Kong Disneyland Falls Further into Red as Losses Double in 2017 to Hit HK$345 Million," *South China Morning Post,* February 20, 2018, www.scmp.com.

16. Thomas Burrows, "How's This for a Magic Kingdom?" *Daily Mail*, February 8, 2015, www.dailymail.co.uk; Kimberley Choi, "Disneyfication and Localisation: The Cultural Globalisation Process of Hong Kong Disneyland," *Urban Studies* 49, No. 2 (2012), pp. 383–397; Tsang and Yau, 2018.

17. "Beyond the Green Corporation," *BusinessWeek*, January 29, 2007, pp. 50–64; Deroy Murdock, "For Corporate Social Hypocrisy. See Unilever's CEO," *National Review.* April 1, 2017, www.nationalreview.com; Vivienne Walt, "Unilever CEO Paul Polman's Plan to Save the World," *Fortune,* February 17, 2017, www.fortune.com.

18. John Dunning, *International Production and the Multinational Enterprise* (London: Allen and Unwin, 1981); Pavida Pananond, "Motives for Foreign Direct Investment: A View from Emerging Market Multinationals," *Multinational Business Review* 23, No. 1 (2015), pp. 77–86.

19. Farok Contractor and Peter Lorange, eds., *Cooperative Strategies in International Markets* (Lexington, MA: Lexington Books, 1988); Gary Hamel, Yves Doz, and C. K. Prahalad, "Collaborate with Your Competitors—and Win," *Harvard Business Review* 67 (January–February 1989), pp. 133–139; *International Construction,* "Equipment Revenues Down –2.6% in 2014." April 2015, p. 6; Luiz F. Mesquita and Roberto Ragozzino, *Collaborative Strategy: Critical Issues for Alliances and Networks* (Cheltenham, UK: Edward Elgar, 2017).

20. Peter Buckley, Peter Enderwick, and Adam Cross, *International Business* (Oxford, UK: Oxford University Press. 2018); Caf Dowlah, *Transformations of Global Prosperity: How Foreign Investment, Multinationals, and Value Chains Are Remaking Modern Economy* (London: Palgrave Macmillan, 2018); Lilach Nachum and Srilata Zaheer, "The Persistence of Distance? The Impact of Technology on MNE Motivations for Foreign Investment," *Strategic Management Journal* 26 (2005), pp. 747–767.

21. *Europetrole*, "CNPC Takes Over Changbei Phase I Project from Shell as the Operator," January 22, 2016, www.euro-petrole.com; Stanley Reed and Dexter Roberts, "What's Shell Doing in China?" *Bloomberg Businessweek*, November 21–27, 2011, pp. 88–93.

22. Buckley, Enderwick, and Cross, 2018; Dowlah, 2018.

23. Ernst & Young, *Biotechnology Report 2017: Beyond Borders: Staying the Course,*, 2017, www.ey.com.

24. Buckley, Enderwick, and Cross, 2018; Dowlah, 2018; Lilach Nachum and Cliff Wymbs, "Product Differentiation, External Economies and MNE Location Choices: M&As in Global Cities," *Journal of International Business Studies* 36 (2005), pp. 415–423.

25. Buckley, Enderwick, and Cross, 2018; Dowlah, 2018; Nachum and Zaheer, 2005.

26. Martin Christopher, *Logistics & Supply Chain Management* (London: Financial Times Publishing, 2016).

27. Mariasole Bannò, Lucia Piscitello, and Celeste Varum, "Determinants of the Internationalization of Regions: The Role and Effectiveness of Public Policy Measures," *Regional Studies* 49, No. 7 (2015), pp. 1208–1222; Theodore H. Moran, "How to Encourage Foreign Investment," *World Economic Forum,* January 30, 2015, www.weforum.org.

28. Andres Schipani, "Body Shop Owner Natura Targets Global Growth," *Financial Times,* February 4, 2018, www.ftu.com.

29. Eva Dou, "Lenovo to Focus on Integrating Acquisitions," January 7, 2015, *Wall Street Journal*, www.wsj.com.

30. UNCTAD, *World Investment Report* (Geneva: UNCTAD, 2018, www.unctad.org).

31. Brent Snavely, "Foreign Automakers Vie to Appear More American," *USA Today,* July 12, 2017, www.usatoday.com.

32. In this chapter, we adopt the customary definition of "joint venture" when it is assumed to carry equity interest by the parent firms that founded it. That is, a joint venture is always an equity venture. Nevertheless, in popular literature, the term *equity venture* incorrectly refers to all types of collaborative ventures, including project-based collaborations. Therefore, we will use the term *equity joint venture* rather than simply *joint venture* to avoid miscommunication.

33. Paul Kaihla, "Why China Wants to Scoop Up Your Company," *Business 2.0*, June 2005, pp. 29–30.

34. *Air Conditioning Heating & Refrigeration News*, "Samsung Electronics America to Acquire Quietside," September 8, 2014, pp. 1–14; *Appliance Design*, "News Watch," February 2010, pp. 4–10.

35. Mesquita and Ragozzino, 2017; Janell Townsend, "Understanding Alliances: A Review of International Aspects in Strategic Marketing," *Marketing Intelligence & Planning* 21 (2003), pp. 143–158.

36. Mesquita and Ragozzino, 2017; Aimin Yan and Yadong Luo, *International Joint Ventures: Theory and Practice* (New York: Routledge, 2016).

37. Piyush Pandey, "Tata, Starbucks to Extend Their Partnership Beyond India," *The Hindu,* June 27, 2016, www.thehindu.com; *The Economic Times,* "Starbucks Expects India to Be Among Its Top 5 Markets Globally," October 25, 2017, www.economictimes.com.

38. "Business Digest," *Chemistry & Industry,* January 2012, p. 14; Y. Kim and K. Ahn, "Samsung Tesco Homeplus and Corporate Social Responsibility," *Richard Ivey School of Business Case Collection,* July 29, 2009; Tess Stynes, "Corning and Samsung in Accord," *Wall Street Journal,* October 23, 2013, p. B7; *Yonhap News,* "Samsung SDS Establishes Joint Venture with Chinese Firm," May 16, 2017, www.yonhapnews.co.kr.

39. Don Clark, "Chip Start-Up Joins with Russia in Memory Deal," *Wall Street Journal,* May 17, 2011, p. B7.

40. Eva Dou, "H-P, Foxconn Start Server Joint Venture," *Wall Street Journal,* May 1, 2014, p. B5; *Fox Business,* "HP, Foxconn Launch Cloud Server Joint Venture," January 8, 2016, www.foxbusiness.com.

41. Suresh Kotha and Kannan Srikanth, "Managing a Global Partnership Model: Lessons from the Boeing 787 'Dreamliner' Program," *Global Strategy Journal* 3, No. 1 (2013), pp. 41–66; Sonal Patel, "New Construction Milestones for AP1000 Units," *Power,* March 1, 2017, www.powermag.com; Power Engineering, "Pressure Vessel for AP1000 Nuclear Reactor in China Put in Place," November 2011, Special section p. 6.

42. Gang Li, Huan Fan, Peter Lee, and T. Cheng, "Joint Supply Chain Risk Management: An Agency and Collaboration Perspective," *International Journal of Production Economics* 164 (June 2015), pp. 83–94; Mesquita and Ragozzino, 2017.

43. *Economist,* "A Glowing Future: China Wants Its Nuclear Industry to Grow Dauntingly Fast," September 22, 2016, www.economist.com; Dexter Roberts and Stanley Reed, "China Wants Nuclear Reactors—Fast," *Bloomberg Businessweek,* December 6–12, 2010, pp. 15–17.

44. S. Tamer Cavusgil, "International Partnering: A Systematic Framework for Collaborating with Foreign Business Partners," *Journal of International Marketing* 6 (1998), pp. 91–107.

45. "Asian Alliances: New Ties for VW, GM and Peugeot Citroen," *Economist,* December 12, 2009, p. 72; "China: The Great Internet Race," *BusinessWeek,* June 13, 2005, pp. 54–55; Nikolaus Lang et al, "How to Successfully Manage Joint Ventures in China," *BCG,* March 1, 2016, www.bcg.com.

46. Cavusgil, 1998; Kandemir, Yaprak, and Cavusgil, 2006; Patrick Hatch, "Virgin Samoa Closure Puts Non-stop Flights from Australia in Doubt," *Sydney Morning Herald,* May 24, 2017, www.smh.com; Brian Tjemkes, Pepijn Vos, and Koen Burgers, *Strategic Alliance Management* (London: Routledge, 2017).

47. James Areddy, "Danone Pulls Out of Disputed China Venture," *Wall Street Journal,* October 1, 2009, p. B1; *Nikkei Asian Review,* "What to do When you Fail in China," November 24, 2015, www.asia.nikkei.com.

48. Charles Clover, "Foreign Carmakers on Edge Despite China Tech Transfer Assurances," *Financial Times,* March 29, 2017, www.ft.com; *Reuters,* "Volkswagen Won't Make Audi Cars with SAIC in China Before 2018," January 17, 2017, www.reuters.com.

49. Laurie Burkitt and Sarah Nassauer, "Wal-Mart Says It Will Go Slow in China," *Wall Street Journal,* April 30, 2015, p. B3; Rachel Change, "Wal-Mart Already Has a Thriving Online Grocery Business—in China," *Bloomberg Businessweek,* November 30, 2017, www.bloomberg.com; Mei Fong, "Retailers Still Expanding in China," *Wall Street Journal,* January 22, 2009, p. B1.

50. *Floor Daily,* "Home Depot Looking at Europe, Asia," September 2, 2017, www.floordaily.net; Andrew Ward, "Home Depot in Mexico," *Financial Times,* April 6, 2006, p. 8.

51. Bryan Pearson, "Expanding Retail Overseas: 3 Lessons from Best Buy, Walmart and Home Depot," *Forbes,* June 10, 2016, www.forbes.com; Andrew Roberts and Carol Matlack, "Once Wal-Mart's Equal, Carrefour Falls Behind," *Bloomberg Businessweek,* October 24–30, 2011, pp. 22–23.

52. *Agence French Press,* "Walmart Is Closing 269 Stores, Including 115 in Latin America," January 15, 2016, www.pri.org; David Agren, Thierry Ogier, and Joachim Bamrud, "Walmart: Latin American Success," *Latin Trade,* July/August, 2011, pp. 24–27; Pearson (2016); WWD: Women's Wear Daily, "Wal-Mart Alters Course in Latin America," April 21, 2014, p. 2.

53. *BMI Research,* "Challenges Persist In Walmart's International Operations," June 21, 2017, www.bmiresearch.com; Amol Sharma, "IKEA Wary of Entering India," *Wall Street Journal,* January 24, 2012, p. B4.

54. Ming-Ling Chuang, James Donegan, Michele Ganon, and Kan Wei, "Walmart and Carrefour Experiences in China: Resolving the Structural Paradox," *Cross Cultural Management* 18, No. 4 (2011), pp. 443–463; Dominique Vidalon, "Auchan/Alibaba Deal Turns Up the Heat on Carrefour in China," *Reuters,* November 21, 2017, www.reuters.com.

55. David Agren, Thierry Ogier, and Joachim Bamrud, "Walmart: Latin American Success," *Latin Trade* 19, No. 4 (July/August 2011), pp. 24–27; *Forbes,* "Home Depot invertirá 1,700 mdp en abrir nuevas unidades en México," January 16, 2018, www.forbes.com.mx; MarketLine, "Wal-Mart Stores Inc.," August 18, 2017, pp. 1–26; Mallory Schlossberg, "While the Rest of the Industry Struggles, This Store Has Created the 'Best Business Model in Apparel' — and Millennials Are Flocking to It," *Business Insider,* June 16, 2016, www.businessinsider.com; Ward (2006).

56. Valerie Chu, Alka Girdhar, and Rajal Sood, "Couching Tiger Tames the Dragon," *Business Today,* July 21, 2013, pp. 92–96; Michael Jarrett and Quy Nguyen Huy, "IKEA's Success Can't Be Attributed to One Charismatic Leader," *Harvard Business Review,* February 2, 2018, www.hbr.org; Beth Kowitt, "It's IKEA's World," *Fortune,* March 15, 2015, pp. 166–175; Carol Matlack, Sam Chambers, and Anna Molin, "IKEA Tries Breaking Out of the Big Box," *Bloomberg Businessweek,* January 15, 2018, pp. 20–21; Hilary Potkewitz, "Can Your Relationship Handle IKEA?" *Wall Street Journal,* April 23, 2015, pp. D1–D2.

CHAPTER

# 8 Implementing Strategy
Small Businesses, Global Alliances,
Emerging Market Firms

## OUTLINE

## OBJECTIVES

**8-1.** To become familiar with the types of strategic alliances for international business, the challenges in implementing them, and guidelines for success in alliances.

**8-2.** To understand what is involved in implementing strategies, including those for small businesses and those involved in emerging economies.

**8-3.** To consider how to manage the firm's performance in international joint ventures, with attention to knowledge management, government and cultural influence, role of e-commerce.

## Opening Profile: TAG Heuer in Smartwatch Alliance with Google and Intel

ADAM THOMSON - PARIS, FT.com, March 20, 2015

TAG Heuer has announced a partnership with Google and Intel to develop a smartwatch, signalling that they want to take the fight to Apple as the Californian company prepares to roll out its Apple Watch.

The Swiss watchmaker, owned by Paris luxury goods conglomerate LVMH, said that the alliance would create "a product that is both luxurious and seamlessly connected to its wearer's daily life'.

The move marks the first time a top-end brand from the Swiss watch industry has joined the competition for smartwatches and leaves no doubt as to Google's determination to follow Apple into the high-end segment of wearable technology.

For chipmaker Intel, the alliance is an opportunity to make up for its failure in the smartphone market by leapfrogging into wearables.

Jean-Claude Biver, who heads LVMH's watches division, said yesterday that the transatlantic partnership between 155-year-old TAG Heuer and 17-year-old Google was "a marriage of technical innovation and watchmaking credibility".

Some industry analysts will see the irony of Mr Biver moving into the smartwatch business. He is largely credited with having saved the Swiss watch industry from the proliferation of quartz movements in the 1970s and 1980s by emphasising the virtues of handmade mechanical timepieces.

A 1980s campaign he launched as head of the Blancpain watchmaker he revived stated defiantly: "Since 1735 there has never been a quartz Blancpain watch. And there never will be."

But Mr Biver told the Financial Times yesterday: "We believe that TAG Heuer is an avant-garde brand and our customers belong to the younger generation. There is a demand for luxury connected watches and we want to satisfy that demand."

He said that the new watch, which will run on Google's operating platform, would probably go on sale in November. Mr Biver declined to give prices or any technical details. The average price of a conventional TAG Heuer watch is about €3,500.

Smartwatches have so far been relatively slow to catch on with activity-tracking wristbands from the likes of Jawbone and Fitbit proving more popular. But that could change next month as Apple prepares to launch its Watch, which it first unveiled last year.

Analysts have estimated that only watchmakers competing at lower price points - up to about €900 - could be affected by the product launch.

## STRATEGIC ALLIANCES

As illustrated in the opening profile, sometimes it takes global strategic alliances to compete with behemoths such as Apple. **Strategic alliances** are partnerships between two or more firms that decide they can pursue their mutual goals better by combining their resources—financial, managerial, and technological—as well as their existing distinctive competitive advantages. Alliances—often called *cooperative strategies*—are transition mechanisms that propel the partners' strategies forward in a turbulent environment faster than would be possible for each company alone. The explosion of international strategic alliances (ISAs) in the past has been caused by the need for organizations to respond to the globalization of markets and the opportunities presented by technological advances. However, the rush to take advantage of those opportunities has resulted in an estimated half of ISAs experiencing poor results or failing.[2] (These problems will be discussed later in this chapter.)

Alliances typically fall under one of three categories: joint ventures, equity strategic alliances, and non-equity strategic alliances, and they can be for various purposes such as sharing technology, marketing, or production joint ventures. Cross-border alliances frequently necessitate acquiring a local partner to counteract political risk factors and to take advantage of local knowledge and contacts. Indeed, Eli Lilly, realizing the need for a local partner in China, made an unprecedented deal between a Western drug manufacturer and a Chinese biotech company to co-develop and commercialize three cancer drugs and market to the growing consumer base there:

> *Indianapolis-based Lilly said it would pay $56 million upfront to Innovent Biologics Inc., a four-year-old startup near Shanghai, to co-develop at least three experimental cancer drugs—including one from Lilly's research labs and two from Innovent.*
>
> WALL STREET JOURNAL,
> *MARCH 20, 2015*[3]

It should be noted, however, that although the past decades brought a surge in companies seeking growth through mergers and acquisitions (M&As), joint ventures, and other alliances, the global economic downturn in 2008–2009 caused many companies to postpone or cancel such plans, often instead retrenching or de-merging. Examples were General Motors and Citigroup having to spin off partners as well as retrench operations to maintain sufficient cash flow. The rate of deals collapsing increased amid the credit crisis and global equity market volatility. Still other deals, made under duress, involved government alliances in an attempt to save companies and industries from default, as with a number of banks that become subject to partial nationalization.

## Joint Ventures

> *MUMBAI, India—After years of studying the Indian market, Starbucks Coffee said Monday that it would open its first store here by September (2012) through a 50-50 joint venture with Tata Global Beverages, a unit of the largest business group in India.*
>
> NEW YORK TIMES
> *JANUARY 20, 2012*[4]

A **joint venture (JV)** is a new independent entity jointly created and owned by two or more parent companies. The JV agreement for a firm may comprise a majority JV (in which the firm has more than 50 percent equity), a minority JV (less than 50 percent equity), or a 50-50 JV (when two firms have equal equity). An international joint venture (IJV) is a joint venture among companies in different countries. In that case, the firm shares the profits, costs, and risks with a local partner (or a global partner) and benefits from the local partner's local contacts and markets. The Starbucks agreement with Tata Global Beverages is an example of a 50-50 equity IJV. "The announcement came a year after the company said it was going to enter the market and nearly two months after the Indian government fumbled an effort to attract more foreign investment in its retailing industry."[5]

Another example of a 50–50 equity IJV is that between France's PSA Peugeot-Citroen Group and Japan's Toyota at Kolin in the Czech Republic. As noted by Fujio Cho, president of Toyota Motors, the world's richest carmaker:

> *Each company has brought its own style, culture and way of thinking to this partnership—but our different approaches have benefited our joint venture enormously.*[6]

Among the benefits noted by the two companies are that Toyota "gains an insight into the mindset of one of Europe's biggest indigenous carmakers and knowledge of its suppliers and their capabilities."[7] And Peugeot-Citroen can gain experience from Toyota's lean manufacturing system. The companies acknowledge that the IJV has resulted in faster development and increased production capacity and that costs are shared without either company renouncing its independence.[8]

## Equity Strategic Alliances

*Brazilian firm 3G Capital and Buffett mastermind latest takeover in 7 year campaign. Heinz is to take over Kraft Foods to create one of North America's largest food companies.... The deal—the world's largest M&A transaction this year— marks another step in the conquest of the U.S. food industry by a Brazilian private equity group.*

WWW.FT.COM
MARCH 26, 2015[9]

Two or more partners have different relative ownership shares (equity percentages) in the new venture in an equity strategic alliance. In the merger with Heinz and Kraft, which will create the fifth largest food and beverage company globally, Heinz will control 51 percent and Kraft 49 percent. Most global manufacturers have equity alliances with suppliers, sub-assemblers, and distributors, forming a network of internal family and financial links. Risk-sharing is often the motive behind equity alliances. Sometimes an international, or global, joint venture is part of a desperate strategy. This was the case in January 2009 when Chrysler reached for another lifeline in its equity deal to join forces with Italy's Fiat. The plan was for Fiat to get a 35 percent ownership stake in Chrysler with the goal of bringing its Fiat and Alfa Romeo brands back to the United States through Chrysler's dealership network. In return, Chrysler would try to stay alive by presenting a strategic partnership as part of its plan to the U.S. government in its quest for an additional $3 billion loan to allow it to stay in business.[10] However, further developments led to a change in plans when some creditors did not make concessions, and—as reported in the New York Times, President Obama announced on April 30, 2009:

> *Chrysler, the third-largest American auto company, will seek bankruptcy protection and enter an alliance with the Italian automaker Fiat, the White House announced Thursday.*[11]

However, the deal with Fiat would be intact after bankruptcy, with Fiat to take part in running Chrysler, provide technical operations, and build at least one vehicle in a Chrysler plant. Fiat did not put up any financing as part of the agreement. Considerable additional financing from the U.S. government was planned after Chrysler's restructuring, with the Canadian government also offering some financing.[12]

## Non-equity Strategic Alliances

*Uber Technologies Inc.'s biggest rivals around the world are banding together to launch a counterattack by linking their apps and effectively creating an international ride-hailing service.*

WALL STREET JOURNAL,
17 SEPTEMBER, 2015[13]

As illustrated by the global ride-hailing alliance to defend their turf against Uber, agreements are carried out through contract rather than ownership sharing in a non-equity strategic alliance. Such contracts are often with a firm's suppliers, distributors, or manufacturers, or they may be for purposes of marketing and information sharing, such as with many airline partnerships. UPS, for example, is a global supply-chain manager for many companies around the world, such as Nike, that essentially do not touch their own products but contract with UPS to arrange the entire delivery process from factory to warehouse to customer to repair, even collecting the money.[14]

## Global Strategic Alliances

Working partnerships between companies (often more than two) across national boundaries and increasingly across industries are referred to as global strategic alliances. A glance at the global airline industry, for example, tells us that global alliances have become a mainstay of competitive strategy. Not one airline is competing alone; each major U.S. carrier has established strategic links with non-U.S. companies. The Star Alliance, for example, has code sharing among 26 member airlines around the world.

Alliances are also sometimes formed between a company and a foreign government or among companies and governments. In addition, changing regulations and policies by governments and institutions lead to new opportunities for alliances with national industries abroad. Alliances may comprise full global partnerships, which are often joint ventures in which two or more companies, while retaining their national identities, develop a common, long-term strategy aimed at world leadership. The European Airbus Industrie consortium, for example, comprises France's Aerospatiale and Germany's Daimler-Benz Aerospace, each with 37.9 percent of the business; British Aerospace with 20 percent; and Spain's Construcciones Aeronauticas with 4.2 percent.

Whereas such alliances have a broad agenda, others are formed for a narrow and specific function such as production, marketing, research and development, or financing. More recently, these have included electronic alliances, such as Covisint, which is redefining the entire system of car production and distribution through a common electronic marketplace, as well as linking partners in other major industries involved in Business-to-Partner (B2P), Business-to-Customer (B2C) and Business-to-Enterprise (B2E) relationships.

> *Our customers have deployed our B2B Cloud Platform to connect to over 212,000 of their business partners and customers – transacting in excess of $1 trillion per year.*
>
> WWW.COVISINT.COM
> *MARCH 24, 2015*[15]

## Global and Cross-Border Alliances: Motivations and Benefits

Some of the typical reasons behind cross-border alliances are as follows.

- ***To avoid import barriers, licensing requirements, and other protectionist legislation:*** Japanese automotive manufacturers, for example, use alliances such as the GM–Toyota venture, or subsidiaries, to produce cars in the United States to avoid import quotas.

- ***To share the costs and risks of the research and development of new products and processes:*** In the semiconductor industry, for example, in which each new generation of memory chips is estimated to cost more than $1 billion to develop, those costs and the rapid technological evolution typically require the resources of more than one (or even two) firms. Intel, for example, has alliances with Samsung and NMB Semiconductor for technology (DRAM) development. Toshiba, Japan's third-largest electronics company, has more than two dozen major joint ventures and strategic alliances around the world, including partners such as Olivetti, Rhone-Poulenc, GEC Alstholm in Europe, LSI Logic in Canada, and Samsung in Korea. Fumio Sato, Toshiba's CEO, recognized long ago that a global strategy for a high-tech electronics company such as his necessitated joint ventures and strategic alliances.

- ***To gain access to specific markets, such as China and Russia, where regulations favor domestic companies:*** Firms often find that the only way—or, at least, the best way—to enter markets such as China and Russia is through alliances, as discussed elsewhere. In addition, in spite of the economic problems in the EU, firms around the world are still investing there and forming strategic alliances with European companies to bolster their chances of competing in the European Union (EU) and to gain access to markets in Eastern European countries as they further develop their businesses. Chun Joo Bum, chief executive of the Daewoo Electronics unit, acknowledged his desire for local partners in Europe for two reasons: (1) to provide sorely needed capital and (2) to help Daewoo navigate Europe's still disparate markets, saying, "I need to localize our management. It is not one market."[16]

- ***To reduce political risk while making inroads in a new market:***

  > *Carefully orchestrated partnerships with governments and other business groups are crucial to the [Disney] entertainment group's thrust into China and the rest of south-east Asia.*
  >
  > BOB IGER
  > PRESIDENT AND COO, WALT DISNEY[17]

Hong Kong Disneyland is jointly owned by the Chinese government with a 57 percent stake. Beijing is especially interested in promoting tourism through the venture and in facilitating employment for the 5,000 workers Disney employs directly as well as the estimated 18,000 workers in related services.[18] Coca-Cola—a global player with large-scale alliances—is not beyond using some very small-scale alliances to be political in China. The company uses senior citizens in the Chinese Communist Party's neighborhood committees to sell Coke locally.

- ***To gain rapid entry into a new or consolidating industry and to take advantage of synergies:***
  Technology is rapidly providing the means and products—such as the iPad—for the overlapping and merging of traditional industries such as entertainment, computers, and telecommunications in new digital-based systems. Disney's business model of cellular partnerships and content sales, for example, created Disney mobile operations in Hong Kong, Taiwan, South Korea, Singapore, and the Philippines.[19] The company uses joint venture partners such as the Hong Kong government or licensees and distributors such as Oriental Land and NTT DoCoMo.[20]

In many cases, technological developments are necessitating strategic alliances across industries for companies to gain rapid entry into areas in which they have no expertise or manufacturing capabilities. Such was the case when Apple announced in September 2015 that it had acquired a "big data" analytics company, Mapsense, that will allow it to analyze the huge mass of location and mapping services required in cars.[21] Competition is so fierce that they cannot wait to develop those resources alone. Many of these objectives, such as access to new technology and new markets, are evident in AT&T's network of alliances around the world. Agreements with Japan's NEC, for example, gave AT&T access to new semiconductor and chip-making technologies, helping it learn how to integrate computers with communications better.

## Challenges in Implementing Global Alliances

Effective global alliances are usually tediously slow in the making but can be among the best mechanisms to implement strategies in global markets. In a highly competitive environment, alliances present a faster and less risky route to global expansion and efficiency. It is extremely complex to fashion such linkages, however, especially when many interconnecting systems are involved, forming intricate networks. Many alliances fail for complex reasons. Many also end up in a takeover in which one partner swallows the other. McKinsey & Company, a consulting firm, surveyed 150 companies that had been in alliances and found that 75 percent of them had been taken over by Japanese partners. Problems with shared ownership, differences in national cultures, the integration of vastly different structures and systems, the distribution of power between the companies involved, and conflicts in their relative locus of decision making and control are but a few of the organizational issues that must be worked out. The *Financial Times* observed that "joint ventures start with smiles, but often end in tears."[22]

Often, the form of governance chosen for multinational firm alliances greatly influences their success, particularly in technologically intense fields such as pharmaceuticals, computers, and semiconductors. Thus, joint ventures are often the chosen form for such alliances because they provide greater control of proprietary technology as well as increased coordination in high-technology industries.

Cross-border partnerships, in particular, often become a race to learn—with the faster learner later dominating the alliance and rewriting its terms. In a real sense, an alliance becomes a new form of competition. In fact, according to researcher David Lei,

> *Perhaps the single greatest impediment managers face when seeking to learn or renew sources of competitive advantage is to realize that co-operation can represent another form of unintended competition, particularly to shape and apply new skills to future products and businesses.*[23]

All too often, cross-border allies have difficulty collaborating effectively, especially in competitively sensitive areas; this creates mistrust and secrecy, which then undermine the purpose of the alliance. The difficulty that they are dealing with is the dual nature of strategic alliances—the benefits of cooperation versus the dangers of introducing new competition through sharing their knowledge and technological skills about their mutual product or the manufacturing process. Managers may fear that they will lose the competitive advantage of the firm's proprietary technology or the specific skills that their personnel possess.

The cumulative learning that a partner attains through the alliance could be applied to other products or even other industries that are beyond the scope of the alliance and, therefore, would hold no benefit to the partner holding the original knowledge.[24] Some of the trade-offs of the duality of cross-border ventures are shown in Exhibit 8-1 and are illustrated by the 2011 joint venture between General Electric (GE) and Avic, a state-owned Chinese company. The alliance shows the tricky risk-and-reward calculations American corporations must increasingly make in their pursuit of the lucrative markets in China. This is a 50–50 venture with Avic planned for a 50-year duration. Additional risks are that such technology-sharing could advance the Chinese military-aviation status.

EXHIBIT 8-1 **EXHIBIT 8-1**  **The Dual Role of Strategic Alliances**

| Cooperative | Competitive |
|---|---|
| Economies of scale in tangible assets (e.g., plant and equipment). | Opportunity to learn new intangible skills from partner, often tacit or organization-embedded. |
| Upstream–downstream division of labor among partners. | Accelerate diffusion of industry standards and new technologies to erect barriers to entry. |
| Fill out product line with components or end products provided by supplier. | Deny technological and learning initiative to partner via outsourcing and long-term supply arrangements. |
| Limit investment risk when entering new markets or uncertain technological fields via shared resources. | Encircle existing competitors and preempt the rise of new competitors with alliance partners in "proxy wars" to control market access, distribution, and access to new technologies. |
| Create a "critical mass" to learn and develop new technologies to protect domestic, strategic industries. | Form clusters of learning among suppliers and related firms to avoid or reduce foreign dependence for critical inputs and skills. |
| Assist short-term corporate restructurings by lowering exit barriers in mature or declining industries. | Alliances serve as experiential platforms to "demature" and transform existing mature industries via new components, technologies, or skills to enhance the value of future growth options. |

*Source:* David Lei, "Offensive and Defensive Uses of Alliances," in Heidi Vernon-Wortzel and L. H. Wortzel, *Strategic Management in Global Economy*, 3rd ed. (New York: John Wiley & Sons, 1997), used with permission.

*But doing business in China often requires Western multinationals like G.E. to share technology and trade secrets that might eventually enable Chinese companies to beat them at their own game—by making the same products cheaper, if not better.*[25]

The enticing benefits of cross-border alliances often mask the many pitfalls involved. In addition to potential loss of a company's technology and knowledge or skills base, other areas of incompatibility often arise such as conflicting strategic goals and objectives, cultural clashes, and disputes over management and control systems. Sometimes it takes a while for such problems to present themselves, particularly if insufficient homework has been done in meetings between the two sides to work out the implementation details.

## Implementing Alliances between SMEs and MNCs

All countries have a large proportion of business enterprises, as well as NGOs, that are small or medium-sized enterprises (SMEs). But, increasingly, MNCs are dominating the markets in which SMEs operate, often crowding them out of business altogether. However, astute managers of SMEs can often find opportunities for alliances with those multinationals, providing "complementary resources and capabilities that can lead to, for instance, an innovative product offering being rolled out on a global scale, or a worldwide licensing agreement."[26] For example, MNCs often partner with local small enterprises to capture new ideas and innovations. Sun Microsystems, for instance, engaged with a number of small enterprises in Scotland on radio frequency identification (RFID) projects to bolster its competitiveness in this emerging area.[27] SMEs should seek out those opportunities to offer MNCs complementary technologies as well as local market networks. SABMiller, for example, helps the many small shop owners in Latin America with training and financing, which boosts beer sales for both the company and the *tiendas*.

## Guidelines for Successful Alliances

As discussed earlier, many global companies, such as IBM, the Tata Group, and Toyota, build extensive alliance portfolios that involve multiple concurrent alliances. Oracle's Partner Network, for example, includes 19,500 partners. Alliance partners can provide synergies and value to corporate performance by providing access to new resources and markets, generating economies of scale and scope, reducing costs, sharing risks, and enhancing flexibility.[28] Unfortunately, the complexities involved in managing many alliances often means that many—around half by most estimates—are unsuccessful, often because of poor partner selections initially and then also because of poor management to ensure that the expected competencies and synergies are realized. Research by Dovev Lavie of 20,000 alliances involving about 8,800 unique partners provides some insight into how managers can manage their alliances in ways that will increase the likelihood of success. The results enabled the identification of "value-creation and value-capture strategies that can guide partner selection decisions, and developed alliance portfolio management practices to help managers extract more value from their alliance portfolios."[29] Value creation strategies include, for example, the importance of assimilating network resources to acquire new skills and capabilities. Value capture strategies caution that it is important to "avoid partners that compete in your industry if they enjoy superior bargaining power."[30] One key factor in managing alliance portfolios is to consider not only what each alliance partner will bring to the company but also how that partner will affect other partners in the portfolio.

It is clear that many difficulties arise in cross-border alliances in melding the national and corporate cultures of the parties, in overcoming language and communication barriers, and in building trust between the parties over how to share proprietary assets and management processes. Some basic guidelines, as follows, will help to minimize potential problems. However, nothing is as important as having a long courtship with a potential partner to establish compatibility strategically and interpersonally and set up a plan with the prospective partner. Even setting up some pilot programs on a short-term basis for some of the planned combined activities can highlight areas that may become problematic.

- Choose a partner with compatible strategic goals and objectives and with whom the alliance will result in synergies through the combined markets, technologies, and management cadre.
- Seek alliances where complementary skills, products, and markets will result. If each partner brings distinctive skills and assets to the venture, there will be reduced potential for direct competition in end products and markets. In addition, each partner will begin the alliance in a balanced relationship.[31]
- Work out with the partner how you will each deal with proprietary technology or competitively sensitive information—what will be shared, and what will not, and how shared technology will be handled. Trust is an essential ingredient of an alliance, particularly in these areas; but this must be backed up by contractual agreements.
- Recognize that most alliances last only a few years and will probably break up once a partner feels it has incorporated the skills and information it needs to go it alone. With this in mind, managers need to "learn thoroughly and rapidly about a partner technology and management: transfer valuable ideas and practices promptly into one's own operations."[32]

Some of the opportunities and complexities in cross-border alliances are illustrated in the following Comparative Management in Focus on joint ventures in the Russian Federation. Such alliances are further complicated by the different history of the two parties' economic systems and the resulting business practices, as well as political issues.

# IMPLEMENTING STRATEGY

### Implementing Strategy McDonald's Style

- *Form paradigm-busting arrangements with suppliers.*
- *Know a country's culture before you hit the beach.*
- *Hire locals whenever possible.*
- *Maximize autonomy.*
- *Tweak the standard menu only slightly from place to place.*
- *Keep pricing low to build market share. Profits will follow when economies of scale kick in.*[33]

## Comparative Management in Focus

### *Joint Ventures in the Russian Federation*

*Russia ranks 53rd out of 139 countries covered by the 2014–2015 Global Competitiveness Index.*

WORLD ECONOMIC FORUM[34]

*GM says it will shut Russian plant; wind down Opel brand.*

WWW.NYTIMES.COM
*MARCH 18, 2015*

*"We are doing everything we can to continue development despite the slowdown of the Russian economy. We are still confident in Russia's long-term prospects."*

MAURIZIO PATARNELLO, NESTLÉ RUSSIA CEO
WWW.NYTIMES.COM
*MARCH 24, 2015*[35]

Judging by the preceding quotes, it seems that Russia poses a number of contradictions to would-be investors. In 2011, as Disney pushed into Russia with a new Disney television channel, its CEO Bob Iger said "we really believe in Russia as a growth market."[36] However, as of 2015, both potential investors and those firms already in Russia were very concerned about Russia's continuing involvement in Ukraine and the negative impact on the economy of the stringent western sanctions. It has been clear for some time that foreign companies have started to think twice about investing in international joint ventures (IJVs) in Russia since President Putin's moves to take control of key industries, including banks, newspapers, and oil assets. In May 2008, President Putin signed the Strategic Industries Bill, which regulates foreign investment. The new law identifies 42 strategic sectors (compared to 16 in 2005) in which foreign investors have to seek special permission before investing.

In September 2014, the U.S. private equity investment group Blackstone gave up on Russia, citing a lack of investors' interest and limited investment opportunities after the widespread impact of the sanctions.[37] In spite of the recent negative climate, Russia—the world's largest country (see Map 8.1), spanning 11 time zones, clearly offers substantial opportunity for companies willing to go for the risk–return

MAP 8.1  **Russia**

*(Continued)*

trade-off. However, its significant growth over the past decade has slowed considerably since the global economic downturn, making it less competitive than the other BRIC countries. According to the 2011 World Economic Forum Russia report, the most important single element explaining a country's medium-term growth performance is productivity; labor productivity in Russia is less than half the value achieved by workers in the OECD member states. The decline in manufacturing competitiveness in Russia "is due to the combination of an increase in real wages and shortcomings of the business climate, which puts Russia at a disadvantage in international comparison."[38] In addition, there is concern that the long-term business climate will remain for some time as an unbalanced, corruption-ridden, natural resource–based economy because of the persistent lack of formal institutions.

> *Russian managers have relied excessively on informal institutions, including personal networks, to conduct business due to the void created by the weak legitimacy of the country's formal institutions.*[39]

All in all, investors are confused, though many are determined to take advantage of the vast, underexploited natural-resource potential; a skilled, educated population; and a huge market. Indeed the abundance of technically skilled Russians has attracted a number of companies in the past, such as Intel, Cisco, Sun Microsystems, and Microsoft. Many MNCs claim that they must have a presence in Russia to be globally competitive.

In addition to the potential for corruption and the constant uncertainty in the business environment, firms doing business in Russia find that implementing a joint venture is very frustrating and time-consuming due to the all-consuming regulations and bureaucracy there. For these reasons, many foreign firms pick a local partner to help them navigate the myriad of negotiations to obtain permissions, get visas, acquire property, and so on. Other firms hire a security firm (Krisha), which smooths the way through the bureaucracy, often with payments.[40]

Until recently Moscow and other major cities have been experiencing a consumer boom, spurred on by rising incomes in the middle class, making Russia one of the fastest growing regions for global consumer giants such as Coca-Cola, Procter & Gamble, and Nestlé.[41] Indeed, the Swiss food giant, Nestlé confirmed its faith in the long-term prospects in Russia and that it would try to use more local content and ingredients to try to offset the currency problems, reinforcing the importance of local suppliers.[42] Nestlé has nine manufacturing facilities in Russia and opened a new factory for baby food in 2014. Many, like Bell Labs, have been involved in research and development, taking advantage of the Russians' high-level education and technical capabilities. Nevertheless,, Western managers need to recognize that cultural factors affect cross-border business, in particular, that Russians are distrustful of outsiders; managers attempting to develop joint ventures must understand that they will need to spend considerable time communicating and developing a trusting relationship. Reliance on their own networks and the use of favors (*blat*) present obstacles to business relations between Russians and outsiders.[43]

Overall, managers of foreign companies who are looking past the current economic problems in Russia and hoping to set up business in the future should carefully consider the following.

- Investigate whether a joint venture is the best strategy. If a lot of real estate is needed, it may be better to acquire a Russian business because of the difficulties involved in acquiring land.
- Set up meetings with the appropriate ministry and regional authorities well in advance. Have good communication about your business needs and build local relationships.
- Be sure to be totally above board in paying all relevant taxes to avoid crossing the Russian authorities.
- Set up stricter controls and accountability systems than usual for the company.
- Communicate clearly up front that your firm does not pay bribes.
- Assign the firm's best available managers and delegate to them enough authority to act locally.
- Take advantage of local knowledge by hiring appropriate Russian managers for the venture.
- Designate considerable funds for local promotion and advertising to establish the corporate image with authorities and consumers.[44]

Foreign managers' alliance strategy must also take into account the goals of potential Russian partners. An awareness and acceptance of the motivations of Russian firms for alliances with foreign companies will aid in finding and achieving a cooperative joint venture.

Researchers for the *Wall Street Journal* reported their findings about what local Russian firms want from an alliance with a foreign firm; they made it clear that they expect assistance with market entry through forming an alliance and that they need assistance in solving bribes, kickbacks, and other under-the-table transactions.[45]

Decisions regarding global alliances and entry strategies must now be put into motion with the next stage of planning: strategic implementation—also known as functional level strategies. Implementation plans are detailed and pervade the entire organization because they entail setting up overall policies, administrative responsibilities, and schedules throughout the organization to enact the selected strategy and to make sure it works. In the case of a merger or IJV, this process requires compromising and blending procedures among two or more companies and is extremely complex. The importance of the implementation phase of the strategic management process cannot be overemphasized. Until they are put into operation, strategic plans remain abstract ideas: verbal or printed proposals that have no effect on the organization.

Successful implementation requires the orchestration of many variables into a cohesive system that complements the desired strategy—that is, a *system of fits* that will facilitate the actual working of the strategic plan. In this way, the structure, systems, and processes of the firm are coordinated and set into motion by a system of management by objectives (MBO) whose primary objective is the fulfillment of strategy. Managers must review the organizational structure and, if necessary, change it to facilitate the administration of the strategy and coordinate activities in a particular location with headquarters. In addition to ensuring the strategy-structure fit, managers must allocate resources to make the strategy work, budgeting money, facilities, equipment, people, and other support. Increasingly, that support necessitates a unified technology infrastructure to coordinate diverse businesses around the world and satisfy the need for current and reliable information. An efficient technology infrastructure can provide a strategic advantage in a globally competitive environment. Jack Welch, while CEO of General Electric (he retired in late 2001), was prescient when he referred to his e-commerce initiative, saying, "It will change relationships with suppliers. Within 18 months, all our suppliers will supply us on the Internet, or they won't do business with us."[46]

An overarching factor affecting all the other variables necessary for successful implementation is that of leadership; it is people, after all, who make things happen. The firm's leaders must skillfully guide employees and processes in the desired direction. Managers with different combinations of experience, education, abilities, and personality tend to be more suited to implementing certain strategies. In an equity-sharing alliance, sorting out which top managers in each company will be in which position is a sensitive matter. Who in which company will be CEO is usually worked out as part of the initial deal in alliance agreements. This problem seems to be frequently settled these days by setting up joint CEOs, one from each company. Setting monitoring systems into place to control activities and ensure success completes, but does not end, the strategic management process. Rather, it is a continuous process, using feedback to reevaluate strategy for needed modifications and updating and recycling plans.

Of particular note here, we should consider what is involved in implementing strategies for SMEs and the issues involved in the effective management of the global sourcing strategy. Then we will review what is involved in managing performance in international joint ventures because they are such a common form of global alliance, and yet they are fraught with implementation challenges.

## Implementing Strategies for SMEs

For small businesses venturing abroad, however, the first step is often that of exporting. This can be a daunting task; however, many sources are available to help small-business managers embark on exporting, as discussed in the nearby feature, Under the Lens: Breaking Down Barriers for Small-Business Exports. Of particular note, China offers substantial opportunities for exports for SMEs (businesses with fewer than 500 employees), which have accounted for an estimated third of exports to China in recent years. Most exports to China include agricultural products leading the way, followed by computers and electronics, chemicals, non-electrical machinery, and waste and scrap.[47] China is the third largest export market for U.S. companies, after Canada and Mexico and followed by Japan and the United Kingdom. Further opportunities for SMEs will emerge once the new Trans Pacific Partnership Trade Deal between the U.S. and eleven Pacific Rim nations (announced October 2015) is ratified and in force.

For SME firms wishing to expand beyond their domestic markets and exporting, they typically need to find a market niche in the chosen countries between the MNCs and the local firms where they know they can compete. While they do not have the economies of scale and financial

## UNDER THE LENS

*Breaking Down Barriers for Small-Business Exports*

Approximately 300,000 small or medium-sized businesses in the United States export goods or services abroad. Small businesses make up 97 percent of American companies that export, according to the U.S. Census Bureau, and their numbers are growing. The U.S. government is looking to boost small-business exports with the National Export Initiative (NEI)—an initiative started in January 2010 by U.S. President Barack Obama—which aimed to double U.S. exports and create millions of jobs in the United States by the end of 2015.

"To double exports we need to increase the number of small business exporters,' said Richard Ginsburg, an international trade specialist with the U.S. Small Business Administration (SBA). Fifty-eight percent of roughly 250,000 U.S. small and medium-sized enterprise (SME) exporters ship to just one market. Ginsburg says one of the key goals of NEI is to help those firms ship to multiple markets.

China has been a growing market for American SMEs—companies with fewer than 500 employees. According to the U.S. International Trade Administration, the number of American SMEs exporting to China increased by 776 percent from 1992 to 2009. But there is still room for growth. Successful exporters to China emphasize the complexity, and that it is essential to meet your clients face-to-face at the beginning.

### U.S. EXPORT ASSISTANCE CENTERS

Of the 20 U.S. government agencies involved in export assistance, SBA specifically aims to increase the number of small business exporters through programs delivered through U.S. Export Assistance Centers. Senior SBA trade and finance specialists—along with employees from the U.S. Commercial Service and the U.S. Export-Import (Ex-Im) Bank—staff 20 of more than 100 U.S. Export Assistance Centers in metropolitan areas around the country. The centers help "export-ready" companies begin to export or expand to new markets abroad by providing counseling, training, export insurance, and loans to these businesses; conducting market research; and facilitating contracts between U.S. exporters and foreign buyers.

Ginsburg says small business owners usually approach an Export Assistance Center when they want to make a deal with a foreign buyer or when they receive an order from a foreign buyer and have never exported before. The centers can help companies understand payment terms and conditions, help them handle logistics such as shipping, and refer them to translators. These transactions are often simple when doing business in the United States, but they can be complicated when crossing international borders.

Counseling, outreach, and loan programs help break down what Ginsburg calls the "psychological trade barriers" that prevent small businesses from exporting. "There are people who feel they can lose their business if they export," Ginsburg says. "The risks are so much more than shipping across town or across the state or across the country." For example, small-business owners sometimes fear that they will not be able to collect payments from overseas buyers.

Companies that want to export face barriers such as language and lack of knowledge of the foreign regulatory environment, and—specifically for businesses exporting to China—fear of intellectual property rights infringement, Ginsburg says.

### EXPORT LOANS FOR SMALL BUSINESSES

In addition to counseling and training, SBA guarantees loans of up to $5 million, and the Ex-Im Bank provides export financing for amounts over $5 million. "It's a success story for SBA when we're working with a small-business exporter and they outgrow the small loan amount and need more than the $5 million SBA threshold," Ginsburg says.

SBA runs four loan programs for small-business exporters: the Export Express Program, the Export Working Capital Program, International Trade Loan Program, and SBA and Ex-Im Bank Co-Guarantee Program. The Export Express Program, formerly a pilot program, was made permanent in 2010 with the passage of the Small Business Jobs Act of 2010 to support the NEI goal of increasing small business exports. The program aims to streamline the export loan process for small businesses. SMEs that have been operating for at least 12 months can receive up to $500,000 to finance export activities, such as participating in foreign trade shows, purchasing equipment, and translating product literature. The law also permanently increased loan limits on export working capital and international trade loans.

Companies can obtain more information on export loans from the nearest Export Assistance Center and apply directly for loans through SBA lenders. Visit www.export.gov/eac to contact the nearest center or www.sba.gov/content/us-export-assistance-centers for a list of centers with SBA representatives.

CHRISTINA NELSON

Christina Nelson (cmnelson@uschina.org) is associate editor of the *CBR*.

*Source:* "U.S. Exports in China Rebound in 2010." This article first appeared in the July–September 2011 *China Business Review*. Used with the permission of the *China Business Review*. Updated from Christina Nelson, "Exporting to China is Not for the Faint of Heart," *China Business Review*, November 19, 2015.

and marketing resources of the MNCs; they also do not have the local connections, suppliers, and consumer knowledge of the small local companies. If those SMEs can find an opportunity, or niche, that the MNCs find too minor to bother with, and also that are not being targeted by local firms, they may be able to gain a foothold and establish their own reputation as leaders. Then, too, a later opportunity may arise with an MNC wanting to use that firm to gain inroads or to use the acquired knowledge or technology, as discussed earlier. Alternatively, seeking an alliance with a local partner would provide early access to hiring local talent, to local connections and suppliers, etc. In their research of successful Israeli small firms going global, Jonathan Friedrich, et al concluded first, that SMEs can take care not to awaken the gorillas by targeting a sufficiently minor opportunity that the MNCs decide is not worth their while, but which can be leveraged profitably across several international regions; and secondly, by bringing in superior technology and processing capabilities to keep out local players.[48]

## Implementing a Global Sourcing Strategy: From Offshoring to Next-Shoring?

Outsourcing abroad—alliances with firms in other countries to perform specific functions for the firm (offshoring)—is often in the news because of the politically charged issue of domestic jobs apparently being lost to others overseas. Beyond finding lower-paid workers, however, the strategic view of global sourcing is to develop into transformational outsourcing—the view that, properly implemented, global sourcing can produce gains in efficiency, productivity, quality, and profitability by fully leveraging talent around the world.[49] Procter & Gamble, for example, having outsourced everything from IT infrastructure and Human Resource Department functions, such as staffing, training, compensation, and so on, around the world, announced that CEO Alan G. Lafley wanted 50 percent of all new P&G products to come from other countries.[50] However, implementing such a strategy is more difficult than it is made to seem in the press, because many companies have encountered unexpected problems when outsourcing. Advice on implementation from experiences by companies such as Dell, IBM, and Reuters Group PLC lead us to the following guidelines:

- *Examine your reasons for outsourcing:* Make sure that the advantages of efficiency and competitiveness will outweigh the disadvantages from your employees, customers, and community; don't outsource just because your competitors are doing it.

- *Evaluate the best outsourcing model:* Opening your own subsidiary in the host country (a captive operation) may be better than contracting with an outside firm if it is crucial for you to keep control of proprietary technology and processes.

- *Gain the cooperation of your management and staff:* Open communication and training is essential to get your domestic managers on board; uncertainty, fear, and disagreement from them can jeopardize your plans.

- *Consult your alliance partners:* Consult with your partners and treat them with the respect that made you decide to do business with them.

- *Invest in the alliance:* Plan to invest time and money in training in the firm's business practices, in particular those to deal with quality control and customer relations.[51]

Further advice comes from Josh Green, CEO of Panjiva, which is an information resource for companies doing business across borders. Green asks, "How healthy is your global partner?" because he noted that an increasing number of firms in developed economies were finding that their suppliers in Asia had gone out of business following the protracted global economic downturn that caused firms to reduce their demand from their suppliers. He notes that both buyers and suppliers have learned the hard way that in the future they need to investigate and evaluate their potential partners carefully. He suggests, for example, that both sides should do a background check on the financial health and future viability of the company; get references from other partners of the firm; be prepared to give those assurances and data about their own companies; and be prepared for problems by having alternate partners ready to fill in.[52] The need to be prepared for the unexpected was suddenly brought home on March 11, 2011, when the Japanese earthquake and tsunami struck—a disaster for the Japanese people and a problem for supply chains of companies around the world (see *Under the Lens: Global Supply Chain Risks—The Japanese Disaster*). The quake and tsunami left nearly 28,000 people dead or missing, thousands homeless, and Japan's northeast coast devastated. Clearly, the first responsibility for Japan was to its people, but this disaster also threatened the country economically—not the least because 15 percent of its GDP was in its supply chain business to global firms ranging from semiconductor makers to shipbuilding.[53]

## UNDER THE LENS

*Global Supply Chain Risks—The Japanese Disaster* [54]

With different component parts for everything from cell phones to cars being sourced from various countries, supply chains have become longer and far more complex to manage than in the past. It is not surprising, then, that companies around the world, from Lenovo to General Motors, had to scramble to find alternate supply sources after the Japanese earthquake and tsunami on March 11, 2011, disrupted supplies. As well as being a disaster for the Japanese people, major problems arose due to the nuclear alert, power shortages, damaged infrastructure, and loss of port access. At Hewlett Packard, for example, Tony Prophet, senior VP for Operations, gathered his team in the wee hours of the morning to brainstorm back-up plans for its $65 billion a year global supply chain, saying,

*"It's like being in an emergency room, doing triage."*[55]

The auto industry in particular was hard hit. Japan exports 2.5 million engines and 8.5 million transmissions annually to assembly plants around the world, and 2,200 parts are used in the typical vehicle. Ironically, it was the Japanese automakers with plants in the U.S. and Europe who were the most disrupted, not expecting to be able to get up to full production again for several months. Toyota, for example, which sources about 15 per cent of its parts from Japan for its U.S. plants, was reduced to about 30 percent of its normal production capacity.

General Motors set up its disaster response teams in three crisis rooms at its Vehicle Engineering Center in Warren, Michigan. Problems included being able to identify tiers of sub-suppliers and what parts were affected. Shortages led to temporary plant shutdowns. Lack of information due to communication outages was a problem, so GM sent 40 employees to Japan to visit suppliers; determine what parts were being held up and why, such as the supplier's inability to get the steel it needed to make the parts or to acquire enough electricity to run its factories; and to offer help.

These days, sourcing risk is somewhat reduced because sourcing is done globally, and technological developments have enabled the ability to management of these complex networks through Internet communications, RFID tags, and sensors attached to valued parts. In addition, sophisticated software can now be used for tracking and orchestrating the flow of goods worldwide. However, as supply chains become longer—that is suppliers of suppliers of suppliers—control is more difficult and, therefore, the risk is greater. A further difficulty is the lack of alternative sources for the thousands of tiny specialized parts for those ubiquitous electronics such as connectors, speakers, microphones, batteries, and sensors. If any of these parts cannot be sourced, the entire plant might be put on hold. Five parts in the Apple iPad, for example, come from Japanese suppliers.

Clearly executives around the world have learned that there are unforeseen risks in implementing a global sourcing strategy—in particular combined with the just-in-time inventory practice. As a result, they realize that they need to have backup sourcing plans to manage the risk of supply chain disruption.

## THE NEXT WAVE

Elsewhere we pointed out that many companies are moving from a single strategy of outsourcing—or offshoring—manufacturing or service operations, towards nearshoring to closer geographic regions and markets, or to reshoring to the 'home' country. Increasing labor costs overseas, as well as the distance and risks of supply chains and transportation, have made offshoring less competitive overall. Two trends are converging towards this next strategy of global sourcing—which McKinsey Consultants call 'next-shoring'—the trend away from labor cost arbitrage, and the trend towards robotics as technological advances provide the opportunity to digitize operations through the Internet of Things.[56] In this way, companies can use the advantages of production facilities which are geographically closer to their markets so as to adapt products locally, while at the same time using innovation and technology to offset the previous advantages of economies of scale through distant outsourcing.

*Nextshoring strategies encompass elements such as a diverse and agile set of production locations, a rich network of innovation-oriented partnerships, and a strong focus on technical skills.*

McKinsey Quarterly,
January 2014[57]

## Implementing Strategies for Emerging Economy Firms

Firms from emerging economies have, out of necessity, expanded globally through different paths and strategies than the traditional paths firms in the developed world followed. Their motives for expansion into developed countries often include the need to acquire specific resources, such as technological know-how, R&D capability, managerial skills, and global brands to make them competitive with established firms. It is interesting to observe how those firms are coping with strategic implementation. Rather than the gradual, staged internationalization process typical of traditional firms from the developed world, the emerging firms—of all sizes—are finding that they have to move quickly or skip various stages to expand into both developed as well as developing markets.[58] As a result, firms such as Brazil's Natura Cosmeticos, China's Lenovo, and Argentina's Tenaris—now significant global players—have tended to expand globally through acquisitions and alliances and have had to be more flexible organizationally. Mauro F. Guillén and Estaban García-Canal point out from their research that firms from emerging and developing countries "face a significant dilemma when it comes to international expansion because they need to balance the desire for global reach with the need to upgrade their capabilities. They can readily use their home-grown competitive advantages in other emerging or developing countries, but they must also enter more advanced countries in order to expose themselves to sophisticated, cutting-edge demand and develop their capabilities."[59] As Guillén and García-Canal demonstrate in Exhibit 8-2, those firms must decide how to balance their geographic expansion with their ability to upgrade their capabilities in the market because they lack the resources and capabilities of established MNEs; they must realize that "prioritizing global reach without improving firm competencies jeopardizes the capability upgrading process."[60] (This puts them in the Unsustainable region in the exhibit.) Huei-Ting Tsai and Eisingerich also note "the dual challenge faced by emerging market firms, namely, market creation and/or R&D knowledge creation."[61] They note that firms with less technological and selling capabilities tend to enter new markets one at a time. In addition, firms with strong technological capabilities often expand to overseas markets shortly after the firm is established, as with Infosys (featured in the Management in Action feature nearby) They found from the firms in their sample that those that were stronger technologically and had more financial resources would compete in the developed markets, whereas those with a smaller stable of competitive resources pursued less-competitive markets during the early stages of their internationalization.

**EXHIBIT 8-2** Expansion Paths for Emerging Economy Firms

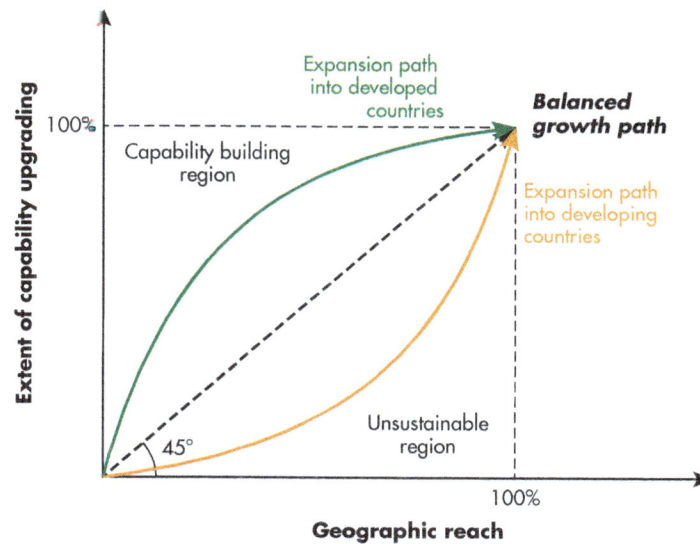

*Source:* Based on Mauro F. Guillén and Estaban García-Canal, "The American Model of the Multinational Firm and the 'New' Multinationals from Emerging Economies," *Academy of Management Perspectives*, May, 2009, pp. 23–35.

## MANAGEMENT IN ACTION

*Infosys's Path From Emerging Start-up to EMNE* [62]

Infosys is one of the most fascinating success stories to come out of India—one of a start-up valued at $250 in 1981 to the over $36.1 billion (market cap as of Q3 2015) emerging market national enterprise (EMNE). It's path from a "born global" IT-services company to strategic alliances around the world is widely admired and reported.

Infosys was established by N. R. Narayana Murthy and six engineers in Pune, India, with an initial capital of $250. A central goal of Narayana Murthy's global strategy was the "global delivery model (GDM)," which focused on producing where it is most cost effective to produce and selling where it is most profitable to sell. As such, most of the software development work was done in India and the sales focused on the United States and other foreign markets. However, this model was competing with both foreign and Indian software companies such as Accenture, IBM Global Services, EDS, and TCS. From the beginning, Infosys focused the company on positioning it as a truly global company—global clients, global operations, global staff, and a global brand image. In 1987 the company opened its first international office in Boston, and in 1995 moved into the United Kingdom and Toronto, Canada. From there, global expansion happened rapidly as the company opened offices in Germany, Sweden, Belgium, Australia, and two development centers in the United States. As of 2015, Dr. Vishal Sikka is Infosys's CEO and Managing Director. The company has been a leader in establishing the Indian Business Process Outsourcing industry (BPO), now a global business. It is now the global leader in consulting, technology, and outsourcing solutions with 165,000 employees and clients in over 50 countries. The company's website emphasizes that its mission is based on "nurturing relationships that reflect our culture of unwavering ethics and mutual respect." In addition, Infosys is well recognized as a leader in sustainability efforts. Much of the company's success is attributed to its hybrid business models to include the best of the Indian culture and expectations, along with adapting to local business practices, and to the alliances and trust in developing new models with partners around the world.

In February 2015, Infosys bought U.S.-based Panaya in a $200 million deal in an effort to diversify away from its traditional outsourcing business into more lucrative opportunities in big data, cloud computing, and artificial intelligence.

## Challenges in Implementing Strategies in Emerging Markets

Firms expanding into emerging, or developing, market countries are often unaware of the considerable differences from their home markets and the challenges they face in getting started. Because of their lack of familiarity and preparation for those challenges, foreign firms are often surprised that they cannot compete successfully with local firms. They may be operating under assumptions that firms from more developed countries have better experience, management knowledge, technology, and other resources than those in the target regions. Unfortunately, that mindset might lead foreign firms to enter those new markets without sufficient research and preparation for the differences and difficulties they may face. However, that is not the case with IKEA, the Swedish home furnishings giant. The company is absolutely committed to not expanding too rapidly; instead, it does extensive research on new locations. For example, it took six years before it opened its first store in South Korea.[63] The care the company takes to get familiar with the local area and the needs of the people there has certainly paid off; the company has 318 stores and around 50 franchised locations around the world and is one of the most profitable in the retail industry.

The initial challenge is likely to be how to navigate poor infrastructures, supply chains, and distribution networks—problems that local firms know how to navigate through experience and contacts. The same edge is enjoyed by local firms when dealing with the myriad regulations and bureaucracies prevalent in some developing economies.

Expansion into emerging markets also brings personnel challenges, especially at management levels. Here too, often the domestic companies have the advantage of knowing how to source, attract, and train local talent; those employees also tend to prefer to work for local companies that are perceived to be more invested in their future.[64] On the other hand, those employees often do not have the experience or familiarity with cross-border business compared with the foreign firms that may bring in their own talent.

Clearly, firms going into developing markets need to explore thoroughly how to navigate the infrastructure and institutions, evaluate the area for their personnel needs, and make local contacts to assess the feasibility of operating there and competing with local firms.

One firm, the global English-language social network LinkedIn, has found that it can make inroads in China through compromising on China's free-expression rules and developing local alliances with two Chinese venture-capital firms. Having local partners placates Chinese authorities and provides an incentive for the partners to make the venture a success. LinkedIn added a Chinese-language version, thereby adding about a million new members to the over four million it already had there.[65] Other technology firms, such as Facebook and Twitter, have been blocked from China, and Google is now in the authorities' bad books because of its about-face on its freedom of speech policies in 2010, as in no longer "cooperating" with the Chinese on what is allowed on the website. LinkedIn faced considerable backlash in the West for bowing to Chinese demands to take down content connected with the anniversary of the Tianamen Square uprising.[66]

## Managing Performance in International Joint Ventures

Much of the world's international business activity involves international joint ventures (IJVs) in which at least one parent is headquartered outside the venture's country of operation. IJVs require unique controls. Ignoring these specific control requisites can limit the parent company's ability to use its resources efficiently, coordinate its activities, and implement its strategy.

The term **IJV control** refers to the processes that management puts in place to direct the success of the firm's goals. Most of a firm's objectives can be achieved by careful attention to control features at the outset of the joint venture, such as the choice of a partner, the establishment of a strategic fit, and the design of the IJV organization. Howard Schultz, CEO of Starbucks, attributes its success in India to its joint venture with Tata Group, the largest coffee producer in Asia. This process followed a complicated six-year journey. Schultz acknowledged that Tata helped with finding highly desired locations, and the complex logistics and supply infrastructure, as well as the menus. Schultz admits there was much to learn, and that the key was finding a partner he could trust and with whom the firm could collaborate.[67]

Clearly the most important single factor determining IJV success or failure is the choice of a partner. Most problems with IJVs involve the local partner, especially in less-developed countries. In spite of this fact, many firms rush the process of partner selection because they are anxious to get on the bandwagon in an attractive market. In this process, it is vital to establish whether the partners' strategic goals are compatible. The strategic context and the competitive environment of the proposed IJV and the parent firm will determine the relative importance of the criteria used to select a partner.[68] IJV performance is also a function of the general fit between the international strategies of the parents, the IJV strategy, and the specific performance goals that the parents adopt.[69] Research has shown that, to facilitate this fit, the partner selection process must determine the specific task-related skills and resources needed from a partner as well as the relative priority of those needs.[70] To do this, managers must analyze their own firms and pinpoint any areas of weakness in task-related skills and resources that can be overcome with the help of the IJV partner.

Partnerships with companies in India present both positive and negative examples of IJV performance, although, overall, IJVs there run into considerable problems. McDonald's has had both experiences so far there. The company reported in February 2015 an ongoing legal battle with its 50–50 joint venture partner, Mr. Bakshi, in the north and east of the country due to a clash of business cultures and expectations which could take years to play out. However, its relationship with its 50–50 joint venture partner in the south and west, Amit Jatia, has been positive. In fact, Mr Jatia's Hardcastle Restaurants have now become a full franchisee, through a friendly buy-out of McDonald's share in the venture. Today, Hardcastle has 185 outlets, 85 of which opened in the past three years, and it plans to open between 175 and 250 more by 2020.[71] Of course both ventures were plagued in the early years by difficulty in adapting the menu to local tastes. Although India still insists on joint ventures in sectors such as telecommunications, agriculture, and insurance, it has lifted restrictions for other industries, allowing wholly owned operations in them. However, a number of recent IJVs have done poorly, especially for the Indian partner. On the other hand, an IJV between Indian engineering group Kirloskar and Japan's Toyota, for vehicle production, has had more positive results, with Mr. Kirloskar acknowledging that Toyota has been open in sharing ideas and improving the productivity of his firm.

Organizational design is another major mechanism for factoring in a means of control when an IJV is started. Beamish et al. discuss the important issue of the strategic freedom of an IJV. This refers to the relative amount of decision-making power that a joint venture will have, compared with the parents, in choosing suppliers, product lines, customers, and so on.[72] It is also crucial to consider beforehand the relative management roles each parent will play in the IJV because such decisions result in varying levels of control for different parties. An IJV is usually easier to manage if one parent plays a dominant role and has more decision-making responsibility than the other in daily operations. Alternatively, it is easier to manage an IJV if the local general manager has considerable management control, keeping both parents out of most of the daily operations.

International joint ventures are like a marriage: the more issues that can be settled before the merger, the less likely it will be to break up. Control over the stability and success of the IJV can be largely built into the initial agreement between the partners. The contract can specify who has what responsibilities and rights in a variety of circumstances, such as the contractual links of the IJV with the parents, the capitalization, and the rights and obligations regarding intellectual property. Of course, we cannot assume equal ownership of the IJV partners; where ownership is unequal, the partners will claim control and staffing choices proportionate to the ownership share. The choice of the IJV general manager, in particular, will influence the relative allocation of control because that person is responsible for running the IJV and for coordinating relationships with each of the parents.[73]

Where ownership is divided among several partners, the parents are more likely to delegate the daily operations of the IJV to the local IJV management—a move that resolves many potential disputes. In addition, the increased autonomy of the IJV tends to reduce many common human resource problems: staffing friction, blocked communication, and blurred organizational culture, to name a few, which all result from the conflicting goals and working practices of the parent companies.[74] Regardless of the number of parents, one way to avoid such potential problem situations is to provide special training to managers about the unique nature and problems of IJVs. The extent of control exercised over an IJV by its parent companies seems to be primarily determined by the decision-making autonomy that the parents delegate to the IJV management—which largely depends on staffing choices for the top IJV positions and thus on how much confidence the partners have in these managers. In addition, if top managers of the IJV are from the headquarters of each party, the compatibility of the managers will depend on how similar their national cultures are. This is because there are many areas of control decisions where agreement will be more likely between those of similar cultural backgrounds.[75]

## Knowledge Management in IJVs

*The most effective strategic leadership practices in the 21st century will be ones through which strategic leaders find ways for knowledge to breed still more knowledge.*[76]

Managing the performance of an IJV for the long term, as well as adding value to the parent companies, necessitates managing the knowledge flows within the IJV network. When managed correctly, "alliances serve as a source of new knowledge for the firm."[77] Sirmon et al. contend that if firms can access and absorb this new knowledge, it can be used to alter existing capabilities or create new ones.[78] Yet, as found by Hitt et al., "cultural differences and institutional deficits can serve as barriers to the transfer of knowledge in alliance partnerships"[79] Clearly, then, managers need to recognize that it is critical to overcome cultural and system differences in managing knowledge flows to the advantage of the alliance.

**Knowledge management**, then, is "the conscious and active management of creating, disseminating, evolving, and applying knowledge to strategic ends."[80] Research on eight IJVs by Berdrow and Lane led them to define these processes as follows.

- *Transfer:* Managing the flow of existing knowledge between parents and from the parents to the IJV
- *Transformation:* Managing the transformation and creation of knowledge within the IJV through its independent activities
- *Harvest:* Managing the flow of transformed and newly created knowledge from the IJV back to the parents[81]

In particular, the sharing and development of technology among IJV partners provides the opportunity for knowledge transfer among individuals who have internalized that information, beyond any tangible assets; the challenge is to develop and harvest that information to benefit the parents through complementary synergies. IJVs that were successful in meeting that challenge were found to have personal involvement by the principals of the parent company in shared goals, in the activities and decisions being made, and in encouraging joint learning and coaching.[82]

The many operational activities and issues involved in strategic implementation—such as negotiating, organizing, staffing, leading, communicating, and controlling—are the subjects of this chapter. Elsewhere, we include discussion of the many variables involved in strategic implementation that are specific to a particular country or region, such as goals, infrastructure, laws, technology, ways of doing business, people, and culture. In the following sections, the focus is on three pervasive influences on strategy implementation: government policy, societal culture, and the Internet.

## Government Influences on Strategic Implementation

Host governments influence, in many areas, the strategic choices and implementations of foreign firms. The family-run Vermeer Company, for example, with its equipment-manufacturing factory in Pella, Iowa, earns about a third of its revenues from exports. However, the company realized its share of the market was falling rapidly due to competition from China, so it decided to open a plant in Beijing, taking a Chinese partner and drawing help for the venture from the Chinese. The chief executive, Ms. Mary Vermeer Andringa, noted that:

*If we wanted to stay in the Chinese market, we needed to be there. That was the reality.*[83]

The profitability of firms that set up operations abroad is greatly influenced, for example, by the level of taxation in the host country and by any restrictions on profit repatriation. Other important influences are government policies on ownership by foreign firms, on labor union rules, on hiring and remuneration practices, on patent and copyright protection, and so on. For the most part, however, if the corporation's managers have done the groundwork, all these factors are known beforehand and are part of the location and entry strategy decisions. However, what hurts managers is to set up shop in a host country and then have major economic or governmental policy changes after they have made a considerable investment. Vodafone, for example, the British mobile phone giant, bought an Indian wireless company in 2007 for $11 billion. However, it soon found the market was full of hazards—including a surprise tax bill of $2.5 billion and a corruption scandal over awarding contracts for additional wireless capacity.

> In emerging markets "there are new hurdles every day, and they can change the rules of the market as you are playing it," Marten Pieters, the chief executive of Vodafone's India business, said.

> The lesson from India? "If you don't have the stomach for that," Mr. Pieters said, "please don't come."

WWW.NYTIMES.COM
*MARCH 27, 2011*

Unpredictable changes in governmental regulations can be a death knell to businesses operating abroad. Recent changes in Russia causing uncertainty for foreign investors were already discussed. Another country that is often the subject of concern for foreign firms is China. Already one of the toughest countries for mergers and acquisitions, China recently added new restrictions on foreign investors, thus prolonging the time that a number of firms have to continue to wait to find out whether their deals will go through. "Acquisitions that will require the ministry's approval include companies with a well-known brand or those that could have an impact on 'China's economic security.'"[34] Although China contends it is more committed to a market economy since it joined the World Trade Organization (WTO) in November 2001, history shows that foreign firms need to be cautious about entering China, as illustrated in the chapter end case.

Running afoul of both governmental and cultural traditions is getting common among new-age companies, as exemplified by Uber, the $50 billion car-ride service operating in 60 countries:

> *Uber Collides With France—Company's growth snarled by entrenched business culture; 'a mockery of the French Republic'*

SAM SCHECHNER, WALL STREET JOURNAL,
*SEPTEMBER 19, 2015*[85]

Uber has created conflicts by rapidly entering markets and asking questions later, and, in the case of France, trying to overturn laws. After taxi drivers in Paris burned tires and stopped traffic, Uber managers realized the strength of the French business culture that favors government and local companies, when two of their executives were arrested for providing illegal taxi services. Beijing has another approach by launching a state-backed car-hailing app to compete with Uber.[86]

## Cultural Influences on Strategic Implementation

When managers are responsible for implementing alliances among partners from diverse institutional environments, such as transition- and established-market economies, they are faced with the critical challenge of reconciling conflicting values, practices, and systems. Research by Danis shows how those important differences among Hungarian managers and Western expatriates can affect implementation. When considering key differences in practices, for example, Danis found that the Western expatriates evinced a team orientation, a consensual management style, and a future-planning mentality. This compared with the findings for the Hungarian managers, who showed an individual orientation, an autocratic management style, and a survival mentality.[87] Such advance knowledge can provide expatriate managers with valuable information to help them in successful local operations.

In other situations, the culture variable is often overlooked when deciding on and implementing entry strategies and alliances, particularly when we perceive the target country to be familiar to us and similar to our own. However, cultural differences can have a subtle and often negative effect. In fact, in a study of 129 U.K. cross-border acquisitions in continental

Europe, Schoenberg found that 54 percent of the acquiring firms cited poor performance resulting from the implementation of their acquisitions compared to their domestic mergers.[88] The researchers' study of those firms revealed six dimensions of national and corporate cultural differences between the management styles of the U.K. firms and the continental European firms.

## CULTURAL DIFFERENCES IN U.K.–EUROPEAN ALLIANCES

- Organizational formality
- The extent of participation in decision making
- Attitude toward risk
- Systemization of decision making
- Managerial self-reliance
- Attitudes toward funding and gearing (financial leveraging)[89]

Among these dimensions, risk orientation was the key factor that affected the performance of the combined firm because risk-taking propensity affects managers' approach toward strategic options. Overall, risk-taking firms are likely to pursue aggressive strategies and deal well with change, whereas risk-averse companies are likely to tread more carefully and employ incremental strategies. Clearly, for companies entering into an IJV, successful implementation will depend largely on careful planning to take account of such differences, in particular that of risk orientation, to improve organizational compatibility. The greater the cultural distance between the allied firms, the more likely problems will emerge such as conflict regarding the level of innovation and the kinds of investments each firm is willing to pursue.

Because many of Europe's largest MNCs—including Nestlé, Electrolux, Grand Metropolitan, and Rhone-Poulenc—experience increasing proportions of their revenues from their positions in the United States and employ more than 2.9 million Americans, they have decided to shift the headquarters of some product lines to the United States. As they have done so, however, there is growing evidence that managing in the United States is not as easy as they anticipated it would be because of their perceived familiarity with the culture. Rosenzweig documents some reflections of European managers on their experiences of managing U.S. affiliates. Generally, he has found that European managers appreciate that Americans are pragmatic, open, forthright, and innovative. However, they also say that the tendency of Americans to be informal and individualistic means that their need for independence and autonomy on the job causes problems in their relationship with the head office Europeans. Americans simply do not take well to directives from a foreign-based headquarters.[90] Rosenzweig presents some comments from French managers on their activities in the United States.

## FRENCH MANAGERS COMMENT ON THEIR ACTIVITIES IN THE UNITED STATES

- Americans see themselves as the world's leading country, and it's not easy for them to accept having a European in charge.
- It is difficult for Americans to develop a world perspective. It's hard for them to see that what may optimize the worldwide position may not optimize the U.S. activities.
- The horizon of Americans often goes only as far as the U.S. border. As a result, Americans often don't give equal importance to a foreign customer. If a foreign customer has a special need, the response is sometimes: It works here, why do they need it to be different?
- It might be said that Americans are the least international of all people, because their home market is so big.[91]

Other European firms have had more successful strategic implementation in their U.S. plants by adapting to U.S. culture and management styles. When Mercedes-Benz of Germany launched its plant in Tuscaloosa, Alabama, U.S. workers and German trainers had doubts. Lynn Snow, who works on the car-door line of the Alabama plant, was skeptical of whether the Germans and the

Americans would mesh well. Now, she proudly asserts that they work together, determined to build a quality vehicle. As Jürgen Schrempp, then CEO of Mercedes's parent, Daimler-Benz, observed, "'Made in Germany'—we have to change that to 'Made by Mercedes,' and never mind where they are assembled."[92]

The German trainers recognized that the whole concept of building a Mercedes quality car had to be taught to the U.S. workers in a way that would appeal to them. They abandoned the typically German strict hierarchy and instead designed a plant in which any worker could stop the assembly line to correct manufacturing problems. In addition, taking their cue from Japanese rivals, they formed the workers into teams that met every day with the trainers to problem solve. Out the window went formal offices and uniforms, replaced by casual shirts with personal names on the pocket. To add to the collegiality, get-togethers for a beer after work became common. "The most important thing is to bring together the two cultures," says Andreas Renschler, who has guided the M-Class since it began in 1993. "You have to generate a kind of ownership of the plant."[93] The local community has also embraced the mutual goals, often having beer fests and including German-language stations on local cable TV.

The impact of cultural differences in management style and expectations is perhaps most noticeable and important when implementing international joint ventures, mergers, or acquisitions. The complexity of such alliances requires managers from each party to learn to compromise to create a compatible and productive working environment, particularly when operations are integrated.

In China, too, strategic implementation necessitates an understanding of the pervasive cultural practice of *guanxi* in business dealings. Discussed in previous chapters, *guanxi* refers to the relationship networks that "bind millions of Chinese firms into social and business webs, largely dictating their success."[94] Tapping into this system of reciprocal social obligation is essential to get permits, information, assistance to access material and financial resources, and tax considerations. Nothing gets done without these direct or indirect connections. In fact, a new term has arisen—*guanxihu*—which refers to a bond between specially connected firms that generates preferential treatment for members of the network. Without *guanxi*, even implementing a strategy of withdrawal is difficult. Joint ventures can become hard to dissolve and as bitter as an acrimonious divorce. Problems include the forfeiture of assets and the inability to gain market access through future joint venture partners—all experienced by Audi, Chrysler, and Daimler-Benz. For example:

*Audi's decision to terminate its joint venture prompted its Chinese partner, First Automobile Works, to expropriate its car design and manufacturing processes. The result was an enormously successful, unauthorized Audi clone, with a Chrysler engine and a First Automobile Works nameplate.*[95]

## E-Commerce Impact on Strategy Implementation

*With subsidiaries, suppliers, distributors, manufacturing facilities, carriers, brokers, and customers all over the globe, global trade is complicated and fragmented. Shipments cross borders multiple times a day. Are they compliant with all the latest trade regulations? Are they consistently classified for each country? Can you give your buyers, customers, and service providers the latest information, on demand?*[96]

As indicated in this quote, global trade is extremely complicated. Deciding on a global strategy is one thing; implementing it through all the necessary parties and intermediaries around the world presents a whole new level of complexity. Because of that complexity, many firms decide to implement their global e-commerce strategy by outsourcing the necessary tasks to **e-commerce enablers**, companies that specialize in providing the technology to organize transactions and follow through with the regulatory requirements. These specialists can help companies sort through the maze of different taxes, duties, language translations, and so on specific to each country. Such services allow small and medium-sized companies to go global without the internal capabilities to carry out global e-commerce functions These kinds of web-based services allow a company to manage an entire global trade operation, including automation of imports and exports by screening orders and generating the appropriate documentation, paying customs charges, complying with trade agreements, and so on.[97]

# CONCLUSION

Cross-border strategic alliances are becoming increasingly common as innovative companies seek rapid entry into foreign markets and as they try to reduce the risks of going it alone in complex environments. Companies that do well are those that do their groundwork and pick complementary strategic partners. Too many, however, divorce because the devil is in the details—which is what happens when a marriage made in heaven runs into unanticipated problems, such as cultural clashes and government restrictions, during actual strategic implementation. Alliances in various forms are particularly important for emerging market firms to expand to developed economies. For SMEs, they too can work to ally with MNCs in the target locations to internationalize quickly.

## Summary of Key Points

- Strategic alliances are partnerships with other companies for specific reasons. Cross-border, or global, strategic alliances are working partnerships between companies (often more than two) across national boundaries and, increasingly, across industries.
- Cross-border alliances are formed for many reasons, including market expansion, cost- and technology-sharing, avoiding protectionist legislation, and taking advantage of synergies.
- SMEs can overcome their resource constraints and accelerate their internationalization process by leveraging their network relationships with other companies—such as key clients or strategic partners. Strategies include forming MNC relationships, consolidating those relationships with MNCs, and then extending the relationships to other endeavors.
- Alliances may be short or long term; they may be full global partnerships, or they may be for more narrow and specific functions such as research and development sharing.
- Alliances often run into trouble in the strategic implementation phase. Problems include loss of technology and knowledge skill-base to the other partner, conflicting strategic goals and objectives, cultural clashes, and disputes over management and control systems.
- Emerging economy firms are finding that they have to move quickly or skip various stages to expand into both developed as well as developing markets. They tend to expand globally through acquisitions and alliances and have had to be more flexible organizationally. Their motives in developing alliances often include the need to access specific resources such as technology or management skills to compete globally.
- Successful alliances require compatible partners with complementary skills, products, and markets. Extensive preparation is necessary to work out how to share management control and technology and to understand each other's culture.
- Strategic implementation—also called *functional level strategies*—is the process of setting up overall policies, administrative responsibilities, and schedules throughout the organization. Successful implementation results from setting up the structure, systems, and processes of the firm as well as the functional activities that create a *system of fits* with the desired strategy.
- Differences in national culture and changes in the political arena or in government regulations often have unanticipated effects on strategic implementation.
- Strategic implementation of global trade is increasingly being facilitated by *e-commerce enablers*—companies that specialize in providing the software and Internet technology for complying with the specific regulations, taxes, shipping logistics, translations, and so on for each country with which their clients do business.

## Discussion Questions

**8-1.** Discuss the reasons that companies embark on cross-border strategic alliances. What other motivations may prompt such alliances? What are the driving forces for firms in emerging economies to embark on strategic alliances? How can SMEs expand abroad through relationships with MNCs?

**8-2.** Why are there an increasing number of mergers with companies in different industries? Give some examples. What industry do you think will be the next for global consolidation?

**8-3.** Discuss the problems inherent in developing a cooperative alliance to enhance competitive advantage, which also incurs the risk of developing a new competitor.

**8-4.** What are the common sources of incompatibility in cross-border alliances? What can be done to minimize them?

**8-5.** Explain what is necessary for companies to implement a global sourcing strategy successfully.

**8-6.** What is an international joint venture? What are the reasons that companies are setting up international joint ventures with local partners when they have different styles, cultures, and ways of thinking?

**8-7.** What are the major factors to be considered when an MNE aims to implement its strategies effectively?

**8-8.** Explain how the host government may affect strategic implementation—in an alliance or another form of entry strategy.

**8-9.** What are the major challenges that a MNE needs to face when it is considering implementing its strategies in emerging markets? In particular, what are the challenges in human resource management?

**8-10.** What is knowledge management? Why is effective knowledge management important to international joint ventures?

## Application Exercise

**8-11.** Research some recent joint ventures with foreign companies situated in India or Russia. How are they doing? Bring your information to class for discussion. What is the climate for foreign investors in developing economies at the time of your reading this chapter?

## CASE STUDY

### Foreign Companies in China Under Attack[1]

Geoff A Howard/Alamy

**Century Square, Nanjing Road, China**

While China is still a very attractive and growing market for foreign businesses, a number of prominent companies are experiencing a sharp increase in problems while operating there. This was confirmed by the AmCham China Business Survey in 2014, which indicated that 60 percent of members feel less welcome than before, up from 41 percent a year ago. Their member firms report continuing challenges, including rising labor costs, inconsistent application of laws, confusing information, pressure from government-owned departments, political tensions, and slowing growth. In addition, a number of targeted attacks on foreign firms have deterred many European and U.S. firms from either new or increased investment in China.

In targeting technology companies through an antitrust investigation, China's National Development and Reform Commission concluded that the U.S. chip manufacturer Qualcomm had used monopoly tactics to set preferable licensing fees. The move was seen as giving preference to local companies, and the U.S. Chamber of Commerce has accused the Chinese government of protectionism and violating its commitments according to the World Trade Organization, which China joined in 2001. Microsoft was also the subject of yet another investigation in early September as Chinese officials made unannounced inspections of Microsoft's offices in Beijing, Shanghai, Guangzhou, and Chengdu. This move followed a purchasing ban on Microsoft's Windows 8 PC software in May by the Chinese government, supposedly over security concerns following the revelations of spying by the United States made by Edward Snowden.

Targeting other industries, the U.S. food processor OSI Group, supplier to a number of fast-food chains in China for over 20 years, was accused of using expired meat. Chinese regulators and persistent reporting of alleged problems on state media put a sudden halt to OSI's operations. The authorities closed down the plant, and restaurants such as McDonald's and Burger King cancelled further orders with OSI. While there may have been a problem, the company was treated very harshly given that no test results were given and there were no reports of illness from the OSI products.

Chinese regulators have been targeting various industries, as well as technology and food processing, including pharmaceuticals, car companies, and in particular, high-profile companies. The U.S. Chamber of Commerce has accused China of using the antimonopoly law to force foreign companies to cut prices. Mercedes-Benz staff, for example, were shocked when ten men from the antitrust investigators from China's National Development and Reform Commission (NDRC) roughly entered the company's east China sales office near Shanghai's Hongqiao international airport and subjected employees to intense questions for ten hours, rifling through the offices and demanding data and other information. More and more foreign companies have been subjected to early morning raids and had their desks, computers, safes, files, and so on inspected and "evidence" taken away, often downloading data from the companies' computers. Legal rights typical in Europe and North America are not acknowledged in China, and information is difficult to acquire about the processes there. It seems that China's antitrust enforcement agencies, the NDRC, and the State Administration for Industry and Commerce (SAIC), has become increasingly aggressive in seizing all evidence that could give them leads to other companies for antitrust violations or corruption.

For their part, the Chinese authorities claim that the investigations are to keep competition fair and to protect consumer rights. However, often the investigators advise foreign companies not to seek legal advice; in addition, European companies reporting to the European Chamber of Commerce claim that they have been intimidated into accepting punitive measures without requesting a court hearing. In fact, 61 percent of European companies that have a long tenure operating in China now say that doing business there is getting more difficult.

A number of Western firms blame poor regulation in the supply chains and stricter imposition of regulations than on Chinese firms. As a result, firms such as Walmart and others involved in food have set up their own supply sources and implemented their own inspection and oversight of their supply chains. These moves, however, raise the overall costs of their products.

While there are many challenges for foreign companies operating in China, the activities described here are blatant and have resulted in a considerable decline in firms wanting to operate there, according to the AmCham survey. The survey concluded that further deterioration of the investment climate would harm ventures and linkages among countries for some time.

## Notes

1. **Andrew Browne, Laurie Burkitt**, "U.S. Firms Feel Unwelcome in China, According to Survey; U.S. Companies Say They Have Become Targets of China's Antimonopoly and Anticorruption Campaigns," *Wall Street Journal*, September 2, 2014; AmCham China 16th Annual Business Climate Survey, *http://www.amchamchina.org/businessclimate2014*, accessed September 2, 2014; Richard Waters, "China Probe Targets Microsoft," *Financial Times*, July 29, 2014; Laurie Burkitt, Andrew Browne, "After China Meat Scandal, Troubles for OSI Reflect Broader Perils for Business; Beijing's Scrutiny Increases as Bad Publicity's Effects Move Swiftly," *Wall Street Journal*, September 2, 2014; Michelle Price and Norihiko Shirouzu, "Food and flirting; how firms learn to live with China antitrust raids," *Reuters*, August 10, 2014; Laurie Burkitt, "China's Use of Antimonopoly Law May Violate Its WTO Commitments; U.S. Chamber of Commerce Report Says China's Use of Its Antimonopoly Law Has Been Subjective," *Wall Street Journal (Online) [New York, N.Y] 08 Sep 2014.*

## Case Questions

8-12. What factors do you think are behind these events? Do some research to find out whether there have been more such problems since this writing. Is it just American companies that are being targeted?

8-13. What can firms currently operating in China, or considering investment there, do to lessen the likelihood of these problems for their managers?

## Endnotes

1. D. Lei and J. W. Slocum, Jr., "Global Strategic Alliances: Payoffs and Pitfalls," *Organizational Dynamics* (Winter 1991).
2. Jung-Ho Lai, Shao-Chi Chang, and Sheng-Syan Chen, "Is Experience Valuable in International Strategic Alliances?" *Journal of International Management* 16 (2010), pp. 247–261; J. Walter, C. Lechner, F. W. Kellermanns, "Disentangling Alliance Management Processes: Decision Making, Politicality, and Alliance Performance," *Journal of Management Studies* 45, No. 3 (2008), p. 530.
3. Peter Loftus, "Lilly Joins with Chinese Biotech to Develop, Market Cancer Drugs," *Wall Street Journal*, March 20, 2015.
4. Vikas Bajaj, "After a Year of Delays, the First Starbucks Is to Open in Tea-Loving India This Fall," *New York Times*, January 20, 2012.
5. Ibid.
6. J. Griffiths, "A Marriage of Two Mindsets," *Financial Times*, March 16, 2005.
7. Ibid.
8. Ibid.
9. James Fontanella, "Buffett backs Brazil Private Equity Conquest of U.S. Food Industry," www.ft.com, March 26, 2015.
10. Bill Vlasic and Nick Bunkley, "Alliance with Fiat Gives Chrysler Another Partner and Lifeline," www.nytimes.com, January 21, 2009.

11. Micheline Maynard, "Chrysler Bankruptcy Plan Is Announced," www.nytimes.com, April 30, 2009.

12. Ibid.

13. Douglas Macmillan, Rick Carew, "Uber rivals form Global Alliance in Counterattack," Wall Street Journal, September 17, 2015.

14. Thomas Friedman, *The World Is Flat* (New York: Farrar, Straus and Giroux, 2005), p. 144.

15. www.covisint.com, accessed March 24, 2015.

16. www.e4engineering.com, January 4, 2001.

17. Tim Burt, "Disney's Asian Adventure," *Financial Times*, October 30, 2003.

18. Ibid.

19. Ibid.

20. Ibid.

21. Tim Bradshaw, "Apple Buys Big Data Analyser, Mapsense," FT.com, September 17, 2015.

22. Andres Parker and Gerrit Wiesmann, "Cross-border Sensitivities Give Grounds for Pessimism," *Financial Times*, September 9, 2009.

23. David Lei, "Offensive and Defensive Uses of Alliances," in Heidi Vernon-Wortzel and L. H. Wortzel, *Strategic Management in Global Economy*, 3rd ed. (New York: John Wiley & Sons, 1997).

24. Lei, 1997.

25. *New York Times*, January 17, 2011.

26. Shameen Prashantham and Julian Birkinshaw, "Dancing with Gorillas: How Small Companies Can Partner Effectively with MNCs," *California Management Review* 51, No. 1 (2008), pp. 6–23.

27. Ibid.

28. Dovev Lavie, "Capturing Value from Alliance Portfolios," *Organizational Dynamics* 38, No. 1 (2009), pp. 26–36.

29. Ibid.

30. Ibid.

31. Lei, 1997.

32. Wheelen and Hunger.

33. A. E. Serwer, "McDonald's Conquers the World," *Fortune*, October 17, 1994.

34. http://www3.weforum.org/docs/WEF_GCR_Russia_Report_2014.

35. Maria Kiselyova, "Nestle Keeps Faith with Russia Despite Turmoil," www.nytimes.com, March 24, 2015.

36. Ibid.

37. Henry Sender, Anne Sylvaine Chassaney, "Blackstone Calls it a Day in Russia After Sanctions Freeze Investor Appetite," *Financial Times*, September 22, 2015

38. http://www3.weforum.org/docs/WEF_GCR_Russia_Report_2011.

39. Sheila M. Puffer and Daniel J. McCarthy, "Two Decades of Russian Business and Management Research: An Institutional Theory Perspective," *Academy of Management Perspectives*, May 2011, pp. 21–36.

40. "Russia's Retail Revolution," www.managementtoday.co.uk, June 1, 2008.

41. N. Buckley, "An Unmissable Opportunity," *Financial Times*, April 5, 2005.

42. Maria Kiselyova, "Nestle Keeps Faith with Russia Despite Turmoil," www.nytimes.com, March 24, 2015

43. Puffer and McCarthy, May 2011.

44. N. Buckley, "Huge Gains but Also a Lot of Pain," *Financial Times*, October 11, 2005.

45. Garry Bruton, David Ahlstrom, Michael Young, and Yuri Rubanik, "In Emerging Markets, Know What Your Partners Expect," December 15, 2008.

46. Jack Welch (then CEO of GE) interviewed in *Fortune*, March 8, 1999.

47. "U.S. Exports to China Rebound in 2010," *China Business Review*, July–September, 2011.

48. Jonathan Friedrich, Amit Noam, Elie Norek, "Right Up the Middle: How Israeli Firms Go Global," *Harvard Business Review*, May 2014.

49. P. Engardio, "The Future of Outsourcing," *BusinessWeek*, January 30, 2006, p. 50.

50. Ibid.

51. Based on M. Kripalani, D. Foust, S. Holmes, and P. Enga, "Five Offshore Practices That Pay Off," *BusinessWeek*, January 30, 2006, p. 60.

52. Josh Green, *Harvard Business Review* 87, No. 7/8 (2009), p. 19.

53. "Japan Seeks Russian Help to End Nuclear Crisis," *Financial Post* (Karachi), April 6, 2011.

54. Steve Lohr, "Stress Test for the Global Supply Chain," www.nytimes.com, March 19, 2011; Nick Bunkley, "G.M. Pieces Together a Japanese Supply Chain," www.nytimes.com, May 12, 2011; Anonymous, "Japan Earthquake: Global Supply Chains to Suffer Extensive Disruption," *Business Wire* (New York), March 17, 2011; Nigel Davis, "Japan's Crisis Affects Global Supply Chains," *ICIS Chemical Business*, March 28–April 3, 2011.

55. Steve Lohr.

56. Katy George, Sree Ramaswamy, and Lou Rassey, "Next-Shoring: A CEO's Guide," *McKinsey Quarterly*, January 2014.

57. Ibid.

58. Huei-Ting Tsai and Andreas B. Eisingerich, "Internationalization Strategies of Emerging Market Firms," *California Management Review*, 53, No. 1 (Fall 2010.).

59. Mauro F. Guillén and Estaban García-Canal, "The American Model of the Multinational Firm and the 'New' Multinationals from Emerging Economies," *Academy of Management Perspectives*, May 2009, pp. 23–35.

60. Ibid.

61. Huei-Ting Tsai, 2010.

62. www.infosys.com, accessed March 24, 2015; Sudheer Gupta and Daniel Shapiro, "Building and Transforming An Emerging Market Global Enterprise: Lessons from the Infosys Journey," *Business Horizons*, (2014) 57, 169–179.; James Crabtree, "Infosys Buys U.S. Technology Group Panaya," *FT.com*, February 17, 2015; http://www.icmrindia.org/free%20resources/casestudies/Narayana, accessed March 24, 2015.

63. Beth Kowitt, "It's Ikea's World," *Fortune*, March 15, 2015, 166–175.

64. "Mahindra and Mahindra (B): An Emerging Global Giant?" Case study from IBSCDC India.

65. Paul Mozur and Vindu Goel, "To Reach China LinkedIn Plays by Local Rules," www.nytimes.com, October 5, 2014.

66. "LinkedIn Faces Flak for Censoring onBehalf of China," Asia News Monitor [Bangkok] 06 June 2014.

67. Howard Schultz, "The Power of Partnership," in R*eimagining India: Unlocking the Potential of Asia's Next Superpower.* Copyright © 2013 by McKinsey & Company. Published by Simon & Schuster, Inc.

68. J. M. Geringer, "Strategic Determinants of Partner Selection Criteria in International Joint Ventures," *Journal of International Business Studies* (First Quarter 1991), pp. 41–62.

69. J. M. Geringer and L. Hebert, "Control and Performance of International Joint Ventures," *Journal of International Business Studies* 20, No. 2 (1989).

70. Geringer, 1991.

71. Amy Kazmin, "Indian Partnership Leaves Sour Taste for McDonald's: Culture Clash," *Financial Times*, February 13, 2015.

72. P. W. Beamish et al., *International Management* (Homewood, IL: Irwin, 1991).

73. J. L. Schaan and P. W. Beamish, "Joint Venture General Managers in Less Developed Countries," in *Cooperative Strategies in International Business*, F. Contractor and P. Lorange, eds. (Toronto: Lexington Books, 1988), pp. 279–299.

74. Oded Shenkar and Yoram Zeira, "International Joint Ventures: A Tough Test for HR," *Personnel* (January 1990), pp. 26–31.

75. R. Mead, *International Management* (Cambridge, MA: Blackwell Publishers, 1994).

76. R. Duane Ireland and M. A. Hitt, "Achieving and Maintaining Strategic Competitiveness in the 21st Century: The Role of Strategic Leadership," *Academy of Management Executive* 19, Nno. 4 (2005), p.: 63.

77. R. S. Bhagat, B. L. Kedia, P. D. Harveston, and H. C. Triandis, "Cultural Variations in the Cross-Border Transfer of Organizational Knowledge: An Integrative Framework," *Academy of Management Review* 27, No. 2 (2002), pp. 204–221.

78. D. G. Sirmon, M. A. Hitt, R. D. Ireland, in press. "Managing Firm Resources in Dynamic Environments to Create Value: Looking Inside the Black Box," *Academy of Management Review* 32., No. 1 (January 2007), pp. 273–292.

79. M. H. Hitt, V. Franklin, and Hong Zhu, "Culture, Institutions and International Strategy," *Journal of International Management* 12, No. 2 (2002), pp. 222–234.

80. I. Berdrow and H. W. Lane, "International Joint Ventures: Creating Value through Successful Knowledge Management," *Journal of World Business* 38, No. 1 (2003), pp. 15–30.

81. Ibid.

82. Ibid.

83. Louis Uchitelle, "Is Manufacturing Falling off the Radar?" *New York Times*, September 10, 2011.

84. "China's New Restrictions on Deals," *Financial Times*, August 10, 2006.

85. Sam Schechner, "Uber Collides With France—Company's Growth Snarled by Entrenched Business Culture; 'A Mockery of the French Republic,'" *Wall Street Journal* 19 Sep 2015: A.1.

86. Patti Waldmeir, "Beijing Joins Ranks of Car-Hailing Apps," FT.com, September 19, 2015.

87. W. M. Danis, "Differences in Values, Practices, and Systems among Hungarian Managers and Western Expatriates: An Organizing Framework and Typology," *Journal of World Business* (August 2003), pp. 224–244.

88. R. Schoenberg, "Dealing with a Culture Clash," *Financial Times*, September 23, 2006.

89. Ibid.

90. P. Rosenzweig, "Why Is Managing in the United States so Difficult for European Firms?" *European Management Journal* 12, No. 1 (1994), pp. 31–38.

91. Ibid.

92. "In Alabama, the Soul of a New Mercedes?" *BusinessWeek*, March 31, 1997.

93. Ibid.

94. J. A. Pearce II and R. B. Robinson Jr., "Cultivating *Guanxi* as a Foreign Investor Strategy," *Business Horizons* 43, No. 1 (2000), pp. 31.

95. Ibid.

96. www.NextLinx.com, September 10, 2001.

97. Ibid.

CHAPTER

# 9 Staffing, Training, and Compensation for Global Operations

## OBJECTIVES

**9-1.** To understand the strategic importance to the firm of the IHRM function and its various responsibilities.

**9-2.** To learn about the major staffing options for global operations and the factors involved in those choices.

**9-3.** To emphasize the need for managing the performance of expatriates through careful selection, training, and compensation.

**9-4.** To discuss the role of host country managers and the need for their training and appropriate compensation packages.

# Opening Profile: Staffing Company Operations in Emerging Markets[1]

Frontpage/Shutterstock

In the 2015 Brookfield Global Relocation Trends Survey (GRTS), firms' human resources (HR) staffs from 143 MNCs were asked to identify the top three countries that represented new assignment locations for them. They were China, Brazil, and the UAE. Those that were considered the most challenging for assigning people, as well as for the assignees, were Brazil, India and China, followed by Russia.[2] However, distinction was made between relatively developed cities, such as Mexico City, pictured here, and less-developed locations in other areas of those countries.

In addition to the challenge of assigning and maintaining expatriates in emerging market economies, the ability to staff subsidiaries in emerging market economies with local managers has become a major challenge in the race for recruiting and retaining local talent. Emerging economies such as Brazil, Russia, India, and China have been developing so rapidly and have so attracted increasing overseas investment that they have outpaced the supply of suitable mid- and upper-level managers in their own markets. Foreign firms wishing to expand their investments in such economies are competing for what talent is available with both local companies and other global companies; however, they are falling behind the curve in not recognizing that they need different approaches than those they use domestically.

The problem is so acute that many companies have had to reconsider how fast they can expand in developing economies. According to *The Economist*:

> *In a recent survey, 600 chief executives of multinational companies with businesses across Asia said a shortage of qualified staff ranked as their biggest concern in China and South-East Asia. It was their second-biggest headache in Japan (after cultural differences) and the fourth-biggest in India (after problems with infrastructure, bureaucracy and wage inflation).*[3]

Reasons for the shortage of upper-level managers vary by country. Research by Ready et al. shows that although Brazil has an influx of new graduates available to staff at the low- to mid-management level, there is a deficit at the upper levels. In India, there is also a surplus at the lower level but a deficit starting at the middle levels; one additional explanation is the brain drain, in particular in the technology industry. In Russia, there is a deficit at all management levels because of decades of operating under a planned economy, together with the great increase in demand by foreign companies. In China, there is a sizable surplus at the entry level—though of varying quality—but a considerable deficit at all levels up from there.[4]

> *Competition for talent in emerging markets is heating up. Global companies should groom local highfliers—and actively encourage more managers to leave home.*[5]

Clearly, the competition for talent has become global, as has the competition for jobs. The brain drain from emerging economies has contributed to the dearth of local talent available. Over a million Chinese went to the United States to study between 1978 and 2006, and 70 percent of them did not go back. Exacerbating the problem is the high turnover of those highly sought managers and, because of that, the escalating salary requirements.[6] In addition, local firms in developing economies such as China are growing rapidly and becoming global themselves, thereby attracting local talent for their own companies. Added to these variables, as of 2015, there has been a decline in the willingness of managers from developed economies to take assignments abroad, perhaps because of global turmoil and uncertainty and concerns for their families' safety in some areas, as well as a growing concern

*(Continued)*

about the spouse/partner's career. For these reasons, the challenge to companies operating around the world is not only to recruit capable local managers but also to retain them. Problems regarding immigration and cultural adaptation persist.[7] Advice from professionals includes growing your own—that is, to provide sufficient training and career mentoring to elicit loyalty with managers; and, in particular, to balance local human resource needs with global standards. This may require tailoring employment packages to local markets to attract and keep top talent rather than applying global policies for the sake of global consistency.[8]

Ready et al. suggest a framework for attracting and retaining talent that recognizes that managers in developing markets are motivated by factors that are a function of their culture, business practices, and personal goals and usually dissimilar to what is expected in the home office. They conclude that successful companies offer more than a good salary and comprise four distinguishing characteristics that provide meaning for potential recruits in emerging markets:[9]

- *Brand:* That is, a global name brand known for its excellence and with a distinctive competence in a particular area, for example, technology, in which new recruits would have confidence in their future.
- *Purpose:* That is, a company that is breaking into new markets with new models and strategy, giving new employees a chance to be part of something meaningful.
- *Opportunity:* That is, a company that provides a fast-track training and career path for new recruits.
- *Culture:* That is, a company that has an organizational culture of openness and transparency for employees, with support for their work and career development.[10]

# THE ROLE OF IHRM IN GLOBAL STRATEGY IMPLEMENTATION

*We believe the war for talent will continue to be the major human resource issue to 2020, when the people pipeline looks to be the most crucial variable separating winners and losers in the marketplace.... Global mobility will play a key role in solving the labor availability conundrum.*

PRICEWATERHOUSECOOPERS' 14TH
ANNUAL CEO SURVEY[11]

*Hello? Anyone in HQ Listening? Why Asian Executives of Western Multinationals So Often Quit.*

HARVARD BUSINESS REVIEW
APRIL 1, 2015[12]

This chapter's opening profile describes the challenges involved in assigning, recruiting, and retaining suitable managers to staff operations in emerging markets, where the burgeoning demand by both foreign and local companies is outstripping the supply. In addition, retention of local managers requires continuing effort; the high turnover rate in Asia, for example, is largely attributable to local managers feeling that those in the firm's headquarters don't understand them and their roles.[13] Other challenges for companies around the world include growing workforce mobility and the increasing trend of outsourcing service and professional jobs, which have now joined manufacturing jobs in the category of boundaryless human capital.

The need to outsource employees is just one of the complex issues for international human resource (IHR) managers as they seek to support strategic mandates. Global firms are finding that their practices of outsourcing skilled and professional jobs have implications for their human resource practices at home and around the world. Consequently, a firm such as Infosys, one of India's top outsourcing companies, also experiences complex human resource challenges involved in recruiting, training, and compensating increasingly sophisticated employees in its attempt to meet the escalating demand for its services; in addition, Infosys has the same challenges with its operations abroad.

It is clear, then, that a vital component of implementing global strategy is *international human resource management* (IHRM). Executives questioned about the major challenges the HR function faces in the global arena cited "(1) enhancing global business strategy, (2) aligning HR issues with business strategy, (3) designing and leading change, (4) building global corporate cultures, and (5) staffing organizations with global leaders."[14] IHRM is therefore increasingly being recognized as a major determinant of success or failure in international business. In a highly competitive global economy, where the other factors of production—capital, technology, raw materials, and information—can increasingly be duplicated, "the caliber of the people in an organization will be the only source of sustainable competitive advantage available to U.S. companies."[15] Corporations operating overseas need to pay careful attention to this most critical resource—one that also provides control over other resources. In fact, increasing recognition is being given to the role of *strategic human resource management (SHRM)*—that is, the two-way role of HRM in both helping to determine strategy and implementing it. That role in helping the organization develop the necessary capabilities to enact the desired strategy includes the reality that strategic plans are developed in large part based on the resources the firm possesses, including the human resources capabilities.[16] IBM is one company that clearly uses its global workforce to convey and implement its strategy of a globally integrated company—doing business with clients in whatever location is appropriate rather than in its previous structure of 160 subsidiaries.[17] The majority of IBM's employees are in countries such as India, Japan, Britain, and Brazil. The company uses various staffing modes and considers international assignments important to its goal of global integration.

The IHRM function comprises varied responsibilities involved in managing human resources in global corporations, including recruiting and selecting employees, providing preparation and training, and setting up appropriate compensation and performance management programs. Although firms would like to harmonize their IHRM practices around the world, considerable and powerful variables confound that goal, making it either impractical or undesirable for many localities. Among these are the complexities of local government laws and regulations, varying cultural norms and practices, and the long-entrenched and accepted business practices in the local area. Some examples are shown in Exhibit 9-1. These

**EXHIBIT 9-1** Influences on Local HRM Practices

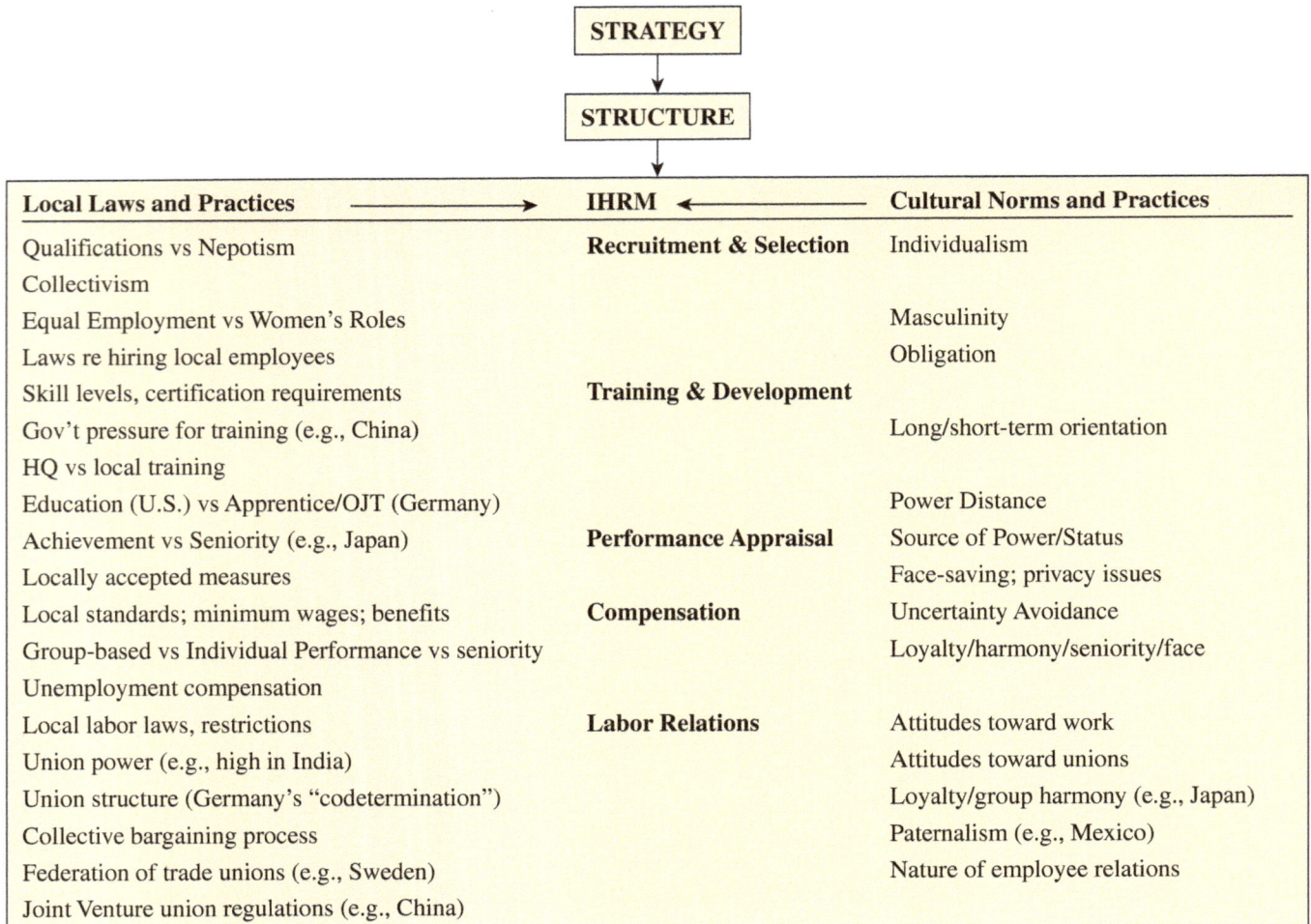

STRATEGY → STRUCTURE →

| Local Laws and Practices | IHRM | Cultural Norms and Practices |
|---|---|---|
| Qualifications vs Nepotism | **Recruitment & Selection** | Individualism |
| Collectivism | | |
| Equal Employment vs Women's Roles | | Masculinity |
| Laws re hiring local employees | | Obligation |
| Skill levels, certification requirements | **Training & Development** | |
| Gov't pressure for training (e.g., China) | | Long/short-term orientation |
| HQ vs local training | | |
| Education (U.S.) vs Apprentice/OJT (Germany) | | Power Distance |
| Achievement vs Seniority (e.g., Japan) | **Performance Appraisal** | Source of Power/Status |
| Locally accepted measures | | Face-saving; privacy issues |
| Local standards; minimum wages; benefits | **Compensation** | Uncertainty Avoidance |
| Group-based vs Individual Performance vs seniority | | Loyalty/harmony/seniority/face |
| Unemployment compensation | | |
| Local labor laws, restrictions | **Labor Relations** | Attitudes toward work |
| Union power (e.g., high in India) | | Attitudes toward unions |
| Union structure (Germany's "codetermination") | | Loyalty/group harmony (e.g., Japan) |
| Collective bargaining process | | Paternalism (e.g., Mexico) |
| Federation of trade unions (e.g., Sweden) | | Nature of employee relations |
| Joint Venture union regulations (e.g., China) | | |

factors, in turn, are influenced by national variables in the political, economic, legal, and institutional arena as well as by competitive factors. Of particular importance to the IHRM function is the management of expatriates—employees assigned to a country other than their own, discussed in this chapter and the next and working within host-country practices and laws are discussed in the following chapter.

At the first level of planning, decisions are required on the staffing policy suitable for a particular kind of business, its global strategy, and its geographic locations. Key issues involve the difficulty of control in geographically dispersed operations, the need for local decision making independent of the home office, and the suitability of managers from alternate sources.

The interdependence of strategy, structure, and staffing is particularly worth noting. Ideally, the desired strategy of the firm should dictate the organizational structure and staffing modes considered most effective for implementing that strategy. In reality, however, there is usually considerable interdependence among those functions. Existing structural constraints often affect strategic decisions; similarly, staffing constraints or unique sets of competencies in management come into play in organizational and, sometimes, strategic decisions. It is thus important to achieve a system of fits among those variables that facilitates strategic implementation.

# STAFFING FOR GLOBAL OPERATIONS

*Globalization in the 21st century has resulted in an even higher demand for businesses to send the right talent to the right place at the right time.*

KPMG 2012 GLOBAL ASSIGNMENT SURVEY[18]

*WWW.KPMG.COM*

Despite concerns about the weaker global economy and the costs of international assignment programs, the results of the PricewaterhouseCoopers' CEO Survey found that CEOs forecast a 50 percent growth of assignments over the next decade.[19] Those executives made it clear that when competing in global markets, global experience and expertise are critical to the success of the organization and employee. Colgate, for example, requires all new hires in its marketing field to have international experience.

In addition to the global war for talent, there are now considerable strategic competitive challenges for some firms regarding the need to "(a) reduce and remove talent in order to lower the costs of operations, (b) locate and relocate operations around the world, and (c) obtain equally competent talent anywhere in the world at lower wages."[20] Firms use short-term assignments and commuter assignments to nearby countries to reduce costs.[21]

Depending on the firm's primary strategic orientation and stage of internationalization, as well as situational factors, managerial staffing abroad falls into one or more of the following staffing modes—ethnocentric, polycentric, regiocentric, and global. When the company is at the internationalization stage of strategic expansion, and has a centralized structure, it will likely use an **ethnocentric staffing approach** to fill key managerial positions with people from headquarters—that is, **parent-country nationals (PCNs)**. Among the advantages of this approach, PCNs are familiar with company goals, products, technology, policies, and procedures—and they know how to accomplish things through headquarters. This policy is also likely to be used when a company notes the inadequacy of local managerial skills and determines a high need to maintain close communication and coordination with headquarters. For German companies, the most important reason for assigning expatriates was "to develop international management skills." For companies in Japan and the United Kingdom, it was "to set up a new operation," and in the United States, it was "to fill a skill gap."[22]

Frequently, companies use PCNs for the top management positions in the foreign subsidiary—in particular, the chief executive officer (CEO) and the chief financial officer (CFO)—to maintain close control. PCNs are usually preferable when a high level of technical capability is required. They are also chosen for new international ventures requiring managerial experience in the parent company and when there is a concern for loyalty to the company rather than to the host country—such as when proprietary technology is used.

In addition, the strategic goal of understanding the needs and opportunities in emerging markets has led an increasing number of top-level executives, including board members and CEOs, to assign themselves to Asia. As an example, in 2011, John Rice, vice chairman of GE and president and chief executive of global growth and operations, relocated to Hong Kong with his wife. Saying his motives were part substance and part symbolism, Mr. Rice conceded that, "Being outside the United States makes you smarter about global issues. It lets you see the world through a different lens."[23] He noted that he had learned more about China since moving there 18 months ago than he had in the 100 or so times he had visited before. According to a survey by the Economist Corporate Network, 45.3 percent of respondents expected to have board members in Asia by 2016.[24] Others in the survey noted that their continuing presence gave them more access to key leaders who regarded them as more committed to the region.

Generally speaking, however, there can be important disadvantages to the ethnocentric approach, including (1) the lack of opportunities or development for local managers, thereby decreasing their morale and their loyalty to the subsidiary; and (2) the poor adaptation and lack of effectiveness of expatriates in foreign countries. Procter & Gamble, for example, routinely appointed managers from its headquarters for foreign assignments for many years. After several unfortunate experiences in Japan, the firm realized that such a practice was insensitive to local cultures and underused its pool of high-potential, non-American managers.[25] Furthermore, an ethnocentric recruiting approach does not enable the company to take advantage of its worldwide pool of management skill. This approach also perpetuates particular personnel selections and other decision-making processes because the same types of people are making the same types of decisions.

With a **polycentric staffing approach**, local managers—**host-country nationals (HCNs)**—are hired to fill key positions in their own country. This approach is more likely to be effective when implementing a multinational strategy. If a company wants to act local, staffing with HCNs has obvious advantages. These managers are naturally familiar with the local culture, language, and ways of doing business, and they already have many contacts in place. In addition, HCNs are more likely to be accepted by people both inside and outside the subsidiary, and they provide role models for other upwardly mobile personnel. For example, HSBC in the UAE has faced various issues in their staffing policies, as detailed in the accompanying Under the Lens section.

With regard to cost, it is usually less expensive for a company to hire a local manager than to transfer one from headquarters, frequently with a family and often at a higher rate of pay. Transferring from headquarters is a particularly expensive policy when the manager and her or his family do not adjust and have to be transferred home prematurely. Rather than opening their own facilities, some companies acquire foreign firms as a means of obtaining qualified local personnel. Local managers also tend to be instrumental in staving off or more effectively dealing with problems in sensitive political situations. Some countries, in fact, legally require a specific proportion of the firm's top managers to be citizens of that country.

One disadvantage of a polycentric staffing policy is the difficulty of coordinating activities and goals between the subsidiary and the parent company, including the potentially conflicting loyalties of the local manager. Poor coordination among subsidiaries of a multinational firm could constrain strategic options. An additional drawback of this policy is that the headquarters managers of multinational firms will not gain the overseas experience necessary for any higher positions in the firm that require the understanding and coordination of subsidiary operations.

In the **global staffing approach**, the best managers are recruited from within or outside of the company, regardless of nationality. This practice—recruiting **third country nationals (TCNs)**—has been used for some time by many European multinationals. Now, HRM professionals everywhere are realizing that "the emergence of a global talent pool following China and India's decade of growth will increasingly influence talent development and acquisition."[26]

## UNDER THE LENS

*HSBC's Staffing Challenges in the UAE*

HSBC is a British multinational banking and financial services company headquartered in London. It has 6,100 offices in 72 countries and territories across Africa, Asia, Europe, North America, and South America. It sends thousands of employees abroad to work in client locations and also makes use of the available local workforce. This presents more of a challenge in some areas than in others; the United Arab Emirates (UAE) is one of the former. HSBC Middle East employs around 48 000 people in the UAE.

Factors affecting HSBC's staffing practices in the UAE include a unique characteristic of the area: UAE citizens only account for 11.32 percent of the total population. The remainder consists of expatriates on residence visas, mostly attained from sponsorship through an employer, a business partner, or ownership of a freehold property. This is a legacy of ambitious plans to transform the country into a regional economic power through the use of a large number of qualified outsiders. A further defining detail is the age distribution among nationals, of whom, according to the 2015 census, 44.4 percent are less than 25 years old.

For the banking sector, there are additional advantages in employing nationals beyond that of mere local knowledge. Many parts of the business interface directly with customers, and the public can observe on a daily basis the extent to which the bank is localized. Indeed, research has shown that the most profitable banking business is done with locals and that they prefer to deal with local people. This is not the case in the business-to-business sector, where public interaction is minimal. However, despite this need for a significant number of local employees and despite pressure from the UAE authorities on foreign firms to employ nationals, this is not always an easy strategy to follow. Multinational corporations such as HSBC compete against a multitude of local banks, many owned by different powerful families from the area, that also want to appeal to local customers. It can take time to recruit and train a local workforce, particularly when there are not enough potential employees to fill available positions.

*Source:* "HSBC's UAE Boss Takes On the Critics," Arabianbusiness.com; "Gaining Legitimacy Through Hiring Local Workforce at a Premium: MNEs in the United Arab Emirates," Academia.edu; and "HSBC Cuts 2 Percent of UAE Staff," A1SaudiArabia.com.

A global staffing approach has several important advantages. First, this policy provides a greater pool of qualified and willing applicants from which to choose, which, in time, results in further development of a global executive cadre. As discussed further in Chapter 10, the skills and experiences those managers use and transfer throughout the company result in a pool of shared learning that is necessary for the company to compete globally.

Second, where third country nationals are used to manage subsidiaries, they usually bring more cultural flexibility and adaptability to a situation, as well as bilingual or multilingual skills, than parent-country nationals, especially if they are from a similar cultural background as the host-country coworkers, and are accustomed to moving around. In addition, when TCNs are placed in key positions, employees perceive them as acceptable compromises between headquarters and local managers; thus, appointing them works to reduce resentment.

Third, it can be more cost-effective to transfer and pay managers from some countries than from others because their pay scale and benefits packages are lower. Indeed, those firms with a truly global staffing orientation are phasing out the entire ethnocentric concept of a home or host country. In fact, as globalization increases, terms such as *TCNs, HCNs,* and *expatriates* are becoming less common because of the kind of situation in which a manager may leave her native Ireland to take a job in England, then be assigned to Switzerland, then to China, and so on, without returning to Ireland. As part of that focus, the term **transpatriate** is increasingly replacing the term *expatriate*. Firms such as Philips, Heinz, Unilever, IBM, and ABB have a global staffing approach, which makes them highly visible and seems to indicate a trend.

Overall, firms still tend to use expatriates in key positions in host countries that have a less familiar culture and in less-developed economies. Clearly, this situation arises out of concern about uncertainty and the ability to control implementation of the corporation's goals. However, given the generally accepted consensus that staffing, along with structure and systems, must fit the desired strategy, firms desiring a truly global posture should adopt a global staffing approach. That is easier said than done. As shown in Exhibit 9-2, such an approach requires the firm to overcome barriers such as the availability and willingness of high-quality managers to transfer frequently around the world, dual-career constraints, time and cost constraints, conflicting requirements of host governments, and ineffective human resource management policies.

In a **regiocentric staffing approach**, recruiting is done on a regional basis—say, within Latin America for a position in Chile. This staffing approach can produce a specific mix of PCNs, HCNs, and TCNs, according to the needs of the company or the product strategy.

More recently, a staffing option known as **inpatriates** has been used to provide a linking pin between the company's headquarters and local host subsidiaries. Inpatriates are managers with global experience who are transferred to the organization's headquarters country so that their overseas business and cultural experience and contacts can facilitate interactions among the country's far-flung operations.[27]

> *Because power will always reside at world headquarters, you have to "inpatriate" foreign executives if you want to ensure that those in leadership positions know and trust them.*
>
> HARVARD BUSINESS REVIEW
> SEPTEMBER 2010[28]

Inpatriate managers can provide communication of strategic goals, change processes, and provide continuity among revolving expatriates and host nationals; in addition, they can facilitate multicultural management teams in global organizations.[29] Nestlé, for example, brings in managers at all levels from around the world to its Swiss headquarters to ensure that its executives become acquainted with the firm's best talent. The inpatriates are also happy to do this because they gain relationships all around and can network with one another in addition to gaining the knowledge and familiarity with the firm's headquarters people and processes.[30] Other companies that have brought inpatriate managers into their headquarters operations are Quaker Chemical Company (Guus Lobsen, Holland); Coca-Cola Co. (John Hunter, Australia); and Sara Lee Corporation (Cornelis Boonstra, Holland).

A critical success factor in the use of an inpatriate is the ability of that person to develop acceptance and trust among the people in the various locations, making it imperative for the

**EXHIBIT 9-2**  Maintaining a Globalization Momentum

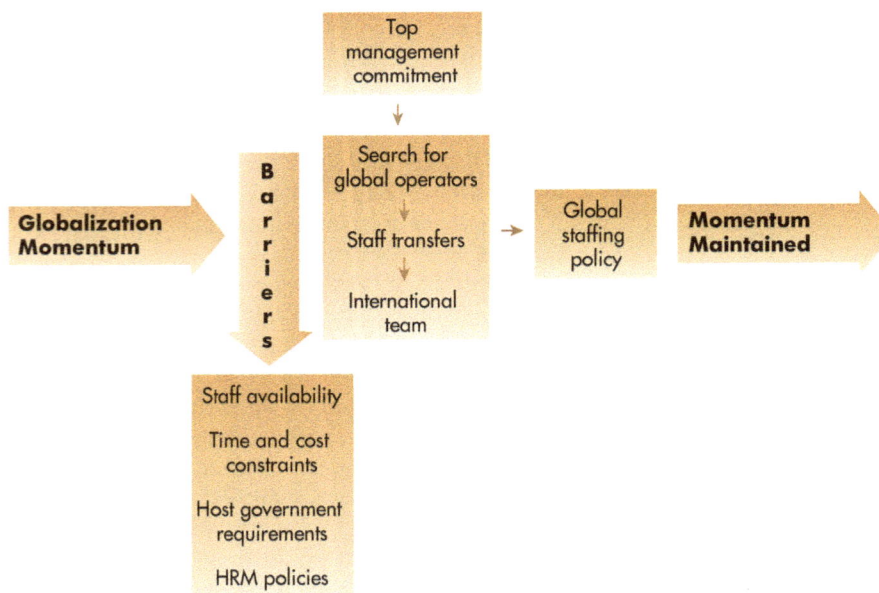

*Source:* Based on and adapted from D. Welch, "HRM Implications of Globalization," *Journal of General Management* 19, No. 4 (Summer 1994), pp. 52–69, used with permission of Braybrooke Press, 2011.

**EXHIBIT 9-3**  Key Advantages and Drawbacks of Global Staffing Practices

| | Advantages | Drawbacks |
|---|---|---|
| **PCNs** | • Transfer and control firm strategy | • Costly to relocate family |
| | • Assignments abroad develop managers | • Little development of HCNs |
| | • Integrate knowledge firm-wide | • Lack local familiarity/contacts |
| | • Suitable managers not available locally | • PCN/family adaptation problems |
| | • Protect proprietary technology | • Limits use of global skills/ideas |
| **HCNs** | • Firm "acts local"; develops HCNs | • May have short-term loyalty |
| | • Familiarity with culture, procedures, politics, language, contacts, laws | |
| | • Fulfill government hiring requirements | |
| | • Can hit the ground running vs PCNs | |
| | • Likely to be less costly | • Less firm-wide coordination |
| | • Local role model; employee morale | • Possible conflict of interests |
| | • Business may be more accepted | |
| **TCNs** | • Broad global experience | • Little development of HCNs |
| | • Pool of shared learning | • May lack local contacts |
| | • Cultural flexibility and adaptability | • Complex to manage and harmonize |
| | • Language skills | |
| | • Often more acceptable than PCNs | • Less acceptable than HCNs |
| | • Often less-costly transferees | • Costly compared to HCNs |
| | • Liaison between HQ and local firm | |
| **Inpatriates** | • Linking pin between firm HQ and local host subsidiaries | • Does not replace need for PCNs or HCNs |
| | • Utilizes overseas experience and contacts to coordinate global operations | • Probably still perceived as an HQ manager |
| | • Provide continuity among revolving PCNs and HCNs | • Difficulty in gaining trust |
| | • Facilitate global multicultural teams | |

firm to retain him or her on a long-term basis.[31] For her part, there is considerable challenge in that "the inpatriate is expected to become a parent country manager in language and lifestyle, yet play a double role as a host country national when returning to her or his home country."[32]

Some of the pros and cons of the different staffing practices are shown in Exhibit 9-3.

What factors influence the choice of staffing policy? Among them are the strategy and organizational structure of the firm as well as the factors related to the particular subsidiary (such as the duration of the particular foreign operation, the types of technology used, and the production and marketing techniques necessary). Factors related to the host country also play a part (such as the level of economic and technological development, political stability, regulations regarding ownership and staffing, and the sociocultural setting).[33] Clearly, there are many complex factors and interactions to consider. As a practical matter, however, the choice often depends on the availability of qualified managers in the host country. Most MNCs use a greater proportion of PCNs (also called expatriates) in top management positions, staffing middle and lower management positions with increasing proportions of HCNs (locals) as one moves down the organizational hierarchy. The choice of staffing policy has a considerable influence on organizational variables in the subsidiary, such as the locus of decision-making authority, the methods of communication, and the perpetuation of human resource management practices. These variables are illustrated in Exhibit 9-4. The ethnocentric staffing approach, for example, usually results in a higher level of authority and decision making in headquarters compared to the polycentric approach.[34]

**EXHIBIT 9-4**  Relationships among Strategic Mode, Organizational Variables, and Staffing Orientation[35]

| Aspects of the Enterprise | Orientation | | | |
|---|---|---|---|---|
| | **Ethnocentric** | **Polycentric** | **Regiocentric** | **Global** |
| Primary strategic orientation/stage | International | Multidomestic | Regional | Transnational |
| Perpetuation (recruiting, staffing, development) | People of home country developed for key positions everywhere in the world | People of local nationality developed for key positions in their own country | Regional people developed for key positions anywhere in the region | Best people everywhere in the world developed for key positions everywhere in the world |
| Complexity of organization | Complex in home country; simple in subsidiaries | Varied and independent | Highly interdependent on a regional basis | "Global Web": complex, worldwide alliances/network |
| Authority; decision | High in headquarters | Relatively low in headquarters | High in regional headquarters and/or high collaboration among subsidiaries | Collaboration of headquarters and subsidiaries around the world |
| Evaluation and control | Home standards applied to people and performance | Determined locally | Determined regionally | Globally integrated |
| Rewards | High in headquarters; low in subsidiaries | Wide variation; can be high or low rewards for subsidiary performance | Rewards for contribution to regional objectives | Rewards to international and local executives for reaching local and worldwide objectives based on global company goals |
| Communication; information flow | High volume of orders, commands, advice to subsidiaries | Little to and from headquarters; little among subsidiaries | Little to and from corporate headquarters, but may be high to and from regional headquarters and among countries | Horizontal; network relations; "virtual" teams |
| Geographic identification | Nationality of owner | Nationality of host country | Regional company | Truly global company, but identifying with national interests ("glocal") |

Without exception, all phases of IHRM should support the desired strategy of the firm. In the staffing phase, having the right people in the right places at the right times is a key ingredient of success in international operations. An effective managerial cadre can be a distinct competitive advantage for a firm.

The initial phase of setting up criteria for global selection, then, is to consider which overall staffing approach or approaches would most likely support the company's strategy, as previously discussed—such as HCNs for localization, the (multilocal) strategic approach, and transpatriates and inpatriates for a global strategy. These are typically just starting points using idealized criteria, however. In reality, other factors creep into the process, such as host-country regulations, stage of internationalization, and—most often—who is both suitable and available for the position. It is also vital to integrate long-term strategic goals into the selection and development process, especially when rapid global expansion is intended. Insufficient projection of staffing needs for global assignments will likely result in constrained strategic opportunities because of a shortage of experienced managers suitable to place in those positions.

The selection process is set up as a decision tree in which the progression to the next stage of selection or the type of orientation training depends on the assessment of critical factors regarding the job or the candidate at each decision point. The simplest selection process involves choosing a local national because minimal training is necessary regarding the culture or ways of doing business locally.[36] However, to be successful, local managers often require additional training in the MNC company-wide processes, technology, and corporate culture. If a local national cannot fill the position, yet the job requires a high level of interaction with the local community, careful screening of candidates from other countries and a vigorous training program are necessary.

Most MNCs tend to start their operations in a particular region by selecting primarily from their own pool of managers. Over time, and with increasing internationalization, they tend to move to a predominantly polycentric or regiocentric policy because of (1) increasing pressure (explicit or implicit) from local governments to hire locals (or sometimes legal restraints on the use of expatriates) and (2) the greater costs of expatriate staffing, particularly when the company has to pay taxes for the parent-company employee in both countries.[37] In addition, in recent years, MNCs have noted an improvement in the level of managerial and technical competence in many countries, negating the chief reason for using a primarily ethnocentric policy in the past. One researcher's comment represents a growing attitude: "All things being equal, a local national who speaks the language, understands the culture and the political system, and is often a member of the local elite should be more effective than an expatriate alien."[38] However, concerns about the need to maintain strategic control over subsidiaries and to develop managers with a global perspective remain a source of debate about staffing policies among human resource management professionals. A globally oriented company such as ABB (Asea Brown Boveri), for example, has 500 roving transpatriates who are moved every two to three years, thus developing a considerable management cadre with global experience.[39]

For MNCs based in Europe and Asia, human resource policies at all levels of the organization are greatly influenced by the home-country culture and policies. For Japanese subsidiaries in Singapore, Malaysia, and India, for example, promotion from within and expectations of long-term loyalty to and by the firm are culture-based practices transferable to subsidiaries.

## MANAGING EXPATRIATES

*The survey identified three significant challenges facing corporations: finding suitable candidates for assignments, helping employees—and their families—complete their assignments, and retaining these employees once their assignments end.*[40]

*If some of your expatriates are about to jump ship because they are not getting paid on time, their families are miserable or their taxes are fouled up, it may be time to move beyond low-tech tools.*

HR MAGAZINE,
APRIL 2015[41]

An important responsibility of IHR managers is that of managing expatriates—employees they assign to positions in other countries—whether from the headquarters country or third countries. Most multinationals underestimate the importance of the human resource function in the selection, training, acculturation, and evaluation of expatriates. However, although the number of employers sending staff abroad is on the rise, only half actually have policies in place to govern these assignments, research shows. In fact, the Brookfield Global Relocation Trends Survey in 2014 concluded that, although career management was stated as a challenging international assignment management issue by company respondents, only 22 percent indicated that they had a formal career management process in place, and only 19 percent had an international assignment candidate pool in place.[42]

In addition, too often, HR managers are not aware that expatriates are unhappy until they find out they are losing valuable, experienced managers to another company. So, in addition to ensuring that there is personal contact with expatriates, a number of firms are turning to technological applications to keep track of visas and immigration status, payroll and compensation packages, taxes, housing, and so on, which can make or break the family's situational satisfaction.[43]

## Expatriate Selection

The selection of personnel for overseas assignments is a complex process. While matching the firm's criteria for selection with the motivation and suitability of potential candidates, it is also useful to bear in mind the reasons candidates might have for taking the assignment. In their survey of reasons people would consider a foreign assignment, the Boston Consulting Group (BCG), with a sample size of 203,756 from respondents around the world, found a high level of willingness to work abroad (64 percent) among those looking for new job opportunities; the top ten reasons were: broaden personal experience, acquire work experience, better career opportunities, an overall attractive job offer, improved salary prospects, better standard of living, ability to live in a different culture, for the challenge, learn a new language, and meet new people to build new networks.[44]

From the firm's perspective, criteria for selection are based on the same success factors as in the domestic setting, but additional criteria must be considered, relative to the specific circumstances of each international position. Unfortunately, many HRM directors have a long-standing, ingrained practice of selecting potential expatriates simply on the basis of their domestic track records and their technical expertise.[45] The need to ascertain whether potential expatriates have the necessary cross-cultural awareness and interpersonal skills for the position is too often overlooked.

Research by Mansour Javidan points to three major global mind-set attributes that successful expatriates possess.

- Intellectual capital, or knowledge, skills, understanding, and cognitive complexity
- Psychological capital, or the ability to function successfully in the host country through internal acceptance of different cultures and a strong desire to learn from new experiences
- Social capital, or the ability to build trusting relationships with local stakeholders, whether they are employees, supply chain partners, or customers[46]

It is also important to assess whether the candidate's personal and family situation is such that everyone is likely to adapt to the local culture. Studies have shown that there are five categories of success for expatriate managers: job factors, relational dimensions such as cultural empathy and flexibility, motivational state, family situation, and language skills. However, deciding before the expatriate goes on assignment whether he or she will be successful in those dimensions poses considerable problems for recruitment and selection purposes. Whereas language skills, for example, may be easy to ascertain, characteristics such as flexibility and cultural adjustment—widely acknowledged as most vital for expatriates—are difficult to judge beforehand. To address the problem of predicting how well an expatriate will perform on an overseas assignment, Tye and Chen studied factors that HR managers used as predictors of expatriate success. They found that the greatest predictive value was in the expatriate characteristics of stress tolerance and extraversion and less in domestic work experience, gender, or even international experience. The results indicate that a manager who is extraverted (sociable, talkative) and who has a high tolerance for stress (typically experienced in new, different contexts such as in a foreign country) is more likely to be able to adjust to the new environment, the new job, and interaction with diverse people than those without those characteristics. HR selection procedures, then, often include seeking out managers with those characteristics because they know there will be a greater chance for successful job performance and less turnover likelihood.[47]

These expatriate success factors are based on studies of American expatriates. One could argue that the requisite skills are the same for managers from any country—and particularly so for third-country nationals. A study of expatriates in China, for example, found that expatriate success factors included performance management, training, organizational support, willingness to relocate, and strength of the relationship between the expatriate and the firm.[48]

## Expatriate Performance Management

Deciding on a staffing policy and selecting suitable managers are logical first steps, but they do not alone ensure success. When staffing overseas assignments with expatriates, for example, many other reasons, besides poor selection, contribute to *expatriate failure* among U.S. multinationals. A large percentage of these failures can be attributed to poor preparation and planning for the entry and reentry transitions of the manager and his or her family. One important variable, for example, often given insufficient attention in the selection, preparation, and support phases, is the suitability and adjustment of the spouse (discussed further in Chapter 10). The inability of the spouse to adjust to the new environment has been found to be a major—in fact, the most frequently cited—reason for expatriate failure in U.S. and European companies.[49] Despite these obvious concerns, few companies include the spouse in the interviewing process. The following is a synthesis of the factors researchers and firms frequently mention as the major causes of expatriate failure.

- Selection based on headquarters criteria rather than assignment needs
- Inadequate preparation, training, and orientation prior to assignment
- Alienation or lack of support from headquarters
- Inability to adapt to local culture and working environment
- Problems with spouse and children—poor adaptation, family unhappiness
- Insufficient compensation and financial support
- Poor programs for career support and repatriation

In considering the overall family adjustment and happiness, it is important to pay attention to the trailing spouse—that is, the spouse or partner of the person taking the assignment overseas. Whether the situation is that the spouse wants to work in the new location but has not found a position or that the couple has made a decision for the spouse to devote the time to the children and household, HR should attempt to help the couple, or family, have a positive experience and thus retain the employee and facilitate a successful assignment. Although most assignees are still men, especially expats from the more masculine cultures, women are increasingly taking the position, and the husband becomes the trailing spouse, creating a unique situation for him to settle into, as illustrated in the following Under the Lens section describing how some men created their own solutions.

## UNDER THE LENS

*Tales from Trailing Husbands*

Stay-at-home men who accompany their wives on overseas postings are looking for support, writes Alicia Clegg.

It is Friday lunchtime. Inside Le Baron, a bar on the outskirts of Brussels, George from Canada and Henri from South Africa are setting the world to rights over cappuccino and Jupiler beer. Among their companions the talk is of iPhones, golf and Prince Harry. Welcome to Spouses Trailing Under Duress Successfully, an expatriate network-cum-social club for men who follow their wives on overseas postings, otherwise known as STUDS.

Once a rarity, women now comprise 23 per cent of workers on overseas assignments according to the latest report from U.S.-based Brookfield Global Relocation Services. But while many international cities have long-established clubs for expat wives, the social needs of accompanying husbands have traditionally been overlooked. STUDS aims to change that, creating a space in which businessmen-turned-stay-at-home-spouses can swap war stories and indulge in some man talk.

The group began in the mid-1990s, when Brussels's expatriate population was expanding. Groups of trailing males can also be found, from Switzerland to China. Eric Johnson, co-organiser of Shanghai-based Guy Tai—a play on taitai, Chinese for "lady who lunches"—says he knows of trailing male groups in the early stages in Beijing, Hong Kong and Zurich. "As [expat spouses] move on to other cities, they start to form local groups. Someone knows someone else and they say, 'let's do things together.'"

Michael Shevlin, a British national, put his career as an animator on hold to look after his two toddlers when his wife had a chance to work in Geneva. As the only man in weekday playgrounds, he hankered for weekends when he could push his kids on the swings without feeling "judged"; he says: "There's a certain look that [says] 'why aren't you at work?'"

He hoped the expat mothers whom he overheard arranging coffee dates around their offspring's play dates would invite him into their circle. But the invitations never came. Instead, with the help of Catherine Nelson-Pollard, an expat blogger and broadcaster, who knew of other expat husbands scattered across the region, he set up a trailing spouse group for men. Two years on, the group still meets in a microbrewery in Nyon, pulling in trailing males from nearby Geneva, Lausanne and across the French border.

In an alien environment, says Yvonne McNulty, author of *Managing Expatriates: A Return on Investment Approach*, people seek out others with whom "they might have something in common." This puts trailing husbands, who will typically be far outnumbered by trailing wives, at an immediate disadvantage. "When it turns out that you're the stay-at-home and your wife has the big career … people can feel awkward because they don't quite know where you fit in."

Differences between gender roles today and the norms with which people grew up create other problems, says David Schiesher, a Geneva-based psychotherapist, recalling a couple who consulted him. The wife's job involved repeated overseas postings, hindering the husband's career. He became resentful and depressed; she thought he needed to make a bigger effort. "Even though she was comfortable being the provider, there was still this old programming that told her that he should be doing more."

Mr. Shevlin says meeting other men who had also come to Switzerland "on the back of their wives' contracts" made his life less lonely. However, having sat in on a few gatherings of expat wives in which—on more than one occasion—a mother "going through hell" began crying, he thinks the emotional lows that both sexes go through are more on display when women get together.

Although some men will share their insecurities with peers, he says, others do not want to. Some become "ultra-blokey" when the conversation takes a personal turn, possibly to signal to the group that emotional matters are off-limits: "In a guys' group you just wouldn't see [tears]."

Likewise, Mr. Johnson—a part-time international development consultant and stay-at-home father from the U.S., who is married to a corporate lawyer—says the emphasis at Guy Tai is on sharing local know-how rather than giving each other overt emotional support: "Because we are in a novel situation we spend a lot of time [helping each other] figure things out." Subjects include bureaucracy or what air purifier to choose. Like the group in Nyon, Guy Tai meets in a microbrewery. It also organises sports activities, factory tours and lunches.

Such groups can also help uprooted spouses restart careers. Mr. Johnson says some Guy Tais have sidelines, but few look for regular employment. Settling in a family in China is a job in itself and opportunities for highly qualified westerners are scarce. By contrast, Mr. Shevlin, who now teaches animation, says that among his group trailing spouses who find jobs act as a grapevine, providing tip-offs when employers are recruiting, for instance.

One risk with any expat spouse group is that members do not learn the local language or make friends and contacts outside the coterie. When you are newly arrived and know nobody, joining a ready-made buddy group may seem like "a cure for social isolation," says Mr. Schiesher, especially if you are the only male at the school-gate and rarely get the chance to talk to other men. He advises trailing males to look upon spouse groups as stepping stones to exploring local life.

This is the approach that Kevin Anderson, a retired high-school band director who followed his accountant wife from Texas to Brussels, has taken. When their radiators sprang a leak, Mr. Anderson found an English-speaking plumber through STUDS, but he is learning French and asks members to suggest cultural events, such as jazz festivals, to help him connect to the local scene.

As more women are posted abroad, some male spouse groups see opportunities to recruit members through HR departments, and thereby solve a problem for employers. When assignments go badly, one frequent explanation is that the family failed to adjust. Yet, according to research done for Lloyds TSB International, only 10 per cent of expat employers provide networking opportunities for spouses. "My impression is that employers like [us] because if spouses feel comfortable, employees are more likely to be happy," says Mr. Johnson, adding that Guy Tai has a flyer that relocation agencies and employers are starting to give to newly arrived female staff.

Alan Welch, a former British naval officer who joined STUDS when his wife's career took them to Brussels, thinks employers would do better to publicise groups such as Guy Tai and STUDS than host socials of their own. "[At your spouse's workplace], you need to keep in mind to whom you're talking.… With a group like STUDS it's more like meeting [friends] in the pub—and you're not relying on your wife for a social life," he says.

### Starting a men's group

- Look for clever locations. Meeting in centrally situated Nyon, rather than Geneva or Lausanne, allows Michael Shevlin's group to pull in trailing males from both cities.

- Keep to the same day, time and place, so people don't get confused. Fit around school runs and office hours so that working wives can relieve stay-at-home dads.

- Publicise meetings through expat forums, establish an email list and do not assume everyone is on Facebook or Twitter. Many older spouses aren't (yet).

- Offer something extra. Guy Tai and the Nyon group both meet in microbreweries with unusual ales. Le Baron overlooks a popular farmer's market selling cheese, fish and patisserie. It also sells fresh flowers—"handy if you're in the doghouse" at home, says Kevin Anderson.

*Source:* Alicia Clegg, *Financial Times* [London (UK)], June 11, 2013, p. 14.

After careful selection based on the specific assignment and the long-term plans of both the organization and the candidates, plans must be made for the preparation, training, and development of expatriate managers. In the following sections, we discuss training and development and then compensation. However, it is useful to note that these should be components of an integrated performance management program, specific to expatriates, which includes goal setting, training, performance appraisal, and performance-related compensation. Some insight into the variability of performance management functions can be gleaned from the accompanying Comparative Management in Focus feature.

## Global Team Performance Management

Global teams are discussed more fully in Chapter 10. But here, we must recognize that expatriate performance often includes performance as a team, typically based on discussions and decisions made with team members in various countries, cultures, and time zones, thus most often conducted virtually through teleconferencing, Skyping, and various social media, but also sometimes personally. As with any HR decision, care must go into the selection and training of the people who will comprise the team so that the advantages of insight, local knowledge, and group creativity will support the firm's strategic plans. Clearly, a first is to include cross-cultural training specific to team members with whom the interactions will take place. This can be followed up by an initial face-to-face group meeting to develop trust, feel out communication styles, and iron out practical matters such as the language to use and the time of day for virtual meetings that would work for everyone. From the team leader's perspective, it is also important to find a way to mesh leadership styles and be creative about how the team as a whole can adapt to one another.[50] Often, differences in the relative emphasis and leadership styles depend on the stage of the project at hand. For example, as concluded from a study by Zhang et al. on the scope of the project management process, team members from the Netherlands wanted a very pre-determined and formal process, compared with team members from China, who preferred flexibility in the project goals and scope.[51]

# EXPATRIATE TRAINING AND DEVELOPMENT

It is clear that preparation and training for cross-cultural interactions are critical. A Global Relocation Trends Survey revealed that attrition rates for expatriates were more than double the rate of non-expatriates. It found that 21 percent of expatriates left their companies during the assignments, and another 23 percent left within a year of returning from the assignment.[52] Moreover, about half of those who remain longer in their overseas assignment function at a low

## Comparative Management in Focus

*Expatriate Performance Management Practices: Samples from Five Countries*

Hsi-An Shih et al. conducted a study in which they interviewed expatriates and human resource professionals in global information technology companies headquartered in five countries. These were Applied Materials (American) with 16,000 employees in 13 countries, Hitachi High Technologies (Japanese) with 470,000 employees in 23 countries, Philips Electronics (Dutch) with 192,000 employees in 60 countries, Samsung (Korean) with 173,000 employees in 20 countries, and Winbond Electronics (Taiwanese) with 47,000 employees in six countries. Shih et al. found that those companies used standardized forms from headquarters rather than tailoring them to the host environment; as such, they reflected the company culture but not the local culture in which those expatriates were operating. There also was lack of on-the-job training from those companies.[53] The differences in procedures for goal setting, performance appraisal, training, and performance-related pay among those five companies are detailed in Exhibit 9-5.

**EXHIBIT 9-5** Expatriate Performance Management from MNEs of Five National Origins

| Company | Goal Setting | Performance Appraisal | Training and Development | Performance-related Pay |
|---|---|---|---|---|
| **AMT (American)** | Short-term: sending unit's general manager. Long term: host country's general manager | Annual performance appraisal. Open feedback. Interview | Applied global university. Seldom take training programs while on assignment. No clear connection between performance result and career development | Clear link between performance and compensation. Cash bonuses and stock options |
| **Hitachi (Japanese)** | Self-setting, then finalized by host-country manager | Annually for managerial purposes, biannually for development purposes; One-way feedback discussion. Seldom take training programs while on assignment | Orientation. Language training. Can apply to host location supervisor. No clear connection between performance result and career development | Link between performance and compensation not clear. Seniority-based pay system. Cash bonuses |
| **Philips (Dutch)** | Self-setting, then finalized by host-country manager | Biannual performance appraisal; Open feedback in interview | Orientation. Seldom take training programs while on assignment. No clear connection between performance result and career development | Clear link between performance and compensation. Cash bonuses and stock options |
| **Samsung (Korean)** | Self-setting, then finalized by host-country manager | Biannually for managerial purposes, annually for development purposes; Open feedback in interview | Orientation. Language training. Can apply to host location supervisor. No clear connection between performance result and career development | Clear link between performance and compensation. Senior managers: cash bonuses and stock options. Ordinary expatriates: cash bonuses |
| **Windbond (Taiwanese)** | Self-setting, then finalized by host-country manager | Biannual performance appraisal; Feedback depends on manager | Orientation. Seldom take training programs while on assignment. Can apply to host location supervisor. No clear connection between performance result and career development | Clear link between performance and compensation. Cash bonuses and stock options |

*Source:* Adapted from His-An Shih, Yun-Hwa Chiang, and In-Sook Kim, "Expatriate Performance Management from MNEs of Different National Origins," *International Journal of Manpower* 26, No. 2 (2005), pp. 161–162. Reprinted with permission of Emerald Group Publishing Ltd, 2011.

level of effectiveness. The direct cost alone of a failed expatriate assignment is estimated to be from $200,000 to $1.2 million. The indirect costs may be far greater, depending on the expatriate's position. Relations with the host-country government and customers may be damaged, resulting in a loss of market share and a poor reception for future PCNs.

Both cross-cultural adjustment problems and practical differences in everyday living present challenges for expatriates and their families. Examples are evident from a survey of expatriates in which they ranked the countries that presented the most challenging assignments to them, along with some pet peeves from their experiences.

*China:* A continuing problem for expatriates; one complained that at his welcome banquet, he was served duck tongue and pigeon head.

*Brazil:* Expatriates stress that cell phones are essential because home phones don't work.

*India:* Returning executives complain that the pervasiveness of poverty and street children is overwhelming.

*Indonesia:* Here you need to plan ahead financially because landlords typically demand rent two to three years in advance.

*Japan:* Expatriates and their families remain concerned that, although there is excellent medical care, the Japanese doctors reveal little to their patients.[54]

Even though cross-cultural training has proved to be of high value in making the assignment a success, only 20 percent of companies surveyed had formal cross-cultural training for expatriates.[55] Much of the rationale for this lack of training is an assumption that managerial skills and processes are universal. In a simplistic way, a manager's domestic track record is used as the major selection criterion for an overseas assignment.

In most countries, however, the success of the expatriate is not left so much to chance. Foreign companies provide considerably more training and preparation for expatriates than U.S. companies do. Therefore, it is not hard to understand why Japanese expatriates experience significantly fewer incidences of failure than their U.S. counterparts, although this may be partially because fewer families accompany Japanese assignees. Japanese multinationals typically have recall rates of below 5 percent, signifying that they send abroad managers who are far better prepared and more adept at working and flourishing in a foreign environment.[56] The demands on expatriate managers have always been as much a result of the multiple relationships that they have to maintain as they are of the differences in the host-country environment. Those relations include family relations; internal relations with people in the corporation, both locally and globally, especially with headquarters; external relations (suppliers, distributors, allies, customers, local community, etc.); and relations with the host government. It is important to pinpoint any potential problems that an expatriate may experience with those relationships so that these problems may be addressed during predeparture training. Problem recognition is the first stage in a comprehensive plan for developing expatriates. The three areas critical to preparation are cultural training, language instruction, and familiarity with everyday matters.[57] In the model shown in Exhibit 9-6, various development methods are used to address these areas during predeparture training, postarrival training, and reentry training. These methods continue to be valid and used by many organizations. Two-way feedback between the executive and the trainers at each stage helps to tailor the level and kinds of training to the individual manager. The desired goal is the increased effectiveness of the expatriate because of familiarity with local conditions, cultural awareness, and his or her family's needs in the host country.

### Cross-Cultural Training

Training in language and practical affairs is quite straightforward, but cross-cultural training is not; it is complex and deals with deep-rooted behaviors. The actual process of cross-cultural training should result in the expatriate learning both content and skills that will improve interactions with host-country individuals by reducing misunderstandings and inappropriate behaviors.

### CULTURE SHOCK

The goal of training is to ease the adjustment to the new environment by reducing **culture shock**, a state of disorientation and anxiety about not knowing how to behave in an unfamiliar culture. The cause of culture shock is the trauma people experience in new and different cultures, where they lose the familiar signs and cues that they had used to interact in daily life and where they must learn to cope with a vast array of new cultural cues and expectations.[58]

**EXHIBIT 9-6** **IHRM Process to Maximize Effectiveness of Expatriate Assignments**

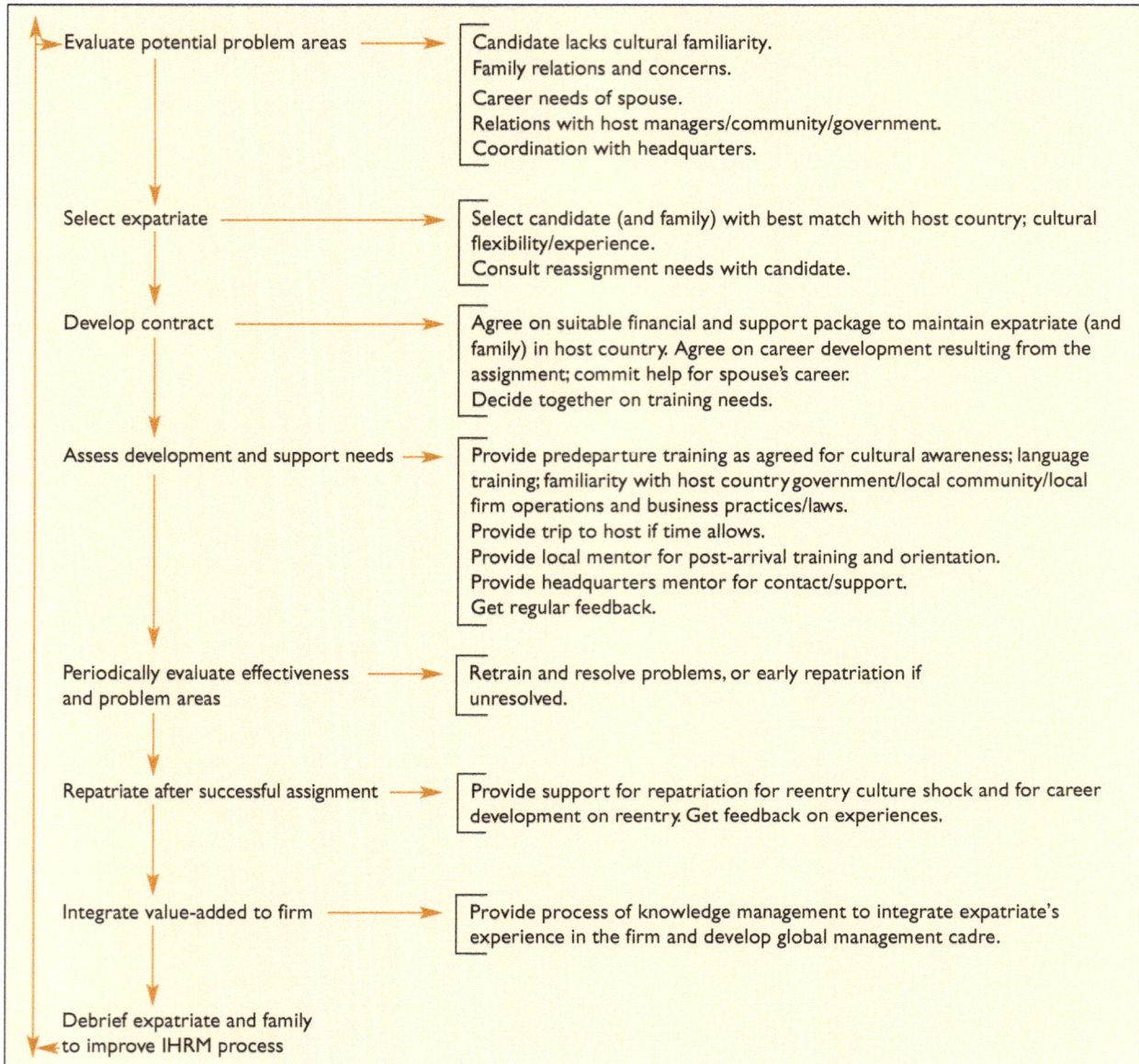

Evaluate potential problem areas ⟶ Candidate lacks cultural familiarity.
Family relations and concerns.
Career needs of spouse.
Relations with host managers/community/government.
Coordination with headquarters.

Select expatriate ⟶ Select candidate (and family) with best match with host country; cultural flexibility/experience.
Consult reassignment needs with candidate.

Develop contract ⟶ Agree on suitable financial and support package to maintain expatriate (and family) in host country. Agree on career development resulting from the assignment; commit help for spouse's career.
Decide together on training needs.

Assess development and support needs ⟶ Provide predeparture training as agreed for cultural awareness; language training; familiarity with host country government/local community/local firm operations and business practices/laws.
Provide trip to host if time allows.
Provide local mentor for post-arrival training and orientation.
Provide headquarters mentor for contact/support.
Get regular feedback.

Periodically evaluate effectiveness and problem areas ⟶ Retrain and resolve problems, or early repatriation if unresolved.

Repatriate after successful assignment ⟶ Provide support for repatriation for reentry culture shock and for career development on reentry. Get feedback on experiences.

Integrate value-added to firm ⟶ Provide process of knowledge management to integrate expatriate's experience in the firm and develop global management cadre.

Debrief expatriate and family to improve IHRM process

The symptoms of culture shock range from mild irritation to deep-seated psychological panic or crisis. The inability to work effectively, stress within the family, and hostility toward host nationals are the common dysfunctional results of culture shock—often leading to the manager giving up and going home.

It is helpful to recognize the stages of culture shock to understand what is happening. Culture shock usually progresses through four stages, as described by Oberg: (1) *honeymoon*, when positive attitudes and expectations, excitement, and a tourist feeling prevail (which may last up to several weeks); (2) *irritation and hostility*, the crisis stage when cultural differences result in problems at work, at home, and in daily living—expatriates and family members feel homesick and disoriented, lashing out at everyone (many never get past this stage); (3) *gradual adjustment*, a period of recovery in which the expatriate gradually becomes able to understand and predict patterns of behavior, use the language, and deal with daily activities, and the family starts to accept its new life; and (4) *biculturalism*, the stage in which the manager and family members grow to accept and appreciate local people and practices and become able to function effectively in two cultures.[59] Many never get to the fourth stage—operating acceptably at the third stage—but those who do report that their assignment is positive and growth oriented. In recognition of the importance of helping expatriates adapt to the local environment, companies such as PepsiCo provide a number of localized programs to aid the transition. PepsiCo's 600 expats and their families are encouraged to join the company's health and wellness programs and various local sports programs such as soccer in Dubai, ping-pong in China, and Zumba in Latin countries. The company believes such activities help their people adjust to the new culture and get involved in the local community. In addition, the company provides families language lessons and help with child tuition.[60]

In addition to family and organizational support, HCN coworkers can provide considerable help for expatriate adjustment. A recent study by Ashish Mahajan and Soo Min Toh concluded that expatriates who sought advice from HCN coworkers whom they felt were credible and likeable reported greater satisfaction with their work and adjustment.[61] Clearly, most expatriates have a number of avenues at their disposal to help in the adjustment process for them and their families if they seek them out and take advantage of the local coworkers and friends.

## SUBCULTURE SHOCK

Similar to culture shock, though usually less extreme, is the experience of **subculture shock**. This occurs when a manager is transferred to another part of the country where there are cultural differences—essentially from what she or he perceives to be a majority culture to a minority one. The shock comes from feeling like an immigrant in one's own country and being unprepared for such differences. For instance, someone going from New York to Texas will experience considerable differences in attitudes and lifestyle between those two states. These differences exist even within Texas, with cultures that range from roaming ranches and high technology to Bible-belt attitudes and laws and to areas with a mostly Mexican heritage.[62] As with other regions in the world, expatriates coming to the United States might need considerable adjustment after working in, say, San Francisco, California, and then being posted to somewhere in Alabama.

## Training Techniques

Many training techniques are available to assist overseas assignees in the adjustment process, although too often programs include only some language coaching and introduction to the host country.

Most training programs take place in the expatriate's own country prior to leaving. Although this is certainly a convenience, the impact of host-country programs can be far greater than those conducted at home because there is no better way for someone to experience the culture and the local people than actually being there. Some MNCs are beginning to recognize that there is no substitute for on-the-job training (OJT) in the early stages of the careers of managers they hope to develop into senior-level global managers. Exhibit 9-7 shows some global management development programs for junior employees.

**EXHIBIT 9-7** Corporate Programs to Develop Global Managers

- ABB (Asea Brown Boveri) rotates about 500 managers around the world to different countries every two to three years in order to develop a management cadre of transpatriates to support their global strategy.
- PepsiCo has an orientation program for its foreign managers, which brings them to the United States for one-year assignments in bottling division plants.
- British Telecom uses informal mentoring techniques to induct employees into the ways of their assigned country; existing expatriate workers talk to prospective assignees about the cultural factors to expect (www.FT.com).
- Honda of America Manufacturing gives its U.S. supervisors and managers extensive preparation in Japanese language, culture, and lifestyle and then sends them to the parent company in Tokyo for up to three years.
- General Electric likes its engineers and managers to have a global perspective whether or not they are slated to go abroad. The company gives regular language and cross-cultural training for them so that they are equipped to conduct business with people around the world (www.GE.com).

In addition, according to Eduardo Caride, Telefonica's regional manager in Latin America, there is no better training than the experience managers get by working in one country and then being able to use that knowledge and experience in another country; in addition, the relationships that are made around the world greatly facilitate business transactions.[63] After assignments in Miami, Telefonica's head office in Spain, and then Argentina, he says:

> *I can tell you, it helps to have been on both sides of the world.*
>
> EDUARDO CARIDE TELEFONICA, HARVARD BUSINESS REVIEW
> SEPTEMBER 2014[64]

## INTEGRATING TRAINING WITH GLOBAL ORIENTATION

In continuing our discussion of strategic fit, it is important to remember that training programs, like staffing approaches, should be designed with the company's strategy in mind. Although it is probably impractical to break down those programs into many variations, it is feasible at least to consider the relative level or stage of globalization that the firm has reached, because obvious major differences would be appropriate—for example, from the initial export stage to the full global stage. Exhibit 9-8 suggests levels of rigor and types of training content appropriate for the firm's managers, as well as those for host-country nationals, for four globalization stages—export, multidomestic, multinational, and global. It is noteworthy, for example, that the training of host-country nationals for a global firm has a considerably higher level of scope and rigor than that for the other stages and borders on the standards for the firm's expatriates.

As a further area for managerial preparation for global orientation—in addition to training plans for expatriates and for HCNs separately—there is a particular need to anticipate potential problems with the interaction of expatriates and local staff. In a study of expatriates and local staff (inpatriates) in Central and Eastern European joint ventures and subsidiaries, Peterson found that managers reported a number of expatriate behaviors that helped them integrate with

**EXHIBIT 9-8**  Stage of Globalization and Training Design Issues[65]

| Export Stage | MNC Stage |
|---|---|
| *Training Need:* Low to moderate | *Training Need:* High moderate to high |
| *Content:* Emphasis should be on interpersonal skills, local culture, customer values, and business behavior. | *Content:* Emphasis should be on interpersonal skills, two-way technology transfer, corporate value transfer, international strategy, stress management, local culture, and business practices. |
| *Host-Country Nationals:* Train to understand parent-country products and policies. | *Host-Country Nationals:* Train in technical areas, product and service systems, and corporate culture. |
| **MDC Stage** | **Global Stage** |
| *Training Need:* Moderate to high | *Training Need:* High |
| *Content:* Emphasis should be on interpersonal skills, local culture, technology transfer, stress management, and business practices and laws. | *Content:* Emphasis should be on global corporate operations and systems, corporate culture transfer, customers, global competitors, and international strategy. |
| *Host-Country Nationals:* Train to familiarize with production and service procedures. | *Host-Country Nationals:* Train for proficiency in global organization production and efficiency systems, corporate culture, business systems, and global conduct policies. |

**EXHIBIT 9-9** Factors That Facilitate or Hinder the Integration of Expatriate Staff with Local Staff

| Facilitates Integration | Hinders Integration |
|---|---|
| Relationship-building | Not using team concept |
| Speaking the local language | Not learning local language |
| Knowledge sharing | Withholding useful information |
| Cultural adaptability/flexibility | Spouse and family problems in adjusting |
| Respect | Superior and autocratic behavior |
| Overseas experience | Limited time in assignment |
| Develop local value-added from venture | Headquarters mentality |
| Encourage local innovation | Dominate from head office |

*Source:* Based on R. B. Peterson, "The Use of Expatriates and Inpatriates in Central and Eastern Europe Since the Wall Came Down," *Journal of World Business* 38 (2003), pp. 55–69.

local staff but also some that were hindrances (see Exhibit 9-9).[66] Clearly, this kind of feedback from MNC managers in the field can provide the basis for expatriate training and help HCNs anticipate and work with the expatriates to meet joint strategic objectives.

### Compensating Expatriates

*If you're an expatriate working alongside another expatriate and you're being treated differently, it creates a lot of dissension.*

CHRISTOPHER TICE
MANAGER, *GLOBAL EXPATRIATE OPERATIONS, DUPONT INC*[67]

The significance of an appropriate compensation and benefits package to attract, retain, and motivate international employees cannot be overemphasized. Compensation is a crucial link between strategy and its successful implementation. There must be a fit between compensation and the goals for which the firm wants managers to aim. So that they will not feel exploited, employees need to perceive equity and goodwill in their compensation and benefits, whether they are PCNs, HCNs, or TCNs. The premature return of expatriates or the unwillingness of managers to take overseas assignments can often be traced to their knowledge that the assignment is detrimental to them financially and usually to their career progression. One company that recognizes the need for a reasonable degree of standardization in its treatment of expatriates is DuPont. The company has centralized programs in its Global Transfer Center of Expertise for its approximately 400 annual international relocations so its expatriates know that everyone is getting the same package.

From the firm's perspective, the high cost of maintaining appropriate compensation packages for expatriates has led many companies—Colgate-Palmolive, Chase Manhattan Bank, Digital Equipment, General Motors, and General Electric among them—to find ways to cut the cost of PCN assignments as much as possible. "Transfer a $100,000-a-year American executive to London—and suddenly he [or she] costs the employer $300,000," explains the *Wall Street Journal.* "Move him to Stockholm or Tokyo, and he [or she] easily becomes a million-dollar [manager]."[68]

Firms try to cut overall costs of assignments by either extending the expatriate's tour, since turnover is expensive—especially when there is an accompanying family to move—or assigning expatriates to a much shorter tour as an unaccompanied assignment.

Designing and maintaining an appropriate compensation package is more complex than it would seem because of the need to consider and reconcile parent- and host-country financial, legal, and customary practices. The problem is that although little variation in typical executive salaries at the level of base compensation exists around the world, a wide variation in net spendable income is often present. U.S. executives abroad may receive more in cash and stock, but they have to spend more for what foreign companies provide, such as cars, vacations, and entertainment allowances. In addition, the manager's purchasing power with that net income is affected by the relative cost of living. The cost of living is considerably higher in most of Europe than in the United States. In designing compensation and benefit packages for PCNs, then, the challenge to IHRM professionals is to maintain a standard of living for expatriates equivalent to their colleagues at home, plus compensating them for any additional incurred costs. This policy is referred to as "keeping the expatriate whole."[69]

To ensure that expatriates do not lose out through their overseas assignment, the **balance sheet approach**, or **home-based method** (see Exhibit 9-10 for an example), is often used to equalize the standard of living between the host country and the home country and add some compensation for inconvenience or qualitative loss. In fact, 78 percent of the firms in the 2015 Brookfield survey stated that they used the home-based approach for long-term assignments.[70] However, recently, some companies have begun to base their compensation package on a goal of achieving a standard of living comparable to that of host-country managers, which does help resolve some of the problems of pay differentials.

In fairness, the MNC is obliged to make up additional costs that the expatriate would incur for taxes, housing, and goods and services. The tax differential is complex and expensive for the company, and MNCs generally use a policy of tax equalization. This means that the company pays any taxes due on any type of additional compensation that the expatriate receives for the assignment; the expatriate pays in taxes only what she or he would pay at home. The burden of foreign taxes can be lessened, however, by efficient tax planning—a fact small firms often overlook. The timing and methods of paying people determine what foreign taxes are incurred. For example, a company can save on taxes by renting an apartment for the employee instead of providing a cash housing allowance. All in all, MNCs have to weigh the many aspects of a complete compensation package, especially at high management levels, to effect a tax equalization policy. The total cost to the company can vary greatly by location; for example:

> Expatriates in Germany may incur twice the income tax they would in the U.S., and they are taxed on their housing and cost-of-living allowances as well. This financial snowball effect is a great incentive to make sure we really need to fill the position with an expatriate.[71]

Managing expatriate compensation is a complex challenge for companies with overseas operations. All components of the compensation package must be considered in light of both home- and host-country legalities and practices. Those components include:

*Salary:* Local salary buying power and currency translation, as compared with home salary; bonuses or incentives for dislocation

*Taxes:* Equalizing any differential effects of taxes as a result of expatriate's assignment

**EXHIBIT 9-10** The Balance Sheet Approach to Expatriate Compensation Package—Hypothetical Examples (Estimates in U.S. Dollars)

| Sample Components for Expat | Chicago | Tokyo | Mexico City |
|---|---|---|---|
| Base Salary + COLA | $100,000 | $150,000 | $75,000 |
| Relocation Allowance (20%) | | 30,000 | 15,000 |
| Housing Allowance (20%) | | 30,000 | 15,000 |
| Private Education for two children | | 30,000 | 20,000 |
| Two trips per year home for four | | 12,000 | 10,000 |
| | $100,000 | 252,000 | 135,000 |

Additional costs not estimated here include any local tax differential, health insurance, placement services for spouse, moving expenses and home sale, predeparture training and preparation, etc., as well as other negotiated items. In some "dangerous" locales, there will be additional costs pertaining to the safety of personnel, such as insurance, security guards, etc.

*Allowances:* Relocation expenses; cost-of-living adjustments (COLA); housing allowance for assignment and allowance to maintain house at home; trips home for expatriate and family; private education for children

*Benefits:* Health insurance; stock options

The **localization,** or **going-rate, approach** pays the expatriate the going rate for similar positions in the host country, plus whatever allowances and benefits for the assignment that the manager negotiates. With the basic pay similar to other managers in the host country, no matter where they come from, there is less resentment and more opportunity for open cooperation. However, when the going rate in a location is less than that in the home country—which is likely the case of a U.S.-based expatriate—she or he is likely to be reluctant to accept that assignment unless there are considerable perks in addition to the salary.

With the increasing number of companies that operate around the world and assign and move personnel (whether one calls them expatriates, transpatriates, or inpatriates) from one country to another, the design of equitable pay scales has become exceedingly complex. In an International Assignments Policies and Practices Survey by KPMG, companies noted the need to "review mobility policies to focus on harmonization of the treatment of globally mobile employees."[72] Should those managers in similar positions who come from different countries to a host country be paid according to the MNE headquarters location, or the host location, or that manager's home location? Or should they all be paid the same according to a globally determined rate for that job? Further complications arise from any legal or cultural restrictions on compensation in a particular location.

Most important, to be strategically competitive, the compensation package must be comparatively attractive to the kinds of managers the company wishes to hire or relocate. Some of those managers will, of course, be local managers in the host country. This, too, is a complex situation requiring competitive compensation policies that can attract, motivate, and retain the best local managerial talent. In many countries, however, it is a considerable challenge to develop compensation packages appropriate to the local situation and culture while also recognizing the differences between local salaries and those expatriates or transpatriates expect (that difference itself often being a source of competitive advantage).

## TRAINING AND COMPENSATING HOST-COUNTRY NATIONALS

### Training HCNs

The continuous training and development of HCNs and TCNs for management positions is also important to the long-term success of multinational corporations. As part of a long-term staffing policy for a subsidiary, the ongoing development of HCNs will facilitate the transition to an indigenization policy. Furthermore, multinational companies like to have well-trained managers with broad international experience available to take charge in many intercultural settings, whether at home or abroad, and, increasingly, in developing countries. Kimberly-Clark, for example, with more than 60,000 employees around the world, has steadily increased its talent development and training programs in all countries but, more recently, has focused on developing markets. "In Latin America, the average employee has gone from receiving practically no training time to about 38 hours each year. By contrast, workers in Europe now receive 40 hours per year—eight hours more than in 1996."[73]

Training for HCNs by foreign companies operating in the United States can be quite surprising for managers operating in their own country when they have to learn new ways. Toyota is an example of how employees at all levels must be trained in the Toyota Way. As recounted by Ms. Newton, a 38-year-old Indiana native who joined Toyota after college 15 years ago and now works at the North American headquarters in Erlanger, Kentucky:

> *For Americans and anyone, it can be a shock to the system to be actually expected to make problems visible. Other corporate environments tend to hide problems from bosses.*[74]

What Ms. Newton is referring to are the colored bar charts against a white bulletin board, which represent the work targets of individual workers, visibly charting their successes or failures to meet those targets. This is part of the Toyota Way. The idea is not to humiliate but to alert coworkers and enlist their help in finding solutions. Ms. Newton, now a general manager in charge of employee training and development at Toyota's North American manufacturing subsidiary, said it took a while to accept that fully, but now she is a firm believer.[75]

Certainly, there is no arguing with success—in 2009, Toyota became the largest global automaker in sales. The training institute in Mikkabi has trained more than 700 foreign executives, including cultural orientation with the same intensity as its training in the production processes. Core concepts such as ownership of problems and visibility are impressed upon new employees. A sense of shared purpose is conveyed with open offices—often without even cubicle partitions between desks.[76]

Many multinationals, in particular chains, wish to train their local managers and workers to bridge the divide between, on the one hand, the firm's successful corporate culture and practices and, on the other, the local culture and work practices. One example of how to do this in China is the Starbucks firm described in the *Management in Action feature, "Success! Starbucks' Java Style Helps to Recruit, Train, and Retain Local Managers in Beijing."*

# MANAGEMENT IN ACTION

*Success! Starbucks' Java Style Helps to Recruit, Train, and Retain Local Managers in Beijing*

*When we first started, people didn't know who we were and it was rough finding sites. Now landlords are coming to us.*

DAVID SUN,
PRESIDENT OF BEIJING MEI DA COFFEE COMPANY (FORMER STARBUCKS' PARTNER FOR NORTHERN CHINA) ECONOMIST *OCTOBER 6, 2001*

As we see from the preceding quote, Starbucks has achieved a remarkable penetration rate in China, given that it is a country of devoted tea drinkers who do not take readily to the taste of coffee.

Starbucks is no stranger to training leaders from around the world into the Starbucks style. As of June 2015, Starbucks has 22,519 both store-owned and licensed locations in 66 countries, as detailed here:

## Starbucks' Global Presence
### United States Stores

**50** states, plus the District of Columbia
**7,087** company-operated stores
**4,081** licensed stores

### International Stores

**65** countries outside the United States

### Company Operated

Australia, Canada, Chile, China (Northern China, Southern China), Germany, Ireland, Puerto Rico, Singapore, Thailand, and the United Kingdom

### Joint Venture and Licensed Stores

Austria, the Bahamas, Bahrain, Brazil, Canada, China (Shanghai/Eastern China), Cyprus, Czech Republic, Denmark, Egypt, France, Greece, Hong Kong, Indonesia, Ireland, Japan, Jordan, Kuwait, Lebanon, Macau S.A.R., Malaysia, Mexico, the Netherlands, New Zealand, Oman, Peru, the Philippines, Qatar, Romania, Russia, Saudi Arabia, South Korea, Spain, Switzerland, Taiwan, Turkey, the United Arab Emirates, and the United Kingdom.[77]

*(Continued)*

**FIGURE 9-1  A Starbucks Coffee Shop in Old Beijing-Style Building in Beijing, China**

*Source:* © Jack Young-Places/Alamy

Company managers nevertheless have had quite a challenge in recruiting, motivating, and retaining managers for its Beijing outlets (and, more recently, in its Qunguang Square outlet in Central China). Starbucks' primary challenge has been to recruit good managers in a country where the demand for local managers by foreign companies expanding there is far greater than the supply of managers with any experience in capitalist-style companies. Chinese recruits have stressed that they are looking for opportunity to train and advance in global companies rather than for money. They know that managers with experience in Western organizations can always get a job. The brand's pop-culture reputation is also an attraction to young Beijingers.

To expose the recruits to java-style culture as well as to train them for management, Starbucks brings them to Seattle, Washington, for three months to give them a taste of the West Coast lifestyle and the company's informal culture, such as Western-style backyard barbecues.

Then they are exposed to the art of cappuccino making at a real store before dawn and concocting dozens of fancy coffees. They get the same intensive training as anyone else anywhere in the world. One recruit, Mr. Wang, who worked in a large Beijing hotel before finding out how to make a triple grande latte, said that he enjoys the casual atmosphere and respect. The training and culture are very different from what one would expect at a traditional state-owned company in China, where the work is strictly defined and has no challenge for employees.

Starbucks has found that motivating their managers in Beijing is multifaceted. They know that people won't switch jobs for money alone. They want to work for a company that gives them an opportunity to learn. They also want to have a good working environment and a company with a strong reputation. The recruits have expressed their need for trust and participation in an environment where local nationals traditionally are not expected to exercise initiative or authority. In all, what seems to motivate them more than anything else is their dignity.

*Source:* www.Starbucks.com, Corporate Information: June 28, 2015; Associated Press, "Starbucks Reorganizes for Growth," www.nytimes.com; J. Adamy, "Starbucks Raises New-Stores Goal, Enters iTunes Deal," *Wall Street Journal*, October 6, 2006; "China: Starbucks Opens New Outlet in Beijing," Info-Prod (Middle East) Ltd., July 20, 2003; "Coffee with Your Tea? Starbucks in China," *Economist*, October 6, 2001.

Many HCNs are, of course, receiving excellent training in global business and Internet technology within their home corporations. For example, the German media company Bertelsmann has specialized training programs to develop and retain local managers. In India, for example, its high-potential employees can apply for an INSEAD Global Executive MBA.[78]

Whether in home corporations, MNC subsidiaries, or joint ventures in any country, managerial training to facilitate e-business adoption is taking on increasing competitive importance to take advantage of new strategic opportunities. Although large companies are well ahead of the curve for information and communication technologies (ICT), there is considerable need for small and medium-sized enterprises (SMEs) to adopt such knowledge-creating capabilities.

Managerial training in ICT is particularly critical for firms in new economy and emerging markets and, taken together, can provide advantage for rapid economic growth in regions such as Eastern Europe. Research by Damaskopoulos and Evgeniou addressed these needs by surveying more than 900 SME managers in Slovenia, Poland, Romania, Bulgaria, and Cyprus. Although most managers recognized the opportunities in implementing e-business strategies, they also noted the urgent need for training to take advantage of those opportunities. Some of the training needs and issues those SME managers perceived are shown below. Some of these factors are at the firm level, whereas other issues relate to the market and regulatory levels, such as the need to increase security for commercial activity on the Internet.[79] Such findings highlight the need to recognize the strategy-staffing-training link and its importance to the overall growth of emerging economies.

## Training Priorities for E-Business Development[80]

- How to develop a business plan and an e-business strategy
- How to develop the partnerships and in-house expertise for e-business
- How to finance e-business initiatives
- Addressing security and privacy concerns
- How to set up electronic payments
- How to develop good customer relations on the Internet
- Training in technology management
- How to collect marketing intelligence online

In another common scenario also requiring the management of a mixture of executives and employees, American and European MNCs presently employ Asians as well as Arab locals in their plants and offices in Saudi Arabia, bringing together three cultures: well-educated Asian managers living in a Middle Eastern, highly traditional society who are employed by a firm reflecting Western technology and culture. This kind of situation requires training to help all parties effectively integrate multiple sets of culturally based values, expectations, and work habits.

## Compensating HCNs

How do firms deal with the question of what is appropriate compensation for host-country nationals, given local norms and the competitive needs of the firm? For the most part, firms adjust pay according to market conditions and design methods for job grading and incentive plans.[81]

Of course, no one set of solutions can be applicable in any country. Many variables apply—including local market factors and pay scales, government involvement in benefits, the role of unions, the cost of living, and so on. In Eastern Europe, for example, Hungarians, Poles, and Czechs spend a considerable portion of their disposable income on food and utilities.Therefore, East European managers must have cash for about 65 to 80 percent of their base pay, compared to about 40 percent for U.S. managers (the rest being long-term incentives, benefits, and perks). In addition, they still expect the many social benefits the old government provided. To be competitive, MNCs can focus on providing goods and services that are either not available at all or are extremely expensive in Eastern Europe. Such upscale perks can be used to attract high-skilled workers.

In Japan, in response to a decade-long economic slump, companies are revamping their HRM policies to compete in a global economy. The traditional lifetime employment and guaranteed tidy pension are giving way to the more Western practices of competing for jobs, of basing pay on performance rather than seniority, and of making people responsible for their own retirement fund decisions.[82]

A key concern of Western managers in China and India, as well as of the firms that outsource there, are the rapidly rising pay rates in those countries and a shortage of top talent. This shortage of talent is especially problematic in India. With the considerable growth in emerging markets, foreign firms trying to get on the bandwagon there are finding themselves in a war for talent. With that kind of supply–demand ratio for local skilled managers, salaries are being pushed up; that situation then lowers the rationale for hiring local managers instead of sending expatriates.

According to Citigroup, it is also imperative to make clear what benefits, as well as salary, come with a position because of the way compensation is perceived and regulated around the world.[83] In Latin America, for example, an employee's pay and title are associated with what type of car he or she can receive.

## CONCLUSION

The IHRM function is a vital component of implementing the global strategy of a firm. In particular, managing the IHRM functions for and in emerging and developing markets presents complex challenges at all employee levels; these include the war for talent for managerial and professional people and the issues of outsourcing employees in those markets. Careful decisions regarding the appropriate staffing policy for foreign locations are crucial to the success of the firm's operations, particularly because of the lack of proximity to and control by headquarters executives. In particular, the ability of expatriates to initiate and maintain cooperative relationships with local people and agencies will determine the long-term success, even the viability, of the operation. In a real sense, a company's global cadre represents its most valuable resource. Proactive management of that resource by headquarters will result in having the right people in the right place at the right time, appropriately trained, prepared, and supported. MNCs using these IHRM practices can anticipate the effective management of the foreign operation, the fostering of expatriates' careers, and, ultimately, the enhanced success of the corporation.

## Summary of Key Points

- Global human resource management is a vital component of implementing global strategy and is increasingly recognized as a major determinant of success or failure in international business.
- The main staffing alternatives for global operations are the ethnocentric, polycentric, regiocentric, and global approaches; the use of inpatriates supplements those choices. Each approach has its appropriate uses, according to its advantages and disadvantages and, in particular, the firm's strategy.
- The causes of expatriate failure include the following: poor selection based on inappropriate criteria, inadequate preparation before assignment, alienation from headquarters, inability of manager or family to adapt to local environment, inadequate compensation package, and poor programs for career support and repatriation.
- The three major areas critical to expatriate preparation are cultural training, language instruction, and familiarity with everyday matters.
- Appropriate and attractive compensation packages must be designed by IHRM staffs to sustain a competitive global expatriate staff. Compensation packages for host-country managers must be designed to fit the local culture and situation as well as the firm's objectives.

## Discussion Questions

9-1. What are the major alternative staffing approaches for international operations? Explain the relative advantages of each and the conditions under which you would choose one approach over another.

9-2. Why is the HRM role so much more complex, and important, in the international context?

9-3. What are the advantages and disadvantages of the use of inpatriates for MNEs?

9-4. Explain the common causes of expatriate failure. What are the major success factors for expatriates? Explain the role and importance of each.

**9-5.** What is culture shock? Why is it important for MNEs to provide cross-cultural training to their expatriate managers?

**9-6.** Explain the balance sheet approach to international compensation packages. Why is this approach so important? Discuss the pros and cons of aligning the expatriate compensation package with the host-country colleagues compared to the home-country colleagues.

**9-7.** Discuss the importance of a complete program for expatriate performance management. What are the typical components for such a program?

## Application Exercises

**9-8.** Make a list of the reasons you would want to accept a foreign assignment and a list of reasons you would want to reject it. Do they depend on the location? Compare your list with a classmate and discuss your reasons.

**9-9.** Research a company with operations in several countries and ascertain the staffing policy used for those countries. Find out what kinds of training and preparation are provided for expatriates and what kinds of results the company is experiencing with expatriate training.

## Experiential Exercise

Form a group of three to four students. Have a discussion with your group members to agree on a specific country (preferably an emerging economy in Asia or South America) for analysis. Summarize the ideas and present them to the rest of the class.

Assume that you are a middle-level manager in a large MNE in the United Kingdom. You are married with two children. You are given a special assignment in the overseas subsidiary of the MNE in the country you and your group members have just identified and agreed on. There are 20 employees in the subsidiary, all locally employed. Although you are merely a middle-level manager in the UK headquarters, you will become the CEO of the designated overseas subsidiary responsible for all the logistics, finance, marketing and HRM operations. You plan to take up the new assignment.

**9-10.** Set out a plan for yourself to settle in the new assignment. In your plan, identify the potential cultural conflicts that you will need to face as well as possible solutions to overcome these conflicts.

**9-11.** You will bring your family (including the children) to work in the overseas subsidiary. You plan to talk to your spouse and children before you agree to take up the assignment. What are you going to tell them? How are you going to settle your family in the country?

## CASE STUDY

### Kelly's Assignment in Japan

Well, it's my job that brought us here in the first place ... I am going to have to make a decision to stick with this assignment and hope I can work things out or to return to the United States and probably lose my promised promotion after this assignment—maybe even my job.

As she surveyed the teeming traffic of downtown Tokyo from her office window, Kelly tried to assess the situation her family was in, how her job was going, and what could have been done to lead to a better situation four months ago when she was offered the job.

As a program manager for a startup Internet services company, she had been given the opportunity to head up the sales and marketing department in Tokyo. Her boss said that "the sky's the limit" as far as her being able to climb the corporate ladder if she was successful in Tokyo. She explained that she did not speak Japanese and that she knew nothing about Japan, but he said he had confidence in her because she had done such a great job in Boston and in recent short assignments to London and Munich. Moreover, the company offered her a very attractive compensation package that included a higher salary, bonuses, a relocation allowance, a rent-free apartment in Tokyo, and an education allowance for their two children, Lisa and Sam, to attend private schools. She was told she had two days to decide, and that they wanted her in Tokyo in three weeks because they wanted her to prepare and present a proposal for a new account opportunity there as soon as possible. Her boss said they would hire a relocation company to handle the move for her.

That night Kelly excitedly discussed the opportunity with her husband, Joe. He was glad for her and thought it would be an exciting experience for the whole family. However, he was concerned about his own job and what the move would do to his career. She told him that her boss had said that Joe would probably find something or be transferred there, but that her boss did seem unconcerned about that. In the end, Joe felt that Kelly should have this opportunity, and he agreed to the move. He talked to his boss about a transfer and was told that the manager would look into that and get back to him. However, he knew that his company was having layoffs because of the economic decline that was taking its toll on profits. The problem was that Kelly had to make a decision before he could fully explore his options, so Kelly and Joe decided to go ahead with the plans. To sweeten the deal, Kelly's company had offered to buy her house in Boston since the housing market decline had her concerned about whether she could sell without taking a loss.

After the long trip, they arrived at their apartment in Tokyo; they were tired but excited, but did not anticipate that the apartment would be so tiny, given the very high rent that the company was paying for it. Kelly realized at once that they had included way too much in their move of personal belongings to be able to fit into this apartment. Undaunted, they planned to spend the weekend sightseeing and looked forward to some travel. Japan was beautiful in the spring, and they were anxious to see the area.

On Monday, Kelly took a cab to the office. She had emailed requesting a staff meeting at 9 A.M. She knew that her immediate staff would include seven Japanese, two Americans, and two Germans—all men. Her assistant, Peter, to whom she had not yet spoken, was an American who had also just arrived, coming from an assignment in London. He greeted her at the elevator, looking surprised, and they proceeded to the conference room, where everyone was awaiting the new boss. Kelly exchanged the usual handshake greetings with the Westerners and then bowed to the Japanese; an awkward silence and exchange took place, with the Japanese looking embarrassed. While she attempted a greeting in her limited Japanese that she had studied on the plane, she was relieved to find that the Japanese spoke English, but they seemed very quiet and hesitant. Peter then told her that they all thought that "Kelly" was a man, and they all attempted a laugh.

After that, Kelly decided that she would just meet with Peter and postpone the general meeting until the next day. She asked them each to prepare a short presentation for her on their ideas for the new account. Whereas the Americans and Germans said they would have it ready, the Japanese seemed reluctant to commit themselves.

Meanwhile, at home Joe was looking into the schools for the children and trying to make some contacts to look for a job. Travelling, getting information, and shopping for groceries proved bewildering, but they decided that they would soon get acquainted with local customs.

At the office the next day, Kelly received a short presentation from the Westerners on the staff, but when it came to the Japanese, they indicated that they had not yet had a chance to meet with their groups and other contacts to come to their decisions. Kelly asked them why they had not told her the day before that they needed more time, and when could they be ready. They seemed unwilling to give a direct answer and kept their eyes lowered. In an attempt to lighten the atmosphere and get to know her staff, Kelly then began chatting casually and asked several of them about their families. The Americans chatted on about their children's achievements, the Germans talked about their family positions, and the Japanese went silent, seemingly very confused and offended.

Still attempting to get everyone's ideas for an initial proposal to the potential new client, Kelly later asked one of the Americans who had been there for some time what he thought was the problem and delay in getting presentations from the Japanese. He told her that they did not like to do individual presentations, but rather wanted to gain consensus among themselves and their contacts and present a group presentation. Having learned her lesson, but feeling irritated, she asked him to intervene and have the presentations ready for the next week. When that time came, the Japanese made the rest of the presentations but, oddly, they seemed to be addressed primarily to Peter. Later, Kelly decided to finalize her own presentation to put forth a proposal for the client, which she set up for the following week.

At home, Joe said that he had not heard anything from his company in Boston and asked Kelly to contact her company again to request some networking in Tokyo that might lead to job opportunities for him. Kelly said she would do that, but that there didn't seem to be any one person back home who was keeping up with her situation or giving any support about that or about her job.

The children, meanwhile, complained that, although their schools were meant to be bilingual English–Japanese, a majority of the children were Japanese and did not speak English; Lisa and Sam felt confused and left out. They were disoriented by the different customs, classes, and foods for lunch. At home, they complained that there was no backyard to go out to play, and they could not get their programs on the television or understand the Japanese programs.

Back at the office, Kelly worked with her staff to finalize the proposal but noticed a strained atmosphere. Peter told her that some of them would drop by a local bar for a drink after work, which helped the whole group to relax together. However, she felt that she could not do that, nor that she would be accepted as a female.

The next week, as arranged, Kelly and Peter went to the offices of the client; she knew that a lot was riding on getting this big new contract. She had asked Peter to let them know ahead of time that she is a woman, yet the introductions still seemed strained. She planned to get straight down to business, so when the client company's CEO handed her his business card, she put it in her pocket without a glance and did not give him her card. Again, she noticed some shock and embarrassment all around. (She found out much later that a business card is very important to a Japanese businessman because it conveys all his accomplishments and position without having to say it himself.) Flustered, she tried to make light of the situation, patted him on the back, and asked him what his first name was, saying, rather loudly, that hers was Kelly. He went quiet again, backed away from her, and, with his head bowed, whispered, "Michio." He glanced around at his Japanese colleagues rather nervously.

After a period of silence, Michio pointed to the table of refreshments, and indicated that they sit and eat; however, Kelly was anxious to present her power-point slides and went to the end of the table where the equipment was and asked Peter to set up the slides. As she proceeded to go through the proposal, telling them what her company could do for them, she paused and asked for questions. However, when Michio and his two colleagues asked questions, they directed them to Peter, not to her. In fact, they made little eye contact with her at all. She tried to remain cool, but insisted on answering the questions herself. In the end, she sat down and asked Michio what he thought of the proposal. He bowed politely and said, "Very good," and that he would discuss it with his colleagues and get back to her. However, Kelly did not hear from them, and after a couple of weeks, she asked Peter to follow up with them. He did that but reported that they were not going to pursue the contract. Frustrated, she said, "Well, why did Michio say that it looked very good, then?" She knew that it was a very competitive proposal and felt that something other than the proposed contract was to blame for the loss of the contract.

Disillusioned, but determined not to give up without success in the assignment, Kelly took a cab to go home and think about it, but the driver misunderstood her and went the wrong way and got stuck in traffic. She felt discouraged and wished that she had some female American friends to whom she could confide her problems.

When Kelly got home, Peter was angrily trying to fix dinner, complaining about the small appliances and inability to understand the food packages or how to prepare the food. He said he needed something else to do, but that a job did not seem to be on the horizon for him. He was also concerned about continuing to live in such a high-cost city on only one salary.

Kelly went to the other room to see the children; they were fighting and complaining that they had nothing to do and wanted to go home. Kelly felt that the three months they had been there was not a fair trial and was wondering what to do. She wished she had had more time to prepare for this assignment, and whenever she contacted the home office, no one seemed able to advise her.

## Case Questions

**9-12.** Explain the clashes in culture, customs, and expectations that occurred in this situation.

**9-13.** What stage of culture shock is Kelly's family experiencing?

**9-14.** Turn back the clock to when Kelly was offered the position in Tokyo. What, if anything, should have been done differently and by whom?

**9-15.** You are Kelly. What should you do now?

## Endnotes

1. 2015 Brookfield Global Relocation Trends Survey, www .brookfieldgrs.com, accessed August 24, 2015; www.McKinsey. com/mgi/; "Capturing Talent," *Economist*, August 18, 2007, pp. 59–61; Douglas A. Ready, Linda A. Hill, and Jay A. Conger, "Winning the Race for Talent in Emerging Markets," *Harvard Business Review* (November 2008); Harold L. Sirkin, "Need Global Talent? Grow Your Own," *BusinessWeek* Online, September 17, 2008; "Talent Retention: Ongoing Problem for Asia-Pacific Region," T+D 61, No. 3 (2007), p. 12.
2. 2015 Brookfield Global Relocation Trends Survey, www .brookfieldgrs.com, accessed August 24, 2015.
3. www.McKinsey.com/mgi/; "Capturing Talent," *Economist,* August 18, 2007, pp. 59–61.
4. Douglas A. Ready, Linda A. Hill, and Jay A. Conger, "Winning the Race for Talent in Emerging Markets," *Harvard Business Review* (November 2008).
5. Martin Dewhurst, Matthew Pettigrew, and Ramesh Srinivasan, "How Multinationals Can Attract the Talent They Need," *McKinsey Quarterly*, June 2012.
6. Sirkin, 2008.
7. 2015 Brookfield Global Relocation Trends Survey, www .brookfieldgrs.com, accessed August 24, 2015.
8. Sirkin, 2008.
9. Ready et al., 2008.
10. Ibid.
11. www.pricewaterhousecoopers.com, accessed November 19, 2011.
12. "Retention: Hello? Is Anyone at HQ Listening?" *Harvard Business Review*, April 1, 2015.
13. Ibid.
14. J. E. Mendenhall, R. J. Jensen, J. S. Black, and H. B. Gregerson, "Seeing the Elephant: Human Resource Management Challenges in the Age of Globalization," *Organizational Dynamics* 32, No. 3 (2003), pp. 261–274.
15. J. L. Laabs, "HR Pioneers Explore the Road Less Traveled," *Personnel Journal* (February 1996), pp. 70–72, 74, 77–78.
16. Friso Den Hertog, Ad Van Iterson, and Christian Mari, "Does HRM Really Matter in Bringing about Strategic Change? Comparative Action Research in Ten European Steel Firms," *European Management Journal* 28, No. 1 (2010), pp. 14–24.
17. www.ibm.com, accessed December 1, 2011; S. Hamm, "International Isn't Just IBM's First Name," www.businessweek .com, January 28, 2008, pp. 36–40.
18. KPMG 2012 Global Assignment Survey, www.kpmg.com, accessed August 9, 2012.
19. *The 2011 PricewaterhouseCoopers' 14th Annual CEO Survey.*
20. J. Stewart Black and Allen J. Morrison, "A Cautionary Tale for Emerging Market Giants," *Harvard Business Review*, September 2010.
21. Ibid.; "International Assignments Remain on the Upswing Despite Economic Concerns, Says KPMG," Anonymous, *PR Newswire*, December 3, 2008.
22. Ibid.
23. Bettina Wassener, "Living in Asia Appeals to More Company Leaders," *New York Times* [New York, NY] June 21, 2012, p. B.3.
24. Ibid.
25. C. A. Bartlett and S. Ghoshal, "Matrix Management: Not a Structure, a Frame of Mind," *Harvard Business Review* (July–August 1990).
26. Lynda Gratton, "Workplace 2025—What Will It Look Like?" *Organizational Dynamics* 40 (2011), pp. 246–254.
27. M. Harvey et al., "Developing Effective Global Relationships through Staffing with Inpatriate Managers: The Role of Interpersonal Trust," *Journal of International Management*, 2011, doi:10.1016/j.intman 2011.01.02.
28. J. Stewart Black and Allen J. Morrison, "A Cautionary Tale for Emerging Market Giants," *Harvard Business Review*, September 2010.
29. M. Harvey, M. M. Novivenic, C. Speier, "Strategic Global Human Resource Management: The Role of Inpatriate Managers," *Human Resource Management Review*, 10, No. 2 (2000), pp. 153–175.
30. Ibid.
31. M. Harvey, 2011.
32. Michael Harvey, Helene Mayerhofer, Linley Hartmann, and Miriam Moeller, "Corralling the 'Horses' to Staff the Global Organization of the 21st Century," *Organizational Dynamics*, 39, No. 3 (2010), pp. 258–268.
33. S. B. Prasad and Y. K. Krishna Shetty, *An Introduction to Multinational Management* (Upper Saddle River, NJ: Prentice Hall, 1979).
34. Rochelle Kopp, "International Human Resource Policies and Practices in Japanese, European, and United States Multinationals," *Human Resource Management* 33, No. 4 (1994), pp. 581–599.
35. Based on, updated, and adapted by H. Deresky, from original work by D. A. Heenan and H. V. Perlmutter, *Multinational Organization Development* (Reading, MA: Addison-Wesley, 1979), pp. 18–19.
36. R. L. Tung, "Selection and Training of Personnel for Overseas Assignments," *Columbia Journal of World Business* (Spring 1981), pp. 68–78.
37. P. Dowling and R. S. Schuler, *International Dimensions of Human Resource Management* (Boston: PWS-Kent, 1990).
38. S. J. Kobrin, "Expatriate Reduction and Strategic Control in American Multinational Corporations," *Human Resource Management* 27, No. 1 (1988), pp. 63–75.
39. Company information, www.ABB.com, accessed July 26, 2004.
40. www.GMACGlobalrelocation.com, accessed March 1, 2009.
41. Ed Hannibal, Yvonne Traber, Paul Jelinek, "Tracking Your Expatriate Workforce," *HRMagazine* 60, No. 3 (April 2015), pp. 63–65.
42. 2014 Global Mobility Talent Trends Survey, Brookfield Global Relocation Services, www.brookfieldgrs.com, accessed April 21, 2015.
43. *HRMagazine* 60, No. 3 (April 2015), pp. 63–65.
44. "Decoding Global Talent," *Boston Consulting Group*, The Network, 2014.
45. M. Mendenhall and G. Oddou, "The Dimensions of Expatriate Acculturation: A Review," *Academy of Management Review* 10, No. 1 (1985), pp. 39–47.
46. Theresa Minton-Eversole, "Best Expatriate Assignments Require Much Thought, Even More Planning," SHRM's 2009 Global Trend Book, *HRMagazine* (2009), pp. 74–75.
47. M. G. Tye and P. Y. Chen (2005), "Selection of Expatriates: Decision-Making Models Used by HR Professionals," *Human Resource Planning* 28, No. 4, pp. 15–20.

**48.** D. Erbacher, B. D'Netto, and J. Espana, "Expatriate Success in China: Impact of Personal and Situational Factors," *Journal of American Academy of Business* 9, No. 2 (2006), p. 183.

**49.** Rosalie Tung, "American Expatriates Abroad: From Neophytes to Cosmopolitans," *Journal of World Business* 33 (1998), pp. 125–144.

**50.** His-An Shih, Yun-Hwa Chiang, and In-Sook Kim, "Expatriate Performance Management from MNEs of Different National Origins," *International Journal of Manpower* 26, No. 2 (2005), pp. 161–162.

**51.** "Managing Global Virtual Teams," http://executive-education. insead.edu/managing_global_virtual_teams, accessed April 26, 2015.

**52.** Ying Zhang, Christopher Marquis, Sergey Filippov, Henk-Jan Haasnoot, Martijn van der Steen, "The Challenges and Enhancing Opportunities of Global Project Management: Evidence from Chinese and Dutch Cross-Cultural Project Management," Harvard Business School Working Paper 15-063-February 11, 2015.

**53.** *Business Wire*, 2006.

**54.** Ibid.

**55.** Ibid.

**56.** Tung, 1998.

**57.** Mendenhall and Oddou.

**58.** K. Oberg, "Culture Shock: Adjustments to New Cultural Environments," *Practical Anthropology* (July–August 1960), pp. 177–182.

**59.** Ibid.

**60.** Lynette Clemetson, "The Pepsi Challenge: Helping Expats Feel At Home," *Workforce Management* 89, No. 12 (December 2010), p. 36.

**61.** Ashish Mahajan and Soo Min Toh, "Facilitating Expatriate Adjustment: The Role of Advice-Seeking from Host Country Nationals," *Journal of World Business* 49 (2014), pp. 476–487.

**62.** Ibid.

**63.** Eduardo Caride, "Diversifying Talent to Suit the Market," *Harvard Business Review*, September 2014.

**64.** Ibid.

**65.** R. B. Peterson, "The Use of Expatriates and Inpatriates in Central and Eastern Europe since the Wall Came Down," *Journal of World Business* 38 (2003), pp. 55–69.

**66.** Based on J. S. Black, Mark. E. Mendenhall, Hal B. Gregersen, and Linda K. Stroh, *Globalizing People through International Assignments* (Reading, MA: Addison Wesley Longman, 1999).

**67.** Christopher Tice, Manager, Global Expatriate Operations, DuPont Inc., quoted in Mark Schoeff, "International Assignments Best Served by Unified Policy," *Workforce Management* 85, No. 3 (2006), p. 36.

**68.** "Living Expenses," www.economist.com, July 22, 2000; "Runzheimer International Compensation Worksheet," www.runzheimer.com, 2000.

**69.** B. W. Teague, *Compensating Key Personnel Overseas* (New York: Conference Board, 1992).

**70.** 2015 Brookfield Global Relocation Trends Survey, www.brookfieldgrs.com, accessed August 24, 2015.

**71.** S. F. Gale, "Taxing Situations for Expatriates," *Workforce* 82, No. 6 (2003), p. 100.

**72.** International Assignment Policies and Practices Survey, 2011, www.kpmg.com, accessed November 11, 2011.

**73.** Gina Ruiz, "Kimberly-Clark: Developing Talent in Developing World Markets," *Workforce Management* 85, No. 7 (2006), p. 34.

**74.** Martin Fackler, "The 'Toyota Way' Is Translated for a New Generation of Foreign Managers," www.nytimes.com, February 17, 2007.

**75.** Ibid.

**76.** Ibid.

**77.** Company website, www.starbucks.com, accessed March 5, 2012.

**78.** Martin Dewhurst, Matthew Pettigrew, and Ramesh Srinivasan, "How Multinationals Can Attract the Talent They Need," *McKinsey Quarterly*, June 2012.

**79.** P. Damaskopoulos and T. Evgeniou, "Adoption of New Economy Practices by SMEs in Eastern Europe," *European Management Journal* 21, No. 2 (2003), pp. 133–145.

**80.** Based on Damaskopoulos and Evgeniou, 2003.

**81.** Fay Hansen, "The Great Global Talent Race: One World, One Workforce: Part 1 of 2," *Workforce Management* 85, No. 7 (2006), p. 1.

**82.** Y. Ono and W. Spindle, "Japan's Long Decline Makes One Thing Rise: Individualism," *Wall Street Journal*, January 3, 2001.

**83.** "Personnel Demands Attention Overseas," *Mutual Fund Market News* (March 19, 2001), p. 1.

# 10 Developing a Global Management Cadre

## OUTLINE

## OBJECTIVES

**10-1.** To appreciate the importance of international assignments in developing top managers with global experience and perspectives

**10-2.** To recognize the need to design programs for the careful preparation, adaptation, and repatriation of the expatriate and any accompanying family, as well as programs for career management and retention, thereby also transferring knowledge to and from host operations

**10-3.** To become familiar with the use of global management teams to coordinate host country and cross-border business

**10-4.** To recognize the varying roles of women around the world in international management

**10-5.** To understand the variations in host-country labor relations systems and the impact on the manager's job and effectiveness

## Opening Profile: The Expat Life[1]

*Expats Flee Moscow as Tensions Flare*

WALL STREET JOURNAL, JUNE 10, 2015.

What is it like to take an assignment abroad? Well, if you were one of the expats from the west who were living the good life in Moscow, for example, life took an abrupt turn when they were recalled in 2014–2015 because so many western companies were pulling out as a result of the sanctions on Russia. This situation makes it clear that expat lives are vulnerable to sudden changes in the political and business climate around the world. But, if you were an expat from China you were one of the sudden surge of people moving to Moscow to take up the slack in business opportunities left open by western companies.

Would you like to be an expat (expatriate)? Is it an adventure or a hardship? (The young man from Asia pictured in Fig. 10-1 seems to be excited about his assignment in London.) Experiences of those who have done a stint abroad are mixed, but it is clear that it is very likely an opportunity that will present itself at some point during your career. Most companies with global business transactions want their top employees to have overseas experience. At Procter & Gamble, for example, 39 of the company's top 44 global officers have had an international assignment, and 22 were born outside the United States. According to the 2015 Brookfield Relocation Trends Survey of 143 firms, 43 percent of assignees were relocated to or from a non-headquarters country.

Experiences vary by job type, especially by location. Adjustment is easier for those who go to places where the culture and business practices are similar to their own. Those transitioning between Western Europe and the United States or Canada, for example, typically adapt easier than those going to China or Yemen, as related below. Some expatriates enjoy perks that they do not get at home, and others find they fare worse financially, either while overseas or when they return home. In addition, with more firms expanding operations in emerging economies, expats often face considerable challenges such as inefficient infrastructure; limited housing, medical, or educational facilities; security risks; and political instability. Such conditions often mean that the assignment is turned down or that the manager will decide to go without his or her family. In most places, assignees expect the assignment to be career-broadening and hope it will leverage them to a promotion. Some expat experiences are described below.

As an example of how quickly the changing global environment can affect expats, we can look at the typical expat life for Wall Street executives as described in the *New York Times* in 2008: "When Wall Streeters pack their bags for Dubai or Shanghai, for example, they get much more than a plane ticket and coverage of per-diem expenses. These days, moving abroad can mean scoring a nanny, a driver, or even a bodyguard."[2] In Shanghai, there are 70,000 expatriates from around the world, in various capacities. For those in the finance industry, the expat package typically includes round trips home a year; fees for a real estate agency; moving expenses; at least one month of temporary

**FIGURE 10-1** Enjoying London

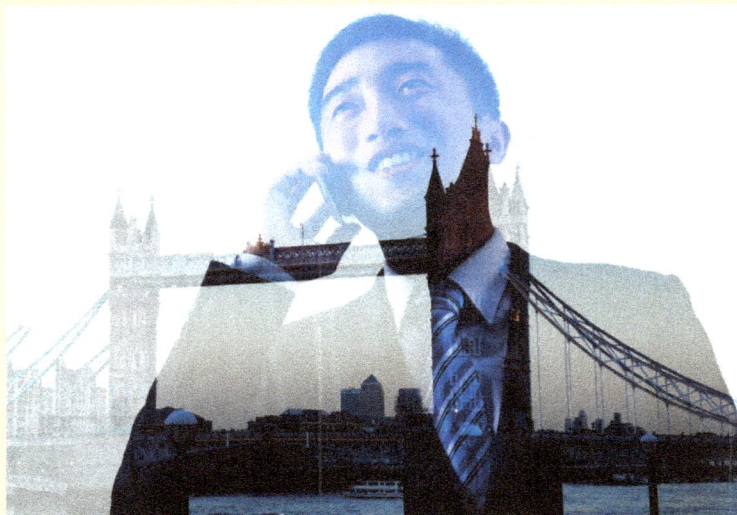

Rawpixel/Fotolia

accommodation; and language classes if required. For an accompanying family, fees for private schools, for example, are usually included as well as help for the spouse to find a job. A cost of living adjustment is typically included as well as an adjustment for tax equalization. A very nice assignment—however, in spring 2009, the *New York Times* was then reporting about the number of expats in the banking and finance industry who were being laid off.

> *Losing your job anywhere is disorienting, but imagine being laid off when you work in a foreign country. Not only is your source of income, and perhaps a good part of your identity, suddenly yanked away, but often you lose your right to remain in the country.*[3]

That, however, was an unusual development; for most expats, the overseas assignment has been very rewarding in terms of both personal and job experience.

In many circumstances, the adventure that started out with many concerns turns out to be one that the expats and their families do not want to end. According to the Global Relocation Trends Survey, 26 percent of expats opt to continue their overseas assignment when the original term ends. Those people have settled in to their position and life in the host country and enjoy their situations.

One reporter assigned to Beijing commented, "That's why we recently decided to extend our stay for a fourth year. For me, it was an easy decision. The three years that seemed so ominous turned out to be not nearly enough time to settle into a new life." The family wanted to do more travelling as well as really understand and enjoy the culture of Beijing.[4]

Assignments in some locations can turn out to be more challenging. One example is that of Mr. Deffontaines, who moved to Yemen in 2008 as the local manager for Total, the French oil giant, along with his family. Since then, Mr. Deffontaines has seen his main export pipeline damaged by terrorists, endured devastating flash floods, and sent expatriate families back home because of security concerns.

Recounting some of the interesting challenges he had faced there, Mr. Deffontaines, a 43-year-old Parisian, described "negotiating with tribal leaders and sending actors to remote villages to stage a play about the hazards of gas pipelines. In meetings with government officials to thrash out problems, participants typically chew khat, a mildly narcotic plant that is widely consumed in Yemen but banned in many places around the world."[5]

A particularly difficult decision, in response to growing security concerns, was to send the families of his workers back to France. His own wife, son, and twin daughters were among those forced to depart.

Robert Kneupfer, a lawyer, reflects that, in spite of inconveniences such as the 17-year wait for a telephone line and the absence of any McDonald's restaurants, the five years he spent in Budapest with his family on behalf of the international law firm Baker & McKenzie were a "defining moment both personally and professionally." The 56-year-old partner, now based in Chicago, didn't speak the language, and his children had been reluctant to leave family and friends. His advice: "Don't sweat the small stuff. You need to appreciate the bigger-picture experience."[6] To do that, he makes it clear that preparation is important for a positive experience. His advice follows that of many others as discussed throughout this chapter and the preceding chapter. First and foremost, you and any accompanying family members must familiarize yourselves ahead of time with the local people and their culture, their language and communication style, and their ways of living and doing business. Most important, prepare your family for the stages of adjustment they will go through so that they know what to expect; plans must be made to integrate them as quickly as possible into the local schools, church, social life, and so on. It also helps if you can meet with other expat families in the area who will provide both practical and emotional support. In addition, research shows that part of the pre-departure training should include setting up a mentor in the headquarters office or in the local area so that regular support will be available as well as some visibility for your career continuity.

Further advice from a well-travelled expat comes from Philip Shearer, Group President, Clinique, Estee Lauder. His mother was French, his father British, and he was born in Morocco. After going to college in France and then business school in the United States, he worked at a pharmaceutical company in Minneapolis. Then he worked in France, Mexico, Britain, Japan, and again in the United States for companies such as L'Oréal and the Elizabeth Arden division of Eli Lilly.

Shearer's advice melds with that of other successful expats who seem to be able to distill their experiences and travels to arrive at common themes. They recommend that, above all, you should be yourself and gain a reputation for being trustworthy. In that way, people will trust you and relate to you no matter where you are from. Shearer warns, however, that Americans generally show off too much. "But in the end, you have to deliver. And that's the same all over the world."[7]

*After investing over a million dollars in my overseas experience, I thought someone, somewhere in the organization would want to know what I have learned. I was wrong.*

INTERNATIONAL MANAGER[8]

A crucial factor in global competitiveness is the ability of the firm to maximize its global human resources in the long term. In the globalized economy, the knowledge and management resources, as well as the skilled and non-skilled employee resources, required for the firm to succeed are no longer concentrated in a single region but are distributed around the world. There are various categories of those resources—both people and processes—that IHR managers and others must develop and maintain; in particular it is essential for them to:

- Maximize long-term retention and benefits of an international cadre through career management so that the company can develop a top management team with global experience.
- Develop effective global management teams.
- Understand, value, and promote the role of women in international management to maximize those underused resources.
- Work with the host-country labor relations system to effect strategic implementation and employee productivity.

# EXPATRIATE CAREER MANAGEMENT

*Martin Walker, senior director of the Global Business Policy Council at A. T. Kearney, a consultancy, maintains that the dearth of talent is mainly evident at the very top: "Shortages do exist—most notably, of people with the internationalized business skills to thrive at senior management level in global companies.*

THE GLOBAL TALENT INDEX REPORT: THE OUTLOOK TO 2015
HEIDRICK & STRUGGLES [9]

It is clear from the preceding quote that the road to the top necessitates managers to have overseas experience. For the firm, the ability to develop a top management team, globally experienced, depends largely on the success of expatriates' assignments—and that depends on the ability to manage the transitions for the expatriate and any accompanying family members well. The importance of this was determined by the 2015 Global Relocation Trends Survey, which found that "only 18% of respondents had formal career-management processes for international assignees and 19% of respondents had a formal candidate pool for international assignments." [10]

## Preparation, Adaptation, and Repatriation

*The top family challenges identified as very critical to companies were partner resistance (40%), family adjustment (40%), children's education (40%).* [11]

THE 2015 BROOKFIELD GLOBAL RELOCATIONS TRENDS SURVEY

Effective human resource management of a company's global cadre does not end with the overseas assignment. It ends with the successful repatriation of the executive into company headquarters. A study by Heidrick & Struggles, the international headhunting firm, revealed that international experience has become much more important to get to the top of the FTSE (London Stock Exchange) 100 companies than a decade ago. "Chief executives such as Mark Tucker at Prudential, who has experience in the United States and Asia, and Unilever's Patrick Cescau, who has worked in Europe, Asia and the United States, are becoming the norm in top companies." [12] Clearly, those executives and their companies have paid careful attention to what is necessary for successful assignments, career management, and repatriation of their experiences and skills. Such firms realize that long-term, proactive management of such critical resources should begin with the end of the current assignment in mind—that is, it should begin with plans for the repatriation of the executive as part of his or her career path. The management of the reentry phase of the career cycle is as vital as the management of the cross-cultural entry and training. Otherwise, the long-term benefits of that executive's international experience may be negated. Shortsightedly, many companies do little to minimize the potential effects of **reverse culture shock** (return shock). In fact, a KPMG survey concluded that "25 percent of organizations surveyed do not know if assignees have left the organization within 12 months of returning from international assignment. For repatriated assignees that are tracked as leaving the organization soon after returning from assignment, the overriding reason cited is the lack of an appropriate job after repatriation."[13] For smaller companies, little, if any pre- or post-assignment counseling was provided.

A study by Lazarova and Caligiuri with 58 expatriates from four North American companies found that repatriates who received supportive practices from their firms felt that their companies had an interest in their careers and well-being and so were more likely to stay with the firm upon reentry. The expatriates cited the following HRM practices as important to them.

- Visible signs that the company values international experience
- Career planning sessions
- Communications with home office of details of the repatriation process
- Continuous communications with the home office
- Agreement about position upon repatriation[14]

Reverse culture shock occurs primarily because of the difficulty of reintegrating into the organization but also because, generally speaking, the longer a person is away, the more difficult it is to get back into the swing of things. Not only might the manager have been overlooked and lost in the shuffle of reorganization, but her or his whole family might have lost social contacts or jobs and feel out of step with their contemporaries. These feelings of alienation from what has always been perceived as home—because of the loss of contact with family, friends, and daily life—delay the resocialization process. Such a reaction is particularly serious if the family's overall financial situation has been hurt by the assignment and if the spouse's career has also been kept on hold while he or she was abroad.

For companies to maximize the long-term use of their global cadre, they need to make sure that the foreign assignment and the reintegration process are positive experiences. This means careful career planning, support while overseas, and use of the increased experience and skills of returned managers to benefit the home office

## The Role of the Expatriate Spouse

*We began to realize that the entire effectiveness of the assignment could be compromised by ignoring the spouse.*

STEVE FORD
*CORPORATION RELOCATIONS, HEWLETT-PACKARD*[15]

Many companies are beginning to recognize the importance of providing support for spouses and children—in particular because both spouses are often corporate fast-trackers and demand both sets of needs to be included on the bargaining table. Research shows that 83 percent of married expatriates were accompanied by their spouses. However, although about half of the spouses were employed before the assignment, only 11 percent were employed during the assignment.[16] "That's underscored by the fact that 61 percent of respondents noted that the impact of family issues on early returns from assignment was very critical or of high importance."[17] The 2015 Brookfield Survey found that candidates' "knowledge of career concerns is the second most noted reason for assignment refusal, and 35% of respondents indicated that spouse/partner career concerns were having an impact on their ability to attract employees for international assignments."[18]

Firms often use informal means, such as intercompany networking, to help find the trailing spouse a position in the same location. They know that with the increasing number of dual-career couples, if the spouse does not find a position, the manager will very likely turn down the assignment. They decline because they cannot afford to lose the income or because the spouse's career may be delayed entirely if he or she is out of the workforce for a few years. As women continue to move up the corporate ladder, the accompanying (trailing) spouse is often male. Companies such as Hewlett-Packard, Shell, Medtronic, and Monsanto offer a variety of options to address the dual-career dilemma.

Clearly, then, the selection process must include spouses, partners, and entire families. Global assignments must take account of the expatriate's personal concerns and future career; otherwise, the company will face the possibility of early return and a possible doubling of the chances for employee attrition. The GMAC survey revealed that the annual turnover rate is 13 percent for all employees but 25 percent for expatriate employees during assignments and 27 percent within one year of completing assignments. Those assignees indicated that they felt their firms did not appreciate the difficulties of their overseas stints; nor did they fully use the expatriates' skills on return to the home country.[19]

At Procter & Gamble, employees and spouses destined for China are sent to Beijing for two months of language training and cultural familiarization. Nissho Iwai, a Japanese trading company, gets together managers and spouses who are leaving Japan with foreign managers and spouses who are on their way there. In addition, the firm provides a year of language training and information and services for Japanese children to attend schools abroad.

## Expatriate Retention

*Managers returning from expatriate assignments are two to three times more likely to leave the company within a year because attention has not been paid to their careers and the way they fit back into the corporate structure back home.*[20]

Firms must design support services to provide timely help for the manager and, therefore, are part of the effective management of an overseas assignment. The overall transition process experienced by the company's international management cadre over time comprises three phases of transition and adjustment that must be managed for successful socialization to a new culture and resocialization back to the old culture. These phases are (1) the exit transition from the home country, the success of which will be determined largely by the quality of preparation the expatriate has received; (2) the entry transition to the host country, in which successful acculturation (or early exit) will depend largely on monitoring and support; and (3) the entry transition back to the home country or to a new host country, in which the level of reverse culture shock and the ease of re-acculturation will depend on previous stages of preparation and support.[21]

A company may derive many potential benefits from carefully managing the careers of its expatriates. By helping managers make the right moves for their careers, the company will be able to retain people with increasing global experience and skills.

However, from the individual manager's perspective, most people understand that no one can look out better for one's interests than oneself. With that in mind, managers must ask themselves, and their superiors, what role each overseas stint will play in career advancement and what proactive role each will play in one's own career. Retaining the returning expatriate within the company (assuming he or she has been effective) is vitally important to gain the knowledge and benefit from the assignment. Yet, as discussed earlier, the attrition rate for expatriates is about double that of non-expatriates for the following reasons.

- Expatriates are more marketable and receive more attractive offers from other employers.
- Expatriates find that their compensation packages on overseas assignments are more generous than at home and go from one company to another to take advantage of that.
- Expatriates feel unappreciated and dissatisfied both during and after the assignment and leave the company.[22]

It is essential, therefore, for the company to pay careful attention to maintaining and retaining the expatriate by managing both the assignment and the repatriation of the expatriate and the family.

# THE ROLE OF REPATRIATION IN DEVELOPING A GLOBAL MANAGEMENT CADRE

In the international assignment, both the manager and the company can benefit from the enhanced skills and experience the expatriate gains. Many returning executives report an improvement in their managerial skills and self-confidence. Some of these acquired skills, as reported by Adler, include the following.

- **Managerial skills, not technical skills:** Learning how to deal with a wide range of people, to adapt to their cultures through compromise, and not to be a dictator
- **Tolerance for ambiguity:** Making decisions with less information and more uncertainty about the process and the outcome
- **Multiple perspectives:** Learning to understand situations from the perspective of local employees and businesspeople
- **Ability to work with and manage others:** Learning patience and tolerance—realizing that managers abroad are in the minority among local people; learning to communicate more with others and empathize with them[23]

## Knowledge Transfer

In addition to the managerial and cross-cultural skills expatriates acquire, the company benefits from the knowledge and experience those managers gain about how to do business overseas and about new technology, local marketing, and competitive information. Expatriates have long served as facilitators of intra-firm knowledge transfer and application. Traditionally, it has been assumed that the role of expatriates is partly to bring knowledge from the corporate headquarters to subsidiaries; however, it is clear that there is a potential strategic advantage when expatriates acquiring knowledge while on international assignment bring it back to the center of the organization or disseminate it across other subsidiaries.[24] Consider, for example, Claire Molyneux, Associate Marketing Director for P&G West Africa. Claire, who was born and raised in England, started her P&G career there in 1998 as an assistant brand manager. Over the years, she worked for P&G in Geneva and Israel. In 2008, Claire was assigned to Nigeria as marketing director for Ariel detergent, Duracell batteries, and Gillette razors and to lead research into West Africa's consumers. Claire has taken up the challenge, saying, "Africa has this huge diversity. Our job is to find the similarities."[25] Consider the wealth of knowledge and information she has gathered in those ten years—cultural, consumer- and product-related, and technical as well as her contacts around the world—that she is transferring across subsidiaries and benefiting the organization. Claire's situation is an example of the five types of knowledge gained abroad that Berthoin discusses.

- Knowledge about **what** (such as differences in customer preferences)
- Knowledge about **why** (e.g., understanding how cultural differences affect cross-cultural understanding)
- Knowledge about **how** (e.g., management skills such as delegating responsibilities)
- Knowledge about **when** (e.g., knowledge about the effect of timing)
- Knowledge about **who** (e.g., relationships created over the life of an assignment)[26]

Berthoin also points out that expatriate experience not only brings knowledge about culture differences but also creates insights about HQ–subsidiary relations, from which ideas about improving business could be derived.[27] However, as Lazarova and Tarique found, "repatriates' motivation to contribute to collective organizational learning is primarily driven by the fit between their individual career objectives and the career development opportunities offered by the organization upon return."[28] They found that several conditions have to be met to transfer knowledge successfully. First, the repatriates have to (a) have valuable knowledge to transfer and (b) be motivated to transfer that knowledge; secondly, organizations need to (a) have the right tools to capture knowledge, and (b) create the right incentives for repatriates to share their knowledge. Knowledge transfer is optimized when the type of knowledge repatriates gain is matched by the right knowledge transfer mechanisms—for example, by assigning repatriates to strategic teams—and when career opportunities the organization provides are congruent with

**EXHIBIT 10-1** Variables Influencing Success of Knowledge Transfer from Repatriated Manager

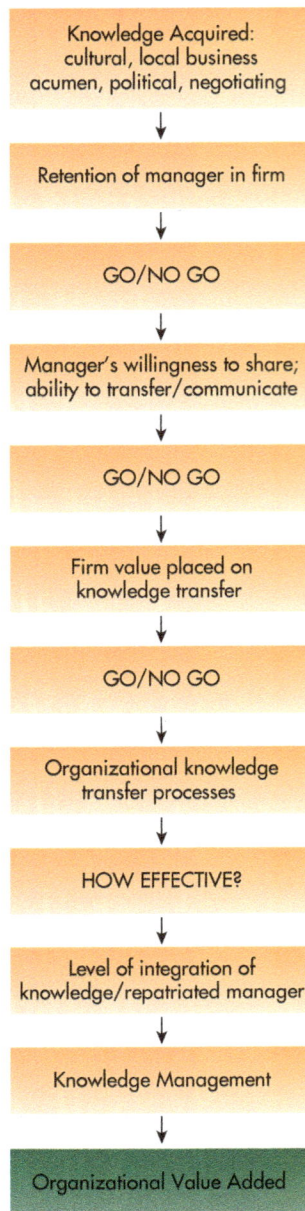

*Source:* Based on M. Lazarova and Ibraiz Tarique, "Knowledge Transfer Upon Repatriation," *Journal of World Business*, 40, 4 (2005): 361–373.

repatriate career goals and aspirations.[29] Exhibit 10-1 illustrates the conditions and process by which knowledge may be successfully integrated into the organization.

The company should therefore position itself to benefit from that enhanced management knowledge if it wants to develop a globally experienced management cadre—an essential ingredient for global competitiveness—in particular when there is a high degree of shared learning among the organization's global managers. If the company cannot retain good returning managers, their potential shared knowledge is not only lost but also conveyed to another organization that hires that person. This can be very detrimental to the company's competitive stance. Some companies are becoming quite savvy about how to use technology to employ shared knowledge to develop their global management cadre, to service their customers better, and—as a side benefit—to store the knowledge and expertise of their managers around the world in case they leave the company. That knowledge, it can be argued, is an asset in which the company has invested large amounts of resources. A successful repatriation program, then, starts before the assignment. The company's top management must set up a culture that conveys the message that the organization regards international assignments as an integral part of continuing career development and advancement and that it values the skills of the returnees. The company's objectives should be reflected in its long-range plans, commitment, and compensation on behalf of the expatriate. Unfortunately, as indicated by the respondents in the 2015 Brockfield survey, most companies do very little to minimize attrition by returning international assignees, with only 14 percent guaranteeing a position upon the assignee's return.[30] However, GE is one company that sets a model for effective expatriate career management. With its 500 expatriates worldwide, it takes care to select only the best managers for overseas jobs and then commits to placing them in specific positions upon reentry. The following Under the Lens section illustrates some expatriates' experiences that contribute to their firms' store of knowledge.

## UNDER THE LENS

### Expatriates' Careers Add to Knowledge Transfer[31]

*Brazil's distinctive culture, the lack of English spoken at street level and the country's labyrinthine politics and bureaucracy make it hard to import foreign talent. Meanwhile, the global financial crisis is also prompting more Brazilian expatriates to consider going back.*[32]

Developments around the world and in an expatriate's original country can redirect an expatriate's career choices in unexpected ways and, at the same time, affect the firms involved. Such was the case for Casio Calil. As reported in the *Financial Times*, he left Brazil in 1987, in very poor economic times, to seek his fortune elsewhere. After stints in Japan, Australia, and Ireland, he went to New York and, in 2005, took a job with J. P. Morgan's investment bank. Since then, through his business contacts in Brazil, he realized that the expanding economy and opportunities in Brazil made a move back home very attractive. Therefore, in 2011, he found himself head of J. P. Morgan Asset Management in Sao Paulo. He is now one of many Brazilians bringing their international experience and knowledge back to help a rapidly growing country with a shortage of management talent.[33]

Sometimes those world developments are less positive, causing unwanted upheaval to the lives of expats and their families. Such has been the case in Libya. After booming with international businesses taking advantage of the oil-rich country, the war to overthrow Col. Gaddafi drove out foreign businesses and their expatriates and families, some of whom had come to regard it as home. In 2012, after a year of disrupted lives, those expatriates were gradually going back and hoping that the business climate would improve after elections in June 2012. If not:

*The challenges for conducting business in Libya under its old rules are daunting. Regulators required companies to hire large proportions of Libyan workers and managers even if they were unqualified. Land ownership was impossible. Even majority ownership in joint ventures did not translate into authority over strategic decisions.*[34]

Similar upheavals were experienced by expatriates in Japan and, of course, the Japanese themselves during their triple disaster in 2011 composed of the earthquake, tsunami, and nuclear meltdown. Foreign companies naturally wanted to bring their staff out of danger, and the expatriates wanted to get their families out of harm's way, when the U.S. embassy sent in planes to ferry them out. However, the Japanese felt betrayed by the expatriates leaving while they worked through the crisis. In their anger, they were calling those who left *flyjin* as a take-off on their term *gaijin*, meaning foreigner. The anger the Japanese felt toward those who left is largely based on the difference between the cultural attitude of the Japanese that the company and the family are almost one entity, compared with that in the West, where family comes before the company. One expat clearly recognized this.

*If I had left as the president, my role as a leader would have been diminished," said Gerry Dorizas, the president of Volkswagen AG's operations in Japan, who has been in that role four years. "We've been very transparent."*[35]

There is no doubt that the events in Japan and Libya, rare as they are, have proven to add valuable experience and knowledge transfer for those expatriates and their companies about how to prepare for and deal with such events and their repercussions.

# GLOBAL MANAGEMENT TEAMS

MNCs realize it is essential to maximize their human assets in the form of global management teams so they can share resources and manage the transnational transfer of knowledge. The term **global management team** describes a collection of managers in or from several countries who must rely on group collaboration if each member is to experience optimum success and goal achievement. Whirlpool International, for example, is a U.S.–Dutch joint venture with administrative headquarters in Comerio, Italy, where it is managed by a Swede and a six-person management team from Sweden, Italy, Holland, the United States, Belgium, and Germany. To achieve the individual and collective goals of the team members, international teams must have a global perspective but at the same time share the expectations of the corporate culture; they also must be glocal—able to respond to the local market while still be adept at coordinating the parts of the firm. The role and importance of international teams increase as the firm progresses in its scope of international activity. Similarly, the manner in which multicultural interaction affects the firm's operations depends on its level of international involvement, its environment, and its strategy.

The team's ability to work effectively together is crucial to the company's success. In addition, technology facilitates effective and efficient teamwork around the world. This was found by the Timberland U.K. sales conference planning team. In the past, the company's large sales conferences were cumbersome to organize because their offices were in France, Germany, Spain, Italy, and the United Kingdom. Then the team started using the British Telecom (BT) Conference Call system for the arrangements, which saved them much travel and expense. The company subsequently adopted the BT Conference Call system for the executive team's country meetings. Teleconferencing and videoconferencing are now much of the way of life for global businesses. However, research indicates that face-to-face meetings are the best way to kick off a virtual team project so that the members can agree on goals and schedules and who is responsible for what. IBM project teams start with all members in a personal meeting to help to build an understanding of the other members' cultures and set up a trusting relationship.[36]

For global organizations and alliances, the same cross-cultural interactions hold as in MNCs and, in addition, considerably more interaction takes place with the external environment at all levels of the organization. Therefore, global teamwork is vital, as are the pockets of cross-cultural teamwork and interactions that occur at many boundaries.[37] For the global company, worldwide competition and markets necessitate global teams for strategy development, both for the organization as a whole and for the local units to respond to their markets.

When a firm responds to its global environment with a global strategy and then organizes with a networked glocal structure, various types of cross-border teams are necessary for global integration and local differentiation. These include teams between and among headquarters and subsidiaries; transnational project teams, often operating on a virtual basis; and teams coordinating alliances outside the organization.[38] In joint ventures, in particular, multicultural teams work at all levels of strategic planning and implementation as well as on the production and assembly floor. Clearly, the team's success is highly dependent on the members' ability to understand the culture and communication style of members in other countries. The United Kingdom is one example where considerable differences in behavior, expectations of business protocol, and communication are often dismissed by other Westerners because of the assumption of similarity between English-speaking countries. This brings to mind a quote often attributed to Winston Churchill, "Britain and America are two nations divided by a common language."

## Virtual Transnational Teams

*Virtual groups, whose members interact through computer-mediated communication systems (such as desktop video conferencing systems, email, group support systems, the Internet, and intranets), are linked across time, space, and organizational boundaries.[39]*

As illustrated in the diagram, advances in communication now facilitate virtual global teams formed of people working from home or work, while travelling, or anywhere in the world, using their laptops or tablets, Wi-Fi, and smartphones. **Virtual global teams**, a horizontal networked structure with people around the world conducting meetings and exchanging information through the Internet, enable the organization to capitalize on 24-hour productivity. In this way, too, knowledge is shared across business units and across cultures.[40] The advantages and cost savings of virtual global teams are frequently offset by their challenges—including cultural misunderstandings and the logistics of differences in time and space, as shown in Exhibit 10-2. Group members must build their teams while bearing in mind the group diversity and the need for careful communication.[41]

**Virtual Transnational Teams**

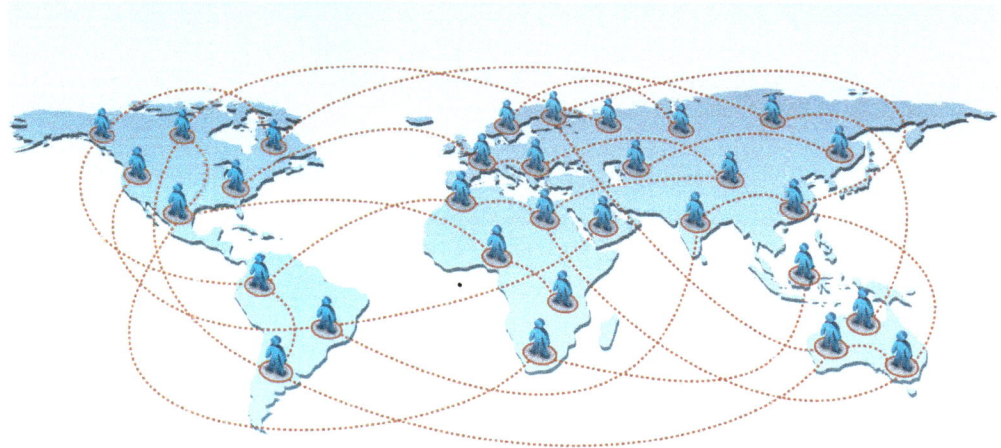

*Source:* Janos Levente/Shutterstock

**EXHIBIT 10-2** Operational Challenges for Global Virtual Teams

| | |
|---|---|
| Geographic Dispersal: | The complexity of scheduling communications such as teleconferences and video conferences across multiple time zones, holidays, and so on. Lack of face-to-face meetings to establish trust or for cross-interaction processes such as brainstorming. |
| Cultural Differences: | Variations in attitudes and expectations toward time, planning, scheduling, risk taking, money, relationship building, and so on. Differences in goal sets and work styles arising out of such variables as individualism/ collectivism; the relative value of work compared with other life factors; and variable sets of assumptions, norms, patterns of behavior. |
| Language and Communications: | Translation difficulties, or at least variations in accents, semantics, terminology, or local jargon. Lack of personal and physical contact, which greatly inhibits trust and relationship building in many countries; the social dynamics change. Lack of visibility of nonverbal cues makes interpretation difficult and creates two-way noise in the communication process. |
| Technology: | Variations in availability, speed, acceptability, and cost of equipment necessary for meetings and communications through computer-aided systems. Variable skill levels and willingness to interact through virtual media. |

*Source:* Some of this content is based on Kenneth W. Kerber and Anthony F. Buono, "Leadership Challenges in Global Virtual Teams: Lessons from the Field," *SAM Advanced Management Journal* 69, no. 4 (2004): 4–10.

Virtual team leaders from Alcoa Company's operations in 20 diverse countries have noted many of these challenges. (Alcoa is the world leader in the production of aluminum and has 63,000 employees in 31 countries.) The teams are called parallel Global Virtual Teams (pGVTs)—teams that operate outside the formal structure, focusing on innovation and improvement. All their meetings are conducted electronically through videoconferencing, teleconferencing, discussion boards, email, instant messaging, knowledge repositories, and planning and scheduling tools.

*There is clearly a cross-cultural issue here—one that is particularly important to the success of pGVTs as, more than other forms of team, their success vitally depends on all members contributing and debating ideas.*

"LESSONS FROM ALCOA,"
*ORGANIZATIONAL DYNAMICS*[42]

Cordery et al.'s studies of Alcoa's teams highlighted leadership problems. One GVT leader described the problems in not always being able to interpret or understand the subtleties of language being expressed and respond accordingly when sharing ideas because of the inability to observe the body language of members. She observed, "People from some cultures will say, 'yes' even if they have not understood. They do not feel comfortable asking you to repeat what they have not understood, being in such a large group. Others will commit to do almost anything (quite willingly) in the meeting, but it doesn't get done."

A survey of 200 of Alcoa's virtual team members by Cordery et al. revealed that they view successful team leaders as having the following skills: *interpersonal facilitation*—the ability to build teams and resolve conflicts; *task facilitation*—the ability to convey goals and train team members to use the collaborative technology effectively; *resource acquisition;* and *external alignment/vision*—that is, the ability to mesh the team's activities with the organization's goals.[43]

In a separate survey of 440 training and development professionals across a variety of industries conducted by Rosen, Furst, and Blackburn, the respondents indicated which training techniques for virtual teams were more effective than others and reported which of those programs were most needed in the future. The relative priority of the training modules is shown in Exhibit 10-3.[44]

**EXHIBIT 10-3** Virtual Team Training

| **Importance of Virtual Team Training Modules (in order of value and effectiveness)** |
|---|
| Training on how to lead a virtual team meeting |
| Leader training on how to coach and mentor team members virtually |
| Training on how to monitor team progress, diagnose team problems, and take corrective actions |
| Training to use communications technologies |
| Leader training on how to manage team boundaries, negotiate member time commitments with local managers, and stay in touch with team sponsors |
| Training on how to establish trust and resolve conflicts in virtual teams |
| Communications skills training—cultural sensitivity, etc. |
| Team-building training for new virtual teams |
| Training to select the appropriate technologies to fit team tasks |
| Leader training on how to evaluate and reward individual contributions on the virtual team |
| Training on how to select virtual team members, establish a virtual team charter, and assign virtual team roles |
| Realistic preview of virtual team challenges |
| Training on what qualities to look for in prospective virtual team members and leaders |

*Source:* Based on B. Rosen, S. Furst, and R. Blackburn, "Training for Virtual Teams: An Investigation of Current Practices and Future Needs," *Human Resources Management* 45, No. 2 (2006), pp. 229–247.

### Managing Transnational Teams

The ability to develop and lead effective transnational teams (whether they interact virtually, physically, or, as is most often the case, a mixture of both) is essential in light of the increasing proliferation of foreign subsidiaries, joint ventures, and other transnational alliances. The primary corporate question is how to integrate a diverse pool of cultural values, traditions. and norms in order to be competitive. These challenges were experienced when Nomura, Japan's largest investment bank, acquired most of Lehman Brothers' operations in Asia, Europe, and the Middle East in October 2008, after Lehman's collapse. Nomura had to absorb hundreds of Lehman employees immediately. Although Nomura is the acquirer, it is trying to transform its own culture to be more globally competitive. As observed by one manager:

> Nomura has "a completely domestic culture"... one based on Japanese customs of employment, and where company loyalty is strong, decision-making is slow and tolerance for risk is low.[45]

Both the Japanese and the Americans trying to work together felt the cultural divide. In particular, the Japanese were shocked when Nomura's management introduced American-style pay and career structures.[46]

Teams comprising people located in far-flung operations are faced with often-conflicting goals of achieving greater efficiency across those operations, responding to local differences, and facilitating organizational learning across boundaries; conflicts arise based on cultural differences, local work norms and environments, and varied time zones. A study by Joshi et al. of a 30-member team of human resource (HR) managers in six countries in the Asia-Pacific region showed that network analysis of the various interactions among team members can reveal when and where negative cross-cultural conflicts occur and, thus, provide top management with information for conflict resolution so that a higher level of synergy may be attained among the group members. The advantages of synergy include a greater opportunity for global competition (by being able to share experiences, technology, and a pool of international managers) and a greater opportunity for cross-cultural understanding and exposure to different viewpoints. The disadvantages include problems resulting from differences in language, communication, and varying managerial styles; complex decision-making processes; fewer promotional opportunities; personality conflicts, often resulting from stereotyping and prejudice; and greater complexity in the workplace.[47] In the Joshi study, the greatest conflict and, therefore, lack of synergy, was not, as one would expect, resulting from the headquarters subsidiary power divide. Rather, the critical conflicts were between the Country A subsidiary and Country B subsidiary, given the required communication and workflow patterns between them. What are other ways that management can ascertain how well its international teams are performing and what areas need to be improved? In recognizing the areas needing better team management, executives in a study by Govindarajan and Gupta ranked five key tasks based on their level of importance, as follows.

### Tasks for Global Business Teams[48]

- Cultivating trust among members
- Overcoming communication barriers
- Aligning goals of individual team members
- Obtaining clarity regarding team objectives
- Ensuring that the team possesses necessary knowledge and skills

The managers also rated the level of difficulty to accomplish that task. The researchers concluded from their study that the ability to cultivate trust among team members is critical to the success of global business teams if they want to minimize conflict and encourage cooperation.[49]

Following are some general recommendations the researchers make for improving global teamwork.

- Cultivate a culture of trust; one way to do this is by scheduling face-to-face meetings early on, even if later meetings will be virtual.
- Rotate meeting locations; this develops global exposure for all team members and legitimizes each person's position.
- Rotate and diffuse team leadership.
- Link rewards to team performance.
- Build social networks among managers from different countries.[50]

What other techniques do managers actually use to deal with the challenge of achieving cross-cultural collaboration in multinational horizontal projects? A comparative study of European project groups in several countries by Sylvie Chevrie revealed three main strategies.[51]

- **Drawing upon individual tolerance and self-control:** In this R&D consortium, the Swiss manager treated all team members the same, ignoring cultural differences, and the team members coexisted with patience and compromise. Many of the members said they were used to multinational projects and just tried to focus on technical issues.
- **Trial-and-error processes coupled with personal relationships:** This is a specific strategy in which the project manager sets up social events to facilitate acquaintance of the team members with one another. Then, they discover, through trial and error, what procedures will be acceptable to the group.
- **Setting up transnational cultures:** Here the managers used the common professional, or occupational, culture, such as the engineering profession, to bring the disparate members together within a common understanding and process.

The managers in the study admitted their solutions were not perfect but met their needs as best they could in the situation. Chevrie suggests that, where possible, a "cultural mediator" should be used who helps team members interpret and understand one another and come to an agreement about processes to achieve organizational goals.[52]

# THE ROLE OF WOMEN IN INTERNATIONAL MANAGEMENT

Whether in global management teams, as expatriates, or as host-country nationals, the importance of women as a valuable, and often-underused resource should not be overlooked in IHRM efforts to maximize the company's global management cadre. On February 26, 2015, Christine Lagarde, Managing Director of the International Monetary Fund (IMF), explained on various news programs its committee's action plan to discuss with heads of state what can be done to improve their country's economic progress by removing or lessening the roadblocks to females working there—cultural and practical. For example, in Japan, she proposed that more women could take jobs if the government instituted a child-care plan. And, in fact, in August 2015, Prime Minister Shinzo Abe announced a new law requiring companies with over 300 employees to set targets for hiring more women managers - although child-care was not addressed and remains an obstacle; at that time women comprised only 11 percent of supervisory or management positions. This move was heralded as:

*A Step Forward for 'Womenomics' in Japan.*

THE WALL STREET JOURNAL
*AUGUST 28, 2015*[53]

The changing roles of women in management is explored in the following Management in Action feature.

## MANAGEMENT IN ACTION
*Women in Management Around the World*

*More CEOs, More Industries, More Power, More Challenges*

FORTUNE.COM[54]

Although it is clear that women are increasingly making their way into the international management cadre, their numbers and clout vary greatly around the world.

The 2015 ranking by *Fortune* magazine of the most powerful women in business in the United States includes a record 27 CEOs of large companies. At the top of the list are Mary Barra, CEO of General Motors; and Indra Nooyi, PepsiCo Chairman and CEO, the Indian-born strategist and former CFO and president, followed by Ginni Rommetty, Chairman, CEO, and President of IBM—and at number 51—Taylor Swift, singer, Music and Technology Industry Disrupter! The article also includes a separate list of "Most Powerful Women: International." For the EMEA region, with 10 of the top 25 based in England, the list includes Ana Botin, Chairman Banco Santander, Spain; and Maria Ramos, Group CEO, Barclays Africa. For the Asia-Pacific region, first was Chanda Kochhar, Managing Director and CEO, ICICI Bank, India, and includes Chua Sock Koon, Group CEO of Singapore Telecommunications, along with eleven from Mainland China.' Eighteen of the top 25 most powerful women of the Asia-Pacific region were in India or China. *Fortune* also pointed out that Alibaba is a great company for fostering talented women and featured Maggie Wu, CFO of Alibaba, and Lucy Peng, Alibaba's head of HR and the affiliated Small and Micro Financial Services Co, which owns Alipay.[55]

However, although women's advancement in some global companies is impressive, it is still true that there are limitations on managerial opportunities for many women in their own country—some more than others—and there are even more limitations on their opportunities for expatriate assignments

A report by the World Economic Forum stated that companies in the United States, Spain, Canada, and Finland lead the world in employing the largest numbers of women from entry level to senior management. Yet the report also found that, "despite increasing awareness of gender disparities in the workplace, women at many of the world's top companies continued to lag behind their male peers in many areas, including pay and opportunities for professional advancement."[56] In addition, the study found that overall only 5 percent of the chief executives of the 600 companies surveyed were women. Finnish companies were at the top with 13 percent, Norway and Turkey with 12 percent, and Italy and Brazil with 11 percent.[57]

> *Gender diversity is gaining ground in Latin America, yet women in the region are still greatly under-represented in top management—even though they are more likely than men to say they want to advance their careers.*

MCKINSEY GLOBAL SURVEY RESULTS
*AUGUST 2013*[58]

The reasons for the different opportunities for women among various countries can often be traced to the cultural expectations of the host countries—the same cultural values that keep women in these countries from the managerial ranks. For example, in a McKinsey 2013 survey of what gender-diversity measures CEOs are taking, the results for Latin America showed a considerable discrepancy by country. In Brazil, 59 percent say they have programs to recruit and retain women; in Chile, only 10 percent acknowledge they have taken such steps.[59]

Cultural expectations may also contribute to different opportunities for women at the top levels between northern and southern Europe. For example, Maitland reported in an article entitled "the North–South Divide in Europe, Inc.", that "[w]omen are far more likely to serve on the boards of Scandinavia's biggest companies than Italy's or Spain's, and attitudes to their promotion remain deeply split."[60]

In their research in 32 countries on the cultural indicators of the reasons for the variation in the participation of women in management around the world, Toh and Leonardelli found a relationship between loose and tight cultures and the presence of women in the firms of those countries. They conclude that in tight cultures, such as Germany and South Korea, the norms of expected behavior are more clear and rigid, with norms of traditional male attitudes, and thus have far fewer women in leadership positions than those in loose cultures such as New Zealand and Hungary.[61] In loose cultures, people are more open to change and variations in expectations, so the general attitude in the leadership of firms in those cultures is one of a more open and positive perspective of women leaders.

> *Men from Australia, a looser culture, were more likely to rate the leadership styles of women leaders as effective, compared to men from Malaysia, a tighter culture.*

SOO MIN TOH AND GEOFFREY J. LEONARDELLI
*2013*[62]

The problem is even more acute at the boardroom level. Whereas in top boardrooms only 5 percent were female in Italy, and 10 percent in Spain, women occupied 32 percent of board seats in the largest companies in Norway and 27 percent in Sweden. Overall, over half of major European companies have no female representation on their executive committees.[63] The female composition on executive committees in 2010 was similarly divided although overall lower than the female board composition. Whereas Sweden had 17 percent representation, followed by the United States and Britain with 14 percent, at low end was Brazil with 6 percent and Germany with 2 percent.[64]

Given the powerful figure at the top in Germany—Chancellor Angela Merkel—it seems surprising to see the low female participation at the top levels, "but a decade of earnest vows from the corporate sector has not dented male-dominated Deutschland AG…all 30 DAX companies are run by men."[65] Clearly, traditional cultural values about gender roles in Germany, as well as lifestyle and laws, can account for much of the disparity in Germany. For example, most children attend school only in the mornings, which restricts the ability for both parents to work. Nevertheless, in spite of considerable recent government encouragement in its attempts to capitalize on females as an economic resource, only about 14 percent of German mothers with one child resume full-time work and only 6 percent of those with two children. Even though the German birthrate—at 1.39—is the lowest in Europe, and even though there is a generous 14-month shared parental leave after childbirth, conservative family values that expect mothers to stay home with their children still predominate.

Opportunities for indigenous female employees to move up the managerial ladder in a given culture depend on the values and expectations regarding the role of women in that society. In Japan, for example, the workplace has traditionally been a male domain as far as managerial careers are concerned (although rapid changes are now taking place, as previously pointed out). To the older generation, a working married woman represented a loss of face to the husband because it implied that he was not able to support her. The younger generation and increased global competitiveness have brought some changes to traditional values regarding women's roles in Japan. More than 60 percent of Japanese women are now employed, including half of Japanese mothers, but largely in part-time and temporary positions. How and when the new law, and cultural changes will affect the number of Japanese women in managerial positions remains to be seen. Currently, only about 11 percent are in managerial positions, compared with about 45 percent in the United States and 30 percent in Sweden, for example. One can understand the problems Japanese women face when trying to enter and progress in managerial careers when we review the experiences of Yuko Suzuki, who went into business for herself after the advertising company she worked for went bankrupt. However, she could not gain respect or even attention from customers, who often asked her who her boss was after she finished a presentation. She eventually hired a man to accompany her, which increased her sales, but, to her dismay, customers would only establish eye contact with him, even though she was doing the talking and he had nothing to do with the company.[66] Japanese labor economists observe that, "Japan has gone as far as it can go with a social model that consists of men filling all of the economic, management and political roles."[67]

Although the variation in women's roles around the world can be attributed to complex social and cultural issues, firms ought to be aware of the effects on their bottom line. Research by Catalyst showed that—of the 353 Fortune 500 companies they surveyed—the quartile with the largest proportion of women in top management had a return on equity of 35.1 percent higher than the quartile with the lowest female representation.[68]

The lack of expatriates who are female or represent other minority groups does not reflect their lack of desire to take overseas assignments. Indeed, studies indicate women's strong willingness to work abroad and their considerable success on their assignments. For example, Adler's major study of North American women working as expatriate managers in countries around the world showed that they are, for the most part, successful.[69]

Women and minorities represent a significant resource for overseas assignments—whether as expatriates or as host-country nationals—a resource that U.S. companies underuse. Adler studied this phenomenon regarding women and recommends that businesses (1) avoid assuming that a female executive will fail because of the way she will be received or because of problems female spouses experience; (2) avoid assuming that a woman will not want to go overseas; and (3) give female managers every chance to succeed by giving them the titles, status, and recognition appropriate to the position—as well as sufficient time to be effective.[70]

# WORKING WITHIN LOCAL LABOR RELATIONS SYSTEMS

*If you have to close a plant in Italy, in France, in Spain or in Germany, you have to discuss the possibility with the state, the local communities, the trade unions; everybody feels entitled to intervene…even the Church.*

JACOB VITTORELLI
*FORMER DEPUTY CHAIRMAN OF PIRELLI*[71]

An important variable in implementing strategy and maximizing host-country human resources for productivity is that of the labor relations environment and system within which the managers of a multinational enterprise (MNE) will operate in a foreign country. Differences in economic, political, and legal systems result in considerable variation in labor relations systems across countries. It is the responsibility of the IHRM function to monitor the labor relations systems in host countries and advise local managers accordingly. In fact, that information should be considered one input to the strategic decision of whether to operate in a particular country or region.

### The Impact of Unions on Businesses

European businesses, for example, continue to be undermined by their poor labor relations and by inflexible regulations. As a result, businesses have to move jobs overseas to cut labor costs, resulting from a refusal of unions to grant any reduction in employment protection or benefits to keep the jobs at home. In addition, non-European firms wishing to operate in Europe have to weigh carefully the labor relations systems and their potential effect on strategic and operational decisions, as illustrated by Ford's experiences, described in the accompanying Under the Lens feature.

## UNDER THE LENS

*Ford's Bitter Struggle to Close a Plant in Belgium*[72]

When Ford announced that it would close its factory in Genk, Belgium, at the end of 2014, and move its production to Spain, its 4,300 employees, the approximately 5,000 associated suppliers and works, the community, and Ford, paid a high price.

The economic downturn in Europe severely restricted consumer demand for cars, resulting in the need to close three European plants, including Genk, to cut about 18 percent of its productive capacity. (Ford also has plants in Germany, Spain, and the United Kingdom, totaling 15,000 employees.) The news triggered violent protests in Cologne, Germany, at the site of Ford's European headquarters. At the Genk factory, union representatives announced the decision over loudspeakers as soon as it was announced, resulting in workers barricading factory gates, thus restricting any movement of about 6,000 newly built Mondeo cars, S-Max minivans, and Galaxy vans that had already been ordered. This caused a backlog, which halted production for months. About 20,000 people staged a protest in Genk; the factory workers there were joined by workers from other factories who traveled to join the protest. The proposal was met with shock throughout Belgium because of the likely negative impact on the Belgian economy and because Ford had committed to operating there until 2020. The proposal also sparked criticism because a statute in Belgium requires firms planning large cutbacks to consult with employees to seek other options.

The three trade unions decided right away to accept the closure in favor of securing a favorable deal, but the workers disagreed and staged walkouts, angry that they had been left out of the negotiations between management and unions, resulting in the assignment of a government arbitrator. The workers did not accept the proposals. Protests and picketing by the workers and suppliers followed. As of January 2013, the Genk plant had been shut for three months due to no resolution with the workers, and Ford tried to meet orders from existing inventory. Even after management and unions had an agreement that the workers approved, production could not resume because protestors blocked access to supply deliveries. Other staged protests blocked the union leaders from leaving the building after a meeting at Ford's headquarters in Cologne.

In the end, Ford settled with a labor agreement that allowed the company to close the plant, but at a high price. In all, five unions were involved in the protracted negotiations, and Ford ended up paying $750 million in severance pay to its workers at the Genk plant—about 11,000 workers, including suppliers. The Genk workers received about $190,000. In all, Ford's bill for closing the Genk plant and two in England was estimated at about $1 billion, but it compared that to the losses of about $1 billion in 2013, which would have continued.

Ford is one of few companies to go up against the fierce resistance of Europe's powerful unions and its politicians, illustrating the difficulty and expense of closing auto plants in Europe compared with those in the United States. Few companies dared close plants in Europe after the 2008–2009 financial crisis, compared with more than a dozen plants in the United States. The European labor laws support unions, even in their protests, far more than in the United States.

These situations raise a number of issues for managers regarding strategic decisions for overseas plant locations, relationships with host unions and communities, and sustainability and social responsibility.

With the economic downturn in Europe, however, recent changes bring relief to businesses in Europe as some unions grant concessions to firms to keep their jobs. Unions in Germany, France, and Italy have been losing their battle to derail labor-market reforms by the governments in those countries, which are increasingly concerned that excess regulation and benefits to workers are smothering growth opportunities. Firms such as the Swedish furniture company IKEA, for example, have set up plants abroad. IKEA opened its non-unionized plant in Danville, southern Virginia, where the unemployment rate is very high, and received incentive grants of $12 million. However, in July 2011, employees at the plant voted 221 to 69 to allow the International Association of Machinists and Aerospace Workers union to negotiate salary and benefits with the retailer's manufacturing subsidiary, Swedwood. The union organizers claimed that IKEA's high corporate standards for employees stopped at the U.S. border and that employees were "grossly underpaid compared to their Swedish counterparts, suffer high injury rates, are forced to work overtime, and demoted or fired for expressing union sympathies."[73]

The term **labor relations** refers to the process through which managers and workers determine their workplace relationships. This process may be through verbal agreement and job descriptions or through a union's written labor contract, which has been reached through negotiation in **collective bargaining** between workers and managers. The labor contract determines rights regarding workers' pay, benefits, job duties, firing procedures, retirement, layoffs, and so on.

The prevailing labor relations system in a country is important to the international manager because it can constrain the strategic choices and operational activities of a firm operating there. The three main dimensions of the labor-management relationship that the manager will consider are (1) the participation of labor in the affairs of the firm, especially as this affects performance and well-being; (2) the role and impact of unions in the relationship; and (3) specific human resource policies in terms of recruitment, training, and compensation.[74] Constraints take the form of (1) wage levels that are set by union contracts and leave the foreign firm little flexibility to be globally competitive, (2) limits on the ability of the foreign firm to vary employment levels when necessary, and (3) limitations on the global integration of operations of the foreign firm because of incompatibility and the potential for industrial conflict.[75]

## Organized Labor around the World

The percentage of the workforce in trade unions in industrialized countries has declined in the past decade, most notably in Europe. In the United States, union membership fell from a 20.1 percent in 1983 to 11.1 percent in 2014.[76] This global trend is attributable to various factors, including an increase in the proportion of white-collar and service workers to manufacturing workers, a rising proportion of temporary and part-time workers, offshoring of jobs to gain lower wage costs, and a reduced belief in unions by the younger generations. In addition, the global economic decline and loss of jobs has put downward pressure on union demands and power when the focus changed to job retention rather than increased benefits.

The numbers do not show the nature of the system in each country. In most countries, a single dominant industrial relations system applies to almost all workers. Both Canada and the United States have two systems—one for the organized and one for the unorganized. Each, according to Adams, has "different rights and duties of the parties, terms and conditions of employment, and structures and processes of decision making." In North America, an agent represents unionized employees, whereas unorganized employees can only bargain individually, usually with little capability to affect major strategic decisions or policies or conditions of employment.[77]

The traditional trade union structures in Western industrialized societies have been in *industrial unions*, representing all grades of employees in a specific industry, and *craft unions*, based on certain occupational skills. More recently, the structure has been conglomerate unions, representing members in several industries—for example, the metalworkers unions in Europe, which cut across industries, and general unions, which are open to most employees within a country.[78] The system of union representation varies among countries. In the United States, most unions are national and represent specific groups of workers—for example, truck drivers or airline pilots—so a company may have to deal with several national unions. A single U.S. firm—rather than an association of firms representing a worker classification—engages in its own negotiations. In Japan, on the other hand, it is common for a union to represent all workers in a company. In recent years, company unions in Japan have increasingly coordinated their activities, leading to some lengthy strikes.

Industrial labor relations systems across countries can be understood only in the context of the variables in their environment and the sources of origins of unions. These include government regulation of unions, economic and unemployment factors, technological issues, and the influence of religious organizations. Any of the basic processes or concepts of labor unions, therefore, may vary across countries, depending on where and how the parties have their power and achieve their objectives such as through parliamentary action in Sweden. For example, collective bargaining in the United States and Canada refers to negotiations between a labor union local and management. However, in Europe, collective bargaining takes place between the employer's organization and a trade union at the industry level.[79] This difference means that North America's decentralized, plant-level, collective agreements are more detailed than Europe's industry-wide agreements because of the complexity of negotiating myriad details in multi-employer bargaining. In Germany and Austria, for example, such details are delegated to works councils by legal mandate.[80]

The resulting agreements from bargaining also vary around the world. A written, legally binding agreement for a specific period, common in Northern Europe and North America, is less prevalent in southern Europe and Britain. In Britain, France, and Italy, bargaining is frequently informal and results in a verbal agreement valid only until one party wishes to renegotiate.[81]

Other variables of the collective bargaining process are the objectives of the bargaining and the enforceability of collective agreements. Because of these differences, managers in MNEs overseas realize that they must adapt their labor relations policies to local conditions and regulations. They also need to bear in mind that, although U.S. union membership has declined by about 50 percent in the past 30 years, in Europe, overall, membership is still quite high, particularly in Italy and the United Kingdom—though it, too, has been falling, but from much higher levels.

Most Europeans are covered by collective agreements, whereas most Americans are not. Unions in Europe are part of a national cooperative culture among government, unions, and management, and they hold more power than in the United States. Increasing privatization will make governments less vulnerable to this kind of pressure. It is also interesting to note that some labor courts in Europe deal separately with employment matters from unions and works councils.

In Japan, labor militancy has long been dead since labor and management agreed 40 years ago on a deal for industrial peace in exchange for job security. Unions in Japan have little official clout, especially in the midst of the Japanese recession. In addition, not much can be negotiated because wage rates, working hours, job security, health benefits, overtime work, insurance, and the like have traditionally been legislated. However, global competition is putting pressure on companies to move away from guaranteed job security and pay. Often, however, the managers and labor union representatives are the same people, a fact that limits confrontation, as does the cultural norm of maintaining harmonious relationships.

In the industrialized world, tumbling trade barriers are also reducing the power of trade unions because competitive multinational companies have more freedom to choose alternative production and sourcing locations. Most new union workers—about 75 percent—will be in emerging nations such as China and Mexico, where wages are low and unions are scarce. However, in some countries, such as India, outmoded labor laws are very restrictive for MNEs, making it difficult to lay off employees under any circumstances and forcing foreign companies to be very careful in their selection of new employees.

In China, for example, in a surprising move, the government passed a new law that will grant power to labor unions, in spite of protests by foreign companies with factories there. The order was in response to a sharp rise in labor tension and protests about poor working conditions and industrial accidents.[82] The All-China Federation of Trade Unions claimed that foreign employers often force workers to work overtime, pay no heed to labor-safety regulations, and deliberately find fault with the workers as an excuse to cut their wages or fine them. The move, which underscores the government's growing concern about the widening income gap and threats of social unrest, is setting off a battle with American and other foreign corporations that have lobbied against it by hinting that they may build fewer factories in China.[83]

Protests arose after Walmart, the world's biggest retailer, was forced to accept unions in its Chinese outlets; other MNCs then joined the effort to get the Chinese government to reverse its decision. State-controlled unions in China have traditionally not wielded much power; however, after years of reports of worker abuse, the government seems determined to give its union new powers to negotiate worker contracts, safety protection, and workplace ground rules.[84] However, in spite of such well-publicized incidences, the union situation in China is generally regarded as *The Economist* states in the following:

> *In name, the All-China Federation of Trade Unions (ACFTU) is a vast union bureaucracy running from the national level to small enterprises. In practice it is controlled by the Communist Party at the national level and, in companies, is mostly a tool of the management.*
>
> THE ECONOMIST[85]

Chinese managers often ignore workers' basic rights for reasonable working conditions, safety, and even the right to be paid.

> *Less than two years after the worker suicides at electronics giant Foxconn and a strike at Honda suppliers in Guangdong province, labor troubles are again roiling China.*[86]
>
> BUSINESS WEEK
> *DECEMBER 19, 2011*

At Foxconn Technology, for example, which is a major supplier to several electronics giants such as Hewlett Packard, Apple, and Microsoft, there were large protests in January 2012 by workers at its Wuhan plant that involved threats from some workers to commit suicide. The employees were protesting that they had been forced to work long hours under poor conditions with little pay. Foxconn resolved the dispute and, under pressure from Apple and other companies, pledged to improve working conditions in China.[87] Increasing protests and strikes across China are partly attributed to more awareness of labor laws as well as to inflationary pressures. The next day, Apple, following the lead of companies such as Intel and Nike, released a list of its major suppliers, including a list of troubling practices at some of those.[88]

> *Apple said in the report that it recently became the first technology company to join the Fair Labor Association, a nonprofit group that aims to improve conditions in factories around the world.*
>
> INTERNATIONAL HERALD TRIBUNE
> *JANUARY 14, 2012*

However, because problems occur in factories from which Apple's suppliers outsource, or that supply parts to the suppliers, retaining control and oversight is very difficult. Perhaps the improved social responsibility of foreign firms operating in China might exert pressure for better working conditions for Chinese employees. Policymakers want 80% of all companies to have collective bargaining agreements by 2013."[89]

Historically, the existence of unions in the West has been linked closely to improved social responsibility toward workers, and countries around the world are beginning to catch up as far as improved conditions for workers. This happens when unions are permitted and have some power or when governments exert pressure to improve life for workers so that unions will not take hold. However, strict adherence to union regulations is often traded off by all parties for the local factory to remain competitive and viable and thus provide jobs and a reasonable level of living conditions compared to those experienced previously. This connection is illustrated in the following Under the Lens feature, "Vietnam: The Union Role in Achieving Manufacturing Sustainability and Global Competitiveness."

## Convergence versus Divergence in Labor Systems

> *The world trade union movement is poised to follow the lead of transnational companies, by extending its reach and throwing off the shackles of national boundaries. Unions are about to go global.*[90]

In October 2006, the International Trade Union Confederation (ITUC) was formed in Vienna, comprising the affiliated organizations of the former ICFTU (International Confederation of Free Trade Unions) and WCL (World Confederation of Labor) and eight other national trade union organizations, to form a global body.[91] The ITUC is the world's largest trade union and, as of 2012, represents 168 million workers through its 308 affiliated organizations in 155 countries and territories.[92] Its objective is to provide "a countervailing force in a society that has changed

## UNDER THE LENS

*Vietnam: The Union Role in Achieving Manufacturing Sustainability and Global Competitiveness*

In most aspects, Vietnam has been gone from the attention of Americans for an entire generation. The country is, however, open for business—and business is booming. Capital is flowing in large amounts from Asia Pacific interests based in Singapore, Japan, Australia, Taiwan, and South Korea. The U.S is Vietnam's seventh-largest foreign direct investment country, primarily through apparel and footwear manufacturing.

### FAST DEVELOPMENT SINCE 2000

Vietnam's appearance as a global competitor is comparatively recent. After the North and South were united in 1975, the country languished for ten years. Finally, in 1986, the Vietnamese government woke up and initiated an overall economic renewal policy, known as *doi moi*. Business privatization was encouraged, commerce restrictions came down, and relations with other countries were normalized. It has only been since 2000 that their stock market has been established. Moving rapidly from there, they have been admitted to the Association of Southeast Asian Nations (ASEAN) Free Trade Area (AFTA) and to the World Trade Organization (WTO). Trade relations with the U.S. were normalized in 2006. The results are that Vietnam has gone from triple-digit annual inflation and the inability to grow enough food even for its own use, to single-digit inflation and becoming a mass exporter of both agricultural and manufactured goods.

Major components of their manufacturing for export are footwear and apparel. Unfortunately, most of what the West sees of these types of manufacturing operations comes through non-governmental organizations (NGOs), whose agendas are often far from being unbiased. The purpose of this author's visit in June, 2011 was to see if low labor costs are synonymous with exploitation of workers.

It is important to note that footwear and apparel manufacturing sites in Vietnam are frequently offshored operations owned by outsourced contractors from Taiwan and South Korea. This puts the actual production and labor management considerably removed from the oversight and control of the companies whose brands are being manufactured. Images of sweatshops and exploitation are generally associated with offshored apparel manufacturing.

### MODERN INDUSTRIAL PARKS

In visiting Ho Chi Minh City in 2011, the industrial developments look quite modern. Closest to the city is the Saigon High Tech Park, which is in the early stages of developing a world-class industrial park. Intel is in the process of a $1 billion investment on those grounds. A few kilometers further out are the Linh Trung Processing Zone, Vietnam Singapore Industrial Park, and Song Than Park. Along with Western firms, such as Siemens and Kimberly Clark, are various apparel and footwear manufacturers owned by Asian outsourcers. The industrial parks are very similar to Western-style developments in terms of the grounds, infrastructure, cleanliness, and the spaciousness of the layouts. The main difference is the size of the buildings, some of which are enormous four-level structures containing as many as 10,000 workers at any given time. At 6:00 a.m. a sea of humanity floods the roadways, mostly on foot but many on motorbikes carrying up to three passengers. Workers clock in for 12-hour shifts, and factories operate on a 24-hour basis when orders and deadlines are high. Employment turnover is very high, but jobs are plentiful. Interestingly, the high turnover and high need for workers has not led to fast wage growth. Employers are finding an adequate supply of workers to keep their lines running.

### WAGES AND HOUSING

The typical factory worker comes from farming provinces in order to earn higher wages. Workers start at $80–85 per month, with more for experience and productivity. This is often double the potential in their home towns. Many workers will take the option to work 7-day weeks and beyond their 12-hour shifts when factory orders are high. They send as much of their wages home as possible. Workers like to take a yearly 20-day holiday to return home, often on a very long bus ride to the north of the country. Research by Dr. Rhys Jenkins found the migrant textile workers to be appreciative of their job situation, as it had raised their standard of living.[93]

In a tour and interview with a Vietnamese housing owner, as well as several current tenants, the workers were observed to have satisfactory living accommodations, although understandably modest. Workers' rooms rent for $30 per month, and are usually shared by four workers, making their housing

FIGURE 10-2 Not the Comfort Inn, But Even the Bosses Don't Live This Well Back on the Rice Farm

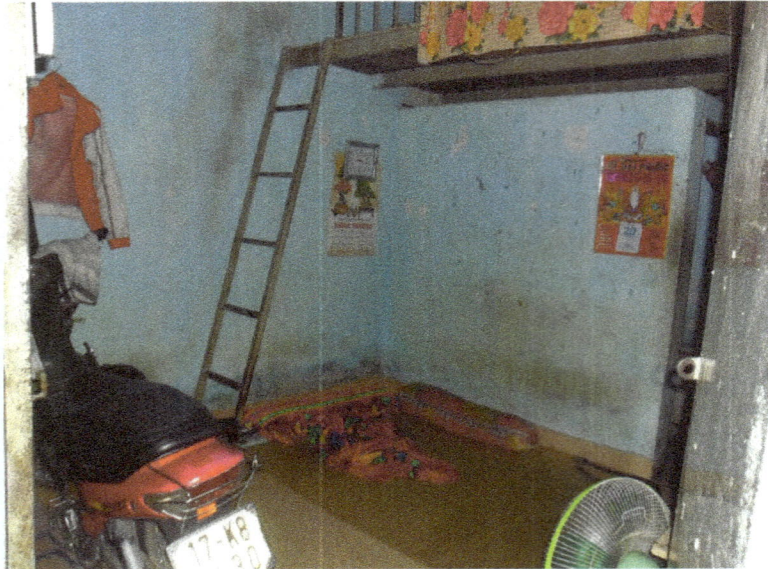

*Source:* © F. Robert Buchanan/Buchanan, F. Robert used with permission.

cost about 25 cents per day or $8 per month. This is just 10% of base wages. The rooms are clean, austere, and approximately the size of a budget hotel room, with an upper deck for sleeping. Residents cook and have running water downstairs, with a communal bathroom down the hall. The rooms are in single-story buildings, situated along covered, secure corridors. Out on the street, a multitude of vendors serve the food and service needs of this demographic. We observed nothing about these living arrangements that would be characterized as inhumane or even depressing. The housing owners are typically hard-working locals who bought the properties from their own savings, live on-site, and have a congenial, patriarchal relationship with their tenants.

## GOVERNMENT OVERSIGHT AND CSR

The general consensus is that the Vietnam government is providing effective levels of oversight and threats to keep factories from being exploitative. Better Work Vietnam is an NGO sponsored by the World Bank and the International Labor Organization (ILO). It has been vocal and credible in its reporting. Their most recent report indicates widespread noncompliance with government overtime standards, as well as health and safety standards. They did not find child labor in any of the large factories. While labor unions are commonplace and protected by law, the reality is that the union officers in many factories are managerial staff. This fails the non-interference test.

Corporate Social Responsibility (CSR) is a luxury that only the largest manufacturers can afford. Nonetheless, the emergence of CSR to benefit Vietnamese workers can be quite similar to those of developed nations. An April, 2011 "Fun Run" in Ho Chi Minh City to raise safety awareness was sponsored by the ILO along with such companies as Abercrombie & Fitch, Levi's, Nike, and The Walt Disney Company. Entertainment, education, and an appearance by a Vietnam Idol winner were sponsored.

## CONCLUSIONS

The upshot of these observations is that Vietnam appears to be a successful model for sustainable low-cost labor manufacturing. While it is debatable whether large apparel manufacturers really contribute much to the country overall, there is no question that the jobs they provide are beneficial to that category of worker. Hopefully unions can improve the conditions further for the workers while those plants can remain competitive and retain the jobs locally.

*Source:* Dr. F. Robert Buchanan, University of Central Oklahoma, used with permission.

enormously, with workers' rights being flouted under the pressure created by the current trajectory of 'race to the bottom' globalization."[94]

Political changes, external competitive forces, increased open trade, and frequent moves of MNCs around the world are forces working toward convergence in labor systems. **Convergence** occurs as the migration of management and workplace practices around the world reduce workplace disparities from one country to another. This occurs primarily as MNCs seek consistency and coordination among their foreign subsidiaries and as they act as catalysts for change by exporting new forms of work organization and industrial relations practices.[95] It also occurs as harmonization is sought, such as for the EU countries, and as competitive pressures in free-trade zones, such as the NAFTA countries, eventually bring about demands for some equalization of benefits for workers.[96] It would appear that economic globalization is leading to labor transnationalism and will bring about changes in labor rights and democracy around the world.

Other pressures toward convergence of labor relations practices around the world come from the activities and monitoring of labor conditions worldwide by various organizations. One of these organizations is the International Labor Organization (ILO)—comprising union, employer, and government representation—whose mission is to ensure that humane conditions of labor are maintained. Other associations of unions in different countries include various international trade secretariats representing workers in specific industries. The activities and communication channels of these associations provide unions and firms with information about differences in labor conditions around the world.[97]

However, there are considerable forces for continued divergence of unions. These include government attitudes toward unions; union competition to attract foreign investment and provide jobs locally; different approaches to structuring unions and how to organize collective bargaining and deal with workers' rights. Exhibit 10-4 shows the major forces for and against convergence in labor relations systems.

## Adapting to Local Industrial Relations Systems

Although forces for convergence are found in labor relations systems around the world (as discussed previously), for the most part, MNCs still adapt their practices largely to the traditions of national industrial relations systems, with considerable pressure to do so. Those companies, in fact, act more like local employers, subject to local and country regulations and practices. Although the reasons for continued divergence in systems seem fewer, they are very strong. Not the least of these reasons are political ideology and the overall social structure and history of industrial practices. In the European Union (EU), where states are required to maintain parity in wage rates and benefits under the Social Charter of the Maastricht Treaty, a powerful defense of cultural identity and social systems still exists, with considerable resistance by unions to comply with those requirements. Managers in those MNCs also recognize that a considerable gap often exists between the labor laws and the enforcement of those laws—in particular in less-developed countries.

**EXHIBIT 10–4**  Trends in Global Labor Relations Systems

| Forces for Global Convergence → | Dynamic Forces Acting on Current System ← | Forces to Maintain or Establish Divergent Systems |
|---|---|---|
| Global competitiveness | | National labor relations systems and traditions |
| MNC presence or consolidation initiatives | | Social systems |
| Political change | | Local regulations and practices |
| New market economies | | Political ideology |
| Free-trade zones: harmonization | | Cultural norms |
| (EU), competitive forces (NAFTA) | | Competition for jobs |
| Technological standardization, IT | | Collective bargaining methods |
| Declining role of unions | | |
| Agencies monitoring world labor practices | | |

## NAFTA and Labor Relations in Mexico

About 40 percent of the total workforce in Mexico is unionized, with about 80 percent of the workers unionized in industrial organizations that employ more than 25 workers. However, government control over union activities is very strong, and although some strikes occur, union control over members remains rather weak. Most labor unions are affiliated with the Institutional Revolutionary Party (PRI) through the Confederation of Mexican Workers (Confederación de Trabajadores Mexicanos—CTM). In April 2011, the Teamsters Union charged that Mexico's oligarchs, led by President Felipe Calderon, were trying to take away workers' collective bargaining rights through various labor law reforms. The union charged that:

> *In reality, the growing power of corporations (enabled by NAFTA) has undermined those rights, especially in the maquiladora district in northern Mexico. Half of all Mexicans live in poverty, and even those with a formal job don't make much money.*[98]

> TEAMSTER NATION
> *APRIL 21, 2012*

MNCs are required by government regulation to hire Mexican nationals for at least 90 percent of their workforce; preference must be given to Mexicans and to union personnel. In reality, however, the government permits hiring exceptions. The HSBC Bank, for example, found the following.

The owner must employ a minimum of 90 percent Mexican workers in accordance with Mexican Federal Labor Law (MFLL). In the case of technicians and professional workers, they must be Mexican; in the event that Mexican technicians or professional workers are not available, the business may temporarily hire a foreign worker, but both will then have the obligation to train a Mexican technician or professional worker in order to comply with the MFLL. For management or director levels, the rule does not apply.[99]

Many foreign firms set up production in Mexico—using the advantages of NAFTA—at least in part for the lower wages and lower overall cost of operating there, as well as low transportation costs to the United States - and the Mexican government wants to continue to attract that investment as it has for many years before NAFTA. Mexican workers claim that some of the large U.S. companies in Mexico violate basic labor rights and cooperate with pro-government labor leaders in Mexico to break up independent unions. Workers there believe that MNCs routinely use blacklists, physical intimidation, and economic pressure against union organizations and independent labor groups that oppose Mexican government policies or the pro-government Confederation of Mexican Workers (CTM).

This example illustrates the complexities of labor relations when a firm operates in other countries—particularly when there are linkages and interdependence among those countries, such as through NAFTA or the EU. Of interest are the differences among NAFTA nations in labor law in the private sector. For example, although the minimum wage in Mexico is far less than that in Canada or the United States, a number of costly benefits for Mexican workers are required, such as 15 days of pay for a Christmas bonus and 90 days of severance pay. For comparison, the accompanying Comparative Management in Focus feature examines labor relations in Germany.

## Comparative Management in Focus
*Labor Relations in Germany*

> *IG Metall yesterday settled on a 3.4 percent pay rise for a year from April for employees in Baden-Württemberg, one of Germany's richest states, where unemployment is just 4.2 per cent. The deal is seen as a bellwether for negotiations in the rest of the country.*

> FINANCIAL TIMES
> *FEBRUARY 25, 2015*[100]

Given the continuing economic problems in Europe at that time, there was considerable commitment to Germany's largest union, IG Metall, at its 2011 annual congress in Karlsruhe. "The union's executive used the occasion to confirm and celebrate its policy of class collaboration. Federal President Christian Wulff and Chancellor Angela Merkel (both from the Christian Democratic Union—CDU) came to the gathering to pay their respects."[101]

*(Continued)*

It is noteworthy that the German economy has done very well over the past few years—while the rest of Europe staggered—leading Angel Gurría, the OECD's secretary general, to say in a speech in Berlin in February 2012 that Germany's "growth model has been so successful in navigating through the stormy waters of the crisis."[102] The German unemployment level fell to the lowest level in decades, whereas it went up in the rest of Europe. Part of that result is because, in the labor system in Germany, companies tend to move employees to part-time status and give them continued training the rest of the time rather than laying them off. In addition, the company often banks the overtime pay of employees to use when times are difficult and they have to reduce employees' hours. Unfortunately, many of the younger generation workers do not have permanent jobs; rather they have contract (temporary) jobs, which makes it easier for companies to let them go when the term of the contract ends.[103]

In spite of the commitment to IG Metall, Germany's **codetermination** law *(mitbestimmung)* is coming under pressure from German companies dealing with global competition and the results of global trends of outsourcing, industrial restructuring, and the expansion of the service sector.[104] That pressure is increasingly taking the form of concession bargaining to keep jobs at home. Still, some companies—tired of restrictions on their strategic decisions and necessary job cuts—are sidestepping those restrictions by registering as public limited companies in the United Kingdom.[105]

*Mitbestimmung* refers to the participation of labor in the management of a firm. The law mandates representation for unions and salaried employees on the supervisory boards of all companies with more than 2,000 employees and works councils of employees at every work site. Companies with 2,000 or more staff have to give employees half the votes; those with 500 employees or more have to give a third of supervisory board seats to union representatives.[106] Unions are well integrated into managerial decision-making and can make a positive contribution to corporate competitiveness and restructuring; this seems different from the traditional adversarial relationship of unions and management in the United States. However, the fact is that German firms, in the form of affiliated organizations of companies, have to contend with negotiating with powerful industry-wide unions. Employment conditions that would be negotiated privately in the United States, for example, are subject to federal mandates in Germany—a model unique in Europe. Germans on average work fewer hours than those in any other country than the Netherlands.[107] Under pressure from global competition, German unions incurred huge membership losses. In 2010, there were 7.9 million members, 40 percent fewer than in 1990, but that includes about 20 percent of retired union members.[108] In fact, only 20 percent of employees in Germany are union members, compared to 28 percent in the United Kingdom and 67 percent in Denmark.[109] As a result, the unions are now more willing to make concessions and trade flexibility for increased job security.

Union membership in Germany is voluntary, usually with one union for each major industry, and union power traditionally has been quite strong. Negotiated contracts with firms by the employers' federation stand to be accepted by firms that are members of the federation, or used as a guide for other firms. These contracts, therefore, result in setting the pay scale for about 90 percent of the country's workers.[110]

The union works councils play an active role in hiring, firing, training, and reassignment during times of reorganization and change.[111] Because of the depth of works council penetration into personnel and work organization matters, as required by law, its role has been described by some as "co-manager of the internal labor market."[112] This situation has considerable implications for how managers of MNCs plan to operate in Germany.

IG Metall (*Industriegewerkschaft Metall*—Industrial Union of Metalworkers) had nearly 3.7 million members as of February 2015, representing workers at Germany's biggest companies. IG Metall has traditionally negotiated guidelines regarding pay, hours, and working conditions on a regional basis. IG Metall's proactive role on change illustrates the evolving role of unions by leading management thinking instead of reacting to it. In addition, management and workers tend to work together because of the unions' structure. Indeed, such institutional accord is a powerful factor in changing deeply ingrained cultural traits. Codetermination has clearly helped to modify German managerial style from authoritarian to something more akin to humanitarian without, it should be noted, altering its capacity for efficiency and effectiveness.[113] This system compares to the lack of integration and active roles for unions in the U.S. auto industry—for example, conditions that limit opportunities for change.

Pay for German production workers has been among the highest in the world, about 150 percent of that in the United States and about ten times that in Mexico. German workers also have the highest number of paid vacation days in the world and prefer short workdays.

Foreign companies operating in Germany also have to be aware that termination costs—including severance pay, retraining costs, time to find another job, and so on—are very high, and that is assuming the company is successful in terminating the employee in the first place, which is very difficult

**MAP 10.1 Germany and Western Europe**

- EU members using the euro
- EU members using own national currency
- Countries not members of the EU
- Cities over 1 million
- Capitals over 1 million

*Source:* Deloitte Services LP

to do in Europe. This was brought home to Colgate-Palmolive when it tried to close its factory in Hamburg. The company offered the 500 employees an average severance of $40,000 each, but the union would not accept, and eventually Colgate had to pay a much higher (undisclosed) amount.

To the extent that the West German unions have established the high-wage, high-skill, and high-value-added production pattern, they have also become dependent on the continued presence of that pattern.[114]

Conflicting opinions over the value of codetermination are increasingly evident as business practices become increasingly subject to EU policies. A major concern was that firms from other countries that were considering cross-border mergers would be discouraged by the EU statute that would oblige them to incorporate codetermination if the new company includes significant German interests.

# CONCLUSION

The role of the IHRM department has expanded to meet the strategic needs of the company to develop a competitive global management cadre. Maximizing human resources around the world requires attention to the many categories and combinations of those people, including expatriates, inpatriates, host-country managers, third-country nationals, global teams, and local employees. Competitive global companies need top managers with global experience and understanding. To that end, attention must be paid to the needs of expatriates before, during, and after their assignments to maximize their long-term contributions to the company.

## Summary of Key Points

- Expatriate career management necessitates plans for retention of expatriates during and after their assignments. Through retention, the firm can benefit from the knowledge and experiences attained on assignments; otherwise, the next firm that hires the returnee will benefit from that knowledge. Support programs for expatriates should include information from and contact with the home organization as well as career guidance and support after the overseas assignment.

- The expatriate's spouse plays a crucial role in the potential retention and effectiveness of the manager in host locations. Companies should ensure the spouse's interest in the assignment, include him or her in the predeparture training, and provide career and family support during the assignment and upon return.

- Global management teams offer greater opportunities for competition—by sharing experiences, technology, and international managers—and greater opportunities for cross-cultural understanding and exposure to different viewpoints. Disadvantages can result from communication and cross-cultural conflicts and greater complexity in the workplace.

- Virtual global teams enable cost-effective, rapid knowledge sharing and collaboration but are fraught with cross-cultural and logistical challenges.

- Women represent an underused resource in international management. One reason for this situation is the assumption that culturally based biases may limit the opportunities and success of female managers and employees.

- The labor relations environment, system, and processes vary around the world and affect how the international manager must plan strategy and maximize the productivity of local human resources.

- Labor unions around the world are becoming increasingly interdependent because of the operations of MNCs worldwide, the outsourcing of jobs around the world, and the leveling of the playing field for jobs.

## Discussion Questions

**10-1.** What appropriate measures can be taken by MNEs to ensure that the overseas assignments of their expatriate managers are performed effectively?

**10-2.** Given the fact that many returning executives from overseas assignments report an improvement in their managerial skills and self-confidence, how can MNEs make sure that the company and the returned managers can both benefit from the enhanced skills and experience of the expatriate assignment?

**10-3.** What are the reasons for the small numbers of female expatriates? What more can companies do to use women as a resource for international management?

**10-4.** What is a virtual global management team? How do the members interact? Discuss the advantages and the challenges these teams face. Suggest some ways to maximize the effectiveness of virtual teams across borders.

**10-5.** Discuss the reasons behind the growing convergence and interdependence of labor unions around the world.

## Application Exercise

**10-6.** Interview one or more managers who have held positions overseas. Try to find a man and a woman. Ask them about their experiences both in the working environment and in the foreign country generally. How did they and their families adapt? How did they find the stage of reentry to headquarters, and what were the effects of the assignment on their career progression? What differences do you notice, if any, between the experiences of the male and the female expatriates?

## Experiential Exercise

Form groups of six students, divided into two teams, one representing union members from a German company and the other representing union members from a Mexican company. These companies have recently merged in a joint venture, with the subsidiary to be located in Mexico. These union workers, all line supervisors, will be working together in Mexico. You are to negotiate six major points of agreement regarding union representation, bargaining rights, and worker participation in management, as discussed in this chapter. Present your findings to the other groups in the class and discuss.

## CASE STUDY

### Expatriate Management at AstraZeneca Plc

Over the years, AstraZeneca Plc (AstraZeneca) has developed a strong reputation for its expatriate management practices. Expatriate management at AstraZeneca went beyond tackling issues such as compensation, housing, issues related to the spouse's career abroad, and so on. It also took care to ensure that employees on international assignment were able to adapt well to the new environment and achieve a work–life balance. With the global economic situation continuing to be grim, AstraZeneca also began placing emphasis on a "more thoughtful planning and selection process" of candidates for international assignments.[1]

*Source:* Deloitte Services LP

AstraZeneca is the world's fifth-largest pharmaceutical company by global sales.[2] It is headquartered in London, UK, and Södertälje, Sweden. For the year 2013, AstraZeneca's revenues were US$25.7 billion, and it employed around 51,500 employees. As of 2013, AstraZeneca had around 350 employees working on international assignments in 140 countries worldwide. These were employees who were on short-term, long-term, or commuter assignments.[3] According to Ashley Daly (Daly), senior manager of international assignments for AstraZeneca in the United States, the company's employees were mainly concentrated in Belgium, the United States, and the United Kingdom, but they "also have a significant presence in the Asia-Pacific and Latin America regions."[4] AstraZeneca's policy stipulates that for any international assignment, there had to be a business rationale. The company saw to it that the costs involved were acceptable and that the career management of the employee during the assignment was consistent with personal development goals as well as business needs. The contractual arrangements for the assignment were also centrally managed.[5] "From the outset, if there is not a clear sense of how the international assignment experience can be applied at the end of the assignment term—at least in broad terms—the business should strongly consider whether an international assignment should even move forward,"[6] said Daly.

Once an assignment offer was made to a potential expat, AstraZeneca paired the employee up with an international assignment manager (IA manager), who briefed him or her on company policy and opportunities for cultural and language training. Before leaving for the international assignment, the employee was trained in a workshop that focused on relevant issues (such as leaving the destination location and returning to the home country). The expat was given information about the culture of the destination country—particularly differences with the home country—as well as social considerations and do's and don'ts. If necessary, the employee and his or her spouse were given training in the local language. Tessi Romell (Romell), research and development projects and HR effectiveness leader at AstraZeneca, said that the company also helped connect new expats with those who had already served in that location.

Sometimes, follow-up workshops were held in the host country. Once on assignment, expats stayed in touch with their IA manager in addition to the manager they reported to in the home country. AstraZeneca saw to it that expats were given the necessary flexibility to achieve a work–life balance. "AstraZeneca is really good at allowing people to manage their own time and being aware that we are working across different time zones. It's always something that we try to take into consideration so we don't have people [taking care of work matters] in the middle of the night,"[7] said Romell.

With AstraZeneca taking various initiatives on this front, there were few complaints about work–life balance among the company's expat population. Romell attributed this to the mechanisms the company had put in place to prepare the employees for life in a different country. "It's a combination of things that the company is doing and having a culture that is supportive of work–life balance, as well as encouraging individuals themselves to think about their own work–life balance,"[8] she said. Experts, too, felt that the practices AstraZeneca followed, such as preparing the employees for international assignments, providing them with support, and assigning IA managers, were effective. They lauded AstraZeneca's practices, which were in contrast to those of many companies that rushed employees to foreign assignments without adequate support. Chris Buckley, manager of international operations for St. Louis–based Impact Group Inc., pointed out that the expats knew that the organization was spending a lot of money on them and they might be wary about coming up with any complaints regarding their new assignment with their boss. In such a scenario, contact with the IA manager was useful because it could encourage them to open up.

With the economic situation around the globe still gloomy, experts felt that organizations would be forced to take a second look at the costs associated with international staffing. Some felt that organizations would send fewer people on international assignments or allot them to shorter terms abroad. They even predicted that the high compensation and benefits generally associated with foreign assignments could also see cuts. While AstraZeneca had also taken measures to cut costs (specifically tax costs) by sending employees on short-term assignments, Daly noted that this was not always possible. When the expat had a family and was being posted for a longer term, Daly pointed out that some of the elements of AstraZeneca's expat packages, such as comprehensive destination support and educational counseling for expatriate children, played a critical role in ensuring the employee's productivity. These supports ensured that the expatriate family could settle down in the host country. Not providing them might prevent employees from focusing on their new job, putting the company's investment at risk, so the company was not looking at this issue in terms of expenditures alone. The company also did not have any plans to decrease the number of its staff deployed internationally. According to Daly, "Our recent focus has been less on reducing numbers of international assignees and more on making the right decisions about who goes on assignment; why they go; and perhaps most important, how the skills and experience gained abroad will be leveraged in their next role, post assignment."[9]

## Notes

1. Tanya Mohn, "When U.S. Home Isn't Home Anymore," www.mydigitalfc.com, March 10, 2009.
2. "The Pharm Exec 50," www.pharmexec.com, May 2009.
3. www.ideas.astrazeneca.com.
4. Susan Ainsworth, "Expatriate Programs," http://pubs.acs.org, April 6, 2009.
5. "AstraZeneca Global Policy: People," www.astrazeneca.com.
6. Susan Ainsworth, "Expatriate Programs," http://pubs.acs.org, April 6, 2009.
7. Julie Cook Ramirez, "Finding Balance Abroad," www.hreonline.com, August 1, 2009.
8. Ibid.
9. Susan Ainsworth, "Expatriate Programs," http://pubs.acs.org, April 6, 2009.

## Case Questions

**10-7.** Critically analyze AstraZeneca's expatriate management practices.

**10-8.** Surveys show that most expats report feeling the strain of managing the demands of work and home while adjusting to the foreign environment, leading to more anxieties at home and at the workplace. What steps can an organization take to mitigate this?

**10-9.** What decisions related to expatriates can organizations take to maximize the benefits to the company despite the economic downturn? Do you think a company that paid more careful attention to selection could further boost its chances of success?

This case was written by Debapratim Purkayastha, ICMR Center for Management Research (ICMR). It was compiled from published sources and is intended to be used as a basis for class discussion rather than to illustrate either effective or ineffective handling of a management situation. © 2010, ICMR. All rights reserved. Used with permission, 2012.

## Endnotes

1. Thomas Grove, "Expats Flee Moscow as Tensions Flare," Wall Street Journal, June 10, 2015, B1. Julia Werdigier, "Paychecks and Passports," *New York Times*, April 2, 2008; Doreen Carvajal, "Paid in Dollars, Some Americans Are Struggling in Europe," *New York Times*, December 15, 2007; Alan Paul, "The Expat Life: Clock Counts Down as Decision Weighs: Should I Stay or Go?" www .wallstreetjournal, February 28, 2008; Monica Ginsburg, "Getting Ahead by Going Abroad," *Crain's Chicago Business* 31, No. 50 (2008), p. 20; Philip Shearer and Abby Ellin, "Foreign from the Start," www.nytimes.com, September 21, 2003; Jad Mouawad, "Total, the French Oil Company, Places Its Bets Globally," www .nytimes.com, February 22, 2009; www.Global Relocation Trends Survey, www.brookfieldgrs.com, accessed March 1, 2009; Keith Bradsher and Julia Werdigier, "Abruptly Expatriate Bankers Are Cut Loose," www.nytimes.com March 4, 2009.

2. Werdigier.

3. Bradsher and Werdigier.

4. *Wall Street Journal*, February 28, 2008.

5. www.nytimes.com, February 22, 2000.

6. Ginsburg.

7. Shearer and Ellin.

8. Garry Oddou et al., "Repatriates as a Source of Competitive Advantage, *Organizational Dynamics* (2013), pp. 42, 257–266.

9. The *Global Talent Index Report: The Outlook to 2015* was written by the Economist Intelligence Unit and published by Heidrick & Struggles.

10. 2015 Global Relocation Trends Survey, www.brookfieldgrs .com, accessed August 26, 2015.

11. Ibid.

12. A. Maitland, "Top Companies Value Overseas Experience," www.Financial Times, July 3, 2006.

13. "International Assignments Remain on the Upswing Despite Economic Concerns, Says KPMG," *PR Newswire*, December 3, 2008; www.kpmglink.com.

14. M. Lazarova and P. Caligiuri, "Retaining Repatriates: The Role of Organizational Support Practices," *Journal of World Business* 36, No. 4 (2001), pp. 389–401.

15. Charlene M. Solomon, "One Assignment, Two Lives," *Personnel Journal* (May 1996), pp. 36–44.

16. 2015 Global Relocation Trends Survey, www.brookfieldgrs .com, accessed August 26, 2015.

17. Ibid.

18. Ibid.

19. 2011 Global Relocation Trends Survey, accessed March 1, 2011.

20. www.FT.com, March 5, 2001.

21. P. Asheghian and B. Ebrahimi, *International Business* (New York: HarperCollins, 1990), p. 470.

22. Global Relocation Trends Survey, 2011.

23. N. J. Adler, *International Dimensions of Organizational Behavior*, 4th ed. (Boston: PWS-Kent, 2002).

24. J. Bonache and C. Brewster, "Knowledge Transfer and the Management of Expatriation," *Thunderbird International Business Review* 43, No. 1 (2001), pp. 145–168.

25. David Holthaus, "P&G at Work: Key Managers in Africa," *Cincinnati Enquirer*, April 16, 2011; www.pg.com, accessed December 9, 2011.

26. Berthoin-Antal, "Expatriates' Contributions to Organizational Learning," *Journal of General Management* 26, No. 4 (2001), pp. 62–84.

27. Ibid.

28. Mila Lazarova and Ibraiz Tarique, "Knowledge Transfer upon Repatriation," *Journal of World Business* 40, No. 4 (2005), pp. 361–373.

29. Ibid.

30. 2015 Global Relocation Trends Survey, www.brookfieldgrs .com, accessed August 26, 2015.

31. Joe Leahy, "Brazil Hosts a Homecoming," *Financial Times*, August 23, 2011, p. 8; Guy Chazan, "Middle East: Oil Firms Suspend Libyan Operations," *Wall Street Journal*, February 22, 2011, p. A.11; Borzou Daragahi, "Expats Trickle Back to Libya but Business Remains Slow," *Financial Times*, London (UK), February 11, 2012, pp. 2; Mariko Sanchanta, "Disaster in Japan: Expatriates Tiptoe Back to the Office," *Wall Street Journal*, March 23, 2011, p. A.7.

32. *Financial Times*, August 23, 2011.
33. Ibid.
34. *Financial Times*, February 11, 2012.
35. *Wall Street Journal*, March 23, 2011.
36. J. Conger and E. Lawler, "People Skills Still Rule in the Virtual Company," *Financial Times*, August 26, 2005.
37. Based largely on Adler, 2002.
38. T. Gross, E. Turner, and L. Cederholm, "Building Teams for Global Operations," *Management Review* (June 1987), p. 34.
39. T. R. Kayworth and D. E. Leidner, "Leadership Effectiveness in Global Virtual Teams," *Journal of Management Information Systems* 18, No. 3 (2001–2002), pp. 7–40.
40. C. Solomon, "Building Teams across Borders," *Global Workforce* (November 1998), pp. 12–17.
41. Ibid.
42. J. Cordery, C. Soo, B. Kirkman, B. Benson, and J. Mathieu, "Leading Parallel Virtual Teams: Lessons from Alcoa," *Organizational Dynamics* 38, No. 3 (2009), pp. 204–216.
43. Ibid.
44. B. Rosen. S. Furst, and R. Blackburn, "Training for Virtual Teams: An Investigation of Current Practices and Future Needs," *Human Resources Management* 45, No. 2 (2006), pp. 229–247.
45. Michiyo Nakamoto, "Cultural Revolution in Tokyo," www.ft.com, September 17, 2009.
46. Ibid.
47. A. Joshi, G. Labianca, and P. M. Caligiuri, "Getting along Long Distance: Understanding Conflict in a Multinational Team through Network Analysis," *Journal of World Business* 37 (2002), pp. 277–284.
48. V. Govindarajan and A. K. Gupta, "Building an Effective Global Business Team," *MIT Sloan Management Review* 42, No. 4 (2001), p. 63.
49. Ibid.
50. Ibid.
51. S. Chevrier, "Cross-Cultural Management in Multinational Project Groups," *Journal of World Business* 38, No. 2 (2003), pp. 141–149.
52. Ibid.
53. Eleanor Warnok, "A Step Forward for Economics in Japan," *The Wall Street Journal*, August 28, 2015.
54. "The Most Powerful Women in Business 2015," *Fortune.com*, accessed September 20, 2015.
55. Ibid.
56. Nicola Clark, "Awareness Rises, but Women Still Lag in Pay," www.nytimes.com, March 8, 2010.
57. Ibid.
58. "Why Top Management Eludes Women in Latin America," *McKinsey Global Survey Results*, August 2013.
59. Ibid.
60. Alison Maitland, "The North–South Divide in Europe, Inc.," *Financial Times*, June 14, 2004.
61. Soo Min Toh and Geoffrey J. Leonardelli, "Cultural Constraints on the Emergence of Women Leaders: How Global Leaders Can Promote Women in Different Cultures," *Organizational Dynamics* (2013), pp. 42, 191–197.
62. Ibid.
63. Katrin Bennhold, "Women Nudged Out of German Workforce," www.nytimes.com, June 28, 2011.
64. Based on selected data from Bennhold, June 28, 2011, and McKinsey's 2010 "Women Matter" Report

65. Bennhold.
66. Japan's Neglected Resource—Female Workers," www.nytimes.com, July 24, 2003.
67. Ibid.
68. Maitland, 2004.
69. M. Jelinek and N. Adler, "Women: World Class Managers for Global Competition," *Academy of Management Executive* 11, No. 1 (February 1988), pp. 11–19.
70. Ibid.
71. Jacob Vittorelli, Former Deputy Chairman of Pirelli.
72. Deepa Seetharaman, "Ford to Pay $750 Million Severance to Workers at Belgium Plant," www.reuters.com, March 19, 2013; Jack Ewing, "Ford Pays a High Price for its Factory Closing in Belgium," www.nytimes.com, November 5, 2013; Dietmar Henning, "Unions Suppress Opposition to Closure of Belgian Ford Plant," http://www.wsws.org/en/articles/2013/02/14/genk-f14.html; "Ford Confirms Plans to Close Belgian Factory," http://www.bbc.com/news/business-20054924, October 24, 2012; John Reed in London and James Fontanella-Khan in Brussels, "Ford to Close Belgian Plant," www.ft.com, October 24, 2012; Chris Reiter and Keith Naughton, "Ford's Genk Plant Remains Shut on Strikes at Suppliers," www.bloomberg.com/news, January 18, 2013; Mike Ramsey and Marietta Cauchi, "Vote Nears at Troubled Ford Plant in Belgium," *Wall Street Journal*, March 13, 2013.
73. Stuart Pfeifer, "Workers at IKEA's First U.S. Factory O.K. Union," *Los Angeles Times*, July 29, 2011.
74. "A New Deal in Europe?" www.businessweek.com, July 14, 2003.
75. M. R. Czinkota, I. A. Ronkainen, and M. H. Moffett, *International Business*, 3rd ed. (New York: Dryden Press, 1994).
76. Bureau of Labor Statistics news release, January 23, 2014.
77. R. J. Adams, *Industrial Relations under Liberal Democracy* (University of South Carolina Press, 1995).
78. J. S. Daniels and L. H. Radebaugh, *International Business*, 10th ed. (Reading, MA: Addison-Wesley. 2004).
79. P. J. Dowling, R. S. Schuler, and D. E. Welch, *International Dimensions of Human Resource Management*, 2nd ed. (Belmont CA: Wadsworth, 1994).
80. Adams.
81. Ibid.
82. D. Barboza, "China Passed Law to Empower Unions and End Labor Abuse," *New York Times*, October 12, 2006.
83. David Barboza, www.nytimes.com, October 12, 2006.
84. Ibid.
85. Anonymous, "Asia: Arbitration Needed: China's Labour Laws," *Economist* 392, No. 8642 (2009), p. 37.
86. Dexter Roberts, "Using Propaganda to Stop China's Strikes," *BusinessWeek* (Dec 19, 2011), p. 1.
87. David Barboza, "Foxconn Resolves a Dispute with Some Workers in China," *International Herald Tribune*, January 12, 2012.
88. Nick Wingfield and Charles Duhigg, "Apple Lists Its Suppliers for the First Time," *International Herald Tribune*, January 14, 2012.
89. *BusinessWeek*, 2011.
90. R. Jenkins, "Globalisation of Production, Employment and Poverty: Three Macro-Meso-Micro Studies," *European Journal of Development Research* 17, No. 4, (2005), pp. 601–625.
91. B. Barber, "Workers of the World Are Uniting," *Financial Times*, December 7, 2004.
92. International Confederation of Free Trade Unions, www.icftu.org, accessed August 29, 2015
93. Ibid.

94. www.ituc-csi.org, accessed August 29, 2015.

95. M. M. Lucio and S. Weston, "New Management Practices in a Multinational Corporation: The Restructuring of Worker Representation and Rights?" *Industrial Relations Journal* 25, No. 2 (2004), pp. 110–121.

96. D. B. Cornfield, "Labor Transnationalism?" *Work and Occupations* 24, No. 3 (August 1997), p. 278.

97. Daniels and Radebaugh.

98. "Mexico Prez Trying to Crush Labor Unions Legally," *Teamster Nation*, April 21, 2011.

99. "Maximum Number of Permitted Foreign Employees," HSBC Bank, www.hsbc.com, accessed October 3, 2011.

100. Claire Jones: Frankfurt, and Jeevan Vasagar: Berlin, "IG Metall-Bellwether Deal: Germany's Largest Union Agrees Above-Inflation Pay Rise," *Financial Times*, February 25, 2015.

101. Dietmar Henning, "IG Metall Union and German Government Reaffirm Their Collaboration," www.wsws.org, October 21, 2011.

102. Floyd Norris, "Germany vs. the Rest of Europe," *New York Times*, February 16, 2012.

103. Ibid.

104. R. Milne and H. Williamson, "Selective Bargaining: German Companies Are Driving a Hidden Revolution in Labour Flexibility," *Financial Times*, January 6, 2006.

105. Gerrit Wiesmann, "Germans Eye U.K. Listings as a Way Out of Worker Law," *Financial Times*, May 24, 2006.

106. Ibid.

107. "A New Deal in Europe?" www.businessweek.com; BW Online, July 14, 2003.

108. http://www.worker-participation.eu/National-Industrial-Relations/Countries/Germany/Trade-Unions, accessed August 22, 2012.

109. http://www.worker-participation.eu, accessed August 22, 2012.

110. J. Hoerr, "What Should Unions Do?" *Harvard Business Review* (May–June 1991), pp. 30–45.

111. H. C. Katz, "The Decentralization of Collective Bargaining: A Literature Review and Comparative Analysis," *Industrial and Labor Relations Review* 47, No. 1 (1993), pp. 3–22.

112. Williamson, *Financial Times*, July 22, 2004.

113. www.nytimes.com, July 24, 2004.

114. Wofgang Streeck, "More Uncertainties: German Unions Facing 1992," *Industrial Relations* (Fall 1991), pp. 30–33.